THE IRONY OF DEMOCRACY

An Uncommon Introduction to American Politics

THE IRONY OF DEMOCRACY

An Uncommon Introduction to American Politics

SIXTEENTH EDITION

Louis Schubert

Thomas R. Dye

Harmon Zeigler, Late

WADSWORTH
CENGAGE Learning

Australia • Brazil • Japan • Korea • Mexico • Singapore • Spain • United Kingdom • United States

WADSWORTH
CENGAGE Learning

The Irony of Democracy: An Uncommon Introduction to American Politics, Sixteenth Edition
Louis Schubert, Thomas R. Dye, Harmon Zeigler, Late

Publisher: Suzanne Jeans

Executive Editor: Carolyn Merrill

Acquisitions Editor: Anita Devine

Development Editor: Jean Findley

Assistant Editor: Patrick Roach

Editorial Assistant: Eireann Aspell

Brand Manager: Lydia LeStar

Market Development Manager: Kyle Zimmerman

Rights Acquisitions Specialist: Jennifer Meyer Dare

Manufacturing Planner: Fola Orekoya

Art and Design Direction, Production Management, and Composition: PreMediaGlobal

Cover Image: Shutterstock

Cover Designer: Riezebos Holzbaur/ Tim Heraldo

For product information and technology assistance, contact us at **Cengage Learning Customer & Sales Support, 1-800-354-9706.**

For permission to use material from this text or product, submit all requests online at **www.cengage.com/permissions**. Further permissions questions can be emailed to **permissionrequest@cengage.com**.

Library of Congress Control Number: 2012951454

ISBN-13: 978-1-133-60725-0

ISBN-10: 1-133-60725-X

Wadsworth
20 Channel Center Street
Boston, MA 02210
USA

Cengage Learning is a leading provider of customized learning solutions with office locations around the globe, including Singapore, the United Kingdom, Australia, Mexico, Brazil, and Japan. Locate your local office at **international .cengage.com/region**.

Cengage Learning products are represented in Canada by **Nelson Education, Ltd.**

For your course and learning solutions, visit **www.cengage.com**.

Purchase any of our products at your local college store or at our preferred online store **www.cengagebrain.com**.

Instructors: Please visit **login.cengage.com** and log in to access instructor-specific resources.

Printed in the United States of America
1 2 3 4 5 6 7 16 15 14 13 12

CONTENTS

TO THE STUDENT

In assigning this book, your instructor wants to do more than teach you the basics of government in the United States. This book has a bit of attitude and a central theme: Only a tiny number of people make the decisions that shape our lives, and, despite the elaborate rituals of parties, elections, and interest-group activity, the vast majority have little direct influence over these decisions. This theme is widely known as *elitism*. Your instructor may not believe completely in this theory but may instead believe that many groups of people share power in the United States, that competition is widespread, that we have checks against the abuse of power, and that the individual citizen can personally affect the course of national events by voting, supporting political parties, and joining interest groups. That theory, widely known as *pluralism*, characterizes virtually every U.S. government textbook now in print—except this one. Your instructor, whether personally agreeing with the elitist or with the pluralist perspective, is challenging you to confront our arguments. He or she wants you to deal critically with some troubling questions about democracy in the United States.

It is far easier to teach the basics of government in the United States—the constitutional powers of the president, Congress, and courts; the function of parties and interest groups; the key cases decided by the Supreme Court; and so on—than to tackle the question, "How democratic is U.S. society?" It is easier to teach the "facts" of the political system than to search for the explanations. Although this book does not ignore such facts, its primary purpose is to present them to you through the critical lens of elite theory—to help you understand why government and politics work as they do.

The Irony of Democracy is not some polemic or even necessarily "antiestablishment." This book challenges the prevailing pluralistic view of democracy in the United States, but it neither condemns nor endorses the reality of political life. Governance by a small, homogeneous elite is subject to favorable or unfavorable interpretation, according to one's personal values. Readers are free to decide for themselves whether we as a society should preserve, reform, or restructure the political system described in these pages. If this book encourages thought about this question, we see it as a success.

The Irony of Democracy is neither a conservative nor a liberal textbook. It does not apologize for elite rule or seek to defend U.S. institutions or any of its leaders. On the contrary, we are critical of politicians, bureaucrats, corporate chieftains, media moguls, lobbyists, and special interests. But we do not advocate fruitless liberal nostrums promising to bring "power to the people" or "citizen movements" that are themselves led by elites with their own self-interests. We note that partisans are happy with the parts of the book that describe their opponents, but unhappy when the same gaze is cast on those they favor. Tough!

The Irony of Democracy is indeed an endorsement of the most fundamental democratic values—individual dignity, limited government, freedom of expression and dissent, equality of opportunity, private property, and due process of law. Our elitist theory of democracy is not an attack on democratic government but rather an effort to understand the realities of politics in a democracy.

TO THE INSTRUCTOR

This 16th edition of *The Irony of Democracy* has two aims: to keep its vigorous classic elite theory approach and to reflect an ever-changing politics. This new edition unapologetically continues to assert that to understand democracy in the United States it is necessary to understand the elites who run the nation. There may be a near-universal acceptance of pluralist ideology in U.S. political science and government texts; that Noble Lie of the empowered masses certainly contains significant truth, but *The Irony of Democracy* unrepentantly remains an elitist introduction to U.S. government. Elite theory is used as an analytic model for understanding and explaining U.S. politics; it is *not* presented as a normative prescription for the nation. The discomfort caused by this approach in instructors or students stems from its being grounded in fact and observation of reality, not in idealism.

Few today still believe that government is run for the benefit of the people. Most see the political system as run by a few big interests for their own benefit, leaving the average person forgotten behind. This reality brings us no pleasure. Over the course of the 43 years of this text's publication, the situation has only gotten worse. Our elitist theory of democracy also recognizes the potential for danger in mass movements and intolerant demagogues. Mass ignorance and apathy do not inspire much hope that "the people" will somehow suddenly gain some newfound commitment to the hard work of democracy. The irony of democracy in the United States is that somehow democracy survives despite and possibly because of these conditions.

This book has provided a framework to understand U.S. politics for over four decades. It has seen many political events and eras come and go: the war in Vietnam, Watergate, Carter-era inflation, the collapse of communism, the rise of globalization, a balanced federal budget for four years, the influx of once unimaginable amounts of money into campaigns, mass death from terrorism, and the wars in Iraq and Afghanistan. Still, the basic analytic model of staying focused on those in power remains critically necessary.

This edition reflects the growing role of the new coauthor to the text who joined last edition: Louis Schubert of City College of San Francisco, a very large, diverse, community college. His affection for the text and its project are deep, and many changes in this new edition reflect him having taught thousands of students using this text for over a decade. He brings fresh blood and new areas of interest to *Irony*, but it is worth noting that the first change he insisted on was restoring material from the first edition. He sees its classic focus as the key to its continuing relevance to political science and usefulness to teaching the politics of the United States.

Each chapter in this new edition has seen updating and improvement. It reflects the consolidation of the major revision begun last edition and the input of reviewers and hundreds of students. Chapter 1, the introduction to elite theory, has clearer presentation of the connection between elitism and pluralism. Chapter 2, concerning the Founders, has added attention to the classical liberal and classical conservative traditions from which they drew. Chapter 3 follows the evolution of U.S. elites, starting with Hamilton's financial vision for the new nation and adding significant new focus on the New Deal and the impact of the expansion of government on the nature of elite power. It includes a new Focus section on the role of hedge funds. Chapter 4, on the masses, gives credit for developments in tolerance over recent decades, but still recognizes the dominance of apathy and ignorance.

The media chapter, Chapter 5, has been revised to reflect the reality of current technology. Just a few decades ago, media required access to considerable capital to reach an audience of any size; now students are publishing to global audiences online with their cell phones (sometimes even during class). The role of social media has been integrated throughout. Chapter 6, on elections and political parties, continues the necessary focus on money in campaigns, the role of the parties, and updates including the 2010 congressional and 2012 presidential races. Speaking of money, Chapter 7 focuses on organized interests and their activities such as lobbying and funding campaigns to attempt to influence the political elites.

Each chapter on political institutions has been updated to reflect a changing Congress, the Obama administration, and a Supreme Court including Justices Sotomayor and Kagan. The sections on lawmaking have been rewritten to better show the "sausage making" nature of the entire process; the introduction to legislation is now called "Kill Bill" to reflect that Congress is far better at preventing laws than making them. The continuing diversification of the Congress is also covered. The impact of President Barack Obama and coverage of his White House has also been added.

Chapter 11 reflects the increased role of the bureaucracy in the political system in a time of a significantly larger government with some vastly greater roles. Chapter 12, federalism, has been revised to include more discussion on the state initiative process and highlights some rising political stars, Newark Mayor Cory Booker and Louisiana Governor Bobby Jindal. It also addresses the tension between the federal and state governments over health care.

Civil rights, Chapter 13, showcases the rapid diversification of the elite in both politics and the economy. The exclusion of minorities and women from power was once a major theme in the study of the elite—now the theme must be the continually growing impact of persons who 40 years ago would have had little if any chance to hold power positions. From the presidency, to governors' mansions, to the corporate boardroom, substantive and qualitative change has occurred in the composition of the elites. This chapter has also been revised to give greater attention to the civil rights of Hispanic-Americans, Asian-Americans, multiracial persons, and gays and lesbians, as well as updated coverage of African-Americans and women.

The last chapter, "The United States as Global Elite," deals with the fact that the United States holds an unprecedented position in the world. It leads economically and militarily, but the cost of functioning as hegemon and "global cop" has led to significant vulnerabilities as well. This chapter covers the role of the United States in the world political system, examines its current security threats, and shows the place of the United States in a globalized economy. New coverage of drone warfare has been added.

We believe that the strength of this textbook comes from its honest presentation of the world as it is, not as how one may wish it. Punches are not pulled, awkward areas are not avoided, and credit is given where it is due even if it is a difficult fit with the central elite theory theme. The text does not talk down to students. Suggestions to "dumb down" vocabulary have been respectfully declined. The Epilogue does not end the book with a warm, fuzzy feeling, but rather gives students some blunt advice on how to preserve democratic values in an elitist system and maybe in the process keep themselves from being rolled over by the elites. We are not concerned if students like this book, but we do hope they find it interesting and have some good arguments with it. For the instructor, whether you agree with the basic elitist approach or not, we hope this text helps get your pedagogical juices flowing and that it makes your classroom experience more enjoyable and rewarding through keeping you and your students intellectually and perhaps emotionally engaged in the wonderful world of U.S. politics.

Louis Schubert
Thomas R. Dye
Harmon Zeigler, Late

ACKNOWLEDGMENTS

In particular, we thank the following reviewers who provided useful comments and suggestions for the sixteenth edition:
Robert Porter, *Ventura College*
Bob Peter, *Tri-County Technical College*
Peter Davies, *California State University, Sacramento*

SUPPLEMENTS FOR INSTRUCTORS

CourseReader

CourseReader: American Government 0-30 Selections
- Printed Access Card ISBN-13: 9781111479954
- Instant Access Code ISBN-13: 9781111479978
- CourseReader: American Government allows you to create your reader, your way, in just minutes. This affordable, fully customizable online reader provides access to thousands of permissions-cleared readings, articles, primary sources, and audio and video selections from the regularly updated Gale research library database. This easy-to-use solution allows you to search for and select just the material you want for your courses.

Each selection opens with a descriptive introduction to provide context, and concludes with critical-thinking and multiple-choice questions to reinforce key points. CourseReader is loaded with convenient tools like highlighting, printing, note-taking, and downloadable MP3 audio files for each reading.

CourseReader is the perfect complement to any Political Science course. It can be bundled with your current textbook, sold alone, or integrated into your learning management system. CourseReader 0-30 allows access to up to 30 selections in the reader.

Please contact your Cengage sales representative for details or for a demo please visit us at **www.cengage.com/coursereader**. To access CourseReader materials go to **www.cengage.com/sso**, click on "Create a New Faculty Account," and fill out the registration page. Once you are in your new SSO account, search for "CourseReader" from your dashboard and select "Course Reader: American Government." Then click "CourseReader 0-30: American Government Instant Access Code" and click "Add to my bookshelf." To access the live CourseReader, click on "CourseReader 0-30: American Government" under "Additional resources" on the right side of your dashboard.

Custom Enrichment Module: Latino-American Politics Supplement
- ISBN-13: 9781285184296
- This revised and updated 32-page supplement uses real examples to detail politics related to Latino Americans and can be added to your text via our custom publishing solutions.

Election 2012: An American Government Supplement
- Printed Access Card ISBN-13: 9781285090931
- Instant Access Code ISBN-13: 9781285420080
- Written by John Clark and Brian Schaffner, this booklet addresses the 2012 congressional and presidential races, with real-time analysis and references.

Free Instructor Companion Website for *The Irony of Democracy*, 16e
- ISBN-13: 9781285058610
- This password-protected website for instructors features all of the free student assets plus an instructor's manual, book-specific PowerPoint® presentations, JoinIn™ "clicker" questions, and a test bank. Access your resources by logging into your account at **www.cengage.com/login**.

The Wadsworth News DVD for American Government 2014
- ISBN: 9781285053455
- This collection of two- to five-minute video clips on relevant political issues serves as a great lecture or discussion launcher.

Government is always government by the few, whether in the name of the few, the one, or the many.

—Harold Lasswell

THE IRONY OF DEMOCRACY

Elites—not masses—govern the United States. Life in U.S. democracy, as in all societies, is shaped by a tiny fraction of the population. Major political, economic, and social decisions are made by this elite minority, not by the masses of people.

Elites are the few who have power; the masses are the many who do not. Power is deciding who gets what, when, and how. Power is meaningful participation in the decisions that shape our lives. The masses are the many whose lives are shaped by institutions, events, and leaders over which they have little direct control. Political scientist Harold Lasswell wrote, "The division of society into elite and mass is universal," and even in a democracy "a few exercise a relatively great weight of power, and the many exercise comparatively little."[1]

Elite theory, or elitism, is an approach to describing society focusing on the few with power, their values, their behavior, and their demographics. Elite theory is not a normative endorsement of elite rule, nor is it an automatic dismissal of it. Elites are not necessarily conspiracies to oppress and exploit the masses. On the contrary, they may be deeply concerned with the welfare of the masses. This is especially true in democracies. Membership in the elite increasingly is open to ambitious and talented individuals from the masses, exemplified by leaders such as Barack Obama and Bill Gates, though it sometimes may still appear a closed group. Elites may compete with each other, or they may largely agree over the direction of domestic and foreign policy. Elites may be responsive to the demands of the masses and influenced by the outcomes of elections or public demands, or they may be unresponsive to mass movements and unaffected by elections. Still, whether elites are public-minded or self-serving, open or closed, competitive or consensual, unified or pluralistic, responsive or unresponsive, it is elites and not the masses who govern the modern nation. *How* elites rule is a separate discussion from the fact that they always do rule.

Democracy is government "by the people," but the responsibility for the survival of democracy rests on the shoulders of elites. This is the irony of democracy: Elites must govern wisely if government "by the people" is to survive. If the survival of the U.S. system depended on an active, informed, and enlightened citizenry, then democracy in the United States would have disappeared long ago, for the masses normally are apathetic and ill-informed about politics and public policy, and they exhibit a surprisingly weak commitment to democratic values—individual dignity, equality of opportunity, the right to dissent, freedom of speech and press, religious toleration, and due process of law. Fortunately for these values and for U.S. democracy, the masses do not lead; they follow. They respond to the attitudes, proposals, and behavior of elites. The abolition of slavery, civil rights for minorities, and religious freedom did not arise because of mass demand—elites led the United States to these important places.

Although the symbols of U.S. politics are drawn from democratic political thought, we can often better understand the reality of U.S. politics from the viewpoint of elite theory. The questions posed by elite theory are the vital questions of politics: Who governs the United States? What are the roles of elites and masses in U.S. politics? How do people acquire power? What is the relationship between economic and political power? How open and accessible are elite ranks? How do U.S. elites change over time? How widely is power shared in the United States? How much real competition takes place among elites? What is the basis of elite consensus? How do elites and masses differ? How responsive are elites to mass sentiments? How much influence do masses have over policies decided by elites?

This book, *The Irony of Democracy*, explains U.S. political life using elite theory. It presents evidence from U.S. political history and contemporary political science describing and explaining how elites function in a modern democratic society. But before we examine U.S. politics, we must understand more about *elitism, democracy*, and *pluralism*.

THE MEANING OF ELITISM

The central idea of elitism is that all societies are divided into two classes: the few who govern and the many who are governed. Italian political scientist Gaetano Mosca expressed this basic concept as follows:

> In all societies—from societies that are very underdeveloped and have largely attained the dawnings of civilization, down to the most advanced and powerful societies—two classes of people appear—a class that rules and a class that is ruled. The first class, always the less numerous, performs all of the political functions, monopolizes power, and enjoys the advantages that power brings, whereas the second, the more numerous class, is directed and controlled by the first, in a manner that is now more or less legal, now more or less arbitrary and violent.[2]

Elites are not a product particular to capitalism or socialism or industrialization or technological development. They govern all societies—democracies and dictatorships, capitalist and socialist, monarchies and theocracies, developing and industrialized. All societies require leaders, and leaders acquire a stake in preserving the organization and their position in it. This motive gives them a perspective different from that of the organization's members. That an elite is inevitable in any social organization is known in political science as the **Iron Law of Oligarchy**.

French political scientist Roberto Michels stated this thesis: "He who says organization, says oligarchy."[3] The "law" holds true for all sizes of organizations, whether family, club, religious congregation, union, business, or society as a whole. In all these, there are the few who hold power and the many who do not.

Elitism also asserts that the few who govern are not typical of the masses who are governed. Elites by definition control resources: power, wealth, education, prestige, status, skills of leadership, information, knowledge of political processes, ability to communicate, and organization. Elites in the United States are drawn disproportionately from wealthy, educated, prestigiously employed, and socially prominent elements of society. This has historically meant that elites were overwhelmingly European-American (or white), Anglo-Saxon, Protestant, and male, although it is clear today that the demographic diversity of the elite is changing significantly. Elites come disproportionately from society's increasingly diverse upper classes, those whose families already network with leaders of economic, professional, and governmental institutions.

Elitism, however, does not necessarily bar individuals of the lower or middle classes from rising to the top. In a democracy, upward mobility is encouraged—the system needs "fresh blood." The term for persons of nonelite origins entering the ranks of the elite is **circulation of elites,** and it is essential for the stability of the elite system. Openness in the system siphons off potentially revolutionary leadership from the lower classes; moreover, an elite system is strengthened when talented and ambitious individuals from the masses enter governing circles. However, social stability requires that movement from nonelite to elite positions be a slow, continuous assimilation rather than a rapid or revolutionary change. Only those nonelites who have demonstrated their commitment to the elite system itself and to the system's political and economic values can be admitted to the ruling class.

Elites share a general consensus about the fundamental norms of the social system. As individuals, they focus on maintaining or enhancing their position as elite. As a group, they agree on the basic rules of the game and on the importance of preserving the political and social system in which they thrive. The system has clearly worked well for them. The stability of the system, even its survival, depends on this consensus by those who have been most successful within the system. Political scientist David Truman writes that elites have "a special stake in the continuation of the system in which their privileges rest."[4] However, elite consensus does not prevent elite members from disagreeing or competing with each other for preeminence. But this competition takes place within a narrow range of issues; elites agree on more matters than they disagree on. Disagreement usually occurs over *means* rather than *ends*.

In the United States, the bases of elite consensus are the sanctity of individual liberty, private property, and limited government. Political historian Richard Hofstadter wrote about U.S. elite struggles:

> The fierceness of political struggles has often been misleading; for the range of vision embodied by the primary contestants in the major parties has always been bounded by the horizons of property and enterprise. However much at odds on specific issues, the major political traditions have shared a belief in the rights of property, the philosophy of economic individualism, the value of competition; they have accepted the economic virtues of capitalist culture as necessary qualities of man.[5]

C. Wright Mills
Website devoted to the works of the author of the classic book on elitism in the United States, *The Power Elite* (1956). *www.cwrightmills.org*

America's Most Wealthy
Wealth is not always a measure of power. But *Forbes* magazine annually lists the richest people and the sources of their wealth. *www.forbes.com*

IN BRIEF | ELITE THEORY

incremental

- Society is divided into the few who have power, called elites, and the many who do not, called masses.
- Elites are not typical of the masses who are governed. Elites are drawn disproportionately from the upper socioeconomic strata of society. The movement of nonelites to elite positions is necessary but must be slow and continuous to maintain stability and avoid revolution. Only nonelites who have accepted the basic elite consensus enter governing circles. Elites share a consensus on the basic values of the social system and the preservation of the system. They disagree only on a narrow range of issues.

- Public policy reflects not the demands of the masses but the prevailing values of the elite. Changes in public policy will be incremental rather than revolutionary.
- Elites may act out of narrow self-serving motives and risk undermining mass support, or they may initiate reforms, curb abuse, and undertake public-regarding programs to preserve the system and their place in it.
- Active elites are subject to relatively little direct influence from the apathetic masses. Elites influence the masses more than the masses influence elites.

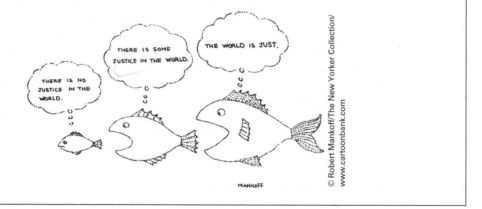

© Robert Mankoff/The New Yorker Collection/ www.cartoonbank.com

Elitism implies that public policy does not reflect demands of "the people" so much as it reflects the interests and values of elites. Changes and innovations in public policy come as elite values slowly evolve to adapt to new challenges to system stability, often caused by new technologies or external events. However, elite interest in preserving the system means that changes in public policy normally will be *incremental* rather than revolutionary. Public policies are often modified but seldom replaced.

Elites may act out of narrow self-serving interests or enlightened, "public-regarding" motives. Occasionally elites abuse their powers and position and undermine mass confidence in their leadership. This threatens the system and requires a punitive response by other members of the elite who are more focused on preserving the system. Unethical business executives get fired for violating the rules, politicians are impeached for breaking their oath to uphold the law, and union officials are expelled for corruption. At other times, elites initiate reforms designed to preserve the system and restore mass support. Elitism does not necessarily mean that the masses are exploited or repressed, although these abuses are not uncommon, especially outside democracies. Elitism means only that the responsibility for mass welfare rests with elites, not with masses.

Finally, elitism assumes that the masses are largely passive, apathetic, and ill-informed. Mass sentiments are manipulated by elites more often than elite values are influenced by the sentiments of the masses. More communication between elites and masses flows downward than upward. Masses seldom make decisions about governmental policies through elections or through thoughtful evaluation of political parties' policy alternatives. For the most part, these "democratic" institutions—elections and parties—have only symbolic value: They help tie the masses to the political system by giving them a ritual role to play on Election Day. Elitism contends that the masses have at best only an indirect influence over the decision-making behavior of elites.

Naturally, elitism is frequently misunderstood in the United States because the prevailing myths and symbols of the U.S. system are drawn from democratic theory rather than elite theory. So let us sum up here what elitism is *not*. Elitism does not mean those who have power are continually locked in conflict with the masses or that powerholders always achieve their goals at the expense of the public interest. Elitism in a democracy is not a conspiracy to oppress the masses, although that myth is common among extremists on the right and left. Elitism does not imply that powerholders constitute a single impenetrable monolithic body or that they always agree on public issues. Elitism does not pretend that power in society does not shift over time and that new elites do not emerge to compete with old elites. Power need not rest exclusively on the control of economic resources but may rest instead upon other leadership resources—organization, communication, or information. Lastly, elitism does not imply that masses have no impact on the attitudes of elites, only that elites influence masses more than masses influence elites.

THE MEANING OF DEMOCRACY

While the term **democracy** has been used in different ways throughout history, at its core it refers to popular participation in the allocation of values in a society. (The Greek roots *demos* and *kratos* translate to "people" and "rule," respectively.) The ruled and the rulers are the same. The Founders looked to classical understandings of the concept of democracy, where the term was used by the Greek political philosopher Aristotle[6] as describing a corrupt form of government in which the masses ruled in their self-interest and not in the interest of the country. The term *demos* was more a synonym for "mob." The modern term *democracy* conflates its negative original meaning with the positive form of government called *polity* (or in Latin, *republic*). We can account for at least some of the ironic gap between the United States as an elite-run political system and the ideals of democracy in the common misunderstanding of the term "democracy" itself. Chapter 2 will clarify this further.

The underlying value in almost any modern understanding of democracy is individual dignity. Traditionally, democratic theory has valued popular participation in politics as an opportunity for individual self-development through civic virtue: Responsibility for governing our own conduct develops character, self-reliance, intelligence, and moral judgment—in short, dignity. The ancients of

Athens and Rome saw political participation as virtuous, or necessary to becoming a good person. The classic democrat would reject even a benevolent despot who could govern in the interest of the masses, as that would deny the opportunity to participate. As the English political philosopher John Stuart Mill asked, "What development can either their thinking or active faculties attain under it?" Thus the argument for citizen participation in public affairs depends not on its policy outcomes but on the belief that it is essential to the full development of human capacities. Ideally, democracy means individual participation in the decisions that affect our lives. Mill argued that people can know truth only by discovering it for themselves.[7]

Procedurally, a democratic society achieves popular participation through majority rule and respect for the rights of minorities. Self-development presumes self-government, and self-government comes about only by encouraging each individual to contribute to the development of public policy and by resolving conflicts over public policy through majority rule. Minorities who have had the opportunity to influence policy but whose views have not won majority support accept the decisions of majorities because of the fairness and openness of the democratic procedure. In return, majorities permit minorities to attempt openly to win majority support for their views. Freedom of speech and press, freedom to dissent, and freedom to form opposition parties and organizations are essential to ensure meaningful individual participation. This freedom of expression is also critical in ascertaining the majority's real views.

Classical liberal theory became the modern expression of democratic theory for the Founders and their European influences. Originally, democratic equality came out of the Biblical idea of humans created in the image of the divine and thus having intrinsic rights and dignity. Human beings, by virtue of their existence, are entitled to life, liberty, and property. A "natural law," or moral tenet, guarantees every person liberty and the right to property, and this natural law is morally superior to human law. John Locke, the English political philosopher whose writings most influenced the United States' founding elites, argued that even in a "state of nature"—that is, a world of no governments—an individual possesses inalienable rights to life, liberty, and property. Locke meant that these rights are independent of government; governments do not give them to individuals, and no government may legitimately take them away.[8]

U.S. State Department Bureau of Democracy, Human Rights, and Labor Official U.S. government definitions of democracy and individual rights. *www.state. gov/g/drl/*

IN BRIEF | DEMOCRATIC THEORY

Democratic theory proposes:

- Popular participation in the decisions that shape the lives of individuals in a society.
- Government by majority rule, with recognition of the rights of minorities to try to become majorities. These rights include the freedoms of speech, press, assembly, and petition as well as the freedoms to dissent, to form opposition parties, and to run for public office.
- A commitment to individual dignity and the preservation of the classical liberal values of life, liberty, and property.
- A commitment to equal opportunity for all individuals to develop their capacities through political participation.

Locke

Locke believed that a government's purpose is to protect individual liberty. People form a "social contract" with one another to establish a government to help protect their rights; they tacitly agree to accept government authority to protect life, liberty, and property. Property has been of particular importance as it provides economic self-sufficiency, rather than a child-like, feudal dependence on the government. Implicit in the social contract and the democratic notion of freedom is the belief that social control over the individual must be minimal. Classical liberal theory sees government as a major threat to human freedom, and governmental authority must be limited. These beliefs call for removing as many external restrictions, controls, and regulations on the individual as possible without harming the freedom of other citizens.

Another vital aspect of classical democracy is a belief in the equality of all people. The Declaration of Independence states that "all men are created equal." Even the Founding Fathers believed that all persons had **equality before the law**, regardless of their personal circumstances. A democratic society's legal system cannot judge a person by social position, economic class, creed, or race. The law should treat all fairly without advantage. Political equality is expressed in the concept of "one person, one vote."

In the United States, the notion of equality has come to include **equality of opportunity** in many aspects of life: social, educational, economic, and, of course, political. Each person should have a reasonably equal chance to develop his or her capacities to the fullest potential. There should be no artificial barriers to the pursuit of happiness or success in life, however each individual may define it. All persons should have the opportunity to make of themselves what they can, to develop their talents and abilities to their fullest, and to be rewarded for their skills, knowledge, initiative, and hard work. Democratic theory has always stressed equality of opportunity over "equality of outcome," which by seeking conformity of result denies the individual right to choose one's goals and happiness.

ELITISM IN A DEMOCRACY

Founders

Democracy requires popular participation in government. To our nation's Founders, whose classical educations included an ambivalence about the wisdom of democracy, it meant the people would have representation in government. The Founders believed government rests ultimately on the *consent* of the governed. Their notion of republicanism envisioned decision making by representatives of the people, rather than direct decision making by the people themselves. These representatives would be expected to use their prudence and wisdom to make decisions based on what was in the best interests of the masses. The Founders were profoundly skeptical of direct democracy, in which the people initiate and decide policy questions by popular vote. They had read about direct democracy in the ancient Greek city-state of Athens, and they were fearful of the "follies" of democracy. James Madison wrote,

> Such democracies have ever been spectacles of turbulence and contention; have ever been found incompatible with personal security of the rights of property and have in general been as short in their lives as they have been violent in their deaths.[9]

Freedom House
Dedicated to expanding freedom worldwide. Provides measures of freedom and classifies nations as "free," "partly free," and "not free." *www.freedomhouse.org*

ISSUES WITH DIRECT DEMOCRACY

Even if it were desirable, mass government is not feasible in a large society. Abraham Lincoln's rhetorical flourish—"a government of the people, by the people, for the people"—has no real-world meaning. What would "the people" look like if all U.S. citizens were brought together in one place?

> Standing shoulder to shoulder in military formation, they would occupy an area of about sixty-six square miles. The logistical problem of bringing [300] million bodies together is trivial, however, compared with the task of bringing about a meeting of [300] million minds. Merely to shake hands with that many people would take a century. How much discussion would it take to form a common opinion? A single round of five-minute speeches would require five thousand years. If only one percent of those present spoke, the assembly would be forced to listen to over two million speeches. People could be born, grow old and die while they waited for the assembly to make one decision.
>
> In other words, an all-American town meeting would be the largest, longest, and most boring and frustrating meeting imaginable. What could such a meeting produce? Total paralysis. What could it do? Nothing.[10]

The U.S. Constitution has no provision for national popular referenda. Only a century later did political support develop in some states for more direct involvement of citizens in policy-making through initiative and referendum. Today voters in only about half the states can express their frustrations with elite governance directly through these mechanisms. The **initiative** is a device whereby a specified number or percentage of voters, through the use of a petition, may have a proposed measure placed on the ballot for adoption or rejection by the electorate of a state. This process bypasses the legislature and allows citizens to propose both state laws and state constitutional amendments. The initiative measures that pass sometimes may hold the elite more accountable and enhance democracy; other times they may circumvent elite efforts to protect democratic values (more on this in Chapter 12). The **referendum** is a device by which the electorate must approve decisions of the legislature before these become law or become part of the state constitution or by which the electorate must approve of proposals placed on the ballot by popular initiative. Voters in 18 states can **recall** elected officials—petition for an election to decide whether or not an incumbent official should be ousted from office before the end of his or her term.[11]

REPRESENTATIVE DEMOCRACY AND ELITES

The Founders were most fearful that unrestrained *majorities* would threaten liberty and property and abuse minorities and individuals, "the weaker party and the obnoxious individual." James Madison framed this concern in *Federalist Paper #10* (see Chapter 2). The Founders recognized the warning found in the classical understanding of the term democracy—that government by majority rule can threaten the life, liberty, and property of minorities and individuals. They saw the notion that a majority must be right simply because it is a majority as logically flawed and historically disproved. The solution to the practical problem of popular government is rule not by the masses but with the consent of the masses through the development

| FOCUS | MASS DISTRUST OF THE U.S. ELITE |

How much trust do the masses have in U.S. leadership? Public opinion polls show a generally declining willingness of the people to "trust the government in Washington to do what is right" (see figure). Defeat and humiliation in war or foreign affairs undermines mass support for a nation's leadership, as seen in the Vietnam War, Iran hostage crisis, or Iraqi occupation, while success such as the Gulf War victory in 1991 can produce greater trust. U.S. adults traditionally "rally 'round the flag" when confronted with serious national threats, such as following the terrorist attacks of September 11, 2001, when mass trust in government skyrocketed to levels not seen since the 1960s.

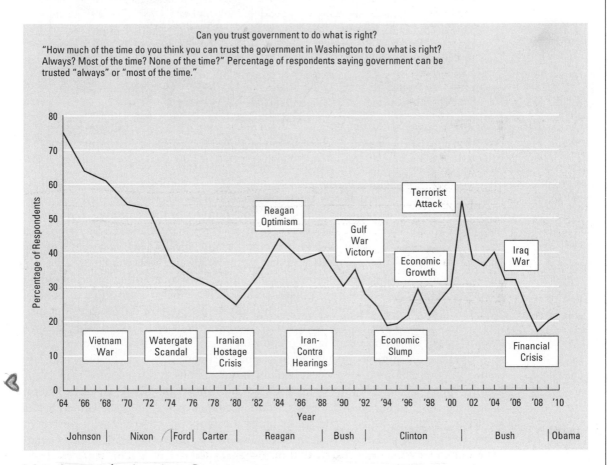

Mass Support for American Government

Source: Prepared by the authors from National Election Surveys, University of Michigan, data. Data from 1996 onward from various polls reported in *The Polling Report*, Washington, D.C.

Documents of U.S. Democracy
Core documents defining U.S. democracy at the official site of the U.S. Government Printing Office. *www.gpo.gov/fdsys/*

of institutions of representation—elections, parties, organized interest groups—as bridges between individuals and their government. This solution is rooted in a commitment to protect democratic values from "the tyranny of the majority," but it leads inevitably to elitism. In U.S. democracy, political elites may be chosen by the masses through elections, but they are no less elite because of this. We can think of the democratic process in the United States as the popular selection of political elites.

Power is the ability to influence people and events by granting or withholding valuable resources. To exercise power, someone must be in a position to control valuable resources. We define resources broadly to include not only wealth but also position, status, celebrity, comfort, safety, and power itself. Most of the nation's resources are concentrated in large organizations and institutions—in corporations and financial institutions; in media; in organized interest groups, lobbies, and law firms; in foundations and policy planning organizations ("think tanks"); in labor unions; in civic and cultural organizations; and, most important, in government. While the classical liberal distrust of government has meant that in the United States a thriving and powerful private sector limits the scope of government, government remains the most powerful of all these organizations, not only because it has accumulated great economic resources but also because it has a monopoly on legal coercion. Only government can legitimately tax, imprison, and execute people.

Elite Competition as the Basis of Pluralism

In a democratic society, unlike a totalitarian one, multiple elites exist. A defining characteristic of democratic nations is the **relative autonomy of elites**, that each segment of the elite is relatively independent of the others and is able to pursue its own interests, whether those elites are governmental, economic, media, civic,

IN BRIEF	WHY ELITISM PREVAILS IN A DEMOCRACY

Founders

- The Founders believed in republicanism—decision making by representatives of the people on behalf of the people, not the people themselves. The democratic process is the popular selection of political elites.
- There is no provision for national referendum, although some states allow initiative, referendum, and recall voting.

- Direct individual participation in decision making by 300+ million people is not possible.
- Decision making by representatives inevitably leads to elitism—the "Iron Law of Oligarchy."
- Democratic values can be preserved only by multiple competitive elites—the media, parties, interest groups, corporations, unions, and other independent institutions.

cultural, and so on.[12] In contrast, a defining characteristic of societies without freedom is the idea that no power should exist outside the unified, elite-run state. Fascism, such as in Nazi Germany or Baathist Iraq, asserts the unity of the state under its leader. Marxism, such as in Cuba or North Korea, asserts government as a "dictatorship of the proletariat" run by a party elite with control of economic as well as political resources. Elites exist in all political systems, but the ability of a society to limit the elite capacity for corruption and violations of human rights resides most strongly in democracies.

In democracies, the relative autonomy of elites exists because elites have multiple institutional bases of power. Not all power is lodged in government, nor is all power derived from wealth. Democracies legitimize the existence of opposition parties and of organized interest groups, which have the freedom to promote alternative policies. The power and independence of a media elite is a distinctive feature of U.S. democracy. Even within U.S. government, relatively autonomous multiple elites were hardwired into the system or have emerged—in Congress, in the judiciary, in the executive, and even within the executive, in a variety of bureaucratic domains. But it is really the power and autonomy of nongovernmental elites—media, corporate, financial, labor, legal, civic, interest groups, and so on—and their recognized and protected legitimacy that distinguishes the elite structures of democratic nations from those of states lacking freedom.

Our discussion of elitism and democracy raises several vital questions: Is power in the United States concentrated in the hands of a small elite, with the masses permanently barred from power? Or is it diffused, with many separate elites exercising power from time to time? Is there a convergence at the top of the U.S. power structure, with a single group dominating decision making in industry, finance, foreign policy, military affairs, and domestic programs? Or are there separate elites in each area of decision making? Do elite members in the United States compete with each other over major questions of public policy? Or do they share a consensus about the direction of public policy and disagree only on minor details? Can masses, through competitive elections and media watchfulness, hold elites accountable for their policy decisions, or are elites free from mass influence?

Social scientists recognize at least two major models of elitism that answer these questions. The **ruling elite model** views power as concentrated in the hands of relatively few people, usually drawn from the corporate, financial, military, and governmental circles, who make the key decisions in all significant areas of life and who are subject to little influence from the masses. In contrast, the **plural elite model** views power as more widely shared among leadership groups representing different segments of society; these separate elites are competitive and are held responsible by the masses through elections, party competition, and interest groups. This is the predominant model for the United States. Pluralism, unlike elitism, focuses on the creation and function of the many groups in society.

THE MEANING OF PLURALISM

No scholar or commentator, however optimistic about life in the United States, would assert that the U.S. political system has fully realized all of the goals of democracy. No one contends that citizens participate in all decisions shaping their lives or that majority preferences always prevail. Nor does anyone argue that the system always protects the rights of minorities; always preserves the values of life, liberty, and property; or always provides every citizen with an equal opportunity to influence public policy. These are ideals toward which the nation has made phenomenal progress, but which it may never perfectly achieve.

Pluralism is the belief that democratic values can be preserved in a system where multiple, competing elites determine public policy through bargaining and compromise, voters exercise meaningful choices in elections, and new elites can gain access to power. But we should not consider pluralism synonymous with democracy, for it does not include *direct* citizen participation in decision making. Pluralists recognize that mass participation in decision making is not possible in a complex post-industrial society and that decision making must be accomplished through elite interaction, rather than individual participation. However, the underlying value of individual dignity still motivates pluralism, for it is the hope of pluralists that countervailing centers of elite power—the competition between business elites, labor elites, and governmental elites—can check each other and keep each interest from abusing its power or oppressing the individual.

Pluralism seeks to affirm that U.S. society is democratic. Pluralist theory begins with the idea that each individual develops as a person by having multiple, or plural, interests.[13] These may be political, social, cultural, ethnic, religious, or situational, but when individuals are able to express their interests (which requires freedom of expression), they can then connect with other individuals to form associations or interest groups based on shared interests (which requires freedom of assembly). These groups will then inevitably generate leaders, but this creates a wellspring of elites that arises from the expression of individual interests.

HOW ELITISM AND PLURALISM DIFFER

Elite theory differs from the prevailing pluralist vision of democracy in several fundamental respects. Both theories agree that societal decision making occurs through elite interaction, not mass participation; that the key political actors are the leaders of large organizations and institutions, not individual citizens; and that public policy generally reflects the interests of large organizations and institutions, not majority preferences. The primary disagreement is not about the facts, but more about which is the better perspective from which to view them: top-down or bottom-up.

First of all, elite theory asserts that the most important division in society is between elites and masses, between the few who govern and the many who do not. Pluralism overlooks this central division of society into elites and masses and emphasizes instead the division and fragmentation of society into interests, and subsequent competition between leadership groups. Elitism emphasizes the importance to leaders of maintaining their positions of power, whereas pluralism emphasizes their devotion to their group interests.

Reflecting the Iron Law of Oligarchy, elite theory asserts that the mass membership of organizations, parties, interest groups, and institutions in society rarely exercises any direct control over the elite leadership. Group membership does *not* ensure effective individual participation in decision making. While corporations, unions, armies, churches, governmental bureaucracies, or professional associations may have internal democratic mechanisms, they are usually run by a small elite of officers and activists. The pluralists offer no evidence that the giant organizations and institutions in U.S. life really represent the views or interests of their individual members, beyond merely that individual membership in a group indicates interest.

Elite theory suggests that accommodation and compromise among leadership groups is the prevailing style of decision making, not competition and conflict. Pluralism contends that competition among leadership groups protects the individual. But why should we assume that leadership groups compete with each other? More likely, each elite group allows other elite groups to govern in their own spheres of influence without interference. According to elite theory, accommodation rather than competition is the prevailing style of elite interaction: "You scratch my back and I'll scratch yours."

Elite theory takes account of *all* powerholders in society, private as well as public, economic as well as political. Pluralism tends to focus on governmental leaders and those who interact directly with them. Because governmental leaders are chosen directly in elections or indirectly by those elected, pluralism asserts that leaders can be held accountable to the people. But even if governmental elites can be held accountable through elections, how can corporate executives, media elites, union leaders, and other persons in positions of private leadership be held accountable? Do they answer to their customers, members, and stockholders?

Elitism emphasizes the shared characteristics of leaders, not only their common interest in preserving the social system and their place in it but also their many shared experiences, values, and goals. Pluralism emphasizes diversity among leaders—differences in backgrounds, ideologies, and viewpoints. Even when elitists show that a disproportionate share of U.S. leadership is composed of wealthy, educated, white, upper- and upper-middle-class males, pluralists respond by asserting that these background characteristics do not preclude leaders from making decisions in the masses' interests. Elitism focuses on leadership consensus regarding the system itself, asserting that elites differ more over the means than the ends of public policy. Pluralism focuses on elite conflict, asserting that elites differ on a wide variety of issues of vital importance to society.

Pluralism and elitism also differ over the nature and extent of mass influences over societal decision making. Elitism asserts that elites influence the masses more

| IN BRIEF | PLURALISM |

- Society is divided into numerous groups, all of which make demands on government and none of which dominate decision making. Although citizens do not directly participate in decision making, their many leaders make decisions through a process of bargaining, accommodation, and compromise.
- Competition among leadership groups helps protect individuals' interests. Countervailing centers of power—for example, competition among business leaders, labor leaders, and government leaders—can check one another and keep each interest from abusing its power and oppressing the individual.
- Although individuals do not participate directly in decision making, they can exert influence through participating in organized groups, as well as parties and elections.
- Leadership groups are open; new groups can form and gain access to the political system.

- Although political influence in society is unequally distributed, power is widely dispersed. Access to decision making is often determined by how much interest people have in a particular decision. Because leadership is fluid and mobile, power depends on one's interest in public affairs, skills in leadership, information about issues, knowledge of democratic processes, and skill in organization and public relations.
- Multiple leadership groups operate within society. Those who exercise power in one kind of decision do not necessarily exercise power in others. No single elite dominates decision making in all issues.
- Public policy does not necessarily reflect majority preference but is an equilibrium of interest interaction—that is, competing interest group influences are more or less balanced, and the resulting policy is therefore a reasonable approximation of society's preferences.

than the masses influence elites. Communication flows primarily downward from the elites to the masses. An enlightened elite may choose to consider the well-being of the masses in decision making, from either ethical principles or a desire to avoid instability and revolution. But even when elites presume to act in the interests of the masses, the elites act on their *own* view of what is good for the masses, not what the masses decide for themselves. In contrast, pluralists, while acknowledging that elites rather than the masses make society's decisions, nonetheless assert that the masses have real influence on policy through their membership in organized interest groups and their participation in elections. Interest groups, parties, and elections, according to the pluralists, provide the means by which the masses can hold elites accountable for their decisions.

In short, although elitism and pluralism share some common views on the preeminent role of elites in a democratic society, they differ in several key respects, as summarized in Table 1.1.

ELITE AND MASS THREATS TO DEMOCRACY

It is the irony of democracy that the survival of democratic values—individual dignity, limited government, equality of opportunity, private property, freedom of speech and press, religious tolerance, and due process of law—depends on enlightened elites. The masses respond to the ideas and actions of elites. When elites abandon democratic principles or the masses lose confidence in elites, democracy is in peril.

TABLE 1.1 | HOW ELITISM AND PLURALISM DIFFER IN THEIR VIEWS OF POWER AND SOCIETY

	Elite Theory	Pluralist Theory
Most important political division(s) in society	*Elites* who have power, and *masses* who do not.	*Multiple competing groups* (economic, identity, religious, ideological, etc.) that individuals join or create and that make demands on government.
Structure of power	*Concentrated* in a relatively small set of institutional leaders who make key social decisions.	*Dispersed* among multiple leadership groups who bargain and compromise over key societal decisions.
Interaction among leaders	*Consensus over values and goals* for society, with disagreements largely limited to means of achieving common goals.	*Conflict and competition over values and goals* as well as means of achieving them.
Sources of leadership	*Common backgrounds and experiences* in control of institutional resources; wealth, education, upper socioeconomic status; slow continuous absorption of persons who accept prevailing values.	*Diversity in backgrounds and experiences* and activism in organizations; continuous formation of new groups and organizations; skills in organizational activity and gaining access to government.
Principal institutions of power	Corporations, banks, investment firms, media giants, foundations, "think tanks," and other *private organizations, as well as government.*	Interest groups, parties, and the legislative, executive, and judicial branches of government. *Focus is on political organizations.*
Principal direction of political influence	*Downward* from elites to masses through mass media, educational, civic, and cultural organizations.	*Upward* from masses to elites through interest groups, parties, elections, opinion polls, new technologies such as email, texting, Twitter, social networking sites.
View of public policy	Public policy reflects *elite preferences*, as modified by both altruism and desire to preserve the political system from mass unrest; policy changes occur incrementally when elites redefine their own interests.	Public policy reflects *balance of competing interest groups*; policy changes occur when interest groups gain or lose influence, including mass support.
Principal protection for democratic values	*Elite commitments* to individual liberty, free enterprise, and tolerance of diversity, and their desire to preserve the existing political system.	*Competition among groups*: countervailing centers of power, each checking the ambitions of others.

Elite theory recognizes several threats to democracy: *elite distemper* (short-sighted and self-interested behavior that undermines popular support for the political system), *mass unrest* (extremist and intolerant political movements, led by appeals to racial hatred, class antagonism, and personal fears), and *elite repression* (limitations on dissent, speech, and assembly in the name of law and order; "political correctness"; and the subversion of democratic values in a paradoxical effort to preserve the system).

ELITE DISTEMPER

Yet democratic elites do not always live up to their responsibilities to preserve the system and its values. Elite behavior is not always enlightened and farsighted but is instead frequently shortsighted and narrowly self-serving. The relative autonomy of separate elites in a democracy—governmental, corporate, financial, media, legal, civic, and cultural—often encourages narrow visions of the common good and a willingness to sacrifice social values for relative advantage.

Examples of narrowly self-serving elite behavior abound. Politicians resort to divisive, racial appeals or to class antagonisms—setting black against white or poor against rich—to win elections, even while knowing these tactics undermine mass confidence in national leadership. Corporate officials sacrifice long-term economic growth for short-term profits, knowing the nation's competitive position is undermined by shortsighted "bottom-line" policies. Elites move factories and jobs out of the United States in search of low-paid workers and higher profits. Global trade and unchecked immigration lower the real wages of U.S. workers. Inequality in the United States increases, and elites and masses grow further apart. Members of Congress in pursuit of personal pay and perks as well as lifetime tenure cater to fat-cat political contributors and well-heeled interest group elites. They devote more energy to running for office than to running the government. Bureaucrats, seeking to expand their powers and budgets, create a regulatory quagmire, disadvantaging the nation in global competition. Politicians have burdened future generations with enormous debts. Interest group leaders pursue their quest for special privileges, treatments, and exemptions from law at the expense of the public interest. Network television executives hype both news and entertainment shows with violence, scandal, sex, corruption, and scares of various sorts, knowing that these stories undermine mass confidence in the nation's institutions. Lawyers and judges pervert the judicial process for personal advantage, drowning the nation in a sea of litigation, clogging the courts and delaying justice, reinterpreting laws and the Constitution to suit their purposes, and undermining mass respect for the law.

In short, elites do not always act with unity and purpose. **Elite distemper** results when they all too frequently put narrow interests ahead of broader, shared values. These behaviors grow out of the relative autonomy of various elites in a democracy. They are encouraged by the absence of any external checks on the power of elites in their various domains. The only effective check on irresponsible elite behavior is their own realization that the system itself will become endangered if such behavior continues unrestrained. This also pits self-serving individuals in the elite against the elite as a whole, which has a clearer stake in system preservation. So periodically elites undertake reforms, mutually agreeing to curb the most flagrant abuses of the system and punish those responsible. The stimulus to reform is the restoration of mass confidence in elite government and ultimately the preservation of the elite system itself. But reforms often succeed only in creating new opportunities for abuse, changing the rules but failing to restrain self-interested elites.

MASS UNREST

Mass politics can also threaten democratic values. Despite a superficial commitment to the symbols of democracy, the masses have surprisingly weak commitments when required to apply these principles to despised or obnoxious groups or individuals. In contrast, elites, and the better-educated groups from which they are recruited, are generally more willing than the masses to apply democratic values to specific situations and to protect the freedoms of unpopular groups.

Masses are dangerously vulnerable to appeals to intolerance, racial hatred, anti-intellectualism, class antagonisms, anti-religious biases, and violence. Demagogues (from the Greek for "mob" and "voice") are mass-oriented leaders who express hostility toward the established order and appeal to such mass sentiments. These counterelites, whether they are on the left or the right, are extremist and intolerant, impatient with due process, contemptuous of individual rights, eager to impose their views by sweeping measures, and often willing to use violence and intimidation to do so. Right-wing speakers talk of "the will of the people," whereas left-wing radicals cry, "Power to the people." Both appeal to mass extremism: the notion that compromise and coalition building and working within the democratic system for change is pointless or even immoral. These counterelites cynically seek to diminish or delegitimize the system, for benefit of their power goals.

Mass unrest must be distinguished from mass protest; the right of peaceable assembly is enshrined in the U.S. Constitution's Bill of Rights. However, frequently mass activism degenerates into mob scenes in which a small number feel that the rights of others do not matter as much as their own emotional views. This has led to violence, including assault, rape, murder, property destruction, blocking others' freedom of movement, and intimidation of less extreme viewpoints. Once a peaceful protest turns ugly, it becomes antidemocratic. This then chills democratic freedom as peaceful protestors become scared off by aggressive rioters.

Democratic values can survive only in the absence of mass political activism. Democratic values thrive best when the masses are absorbed in the problems of everyday life and involved in groups and activities that distract their attention

---

FOCUS | MASS VIEWS OF ELITE GOVERNANCE

Elite theory focuses on the division between masses and elites. Masses themselves are wary of elite governance. They believe their political leaders are distant, insensitive to their needs, and inattentive to their views.

Most U.S. adults believe government pays little attention to their views on public policy, that people in government have little understanding of popular thinking, and that the nation would be better off if elites followed mass views. These numbers stay quite close across gender and race lines.

Over the years, people were asked whether they agreed or disagreed with the following statements.

Public officials don't care much what people like me think.

Agree	60%
Disagree	23%
Neither	17%

People like me don't have a say in what the government does.

Agree	49%
Disagree	40%
Neither	10%

Source: American National Election Survey, 2008.

from mass political movements and demagogues. Political stability depends on mass involvement in work, family, neighborhood, trade union, hobby, religion, group recreation, and other activities.

ELITE REPRESSION

Mass activism inspires elite repression. Mass political movements, if they gain momentum and give rise to hatred and violate the system's democratic values, generate fear and insecurity among elites. Elites respond by limiting freedom and strengthening security, banning demonstrations, demonizing rivals, investigating and harassing opposition, arresting activists, and curtailing speech, internet, and broadcasting—usually under the guise of preserving law and order. Universities, once heralded as society's bastions of free thought and expression, may respond to threats by imposing "speech codes," "sensitivity training," and other repressive measures on students and faculty in the pursuit of tolerance and "diversity." Ironically, elites resort to these repressive actions out of a genuine belief that they are necessary to preserve the democratic values of the system.

AN ELITIST THEORY OF DEMOCRACY

All societies are governed by elites, even democratic societies. The elitist theory of democracy is not an attack on democracy but rather an aid in understanding the realities of democratic politics. Elite theory is not an apology for elite rule; it is not a defense of official misdeeds or repression. These, in fact, threaten elite governance in a democracy and need to be prevented. Rather, elite theory is a realistic explanation of how democracy works, how democratic values are both preserved and threatened, how elites and masses interact, how public policy is actually determined, and whose interests generally prevail.

Fire
The Foundation for Individual Rights in Education advocates for freedom of speech rights on campuses. *www.thefire.org*

Critics of this elitist theory of democracy claim that it legitimizes elite rule, that it obstructs social progress of the masses. But elite theory neither normatively endorses nor reflexively condemns elite governance; rather, it seeks to expose and analyze the way in which elites function in a democracy. As the Iron Law of Oligarchy points out, any alternative political system would also have elites. Critics of elite theory are essentially not criticizing elitism but merely a specific set of elites, one that they would prefer to see replaced with a set of elites more to their liking.

Elite theory poses the central questions of U.S. politics: Who governs the nation? How do people acquire power? How are economic and political power related? How have U.S. elites changed over time? How widely is power shared in the United States? Are leaders in government, business, labor, banking, media, law, foundations, interest groups, and cultural affairs separate, distinct, and competitive—or are they concentrated, interlocked, and consensual? Do the elites or the masses give greater support to democratic values? Are the elites becoming more or less isolated from the masses? Are the masses losing confidence in the nation's elite, and if so, what does this mean for democracy? Can democracy long survive when most people are distrustful of government and cynical toward politics?

Are the masses generally informed, sensible, and considerate—or are they largely ignorant, apathetic, and intolerant? Does public opinion shape elite behavior—or do elites shape public opinion through the mass media? How successful are media elites in molding mass opinion and influencing public debate? Are U.S. political parties "responsible" instruments of popular control of government, or are they weakened oligarchies dominated by ideologically motivated activists? Do elections serve as policy mandates from the people, or are they primarily an exercise in citizenship, choosing personnel, not policy? Are political campaigns designed to inform voters and assess their policy preferences—or are they expensive, commercial adventures in image making? Do organized interest groups fairly represent the views of their members, or do they reflect the views and interests of leaders who are largely out of touch with the members? Does competition among interest groups create a reasonable balance in public policy—or do special interests dominate policy-making at the expense of the mass public?

Power Structure Research Information on how to conduct research on elites, together with a bibliography on power and elites. *www.pages. uoregon.edu/ vburris/whorules/*

How much influence do the masses have over the actions of presidents, Congress, and the courts? What role does the president play in the U.S. elite system? What effect does the president's behavior have on the way the masses view their government? How does presidential popularity with the masses affect the power of the president? Is power shifting from elected officials to "faceless bureaucrats"? What are the sources of bureaucratic power, and can bureaucracy be restrained? Whom do members of Congress really represent? Are members of Congress held accountable for their policy decisions by the voters back home, or are they free to pursue their personal interests in Washington, knowing that their constituents are generally unaware of their policy positions? Why are the nation's most important domestic policy questions frequently decided by the most elitist branch of the government, the unelected, lifetime-tenured justices of the Supreme Court? Can political decentralization—decision making by state and local elites—increase mass involvement in government? How is technology altering the relationships between elites and masses? How do elites respond to mass protest movements? Do mass movements themselves become oligarchic over time and increasingly divorced from the views of the masses?

We will address questions such as these from the perspective of elite theory. But we will also compare and evaluate the answers suggested by pluralist theory, both in the context of democracy. The goal is a better understanding not only of politics in the United States but also of elitism, pluralism, and democracy itself.

NOTES

1. Harold Lasswell and Abraham Kaplan, *Power and Society* (New Haven, CT.: Yale University Press, 1950), p. 219.

2. Gaetano Mosca, *The Ruling Class* (New York: McGraw-Hill, 1939 [1896]), p. 50. Along with the works of Vilfredo Pareto and Roberto Michels, this book forms the basis of "classical elitism."

3. Roberto Michels, *Political Parties: A Sociological Study of the Oligarchical Tendencies of Modern Democracies* (New York: Free Press, 1962 [1911]), p. 70.

4. David Truman, "The American System in Crisis," *Political Science Quarterly* 74 (December 1959): 489.

5. Richard Hofstadter, *The American Political Tradition* (New York: Knopf, 1948), p. viii.

6. Aristotle. *Politics*. Benjamin Jowett, trans. New York: Dover, 2000.

7. John Stuart Mill, *Representative Government* (New York: Dutton, Everyman's Library, 1962), p. 203.

8. For a discussion of John Locke and the political philosophy underlying democracy, see George

Sabine, *A History of Political Theory* (New York: Holt, Rinehart & Winston, 1950), pp. 517–541.

9. James Madison, *The Federalist*, Number 10 (New York: Modern Library, 1937).

10. E. E. Schattschneider, *Two Hundred Million Americans in Search of a Government* (New York: Holt, Rinehart & Winston, 1969), p. 63. The parenthetical update of the U.S. population to 300 million is by the authors.

11. For a discussion of "Democracy in the States" and a list of states that allow initiative, referenda, and recall voting, see Thomas R. Dye and Susan A. MacManus, *Politics in States in Communities* (Upper Saddle River, NJ: Prentice-Hall, 2003), Chapter 2.

12. See Eva Etzioni-Halevy, *The Elite Connection* (Cambridge, MA.: Polity Press, 1993).

13. Avigail Eisenberg. *Reconstructing Political Pluralism*. Albany, SUNY Press, 1995. Eisenberg's work concerns itself with combining democratic theory and pluralism.

All communities divide themselves into the few and the many. The first are the rich and well-born, the other the masses of people.

—Alexander Hamilton

THE ELITE CONSENSUS OF THE FOUNDING FATHERS: U.S. POLITICAL PRINCIPLES

See the Appendix for the complete text of the Constitution of the United States of America.

The Founding Fathers—those 55 men who wrote the Constitution of the United States and founded a new nation—were a truly exceptional elite, not only "rich and well-born" but also educated, talented, and resourceful. When Thomas Jefferson, then the nation's minister in Paris, first saw the list of delegates to the Constitutional Convention of 1787, he wrote to John Adams, the minister to London, "It is really an assembly of demigods."[1] The men at the Convention belonged to the nation's intellectual and economic elites; they were owners of landed estates, important merchants and importers, bankers and financiers, real estate and land speculators, and government bond owners. Jefferson and Adams were among the nation's few notables who were not at the Constitutional Convention.

The Founding Fathers were not typical of the four million members of the new nation, most of whom were small farmers, tradespeople, frontier dwellers, servants, or slaves. However, to say they were not representative or that the Constitution was not a very democratic document does not discredit them or the Constitution. To the aristocratic society of eighteenth-century Europe, the Founding Fathers were dangerous revolutionaries, establishing a government in which men with the talent of acquiring property could rise to political power even though they were not born into the nobility. And the Constitution has survived the test of time, providing the basic framework for an ever-changing society.

ELITES AND MASSES IN THE NEW NATION

Many visitors to the United States from the aristocratic countries of Europe noted the absence of nobility and commented on the spirit of equality that prevailed. Yet class lines existed in the United States. At the top of the social structure, a tiny elite dominated the social, cultural, economic, and political life of the new nation. The

French *chargé d'affaires* reported in 1787 that the United States had "no nobles" but that certain "gentlemen" enjoyed "preeminence" because of "their wealth, their talents, their education, their families, or the offices they hold."[2]

Below this thin layer of educated and talented merchants, planters, lawyers, and bankers was a substantial body of successful farmers, shopkeepers, and independent artisans—of the "middling" sort, as they were known in revolutionary days. This early middle class, while small, stood considerably above the masses of debt-ridden farmers and frontier dwellers who made up most of the population. It had some political power, even at the time of the Constitutional Convention; it was entitled to vote, and its views were represented in governing circles, even if they did not prevail at the Convention. The middle class was better represented in state legislatures and was championed by several men of prominence in the revolutionary period—Patrick Henry, Luther Martin, and Thomas Jefferson.

The great mass of white colonials in the revolutionary period were "freeholders," small farmers who worked their own land, scratching out a bare existence for themselves and their families. They had little interest in or knowledge of public affairs. Usually the small farmers who were not barred from voting by the requirement to own property or pay taxes were too preoccupied with debt and subsistence, or too isolated in the wilderness, to vote anyway. Nearly eight of 10 people farmed; one in 10 worked in fishing or lumbering; and one in 10 worked in commerce in some way, whether as a dockhand, sailor, lawyer, or merchant.

At the bottom of the white social structure in the new republic were indentured servants and tenant farmers; this class, perhaps 20 percent of the population, exercised little if any political power. Finally, still further below, were the black slaves. Although they made up almost another 20 percent of the population and were an important component of the U.S. economy, they were considered property, even in a country that proclaimed the natural rights and equality of "all men."

ELITE PREFERENCES: INSPIRATION FOR A NEW CONSTITUTION

Our Documents
National Archives website with access to 100 "milestone documents" in U.S. history. *www. ourdocuments.gov*

In July 1775, Benjamin Franklin proposed to the Continental Congress a plan for a "perpetual union"; following the Declaration of Independence in 1776, the Congress appointed a committee to consider the Franklin proposal. This committee made its report in the form of the Articles of Confederation, which the Congress debated and finally adopted on November 15, 1777.

The **Articles of Confederation**, effective from 1781 to 1789, were a treaty between sovereign nations. They established a "firm league of friendship" among the states "for their common defense, the security of their liberties, and their mutual and general welfare." The document reassured each state of "its sovereignty, freedom, and independence, and every power, jurisdiction, and right, which is not by this confederation expressly delegated to the United States, in Congress assembled." The Confederation's delegated powers included power to declare war, to send and receive ambassadors, to make treaties, to fix standards of weights and measures, to regulate the value of coins, to manage Native American affairs, to establish post offices, to borrow money, to build and equip an army and navy, and to make requisitions (requests) to the several states for money and people. However, certain key powers remained with the states, including two of the most important ones of

*"Religious freedom is my immediate goal, but my
long-range plan is to go into real estate."*

government: to regulate commerce and to levy taxes. By failing to provide for the financing of the Confederation, this first attempt toward union by the states was doomed from the start.

FORMATION OF A NATIONAL ELITE

In 1785, the Virginia legislature issued a call for a general economic conference of all the states to meet in Annapolis, but only five states sent representatives. However, these states' 12 delegates saw the opportunity to use the Annapolis meeting to achieve greater political successes. Alexander Hamilton, with masterful political foresight, persuaded the others in attendance to strike out for a full constitutional solution to the new country's ills. The Annapolis Convention adopted a report, written by Hamilton, that outlined the defects in the Articles of Confederation and called on the states to send delegates to a new convention, set for May 1787 in Philadelphia, to remedy them.

Meanwhile, in Massachusetts in summer 1786, a violent uprising known as Shays' Rebellion threatened the property and creditor class and galvanized the elite into action. Bands of debt-ridden farmers, artisans, and laborers led by Daniel Shays, a veteran of the battle of Bunker Hill, captured courthouses in several western districts and briefly held the city of Springfield. The rebellion was put down by

Shay's
Rebellion

IN BRIEF | ELITE DISSATISFACTIONS WITH GOVERNMENT IN 1787

- The confederation government had no tax powers and therefore could not repay the money lent to it by wealthy bankers, planters, merchants, and investors.
- States were imposing tariffs on goods shipped from state to state, inhibiting trade and commerce.
- States were issuing their own paper money and obliging banks and other creditors to accept it as legal tender.
- Open rebellion against tax collectors and creditors repossessing property (such as Shays' Rebellion) threatened property classes.

- The absence of a strong army allowed Native Americans to attack Western land setters, lowering the prices Western land speculators could get for their investments. The absence of a strong navy allowed pirates to attack shipping.
- The absence of federal tariffs and customs duties allowed foreign goods to challenge domestic manufacturers.
- Slaves who ran away to free states threatened the "property" of slave owners.
- U.S. elites were hampered in their dealings in the international community by the absence of a strong central government.

---

a smaller mercenary army, paid for by wealthy citizens who feared a wholesale attack on property rights. Such growing radicalism in the states intimidated the propertied classes, who began to advocate a strong central government to protect them against social upheavals by the large debtor class.

On February 21, 1787, Congress confirmed the call for a convention to meet in Philadelphia,

> for the sole and express purpose of revising the Articles of Confederation and reporting to Congress and the several legislatures such alterations and provisions therein as shall, when agreed to in Congress and confirmed by the states, render the federal Constitution adequate to the exigencies of government and the preservation of the union.

Delegates were appointed by the legislatures of every state except Rhode Island, the only state in which the debtor classes had gained political control of the legislature. The delegates quickly chose George Washington, their most prestigious member—indeed the most prestigious man on the continent—to preside over the assembly. The Convention also decided to hold its sessions behind closed doors and to keep all proceedings a carefully guarded secret, in order to promote free discussion and debate without an appearance of elite division or conflict. Apparently the Founding Fathers were aware that elites are most effective in negotiation, compromise, and decision making when they operate in secrecy.

The Convention was quick to discard its congressional mandate to "revise the Articles of Confederation" and proceeded to write an entirely new constitution. Only men confident of their powers and abilities, men of principle and property, could proceed in this bold fashion. Let us examine the characteristics of the nation's first elite more closely.

GEORGE WASHINGTON'S PRESTIGE

It would be hard to overestimate the prestige George Washington enjoyed at this time in his life. As commander-in-chief of the successful revolutionary army and founder of the new nation, he had overwhelming charismatic appeal among both elites and masses. He was also one of the richest men in the country and often paid his soldiers from his personal fortune, refusing payment for his own services through all the years he spent in the revolutionary cause. In addition to his large estate on the Potomac, he possessed many thousands of acres of undeveloped land in western Virginia, Maryland, Pennsylvania, Kentucky, and the Northwest Territory. He owned major shares in the Potomac Company, the James River Company, the Bank of Columbia, and the Bank of Alexandria. He also held large amounts in U.S. bonds and securities. Washington stood at the apex of U.S. elite structure.

George Washington
Documents, articles, and other resources on the nation's first president. *http://gwpapers. virginia.edu*

THE FOUNDERS' GOVERNING EXPERIENCE

Biographies of the Founding Fathers Brief biographies of each of the 55 delegates to the Constitutional Convention, as well as signers of the Declaration of Independence and the Articles of Confederation. *www.colonialhall. com*

The 55 Founding Fathers had extensive experience in governing. They had made all the key decisions from the Stamp Act Congress to the Declaration of Independence to the Articles of Confederation. They controlled the Congress of the United States and had conducted the Revolutionary War. Eight delegates had signed the Declaration of Independence. Eleven had served as officers in Washington's army. Forty-two had already served in the U.S. Congress. Even at the moment of the Convention, more than 40 held high offices in state governments; Franklin, Livingston, and Randolph were governors. The Founding Fathers were unsurpassed in political skill and experience.

THE FOUNDERS' EDUCATION

In an age when no more than a handful of men on the North American continent had gone to college, the Founding Fathers were conspicuous for their educational attainment. More than half had been educated at Harvard (founded in 1636), William and Mary (1693), Yale (1701), the University of Pennsylvania (1740), Columbia College (1754), or Princeton (1756) or in England. The precedent of legal training for political decision makers, which has continued in the United States to the present, was already evident. About three dozen delegates had legal training, and more than half were serving or had served as lawyers or judges.

The educations of the Founding Fathers clearly help us understand the ideas and principles they brought to the U.S. Constitution. First, the Founders were deeply trained in classical learning in Greek and Latin. The works of political theorists such as Plato, Aristotle, Polybius, and Cicero informed them of classical approaches to government. Both John Adams and James Monroe wrote critical examinations of ancient constitutions, while Jefferson said, "History informs us what bad government is." From Aristotle came the emphasis on a form of government called polity, which mixed elements of aristocracy and democracy, for the best interests of the country. From the Roman experience, the Founding Fathers learned of the importance of checks and balances to limit potential or real corruption in government. The Romans also emphasize the idea of civic virtue, the idea that through participation in governing, we become better people. The Latin-rooted term **republic,** or its Greek equivalent, **polity,** described a political system in which the many participated, but in which the majority was restrained from becoming tyrannical. (The term *democracy* did not become popular and lose its conventional usage as a negative until the 1820s.)

The Founders also studied the history of Britain, in which principles such as a checked executive power, civil rights, and due process of law follow directly from the Magna Carta of 1215. Another inspiration was the British Bill of Rights of 1689, which included each person's inalienable rights to life, liberty, and property. England also provided a strong cautionary example; in the bloody period from 1649 to 1659, its monarchy was overthrown and an attempt at a republic quickly devolved into dictatorship under the demagogic "Lord Protector" Oliver Cromwell. This period demonstrated that an attempt to move power to the people could simply become a disaster. Still, the principles of the American Revolution and the Constitution were rooted in the British history of the colonies. In his speech calling for conciliation with the colonies, British statesman Edmund Burke had defended the colonists, saying, "They are therefore not only devoted to liberty, but to liberty according to English ideas and English principles."

THE FOUNDERS' WEALTH

The men at the Philadelphia Convention formed a major part of the nation's economic elite as well. The finances of the period were chaotic and wealth assumed a variety of forms—land, ships, credit, slaves, business inventories, bonds, and paper money of uncertain worth (even George Washington had difficulty at times converting his land wealth into cash). But at least 40 of the 55 delegates were holders of government bonds; 14 were land speculators; 24 were money-lenders and investors; 11 were engaged in commerce or manufacturing; 35 were slave-holders, and 15 owned large plantations[3] (see Table 2.1). In a sign of the mobility of economic status, the two richest, Robert Morris and James Wilson, died bankrupt, while the poorest, William Few, ended up quite wealthy.

The economic interests of the Founders meant that besides political freedom, economic prosperity and stability were major goals of the new Constitution. Having a new government on a solid financial footing, unlike the government under the Articles of Confederation, was paramount. Issues of trade, debt, taxes, and monetary policy were as important as issues of governing institutions. The Founder most responsible for creating a financially sound nation was ironically born illegitimate and poor in the British West Indies and never achieved significant wealth: Alexander Hamilton.[4]

THE FOUNDERS' NATIONAL VIEW

Perhaps what most distinguished the men in Philadelphia from the masses was their cosmopolitanism. They approached political, economic, and military issues from a national point of view, seeing the colonies more as a single nation than the separate countries they were. Unlike the masses, members of the elite extended their loyalties beyond their states; they experienced the sentiment of nationalism half a century before it would begin to seep down to the masses.[5] They were also concerned about the weakness of the United States as a nation in the international community. Its

TABLE 2.1 | FOUNDERS' MEMBERSHIP IN ELITE GROUPS

Government Bond Holders		Real Estate and Land Speculators	Lenders and Investors	Merchants, Manufacturers, and Shippers	Planters and Slaveholders
Major	Minor				
Baldwin	Bassett	Blount	Bassett	Broom	Butler
Blair	Blount	Dayton	Broom	Clymer	Davie
Clymer	Brearly	Few	Butler	Ellsworth	Jenifer
Dayton	Broom	Fitzsimons	Carroll	Fitzsimons	A. Martin
Ellsworth	Butler	Franklin	Clymer	Gerry	L. Martin
Fitzsimons	Carroll	Gerry	Davie	King	Mason
Gerry	Few	Gilman	Dickinson	Langdon	Mercer
Gilman	Hamilton	Gorham	Ellsworth	McHenry	C. C. Pinckney
Gorham	L. Martin	Hamilton	Few	Mifflin	C. Pinckney
Jenifer	Mason	Mason	Fitzsimons	G. Morris	Randolph
Johnson	Mercer	R. Morris	Franklin	R. Morris	Read
King	Mifflin	Washington	Gilman		Rutledge
Langdon	Read	Williamson	Ingersoll		Spaight
Lansing	Spaight	Wilson	Johnson		Washington
Livingston	Wilson		King		Wythe
McClurg	Wythe		Langdon		
R. Morris			Mason		
C. C. Pinckney			McHenry		
C. Pinckney			C. C. Pinckney		
Randolph			C. Pinckney		
Sherman			Randolph		
Strong			Read		
Washington			Washington		

13 separate states failed to manifest a sense of national purpose and identity. The Confederation was held in contempt not only by Britain, as evidenced by its violations of the Treaty of Paris, but even by the lowly Barbary States. Alexander Hamilton expressed the indignation of U.S. leadership over its inability to swing weight in the world community:

> There is something … diminutive and contemptible in the prospect of a number of petty states, with the appearance only of union, jarring, jealous, and perverse, without any determined direction, fluctuating and unhappy at home, weak and insignificant by their dissentions in the eyes of other nations.[6]

In short, the U.S. elite wanted to assume a respectable role in the international community and exercise power in world affairs. The Founding Fathers believed that only a strong national government, with power to exercise its will directly on

Founding Fathers

the people, could "establish justice, insure domestic tranquility, provide for the common defense, promote the general welfare, and secure the blessings of liberty."

ELITE CONSENSUS IN 1787

The Convention was undoubtedly the site of many conflicting views and innumerable compromises, yet the more striking fact is that the delegates were in almost complete accord on essential political questions.

At the center of their political worldview was an approach to politics that had grown in Britain over the previous two centuries, known today as **classical liberalism**. This ideology was based on the modern idea of human beings as rational beings, free individuals capable of thinking for themselves and determining what was in their own best interest. Classical liberal theory holds that society is created by a social contract, explicit or implicit, among individuals who, rather than deal with a condition Thomas Hobbes described as a "war of all against all," saw that it was rational to give up some freedoms in exchange for some security. Liberal theory also focuses on individual freedoms, civil liberties, and a distrust of government, all concepts that grew in reaction to the miserable conditions of medieval feudalism.

At the same time, the Founders also exhibited **classical conservatism**, a worldview that saw human nature as flawed and prone to weakness. Because of this basic fact, a politics was needed that would mitigate the worst of the damage humans might inflict on themselves. The conservative solution was a reliance on past practices that had proven successful and a focus on the institutions that help individuals control their self-serving natures: family, faith, education, and government. Tradition was to be a guide. The Founders demonstrated this most powerfully in adopting the British legal approach known as common law. **Common law** provided a legal system that did not spring from some contemporary legislature but was built up over generations and even centuries of precedents. The key work on the topic, Sir William Blackstone's 1765 *Commentaries on the Laws of England*, sold as many copies in the colonies as in Britain.[7] To this day, English common law precedents from before the founding of the United States may still be valid in legal arguments in U.S. courts.[8]

PROTECTING LIBERTY AND PROPERTY

The Founders agreed with the core tenet of classical liberalism that the fundamental end of government is the protection of individual liberty. They accepted without debate many of the precedents set by the English constitution and by the constitutions of the new states. Yet they believed in a law of nature with rules of abstract justice to which human laws should conform. They believed this law of nature endowed each person with certain inalienable rights essential to a meaningful existence—the rights to life, liberty, and property—and that these rights should be recognized and protected by law. All people were equally entitled to respect of their natural rights regardless of their station in life. Most of the Founding Fathers were even aware that this belief ran contrary to the practice of slavery and were embarrassed by the inconsistency.

But "equality" did *not* mean to the Founding Fathers that people were equal in wealth, intelligence, talent, or virtue. They accepted inequalities in wealth and property as a natural product of human diversity. They did not believe government had a responsibility to reduce these inequalities; in fact, they saw "dangerous leveling" as a serious violation of the right to property and the right to use and dispose of the fruits of industry. Equality meant equality under the law and equality of opportunity to pursue goals each person defined for himself or herself. Classical liberal theory sees each individual as a rational person capable of determining his or her own goals or "happiness." Equality of outcome, such as equality in material or financial status, is meaningless in classical liberalism because different individuals may choose different goals and make different efforts. The individual who wishes to be a vagabond poet may be as happy as the wealthy stockbroker, even though their material lives will be rather different.

GOVERNMENT AS CONTRACT

The modern era of political thought is based in **social contract theory**. The core concept is that society exists because the free individuals who compose it have made a rational decision that forming society is in their self-interest. Philosopher Thomas Hobbes saw a single inalienable right—the right to life. To survive the conflict of "all against all" in a brutal, anarchic state of nature in which life is "solitary, nasty, brutish, and short," individuals surrender their natural freedom to protect their lives. After this first step, social contract theory evolved to John Locke's idea that human rights go beyond just being alive, to being free and having the economic means to be self-supporting rather than being dependent on the state or another for your livelihood. The focus was the "life, liberty, and property" of the individual. In social contract theory all political power resides with the people unless they choose to delegate it to a government. The Founding Fathers agreed that the origin of government is an implied contract among people. They believed people pledge allegiance and obedience to government in return for protection of their persons and property. They felt the ultimate legitimacy of government— sovereignty—rests with the people and that *the basis of government is the consent of the governed.*

REPUBLICANISM

The Founding Fathers believed in republican government, not democracy, which in their day denoted a corrupt rule by the mob. They opposed hereditary monarchies, the prevailing form of government in the world at the time. Although they believed people of principle and property should govern, they were opposed to an aristocracy or a governing nobility. To them, a "republican government" was a representative, responsible, and nonhereditary government. They certainly did *not* mean mass democracy, with direct participation by the people in decision making. They expected the masses to consent to government by men of principle and property, out of recognition of their abilities, talents, education, and stake in the preservation of liberty and order. The Founding Fathers bickered over how much direct participation was appropriate in selecting decision makers and over the qualifications necessary for public office, but they generally agreed the *masses should have only a limited, indirect role in selecting decision makers, and that decision makers themselves should be men of wealth, education, and proven leadership ability.*

LIMITED GOVERNMENT

The Founding Fathers believed in limited government that could not threaten liberty or property. Because they saw power as a corrupting influence and the concentration of elite power as dangerous, they believed in dividing government power into separate bodies capable of checking, or thwarting, one another should any one branch pose a threat to liberty or property. Honest people could best resolve their differences of opinion, particularly differences among elites in separate states, by balancing representation in the national government and creating a decentralized system that permits local elites to govern their states as they see fit, with limited interference from the national government. The most fundamental classical liberal approach to limiting the government is to leave as much power as possible with the people, in the private sector. We see this principle at work most clearly in the emphasis on private ownership of U.S. business.

ELITE CONSENSUS IN A WORLD CONTEXT

National Constitutional Center
Constitutional museum adjoining Independence Hall in Philadelphia. The website includes a virtual tour. *www. constitutioncenter. org*

Elite consensus in 1787 was conservative in that it sought to preserve the status quo in the distribution of power and property in the United States. Yet at the same time, *this elite consensus was radical compared with the beliefs of elite contemporaries elsewhere in the world.* Nearly every other government adhered to the principles of hereditary monarchy and privileged nobility, whereas U.S. elites were committed to republicanism. Other elites asserted the divine rights of kings, but U.S. elites talked about government by the consent of the governed. While the elites in Europe rationalized and defended a rigid class system, U.S. elites believed in equality and inalienable human rights. The Founders went beyond even the British tradition of liberty on which U.S. ideas were based.

AN ELITE IN OPERATION: CONCILIATION AND COMPROMISE

On May 25, 1787, the Constitutional Convention opened in Independence Hall, Philadelphia. Thus began a long process of negotiation over many key issues that would require elite consensus. The willingness and ability of the elite delegates to work together and compromise show that despite their differences, their general goals were the same. After the delegates had selected Washington as president of the Convention and decided to keep the proceedings of the Convention secret, Governor Edmund Randolph, speaking for the Virginia delegation, presented a draft of a new constitution.[9]

REPRESENTATION COMPROMISE

The Virginia plan gave little recognition to the states in its proposed composition of the national government. The plan suggested a two-house legislature: a lower

IN BRIEF | ELITE CONSENSUS IN 1787

- Natural law endows each person with inalienable rights to life, liberty, and property.
- Government exists by consent of the governed and originates as a contract among individuals to protect their liberty and property. A government that violates this contract is illegitimate and may rightfully be overthrown by virtue of the right to revolution.
- Republican government—a government by representatives of the people—is preferable to

hereditary monarchies and aristocracies. Direct democracy is a dangerous idea. The masses should have only a limited role in selecting decision makers.
- Governmental power should be limited by establishing written constitutional guarantees and dividing and separating governmental powers.
- A strong national government is required to protect liberty and property.

house to be chosen by the people of the states, with representation according to the population, and an upper house to be chosen by the first house. This Congress would have power to "legislate in all cases in which the separate states are incompetent, or in which the harmony of the United States may be interrupted by the exercise of individual legislation." Moreover, Congress would have the authority to nullify state laws it felt violated the Constitution, thus ensuring national supremacy. The Virginia plan also proposed a parliamentary form of government, with Congress choosing members of the executive and judiciary branches.

The most important line of cleavage at the Convention was not economic or ideological; it ran between elites of large states and elites of small states over the representation scheme in the Virginia plan. After several weeks of debate, delegates from the small states presented a counterproposal in a report by William Paterson of New Jersey. The New Jersey plan proposed to retain the representation scheme outlined in the Articles of Confederation, which granted each state a single vote. But it went further, proposing separate executive and judiciary branches and expansion of the powers of Congress to include the right to levy taxes and regulate commerce.

The New Jersey plan was not an attempt to retain the Confederation. Indeed, it included words that later appeared in the Constitution as the famous national supremacy clause, which provides that the U.S. Constitution and federal laws supersede each state's constitution and laws. Thus, even the small states did not envision a confederation. Both the Virginia and New Jersey plans were designed to strengthen the national government; they differed only on how much to strengthen it and on its system of representation. However, the New Jersey plan was set aside after only a week of debate.

On June 29, William Samuel Johnson of Connecticut proposed the obvious compromise: that representation in the lower house of Congress be based on population, whereas representation in the upper house would be equal—two senators from each state. The **Connecticut compromise** also provided that equal representation of states in the Senate could not be abridged, even by constitutional amendment.

Slavery Compromises

A particularly divisive issue was slavery. While most delegates had slaves, others strongly opposed the practice, even many who were slaveholders. The main divide ultimately ran on economic lines: Southern states were more reliant on slaves for labor in agriculture and were unwilling to disrupt their economic system. Whatever success the Constitutional delegates had at finding compromise finally broke down with the Civil War, the one period in U.S. history when elite division was irreconcilable.

The next question requiring compromise at the Convention was the role of slaves in the system of representation, an issue closely related to economic differences among the elite. Planters and slaveholders generally believed that wealth, particularly wealth in slaves, should count in apportioning representation. Non-slaveholders felt "the people" should include only free inhabitants. The decision to levy direct taxes among the states in proportion to population opened the way to compromise, because the attitudes of slaveholders and non-slaveholders were reversed when it came to counting people in order to apportion taxes. The result was the famous **Three-fifths compromise**: Three-fifths of the slaves of each state would be counted for the purpose of both representation and apportioning direct taxes.

A compromise was also necessary on the question of trading in slaves. The men of Maryland and Virginia, states already well supplied with slaves, were able to indulge in the luxury of conscience and support proposals for banning the further import of slaves. But the less-developed southern states, particularly South Carolina and Georgia, wanted additional slave labor. Because the southern planters were themselves divided, the ultimate compromise permitted Congress to prohibit the slave trade—but not before the year 1808. The 20-year delay would allow the undeveloped southern states to acquire all the slaves they needed before the slave trade ended. While the U.S. slave trade did lapse after 20 years, slavery itself, as a domestic institution, was better safeguarded under the new Constitution than under the Articles. Still, as Abraham Lincoln noted in 1858, with this measure, the Founders put "a provision in the Constitution which they supposed would gradually remove the disease by cutting off its source. This was the abolition of the slave trade."

Southern planters and slaveholders also sought protection for their ownership of human "property." Most southern planters were more interested in protecting their existing property and slaves than in extending the slave trade. In 1787, slavery was lawful everywhere except in Massachusetts. Although many leaders in the South as well as the North recognized the moral paradox of asserting in the Declaration of Independence that "all men are created equal" while at the same time owning slaves (as did the author of the Declaration, Thomas Jefferson), nonetheless the nation's Founders were fully prepared to protect "the peculiar institution" of slavery. (Interestingly, they were too embarrassed to use the word *slave* in the new Constitution, preferring the euphemism "persons held to service or labor.") It was especially important to slave owners to guarantee the return of escaped slaves, and the Constitution provided an explicit advantage to slaveholders in Article IV, Section 2:

> No person held to service or labor in one State, under the laws thereof, escaping into another, shall in consequence of any law or regulation therein, be discharged from such service or labor, but shall be delivered up on claim of the party to whom such service or labor may be due.

This provision was an extremely valuable protection for one of the most important forms of property in the United States at the time.

TRADE AND COMMERCE COMPROMISES

The inability of Congress under the Articles of Confederation to regulate commerce among the states and with foreign nations, and the states' practice of laying tariffs on the goods of other states as well as on those of foreign nations, created havoc among commercial and shipping interests. "In every point of view," Madison wrote in 1785, "the trade of this country is in a deplorable condition."[10] The American Revolution had been fought, in part, to defend colonial commercial and business interests from oppressive regulation by the British government. Now the states themselves were interfering with the development of a national economy. Merchants and shippers with a view toward a national market and a high level of commerce were vitally concerned that the national government acquire the power to regulate interstate commerce and to prevent the states from imposing crippling tariffs and restrictions on interstate trade.

Southern planters feared the unrestricted power of Congress over commerce might lead to the imposition of export taxes. Such taxes would bear most heavily on the southern states, which depended on foreign markets to sell the indigo, rice, tobacco, and cotton they produced. However, planters and merchants were able to compromise again in resolving this issue: Articles exported from any state should bear no tax or duty. Only imports could be taxed by the national government. Congress was given the power to tax imports so northern manufacturers could erect a tariff wall to protect U.S. industries against foreign goods.

In the Constitution, Congress has the power to "regulate commerce with foreign nations, and among the several States." The interstate commerce clause, together with the provision in Article I, Section 9, prohibiting the states from taxing either imports or exports, created a free-trade area over the 13 states. This arrangement was beneficial for U.S. merchants.

VOTER QUALIFICATION COMPROMISE

Another important compromise, one that occupied much of the Convention's time, was over qualifications for voting and holding office in the new government. Although no such qualifications appear in the text of the Constitution, members of the Convention generally favored them for holding office. This preference was another rooted in classical ideas of political participation, including Aristotle's principle that a property owner, meaning someone with an agricultural or other ongoing business, would have the necessary skills in management, finance, human relations, and decision making to qualify him to contribute to the governing of the community.

The delegates showed little enthusiasm for mass participation in democracy. Elbridge Gerry of Massachusetts declared that "the evils we experience flow from the excess of democracy." Roger Sherman protested that "the people immediately should have as little to do as may be about the government." Edmund Randolph continually deplored the turbulence and follies of democracy, and George Clymer's notion of republican government was that "a representative of the people is appointed to think for and not with his constituents." John Dickinson considered property qualifications a "necessary defense against the dangerous influence of those multitudes without property and without principle, with which our country like all others, will in time abound." Charles Pinckney later wrote to Madison, "Are you not … abundantly depressed at the theoretical nonsense of an election of Congress by the people; in the first instance, it's clearly and practically wrong, and it will in the end be the means of bringing our councils into contempt." Many more such elitist statements appear in the records of the Convention.[11]

Given these views, how do we explain the absence of property qualifications in the Constitution? Actually a motion was carried in the Convention instructing a committee to fix property qualifications for holding office, but the committee could not agree on what qualifications to impose. Various propositions met defeat on the floor, not because delegates believed they were inherently wrong but, interestingly enough, because the elites at the Convention represented different kinds of property holdings. Madison pointed out that fact in the July debate, noting that a land ownership requirement would exclude from Congress the mercantile and manufacturing classes, who would hardly be willing to turn their money into landed property just to become eligible for a seat in Congress. Madison rightly observed that "landed possessions were no certain evidence of real wealth. Many enjoyed them to a great extent who were more in debt than they were worth." The objections by merchants and investors defeated the "landed" qualifications for congressional representatives.

Thus, the Convention approved the Constitution without property qualifications on officeholders or voters, except those the states themselves might see fit to impose. Failing to come to a decision on the issue of suffrage, the delegates merely returned the question to state legislatures by providing that "the electors in each state should have the qualifications requisite for electors of the most numerous branch of the state legislatures." At the time, this expedient course did not seem likely to produce mass democracy. Only one branch of the new government, the House of Representatives, was to be elected by popular vote. The other three controlling bodies—the president, the Senate, and the Supreme Court—were removed from direct voter participation (see Figure 2.1). The delegates were reassured that nearly all the state constitutions then in force included property qualifications for voters.

Finally, the Constitution did not recognize women as legitimate participants in government. For nearly 100 years, no state accorded women the right to vote. (The newly formed Wyoming Territory first gave women the right to vote and hold public office in 1869.) Not until 1920 was the U.S. Constitution amended to guarantee women the right to vote.

THE CONSTITUTION AS ELITIST DOCUMENT

The text of the Constitution, together with interpretive materials in *The Federalist Papers* written by Hamilton, Madison, and John Jay, provides ample evidence that elites benefited both politically and economically from the adoption of the Constitution. Although both elites and nonelites—indeed, all citizens—have benefited from the Constitution, *elites benefited more directly and immediately than did*

*"You know, the idea of taxation _with_ representation doesn't
appeal to me very much, either."*

nonelites. We can infer the elites would not have developed and supported the Constitution if they had not stood to gain substantially from it.

Let us examine the text of the Constitution itself and its impact on U.S. elites. Article I, Section 8, grants 17 types of power to Congress, followed by a general grant of power to make "all laws which shall be necessary and proper for carrying into execution the foregoing powers."

TAXATION AND THE REPAYMENT OF LOANS

The first and perhaps most important power is the "power to lay and collect taxes, duties, imposts, and excises." The taxing power is the basis of all other powers, and it enabled the national government to end its dependence on states. The inability of Congress to levy taxes under the Articles of Confederation had been a serious threat to those elites who had given financial backing to the new nation during the Revolutionary War by purchasing government bonds. Congress was unable to tax the people to pay off those debts, and the states became less and less inclined, as time passed, to repay the central government. During the last years under the Articles, the national government was unable even to pay interest on its debt. As a result, the bonds and notes of the national government lost most of their value, sometimes selling on the open market for only one-tenth of their original value. Investors who had backed the Revolutionary War effort were left with nearly worthless bonds.

Without the power to tax, and with the credit of the Confederation ruined, the prospects of the central government for future financial support—and survival—looked dim. Naturally, the rich planters, merchants, and investors who owned government bonds had a direct financial interest in helping the national government acquire the power to tax and to pay off its debts. This power was essential to the holders of public securities, particularly when combined with the provision in Article VI, "All debts contracted and engagements entered into, before the adoption of this Constitution, shall be as valid against the United States under this Constitution, as under the Confederation." Thus, the national government was committed to paying off all those investors who held bonds of the United States, and the taxing power guaranteed that commitment would be fulfilled.

The text of the Constitution suggests the Founding Fathers intended Congress to place most of the tax burden on consumers in the form of custom duties and excise taxes rather than direct taxes on individual income or property. Article I, Section 2, states that government can levy direct taxes only on the basis of population; it follows that it could not levy such taxes in proportion to wealth. This provision prevented the national government from levying progressive income taxes; not until the Sixteenth Amendment in 1913 did this protection for wealth disappear from the Constitution.

PROTECTING MONEY AND CREDIT

In the Constitution, following the Article I, Section 8, powers to tax and spend, to borrow money, and to regulate commerce is a series of specific powers designed to enable Congress to protect money and property. Congress is given the power to make bankruptcy laws, to coin money and regulate its value, to fix standards of weights and measures, to punish counterfeiting, to establish post offices and post roads, and to pass copyright and patent laws to protect authors and inventors. Each of these powers is a specific asset to bankers, investors, manufacturers, and shippers. Obviously, the Founding Fathers felt giving Congress control over currency and credit in the United States would result in better protection for financial interests than leaving the essential responsibility to the states. Similarly, they believed control over communication and transportation infrastructure (in the form of post offices and post roads) was too essential to trade and commerce to be left to the states.

State governments under the Articles posed a serious threat to investors and creditors by issuing cheap paper money and passing laws allowing debtors to avoid their contractual obligations. Paper money issued by the states permitted debtors to pay off their creditors with money worth less than the money originally loaned. States were requiring creditors to accept their money as "legal tender"; refusal to do so would abolish the debt. Even the most successful farmers were usually heavily in debt, and many of them were gaining strength in state legislatures, most significantly in Rhode Island. They threatened to pass laws delaying the collection of debts and even abolishing the prevailing practice of imprisonment for unpaid debts. Obviously, creditors had a direct financial interest in establishing a strong central government that could prevent the states from issuing public paper or otherwise interfering with debt collection.

In response, the Constitution provided specific protections to economic elites in the new nation. States could not coin money, issue paper money, or pass legal tender laws that would make any money other than gold or silver coin tender in the payment of debts. They could not pass any law "impairing the obligation of contracts." If state legislatures could relieve debtors of their contractual obligations, relieve indentured servants of their obligations to their masters, prevent creditors from foreclosing on mortgages, declare moratoriums on debt, or otherwise interfere with business obligations, then the interests of investors, merchants, and creditors would be seriously damaged. More broadly, if the new nation did not have a solid monetary system and strong credit, its economy as an independent country might have been stillborn, leading the Founders, particularly Hamilton, to demand steps to establish a solid financial system.[12]

OPENING WESTERN LAND TO SPECULATION

Men of property in the new United States, including Benjamin Franklin, Robert Morris, and even the popular hero Patrick Henry, actively speculated in Western land. As a rich planter and land speculator who owned more than 30,000 acres of Western lands upstream on the Potomac, George Washington was keenly aware of commercial problems under the Articles. During the Revolutionary War, Congress had often paid Continental soldiers with land certificates. After the war, most of the ex-soldiers sold the certificates to land speculators at very low prices. The Confederation's military weakness along its frontiers had kept the value of Western lands low, for Native Americans discouraged immigration to their lands west of the Alleghenies and the British threatened to cut off westward expansion by continuing to occupy several important fur-trading forts in the Northwest (in defiance of the peace treaty).

A strong central government with enough military power to oust the British from the Northwest and protect Western settlers against attack could open the way for the development of the American West. In addition, the protection and settlement of Western land would cause land values to skyrocket and make land speculators rich.

CREATING THE MILITARY

Many of the powers in the Constitution Article I, Section 8, deal with military affairs: raising and supporting armies; organizing, training, and calling up the state militia; declaring war; suppressing insurrections; and repelling invasions. These powers—together with the provisions in Article II that make the president the commander-in-chief of the army and navy and of the state militia when called into the federal service, and that give the president power to make treaties with the advice and consent of the Senate and send and receive ambassadors—centralized diplomatic and military affairs at the national level. Article I, Section 10, confirms this centralization of diplomatic and military powers by prohibiting the states from entering into treaties with foreign nations, maintaining ships of war, or engaging in war unless actually invaded.

Clearly, the Founding Fathers had little confidence in the state militias, particularly when they were under state control. General Washington's painful experiences with state militias during the Revolutionary War were still fresh in his memory. The militias had proved adequate when defending their own states against invasion, but when employed elsewhere they were often a disaster. Moreover, if Western settlers were to open the way to westward expansion, the national government could not rely on state militias but must have an army of its own. Similarly, a strong navy was essential to the protection of U.S. commerce on the seas, because the states seemed ineffective in preventing smuggling and piracy was a real danger and a vital concern of shippers (the first significant naval action under the new government was against the piracy of the Barbary States). Thus, a national army and navy were not so much protection against invasion (for many years the national government continued to rely primarily on state militias for this purpose) as protection and promotion of the government's commercial and territorial ambitions.

PROTECTING AGAINST REVOLUTION

A national army and navy, as well as an organized and trained militia that could be called into national service, also provided protection against class wars and debtor rebellions. In an obvious reference to Shays' Rebellion, Hamilton warned in *The Federalist,* Number 21:

> The tempestuous situation from which Massachusetts has scarcely emerged evinces that dangers of this kind are not merely speculative. Who could determine what might have been the issue of her late convulsions if the malcontents had been headed by a Caesar or a Cromwell? A strong military force in the hands of the national government is a protection against revolutionary action.[13]

We find further evidence of the Founding Fathers' intention to protect the governing elites from revolution in Article IV, Section 4, where the national government guarantees to every state "a republican form of government" as well as protection against "domestic violence." Thus, in addition to protecting western land and commerce on the seas, a strong army and navy would enable the national government to back up its pledge to protect governing elites in the states from violence and revolution.

Finally, protection against domestic insurrection also appealed to the southern slaveholders' deep-seated fear of a slave revolt. Madison drove this point home in *The Federalist,* Number 23:

> I take no little notice of an unhappy species of population abounding in some of the states who, during the calm of regular government were sunk below the level of men; but who, in the tempestuous seeds of civil violence, may emerge into human character and give a superiority of strength to any party with which they may associate themselves.[14]

IN BRIEF | CONSTITUTIONAL PROTECTIONS FOR PROPERTY AND COMMERCE

- The debts of the U.S. government, including those incurred prior to the adoption of the Constitution, must be paid.
- The national government is given the power to tax in order to pay off its debts.
- Taxes must be direct, not proportional or based on wealth or income (a provision not changed until the adoption of the Sixteenth Amendment in 1913).
- No taxes can be placed on exports—goods produced in the United States. The national government may tax imports from other countries—a form of protection for domestic industries.
- States cannot interfere with interstate commerce.

- States cannot issue their own paper money or require its acceptance as legal tender.
- The national government will protect creditors in bankruptcy laws and protect authors and inventors in patent and copyright laws. It will punish counterfeiting and piracy.
- A national army will protect Western landholders, and a national navy will protect merchants and shippers.
- The national government will protect property owners against revolution—"domestic violence."
- The Constitution guarantees slave owners the return of escaped slaves (until the adoption of the Thirteenth Amendment in 1865 ended slavery).

ELITISM AND THE STRUCTURE OF THE NATIONAL GOVERNMENT

The structure of the national government clearly reflects the desire of the Founders to protect liberty and property, especially from **the tyranny of the majority**. Those who criticize the U.S. government for its slow, unwieldy processes should realize that the government's founders deliberately built in this characteristic. These cumbersome arrangements—the checks and balances and the fragmentation of authority that make it difficult for government to realize its potential for corruption or the violation of individual rights—aim to protect private interests from governmental interference and to shield the government from an unjust and self-seeking majority. If the system handcuffs government and makes it easy for established groups to oppose change, then it is working as intended.

This system of intermingled powers and conflicting loyalties is still alive today. Of course, some aspects have changed; for example, voters now elect senators directly, and the president is more directly responsible to the voters than the Founders originally envisioned. But the basic arrangement of **checks and balances** endures. Presidents, senators, representatives, and judges are chosen by different constituencies; their terms of office vary, and their responsibilities and loyalties differ. This system makes majority rule virtually impossible.

NATIONAL SUPREMACY

The heart of the Constitution is the supremacy clause of Article VI:

> This Constitution, and the laws of the United States which shall be made in pursuance thereof; and all treaties made, or which shall be made, under the authority of the United States, shall be the supreme law of the land; and the judges in every State shall be bound thereby, any thing in the Constitution or laws of any State to the contrary notwithstanding.

This sentence made it abundantly clear that laws of Congress would supersede laws of the states, and it made certain that Congress would control interstate commerce, bankruptcy, monetary affairs, weights and measures, currency and credit, communication, transportation, and foreign and military affairs. Thus, the supremacy clause ensures that the decisions of the national elite will prevail over those of the local elites in all vital areas allocated to the national government.

REPUBLICANISM IN OPERATION

The structure of the national government—its republicanism and its system of separated powers and checks and balances—was also designed to protect liberty and property. To the Founding Fathers, a republican government meant the delegation of powers by the people to a small number of citizens "whose wisdom may best discern the true interest of their country, and whose patriotism and love of justice will be least likely to sacrifice it to temporary or partial consideration."[15] Madison explained, in classic elite fashion, "that the public voice, pronounced by representatives of the people, will be more consonant to the public good than if pronounced by the people themselves." The Founding Fathers clearly believed representatives of the people were more likely to be enlightened persons of principle and property than the voters who chose them and thus would be more trustworthy and dependable.

Voters also had a limited voice in the selection of decision makers. Of the four major decision-making entities established in the Constitution—the House of Representatives, the Senate, the presidency, and the Supreme Court—the people were to elect only one (see Table 2.2). The others were to be at least twice removed from popular control. In the constitution of 1787, the people elected only House members, and for short terms of only two years. In contrast, state legislatures were to elect U.S. senators for six-year terms. Electors, selected as state legislatures saw fit, selected the president. The states could hold elections for presidential electors, or the state legislatures could appoint them. The Founding Fathers hoped presidential electors would be prominent men of wealth and reputation in their respective states. Finally, federal judges were to be appointed by the president for life, thus removing those decision makers as far as possible from popular control. (See Figure 2.1.)

SEPARATION OF POWERS AND CHECKS AND BALANCES

The Founding Fathers also intended the system of separated powers in the national government—with separate legislative, executive, and judicial branches—as a bulwark against majoritarianism (government by popular majorities) and an additional safeguard for elite liberty and property. The doctrine derives from the French writer Montesquieu, whose *Spirit of Laws* was a political textbook for these eighteenth-century statesmen. *The Federalist,* Number 51, expressed the logic of the system of checks and balances:

> Ambition must be made to counteract ambition. ... It may be a reflection on human nature, that such devices should be necessary to control the abuses of government. But

TABLE 2.2 | CHECKS AND BALANCES

Who checks whom?	Congress	President/Executive	Courts
Congress	House and Senate must agree on bills	Can override president's veto, Can impeach and remove president, Senate can reject appointments, Senate can refuse to ratify treaties, Can reject president's requests for laws and funds, Can investigate president's actions	Can reject judicial nominees (including Supreme Court), Can create lower federal courts, Can amend laws to change court interpretations of laws, Can propose constitutional amendments to change court interpretations of the Constitution, Can impeach and remove judges
President/ Executive	Can veto bills passed by Congress, Can call special sessions, Can recommend legislation, Vice president presides over Senate and can vote to break ties	Head of bureaucracy	Nominates judges (including Supreme Court justices), Can pardon persons convicted by federal courts,
Courts	Can interpret laws of Congress, Can declare laws unconstitutional	Can declare actions of president unconstitutional	Supreme Court and Appeals courts can overturn rulings by lower courts,

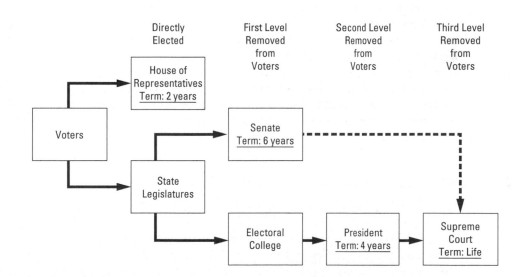

FIGURE 2.1 | LIMITED VOTER VOICE IN SELECTION OF DECISION MAKERS, CONSTITUTION OF 1787

Note: The voice of the voters has since grown far stronger. Both the U.S. Senate and the Electoral College are now elected directly by the people.

what is government itself, but the greatest of all reflections on human nature? If men were angels, no government would be necessary. If angels were to govern men, neither external or internal controls on government would be necessary. In framing a government which is to be administered by men over men, the greatest difficulty lies in this: you must first enable the government to control the governed; and in the next place oblige it to control itself.[16]

As the Founders learned from the historical example of the Roman Republic, checks and balances are necessary because neither elites nor masses are "angels." They shared a general concern that an abuse of power by the many *or* the few might doom the new republic, just as it did that of Rome nearly two millennia earlier.

The Constitution states the **separation of powers** concept in the opening sentences of the first three articles:

[Article I:] All legislative powers herein granted shall be vested in a Congress of the United States, which shall consist of a Senate and House of Representatives. [Article II:] The executive power shall be vested in a President of the United States.... [Article III:] The judicial power of the United States shall be vested in one Supreme Court, and in such inferior courts as the Congress may from time to time ordain and establish.

Insofar as this system divides responsibility and makes it difficult for the masses to hold government accountable for public policy, it achieves one of the purposes intended by the Founding Fathers. Each of the four major decision-making bodies of the national government—House, Senate, president, and Supreme Court—is chosen by a different constituency. Because the terms of these decision-making bodies are of varying length, it is impossible to completely remake the government at one stroke. Thus, the people cannot wreak speedy havoc through direct elections. To make their will felt in all the decision-making bodies of the national government, they must wait years.

Madison's Papers
Biography, correspondence, and papers of James Madison. *www.virginia.edu/ pjm*

The Federalist Papers Numbers 10 and 51 at the Library of Congress. *http:// thomas.loc.gov/ home/histdox/ fedpapers.html*

Checks and balances is also a limitation on elite distemper, actions by members of the elite who might use their positions of power and authority for corrupt self-serving ends. Moreover, each of these decision-making bodies has an important check on the decisions of the others. No bill can become law without the approval of both the House and the Senate (see Table 2.2). The president shares in the legislative power through the veto and the responsibility to "give to the Congress information of the state of the Union, and recommend to their consideration such measures as he shall judge necessary and expedient." The president can also convene sessions of Congress. But the appointing power of the president is shared by the Senate; so is the power to make treaties. Also, Congress can override executive vetoes. The president must execute the laws but cannot do so without relying on executive departments, which Congress must create. The executive branch can spend only money appropriated by Congress. Even the Supreme Court, created by the Constitution, must be appointed by the president with the consent of the Senate, and Congress may prescribe the number of justices. Congress must create lower and intermediate courts, establish the number of judges, and fix the jurisdiction of lower federal courts. Indeed, "separation of powers" is a misnomer, for we are really talking about sharing, not separating, power; each branch participates in the activities of every other branch.

JUDICIAL REVIEW

The final touch on the system of checks and balances came in 1803 with the idea of **judicial review,** an original contribution by the Founding Fathers to the science of government. In the Supreme Court case of *Marbury v. Madison,* Chief Justice John Marshall argued convincingly that the Founding Fathers intended the Supreme Court to have the power to invalidate not only state laws and constitutions but also any laws of Congress that came into conflict with the Constitution. The text of the Constitution nowhere specifically authorizes federal judges to invalidate acts of Congress; at most, it implies this power. (But Hamilton apparently thought that the Constitution contained this power, since he was careful to explain it in *The Federalist,* Number 78, before the ratification of the Constitution.) Thus, the Supreme Court stands as the final defender of the fundamental principles agreed on by the Founding Fathers, against the encroachments of popularly elected legislatures.

Constitutional Law
Cornell University Law School collection of key Supreme Court constitutional decisions. *www. law.cornell.edu/ supct/*

| IN BRIEF | CONSTITUTIONAL LIMITS ON MASS PARTICIPATION IN GOVERNMENT |

- The Constitution, laws, and treaties of the United States are the "Supreme Law of the Land"; "any Thing in the Constitution and or Law of any State to the contrary notwithstanding." This moves political power away from the local to the national.
- Of the four decision-making entities established in the Constitution of 1787—the House of Representatives, the Senate, the presidency, and the Supreme Court—only one, the House of Representatives, was to be elected directly by the people; Senators were selected by state legislatures (not changed until the adoption of the Seventeenth Amendment in 1913); the president is selected by "electors" (by custom and usage beginning in 1800 "electors" pledged to presidential candidates came to be elected by voters in the states); justices of the Supreme Court and other federal judges are appointed for life by the president and confirmed by the Senate.

- Mass movements are frustrated by separation of powers, including differing terms for each decision-making body—the House of Representatives, two years; Senate, six years; president, four years; courts, lifetime.
- Mass movements are frustrated by the need for consensus—both House and Senate must agree to the proposed legislation; the president must sign the legislation; a veto can be overwritten only by a two-thirds vote of both houses; if the legislation is challenged, the courts must decide on its interpretation and whether it is constitutional or not.
- Judicial review can invalidate not only state laws and constitutions but also any laws of Congress; nine justices, appointed not elected, decide conflicts with the Constitution.
- A "republican" government and the principle of representative, not direct, democracy are guaranteed.

FOCUS | JAMES MADISON: SUPPRESSING MAJORITY "FACTIONS"

Perhaps the most important contributor to the Constitution was James Madison (1751–1836). Not only did he play a key role in writing the Constitution, but his insightful and scholarly defense of it also helped immeasurably in securing its ratification. Indeed, Madison is more highly regarded by political scientists and historians as a political theorist than as the fourth president of the United States.

Madison's family owned a large plantation, Montpelier, near present-day Orange, Virginia. Private tutors and prep schools provided the young man with a thorough background in history, science, philosophy, and law. He graduated from the College of New Jersey (now Princeton University) at age 18 and assumed a number of elected and appointed positions in Virginia's colonial government. In 1776, Madison drafted a new Virginia Constitution. While serving in Virginia's Revolutionary assembly, he met Thomas Jefferson; the two became lifetime political allies and friends. In 1787, Madison represented Virginia at the Constitutional Convention and took a leading role in its debates over the form of a new federal government. Madison's *Notes on the Constitutional Convention of 1787,* published 20 years after the event, is the only account of the secret meeting.

Madison's political philosophy is revealed in *The Federalist Papers,* a series of 85 essays published in major newspapers in 1787 and 1788, all signed simply "Publius." Alexander Hamilton and John Jay contributed as well but Madison wrote the two most important: Number 10, which explains the nature of political conflict (faction) and how it can be "controlled," and Number 51, which explains the system of separation of powers and checks and balances.

According to Madison, conflict is part of human nature, and "controlling faction" is the principal task of government. In all societies, we find "a zeal for different opinions concerning religion, concerning government, and many other points" as well as "an attachment to different leaders ambitiously contending for preeminence and power." Even when there are no serious differences among people, these "frivolous and fanciful distinctions" will inspire "unfriendly passions" and "violent conflicts." However, according to Madison,

> the most common and durable source of factions has been the various and unequal distribution of property. Those who hold and those who are without property have ever formed distinct interests in society. Those who are creditors and those who are debtors fall under like discrimination. A landed interest, a manufacturing interest, a mercantile interest, a monied interest, with many lesser interests, grow up of necessity in civilized nations, and divide them into different classes, actuated by different sentiments and views.[17]

In Madison's view, a national government is the most important protection against mass movements that might threaten property. By creating such a government, encompassing a large number of citizens and a great expanse of territory,

> you take in a greater variety of parties and interests; you make it less probable that a majority of the whole will have a common motive to invade the rights of other citizens; or if such a common motive exists it will be more difficult for all who feel it to discover their own strength, and to act in unison with each other.

The structure of the new national government should ensure suppression of "factious" issues (those that would generate factions). And Madison did not hedge in naming these factious issues: "A rage for paper money, for an abolition of debts, for an equal division of property, or for any other improper or wicked project." Note that Madison's factious issues are all challenges to the dominant economic elites. His defense of the new Constitution was that its republican and federal features would help keep certain threats to property from ever becoming public issues.

RATIFICATION: AN EXERCISE IN ELITE POLITICAL SKILLS

When its work ended on September 17, 1787, the Constitutional Convention sent the Constitution to New York City, where Congress was then in session. The Convention suggested the Constitution "should afterwards be submitted to a convention of delegates chosen in each state by the people thereof, under the recommendation of its legislature for their assent and ratification." Convention delegates further proposed that ratification by nine of the 13 states be sufficient to put the new constitution into effect. On September 28, Congress sent the Constitution to the states without further recommendations.

The extraordinary ratification procedure suggested by the Founding Fathers was a skillful political maneuver, because submitting the plan to the state legislatures would have weakened its chances for success. Thus, the struggle for ratification began under ground rules designed by the national elite to give them the advantage over any potential opponents.

In an important and controversial study of the Constitution, Charles A. Beard compiled significant evidence supporting the hypothesis "that substantially all of the merchants, moneylenders, security holders, manufacturers, shippers, capitalists and financiers, and their professional associates are to be found on one side in support of the Constitution, and that substantially all of the major portion of the opposition came from the non-slaveholding farmers and debtors."[18] Beard's economic interpretation differs from an elitist one in that an elitist interpretation asserts only that the masses did not participate in writing or adopting the Constitution and does not depend on showing they opposed it. Most historians concede that only about 160,000 people voted in elections for delegates to state ratifying conventions, and that not more than 100,000 of these voters favored the adoption of the Constitution. This figure represents about one in six of the adult males in the country, and no more than 5 percent of the general population. It is clear that the number of people who participated in any fashion in ratifying the Constitution was an extremely small minority of the population.

THE BILL OF RIGHTS AS AN AFTERTHOUGHT

Some men of property and education did oppose the new Constitution. These were men who had greater confidence in their ability to control state governments than to control the new federal government. They called themselves Anti-Federalists and deplored the undemocratic features of the new Constitution. Their most effective criticism centered on the absence of any bill of rights, a particularly glaring omission as the idea was popular at the time, and most new state constitutions contained one. It is an interesting comment on the psychology of the Founding Fathers that the idea of a bill of rights did not come up in the Convention until the final week of deliberations; even then it received little consideration. The Founding Fathers certainly believed in limited government, and they did write a few liberties into the body of the Constitution, such as protection against bills of attainder and ex post facto laws, a guarantee of the writ of habeas corpus, a limited definition of treason, and a guarantee of jury trial. However, they did not include a bill of rights.

When criticism about the absence of such a bill began to mount during the ratification process, supporters of the Constitution argued to explain the deficiency: (1) the national government was one of enumerated powers and could not exercise any powers not expressly delegated to it in the Constitution; (2) the power to interfere with free speech or press or otherwise to restrain liberty was not among the enumerated powers in the Constitution; (3) it was therefore unnecessary to deny the new government that power specifically. But this logic was unconvincing; the absence of a bill of rights seemed to confirm the suspicion that the Founding Fathers were more concerned with protecting property than with protecting the personal liberties of the people. Many members of the elite and nonelite alike were uncomfortable with the thought that personal liberty depended on a thin thread of inference from enumerated powers. Supporters of the Constitution thus had to retreat from their demand for unconditional ratification. The New York, Massachusetts, and Virginia conventions agreed to the new Constitution only after receiving the Federalists' solemn promise to add a bill of rights as amendments. Thus, the fundamental guarantees of liberty in the Bill of Rights were political concessions by the nation's elite. Whereas the Founding Fathers deserved great credit for the document that they produced in Philadelphia, the first Congress to meet under that Constitution was nonetheless obliged to submit 10 amendments to the states—the Bill of Rights—which were ratified by 1791.

THE CONSTITUTION | AN ELITIST INTERPRETATION

Elite theory provides us with an interpretation of the U.S. Constitution and the basic structure of U.S. government. Our analysis of constitutional policies centers on the following propositions:

1. The Constitution of the United States was not "ordained and established" by "the people." Instead it was written by a small, educated, talented, wealthy elite representative of powerful economic interests.
2. The Constitution and the national government it established had their origins in elite dissatisfaction with the inability of the central government under the Articles of Confederation to pay off bondholders, interference of state governments with the development of a national economy, threats to investors and creditors posed by state issuance of cheap paper money and laws relieving debtors of contractual obligations, the threat to propertied classes arising from post–Revolutionary War radicalism, the inability of the central government to provide an army capable of protecting western development or a navy capable of protecting commercial interests on the high seas, and the inability of the elite to exercise power in world affairs.
3. The elite achieved ratification of the Constitution through astute political skills. The masses of people in the United States did not participate in the writing of the Constitution or in its adoption by the states.
4. The Founding Fathers shared a consensus that the fundamental role of government is the protection of liberty and property. They believed in a

republican form of government by men of principle and property. They opposed an aristocracy or a governing nobility, but they also opposed mass democracy with direct participation by the people in decision making. They feared mass movements seeking to reduce inequalities of wealth, intelligence, talent, or virtue. Such "dangerous leveling" was a serious violation of individual rights to pursue different goals and see different outcomes.

5. Republicanism, the division of power between state and national governments, and the complex system of checks and balances and divided power were all designed as protections against mass movements that might threaten liberty and property.

6. The text of the Constitution contains many direct and immediate benefits to the governing elite. Although both elites and masses have benefited by the adoption of its rights and protections, the benefits to elites were the compelling motives for supporting it.

NOTES

1. Lester Cappon, ed., *The Adams-Jefferson Letters* (Chapel Hill: University of North Carolina Press, 1959), vol. l, p. 106.

2. Max Ferrand, ed., *The Records of the Federal Convention of 1787* (New Haven, CT.: Yale University Press, 1937), vol. 3, p. 15.

3. Charles A. Beard, *An Economic Interpretation of the Constitution of the United States* (New York: Macmillan, 1913), pp. 73–151. Much of this chapter reflects data presented by Beard in this classic work. Beard shows that economic considerations played a major role in the shaping of the Constitution.

4. See Chernow, Ron. *Alexander Hamilton*. New York: Penguin, 2004.

5. John P. Roche, "The Founding Fathers: A Reform Caucus in Action," *American Political Science Review* 55 (December 1961): 799.

6. See Clinton Rossiter, *1787, The Grand Convention* (New York: Macmillan, 1966), p. 45.

7. McClellan, James. *Liberty, Order, and Justice: An Introduction to the Constitutional Principles of American Government*, 3rd ed. (Indianapolis: Liberty Fund, 2000), p. 32.

8. The words *liberal* and *conservative* have changed significantly in meaning since the time of the Founders. Liberals today may still have strong beliefs in individual freedoms but often cast them in terms of group identity. The classical liberal distrust of government has split into one group called liberals with a more accepting attitude toward a more active role of government, and a second group called libertarians who have stuck to the more skeptical view. Meanwhile, conservatism has maintained its strong basis in traditional skepticism of human nature, but it has also incorporated many classical liberal ideas on limited government and individual economic autonomy. Most U.S. adults hold a mixture of liberal and conservative views, just like the Founders.

9. James Madison kept secret notes on the Convention, which he published many years later. Most of our knowledge about the Convention comes from Madison's notes. See Ferrand, *Records*.

10. Ferrand, *Records*, p. 32.

11. See especially Beard, *Economic Interpretation*.

12. Chernow, Alexander Hamilton.

13. James Madison, Alexander Hamilton, and John Jay, *The Federalist* (New York: Modern Library, 1937).

14. Madison, *The Federalist*, Number 10.

15. Madison, *The Federalist*, Number 10.

16. Madison and Hamilton, *The Federalist*, Number 51.

17. Madison, *The Federalist*, Number 10.

18. Beard, *Economic Interpretation*, pp. 16–17. Beard's economic interpretation differs from an elitist interpretation in that Beard believes that the economic elites supported the Constitution and

the masses opposed it. Our elitist interpretation asserts only that the masses did not participate in writing or adopting the Constitution and that elites benefited directly from its provisions. Our interpretation does not depend on showing that the masses opposed the Constitution but merely that they did not participate in its establishment. Attacks on Beard appear in Forrest McDonald, *We the People: The Economic Origins of the Constitution* (Chicago: University of Chicago Press, 1958), and Robert E. Brown, *Charles Beard and the Constitution* (Princeton, NJ: Princeton University Press, 1956). Lee Benson provides a balanced view in *Turner and Beard: American Historical Writing Reconsidered* (New York: Free Press, 1960).

The fierceness of political struggles has often been misleading; for the range of vision embodied by the primary contestants in the major parties has always been bounded by the horizons of property and enterprise.

—**Richard Hofstadter**

ELITES IN AMERICA

CHAPTER **3**

Power in the United States is organized into large institutions. Elite positions at the top of the major institutions in U.S. society are sources of great power. Sociologist C. Wright Mills described the relationship between institutional authority and power in this way:

> If we took the one hundred most powerful men in America, the one hundred wealthiest, and the one hundred most celebrated away from the institutional positions they now occupy, away from their resources of men and women and money, away from the media of mass communication that are now focused upon them—then they should be powerless and poor and uncelebrated. For power is not of a man. Wealth does not center in the person of the wealthy. Celebrity is not inherent in any personality. To be celebrated, to be wealthy, to have power, requires access to major institutions, for the institutional positions men occupy determine in large part their chances to have and to hold these valued experiences.[1]

In this chapter, we introduce the people who occupy elite positions in the major private and governmental institutions of U.S. society. We include the major *private* institutions—in business, finance, media, law, and other nongovernmental institutions—because we believe they allocate resources for our society and shape the lives of all those in it. Remember, we defined an **elite member** as anyone who participates in decisions that allocate resources for society, not just those who participate in decision making as part of the government. The decisions of cell phone companies to raise prices, of banks to raise or lower interest rates, of unions to press for new benefits, of the mass media to determine what is "news," and of universities and colleges to decide what will be taught—all affect our lives as much as government decisions do.[2]

Governmental elites—the president and top executive officials, congressional leaders, and committee chairs—interact closely with corporate, financial, and media elites. Corporate and personal wealth is channeled through foundations to universities and think tanks to undertake policy research and develop policy recommendations. Research reports and policy recommendations are directed toward both media and governmental elites. The media largely set the agenda for discussion and debate of policy directions. Governmental elites are obliged to respond to media definitions of societal "problems," as well as to policy proposals the media receive from foundations, universities, and think tanks. We will examine governmental elites in greater detail in later chapters of this text; this chapter will focus on economic elites.

National policy does not reflect demands of "the people" but rather the preferences, interests, and values of the few who participate in the policy-making process. Elites have little confidence in the judgment of the masses (see Focus: Elite Attitudes toward Mass Governance). Changes or innovations in public policy come about when elites redefine their own interests or modify their own values. Policies decided by elites need not be oppressive or exploitative of the masses. Elites may be paternalistic and public-regarding, and the welfare of the masses may be an important consideration in elite decision making. Yet by definition, it is *elites* who make policy, not the *masses*.

THE EVOLUTION OF U.S. ELITES

A stable elite system depends on the "**circulation of elites**"—the movement of talented and ambitious individuals from the lower strata into the elite. An open elite system that provides for "a slow and continuous modification of the ruling classes" is essential for continuing the system and avoiding revolution. Popular elections, party competition, and other democratic institutions in the United States have not enabled the masses to govern, but they have helped keep the elite system an open one. They have assisted in the circulation of elites, even if they have never been a means of challenging the dominant elite consensus on liberal democracy and its core values.

In this section, a historical analysis of the evolution of U.S. elites, we show that elite membership has evolved slowly, without any serious break in the ideas or values underlying the U.S. political and economic systems. The United States has never experienced a true revolution that forcibly replaced governing elites with nonelites. In fact, historical experience from the French revolution to the Bolshevik takeover of Russia to the theocratic replacement of the Shah in Iran has shown that revolutionary change is far more likely to end in disaster and bloodbath than any real improvement for the masses. There are always elites, and elites that seize power through violence tend to preserve violent methods. As an alternative in the United States, elite membership has been made open to those who acquire wealth and/or prestige and who accept the national consensus about private enterprise, limited government, and individualism. Industrialization, technological change, and other new sources of wealth in the expanding economy have produced new elite members; and the U.S. elite system has permitted, even encouraged, the absorption of the new elites without upsetting the system itself.

Policy changes and innovations in the structure of U.S. government over the decades have been *incremental* (step-by-step) rather than revolutionary. Elites have modified public policies but seldom replaced them. They have made structural adaptations in the constitutional system designed by the Founding Fathers but have kept intact the original framework of U.S. constitutionalism.

Political conflict in the United States has centered on a narrow range of issues. Only once, in the Civil War, were elites deeply divided over the nature of U.S. society. Even the major rearrangement of power from the private sector and the states to the federal government begun in the New Deal period was fundamentally a system-preserving move. The brief review of the evolution of U.S. elites in this chapter is no substitute for the study of U.S. political history.

EARLY ELITE CONSENSUS: HAMILTON'S FINANCIAL VISION

The most influential figure in the early United States was Federalist President George Washington. More than anyone else, Alexander Hamilton, his Secretary of the Treasury, was aware that the new nation had to win the lasting confidence of business and financial elites in order to survive and prosper. Only if the United States was established on a sound financial basis could it attract investors at home and abroad and expand its industry and commerce. Hamilton also favored a strong central government as a means of protecting property and stimulating the growth of commerce and industry.

Hamilton's first move was to pay the Revolutionary War debt at face value. Most of the original bonds were held by speculators who had purchased them for only a fraction of their face value, meaning repayment provided them a spectacular profit. Hamilton's objective was to place the creditor elite under a deep obligation to the central government. This maneuver also created a large pool of capital available for investment in the industrialization of the United States, a vision of Hamilton's at odds with the agrarian vision of Jefferson and the Anti-Federalists.

Hamilton also acted to establish a Bank of the United States, which would issue a national currency, facilitate the sale of national bonds, and tie the national government even more closely to the banking elites. The Constitution did not specifically grant Congress the power to create a national bank, but Hamilton was willing to interpret the **"necessary and proper" clause** broadly enough to include the creation of a bank to help carry out the taxing, borrowing, and currency powers enumerated in the Constitution. Hamilton's broad construction of the clause pointed in the direction of a central government that would exercise powers not specifically enumerated in the Constitution.

Not until 1819 and the famous case of *McCulloch v. Maryland* did the Supreme Court uphold the broad definition of national power suggested by Hamilton under the "necessary and proper" clause.[3] The *McCulloch* case firmly established the principle that Congress has the right to choose any appropriate means for carrying out the delegated powers of the national government. The "necessary and proper" clause is often called the "implied powers" or "elastic" clause, because it gives Congress many powers the Constitution does not explicitly grant, providing legal justification for the continuing expansion of the federal government.

The centralizing effect of Hamilton's programs and their favoring of merchants, manufacturers, and shipbuilders aroused some opposition in elite circles. Southern planters and large landowners benefited little from Hamilton's policies, and they were joined in their opposition by local and state elites who feared a strong central

| FOCUS | ELITE ATTITUDES TOWARD MASS GOVERNANCE |

Since the early days of the Republic, U.S. elites have adopted a democratic rhetoric that obscures their disdain for the masses. Alexander Hamilton may have been the last national leader to publicly acknowledge elitist views:

> The voice of the people has been said to be the voice of God, and however generally this maxim has been quoted and believed, it is not true in fact. The people are turbulent and changing; they seldom judge or determine right.[a]

Today, just as two centuries ago, elites have little confidence in the judgment of the masses. The rhetoric of democracy is so ingrained that elites instinctively recite democratic phrases. But consider the following responses obtained in a special survey of congressional, executive, and bureaucratic elites in Washington conducted by the Princeton Survey Research Associates:

QUESTION: "How much trust and confidence do you have in the wisdom of the American people when it comes to making choices on election day: a great deal, a fair amount, not very much, or none at all?"

	Congress Members	Presidential Staff	Senior Bureaucrats
Great deal	64	34	34
Fair amount	31	51	44
Not very much	1	12	20
None at all	0	1	1
Don't know/ No answer	4	2	1

QUESTION: "Do you think the American public knows enough about the issues you face to form wise opinions about what should be done about these issues, or not?"

	Congress Members	Presidential Staff	Senior Bureaucrats
Yes	31	13	14
No	47	77	81
Maybe/ Depends (vol.)	17	7	3
Don't know/ No answer	5	3	2

[a]Quoted in James McClellan, Liberty, Order, and Justice: An Introduction to the Constitutional Principles of American Government, 3rd ed. (Indianapolis: Liberty Fund, 2000), pp. 151–152.

Source: Pew Research Center/National Journal survey conducted under the direction of Princeton Survey Research Associates, October 1997—February 1998. N = 81 members of Congress, 98 presidential appointees, and 151 members of the Senior Executive Service of the federal government. As reported in Polling Report, May 4, 1998.

government threatened their own powers. These landed elites were first called the Anti-Federalists and then the Democratic Republicans. This dispute was not between elites and masses. It was within elite circles between two propertied classes: merchants and bankers on one side and plantation owners and large slaveholders on the other.[4]

In the election of 1800, the Federalists were defeated and Thomas Jefferson became president. This enabled landed interests to gain power in relation to commercial and industrial interests. Because the vast majority of people won their living from the soil, the landed elites were able to mobilize those masses behind their bid for control of the government. Yet the fact that an "out" party, the Democratic-Republicans, peacefully replaced an "in" party, the Federalists, was testimony to the strength of the consensus among the new nation's elite.

It is interesting that once in office Jefferson made few changes in Federalist and Hamiltonian policy. The Democratic-Republicans did not attack commercial or industrial enterprise; in fact, commerce and industry prospered under their rule as never before. Instead of crushing the banks, the Democratic-Republicans soon supported the financial interests they had sworn to oppose. The party that opposed Hamilton's programs adopted them, demonstrating that a core elite consensus had been reached. As for tax policies, Jefferson wrote in 1816:

> To take from one, because it is thought his own industry and that of his fathers has acquired too much, in order to spare to others, who, or whose fathers, have not exercised equal industry and skill, is to violate arbitrarily the first principle of association, "the guarantee to everyone the free exercise of his industry and the fruits acquired by it."[5]

The Democratic-Republicans had no intention of redistributing wealth in the United States. Indeed, before the end of James Madison's second term in 1817, they had taken over the whole complex of Hamiltonian policies: a national bank, high tariffs, protection for manufacturers, internal improvements, western land development, a strong army and navy, and a broad interpretation of national power. So complete was the elite consensus that by 1820 the Democratic-Republican Party had completely driven the Federalist Party out of existence, largely by taking over its programs.

THE RISE OF THE WEST

The expansion of the United States to the West provided the next challenge to the elite system (Figure 3.1). People went west because of the vast wealth of fertile lands that awaited them there; nowhere else in the world could anyone acquire wealth so quickly. Because aristocratic families of the eastern seaboard seldom had reason to migrate westward, the western settlers were mainly middle- and lower-class immigrants. With hard work and good fortune, penniless migrants could become wealthy plantation owners or cattle ranchers in a single generation. Thus, the West offered rapid upward social mobility. New elites arose in the West and had to be assimilated into the country's governing circles. No one exemplifies the new entrants into the U.S. elite better than Andrew Jackson. Jackson's victory in the presidential election of 1828 was not a victory of the common people against the propertied classes but rather one of the new western elites against established leadership in the East, which was forced to open its ranks.

Frontier society idealized the characteristics of rugged individualism and self-creation. People admired wealth and power won by competitive skill, an ideal that continues in our present-day respect for entrepreneurs such as Bill Gates of Microsoft, Mark Zuckerberg of Facebook, Sergei Brin and Larry Page of Google, Michael Dell, Sean John Combs, and Oprah Winfrey. This ideal demands not absolute equality but a more open elite system—a greater opportunity for the rising middle class to acquire wealth and influence. In their struggle to open the U.S. elite system, the Jacksonians appealed to mass sentiment. Rising elites, themselves often

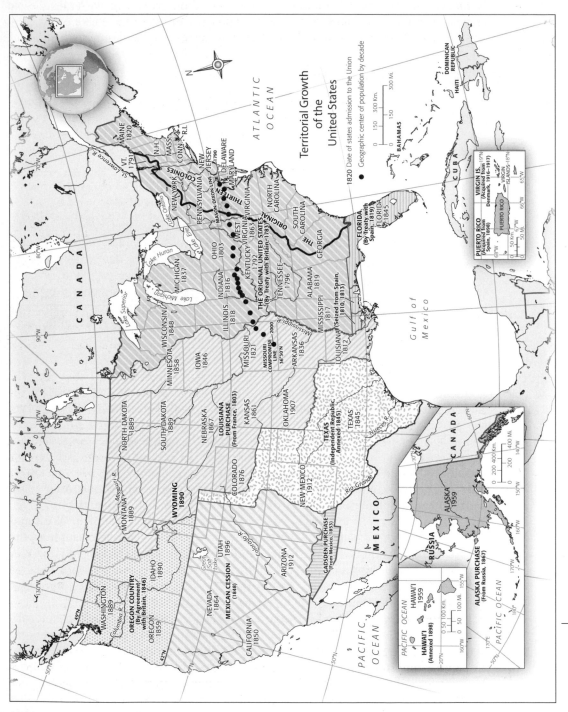

FIGURE 3.1 | U.S. WESTWARD EXPANSION

less than a generation away from the masses, also saw in a widened electorate a chance for personal advancement they could never have achieved under the old regime. Therefore the Jacksonians became noisy and effective advocates of the principle that all (white) men should have the right to vote and to hold public office.

ELITE CLEAVAGE: THE CIVIL WAR

During the nation's first 60 years, elites substantially agreed about the character and direction of the new nation. Conflicts and controversies did not threaten the basic underlying consensus. By the 1850s, however, the status of slaves in U.S. society—the most divisive issue in the history of U.S. politics—drove a wedge among the elites and ultimately led to the nation's bloodiest war. The national political system was unequal to the task of negotiating a peaceful settlement to the slavery problem because the elites were divided deeply over the question.

Southern elites—cotton planters, landowners, exporters, and slave traders—could not profitably produce cotton without slave labor. Cotton accounted for more than half the value of all U.S. goods shipped abroad before the Civil War. "Slave raising" itself also became immensely profitable. It was the white *elites* and not the white *masses* of the South who had an interest in the slave and cotton culture. On the eve of the Civil War, probably no more than 400,000 southern families—approximately one in four—held slaves, and many of those families held only one or two slaves each. The number of great planters—men who owned 50 or more slaves and large holdings of land—was probably not more than 7,000, yet their views dominated southern politics.

The northern elites were merchants and manufacturers who depended on a paid labor market, yet they had no direct interest in abolishing slavery in the South. Both northern and southern elites realized that control of the West was the key to future dominance of the nation. Northern elites wanted a West composed of small farmers who produced food and raw materials for the industrial and commercial East and provided a market for eastern goods. To protect the cotton economy, southern elites believed it was essential to protect slavery in western lands. This conflict over western land eventually precipitated the Civil War.

CLEAVAGE, VIOLENCE, AND SECESSION

Beginning in 1856, proslavery and antislavery forces fought it out in "bleeding Kansas." Intemperate language in the Senate became commonplace, with frequent threats of secession, violence, and civil war. The antislavery Republican Party carried one-third of the vote, including all the North and West, marking the collapse of the Whig Party. For the first time in U.S. history, one of the two major parties failed to compete nationally.

In 1857, the Supreme Court decided, in *Dred Scott v. Sandford*, that the earlier Missouri Compromise was unconstitutional because Congress had no authority to forbid slavery in any territory.[6] The Constitution protected slave property, said Chief Justice Roger B. Taney, as much as any other kind of property.

In 1860, four major parties sought the presidency. While none came close to winning the majority of popular votes, Lincoln, the Republican candidate, v the Electoral College. More important, the cleavage had become so deep that many prominent southern leaders announced they would not accept the outcome of the presidential election if Lincoln won. For the first and only time in U.S. history, prominent elite members were willing to destroy the political system rather than compromise their interests and principles. Shortly after the election, on December 20, 1860, the state of South Carolina seceded from the Union. Within six months, ten other southern states followed. When Southern, or Confederate, forces attacked the Fort Sumter U.S. military base in South Carolina in April 1861, the Civil War began.

LINCOLN AND SLAVERY

Abraham Lincoln had never attacked slavery in the South; his exclusive concern was to halt the spread of slavery in the western territories, which he wanted to tie economically and culturally to the northern system. Lincoln's political posture was essentially conservative: He wished to preserve the long-established order and consensus that had protected U.S. principles and property rights so successfully in the past. He was not an abolitionist, and he did not want to destroy the southern elites or to alter the southern social fabric. His goal was to bring the South back into the Union, to restore orderly government, and to establish that the states cannot resist national authority with force.

Republicans knew the South's power depended on slave labor. Lincoln also knew that if he proclaimed the war was being fought to free the slaves, foreign intervention was less likely. Yet even in late summer of 1862, he wrote:

> My paramount object in this struggle is to save the Union. If I could save the Union without freeing any slaves, I would do it; if I could save it by freeing some and leaving others alone, I would also do that. I shall do less whenever I shall believe what I am doing hurts the cause, and I shall do more whenever I believe doing more will help the cause.[7]

Finally, on September 22, 1862, Lincoln issued his preliminary Emancipation Proclamation. Claiming his right as commander-in-chief of the army and navy, he promised that "on the first day of January 1863, all persons held as slaves within any state or designated part of a state, the people whereof shall then be in rebellion against the United States shall be then, thence forward, and forever free." Thus, one of the great steps forward in human freedom in the United States, the Emancipation Proclamation, did not come about as a result of demands by the people and certainly not as a result of demands by the slaves themselves. It was a political and military action by the president for the sake of helping to preserve the Union. It was not a revolutionary intention but a conservative one.

RISE OF THE NEW INDUSTRIAL ELITE

The economic transformation of the United States from an agricultural to an industrial nation reached its climax after the Civil War. The passage of the Homestead Act in 1862 threw the national domain wide open to settlers, and the Transcontinental Railroad Act of 1862 gave the railroads plentiful incentives to link expanding western markets to eastern industry. The rise of corporations and of stock markets for the accumulation of investment capital upset old-fashioned ideas of property. The introduction of machinery in factories revolutionized the conditions of labor and made urban masses dependent on a new industrial capitalist elite for their livelihood. Civil War profits compounded the capital of the industrialists and placed them in a position to dominate the economic life of the nation. Moreover, when the southern planters were removed from the national scene, the government in Washington became the exclusive domain of the new industrial leaders.

As business became increasingly national in scope, only the strongest, most efficient, or most unscrupulous of the competitors survived. Great producers tended to become the cheapest ones, and little companies tended to disappear. Industrial production rose rapidly, while the number of industrial concerns steadily diminished. Total capital investment and total output of industry vastly increased, while ownership became concentrated. One result was the emergence of "trusts," monopolies and near monopolies in the major industries of the United States. Monopolies are by definition anti-competitive and violate a core elite consensus on free competition in a free marketplace, resulting in elite demand for anti-trust action by the government.

REFORM AS ELITE SELF-INTEREST: THE PROGRESSIVE ERA TO THE NEW DEAL

In 1882, William H. Vanderbilt of the New York Central Railroad expressed the ethos of the industrial elite: "The public be damned." Mostly self-made men, this first generation of great U.S. capitalists had little sense of public responsibility. They had built their empires in the competitive pursuit of profit. They believed their success arose from the immutable laws of natural selection, the survival of the fittest; they believed society was best served by allowing those laws to operate freely. As winners, they approved of the social Darwinist idea that those at the top are better than those in the masses.

The masses, swelled with vast numbers of immigrants from Europe, felt left out. Mass discontent was expressed through populist elites such as William Jennings Bryant. Some saw appeal in radical movements imported by immigrants such as anarchism and socialism. Angry masses are not conducive to a stable system. In 1901, an anarchist assassinated President William McKinley. The elites saw that the system needed to be adjusted in order to remain stable.

PROGRESSIVE ERA

The industrialization and urbanization of the United States that rose to a peak in the late 1800s marked a period of rapid change. For elites, change can be good when it means more wealth and power, but it also represents a threat. Some industrial and financial fortunes became so large they restricted competition, rather than sustaining the free competitive market on which elite consensus rested. This period also brought social disruption, and vast numbers of the masses felt left out by the economic boom they saw around them. Elites in the United States saw that their counterparts in Europe faced similar concerns about system stability. In Great Britain, the Conservative leader and Prime Minister Benjamin Disraeli reduced anti-establishment pressures by pushing social reforms as part of an alliance between the landed aristocracy and the poor who needed the elites' noblesse oblige.

TABLE 3.1 | PROGRESSIVE ERA REFORMS

Year	Name of Law or Action	Purpose
1887	Interstate Commerce Act	Regulate railroads
1890	Sherman Antitrust Act	Stop monopolies
1906	Pure Food and Drug Act	Regulate product safety
1906	Meat Inspection Act	Regulate product safety
1909	Sixteenth Amendment	Introduce federal income tax
1914	Establishment of Federal Trade Commission	Regulate commerce
1914	Child Labor Act (ruled unconstitutional)	Limit child labor

In Prussia, conservative aristocrat Chancellor Otto von Bismarck instituted key welfare state programs such as health insurance and old age and disability insurance specifically to ward off the appeal of socialism. It was clear that elite actions to address at least some of the masses' concerns could preempt much agitation and anger aimed at the elites. In the United States, the federal government instituted a variety of laws and regulations for similar reasons. Some examples appear in Table 3.1.

In the early twentieth century, Presidents Theodore Roosevelt (Republican, 1901–1909) and Woodrow Wilson (Democrat, 1913–1921) showed a new elite ethos and criticized elites for their lack of public responsibility. They urged the U.S. elite to value the welfare of the masses as an aspect of its own long-run welfare (see Focus: The Progressive Era). This was not to upset the established order, but to develop a sense of public responsibility within the establishment. For example, the Federal Reserve Act (1914) placed the nation's banking and credit system under government authority after the Panic of 1907 when the actions of a single member of the elite, J. P. Morgan, saved the nation's banking system. Wilson's administration also established the Federal Trade Commission (1914) and authorized it to function in the "public interest" to prevent "unfair methods of competition and unfair and deceptive acts in commerce." Trustbuster Roosevelt broke up a large number of monopolies, most famously J. D. Rockefeller's Standard Oil. The administration of his successor, William Howard Taft, although less "progressive," prosecuted over 80 anti-trust cases. Both Roosevelt's and Wilson's programs aimed to preserve competition, individualism, enterprise, and opportunity—all considered vital in the U.S. heritage. Both believed elites must function in the public interest and that some government regulation might be required to see that they do so. The size of government grew to reflect this, and the federal budget went from $525 million in 1901 to $3 billion in the 1920s (it hit a peak with World War I at $18.5 billion in 1919).

THE GREAT DEPRESSION AND THE NEW DEAL

The economic collapse of the Great Depression undermined the faith of both elites and nonelites in the ideals of the old order. Following the stock market crash of October 1929, and despite elite assurances that prosperity lay "just around the corner," the U.S. economy virtually came to a halt. Prices dropped sharply, factories closed, real estate values declined, new construction practically ceased, banks went under, wages dropped drastically, and unemployment figures mounted. By 1932, one of every four persons in the United States was unemployed, and one of every five was on welfare. Mass faith in the system was threatened.

The elites recognized that drastic action needed to be taken. Republican President Herbert Hoover decided on multiple government interventions in the economy. Some were to purchase relief for the masses, such as the public works programs of the Emergency Relief and Construction Act and the government's backing of loans through the creation of the Reconstruction Finance Corporation (RFC). Most notoriously, Hoover in 1930 approved the Smoot-Hawley Tariff Act, which sent global trade into a downward spiral. Major errors were made by restricting the money supply in a time of tight credit. These measures did not improve the economy and Hoover was seen as ineffective by the increasingly desperate masses, who thus voted against him by a large margin.

The election of Franklin Delano Roosevelt to the presidency in 1932 ushered in a new era in U.S. elite philosophy. The Great Depression did not result in revolution or the emergence of new elites. The threat to existing elites did drive some new thinking of the nation's governing elites. The models of government-directed economies in Germany, Italy, and the Soviet Union provided examples of centralized elite-driven industrial systems.[8] The growing restlessness of the masses in the United States combined to convince the nation's elite that reform and regard for the public welfare were essential to the continued maintenance of the political system and their dominant place in it.

The New Deal was not new or extreme but rather a necessary reform of the existing capitalist system. Its main innovation was transferring a significant amount of power from economic elites in the private sector to governmental elites. Based on the work of economist John Maynard Keynes, its central idea was that by making the government a major player in the economy, the country could minimize the ups and downs of the business cycle and protect the masses. The New Deal had no consistent unifying plan; it was a series of improvisations, many adopted suddenly and some even contradictory. Roosevelt believed government needed to undertake more careful economic planning to adapt "existing economic organizations to the service of the people." And he believed government must act humanely and compassionately toward those who were suffering hardship. Relief, recovery, and reform—and preventing revolution—were the objectives of the New Deal.

NOBLESSE OBLIGE

For anyone of Roosevelt's background, it would have been surprising indeed to try to do anything other than preserve the existing social and economic order. Roosevelt was a descendant of two of the oldest U.S. elite families, the Roosevelts and the Delanos, patrician clans whose wealth predated the Civil War and the Industrial Revolution. The Roosevelts were not schooled in the scrambling competition of the new industrialists. Like his cousin Theodore, Franklin Roosevelt expressed a more public-regarding philosophy. Soon his personal philosophy of *noblesse oblige*—elite responsibility for the welfare of the masses—became the prevailing ethos of the new liberal establishment. It also generated a belief among the masses that the elites continued to have their best interests at heart.

THE GROWTH OF GOVERNMENT: THE NEW DEAL TO THE COLD WAR

The most important lasting impact of the New Deal was the permanently larger size of the federal government. Except for the short-term expenses of war, the federal budget was well below 5 percent of gross domestic product through 1931. This changed dramatically by 1934 when federal spending passed the 10 percent mark, on its way to hitting over 40 percent of the economy during World War II, before settling into the 18–20 percent range afterward through 2008. Note these statistics are only for *federal* spending; the portion of the economy going to government is significantly higher when state and local spending are included, peaking at well over 50 percent.[9] Figure 3.2 shows the government's expansion into the economy. As money flowed to the federal government, so did power move from the private sector to the public sector. As a result, the relative number and strength of elites shifted. Elite theorist C. Wright Mills reflected that an elite class of government, military, business, and political leaders were running the nation to their mutual benefit.

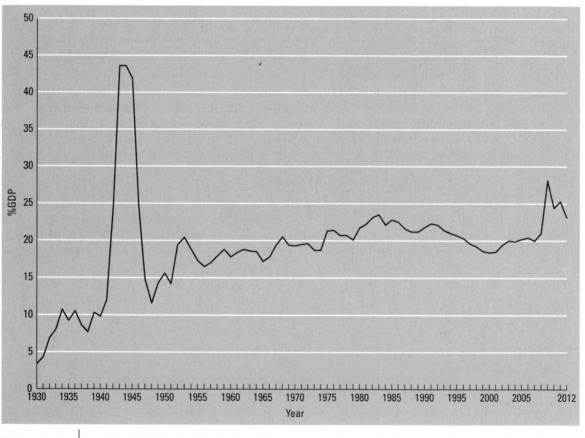

FIGURE 3.2 | FEDERAL SPENDING AS PERCENTAGE OF GROSS DOMESTIC PRODUCT, 1930–2012

Source: *www.gpoaccess.gov/usbudget/fy12/hist.html*

The economic system is inextricably associated with the political system. Often there is no clear line of division between government and business enterprise, or between government elites and business elites. The goals of government and corporate management have largely blurred together: economic stability, a solid currency, an educated workforce, technological development, and continual economic growth. Mills commented that "the decisions of a handful of corporations bear upon military and political as well as economic developments around the world," and that the leaders of government and business form the power elite of the United States.[10] In his farewell address to the nation in 1961, President Dwight Eisenhower warned of a "military-industrial complex" consisting of the government's Department of Defense, private military contractors, and, in the speech's earlier draft, members of Congress.[11]

Frequently, Big Business and Big Government are discussed in conjunction with Big Labor, meaning the labor organizations representing those working for government and government contractors. Big Labor traditionally provided labor market stability to Big Business and a mechanism for mobilizing voters for Big Government. However, Big Labor saw continuing decline from its 1950s peak onward, and it will be focused on primarily as an interest group in Chapter 7.

This new model of the organization of power in the United States, with Big Government at the center and the continued growth of the private sector in Big Business, settled in by the 1950s as the general format of power relations for the country. The expansion of government size with elite support has continued since the New Deal and under the administrations of both parties. The 1960s saw another massive expansion in the role of government in U.S. life, through the introduction of new social welfare programs and increased regulation of the economy. The era of continuing government expansion was not significantly affected by the election in 1980 of President Ronald Reagan (1981–1989), who spoke of smaller government but oversaw its unabated growth. In fact, the only real contraction in government occurred during the administration of President William Clinton (1993–2001), who "reinvented government" and reduced its size and cost. Under President George W. Bush (2001–2009), a program of "compassionate conservatism" provided for even higher levels of government spending and programming, as well as the expense of two wars.

The size of the federal government hit a record high in 2011. In President Barack Obama's first year, the government directly entered the economy by taking over two automobile companies and seizing failing banks. This process started under Bush with the government purchase of the nation's largest insurance company, American International Group (AIG). Unanswered for now is the question whether this expansion is temporary, as was the case after several wars, or permanent, as happened after the New Deal.

GLOBALIZATION

The current phase of the economy and the relationship of government, politics, and business is generally referred to as a period of globalization. Just as the U.S. economy grew from the eastern seaboard across the western frontier, so the United States is the largest player in a global economy. We discuss how globalization has affected the power of elites in the United States in Chapter 14.

FINDING THE ELITES IN THE UNITED STATES

The process of locating which individuals in the United States might be considered members of the elite is straightforward. Elites are elites because they hold positions of power. Power in the United States is found in two overlapping categories: political and economic. Most of the political elite can be found in government, the various portions of which are the subjects of subsequent chapters: the Congress (Chapter 8), the presidency (Chapter 9), the courts (Chapter 10), the bureaucracy (Chapter 11), and the state and local levels of government (Chapter 12). Other members of the political elite are in nongovernmental positions of power: the media (Chapter 5), the political parties (Chapter 6), and organized interest groups (Chapter 7). As the government consumes ever-greater shares of national income, the political elite grow in relative importance of the economic elite. Still, the bulk of power in the United States rests in its dynamic and colossal economy. The remainder of this chapter will focus on economic elites.

ECONOMIC ELITES IN THE UNITED STATES

Economic power in the United States is concentrated in a small number of very large corporations and banks. The men and women who hold positions of power in those businesses, whether as executives or directors, are the **economic elite**. They function under considerable transparency; a basic Internet search of corporate and financial press websites reveals their identities. Public documents filed with the Securities and Exchange Commission (SEC) list their compensation and activities. While not chosen by the masses as politicians are, economic elites are generally held to high levels of accountability by stockholders: to keep their jobs they must show profitable results. It is worth noting that many of the largest institutions that own stocks in corporate America are the public employee pension funds.

Traditionally, pluralism portrays business as just another interest group, competing with all other interest groups to influence public policy. Corporate power, according to the pluralists, depends on the political skills and resources of particular individuals, groups, and industries within the corporate world, on the performance of the economy, on the climate of public opinion, and on the relative strength of competing groups. In contrast, elitism views economic elites as distinctly powerful, not only in shaping government policy but, more important, in making decisions that directly influence all our lives.

Fortune Magazine Rankings Information about corporate and financial institutions, including the largest U.S. ("Fortune 500") and global corporations. *http://money.cnn. com/magazines/ fortune/rankings*

Economic elites decide what will be produced, how it will be produced, how much it will cost, how many people will be employed, who will be employed, and what their wages will be. They decide how goods and services will be distributed, how much money will be available for loans, what interest rates will be charged, and what new technologies will be developed. As President Calvin Coolidge said in 1925, "The chief business of the American people is business."

Of course, these decisions are influenced by governmental regulations, consumer demand, international competition, federal fiscal and monetary policy, and other public and private market forces. The location of power in the U.S. economy shifted significantly toward the government in 2008 and 2009, with federal takeovers of two major automobile manufacturers, the largest insurance company, and countless banks. Still, in a free-market economy, corporate elites, not government officials, typically make most of the key economic decisions.[12]

INDUSTRIAL CONCENTRATION

Formal control of the nation's economic life rests in the hands of a relatively small number of senior officers and directors of the nation's largest corporate institutions. This concentration has occurred chiefly because economic enterprise has increasingly consolidated into a small number of giant corporations. The following statistics only suggest the scale and concentration of modern U.S. corporate enterprise.

The U.S. Internal Revenue Service receives about six million corporate tax returns each year. Only 25,000 (0.4 percent) come from corporations that earn over $50 million in annual revenues. Yet these large corporations account for nearly three-fourths of the total corporate revenues in the nation. The 500 largest U.S. corporations—the "Fortune 500"—collectively took in about $10.8 *trillion* in revenues in 2011, or more than half of all corporate revenue in the nation. Of this, $709 billion was profit. The nation's 20 largest corporations are listed in Table 3.2.

TABLE 3.2 | THE NATION'S LARGEST NON-FINANCIAL CORPORATIONS

Rank	Corporation	Revenue
1	Wal-Mart	$421,849,000,000
2	Exxon Mobil	$354,674,000,000
3	Chevron	$196,337,000,000
4	Conoco Phillips	$184,966,000,000
5	General Electric	$151,628,000,000
6	Berkshire Hathaway	$136,185,000,000
7	General Motors	$135,592,000,000
8	Ford	$128,954,000,000
9	Hewlett-Packard	$126,033,000,000
10	AT&T	$124,629,000,000
11	McKesson	$108,702,000,000
12	Verizon	$106,565,000,000
13	International Business Machines	$99,870,000,000
14	Cardinal Health	$98,602,000,000
15	CVS Caremark	$96,413,000,000
16	UnitedHealth Group	$94,155,000,000
17	Valero Energy	$86,034,000,000
18	Kroger	$82,189,000,000
19	Procter & Gamble	$79,689,000,000
20	AmerisourceBergin	$77,954,000,000

Source: Derived from data provided by *Fortune* at *http://money.cnn.com/magazines/fortune/rankings*. Data from 2011.

(In 2009, the seventh largest company, General Motors, was taken over by and then majority-owned by the U.S. government, with the Canadian government and the United Autoworkers union [UAW] as primary partners. In 2010, the government sold some of its shares, reducing its holding to about 33 percent of the company.)

FINANCIAL CONCENTRATION

The U.S. financial elite is even more concentrated than the industrial elite and becoming more so each year. Table 3.3 lists the 10 largest commercial banks in the nation; together they control nearly half of all banking assets. Due to dramatic changes made in the financial crisis that began in 2007, Citigroup was once 36 percent owned by the U.S. government, although its ownership stake was sold in 2010 at a $12 billion profit. Ally Bank, formerly GMAC (General Motors' finance division), is still 73.8 percent majority-owned by the government (with government-owned General Motors holding almost another 10 percent). Meanwhile, Morgan Stanley, Goldman Sachs, and American Express were forced to change their status from investment banks to commercial banks, which brought them greater access to government funds but also greater regulation.

Giant banking mergers in the last decade have resulted in a greater concentration of banking assets than at any time in recent history. The mergers of JPMorgan with Chase Manhattan and of Bank of America with NationsBank consolidated the nation's financial industry. The federal government forced Bank of America to buy the investment firm Merrill Lynch in 2008, the same year JPMorgan Chase purchased the investment firm Bear Stearns and the commercial bank Washington Mutual under strong government encouragement. Today, three banking corporations—Bank of America, Citigroup, and JPMorgan Chase—control about one-third of all the nation's banking assets.

Beyond banks, other financial companies also have immense power in the U.S. economy. The nation's largest insurance companies invest nearly half of all insurance investment funds, acting on behalf of the millions of consumers who purchase life, home, and auto insurance. As we saw above, the largest insurance company before the crisis, American International Group (AIG), was taken over by the U.S. government in 2008; the government is now in the process of unloading its shares in the company.

The largest U.S. investment firms largely decide how the nation will invest in its future. They decide whether, when, and under what terms U.S. corporations can borrow money from and sell stocks and bonds to the general public. That is to say,

TABLE 3.3 | THE NATION'S LARGEST COMMERCIAL BANKS

Rank	Commercial Bank	Rank	Commercial Bank
1	Bank of America	6	Morgan Stanley
2	JPMorgan Chase	7	American Express
3	Citigroup	8	USBancorp
4	Wells Fargo	9	Capital One
5	Goldman Sachs	10	Ally Bank (GMAC)

Source: Derived from data provided by *Fortune* at *http://money.cnn.com/magazines/fortune/rankings*. Data from 2011.

| HEDGE FUNDS

Much discussion has been made in recent years of hedge funds, special private investment partnerships that frequently produce outstanding investment returns. In 2011, there were 241 hedge funds with over $1 billion in assets under management, totaling $1.4 trillion.[a] They will use leverage, or borrowed funds, as well as purchase derivatives. Due to the risks associated with hedge funds, elites have determined that investing in them should be limited to other elites, so the Securities and Exchange Commission (SEC) limits them to those with over $1 million in investible assets. Some hedge funds specialize in purchasing troubled companies and attempting to turn their businesses around, later to resell them at a profit.

In 2011, the top hedge funds were Bridgewater Associates with $70.3 billion in assets under management, JP Morgan Asset Management ($55.2 billion), Paulson and Company ($35.2 billion), BlackRock Financial Management ($29.6 billion), Och-Ziff Capital Management Group ($29.3 billion), and Soros Fund Management ($25.5 billion). Bain Capital, formerly run by Republican Mitt Romney, invested in almost 200 companies and was able to save about

75 percent of them, in some cases by laying off employees. Hedge funds are a particular favorite of pension funds, thus allowing government employees and others in the masses access to these special investments.[b]

A delight of conspiracy theorists, another "private equity" fund with notable political elite connections is Carlyle Group, whose associates include several prominent former politicians: James Baker (U.S. Secretary of State), George H.W. Bush (U.S. President), Frank Carlucci (U.S. Secretary of Defense), Arthur Levitt (Chair, Securities and Exchange Commission), John Major (U.K. Prime Minister), Fidel Ramos (President of the Philippines), and Thaksin Shinawatra (later to be Prime Minister of Thailand). Carlyle is owned by its partners, the government of Abu Dhabi, and the California Public Employee Retirement System (CalPERS).

[a]Du, Lisa. The 10 Biggest Hedge Funds in America. Business Insider October 5, 2011. *www.businessinsider.com/the-top-ten-hedge-funds-in-america-2011-10##ixzz1mtJ0QlKl*

[b]Full disclosure, your author, Louis Schubert, is in the California Teachers Retirement System (CalSTRS), which invests with Bain, Carlyle, and KKR, among many other hedge funds.

Bank of America
Website of the largest U.S. financial institution.
www.bankof america.com

they decide the allocation of capital in our capitalist system. Of the top five investment firms of 2006, none remained on this list by 2011, having either been forced to convert to a commercial bank (Morgan Stanley and Goldman Sachs), merged into a larger firm (Merrill Lynch and Bear Stearns), or gone into bankruptcy (Lehman Brothers). It is clear that the governmental elites have taken on a greater role in this area.

CORPORATE ELITES

Following the Industrial Revolution in the late nineteenth century and well into the twentieth century, the nation's largest corporations were controlled by the tycoons who created them—Andrew Carnegie (Carnegie Steel, later United States Steel), Andrew Mellon (Alcoa and Mellon banks), Henry Ford (Ford Motor Co.), J. P. Morgan (J. P. Morgan), and, of course, John D. Rockefeller (Standard Oil Company, later broken into Exxon, Mobil, Chevron, Atlantic Richfield, and other large oil companies). While founders still control some firms, especially in technology, by the 1930s control of most large corporations had passed to professional managers. As early as 1932, Adolf Berle and Gardiner Means, in their classic book, *The Modern Corporation and Private Property,* described the separation of ownership from control. The theory of **managerialism**, that general management skills are more important than detailed production-specific knowledge, became the conventional wisdom about corporate governance.[13]

MANAGEMENT POWER

Corporate power does not rest in the hands of the masses of corporate employees or even in the hands of the millions of middle- and upper-class workers who own corporate stock. Rather, it is generally wielded by the top managers of the nation's large industrial corporations and financial institutions. Theoretically, stockholders have ultimate power over management, but in fact individual stockholders seldom have any control over the activities of the corporations they own. When confronted with mismanagement, individual stockholders simply sell their stock rather than try to challenge the powers of the managers. Indeed, most stockholders sign over "proxies" so top management can cast these proxy votes at the annual meetings of stockholders. Management itself usually selects its own slate for the board of directors and easily elects its candidates with the help of proxies. While calls for greater "shareholder democracy" continue, it is still rare for management not to see its wishes confirmed. Even if shareholders wielded more power, the largest blocks of stock still are controlled by a few elite, not the masses.

Large control blocks of stock in corporations are usually held by public, private, and union pension trusts, banks and financial institutions, and mutual funds. Occasionally, the managers of these institutions will demand the replacement of corporate managers who have performed poorly. But more often than not, institutional investors such as banks and trust funds vote their stock for the management slate. Institutional investors usually allow the management of corporations essentially to appoint themselves and their friends to the board of directors and thus to become increasingly unchallengeable.

The formal division of power in a corporation is between the board of directors, elected by the shareholders, and the company executives, hired and fired by the board. The board sets policy; management operates the company. The number

Tribune Media Services Inc.

of board members in major U.S. banks and corporations averages between 12 and 15. Board members are divided among "inside" directors (top executive officers of the corporation itself), "outside" directors (usually top executive officers of other banks or corporations), and "public interest" directors (persons selected to give symbolic representation to consumers, minorities, or civic groups).

INTERLOCKING DIRECTORATES

ExxonMobil
Website of the world's largest corporation, including information about officers and directors. *www. exxonmobil.com*

Corporate power is further concentrated by a system of **interlocking directorates**, in which a director of one corporation also sits on the boards of one or more other corporations. These structures enable key corporate elites to wield influence over a large number of corporations. This influence is particularly noticeable when boards of directors vote on executive compensation, and mutual self-interest in higher pay for corporate officers spreads across interlocking directorates.

GOVERNMENT AND CORPORATE ELITES: REVOLVING DOORS

Apple Inc.
Website of the world's most valuable corporation by market capitalization. *www.apple.com*

Politicians specialize in office seeking. They know how to run for office, but they may not know how to run the government. After victory at the polls, wise politicians turn to experienced executive elites to run the government. Normally, both Democratic and Republican presidents seek essentially the same type of experienced executive elite to staff the key positions in their administrations. Frequently, these top government executives—cabinet members, presidential advisers, special ambassadors—have occupied key posts in private industry, finance, or law or influential positions in education, the arts and sciences, or social, civic, and charitable associations. The classic example is President Eisenhower's Secretary of Defense Charles Wilson, who was CEO of General Motors. When asked at his confirmation hearing whether his position might create a conflict of interest, Wilson responded, "I thought what was good for the country was good for General Motors and vice versa." The executive elites move easily in and out of government posts from their positions in the corporate, financial, legal, and education worlds. They often assume government jobs at a financial sacrifice, and many do so from a sense of public service.

The elitist model of power envisions a single group of people exercising power in many sectors of U.S. life. Elite theory does not expect to see individuals *simultaneously* occupying high positions in both business and government, but they do expect to see a **"revolving door"** by which elites move from power positions in banking, industry, the media, law, the foundations, and education to power positions in government, then frequently return to prestigious private posts after a term of "public service." The Obama administration has been showing itself to be an exception. While many of President Barack Obama's closest advisors are millionaires, the members of his cabinet are remarkable for their lack of business experience. Almost all are career politicians, especially former governors, such as Kathleen Sebelius (Health and Human Services), Thomas Vilsak (Agriculture), and Janet Napolitano (Homeland Security), and senators, such as Hillary Clinton and Kenneth Salazar. This contrasts with the previous administration under President George W. Bush, when most executive department heads had corporate leadership

FOCUS | GREED IN THE BOARDROOM

There is abundant evidence that corporate managers put *personal motives*—especially their own pay, benefits, and perquisites—above the interests of the corporation and its stockholders. The pay of chief executive officers (CEOs) of the largest corporations has mushroomed in recent years, as has the pay of corporate directors. The average CEO in the largest corporations took home nearly $11.4 million in pay and benefits in 2011.[a] As it was put by business professor Edward E. Lawler, "It just seems to get more absurd each year. What is outrageous one year becomes a standard for the next. And no one is in a position to say no."[b]

Boards of directors are supposed to oversee top executive pay and protect stockholders, but CEOs generally win approval for their own salaries from compliant directors. Some argue that superstar athletes and pop music stars are also excessively rewarded, but in those fields a bad season or a failed album release tend to result in less pay, while in many cases massive corporate losses still yield massive compensation for executives.

The pay gap between corporate chieftains and average factory workers in the United States has increased dramatically over the last few decades. In the early 1980s, the median pay package (pay, benefits, and perquisites) of a corporate CEO was approximately 50 times greater than the pay of the average factory worker. By 2000 that gap had become a chasm, with the median CEO hitting 525 times the average worker's pay. This gap had declined by 2010, but to a still-vast multiple of 343. (In Japan, by contrast, the average CEO receives only 17 times the pay of an ordinary worker.) It is difficult to explain to workers, whose average real hourly earnings have continued to stagnate since 1970, why the pay packages of top corporate (and governmental) leaders have skyrocketed.

[a]AFL-CIO, *Executive Paywatch*. Available online at *www.aflcio.org/corporatewatch/paywatch/pay/index.cfm*

[b]Quoted by Thomas A. Stewart, "The King Is Dead," *Fortune* (January 11, 1993), p. 34.

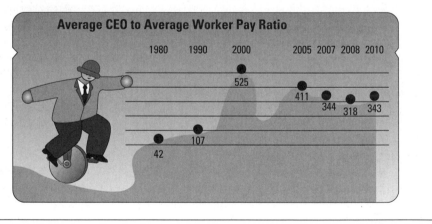

Average CEO to Average Worker Pay Ratio

| 1980 | 1990 | 2000 | 2005 | 2007 | 2008 | 2010 |

525 · 411 · 344 · 318 · 343 · 107 · 42

Center for Responsive Politics. This watchdog group tracks revolving door activities between government and lobbying and corporate jobs. *www.opensecrets. org*

experience, such as Treasury Secretaries Paul O'Neill of Alcoa, John Snow of CSX, and Henry Paulson of Goldman Sachs, as well as Vice President Richard Cheney of Halliburton and Commerce Secretary Carlos Gutierrez of Kellogg's. Bush, the nation's first MBA president, himself had been an officer at several companies before entering public service.

An excellent location for a revolving door appears to be Goldman Sachs, whose executives have held numerous key government positions. Since Goldman is known for its generous compensation, each move to public service also meant severe reductions in pay. Three U.S. Secretaries of the Treasury have worked at this firm: Henry Fowler, Robert Rubin, and Henry Paulson, the latter two first having served as CEO. Another former CEO, Jon Corzine, went on to become a U.S. Senator and Governor of New Jersey. Robert Zoellick went from managing director to U.S. trade representative to president of the World Bank. Another former executive director, Mark Carney, is now governor of the Bank of Canada.

ELITE POLICY-MAKING INSTITUTIONS

The U.S. elite is found not only in the higher echelons of business, banking and investments, insurance, and government itself but, equally important, in the nation's leading foundations, policy-planning organizations or think tanks, mass media, and universities. We can think of these institutions as a "third force" in U.S. society (the other two being business and government) that funds, plans, formulates, and directs the policy-making process.

The most influential institutions have been labeled the **Establishment**. They include the top policy-oriented foundations—the Ford Foundation, the Rockefeller Foundation, and the Carnegie Corporation. They include the nation's leading think tanks—the Brookings Institution, the RAND Corporation, the American Enterprise Institute, the Council on Foreign Relations, and the Cato Institute. Top business and financial leaders look to the Business Roundtable and the Committee for Economic Development for policy advice. Elites communicate with the masses and with each other through the *Washington Post,* the *New York Times,* and especially the *Wall Street Journal* (see Chapter 5). They sit on the boards of trustees, provide financial support, and rely on policy recommendations generated by Harvard University, Yale University, Princeton University, the University of Chicago, and Stanford University. In the nation's financial center, New York City, they support the Metropolitan Museum of Art, the Museum of Modern Art, and the Metropolitan Opera. A fine example of elites' intimate connection with policy-making institutions is President Obama's former chief economic advisor Larry Summers, whose previous employers in the last decade included the U.S. Treasury Department, hedge fund D.E. Shaw Group, and Harvard University (as president).

The Establishment is influential whether the Republicans or the Democrats control the White House or Capitol Hill. "A change of the guard in Washington pulls to the new president those prominent establishmentarians most friendly to his aims, while pushing their counterparts from the previous administration back to the staffs and boards of the Establishment's private institutions."[14]

PUBLIC POLICY AS ELITE PREFERENCE

The major directions of public policy in the United States are determined by a relatively small group of like-minded individuals interacting among themselves and reflecting their own values and preferences in policy making. By contrast, the pluralist model of the policy process portrays public policy as the product of competition, bargaining, and compromise among many diverse groups in society. Interest groups are viewed as the principal actors in the policy-making process— the essential bridges between individuals and government. However, each of these interest groups generates leaders who then work with other elites. Public policy,

Brookings Institution
Washington's most influential think tank, responsible for many significant policy initiatives. *www. brookings.edu*

according to the pluralists, reflects an equilibrium of the relative influence of interest groups. The actual equilibrium is between the relative influence levels of interest group elites.

The elite model of the public policy-making process is presented in Figure 3.3. It suggests that the initial resources for research, study, planning, and formulation of national policy are derived from corporate and personal wealth. This wealth is channeled into foundations, universities, and policy-planning groups in the form of endowments, grants, and contracts. Moreover, corporate presidents, directors, and top wealthholders also sit on the governing boards of the foundations, universities, and policy-planning groups to oversee the spending of their funds. In short, corporate and personal wealth provide both the financial resources and the overall direction of policy research, planning, and development.

THE FOUNDATIONS AND UNIVERSITIES

The foundations provide a link between wealth and the intellectual community. They provide the initial "seed money" to identify social problems, to determine national priorities, and to investigate new policy directions. Universities must respond to the policy interests of foundations, and of course they also try to convince foundations of new and promising policy directions. But research proposals originating from universities that do not fit the emphasis of foundations are usually lost in the shuffle of papers. Although university intellectuals working independently occasionally have an impact on the policy-making process, on the whole, intellectuals respond to policy directions set by the foundations, corporations, and government agencies that underwrite the costs of research. As President Eisenhower stated in his Farewell Address, "The prospect of domination of the nation's scholars by Federal employment, project allocations, and the power of money is ever present—and is gravely to be regarded."[15]

THE THINK TANKS

The policy-planning groups, or think tanks, are the central coordinating points in the policy-making process. They review the relevant university and foundation-supported research on topics of interest, with the goal of developing policy

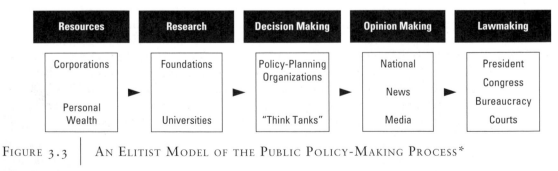

Resources	Research	Decision Making	Opinion Making	Lawmaking
Corporations Personal Wealth	Foundations Universities	Policy-Planning Organizations "Think Tanks"	National News Media	President Congress Bureaucracy Courts

FIGURE 3.3 │ AN ELITIST MODEL OF THE PUBLIC POLICY-MAKING PROCESS*

*For a more detailed model, see Thomas R. Dye, *Who's Running America? The Bush Restoration* (Upper Saddle River, NJ: Prentice Hall, 2002), p. 173.

IN BRIEF	HOW ELITES MAKE POLICY

- Public policy in America primarily reflects the values and preferences of the elite.
- The initial resources for research, planning, and formulation of national policy come from corporate and personal wealth. This wealth is channeled into universities and policy-planning organizations; corporate directors and wealth holders serve on the boards of directors of these organizations.
- The foundations provide the initial seed money to identify social problems, determine national priorities, and investigate policy directions. Universities respond to the availability of grants from foundations.
- The policy-planning organizations, or "think tanks," are central coordinating points in the policy-making process. They undertake their own research, as well as review relevant university and foundation-supported research, with the goal of developing policy recommendations. They also endeavor to build consensus among corporate, financial, media, civic, intellectual, and government elites around major policy directions.
- Media elites set the agenda for policy making by allocating valuable network broadcast time to what they define as societal "problems." The media frequently base their broadcasts on university and think tank research and recommendations.
- The White House, congressional committees, and top executives maintain contact with think tanks and must respond to the issues presented them by the media. Thus, the groundwork is laid for making policy into law.

recommendations—explicit programs designed to resolve or ameliorate national problems. At the same time, they endeavor to build consensus among corporate, financial, media, civic, intellectual, and government leaders around major policy directions. Certain policy-planning groups—notably the Council on Foreign Relations, the American Enterprise Institute, the Heritage Foundation, and the Brookings Institution—are influential in a wide range of key policy areas (see Focus: The Elite Think Tanks). Think tanks cover the political spectrum, from the conservative American Enterprise Institute to the left-progressive Economic Policy Institute. A recent study by the progressive media watchdog FAIR of the most cited think tanks found 48 percent are centrist, 31 percent are conservative, and 21 percent are left-center or progressive.[16] These numbers roughly mirror the ideological preferences of the U.S. people.

Heritage Foundation
Conservative think tank influential in Republican policy initiatives. *www. heritage.org*

THE MEDIA

Policy recommendations of the leading policy-planning groups are distributed to the mass media, federal executive agencies, and Congress. The mass media play a vital role in preparing public opinion for policy change. The media define the "problem" as a problem and thus set the agenda for policy making. They also encourage politicians to assume new policy stances by allocating valuable network broadcast time to those who will speak out in favor of new policy directions. (Chapter 5 will focus on the media elite's role in the United States.)

THE WASHINGTON INSIDERS

The White House staff, congressional committee staffs, and top executive administrators usually maintain close contact with policy-planning groups. Often these groups help prepare legislation for Congress to implement policy decisions. Particular versions of bills will pass between executive agencies, the White House, policy-planning groups, and the professional staffs of the congressional committees that eventually will consider the bills. Thus groundwork is laid for making policy into law.

POWER IN THE UNITED STATES | An Elitist Interpretation

Power in the United States is organized into large institutions, private as well as public: corporations, banks and financial institutions, universities, law firms, religious institutions, professional associations, and military and government bureaucracies. The persons in positions of power in these institutions are the elites.

According to elite theory, the movement of nonelites into elite positions must be slow and continuous in order to maintain stability and avoid revolution. Furthermore, potential elite members must demonstrate their commitment to the basic elite consensus before being admitted to elite positions. Elite theory recognizes competition among elites but contends that elites share a broad consensus about preserving the system essentially as it is. It views public-policy changes as a response to elites' redefinition of their self-interest rather than as a product of direct mass influence. Finally, elite theory views changes in public policy as incremental rather than revolutionary. U.S. political history supports these propositions:

1. Elite membership evolved slowly, with no serious break in the ideas or values of the U.S. political and economic system. When the leadership of Hamilton and the Federalists shifted to that of Jefferson and the Democratic-Republicans, government policies changed little because of the fundamental consensus among elite members.

2. As new sources of wealth opened in an expanding economy, elite membership opened to new groups and individuals who had acquired wealth and property and who accepted the national consensus about private enterprise, limited government, and individualism. This has been true from the arrival of the new elites who arose in the frontier West 200 years ago to the new technology elite today.

3. Elites have been deeply divided on the nature of U.S. society only once. The Civil War was a conflict between southern elites, dependent on a plantation economy, slave labor, and free trade, and northern industrial commercial elites, who prospered under free labor and protective tariffs.

4. The new liberal establishment sought to preserve the existing social and economic order, not to overthrow it. Governing elites—acting on the basis of enlightened self-interest—instituted public-regarding reforms to preserve the system and their prominent place in it. Even the reforms and welfare policies of the New Deal were designed to strengthen the existing social and economic fabric of society while minimally dislocating elites. Franklin Roosevelt's philosophy of noblesse oblige—elite responsibility for the welfare of the masses— won widespread acceptance among established U.S. leadership.

5. The corporate structure of U.S. society concentrates great authority in a relatively small number of positions. The 500 largest industrial corporations

FOCUS | THE ELITE THINK TANKS

The nation's private policy-planning organizations, popularly referred to as think tanks, compose the center of our elitist model of national policy making. There are a host of think tanks in Washington, but among the generally recognized elite organizations are the Brookings Institution, the American Enterprise Institute, and the Heritage Foundation. The leading think tank in the fields of foreign affairs, national security, and international trade is the Council on Foreign Relations, together with its multinational arm, the Trilateral Commission.[a]

The Brookings Institution

This organization has long been the dominant policy-planning group for U.S. domestic policy, despite the growth of other think tanks over the years. It is associated with the Democratic Party. Brookings has been described as the central locus of the Washington "policy network."[b] It was started early in the twentieth century with grants from Robert Brookings, a wealthy St. Louis merchant; Andrew Carnegie, head of U.S. Steel (now USX); John D. Rockefeller, founder of the Standard Oil (now Exxon); and Robert Eastman, founder of Kodak. Its early recommendations for economy and efficiency in government led to the Budget and Accounting Act of 1921, which established the annual unified federal budget. (Before 1921, each department submitted separate budget requests to Congress.) In the 1960s, the Brookings Institution, with grants from the Ford Foundation, helped design the war on poverty. Brookings staffers were influential in developing Clinton's comprehensive, but unsuccessful, health care package, and Brookings economists long pushed for the North American Free Trade Agreement (NAFTA).

The American Enterprise Institute

For many years, Republicans dreamed of a "Brookings Institution for Republicans" that would help offset the liberal bias of Brookings. In the late 1970s, that role was assumed by the American Enterprise Institute (AEI). The AEI attracted many distinguished "neoconservative" scholars who were beginning to have doubts about big government. Their work was influential in shaping Reagan administration efforts in deregulation, tax reduction, and anti-inflationary monetary policy. Today the AEI harbors both moderate Republicans and pro-growth "new" Democrats.

Policy work by AEI scholars laid the groundwork for the Welfare Reform Act of 1996. This work convinced many Democrats as well as Republicans in Congress that federal welfare entitlement programs, notably Aid to Families with Dependent Children, were contributing to family breakdown and welfare dependency. Welfare reform generally followed AEI-sponsored recommendations to eliminate the federal entitlement to cash aid, return welfare policy-making to the states, set limits on the length of time people could be on welfare, and require teenage mothers to stay with their parents and in school as a condition of receiving cash aid.

The Heritage Foundation

Conservatives gradually came to understand that without an institutional base in the capital city they could never establish a strong and continuing influence in the policy network. The result of their efforts to build a "solid institutional base" and establish "a reputation for reliable scholarship and creative problem solving" is the Heritage Foundation. The initial funding came from Colorado brewer Joseph Coors, who was later joined by two drugstore magnates, Jack Eckerd of Florida and Lewis I. Lehrman of New York. Heritage boasts that it accepts no government grants or contracts and has a larger number of individual contributors than any other think tank. Heritage is "unabashedly conservative;" President Ronald Reagan once hailed the foundation as changing "the intellectual history of the West" and testified to its "enormous influence on Capitol Hill—and believe me, I know—at the White House."[c] The Heritage Foundation "is committed to rolling back the liberal welfare state and building an America where freedom, opportunity, and civil society flourish."[d] Heritage has addressed many of the "hot-button" conservative issues: abortion, racial preferences in affirmative action programs, public vouchers for pupils to attend private religious schools, and religion and morality in public life.

[a]The Council on Foreign Relations is described in Chapter 14.

[b]Leonard. Silk and Mark Silk, The *American Establishment* (New York: Basic Books, 1980), p. 160.

[c]Heritage Foundation., *Annual Report* (1985), p. 1.

[d]Heritage Foundation., *Mission Statement*, 2000.

receive over 50 percent of the nation's industrial revenues, and the 10 largest banks control nearly half the nation's banking assets.

6. Top management wields corporate power rather than the mass of employees or individual stockholders. Only occasionally do large institutional investors, such as pension funds, investment firms, banks, and insurance companies, challenge top management.

7. Despite democratic rhetoric, elites doubt that the masses of people have the knowledge or judgment to make wise decisions about public affairs.

8. Public policy reflects the preferences and values of the elites. Elites may consider the welfare of the masses in policy making, but it is the elites, not the masses, who make policy.

9. The initial resources for policy planning are derived from corporations and personal wealth. These resources are channeled through foundations and universities in the form of grants, contracts, and endowments. Elite policy-planning organizations play a central role in preparing policy recommendations and developing policy consensus among corporate, governmental, and media elites.

NOTES

1. C. Wright Mills, *The Power Elite* (New York: Oxford University Press, 1956), pp. 10–11. A classic which focuses on the idea that the individuals who fill the positions within the most powerful institutions form a power elite.

2. Robert A. Dahl and Charles E. Lindblom, *Politics and Economic Welfare*, 2nd ed. (Chicago: University of Chicago Press, 1976). See preface.

3. McCulloch v. Maryland, 4 Wheaton 316 (1819).

4. Richard Hofstadter. *The American Political Tradition* (New York: Knopf, 1948), pp. 32–33. This book is a political history from an elite perspective from the founding to Franklin Roosevelt.

5. Hofstadter, American Political Tradition, p. 38.

6. Dred Scott v. Sandford, 19 Howard 393 (1857).

7. Hofstadter, American Political Tradition, p. 119.

8. See Amity Shlaes. *The Forgotten Man: A New History of the Great Depression* (New York: Harper Perennial, 2007). This book is a detailed review of the New Deal and the Depression, with special attention to the European influences on New Deal elites.

9. See http://www.gpo.gov/fdsys/ for the official numbers from the White House and www.usgovernmentspending.com for more critical data.

10. Mills. *The Power Elite*, pp. 7–8.

11. Dwight D. Eisenhower. *Farewell Radio and Television Address to the American People,* January 17th, 1961. http://www.eisenhower.archives.gov/All_About_Ike/Speeches/ Farewell_Address.pdf

12. Christopher Lasch, *The Revolt of the Elites* (New York: W. W. Norton, 1995), p. 6.

13. John Kenneth Galbraith, *The New Industrial State* (Boston: Houghton Mifflin, 1967), p. 323.

14. Leonard Silk and Mark Silk, *The American Establishment* (New York: Basic Books, 1980), p. 20.

15. Eisenhower, Farewell Address.

16. Michael Dolny. 2009. "The Right Ebbs, Left Gains as 'Media experts'" Fairness and Accuracy in Reporting, http://www.fair.org/index.php?page=3857

Let us transport ourselves into a hypothetical country that, in a democratic way, practices the persecution of Christians, the burning of witches, and the slaughtering of Jews. We should certainly not approve of these practices on the ground that they have been decided on according to the rules of democratic procedure.

—**Joseph Schumpeter**

MASSES IN THE UNITED STATES

Democratic government envisions an active, informed, participating citizenry. It also envisions a citizenry committed to core values—liberty and equality, freedom of speech and the press, tolerance of diversity, property rights, and due process of law. A republic requires much from its citizens: being engaged in politics, staying educated on important political and policy issues, and remaining willing to participate in decision making in a way that places the interests of the community as a whole ahead of narrow self-interest. Perhaps the greatest threat to democracy in the United States is the continuing prevalence of apathy and ignorance among the masses.

Most in the United States are ignorant of public affairs and apathetic about politics. The number of eligible U.S. citizens who vote is over half only in presidential elections; an "off-year" local election may see turnout as low as 15–20 percent. Other more demanding forms of political participation draw even less interest. Poll after poll shows respondents have little knowledge about political matters, and most are not even aware of basic political facts, such as who is their representative in Congress. If a healthy democracy depends on its continuance on investments of time and effort by its citizens, it is fortunate the elites preserve the democratic system. The majority of the masses show little interest in helping democracy to survive.

U.S. Census Bureau Perhaps the single best source for statistical snapshots and in-depth data on the U.S. population. *www.census.gov*

Even in their commitment to the core beliefs of democracy, the masses fall short. Although they may voice superficial agreement with abstract statements of democratic values, they do not translate these values into specific attitudes or behaviors, especially toward people and ideas they despise. Mass commitment to tolerance has certainly improved vastly in the last decades, but major prejudices remain. The real question is how democracy and individual freedom can survive in a society where the masses give only limited support to these values.

Democracy also envisions a people who believe in equality of opportunity, that is, they believe they or their children have a reasonable and fair opportunity to improve their lives if they study and work hard, save and invest wisely, and display initiative and enterprise. The United States describes itself as the "land of opportunity." The promise of freedom to participate in the political process, to speak up and discuss political alternatives with fellow citizens, and to enjoy upward mobility has made the United States the magnet for those seeking liberty.

For many in the United States, economic well-being is more important than politics. The freedom to work hard and enjoy the fruits of one's labor is a value stretching back to colonial days. Almost every year, the masses in the United States have seen an improvement in their quality of life as measured by the standard variables: living space, technology adoption, general consumption, higher education, and life expectancy. However, despite a generally robust economy over the last few decades, many—especially unskilled and semiskilled workers—have seen their average hourly wages stagnate. The nation's private labor force has been deunionized (see "Deunionization" below). Despite mass opposition, illegal immigration has skyrocketed, depressing low-end wages. Income inequality is increasing, as the highly educated and skilled move forward while those without such qualifications have largely stayed still. As a result, income and wealth differences between rich and poor are growing. The masses who expected readily available upward socioeconomic mobility are now doubtful of ever achieving it. The fact that 2012 employment remains six million jobs below the 2007 level after five years has only compounded such feelings.

ELITE GAINS, MASS STAGNATION

The U.S. economy performs very well, but the benefits from that performance are unevenly distributed. The global economy produces growth and profit for the largest U.S. corporations and amply rewards the nation's highest-skilled workers. Indeed, global trade raises aggregate income for the nation. It also lowers costs on goods for consumers. But at the same time, it contributes to a stagnation in average hourly earnings of U.S. workers and worsens income inequality. Elites get richer while the masses stay put.

STAGNATING WORKER EARNINGS

Average hourly and weekly earnings of U.S. workers have stagnated over the past three decades (see Figure 4.1). In real 1982 dollars (controlling for the effects of inflation), average hourly earnings declined from $8.40 in 1970 to a low of $7.50 in 1995, before rising to $8.90 by 2011. Real worker wages are still basically where they were 40 years ago, despite decades of overall economic growth. We can attribute much of this stagnation to the higher costs of benefits, especially health insurance, which account for a large portion of employee compensation (about a third on average). Wage stagnation is also a result of broader economic changes.

Stagnating real wages in the United States have been obscured by the fact that median family income has been rising. In 1970, median family income was

Bureau of Labor Statistics
Official source of information on income, wages, employment, and other economic data. *www.bls.gov*

$43,540 (in constant 2010 dollars); by 2010, this figure had risen to $49,309.[1] But family income rose because more family members entered the workforce, not because workers were paid more. Workforce participation among married women rose from 40 percent in 1970 to 70 percent in 2010.[2] In short, U.S. families raised their incomes despite stagnant hourly wages simply by having more family members go to work.

Wage stagnation occurred simultaneously with the growth of international trade. Although this coincidence does not prove trade is causing earnings to stagnate or decline, it does raise a question: In a global economy, is the huge supply of unskilled labor pushing down the wages of U.S. workers? Increased trade, especially with less developed economies such as Mexico, China, and India with their huge numbers of low-wage workers, creates competition for U.S. workers. It is difficult to maintain wage levels especially in labor-intensive industries in the face of such competition. Moreover, it is not uncommon for U.S. corporations to outsource their manufacturing to low-wage countries where the transportation costs of moving finished products back to the U.S. market are minimal.

The biggest gap in relative earnings of U.S. workers is between stagnant or declining basic labor wages and increasing compensation for the skilled and educated. We can see this most clearly by looking at average incomes and how they relate to education level. In 2011, among householders over the age of 25,[3] average income was $30,232 for those with less than a ninth-grade education; $50,561 for those with only a high school diploma (or equivalent); $67,790 for those with an associate's degree; $94,207 for those with a bachelor's degree; and finally $159,202 for those with a professional degree. The more advanced the level of education, the higher the income. The elites are overwhelmingly drawn from society's most educated classes. The average household income for the over-25 householders is $69,052.

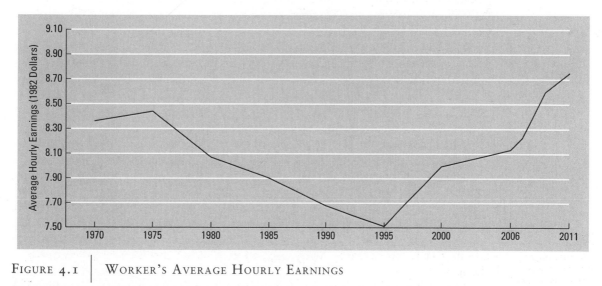

FIGURE 4.1 | WORKER'S AVERAGE HOURLY EARNINGS

Source: U.S. Bureau of Labor Statistics (*www.bls.gov*).

DEUNIONIZATION

Labor unions became a major force in the United States in the 1930s as a result of legislation that made it easier to unionize. Fifty years ago, unions were a significant force in determining workers' wages, especially in manufacturing. Industrial unions such as the United Steel Workers, United Automobile Workers, and United Mine Workers set wage rates that influenced the entire national wage structure. At their peak, unions counted nearly 40 percent of the nation's labor force in their membership. Today only about 13 percent of the nation's labor force is unionized (see Figure 4.2), returning the level of unionization back to where it was in the early 1930s. The major industrial unions have shrunk; only unions of government employees (American Federation of State, County, and Municipal Employees), teachers (who are also government employees; National Education Association), and some transportation and service workers (Service Employees International Union) have gained members in recent years.

AFL-CIO
Home page of the
union federation.
www.aflcio.org

Deunionization is partly a product of the globalization of the economy. Employers can move, or threaten to move, their factories outside the country in response to union demands. Or they can replace striking union members with nonunion workers. Heavy immigration into the United States feeds a large pool of available low-wage workers, especially illegal immigrants, who often accept inferior working conditions and wages below the minimum wage because they fear being deported if they speak out.

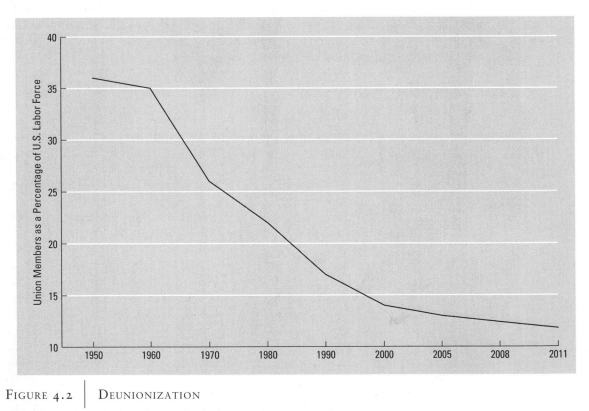

FIGURE 4.2 | DEUNIONIZATION

Source: Data derived from *www.bls.gov*.

Deunionization is also the result of the gap between union elites and union members. In the past, unions were primarily focused on collective bargaining activities that resulted in impressive gains in pay and benefits for their members. However, much union activity has turned to political activism in areas not directly related to collective bargaining, including social policy, where "Joe Six-Pack," the stereotypical union worker and a social conservative, feels alienated by his or her union elite's decisions. In a recent example, in 2009 in California, the United Farm Worker's union opposed an attempt to increase the water supply to the agricultural Central Valley because a broader political coalition objected to the possible environmental impact. Farm workers themselves held that water is needed for crops, and more water would result in more work for union members.

Battles for local control in the Service Employees Union (S.E.I.U.) in the face of moves by union elite leader Andrew Stern to centralize power have also served to magnify the distance between union elites and unionized masses. The AFL-CIO (American Federation of Labor–Congress of Industrial Organizations) is a federation of national unions. Today the AFL-CIO and its members appear to devote more attention to Washington lobbying than to negotiating wage contracts with employers. Indeed, union wage demands have been modest in recent years and nationwide strikes rare.

Polls show that in 2011 barely half the people in the United States approve of labor unions. The majority think unions mostly hurt the U.S. economy overall. Almost two-thirds believe unions help their own members, so it is clear they are still viewed as quite effective in collective bargaining. Still, 62 percent believe unions mostly hurt nonmembers, or the general public.[4]

INEQUALITY IN THE UNITED STATES

Income inequality is and has always been a significant component of the U.S. social structure. The top one-fifth (20 percent) of income recipients in the United States receives nearly 48 percent of all income in the nation, and the bottom fifth receives only about 4 percent (see Table 4.1). The income share of the top fifth has declined since the pre–World War II years, but inequality has risen dramatically since 1970.

We must also recognize that those who earn the most also pay the most taxes. As reported by the Internal Revenue Service (I.R.S.), at the 2007 peak before the recession, filers of the top 1 percent of tax returns paid 40.4 percent of all income taxes, despite earning only 22.8 percent of all income. The top 5 percent paid 60.6 percent, based on having earned 37.4 percent of all reported income.[5] The elite's share of the cost of funding government has grown in direct proportion to the growth in their share of income. From a broader perspective, we see that the top half of all income taxpayers paid 97.1 percent of all income taxes in 2007. In a country in which taxation and representation have historically been intertwined, the connections between earnings, taxes paid, and political participation are significant.

Various theories have been put forward to explain why inequality has worsened: the decline of the manufacturing sector of the economy with its relatively high-paying blue-collar jobs; a rise in the number of two-wage families, making

TABLE 4.1 | DISTRIBUTION OF FAMILY INCOME IN THE UNITED STATES

Quintiles*	Percentage of Total Income Received								
	1929	1936	1950	1962	1972	1980	1990	2000	2010
Lowest	3.5	4.1	4.8	4.6	5.5	5.2	4.6	4.3	3.8
Second	9.0	9.2	10.9	10.9	12.0	11.6	10.8	9.8	9.5
Third	13.8	14.1	16.1	16.3	17.4	17.5	16.6	15.4	15.4
Fourth	19.3	20.9	22.1	22.7	23.5	24.2	23.8	22.7	23.5
Highest	54.4	51.7	46.1	45.5	41.6	41.5	44.3	47.7	47.8
Total	100.0	100.0	100.0	100.0	100.0	100.0	100.0	100.0	100.0
Top 5 percent	30.0	24.0	21.4	19.6	14.4	15.7	17.4	21.1	20.0

*Each quintile is 20 percent of the population.

Source: *Statistical Abstract of the United States*, 2006, p. 464; *www.census.gov*. Table F-2.

single-wage households relatively less affluent; and demographic trends, which include larger proportions of older adults. Among all indicators of poverty in the United States, the strongest correlation is with female heads of households. Others point to the globalization of trade; unskilled and semiskilled U.S. workers compete with very-low-wage workers in nations such as China, Vietnam, Bangladesh, Mexico, and even Botswana. Their pay is pulled down as wages decline to compete or as manufacturing jobs are simply relocated to more wage-competitive areas.

In contrast, our highly skilled workers, entrepreneurs, executives, and investors are well positioned to gain from trade. Income inequality is less the result of a decline of those toward the lower end of the income distribution, for whom wages have been stagnant. Inequality has risen due to those in new areas of technology and finance creating vast new wealth and income through smartphones and derivative trading. The result is that inequality worsens even though the aggregate income of the nation rises.

INEQUALITY OF WEALTH

Wealth is even more unequally distributed than income. (Wealth is the total value of a person's assets—bank accounts, stocks, bonds, mutual funds, business equity, houses, properties, etc.—minus debts, mortgages, and unpaid bills.) Millionaires in the United States are no longer considered rich. To be truly rich today, one must be worth $1 billion. Most of the nation's wealthy are reluctant to reveal their net worth; thus, any listing is only an estimate. *Forbes* lists 400 billionaires in the United States.[6] (See Table 4.2.) All of the twenty richest except those who inherited their wealth from Wal-Mart founder Sam Walton owe their wealth to companies they created and/or run. The top 1.2 percent of wealth holders in the United States currently owns about 20 percent of all net worth.[7]

TABLE 4.2	TOP 20 U.S. WEALTH HOLDERS, 2010
1. William H. Gates III	Microsoft
2. Warren E. Buffet	Berkshire Hathaway
3. Lawrence T. Ellison	Oracle
4. Charles Koch	Koch Industries
5. David Koch	Koch Industries
6. Christy Walton	Wal-Mart Inheritance
7. George Soros	Hedge Funds
8. Sheldon Adelson	Casinos
9. Jim Walton	Wal-Mart Inheritance
10. Alice Walton	Wal-Mart Inheritance
11. S. Robson Walton	Wal-Mart Inheritance
12. Michael Bloomberg	Bloomberg Media
13. Jeffrey Bezos	Amazon.com
14. Mark Zuckerberg	Facebook
15. Sergei Brin	Google
16. Larry Page	Google
17. John Paulson	Hedge funds
18. Michael Dell	Dell Computers
19. Steven Ballmer	Microsoft
20. Forrest Mars	Candy

Source: *www.forbes.com/forbes-400/.*

MASS DISAFFECTION FROM POLITICS

Distrust and cynicism characterize mass attitudes toward government and politics. Surveys of U.S. public opinion since the 1960s have shown dramatic increases in public disdain of politics and politicians. (See Figure 4.3.)

The rise in mass cynicism and decline in mass trust of government deeply concern U.S. elites. If the trust of the masses in government is weakened, "citizens may become less likely to comply with the laws, to support government programs through taxes, and to enter government service. Without those critical resources, government will be unable to perform well, and people will become even more disaffected—a dangerous downward spiral that can weaken democratic institutions."[8]

Studies frequently argue that the underlying causes of declining confidence are complex. While acknowledging that elite actions themselves—such as the Vietnam War and the Watergate scandal—were influential in causing mass disaffection, these studies point to several other underlying factors. First, they bemoan a long-term trend toward disrespect of authority (as elites throughout the ages have done). Second, they acknowledge that globalization of the economy includes some "creative destruction" that disrupts the lives of many people and results in insecurity blamed on government. Third, they contend that changes in the political

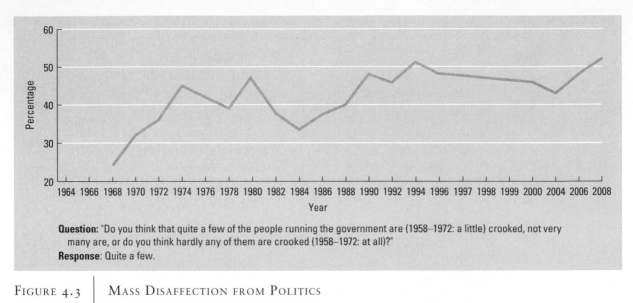

Question: "Do you think that quite a few of the people running the government are (1958–1972: a little) crooked, not very many are, or do you think hardly any of them are crooked (1958–1972: at all)?"
Response: Quite a few.

FIGURE 4.3 | MASS DISAFFECTION FROM POLITICS

Source: National Election Studies to 2000; The Polling Report for 2004, 2006, 2008.

process—the decline in allegiance to political parties, the increased role of television in political campaigns, the banning of wagons loaded with kegs of beer bringing voters to polling places, the professionalization of politics—make average citizens feel they have less control over their elected representatives. Finally, some elite studies have also acknowledged the effect of negative media reporting on popular attitudes toward government and politics.[9]

Core political values in the United States have always included skepticism of government and its role. The cultural belief is that the most important elements in an individual's life are personal and private, rather than public or political. The traditional U.S. approach to politics is that government must be limited by the separation of powers and checks and balances, because at a fundamental level government is not to be trusted. Each scandal or betrayal of the public trust by the political elites only serves to underscore this basic viewpoint. In the midst of the 2011 economic downturn, a Gallup poll asked respondents what was the biggest threat to the country in the future, and a resounding 64 percent answered Big Government (another 26 percent chose Big Business, and 8 percent chose Big Labor).[10] In light of the threat to the economy posed in 2008–2009 by the financial crisis, people were willing to accept a larger role for government, but only on a temporary basis. An April 2009 poll showed 39 percent approved of the expanded role of government but wanted it reduced once the crisis was over. The largest number, 44 percent, disapproved of the expansion of government power to deal with the crisis and a mere 13 percent approved bigger government as permanent.[11]

Polling Report Source for trends in mass opinion, including data from a variety of current polls. *www.pollingreport.com*

The masses continue to distrust governmental elites. Hostility toward government keeps growing. Several factors combine to counter mass dissatisfaction with government. First, a strong economy reduces mass distrust and cynicism. Prosperity

| CONDITIONS AFFECTING THE MASSES

- Average worker earnings have stagnated over time. Family income has risen only because more family members have gone to work.
- Legal and illegal immigration have reached an all-time high. Elites support immigration as a source of low-cost labor.
- Inequality of income has increased over time, with the lowest 20 percent receiving only about

3 percent of the nation's total income, while the highest 20 percent get nearly half.
- Mass distrust and cynicism toward government has grown over the years. Only in crisis periods do the masses "rally 'round the flag."
- Masses view Big Government as the greatest threat to the United States, more than Big Business and Big Labor combined.

appears to moderate mass dissatisfaction with elites, while times of economic weakness are reflected in a decline in support for elites. Second, it is clear the masses want government to play a significant role in many areas of life.

MASS VIEWS ON GOVERNMENT RESPONSIBILITY

QUESTION: *How much responsibility should the government have over this area? (Answers were 5 [Total] or 1 [No] on a 1-to-5 scale.)*

	Total Responsibility	No Responsibility
Protecting Americans from foreign threats	83%	2%
Protecting consumers from unsafe products	51%	3%
Preventing discrimination	47%	8%
Protecting the environment from human actions that can harm it	42%	5%
Making sure that all Americans have adequate health care	42%	20%
Provide a minimum standard of living for all	30%	18%
Upholding moral standards among its citizens	25%	24%
Reducing income difference between the rich and the poor	23%	33%

Source: Frank Newport. "Americans Choose Middle Over Extremes on Gov't Functions." Gallup. October 13, 2010. *www.gallup.com/poll/143636/Americans-Choose-Middle-Extremes-Gov-Functions.aspx.*

Finally, people in the United States are very patriotic, more so than the citizens of most other nations. Mass opinion remains very positive toward the constitutional framework of U.S. government, even though it is critical of the people who run it. The U.S. people are quick to unite behind their leadership when attacked from foreign soil. This was as true following the terrorist attacks in 2001 as it had been after the Imperial Japanese attack on Pearl Harbor 60 years before. Not only does mass support for the nation's leadership skyrocket, but also the masses are quite willing to grant the elites new powers to achieve security. Indeed, mass support for civil liberties diminishes in times of national security crises.

ANTIDEMOCRATIC ATTITUDES AMONG THE MASSES

The masses frequently give only superficial support to fundamental democratic values—freedom of speech and the press, due process of law, and equality for all. People say they believe in those values when they are expressed as abstract principles; for example, they answer yes to the question "Do you believe in freedom of speech for everyone?" However, the public is unable or unwilling to apply the principles to specific situations, especially situations involving despised or obnoxious groups or individuals. In contrast, elites and the well-educated groups from which they are recruited are much more willing than the masses to apply democratic values in specific situations and to protect the freedoms of unpopular groups. Tolerance also appears to be directly correlated to level of education.

After years of studying the differences between the elites and masses in their attitudes toward freedom, political scientists Herbert McClosky and Alida Brill reached the following conclusions regarding the *masses* in the United States:

> If one judges by the responses of the mass public to survey questions, one has little reason to expect that the population as a whole will display a sensitive understanding of the constitutional norms that govern the free exercise of speech and publication. Only a minority of the mass public fully appreciate why freedom of speech and press should be granted to dissenters and to others who challenge conventional opinion.[12]

In contrast, these scholars are much more optimistic regarding freedom and tolerance among *elites*:

> Insofar as these matters are better understood and more firmly believed by those who, in one role or another, help to govern the society, one is tempted to conclude that, owing to the vagaries of the social process, the protection of First Amendment rights rests principally upon the very groups the Amendment was mainly designed to control—the courts, the legislature, political leaders, and the opinion elites of the society.[13]

The irony of democracy appears to us again.

SOCIAL CLASS AND DEMOCRATIC ATTITUDES

Many classic political science studies have shown that the distribution of antidemocratic attitudes among social classes varies greatly. The upper social classes (from which members of the elites are largely recruited) give greater, more consistent support to democratic values than do the lower social classes. Political sociologist Seymour Martin Lipset observed, "extremist and intolerant movements in modern society are more likely to be based on the lower classes than on the middle and upper classes."[14] Analyzing the ideologies of the lower class, Lipset notes the masses are more liberal on economic issues where welfare state measures directly benefit them, but when it comes to non-economic matters, they become more intolerant.[15] This shows not a commitment to democratic values but a commitment to self-interest.

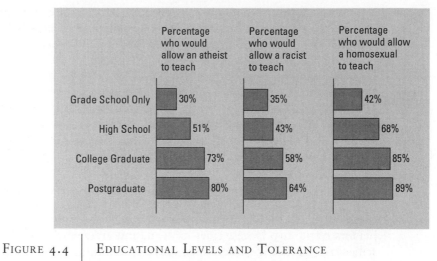

FIGURE 4.4 | EDUCATIONAL LEVELS AND TOLERANCE

Source: General Social Survey, Cumulative Dataset, 2008.

EDUCATION AND DEMOCRATIC ATTITUDES

Public Agenda Online
Mass opinion on a variety of issues.
www.publicagenda.org

Clearly, level of education is related to degree of tolerance and respect for civil liberty in the United States, as illustrated by Figure 4.4. Each increment of education increases respondents' willingness to allow atheists, racists, or homosexuals to teach. Indeed, a lack of education may be more important than any other characteristic in shaping antidemocratic attitudes. Within occupational levels, higher educational status makes for greater tolerance, but increases in tolerance associated with educational level are greater than those related to occupation, and no matter what the occupation, tolerance and education are strongly related.

Education level is closely linked to social trust, the sense that people in general are trustworthy. This indicator is a sign that a faith in a society is strong, which bodes well for democracy. When asked whether people can be trusted, only 35 percent overall answered yes. However, half of all college graduates said yes, while only 28 percent of those with less than a high school education agreed. Similarly, half of those in the professional class answered yes, while only 30 percent of those in the working class did (among those defined as "struggling," the level of social trust was only 18 percent).[16]

ELITE EXPERIENCE AND DEMOCRATIC ATTITUDES

Finally, although education is the most influential factor in promoting tolerance, leadership and activity in public affairs also contribute. In a classic study, McClosky and Brill compared mass attitudes with those of community leaders—local government officials, judges and lawyers, journalists, clergy, school administrators, and leaders of unions and civic organizations. McClosky and Brill asked a variety of questions designed to ascertain support for civil liberty. For example, "Should demonstrators be allowed to hold a mass protest march for some unpopular cause?" with possible answers being "Yes, even if most people in the community do not want it" and "No, not if the majority is against it." Among community leaders, 71 percent said yes, but among the mass public only 41 percent would allow a mass demonstration protest for an unpopular cause.[17]

Perhaps leadership activity socializes people to democratic norms; they may become more familiar with democratic values because they are active in the democratic process. Or perhaps their public activity exposes them to a wider variety of attitudes, opinions, and lifestyles, broadens their perspective, and generates empathy for people different from themselves.

ARE THE MASSES BECOMING MORE DEMOCRATIC?

The United States in 2008 elected a black man president. Barack Obama's primary challenge came from a woman, Hillary Clinton. The Republican candidate for vice president was also a woman, a nursing mother of five named Sarah Palin. The mayors of the two largest cities in the nation are a Jew and a Latino. Few seem to remember the last U.S. Secretary of State who was a white male.[18] The head of Pepsi and the Governors of Louisiana and South Carolina are of Indian descent. Strong evidence suggests that over time the masses in the United States are becoming more tolerant of different social groups (see Table 4.3). This is particularly true of groups that elites themselves have come to accept into their ranks.

Consider, for example, the historic change in white mass attitudes toward school integration that occurred in the years following the landmark Supreme Court decision *Brown v. Board of Education of Topeka, Kansas*, holding that racial segregation violated the equal protection clause of the U.S. Constitution. From 1942 to 1982, a national sample of whites was asked the question "Do you think white and black students should go to the same schools or separate schools?" In 1942, not even a third of whites (30 percent) approved of integrated schools. In 1956, two years after the court decision, white attitudes had shifted markedly and 49 percent approved. By 1963, two of every three whites (67 percent) supported integrated schools, and the upward trend continued until more than 90 percent of whites favored school integration by the 1980s. (Despite increasing tolerance of integration *in principle*, however, white parents do not want their children to become a minority in their schools.) Additional survey information suggests whites are becoming increasingly accommodating toward equal rights for blacks over time in other areas as well. But mass opinion generally *follows* elite-created public policy, rather than leads it.

Another example is increasing acceptance of equal rights for homosexuals. In 1977, the year San Franciscan Harvey Milk, the first openly gay public official, was elected to office, only 56 percent of adults polled felt gays and lesbians should have equal rights in employment (33 percent were opposed). By 2008, a full 89 percent supported such rights and only 8 percent were opposed.[19] Part of this change may have come about because by 2009, well over half the people personally knew someone who identified as gay or lesbian.

The masses are becoming more tolerant in other ways. For example, over time many have become more willing to allow "communists," "atheists," and "homosexuals" to hold meetings, make speeches, and place their books in public libraries. An optimistic interpretation is that increased education as well as increased exposure to media messages of tolerance are having a positive effect. In other ways tolerance

TABLE 4.3 | MASS WILLINGNESS TO VOTE FOR A MEMBER OF A MINORITY FOR PRESIDENT

QUESTION ASKED: *"If your party nominated a generally well-qualified person for president who happened to be _____, would you vote for that person?"*

Group	% Yes in 2007	% No in 2007	% Yes in Older Poll	% No in Older Poll
Black	93	5	38 in 1958	54 in 1958
Hispanic	86	12	No data	No data
a Woman	86	12	33 in 1937	64 in 1937
Homosexual	56	41	26 in 1978	66 in 1978
Catholic	93	4	60 in 1937	30 in 1937
Jewish	91	6	46 in 1937	47 in 1937
Mormon	80	17	75 in 1967	17 in 1967
Atheist	46	48	18 in 1958	77 in 1958

Source: *www.pollingreport.com*, including 2007 and earlier Gallup polls.

seems to have hit certain limits. Polls asking U.S. adults whether they would prefer living in a community of people mainly like themselves showed 20–32 percent preferred *less* diversity. While only 20 percent said they preferred to live with people of the same race, a quarter preferred a community made up of people with the same political views or the same religious faith and almost a third preferred to live with people of their own socio-economic status or class.[20] Tolerance has increased broadly, but intolerance remains, especially for those who hold unacceptable views.

In states with the initiative and referendum, civil rights issues often come up for popular vote. When they do, the restrictive, anti-civil-rights side regularly wins. Indeed, one study of 74 referenda votes in the states on civil rights issues—housing and public accommodation laws protecting minorities, school desegregation, protection for homosexuals, English-only laws, and protection for AIDS victims— reports anti-minority victories on more than three-fourths of the votes.[21] James Madison's concerns about "the tyranny of the majority" appear as well founded today as they were over 200 years ago.

MASS POLITICAL IGNORANCE

If elections are to be a means of popular control over public policy, voters must be reasonably well informed about policy issues and must hold opinions about them. Yet large numbers of the electorate are politically uninformed, have no real opinions on policy issues, and therefore respond inconsistently to policy questions.

IGNORANCE

Thomas Jefferson once wrote, "If a nation expects to be both ignorant and free, it expects what never was and never will be." Jefferson would be alarmed today at

FOCUS	MASS CONFIDENCE IN U.S. INSTITUTIONS

Mass confidence in U.S. institutions is generally higher than mass confidence in the people who run the same institutions. Indeed, mass support for the institutional structure of society is often cited as a barrier to mass attacks on institutions themselves, and even revolution. However, mass confidence in institutions is limited. The strongest support is for the military, which may seem ironic in a democratic society, although perhaps not in light of it being an all-volunteer institution. The church, small business, and the police garner a "great deal" or "quite a lot" of mass confidence, significantly these are local institutions and thus closer to the people. (See figure below.)

Among the branches of the national government, the Supreme Court (the only unelected branch) wins more confidence than the president or Congress. Indeed, mass confidence in Congress is lowest of any institution measured, including labor unions and big business. Compared to 2009, support is up slightly for both small and big business, while the presidency and Congress plummeted (15 and 6 points respectively). Only about one-quarter of the general public expresses confidence in newspapers or television news (see Chapter 5).

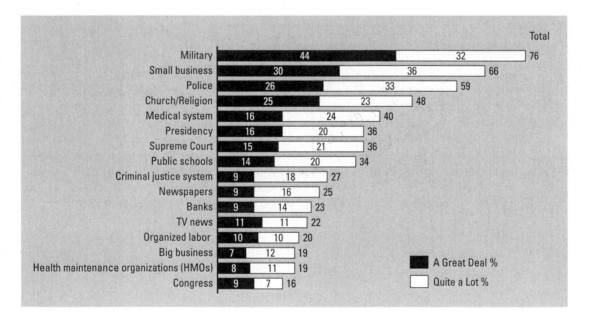

Mass Confidence in American Institutions

Note: Confidence in the presidency usually reflects the personal popularity of the president; in June 2006, the presidency confidence rating was 33, roughly mirroring then-President Bush's own approval rating.

Source: Gallup Poll, June 2009 and November 2010.

the widespread ignorance of U.S. history and basic civics among the U.S. people. Most people know George Washington was the first president of the United States. But beyond such an elementary fact, ignorance of history and government increases alarmingly.

Public opinion surveys regularly report what is now the typical finding of a low level of political information among U.S. adults (see Figure 4.5). More than half do not know the first 10 amendments to the Constitution of the United States are the Bill of Rights. Two-thirds do not recognize the words of the Declaration of Independence or know Martin Luther King Jr. wrote the "Letter from Birmingham Jail."[22] Only about half the public knows the elementary fact that each state has two U.S. senators; fewer still know the terms of members of Congress or the number of Supreme Court justices. Although most can name the president, fewer than half can name their congressional representative, and fewer still can name both their U.S. senators. Knowledge of state and local officeholders is even worse.

For active and influential elites, the stakes of competition in politics are high and the cost of information is cheap; their careers, self-esteem, and prestige are directly, and often daily, affected by political decisions. For them, such ignorance is irrational.

Among the masses, however, political ignorance may be a rational stance—that is, the cost of informing oneself about politics may outweigh the benefits. If others will vote anyway, it may be a rational choice to be a "free rider" who benefits

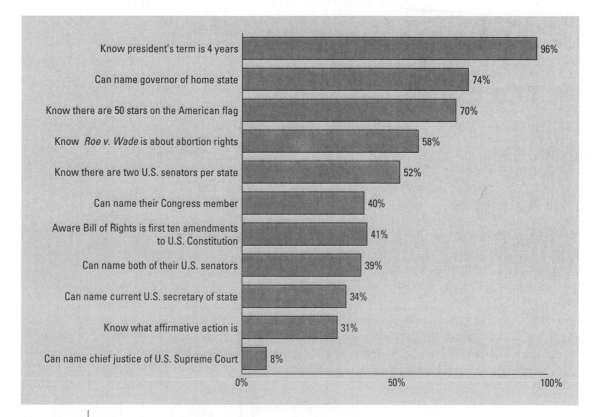

FIGURE 4.5   MASS POLITICAL IGNORANCE

Source: Data from Robrt S. Erikson and Kent L. Tedin, *American Public Opinion*, 6th ed. (New York: Long-man, 2001), p. 55, citing various polls by Gallup, Harris, National Opinion Research Center (NORC), and CBS/*New York Times*.

from other voters' efforts to participate. Most people do not have friends in public office and do not benefit directly from the victory of one candidate or another. Moreover, because one vote among millions seems only infinitesimally influential, to most people it must seem quite reasonable to remain ignorant about politics. The average citizen generally tunes out political information.

PHANTOM OPINIONS AND INCONSISTENT OPINIONS

Because polls ask questions that are meaningless to many people, the answers are often meaningless and sometimes contradictory as well. Many respondents do not wish to appear uninformed, and therefore they offer an "opinion," even if they have never thought about the issue before the interview. They often simply react to question wording, responding positively to positive phrases ("helping poor people," "improving education," "cleaning up the environment," and the like) and negatively to negative phrases ("raising taxes," "expanding governmental power," "restricting choice"). Many respondents succumb to a **halo effect**—giving socially approved responses to questions, regardless of their true feelings.

Because so many people hold no real opinion on political issues, question wording in polls frequently produces inconsistent responses. A study of attitudes toward pornography provides an example. When asked whether they agreed that "people should have the right to purchase a sexually explicit book, magazine, or movie if that's what they want to do," an overwhelming 80 percent of respondents endorsed the statement. However, when the same respondents were also asked

whether they agreed with the opposite view, that "community authorities should be able to prohibit the selling of magazines or movies they consider to be pornographic," 65 percent approved of this statement as well.[23]

IGNORANCE AND PARANOIA: CONSPIRACY THEORY

We can see a particular variety of willful ignorance in the persistence of **conspiracy theories**, which offer easy answers for difficult questions. The idea that a trained marksman alone could kill a president is frightening, so conspiracy theories about the assassination of Kennedy in 1963 abound: mafia, spies, foreign governments, and for the most creative, extraterrestrials. "Birthers" who cannot accept a president they do not support hope against hope that Barack Obama is somehow not qualified to be president and question his "natural born citizen" status. Others, known as "Truthers," cannot accept that all the United States' might was not enough to deter a terrorist attack and so assume 9/11 was some kind of "inside job." In 2009 fully 35 percent of Democrats believed President Bush had advance knowledge of the attack, while 28 percent of Republicans believe Obama was not born in the United States.[24] A 2011 Harris poll showed that 14 percent of Americans think Obama "may be the Anti-Christ." A small but fervent number believe both Bush and Obama are space aliens. This is mass ignorance run amok.

Conspiracy theories are theories about power, and their existence marks places in the political system where segments of the population feel powerless.[25] While such theories are frequently just depositories for class antagonism, racism, and anti-Semitism, each manifestation does point to a real concern about something among the masses. In particular, elites by definition are small numbers of men and women with a great deal of power. If an elite system appears fair and open to new members, it will see mass support. If, however, the elite ranks seem closed and lack transparency, elites may seem so removed from the masses that they might as well be aliens.

MASS POLITICAL APATHY

Political apathy also characterizes mass politics (see Figure 4.6). Nearly half of eligible voters in the United States stay away from the polls, even in presidential elections. Voter turnout is lower yet in off-year congressional elections, when it falls to 35 percent of the voting-age population. City or county elections, when they are held separately from state or national elections, usually produce turnouts of 20–35 percent of eligible voters. Fewer than 1 percent of U.S. adults ever run for public office. Only about 5 percent ever actively participate in parties and campaigns, and about 10 percent make financial contributions. About 15 percent wear political buttons or display bumper stickers. Fewer than 20 percent ever write their congress person or contact any other public official. About one-third of the population belongs to organizations that could be classified as interest groups, and only a few more ever try to convince their friends to vote for a certain candidate.

A significant problem with the pluralist theory that the masses control public policy through elections is that voter turnout is low. Important off-year

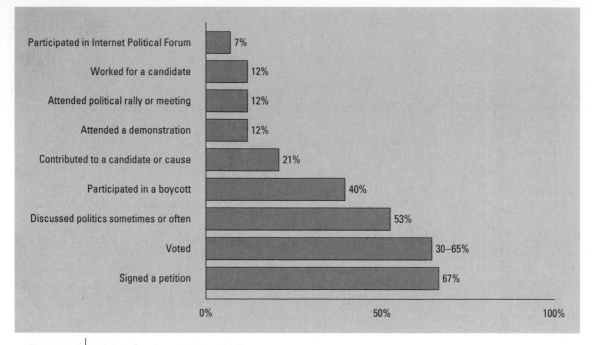

FIGURE 4.6 | MASS POLITICAL APATHY

(nonpresidential) elections bring out fewer than 40 percent of the eligible voters (see Figure 4.7), yet in these contests the nation chooses all its U.S. representatives, one-third of its senators, and about half its governors. Eligible citizens give different reasons for not voting; some of the most popular among the 15 million registered voters who stayed home in 2008 were "not interested" (13.4 percent), "too busy" (17.5 percent), and "didn't like the candidates" (12.9 percent). Another 2.6 percent just "forgot."[26]

The 2004 and 2008 elections each produced a surprisingly high turnout of 64 percent of registered voters, representing record numbers of 126 million in 2004 and 131 million in 2008. In 2004, perhaps the closeness of the 2000 election between Bush and Gore, decided by only 537 votes in Florida, inspired voters to go to the polls. The war in Iraq also may have contributed to the high turnout. The candidacy of African-American Barack Obama inspired many new voters in 2008.

Participation is not uniform throughout all segments of the population (see Table 4.4). Voter turnout relates to such factors as age, race, education, and occupation, and other forms of participation—running for office, becoming active in campaigns, contributing money, and so on—follow substantially the same pattern. Older, white, middle-class, college-educated U.S. adults participate more in all forms of political activity than do their younger, nonwhite, grade-school-educated peers. The high level of turnout among African-Americans in 2008 was attributable to the chance to vote for the nation's first black president.

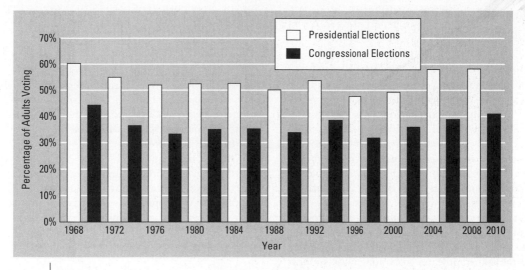

FIGURE 4.7 | PARTICIPATION IN PRESIDENTIAL AND CONGRESSIONAL ELECTIONS

TABLE 4.4 | VOTER TURNOUT BY SELECTED GROUPS IN 2008 PRESIDENTIAL ELECTION

Age	Percentage	Race	Percentage
18–24	49	White, non-Hispanic	66
25–44	60	Hispanics	50
45–64	69	Blacks	65
65–74	72	Asian American	48

Education	Percentage	Gender	Percentage
Eighth grade or less	38	Male	62
Some high school	40	Female	66
High school graduate	55		
Some college	68		
College graduate	77		

Source: U.S. Census Bureau, *www.census.gov/population/twuv/socdemo/voting/cps2008.html*.

Sustained political participation—voting consistently in election after election for state and local offices as well as Congress and the president—is rare. One study of voter participation over 10 elections (including presidential, congressional, gubernatorial, and state and local legislative elections) showed that only 4 percent of the voting-age population voted in nine or all 10 elections; only 26 percent voted in half; and 38 percent did not vote in any election.[27] Age is the best predictor of sustained political activity; older citizens are more likely than young people to be regular voters.

THE DANGERS OF MASS UNREST

It is ironic that democratic ideals survive in the United States because the masses are generally apathetic and inactive, thus leaving the elites with more leeway to protect them. Thus, the masses' capacity for intolerance, authoritarianism, scapegoating, racism, and class antagonism seldom translates into organized, sustained political movements. It is apparently not necessary that most people commit themselves to democracy; all that is necessary is that they fail to support actively radical antidemocratic movements. Occasionally, however, mass apathy gives way to mass unrest. When it reflects mass antidemocratic, extremist, hateful, and violence-prone sentiments, this activism can threaten democratic values.

SOURCES OF MASS UNREST

Mass unrest tends to occur in crises, such as defeat or humiliation in war or economic depression and severe unemployment. Political sociologist William Kornhauser correctly observed:

> There appears to be a close relation between the severity of crises and the extent of mass movements in Western societies. The more severe the depression in industrial societies, the greater the social atomization, and the more widespread are mass movements.... The stronger a country's sense of national humiliation and defeat in war, the greater the social atomization, and the greater the mass action (for example, there is a close association between military defeat and the rise of strong mass movements).[28]

FOCUS | Popular Movements: the Tea Party and Occupy Wall Street

In the past few years, two mass activist groups have formed and reached political significance: the Tea Party movement of 2009–10 and the Occupy Wall Street movement of 2011. Despite almost opposite political views, the two groups show many similarities. The Tea Party movement believes in reducing government spending and cutting taxes. The Occupy Wall Street movement contains a wide variety of people with very diverse policy goals, but it is clearly at core anti-business and advocates greater government control over the private sector and higher taxes.

Both movements were largely without leadership and functioned as separate groups in different states. Both movements relied heavily on the Internet and social media to promote their causes and to organize protests in which large numbers of people showed up to express their views. Both movements began when media elites promoted the idea of a protest movement. The Tea Party movement was able to change Congress through getting its candidates elected in 2010, giving the House of Representatives to the Republicans, although costing the GOP the Senate. The institutional impact of the Occupy movement is still unknown.

The Tea Party movement got underway on February 19, 2009, when a CNBC Business editor had an on-air rant about government bailing out persons who took mortgages they could not pay and suggested a new "tea party" inspired by the 1773 Boston Tea Party. Within days, websites and Facebook pages provided a forum for people who shared views that the government had gone "too far."

The Occupy Wall Street movement was started by a Canadian anti-capitalist magazine called *Adbusters*, whose founder, Kalle Lasn, wished to share his outrage at economic elite excesses. The Twitter hashtag #OccupyWallStreet was introduced in the magazine's July 2011 issue. On July 13, 2011, an email from *Adbusters* announced a Wall Street, New York City protest for September 17, which was Lasn's mother's birthday. The email was widely forwarded and social media saw a rapid expansion in Occupy sites and messages once the protest got underway. The movement grew even more with celebrity endorsements from Kanye West, Joan Baez, and Mark Ruffalo, best known as the Hulk in the 2012 *Avengers* film.

Demographically the movements at their peaks were very similar. Both tend to be more male (61 percent for Occupy, 56 percent for the Tea Party). Both are overwhelmingly white (81 percent each) with a smaller Latino presence (7 percent for the Tea Party, 9 percent for Occupy) and relatively few African-Americans (2 percent for the Tea Party, 3 percent for Occupy). Despite the dearth of blacks participating, the favored Republican presidential candidate of the Tea Party movement in 2011 was African-American Herman Cain, while the Occupy movement has shown strong support for Barack Obama. The difference in demographics is found in age: where the Occupy movement is about a quarter under 25 and overwhelmingly under 50, the Tea Party movement is only 8% under 30 and a majority over 50.

Sources: Pew Research Center. April 18, 2010. "Distrust, Discontent, Anger and Partisan Rancor: The People and Their Government." *www.people-press.org/2010/04/18/section-6-tea-party-and-views-of-government-overreach/*, Sean Captain. November 2, 2011. "Infographic: Who Is Occupy Wall Street?" *www.fastcompany.com/1792056/occupy-wall-street-demographics-infographic*, and Max Chafkin. February 2012. "Revolution Number 99." *Vanity Fair*. Number 618.

Defeat in war, or even failure to achieve any notable victories in a protracted military effort, reduces mass confidence in established leadership and makes the masses vulnerable to the appeals of counterelites. Both fascism in Germany and communism in Russia followed on the heels of national humiliation and defeat in war. The antiestablishment culture of the late 1960s and early 1970s owed a great deal to the mistakes and failures of the nation's leadership in Vietnam.

Mass anxiety and vulnerability to antidemocratic appeals also increase in periods of economic dislocation—depression, unemployment, or technological change—that threaten financial security. Poverty alone causes less anxiety than does change or the threat of change in people's level of affluence. Another source of anxiety among the masses is their perceived level of personal safety. Crime, street violence, and terrorism can produce disproportionately strong anxieties about personal safety. Historically, masses that believe their personal safety is threatened have turned to vigilantes, the Ku Klux Klan, and "law and order" movements.

The masses are most vulnerable to extremism when they are alienated from group and community life and when they feel their own lives are without direction or purpose. Mass participation in the established organizations of the community—church groups, PTAs, Little League, fraternal orders—provides a sense of participation, involvement, and self-esteem. Involvement shields the masses from the despairing appeals of demagogues who play on latent mass fears and hatreds. People who are socially isolated are most likely to become mobilized by totalitarian movements. Thus, a thriving participation in group and community life serves the interest of the elites; it helps protect them from the threat of demagogues who wish to challenge the established system of values.

Monitoring Extremism Jewish Anti-Defamation League: information on anti-Semitic and extremist movements in America. *www.adl.org*

COUNTERELITES

Mass unrest presents potentially serious threats to democratic values. **Counterelites** are generally demagogues who wish to become elite without going through the existing system of achieving power. They rely on an ability to agitate the masses into supporting them and try to leverage this into a claim to power. They seek to exploit the worst attributes of mass politics—intolerance, racial hatred, class antagonism, anti-Semitism, impatience with democratic processes, and the tendency to resort to violence to achieve "the will of the people." Counterelites try to tap populist anger at existing elites. They have arisen in U.S. politics from both the extreme left and the extreme right, but they appeal to similar mass sentiments.

LEFT-WING EXTREMISM

Although left counterelites in the United States are just as antidemocratic, extremist, and intolerant as are right counterelites, their appeal is not as broadly based as is the appeal to the right. Despite defining themselves as champions of the oppressed, left counterelites have no mass following among workers, farmers, or the middle class. Leftist movements in the United States draw most heavily from wealthier, more educated young persons feeling disillusioned with the system. While in the past some leftist groups such as the Weather Underground and the Symbionese Liberation Army have resorted to terrorist violence, they have had no lasting effect. Anarchist groups espousing socialistic views were a significant threat in the early twentieth century, assassinating President McKinley in 1901 and exploding a vehicle bomb on Wall Street in 1920. In contrast, right counterelites in the United States historically have been more successful in appealing to broad mass followings and thus have been a far greater threat to democracy.

RIGHT-WING EXTREMISM

Many changes in U.S. society have contributed to the popular appeal of right counterelites: shifts in power and prestige from the farms to the cities and from agriculture to industry; shifts away from racial segregation toward special emphasis on opportunities for blacks; shifts from religion to secularism; shifts in scale from small to large, from personal to impersonal, from individual to bureaucratic; and increases in crime, racial disorder, and threats to personal safety. The single most enduring and popular right-wing extreme group in U.S. history has been the Ku Klux Klan (KKK), whose peak membership in the 1920s was in the millions. In more recent years, the KKK has claimed to give up endorsing violence in order to focus on its message of hate. The violent end of the white supremacist movement had splintered by the 1980s into a variety of organizations that try to combine racism, anti-Semitism, anti-government paranoia, and extreme distortions of Christianity.

White Supremacists A popular website for adherents of the white supremacist ideology. *www.stormfront.org*

In the 1990s self-styled citizen "militias" cropped up across the nation. Their politics are generally ultranationalistic, occasionally racist, and often conspiracy-minded. They see themselves as modern-day descendants of the patriot militias who fought the Revolutionary War and frequently view federal government agencies as the enemy and the United Nations as a threat to U.S. independence. They emphasize preparation for elite repression through military-style training. At their most extreme, adherents of this radical approach undertook the 1995 bombing of the Oklahoma City federal building, which resulted in the deaths of 168 people and was the largest terrorist attack in the United States before September 11, 2001.

SINGLE-ISSUE EXTREMISM

While left-wing and right-wing extremists have garnered the most attention, the greatest present threat to democracy in the United States is violence from single-issue groups. Though they generally do not result in casualties, the vast majority of terrorist incidents in the United States have been perpetrated by radical animal rights and environmental groups.[29] In the 1990s, a major threat came from violent anti-abortion activists who turned from legitimate protest to terrorist violence

---

IN BRIEF	DANGERS OF MASS UNREST

- The survival of democracy depends on mass apathy. Mass political activism can threaten democratic values.
- Mass unrest can be inspired by economic depressions, defeat in war, and perceived threats to personal safety.
- Mass movements, led by counterelites (demagogues), are frequently intolerant, racist, hateful, anti-Semitic, ultranationalistic, and violence-prone.

- Mass radical activism can lead to political violence or terrorism, whether motivated by ideology of the far left, the far right, or a single issue such as the environment or abortion.
- Elites can become repressive during periods of crisis when they perceive threats from domestic or foreign sources. Both antidemocratic mass unrest and elite repression endanger democratic values.

against abortion providers, including the murder of doctors and nurses. More recently, anti-capitalism rioters in various cities have been able to get attention to their cause, especially in periods of economic recession.

ELITE REPRESSION

Elites may be more committed to democratic values than the masses are, but they frequently abandon these values in periods of crisis and become repressive. Antidemocratic mass activism has its counterpart in elite repression. Both endanger democratic values.

REPRESSION AND THE WAR ON TERRORISM

The current "war on terrorism" was inspired by foreign terrorists rather than by domestic mass activism. In the wake of the attack by Al Qaeda on September 11, 2001, elites adopted various repressive measures, acting with the early enthusiastic support of the masses of the nation, who feared further attacks. Polls taken shortly after September 11 indicated many were prepared to accept new restrictions on their freedom—more surveillance of their papers and communications, more searches of their belongings, roundups of suspect immigrants, and even prolonged detention without recourse to the courts. Indeed, in the months immediately following, almost half of all U.S. adults said the government should take "all steps necessary" to prevent additional acts of terrorism "even if it means your basic civil liberties would be violated." As the initial surprise and fear of terrorist attacks in the United States subsided and effective counterterrorism measures prevented other attacks, concern returned for civil liberties, and willingness to give government the authority to violate liberties to fight terrorism diminished (see Figure 4.8). Still, even by 2007, 43 percent of poll respondents agreed the use of torture to gain information from suspected terrorists was often or sometimes justified.[30]

A BRIEF HISTORY OF ELITE REPRESSION

Repressive behavior is typical of elites who feel threatened in crises. The Alien and Sedition Acts (1798), passed in the administration of John Adams, closed down opposition newspapers and jailed their editors. Although most of these Acts expired in 1801, the Alien Enemies Act is still in effect.[31] Abraham Lincoln suspended the writ of habeas corpus (the requirement that authorities bring defendants before a judge and show cause for their detention) during the Civil War. In the wake of World War I, Congress passed the Espionage Act, which outlawed "any disloyal, profane, scurrilous, or abusive language intended to cause contempt, scorn, contumely, or disrepute" to the government. Socialist presidential candidate Eugene V. Debs was imprisoned for speaking against the war; his conviction was upheld by the U.S. Supreme Court, as were convictions of other antiwar protesters of that period.

Shortly after the Japanese attack on Pearl Harbor, President Franklin Roosevelt authorized removal and internment of Japanese-American citizens living on the West Coast. The U.S. Supreme Court upheld this flagrant violation of the

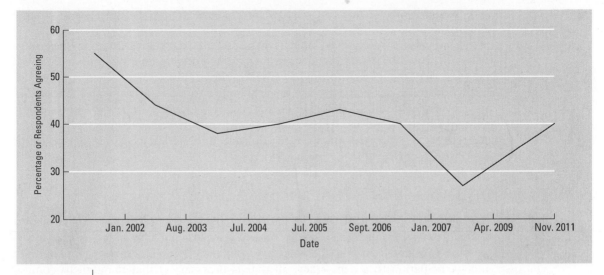

FIGURE 4.8 | CIVIL LIBERTIES AND COUNTERING TERRORISM

QUESTION: Is there a need to sacrifice some civil liberties to curb terrorism?

Source: Pew Research Center for the People and the Press. "27%–Eight Years after 9/11, Fewer See Need to Sacrifice Liberties for Safety." September 17, 2009. *http://pewresearch.org/databank/dailynumber?NumberID= 847* and *www.people-press.org/2011/11/03/section-8-domestic-and-foreign-policy-views/.*

Constitution. Not until 1988 did the U.S. Congress vote to make reparations and public apologies to the surviving victims.

During the Cold War, the U.S. government prosecuted top leaders of the Soviet-allied Communist Party of the United States (CPUSA) for violating the Smith Act, which made it unlawful "to knowingly and willfully advocate, abet, advise, or teach the duty, necessity, or propriety of overthrowing any government in United States by force or violence." Again, the U.S. Supreme Court upheld their convictions. Not until the 1960s did the Court begin to reassert freedom of expression, including the advocacy of revolution.

In response to the terrorist attack in Oklahoma City in 1995, the U.S. Congress passed the Anti-Terrorism and Effective Death Penalty Act of 1996. This law expanded government powers of search, surveillance, and detention in a manner similar to those already granted in the fight against child pornography and organized crime. Following the terrorist attack of September 11, 2001, Congress moved swiftly to further enhance government authority by enacting the USA PATRIOT Act, officially the Uniting and Strengthening America Act by Providing Appropriate Tools Required to Intercept and Obstruct Terrorism of 2001. President Bush and Attorney General John Ashcroft successfully lobbied Congress to increase the federal government's powers of searches, seizures, surveillance, and detention of suspects. The concerns of civil libertarians were largely swept aside. The act was passed nearly unanimously in the Senate (98–1) and overwhelmingly in the House (357–66) with the support of both Democrats and Republicans. Most provisions have been renewed under the Obama administration.

What factors affect a willingness to trade off restrictions on civil liberties in order to provide for safety and security from terrorism? Political science research suggests that the greater people's sense of threat, the greater their support for restrictions on civil liberties.[32] The lower people's trust in government, the less willing they are to trade off civil liberties for security. Liberals are less willing to trade off civil liberties than moderates or conservatives. Overall it seems clear the commitment to civil liberties among U.S. adults is highly contingent on their concerns about threats to national or personal security.

HOW DOES DEMOCRACY SURVIVE?

This chapter's portrait of the elite and the masses indicates that the survival of a democratic system does not depend on a consensus that penetrates to every level of society. It apparently is not necessary that most people commit their attention and participation to a democracy; all that is necessary is that they fail to commit themselves to an antidemocratic system.

We might conclude that democracy in the United States is on shaky foundations. However, it is important to keep in mind that although the masses may have antidemocratic attitudes, they are also inclined to avoid political activity. And those with the most dangerous attitudes are the least involved in politics. As sociologist Herbert Hyman noted, "the normal apathy of the public provided some restraint on violent action against possible victims and also made the public less responsive to appeals to intolerance from national figures."[33] The apathy of the masses acts to counterbalance the radical and potentially irrational nature of their values. Elites also show a willingness to back away from a commitment to democratic values under threatening conditions. Perhaps mass apathy, rather than elite activism, is the key to the survival of democracy.

MASS CONDITIONS | AN ELITIST INTERPRETATION

Democratic theory envisions an active, informed citizenry that believes in equality of opportunity. Democracy is said to thrive in upward social mobility and the absence of extreme differences between rich and poor, and to depend on popular support for individual liberty, freedom of expression, and due process of law. But our analysis of mass conditions and attitudes in the United States today suggests the following propositions:

1. Distrust and cynicism characterize mass attitudes toward government and politics. However, elites have benefited politically from a generally strong economy that has dampened mass enthusiasm for political activism.

2. Income inequality has worsened since 1970 as the earnings of U.S. workers have stagnated over the past three decades while elite incomes have risen, especially those in technology and finance. Earnings declines, especially among unskilled and semiskilled workers, have threatened the ideal of social mobility.

3. Despite mass disaffection for government and politics, the masses expect their government to provide for their economic and physical security.

4. Mass support for democratic values is limited. Elites are more consistent than the masses in applying general principles of democracy to unpopular individuals and groups.

5. Mass tolerance has increased significantly in the last few decades, although a willingness of the masses to deny fundamental liberties to despised groups remains.

6. The survival of democracy depends on elite rather than mass commitment to democratic ideals. Political apathy and nonparticipation among the masses contribute to the survival of democracy. Fortunately for democracy, the antidemocratic masses are generally more apathetic than elites are.

7. Occasionally, mass apathy turns into mass unrest, which is generally extremist, intolerant, antidemocratic, and prone to violence. An unusual demagogue or counterelite can arouse the masses from their apathy and create a threat to the elite consensus.

8. Conditions that encourage mass weakening of support for democratic values include defeat or humiliation in war, economic dislocation, and perceived threats to personal safety.

9. Although left counterelites are as antidemocratic as right counterelites, their appeal is not as broadly based as the appeal of the right. Right counterelites have mobilized mass support among large numbers of farmers, workers, and the middle class.

10. Although more committed to democratic values than the masses are, elites may abandon these values in crises such as war or revolution to maintain the system. They may then cease tolerating dissent, censor mass media, curtail free speech, jail antidemocractic counterelites, and strengthen police and security forces.

NOTES

1. U.S. Bureau of the Census, Historical Income Tables. 2009. Table H-3 http://www.census.gov/hhes/www/income/histinc/h03AR.xls

2. U.S. Bureau of Labor Statistics. 2011 "Women in the Labor Force: a Databook. www.bls.gov/cps/wlf-intro-2011.pdf

3. U.S. Bureau of the Census, Historical Income Tables. Table H-13. Note that we look at the over 25 age group as few under it have advanced degrees and equivalent populations are needed.

4. Jones, Jeffrey M. "Approval of Labor Unions Holds Near Its Low, at 52%." Gallup August 31, 2011. http://www.gallup.com/poll/149279/Approval-Labor-Unions-Holds-Near-Low.aspx and Lydia Saad. "Labor Unions See Sharp Slide in U.S. Public Support." Gallup. September 3, 2009. http://www.gallup.com/poll/122744/labor-unions-sharp-slide-public-support.aspx

5. U.S. Internal Revenue Service. http://www.irs.gov/pub/irs-soi/07in01etr.xls

6. "The *Forbes* Four Hundred," *Forbes*, published annually in the October issue.

7. Brian G. Raub. "Personal Wealth, 2004." United States Internal Revenue Service. http://www.irs.gov/pub/irs-soi/08fallbulpw.pdf

8. Quotations attributed to elites are taken from Harvard professor Joseph S. Nye Jr., "Finding Ways to Improve the Public's Trust in Government," *Chronicle of Higher Education* (January 16, 1998): B6–7. See also Joseph S. Nye Jr., *Why*

People Don't Trust Government (Cambridge, MA.: Harvard University Press, 1997).

9. See Robert S. Erikson and Kent L. Tedin, *American Public Opinion* (New York: Pearson Longman, 2007), Chapter 6.

10. Elizabeth Mendes. "In U.S., Fear of Big Government at Near-Record Level." Gallup. December 12, 2011. www.gallup.com/poll/151490/Fear-Big-Government-Near-Record-Level.aspx

11. Frank Newport. "Americans OK with Short-Term Government Growth." Gallup. April 15, 2009. www.gallup.com/poll/117523/Americans-Short-Term-Government-Growth.aspx

12. Herbert McClosky and Alida Brill, *Dimensions of Tolerance* (New York: Russell Sage Foundation, 1983), p. 249. A report of survey results of support for civil liberties among the mass public and a selected sample of civic leaders. The results reveal consistent differences in levels of tolerance between the mass public and elites in speech and press, due process, fair trial, equal opportunity, privacy, and women's and homosexuals' rights.

13. McClosky and Brill, *Dimensions of Tolerance*, p. 249.

14. Seymour Martin Lipset, *Political Man* (Garden City, NY: Doubleday, 1963), p. 87.

15. Lipset, *Political Man*, p. 92.

16. Pew Research Center. "Americans and Social Trust: Who, Where, and Why?" February 2, 2007. http://pewsocialtrends.org/pubs/414/americans-and-social-trust-who-where-and-why

17. McClosky and Brill, *Dimensions of Tolerance*, p. 249.

18. It was Warren Christopher.

19. Gallup Poll. "Gay and Lesbian Rights." http://www.gallup.com/poll/1651/Gay-Lesbian-Rights.aspx

20. Paul Taylor and Richard Morin. "Americans Say They Like Diverse Communities; Election, Census Trends Suggest Otherwise." Pew Research Center. December 2, 2008. http://www.pewsocialtrends.org/pubs/719/diverse-political-communities

21. See Barbara S. Gamble, "Putting Civil Rights to a Popular Vote," *American Journal of Political Science*, 41 (January 1997): 245–269.

22. Gallup Poll, October 2003. Available online at www.gallup.com

23. *Public Opinion* (September/October 1986): 32; also cited in Robert S. Erikson, Norman R. Luttbeg, and Kent L. Tedin, *American Public Opinion*, 3rd ed. (New York: Macmillan, 1988), p. 55.

24. See David Paul Kuhn. "Both Parties Have Their Fanatics." Real Clear Politics. August 3, 2009. www.realclearpolitics.com/articles/2009/08/03/each_party_has_its_fanatics_97748.html and Rasmussen Reports. 22% Believe Bush Knew about 9/11 Attacks in Advance, May 4, 2007 http://www.rasmussenreports.com/public_content/politics/current_events/bush_administration/22_believe_bush_knew_about_9_l l_attacks_in_advance

25. Mark Fenster. *Conspiracy Theories: Secrecy and Power in American Culture*, 2nd ed. (Minneapolis: University of Minnesota Press, 2008). An excellent examination of what irrational and ignorant views may indicate about U.S. social and political issues.

26. U.S. Census Bureau, www.census.gov/population/www/socdemo/voting/cps2008.html

27. Lee Sigelman et al., "Voting and Nonvoting: A Multi-Election Perspective," *American Journal of Political Science*, 29 (November 1985): 749–765.

28. Kornhauser, *Politics of Mass Society*, p. 174.

29. Federal Bureau of Investigation. *Terrorism 2002–2005*. http://www.fbi.gov/publications/terror/terrorism2002_2005.pdf

30. Pew Center for the People and the Press. "Independents Take Center Stage in Obama Era." May 21, 2009. http://people-press.org/report/?pageid=1525#civil-liberties

31. As *50 U.S.C. 21-23*.

32. Darren W. Davis and Brian D. Silver, "Civil Liberties vs. Security: Public Opinion in the Context of the Terrorist Attacks on America," *American Journal of Political Science*, 48 (January 2004): 28–46.

33. Herbert H. Hyman. "England and America: Climates of Tolerance and Intolerance, 1962." In Daniel Bell (ed.), *The Radical Right* (Garden City, NY.: Doubleday & Co., 1963).

For most people most of the time politics is a series of pictures in the mind, placed there by television news, newspapers, magazines, and discussions.... Politics for most of us is a passing parade of symbols.

—Murray Edelman

THE MEDIA: ELITE–MASS COMMUNICATION

Communication has changed dramatically. Traditionally, the expense of a printing press, radio station, broadcast tower, or audio/visual production equipment created a massive barrier to entry into the communications industry, guaranteeing elite domination of the downward flow of not only information but also values, attitudes, and emotions. Now a video camera is a free bonus feature on a cell phone, video editing is an iPod application, and publishing to a national or even global audience is essentially free on the Internet. In 2012, an obscure human rights group was able to get over 85 million views with a YouTube video.[1] Elite–mass communication has become a two-way street.

Still, while millions of individuals publish blogs, how many get an audience? Some YouTube videos receive hits in the millions, but very few of these do not come from established celebrities. As the masses move to mobile devices for news sources, new elites from technology firms such as Apple and Google interpose themselves in the process of consuming news. The elites still have the edge, though significantly reduced, in controlling the flow of communications. Still, masses frequently misinterpret elite messages to them, and elites cannot always shape mass opinion as they intend.

THE NEWS MAKERS

Elites endeavor to instruct the masses about politics and social values chiefly through television, the major source of information for the vast majority of the United States. Those who control this flow through airwaves, fiber-optic cables, computers, and mobile devices are among the most powerful people in the nation.

Almost all U.S. households have TV sets, and most have cable. Local TV broadcasts, with community news, sports, and weather mixed with national news, are most popular among the masses. Cable news programming audiences

(Fox and CNN especially) regularly surpass the combined nightly network news broadcasts of ABC, CBS, and NBC, which once had a near-monopoly on the news. The elderly (people older than 65) still read newspapers (55 percent), but young people (18–24) rarely do so on a regular basis (15 percent). The Internet is the growing source of news for younger people and older.[2] (See Figure 5.1.)

The power of television arises not only from its mass viewership but also from its ability to communicate emotions. Angry faces in a rioting mob, a parent weeping over a murdered child, wounded soldiers being unloaded from a helicopter—all convey an emotional message. The televised collapse of the World Trade Center buildings on September 11, 2001, united the country in grief and anger, magnifying the response of unity and purpose.

The media elite—television and newspaper executives, reporters, editors, anchors, and producers—do not see themselves as neutral observers of U.S. politics but rather as active participants. They not only report events but also discover events to report, assign them political meaning, and interpret their importance for their mass viewers. They seek to challenge government officials, debate political candidates, and define the problems of society. "TV is the great Legitimator. TV confirms reality. Nothing happens in America, practically everyone seems to agree, until it happens on television."[3]

Pew Research Center for People and the Press Research and information on the media, including opinion polls. *www.people-press. org/*

THE MYTH OF THE MIRROR

How do the media elite see their power? They sometimes claim they do no more than mirror reality, yet they have the power to elevate some national issues and ignore others, to transform obscure people into celebrities, to reward politicians

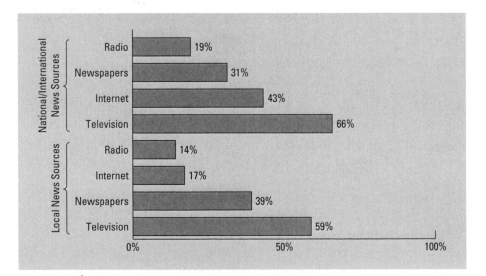

FIGURE 5.1 | WHERE THE MASSES GET THEIR NEWS

Source: Pew Research Center for the People and the Press, July 20–24, 2011. *www.people-press.org/2011/09/22/press-widely-criticized-but-trusted-more-than-other-institutions.*

they favor and punish those they don't. Indeed, at times news makers have credited themselves with the success of the civil rights movement, the end of the Vietnam War, and the forcing of two presidents—Lyndon Johnson and Richard Nixon—from office. These claims more accurately reflect the power of the mass media than the mirror-image theory.

THE CONCENTRATION OF MEDIA POWER

Conglomerate media corporations combine television broadcasting and cable programming, movie production and distribution, magazine and book publication, music recording, sports and recreation, and Internet access and e-commerce. Multinational corporations remain dominant in media and cultural markets: News-Corp, Comcast, Viacom, Time-Warner Disney, and Sony. Older media such as radio and newspapers continue to lose audience, market share, and income. A consistent model for making money by providing Internet content has not been found, except perhaps by the *Wall Street Journal.*

INTER-ELITE COMMUNICATION

The nation's leading television networks (ABC, CBS, NBC, Fox, and CNN), influential national newspapers (*Washington Post, New York Times, Wall Street Journal, USA Today*), and leading news magazines (*Newsweek, Time*) also function as channels of inter-elite communication. These media are monitored by corporate, financial, and government leaders each day and provide the agenda for inter-elite discussion. It is especially important for top government officials to be familiar with the news stories and opinion columns that appear each day in the *Washington Post* and *New York Times*, which mainly serve the political elite, the *Wall Street Journal,* which is more prevalent among the economic elite, and even *USA Today,* whose massive circulation commands respect. (See Table 5.1.)

TABLE 5.1 | TOP 10 NEWSPAPERS BY CIRCULATION, 2011

Rank	Newspaper Title	Daily Circulation
1	*Wall Street Journal*	2,069,169
2	*USA Today*	1,784,242
3	*New York Times*	1,150,589
4	*Daily News* (New York)	601,097
5	*Los Angeles Times*	572,998
6	*New York Post*	512,067
7	*Washington Post*	507,465
8	*Chicago Tribune*	425,370
9	*Newsday* (New York)	404,542
10	*Denver Post*	343,180

Source: Pew Research Center for the People and the Press. *State of the Media 2012. http://stateofthemedia.org/2012/ newspapers-building-digital-revenues-proves-painfully-slow/newspapers-by-the-numbers/.*

THE MEDIA'S POLITICAL FUNCTIONS

The political power of the mass media arises from several of its vital functions: news making, interpretation, socialization, persuasion, and agenda setting.

NEWS MAKING

News making is deciding what and who are newsworthy and allocating valuable television time and newspaper space accordingly. Television producers and newspaper and magazine editors focus attention on certain people, issues, and events, and that attention in turn generates public concern and political action. Without public interest, government officials would not consider the topics important.

The media must select from a tremendous oversupply of information and decide what is news, and this selection process is the root of their power. Television cannot be "a picture of the world" (as some television executives call it) because the whole world cannot squeeze into the 24 noncommercial minutes of the network evening news. Media attention creates events, issues, and personalities; politicians, public relations people, interest group leaders, and aspiring celebrities know the decisions of news executives are vital to their success and even their existence. So they try, sometimes desperately, to attract the media's attention.[4] The result is the "media event"—an activity arranged primarily to stimulate media coverage and attract public attention to an issue or personality. The more bizarre, dramatic, and sensational the event, the more likely it is to attract media attention.

INTERPRETATION

Interpretation of events, issues, and personalities begins when news makers search for an angle on the story—a way to put it into context and speculate about its meaning and consequences. Through interpretation, news makers provide the masses with explanations and meanings for events and personalities.

Most network news broadcasts include a "news special"—two or three minutes of "in-depth" coverage of a particular topic such as gun control, nuclear plant safety, or international terrorism. News staffs prepare the specials in advance and use film or videotape and a script with a lead-in, voice-over, and recapitulation. Interpretation takes place in every news story but is clearest in these.

Many news talk shows or magazine shows present the news in an ideological framework, particularly on cable news such as MSNBC, CNN, and Fox News. Here programmers try to gain audience share by pitching stories and analysis toward viewer biases, whether left, center, or right.

SOCIALIZATION

The media's socialization function is to teach mass audiences the elite's preferred political norms and values through both news and entertainment programming. Election night coverage shows "how democracy works" and reinforces the values of political participation. Entertainment programs introduce social themes and ways of life—for example, racial tolerance, new sexual mores, feminism, and homosexuality. Television executives and producers frequently congratulate themselves on promoting socially progressive themes.

Social media such as Facebook and Twitter also spread societal norms and values, but without elite interference. Personal blogs and other individual-run websites can also reach mass audiences easily. These new media have had profound political impact, including building support for the election of Barack Obama to the White House in 2008, organizing Tea Party protesters against Obama administration policies and as candidates in the 2010 election, and shaping the Occupy movement in 2011.

PERSUASION

Center for Media and Public Affairs
Studies of news and entertainment media, including election coverage.
www.cmpa.com

Persuasion occurs when governments, corporations, unions, political parties, and candidates make deliberate attempts, usually but not always through paid advertising, to affect people's beliefs, attitudes, or behavior. Corporate advertisers ask consumers not only to buy products but also to believe the corporations are concerned with the environment, health, or the nation's economic welfare. We can also consider attempts to influence the masses in political matters as propaganda, although the term carries negative connotations of government media control in fascist or socialist nations and thus is infrequently used in the United States.

The most obvious efforts at political persuasion take place during political campaigns. These are organized advertising campaigns in which the product being sold is a candidate or public policy. Candidates rely less and less on Democratic and Republican party organizations to run their campaigns and instead seek

www.politicalcartoons.com/cartoon/d7ced019-a01b-4830-934d-b5c32ad58859.html.

| IN BRIEF | POLITICAL FUNCTIONS OF THE MEDIA |

- News making—deciding what and who are "newsworthy" and deserving of limited media time and space.
- Interpretation—placing reports into context and providing mass audiences with explanations and meanings.
- Socialization—teaching mass audiences the elite's preferred norms and values in both news and entertainment programming.

- Persuasion—direct attempts, usually through paid advertising, to affect mass beliefs, attitudes, and behaviors.
- Agenda setting—deciding what will be decided, defining issues, and identifying "problems" and "crises."

out advertising and public relations specialists to direct sophisticated media campaigns.

AGENDA SETTING

The real power of the mass media lies in deciding what will be decided. Policy issues do not just happen. Defining the issues, identifying alternative policies, and focusing on political, economic, or social "crises" are critical aspects of national policy-making. We refer to these activities as **agenda setting**. Political leaders, eager to get coverage on the evening news programs, speak out on the issues the mass media have defined as important. Creating an issue, dramatizing it, calling attention to it, turning it into a "crisis," and pressuring government to do something about it are important political tactics. Influential individuals, organized interest groups, political candidates and officeholders, and, perhaps most important, the mass media all employ these tactics. Political elites decide on solutions to problems; media elites determine what the problems are.

BASHING THE UNITED STATES FOR FUN AND PROFIT

Bad news is big news: It is dramatic and sensational. Scandals, rip-offs, violent crimes, threatening budget cuts, sexual deviance, environmental scares all capture audience attention. Good news—improved health statistics, longer life spans, better safety records, higher educational levels, and so on—does not stir audience interest, or build journalistic careers, so easily. The result is an overwhelming bias toward negative news stories in the media, especially on television.

The networks select news for its emotional impact. Topics that inspire mass fear such as bombing and terrorism, mass killings, disease outbreaks, and attacks on children are especially favored. The legendary editor's guideline for choosing a news story is, **"If it bleeds, it leads."** When faced with more complex problems—inflation, government deficits, foreign policy—news makers feel they must simplify, dramatize, or else ignore them altogether.

Entertainment programs reinforce the negative picture of life in the United States. Consider the popularity of crime programs. According to the FBI, fewer

"I think I'll take the murder."

than 3 percent of people will be victims of a violent crime in a year. Murder is the least common crime in the real world but by far the most common crime on television, which averages one killing every two and a half programs. Little wonder that television viewers in the United States and elsewhere tend to greatly overestimate the real amount of crime in society.

SEX SELLS

Historically, reputable newspapers and magazines declined to carry stories about the sex lives of political figures. This unwritten rule of journalism protected Presidents Franklin Roosevelt, Dwight Eisenhower, and John Kennedy among others during their political careers. But today, journalistic ethics do not limit reporting of sexual charges, rumors or innuendoes, or public questioning of candidates and appointees about whether they ever cheated on their spouse, smoked marijuana, or watched pornographic movies.

The media's rationale is that these stories reflect on the *character* of a candidate and deserve reporting as information relevant to the voters' choice for state and national leadership. Yet it seems clear the media pursue scandalous stories primarily for their commercial value. Sex sells; it attracts viewers and readers. But focus on sexual scandal and other misconduct obscures other issues. Politicians defending themselves from personal attack cannot get their political themes and messages across to voters. Otherwise qualified people may stay out of politics to avoid the embarrassment to themselves and their families that results from invasion of personal privacy.

| POLITICAL ENTERTAINMENT

A new form of programming called political entertainment has become popular since 2000 by combining political news and entertainment. It includes television, radio, film, book, and Internet material in which political news and information are the starting point for comedy or feigned drama, both favoring outrage. The two wealthiest practitioners are Michael Moore, whose self-described propaganda film *Fahrenheit 911* earned over $119,000,000, and Rush Limbaugh, whose radio show and books also have made him a rich man.

A classic moment in political entertainment occurred on January 18, 2007, when conservative talk show host Bill O'Reilly appeared on Steven Colbert's *Colbert Report* and said his stage persona was all an act. Colbert, whose stage persona was constructed as a parody of O'Reilly, replied, "If you're an act, what am I?"

Other prominent political entertainers are Ann Coulter, Keith Olberman, Michael Savage, Camille Paglia, Glenn Beck, Lou Dobbs, Michele Malkin, and Rachel Maddow. One of the most famous, Al Franken, author of *Lies and the Lying Liars Who Tell Them: a Fair and Balanced Look at the Right*, is now a member of the United States Senate.

Entertainment too has become increasingly sex-obsessed and profanity-ridden. Recordings, books, television, and films glamorize murder, rape, and suicide. Critic Michael Medved writes:

> Our fellow citizens cherish the institution of marriage and consider religion an important priority in life; but the entertainment industry promotes every form of sexual adventurism and regularly ridicules religious believers as crooks or crazies.[5]

Hollywood claims its movies simply reflect the sex, vulgarity, and violence already present in our culture, that restraints on movie makers would inhibit "creativity," and that censorship would violate freedom of expression. The entertainment industry contends that the popularity of movies, television shows, and albums and the profits they make prove the masses are entertained by Hollywood's current output, regardless of what socially approved responses they give to pollsters. "Movies drenched in gore, gangster rap, even outright pornography are not some sort of alien interstellar dust malevolently drifting down to us, but products actively sought out and beloved by millions."[6]

MASS REACTION

However, media choices can carry high costs for U.S. society. People heavily exposed to political scandal and corruption lose trust and confidence in government and its institutions.[7] Increased mass cynicism and declining voter participation can result from "television malaise"—feelings of distrust, powerlessness, and disaffection stemming from television's emphasis on the negative in politics.[8] The social problem is that while the mainstreaming of violence and sexism may be an expression of freedom for such fare's creators, it ignores the freedom of persons who must now live in a society glorifying brutality and the denigration of women.

BIAS IN TELEVISION NEWS

Overall, network television—through entertainment, newscasts, and news specials—communicates established liberal elite values to the masses. For many years, the media elite was united in its liberal views. The major television networks (ABC,

CBS, NBC, CNN), the leading influential newspapers (*New York Times, Washington Post*), and the national news magazines (*Newsweek, Time*) all reflected the prevailing liberal bias. These are the values of the media elite: liberal reform and social welfare, a focus on the problems of minorities and the poor, skepticism toward organized religion and the traditional family, suspicion of business, hostility toward the military, and an urge to use government power to "do good" (see Focus: The Hollywood Liberals). The liberal bias of the news originates in the values of the news makers. The owners (stockholders) of the major corporations that own the television networks, magazines, and newspaper chains tend to share the moderate conservatism and Republicanism of the business community, but the producers, directors, and reporters are clearly left-leaning and Democratic in their political views. Elite national newsrooms are populated by liberals more than are local newsrooms. Among national media people, self-described liberals outnumber conservatives five to one. Although many describe themselves as moderates, even they are decidedly more liberal in their views than "moderates" in the general public (see Table 5.2).

Conservatives often complained but largely failed to crack the liberal media monopoly, even though polls show 40 percent of people in the United States self-identify as conservative. This audience had no choice but to watch liberal content and complain about the bias in "mainstream media." The 1996 arrival of the Fox television network introduced ideological diversity to television by bringing conservative news reports and commentators to TV viewers.

Billionaire Rupert Murdoch broke the liberal monopoly on the news when he recognized an unfilled market for conservative views on television in the United States. The Fox network slogan is "fair and balanced" news—"We report, you decide." The implication is that Fox is rectifying the liberal bias of the mainstream media; if its reporting appears conservative, the reason is that the country has become so accustomed to left-leaning media that a truly balanced network only seems conservative. In fact, regular news reporting on Fox is not much different from that of other networks. It is the talk and commentary shows that outrage liberals and warm the hearts of conservatives. But whatever its flaws, Fox News has added a diversity of views to U.S. television. Conservatism also prevails on talk radio, both among mass callers and hosts such as Rush Limbaugh, who garners the highest ratings on talk radio. Liberal views still dominate the vast majority of broadcast and cable news programs. The left is also more pronounced on public

TABLE 5.2 | IDEOLOGY IN THE NEWSROOM

	General Public	National Media	Local Media
Ideological Self-Identification			
Liberal	20%	34%	23%
Moderate	41	54	61
Conservative	33	7	12

Source: Pew Research Center for the People and the Press, *State of the New Media*, 2004 and 2007. *www.stateofthemedia.org/2007/journalist_survey_prc4.asp.*

radio and television, which receive government subsidies to present material to their audiences.

In the fall of 2009, Fox News found itself the target of attacks from the Obama White House, which held that its conservative perspective made it an outlet of the Republican party rather than a news organization. In September, Fox was excluded from a series of presidential interviews on health care reform. In October, Fox was blocked from participating in press events with the administration's new "pay czar," a move that led the other news networks to refuse to participate unless their colleagues from Fox were present. Fox had run several stories damaging to the Obama White House including exposés of administration officials and of ACORN, a controversial nonprofit group with links to the administration.[9]

In summarizing the social and political bias of the U.S. mass media, political scientist Doris A. Graber wrote, "Economic and social liberalism prevails, as does a preference for an internationalist foreign policy, caution about military intervention, and some suspicion about the ethics of established large institutions, particularly government."[10]

People for the American Way Website founded by Hollywood "liberals" to combat "right-wing" influence. *www.pfaw.org*

DIVISIONS AMONG MASS AUDIENCES

Thirty years ago, the major networks with a center-left basic orientation, ABC, CBS, NBC, PBS, and CNN, supplied virtually all television news. Center-right Fox News Channel broke this near monopoly and provided an alternative viewpoint on the news. The result has been a "politicization" of news audiences. Increasingly, Democrats and Republicans are choosing different television and radio news sources. A national poll of "regular viewers" indicates that Republicans prefer Fox News, whereas Democrats favor CNN as well as the nightly network news broadcasts of ABC, CBS, and NBC.

Ideology also splits viewers. Fox viewers, especially regular viewers of *The O'Reilly Factor*, Fox's leading show, are decidedly conservative. In contrast, self-described moderates and liberals prefer CNN and MSNBC, including shows such as *The Rachel Maddow Show*. Radio is another news source that has been politicized. Republicans and conservatives are far more likely than Democrats and liberals to listen to news on the radio and radio talk shows, especially Rush Limbaugh (see Table 5.3), although at least some of the programming on NPR public radio as well as that of the Pacifica radio network indicate that the left also has its voice on the airwaves.

Accuracy in Media A self-described watchdog organization critical of liberal bias in the media. *www.aim.org*

HOLLYWOOD LIBERALS

The motion picture and television industry centered in Hollywood has a profound effect on the nation's political culture. Many of the commercial products of Hollywood are directed toward young people, the heaviest watchers of television and the largest buyers of movie tickets. Thus Hollywood plays an important role in socializing them to their political world.

With a few exceptions, Hollywood producers, directors, writers, studio executives, and actors are decidedly liberal in their political views, especially compared with the general public. Of the Hollywood elite, more than 60 percent describe

TABLE 5.3 | POLITICAL DIVISIONS OF NEWS AUDIENCES

Ideology	Conservative	Moderate	Liberal
General public	36	37	19
Network evening news	36	41	15
Fox News	60	26	9
CNN	26	45	23
Daily Show	19	42	35
Colbert Report	19	41	35
O'Reilly Factor	72	21	3
Sean Hannity	80	15	3
Hardball with Chris Matthews	25	39	33
Rachel Maddow Show	21	40	35
Rush Limbaugh	80	13	2

Source: Pew Research Center for People and the Press. Americans Spending More Time Following the News. *www. people-press.org/2010/09/12/americans-spending-more-time-following-the-news/.*

themselves as liberal and only 14 percent as conservative, whereas in the general public, self-described conservatives outnumber liberals by a significant margin. Hollywood leaders are five times more likely to be Democrats than Republicans, although many claim to be independents. And on both economic and social issues, the Hollywood elite is significantly more liberal than the nation's general public or college-educated public.[11]

BIAS AND SLANDER: FREEDOMS OF THE PRESS

Media elites claim the First Amendment's guarantee of freedom of the press gives them a constitutional right to be biased. Certainly the drafters of the Bill of Rights agreed with Thomas Jefferson that a free and critical press was essential to the proper functioning of democracy. The media argue that they must be free to say and print whatever they wish, whether it is biased, unfair, negative, sensational, unfounded, dangerous, or offensive. Generally, the U.S. Supreme Court has agreed.

NO PRIOR RESTRAINT

The Court has interpreted freedom of the press to mean government may place "no prior restraint" (before broadcast or publication) on speech. Originally this doctrine was designed to prevent the government from closing down or seizing newspapers. Today it prevents the government from censoring any news items. For example, the Supreme Court ruled against the federal government and in favor of the *New York Times* in the famous case of the Pentagon Papers. The *New York Times* and the *Washington Post* undertook to publish secret information stolen from the files of the State Department and Department of Defense

MEDIA BIASES

- Negativism—an emphasis on bad news that captures mass audiences' attention, including crime, scandal, environmental scares, terrorism, and other dramatic topics.
- Sensationalism—an emphasis on violence, sex, government corruption, and other themes that lend themselves to dramatic presentations and capture mass audiences.
- Liberalism—a general bias toward content advocating liberal reform, focus on perceived social problems of race and class, skepticism toward organized religion and the traditional family, suspicion of big business and most elites in general, and a propensity to call for expansion of government to use its power to "do good."
- Conservatism—a general bias toward content advocating conservative reforms. The focus is on skepticism toward government, a belief in strong national security, and a propensity to favor family, faith, and tradition in social policy. Fox News and talk radio broke the traditional liberal monopoly and have provided some ideological diversity.

National Association of Broadcasters News and views of the media industry from their trade association. *www. nab.org*

regarding U.S. policy in Vietnam while the war was still in progress. No one disputed that stealing the secret material was illegal. At issue was the ability of the government to prevent its publication to protect national security. But the Supreme Court rejected the national security argument and reaffirmed that the government may place no prior restraint on publication.[12] If the government wishes to keep military secrets, it must not let them fall into the hands of the press or internet publishers such as Wikileaks.

"ABSENCE OF MALICE"

Communications that wrongly damage an individual are known in law as libel (written) and slander (spoken). The injured party must prove in court that the communication caused actual damage and was either false or defamatory. A damaging falsehood, or words or phrases that are inherently defamatory ("This person is a rotten, corrupt, lying no-good"), are libelous and not protected by the First Amendment from lawsuits seeking compensation.

However, media elites have successfully sought over the years to narrow the individual's protection against libel and slander. They were successful in *New York Times v. Sullivan*[13] in depriving public officials of the right to recover damages for false statements unless made with "malicious intent." The "**Sullivan Rule**" requires public officials not only to show the media published or broadcast false and damaging statements but also to prove they did so *knowing at the time* their statements were false and damaging, or did so with "reckless disregard" for the truth or falsehood of their statements. The effect of the Sullivan Rule is to free the media to say virtually anything about public officials. Indeed, the media have sought to expand the definition of "public officials" to "public figures"—that is, virtually anyone the media choose as the subject of a story.

In summary, no effective governmental checks on media power really exist. The constitutional guarantee of freedom of the press is more broadly interpreted in the United States than in any other democracy. The First Amendment guarantees a powerful, independent, and critical media elite.

POLITICS AND THE INTERNET

The Internet provides a powerful channel for mass participation in politics. It is unruly and chaotic by design. It offers a promise of abundant and diverse information, perhaps even information overload. It gives everyone the opportunity for political participation by empowering anyone who can log on and type a blog or upload a video the capacity to spread his or her views to a national and global audience, whether those views are profound and public-spirited, hateful and pornographic, or involving dancing kittens.

The Internet has become a major source of news, particularly for younger and more educated persons. By 2011, 41 percent of poll respondents in the United States said they got most of their national and international news online, behind television at 66% but ahead of newspapers at 31%.[14] Of the top Internet news sources, some are Web outlets for traditional news producers such as the *New York Times*, CNN, or the BBC and others are technology companies such as Google and Yahoo (Table 5.4). Technology company sites are also important feeders to more traditional news sites (Table 5.5).

During the Cold War period, the RAND Corporation, a research think tank, proposed the Internet as a communications network that could survive a nuclear attack. The Internet was deliberately designed to operate without any central authority or organization, although root server systems and Internet address protocols are controlled by ICANN (the Internet Corporation for Assigned Names and

TABLE 5.4 | TOP 20 INTERNET NEWS SITES

Rank	Name	Web Address	Rank	Name	Web Address
1	Yahoo News	news.yahoo.com	11	FoxNews.com	foxnews.com
2	CNN Interactive	cnn.com	12	The Guardian	guardian.co.uk
3	The Huffington Post	huffingtonpost.com	13	Wall Street Journal	online.wsj.com
4	New York Times	nytimes.com	14	Reuters Group PLC	reuters.com
5	BBC	bbc.co.uk/news/	15	The Times of India	timesofindia.indiatimes.com
6	Google News	news.google.com	16	Forbes Magazine	forbes.com
7	The Weather Channel	weather.com	17	Washington Post	washingtonpost.com
8	Reddit	reddit.com	18	Shutterstock	shutterstock.com
9	NBC News and MSNBC News	msnbc.msn.com	19	ABCNews	abcnews.go.com
10	My Yahoo	my.yahoo.com	20	Los Angeles Times	latimes.com

Source: *www.alexa.com/topsites/category/Top/News*.

TABLE 5.5   TOP INTERNET NEWS FEEDER SITES BY MARKET SHARE

Rank	Website
1	Google
2	Yahoo
3	MSN
4	Facebook
5	Yahoo Mail
6	Yahoo Search
7	Bing
8	Drudge Report
9	Google News
10	Windows Live Mail

Source: Hitwise.com, Heather Hopkins. Facebook Largest News Reader? *www.experian.com/blogs/hitwise/2010/2/3/ facebook-largest-news-reader/* Modified by the authors.

Numbers), which was created to allow a private corporation to run the Internet on behalf of the U.S. government (although there is some pressure to share its authority with other nations). Should any part of the system be destroyed, messages will still find their way to their destinations. The later development of the World Wide Web, introduced to the public in 1992, allowed any connected computer in the world to communicate with any other connected computer. The innovation of graphic user interface (GUI) by Microsoft and Apple made using computers vastly simpler as users no longer needed special expertise to communicate. By 1995 U.S. consumers were buying more computers than television sets and sending more e-mail than "snail mail." The United States had 245,203,319 Internet users as of December 2011, a 78.3 percent penetration rate.[15]

POLITICAL WEBSITES

Almost all federal agencies, including the White House, Congress, the federal judiciary, and executive departments and agencies, maintain websites. Individual elected officeholders, including all members of Congress, maintain sites that include personal biographies, committee assignments, legislative accomplishments, issue statements, and press releases. The home pages of the Democratic and Republican parties offer political news, issue positions, opportunities to become active in party affairs, and invitations to send money. No serious candidate for major public office lacks a website containing a flattering biography, press releases, and invitations to contribute money to the campaign online with a credit card. All major interest groups maintain websites—business, trade, and professional groups; labor unions; ideological and issue groups; women's, religious, environmental, and civil rights groups. Indeed, the tidal wave of politics on the Internet may offer so much information in such a fragmented fashion that it simply adds to the apathy and indifference of the masses.[16]

Popular Government Websites *www.whitehouse. gov, www.house. gov, www.senate. gov, www.fbi.gov, www.cia.gov*

THE INTERNET UNCENSORED

The Internet allows unrestricted freedom of expression, from scientific discourses on particle physics and information about the latest developments in medical science to invitations to join paramilitary "militias" and offers to exchange pornographic photos and messages. Commercial sex sites outnumber any other category on the Web.

Drudge Report
Controversial blog that links to stories not always carried by mainstream media, as well as links to all major media outlets. *www.drudgereport. com*

Congress unsuccessfully attempted to outlaw "indecent" and "patently offensive" material on the Internet in its Communications Decency Act of 1996. But the U.S. Supreme Court struck down that act in 1997 and granted the Internet First Amendment protection. Congress had sought to make it a federal crime to send or display indecent material on the Internet to persons under 18 years of age. But the Supreme Court reiterated its view that government may not limit the adult population to consuming "only what is fit for children."[17]

SOCIAL MEDIA

Software making it simple to post messages, pictures, and video to the Internet has spawned myriad individual websites. Many are blogs (short for web logs), highly personal websites which range from diaries of daily activities to scathing political commentary and criticism of the mainstream media. The more reputable bloggers act as journalists, fact-checking stories in the mainstream media or publishing stories overlooked by them, as well as tossing in their own opinions. They have been labeled the media's backseat drivers or watchdogs. Although many offer little more than their own sometimes heated opinions, they frequently succeed in forcing professional journalists to cover stories they would otherwise have ignored.

Facebook, one of the most popular social media websites, has over 150,000,000 users in the United States alone. Facebook allows people to connect as "friends" and share thoughts about anything, including politics. No serious political candidate can be without a Facebook presence. YouTube allows politically themed videos to be easily uploaded to the Internet, so that almost any statement or misstatement by a politician or other elite who appears in public can be captured by smartphone and posted for a wide audience almost immediately.

MEDIA CAMPAIGNS

Television and the Internet have contributed to the decline of political parties, replaced party leaders as "king makers," encouraged voting on the basis of candidate image, fostered the development of media campaigns with professional advertising techniques, and significantly increased the cost of running for office. All these changes limit the influence of the masses in politics, reduce the influence of old-style party bosses, and increase the power of media and media-savvy elites.

THE DECLINE OF PARTIES

The media have replaced the party organizations as the principal link between the candidates and the voters. Candidates can take their campaigns directly to the voters without having to rely on a party hierarchy. Individuals can capture party nominations in primary elections dominated by television advertising. Party organizations have little to say about who wins the party's nomination and next to nothing to say about who wins in the general election. Aspiring candidates no longer begin their quest for public office by calling on party leaders but instead hire professional media advertising firms. Both primary and general elections are now fought largely in the media.

THE MEDIA AS KING MAKERS

The media provide name recognition, the first requirement for a successful candidate. Indeed, heavy media attention can transform unknown figures into instant candidates who no longer need to spend years in political apprenticeship to run for Congress or a governorship. The example of President Obama is informative. A little-known state politician in Illinois who caught the media spotlight in 2004, Obama charmed the media with his stage presence and charisma. News makers select the "serious" candidates for coverage at the beginning of a race. In primary elections, the media even select the "real winner": If the favorite does not win by as large a margin as the media predicted, the media may declare the runner-up the "real winner" even when his or her vote total is less than that of the favorite. People who cannot perform well in front of a camera are no longer feasible candidates for major public office.

IMAGE ELECTIONS

In covering elections, television largely ignores policy questions and focuses on **candidate image**—the personal traits of the candidates and their ability to project a personal image of charm, warmth, compassion, youth and vigor, honesty and integrity, and so forth. Elections are presented on television as struggles between competing personalities. The triumph of the politics of style was the 1960 presidential election debate, when television viewers felt a handsome, cool, and telegenic Jack Kennedy outperformed a feverish, plain Richard Nixon who refused to wear stage makeup (radio audiences thought Nixon won the debate).

The media cover elections as a political game consisting of speeches, rallies, press conferences, travels, and debates. They report who is winning or losing, what their strategies are, how much money they are spending, how they look in their public appearances, the response of their audiences, and so on. It is not surprising that policy issues play a minor role in voters' decisions, because the media do not pay much attention to them.

THE MEDIA CAMPAIGN

Professional media campaigns, usually directed by commercial advertising firms, have replaced traditional party-organized or grassroots political campaigns. Today, expensive media professionals plan an entire campaign; develop mailing lists for fund-raising; select a simple campaign theme and desirable candidate image; monitor progress with continual voter polls; create social media campaigns, produce television, radio, and Internet advertisements, as well as signs, bumper stickers, and T-shirts; select the candidate's clothing and hairstyle; write speeches and schedule appearances that will attract new coverage; and even plan the victory party.[18]

Professional campaign management begins with assessing the candidate's visible strengths and weaknesses, researching those of the opponent, and determining the concerns uppermost in voters' minds. Early polls can test for name recognition, favorable or unfavorable images, and voter concerns; these polls then feed into the campaign strategy. Polls during the campaign chart the candidate's progress, assess the theme's effectiveness, and identify undecided groups as targets for last-minute campaign efforts. Negative campaigns stress the opponent's weaknesses, guided by "opposition research" to dig up dirt on rivals. Most professional campaigning takes the form of paid television commercials, produced by experienced advertising agencies and shown in specific voter markets. But a good media campaign manager also knows how to get the candidate free time on the evening news. Candidates must attract the media and convey a favorable image: They may visit a retirement home, a coal mine, a ghetto, or a pig farm to appeal to specific groups of voters. A candidate may work a day digging ditches (particularly if perceived as a playboy millionaire), walk from city to city (if the opponent flies in a chartered airplane), or participate in a hog-calling contest (if viewed as too intellectual). Such activities are more likely to win a spot on the evening news than a thoughtful speech on nuclear terrorism.

THE COST OF RUNNING FOR OFFICE

The costs of campaigning have risen dramatically because of the high cost of professional ad agencies and television advertising. The first question any aspiring candidate faces today—from city hall to county courthouse to state capital to Washington—is how much money they can raise for the campaign. The candidate must (1) be personally wealthy or have wealthy friends or (2) receive financial support from organized interests, usually the political action committees (or PACs) and SuperPACs established by corporations, banks, professional associations, industry groups, unions, and other special interests. (The power of interest groups is discussed in Chapter 7.)

IN BRIEF | POLITICAL EFFECTS OF THE MEDIA

- The media have replaced parties as the principal link between candidates and voters.
- The media have assumed the "king making" function in their decisions to cover some candidates and ignore others, and to tell audiences who are the "real winners" in primary elections.

- The media, especially television, emphasize candidates' personal traits over their policy positions.
- Media campaigning has dramatically increased the costs of running for office, making candidates more dependent on personal wealth, businesses, unions, and interest groups for campaign contributions.

MEDIA COVERAGE OF PRESIDENTIAL ELECTIONS

Most U.S. voters are exposed to presidential election campaigns through television. But how well does television cover presidential elections?

Horse Race Reporting

For election campaigns, the new media practices **horse race reporting**—reporting on who is ahead or behind, how much money candidates are spending, and their current standing in the polls. Additional stories center on campaign issues—controversies arising on the campaign trail including verbal blunders by the candidates, and character issues such as candidates' sex lives. The media focus early in the 2012 presidential campaign was on strange stories of the candidates and dogs.[19] In contrast, policy issues typically account for only about one-third of television news stories on a presidential election campaign (see Table 5.6). While the 2004

TABLE 5.6 | PRESIDENTIAL ELECTION NEWS COVERAGE ON NETWORK TELEVISION

	2008 ABC-NBC-CBS (Obama-McCain)	2008 Fox News (Obama-McCain)	2004 (Bush-Kerry)	2000 (Bush-Gore)	1996 (Clinton-Dole)	1992 (Clinton-Bush)
Amount of Coverage						
Number of stories	683	524	504	462	483	478
Minutes per day	22	N.A.	27	13	12	25
Focus of Coverage						
Horse race	91	90	48%	71%	48%	58%
Policy issues	31	26	49%	40%	37%	32%
Topic of Coverage (percentage of good press)						
Democratic nominee	68	37	59%	40%	50%	52%
Republican nominee	33	40	37%	37%	33%	29%

Note: Percentages do not add to 100%; some stories were classified in more than one category and some stories did not fit categories shown. Except for the Fox 2008 column, data are for ABC, CBS, and NBC combined.
Source: Derived from *Media Monitor*; Center for Media and Public Affairs, *www.cmpa.com*.

election had significant policy coverage, primarily concerning terrorism and the war in Iraq, the 2008 election returned to a focus on personality.

NEGATIVE COVERAGE

Typically, news stories about both Democratic and Republican presidential candidates are negative. The national news networks—ABC, CBS, NBC—were biased against Bush in 2004 and in favor of Obama in 2008. On-air evaluations of Obama were positive by a two to one margin, whereas evaluations of McCain were negative by the same margin.[20] Only Fox News's evaluations were "fair and balanced," with Obama getting 37 percent positive coverage and McCain 40 percent, a minor difference compared to the bias in the other three networks.

SHRINKING SOUND BITES

Perhaps the most distorting of all television news practices is the reluctance of anchors and reporters to allow candidates to speak for themselves during the campaign. Instead, they discuss the campaigns.[21] Viewers hear almost six times more campaign talk from journalists as from candidates, particularly because journalists often interview each other. The words of the candidates themselves are frequently shown merely as **sound bites**: short, small snippets of a sentence or phrase. The average sound bite for presidential candidates—words actually spoken by the candidates themselves—has shrunk to less than eight seconds.[22]

LATE-NIGHT LAUGHS

The late-night talk shows such as *The Tonight Show* and *The Late Show with David Letterman* continue to play an important role in television campaigning. In 2008, the presidential candidates appeared on late-night programs over 100 times. The Republican ticket was joked about four times as much as the Democrats, the fourth straight election in which comedians have focused their efforts on the GOP. In 2008, Jay Leno's jokes were the most balanced between the parties, while David Letterman was the most partisan (in 2009 Letterman had Obama as his sole guest for an entire program).[23] For younger voters, the *Daily Show with Jon Stewart* and the *Colbert Report* were significant sources of political information.

ASSESSING MEDIA IMPACT

What impact do media elites have on mass opinion and behavior? For many years, political scientists believed the mass media had only minimal effects on political behavior. Of course, wiser business elites never believed this, as the growth of the multibillion-dollar advertising industry attests. Nor did the politicians believe it, as they turned increasingly to expensive television advertising. Presumably, political scientists were basing their theory on the fact that newspaper editorial endorsements seldom changed people's votes.

Media elites influence (1) cognition and comprehension, (2) attitudes and values, (3) public opinion, and (4) behavior. The strongest effects are on cognition and comprehension—in generating awareness and increasing information levels. The media also influence attitudes and values, but the effect is diluted by many other cultural influences. Public opinion, especially on prominent issues, is seldom changed by the media. However, opinion change, when it does occur, is likely to swing in the direction favored by media reporting. Finally, it is most difficult to establish the independent effect of the media on behavior.

COGNITION AND COMPREHENSION

Media elites strongly influence what we know about our world and how we think and talk about it. Bernard Cohen, in the first book to assess the effects of media on foreign policy, put it this way: "The mass media may not be successful in telling people what to think, but the media are stunningly successful in telling their audience what to think about."[24]

The masses generally suffer from **information overload**; so many communications are directed at them that they cannot possibly process them all. The 24-hour news cycle on multiple channels and endless websites offering news and views have diminished the ability of any elite to get the masses to believe anything. Repeated exposure and reinforcement through personal experience aid recall; an individual who has a sibling in the U.S. Army serving in Afghanistan is more likely to be aware of reports from that area. But too many voices with too many messages cause most viewers to block out nearly all information.

Theorist Jean Baudrillard suggested that the production of more information led to a decline in meaning and communication, with the masses resisting elite attempts to influence them by just letting all this information wash over them without absorbing any of it.[25] Information overload may be especially heavy in political news. Television and the Internet tell most viewers more about politics than they want to know. Political scientist Austin Ranney writes: "The fact is that for most Americans politics is still far from being the most interesting and important thing in life. To them, politics is usually confusing, boring, repetitive, and above all irrelevant to the things that really matter in their lives."[26]

ATTITUDES AND VALUES

The media often tell the masses how they should feel about news events or issues—those about which the masses have no prior feelings or experiences. The media also can reinforce values and attitudes the masses already hold. But there is little evidence the media can change existing mass values.

The masses defend against bias in news and entertainment programming by using **selective perception**—mentally screening out information or images with which they disagree. This selectivity reduces the impact of media elites on mass attitudes and behavior. For example, the networks' concentration on scandal, abuse, and corruption in government has not always yielded liberal, reformist notions in viewers' minds but has produced feelings of general political distrust and cynicism toward government and the political system.

PUBLIC OPINION

Can media elites change public opinion? Political scientists Benjamin Page, Robert Shapiro, and Glenn Dempsey performed their classic study of 80 policy issues over 15 years. They examined public opinion polls on various policy issues at a first point in time, then media content over a following interval of time, and finally public opinion on these same issues at the end of the interval. The purpose was to learn whether media content—messages scored by their relevance to the issue, their salience in the broadcast, their pro or con direction, the credibility of the news source, and quality of the reporting—changed public opinion. Although most people's opinions remained constant over time (opinion in the first time period was the best predictor of opinion in the second), opinion changes were heavily influenced by media messages. Page, Shapiro, and Dempsey concluded that "news variables alone account for nearly half the variance in opinion change." They also learned the following:

- *Anchors, reporters, and commentators* had the greatest impact on opinion change. On-air personalities have high credibility with the general public. Their opinions are crucial in shaping mass opinion.
- *Independent experts* interviewed by the media have a substantial impact on opinion but less than that of newscasters.
- A *popular president* can also shift public opinion somewhat. On the other hand, unpopular presidents do not have much success as opinion movers.
- *Interest groups* on the whole have a slightly negative effect on public opinion. "In many instances they seem to actually have antagonized the public and created a genuine adverse effect"; such cases include demonstrators and protesters, even peaceful ones.[27]

BEHAVIOR

Media elites have a difficult task in changing behavior. But television can motivate people who are already predisposed to act in a certain way.

Many studies have examined the effect of the media on behavior—the effect of TV violence, of television on children generally, and of obscenity and pornography. It is difficult to generalize from these studies. However, television appears more likely to reinforce behavioral tendencies than to change them. Nonetheless, we know television advertising sells products. And we know political candidates spend millions to persuade audiences to vote for them. Both manufacturers and politicians create name recognition, employ product differentiation, try to associate with audiences, and use repetition to affect our behavior—in the marketplace and the voting booth.

A voter with a lot of information about both candidates is unlikely to be persuaded by political advertising to change his or her vote. Nor do negative ads change many voters' views, though they do reduce the likelihood a weak supporter will vote for the targeted candidate. But some potential voters are undecided, and the support of many others is "soft." Going to the polls on Election Day requires effort—people have errands to do, it may be raining, they may be tired. Political ads are more successful in motivating a candidate's supporters to go to the polls than in changing opponents into supporters.

THE MEDIA | AN ELITIST INTERPRETATION

Communications in the U.S. political system generally flow downward from elites to masses. Elites influence mass opinion more than masses influence elite opinion, despite the advantages new technologies are giving the masses in reaching large audiences.

1. Television remains the principal means by which elites communicate to masses. Control of the flow of information is highly concentrated. A handful of prestigious news organizations decide what will be the "news."

2. The political functions of the mass media include news making (deciding what to report), interpretation (providing the masses with explanations of events), socialization (teaching about preferred norms, values, and lifestyles), persuasion (making direct efforts to affect behavior), and agenda setting.

3. The most important power of the mass media is agenda setting—deciding which issues will be decided. The media elite choose what to label "crises" or "problems" or "issues" and thereby place these topics on the agenda of political elites.

4. Bias in the news arises from the news makers' liberal-establishment views plus the need to dramatize and sensationalize the news. However, concentration on scandal and corruption in government often produces "television malaise"— social distrust, political cynicism, and feelings of powerlessness—instead of reform.

5. At one time, just four networks—ABC, CBS, NBC, and CNN—monopolized television news and presented a common liberal interpretation of the news. Fox News added ideological diversity by providing a conservative viewpoint. Audiences are increasingly divided by ideology in their viewing habits.

6. The Supreme Court has expanded the First Amendment's guarantee of freedom of the press to remove virtually all checks on media power. The Sullivan Rule renders public officials especially vulnerable to media attacks.

7. The Internet allows the masses to communicate. Any individual with Internet access can use simple software to create a website or blog to express his or her views.

8. The media have largely replaced political parties as the principal link between candidates and voters. The media focus on the personal image of candidates rather than on issues. The high cost of media campaigning adds to the influence of wealthy contributors.

9. The media are most effective at influencing mass cognition and comprehension— what people know, think, and talk about. They are somewhat less effective in shaping attitudes and values; selective perception enables the masses to screen out media messages with which they disagree. The media seldom change public opinion, but when change occurs, it is generally in the direction the media favor. The media are least effective at directly influencing behavior.

NOTES

1. Invisible Children. "Kony 2012," http://www.you tube.com/watch?v=Y4MnpzG5Sqc
2. Pew Project for Excellence in Journalism. *The State of the News Media 2009: An Annual Report on American Journalism*, www.stateofthemedia.org/2009/index.htm and Pew Research Center for People and the Press. 2008 *News Consumption and Believability Survey*, http://people-press.org/reports/pdf/444.pdf
3. William A. Henry, "News as Entertainment," in *What's News: The Media in American Society*, Elie Abel, ed. (San Francisco: Institute for Contemporary Studies, 1981), p. 134.
4. For commentary on this, see Lady Gaga's video "Paparazzi," http://www.youtube.com/watch?v=QQJ9Vi8GLok
5. Michael Medved, *Hollywood vs. America* (New York: Harper, 1992), p. 70.
6. Quoting Katha Pollit, *Time*, June 12, 1995, pp. 33–36.
7. Ion Mihai Pacepa. "Propaganda Redux." *Wall Street Journal*. August 7, 2007. www.opinionjournal.com/editorial/feature.html?id=110010438
8. See Michael J. Robinson, "Public Affairs Television and the Growth of Political Malaise," *American Political Science Review*, 70 (June 1976): 409–132.
9. Jim Ruthenberg. "Behind the War between White House and Fox." *New York Times*. October 22, 2009. www.nytimes.com/2009/10/23/us/politics/23fox.html?_r=l
10. Doris A. Graber, *Mass Media and American Politics* (Washington, DC.: Congressional Quarterly, 1980), p. 41. Currently in its 8th ed. (2009). A wide-ranging description of media effects on campaigns and elections, as well as on social values and public policy.
11. David Prindle, "Hollywood Liberalism," *Social Science Quarterly*, 74 (March 1993): p. 121.
12. New York Times v. United States, 403 U.S. 713 (1973).
13. New York Times v. Sullivan, 376 U.S. 254 (1964).
14. Pew Research Center for the People and the Press. "Internet Gains on Television as Public's Main News Source" January 4, 2011. http://www.people-press.org/2011/01/04/internet-gains-on-television-as-publics-main-news-source/
15. See www.internetworldstats.com/stats14.htm
16. See Arthur Lupia and Tashia S. Philpot, "Views from Inside the Net," *Journal of Politics*, 67 (November 2005): 1122–1142.
17. *Reno v. American Civil Liberties Union*, 521 U.S. 844 (1997).
18. See Darrel M. West. *Air Wars*, 5th ed. (Washington, DC: CQ Press, 2009). An in-depth examination of political advertising in election campaigns from 1952 through 2008.
19. Republican candidate Romney was mocked for driving on a family trip with the dog strapped to the roof of the car in its carrier. Obama had admitted to eating dog meat as a child.
20. Center for Media and Public Affairs. "Election Watch Campaign 2008 Final." *Media Monitor*, Vol. XXIII, No.l. Winter 2009. www.cmpa.com/pdf/media_monitor_jan_2009.pdf
21. See Thomas Patterson, *Out of Order* (New York: Random House, 1993). A devastating attack on television news coverage of political campaigns, its negativism, and the resulting cynicism it inspires among citizens.
22. See Larry Sabato, Mark Stencil, and S. Robert Lichter, *Peepsbow: Media and Politics in an Age of Scandal* (New York: Rowman and Littlefield, 2001).
23. Center for Media and Public Affairs. "The Comedy Campaign: The Role of Late-Night TV Shows in campaign '08." *Media Monitor*. Vol. XXII, No.3. Winter 2008. http://www.cmpa.com/pdf/08winter.pdf
24. Bernard Cohen, *The Press and Foreign Policy* (Princeton, NJ: Princeton University Press, 1963), p. 10.
25. Jean Baudrillard. "The Implosion of Meaning in the Media." in *In the Shadow of the Silent Majorities, and the End of the Social, and Other Essays* (Semiotexte, 1983).
26. Austin Ranney, *Channels of Power* (New York: Basic Books, 1983), p. 11.
27. Benjamin I. Page, Robert Y. Shapiro, and Glenn R. Dempsey, "What Moves Public Opinion," *American Political Science Review*, 81 (March 1987): 23–24, 37.

Democracy substitutes election by the incompetent for appointment by the corrupt few.

—George Bernard Shaw

ELECTIONS, PARTIES, AND DEMOCRACY

Elections function as symbolic reassurance to the masses; by allowing the masses to participate in a political activity, they contribute to the legitimacy of government but do not enable the masses to mandate public policy by voting for one candidate or another. Elected officeholders can claim their selection by the voters legitimizes what they do in office and that the voters' collective decision to install them in office morally binds citizens to obey the laws. The masses' only means to hold the elites responsible for their policy decisions is to wait until the next election and remove politicians who have not produced as expected. Yet even if the incumbents could be thrown out of office (and more than 90 percent are regularly re-elected), there is no guarantee public policy would change.

Traditional political science asserted that parties were necessary instruments of popular control of government. But the two major political parties in the United States usually have little incentive to offer clear policy alternatives. Unlike the parties, Democratic and Republican voters do not divide along neat ideological lines. Party organizations are oligarchic and dominated by activists who are largely out of touch with the voters. Candidates are selected in primary elections in which personal organization and financial assets, not party organizational support, are crucial to victory. Television and the Internet have replaced party organizations as a means of linking candidates to voters. In short, the party system fails to provide the masses with an effective means to direct public policy.

Money-driven elections do not enable voters to direct public policy and most eligible voters stay home on Election Day. What are the purposes of elections? Elite theory views their principal function to be the legitimization of government. Elections are a symbolic exercise to help tie the masses to the established order and obligate them to recognize the legitimacy of government authority and to obey the law. Political scientist Murray Edelman contends that elections are primarily "symbolic reassurance" that serves to "quiet resentments and doubts about particular political acts, reaffirm belief in the fundamental rationality and democratic character of the system, and thus fix conforming habits of future behavior."[1]

Money drives political campaigns in the United States, not policy positions or voting records or even party or ideology. The influence of those interests that provide the money through campaign contributions and related expenditures has grown dramatically in recent decades. The Supreme Court ruled in the 1970s that campaign spending was a form of free speech. The question is, whose voices are heard?

THE FUNCTIONS OF ELECTIONS

ELECTIONS GIVE LEGITIMACY TO GOVERNMENT

Virtually all modern political systems—democratic and authoritarian, capitalist and communist—hold elections. Even dictatorships such as Cuba or Turkmenistan take elections very seriously and strive to achieve 90 to 100 percent voter turnout, despite the fact that the ruling party offers only one candidate for each office. Why do these nations bother to hold elections when the outcome has already been determined? All political regimes seek to tie the masses to the system by holding symbolic exercises in political participation to give the ruling regime an aura of legitimacy. This is the first function of elections. Democratic governments gain the most legitimacy from elections; democratically elected officeholders can claim the voters' participation legitimizes their activities and their laws.

ELECTIONS CHOOSE PEOPLE, NOT POLICY

In democratic nations, elections serve a second function: choosing people to hold public office. The vast majority of people in the world today have never had the opportunity to participate in such a choice. In 2008, U.S. voters decided Barack Obama and not John McCain would occupy the nation's highest office for the next four years. However, this choice was of an individual, not of policy. Few people would think that McCain would have differed from Obama in pursuing Al Qaeda in Afghanistan, ordering the killing of Osama bin Laden, bailing out the big banks, and deporting illegal immigrants. Parties seldom offer clear policy alternatives in election campaigns, voters do not choose the candidates' policy positions, and candidates are not bound by their campaign pledges anyway. Political scientist Gerald M. Pomper explains:

> To choose a government is not to choose governmental policies. Whereas the voters largely do determine the players in the game of American politics, they have far less control over the signals the players will call, the strategies they will employ, or the final score. The popular will, as represented by a majority of voters, does not determine public policy.[2]

ELECTIONS PROVIDE PROTECTION AGAINST OFFICIAL ABUSE

Elections also serve to protect individuals and groups from official abuse. John Stuart Mill wrote, "Men, as well as women, do not need political rights in order that they might govern, but in order that they not be misgoverned."[3] The history of the expansion of suffrage in the United States suggests efforts to ensure voting rights for women, African-Americans, and young adults, so they could better protect themselves from discrimination. While it has proven much more difficult to resolve social and economic inequities through the electoral process than to eliminate discriminatory laws and regulations (see Chapter 13), it is true that voters can defeat officeholders whom they see as acting unethically or abusing their power.

WHY PEOPLE VOTE IN THE UNITED STATES

Voter behavior, or how and why the masses make their ballot decisions, is a central question in political science. To assess the determinants of voters' choice, political science researchers examine the responses of samples of voters in presidential and congressional elections and have derived the following categories as a result:[4]

1. **Policy voters or issues voters** base their decisions on the key issues of greatest importance to them, such as taxation, abortion, or environment. (Sometimes these issues function as markers or "litmus tests" of a candidate's broader ideological beliefs.)

2. **Party voters** (or ideologues) are likely to rely on either liberal or conservative principles in evaluating candidates and issues and generally favor one party over the other. Party identification correlates closely with voter choice; self-identified partisans choose their party's candidates as the "best person."

3. **Group benefits voters** are those who evaluate parties and candidates by expected favorable or unfavorable treatment for specific social groups. Subjects favor candidates they consider sympathetic to a group with which they identify.

4. **Retrospective voters** base their judgment on their perception of the condition of the nation, usually meaning the economy. They blame or praise parties and candidates because of their association with conditions of prosperity or recession. (Sometimes the focus is on war or peace, not economics.)

5. **Candidate image voters** cast their ballots based on a candidate's image as projected through the media—charm, confidence, sincerity, humor, and attractiveness.

Issue and policy voters appear to be a small minority, mainly among the college-educated. Among the masses, party affiliation and candidate image have a stronger grip on voter behavior.

THE MYTH OF THE POLICY-ORIENTED VOTER

For the masses to influence policy through elections, not only would the parties have to offer clear and divergent policy alternatives, but the voters would also have to make their electoral choices on the basis of their policy preferences. Most voters have no information or opinion about many specific policy issues (see Chapter 4) and therefore cannot base their electoral choices on them. Sometimes, voting for specific issue stances is a shortcut to avoid learning more general policy stances, as voters may have broad liberal or conservative policy dispositions they use as a basis for voting.

Victory for a candidate's party does not mean that the voters support all or even most of its programs. Among the voters for a candidate are opponents as well as advocates of the candidate's position on a given issue. A popular majority may be composed of many policy minorities. Frequently candidates make the delusional error of believing the **myth of the policy mandate**, thinking that their positions were what brought electoral victory, when it was most likely some other factor, such as personality or weariness with the opponent.

A policy mandate also would hold that voters actually exercise influence over public policy. This is rare at best, as both parties generally agree on the major direction of most public policy, so the voters cannot influence it by choosing between them. It would be irrational in most cases for either the Democratic or the Republican Party to significantly differentiate its policy positions and risk losing the votes of centrist, independent "swing voters." For a policy mandate to be valid, the electorate must make informed policy-oriented choices; however, most voters are poorly informed on policy questions and have no strong, consistent policy positions. Traditional party ties and candidate personalities influence voters more than policy questions do, diluting voters' influence over policy. Finally, for voters to exercise control over public officials, elected officials would have to be bound by their campaign pledges. However, elected officials frequently ignore these.

American National Election Studies (ANES) Data on voting, public opinion, and political participation in presidential and congressional elections. *www.electionstudies.org*

IDEOLOGY AND VOTING

The masses are less likely to understand the meaning of liberalism or conservatism or to use ideology as a guide to their positions on specific issues. If we ask, "How would you describe your own political philosophy—conservative, moderate, or liberal?" 40 percent of the population describe themselves as conservatives, half as many say they are liberals (21 percent), and almost another 35 percent prefer to think of themselves as moderates (see Figure 6.1).

What do respondents mean when they label themselves liberal, moderate, or conservative? This question has no clear answer. People who label themselves conservative do not consistently oppose social-welfare programs or government regulation of the economy. People who label themselves liberal do not consistently support tax increases or expansion of government services. For many years "conservative" has been a more popular label than "liberal" among the masses, yet government services have continued to expand, civil rights have been strengthened, and the regulation of social conduct has become less restrictive—all ostensibly liberal policy directions. (See Chapter 7 for more on ideological interests.)

In recent years, Democratic and Republican Party activists and leaders have grown further apart ideologically. This **party polarization** is even becoming apparent to the masses.[5] Democratic and Republican *elites* are also ideologically separated from each other and from voters (see Table 6.1). Although exact percentages and specific questions vary from one election to the next, the general pattern is clear: By 2008, Democratic Party elites (represented by delegates to the national Democratic Party convention) were more likely to identify themselves as very liberal (19 percent) than Democratic Party voters (15 percent) or the general public (8 percent). Democratic and Republican delegates were mostly long-term activists, with 59

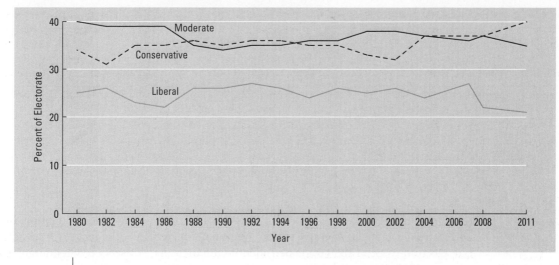

FIGURE 6.1 | LIBERALS, MODERATES, AND CONSERVATIVES IN THE ELECTORATE

Source: Gallup Poll, January 12, 2012. *www.gallup.com/poll/152021/Conservatives-Remain-Largest-Ideological-Group.aspx.*

and 57 percent, respectively, having been active in the party for 20 or more years. Republican Party elites are more likely to identify themselves as very conservative (40 percent) than Republican voters (30 percent) or the general public (15 percent). Both parties are about double the concentration of ideologues as in the general population, the Democrats overall identify as 48 percent liberal versus only 20 percent of the general population, and Republicans as 72 percent conservative compared to 40 percent of the population.[6]

PARTY VOTING

Party identification remains a powerful influence on voter choice, though party ties have weakened over time. More voters today label themselves independents or only weak Democrats or Republicans, or opt to split their tickets or cross party lines,

TABLE 6.1 | PARTY ELITES, PARTY VOTERS, AND MASS AGREEMENT, 2008

Issue	Democratic Party Delegates %	Democratic Voters %	All Voters %	Republican Voters %	Republican Party Delegates %
Abortion: Allowed in all cases	58	33	26	13	5
Iraq: Invasion was the right thing to do	2	14	37	70	80
Tax cuts: Should be permanent	7	34	47	62	91

Source: Adapted from CBS/New York Times Polls August 24 and 30, 2008. *http://20080824.pdf* (Democrats) and *http://graphics8.nytimes.com/packages/pdf/politics/20080901-poll.pdf* (Republicans).

TABLE 6.2 | PARTY AND VOTER CHOICE

Election	1996		2000		2004		2008		2012	
Candidate	Clinton-D	Dole-R	Gore-D	Bush-R	Kerry-D	Bush-R	Obama-D	McCain-R	Obama-D	Romney-R
Democrats	84	10	86	11	90	9	89	10	92	7
Republicans	13	80	8	91	7	92	9	90	6	93
Independents	43	35	45	47	45	48	52	44	45	50

Source: Election exit polls: Voter News Service for 1996–2004, Fox News for 2008–2012. Numbers will not add up to 100 percent due to minor party candidates and rounding.

than in the past. Nevertheless, for those who do join a party, party identification correlates closely with voting choices. Consider, for example, the last four presidential elections (see Table 6.2): Self-identified partisans voted overwhelmingly for their candidate in each. Because self-identified Democrats roughly equal self-identified Republicans in the electorate,[7] both parties' candidates must broaden their appeal to independent and crossover voters to win.

The Democratic and Republican parties reflect prevailing elite consensus on basic democratic values: the sanctity of private property, a free-enterprise economy, individual liberty, majority rule, and due process of law. Both parties have supported the public-oriented, mass-welfare domestic programs of the "liberal establishment": Social Security, Medicare, unemployment compensation, federal highways and infrastructure, countercyclical fiscal and monetary policies, and government regulation of banking, transportation, food and drugs, labor relations, and the environment. Finally, both parties have supported the basic outlines of U.S. foreign and military policy since World War II: international involvement, containment of Soviet expansion during the Cold War, military preparedness, the war on terrorism, and the war in Afghanistan. Both parties voted overwhelmingly to authorize President Bush to use military force in Iraq. Rather than promoting competition over national goals, the parties reinforce social consensus and limit the area of legitimate political conflict.

THE GROUP BASIS OF VOTING

If no social-group influences affected voter choices, we would expect the percentage of each group's vote for Democratic and Republican candidates to be the same as the national percentages. But we readily observe the social-group basis of voting in presidential elections. Different social and demographic groups give disproportionate support to Republican and Democratic candidates. No group is *wholly* within one party or the other, and group differences are not overwhelming, with the exception of the strong Democratic loyalty shown by African-American voters over the years.

Although both parties draw their support from all social groups in the United States, the social bases of the parties are somewhat different. Democratic voters are drawn disproportionately from labor union members (especially government employees) and their families, big-city dwellers, Jews, Catholics, and African-Americans. The core Democratic activists are often government employees or belong to labor and teachers' unions and feminist, civil rights, and environmental organizations. The Democratic Party is more likely to draw its supporters from people earning either below $50,000 or over $200,000 a year.

Republican voters are disproportionately rural, small-town, and suburban Protestants, whites, and businesspeople. Republican activists own small businesses and belong to business organizations, religious and church groups, and civic and service organizations. They are more likely to have annual incomes over $50,000, but less than $200,000.

Democrats tend to do better among the very poor and the very rich, while Republicans do better with the middle class. A significant "gender gap" has also developed between the parties, with Democratic candidates doing better among women, especially single women, than men (see Table 6.3).[8] Party ideology differs to the same degree that each group differs in its general aspirations.

Pluralists argue that social-group differences in voting are evidence of a "responsible" electorate. They may acknowledge that most voters have no knowledge of specific policy issues and do not consistently or accurately apply liberal or conservative policy beliefs to their voting choices. However, pluralists argue, many voters use a *group benefits* standard. For example, many black voters may not follow specific arguments on policy issues, but they have a general idea that since the 1960s the Democratic Party has promoted affirmative action and welfare policies that provide a clear group benefit. Thus, it is not irrational for black voters to give disproportionate support to Democratic candidates, even when most African-Americans tend to be social conservatives.[9] In short, group identification becomes the essential mediating device between the individual voter and electoral choice.

For many years the group basis of voter choice directed political campaign strategy. Candidates conscientiously solicited the support of identifiable social groups—union members, teachers, farmers, small-business owners, religious groups, the young or old, ethnic groups, and so on—by appearing at rallies, securing the endorsement of group elites, pledging to look after a group's interests, or citing their personal (sometimes manufactured) identification with the group they were addressing. Most candidates continue to be sensitive to group identifications among voters. Group identifications in the electorate constitute the strongest arguments in support of pluralist political theory (see Chapter 1).

THE RETROSPECTIVE BASIS OF VOTING

Another function of elections is to give the masses an opportunity to express themselves about the conduct of the public officials who have been in power. Elections do not permit the masses to direct *future* events, but they may allow them to render retrospective judgment about *past* political conduct.[10]

While it is not always easy to decipher what aroused the voters' displeasure, politicians have long understood that *voters tend to hold the incumbent party responsible for hard economic times.* Perhaps politicians have learned no other lesson so well. The economy may not be the only important factor in presidential voting, but economic conditions at election time—recent growth or decline in personal

TABLE 6.3 | GROUP VOTING IN PRESIDENTIAL ELECTIONS

Demographic Factors	1984 Mondale (D)	1984 Reagan (R)	1988 Dukakis (D)	1988 Bush (R)	1992 Clinton (D)	1992 Bush (R)	1996 Clinton (D)	1996 Dole (R)	2000 Gore (D)	2000 Bush (R)	2004 Kerry (D)	2004 Bush (R)	2008 Obama (D)	2008 McCain (R)	2012 Obama (D)	2012 Romney (R)
National (%)	41	59	46	54	43	38	49	41	48	48	48	51	53	46	51	48
Sex																
Male	37	62	41	54	41	38	43	44	42	53	45	54	50	50	45	52
Female	44	56	49	50	45	37	54	38	54	43	52	47	57	43	55	44
Race/ethnicity																
White	35	64	40	59	39	40	43	46	42	54	42	57	44	56	39	59
Black	89	9	86	12	83	10	84	12	90	8	89	11	99		93	6
Hispanic	61	37	69	30	61	25	72	21	62	35	55	42	86	14	71	27
Religion																
Protestant	27	72	33	66	33	47	36	53	42	56	41	58	47	53	42	57
Catholic	45	54	47	52	44	35	53	37	50	47	48	51	53	47	50	48
Jewish	67	31	64	35	80	11	78	16	79	19	76	24	77	23	69	30
Education																
Not high school graduate	50	49	56	43	54	28	59	28	59	38	50	49	63	35	63	35
High school graduate	39	60	49	50	43	36	51	35	48	49	48	51	52	46	51	47
College graduate	41	58	43	56	44	39	47	44	45	51	47	51	50	48	47	51
Union																
Labor union family	53	46	57	42	55	24	59	30	67	30	62	36	68	30	58	40

Source: Gallup and ABC News exits polls, November 2008. *www.abcnews.go.com/PollingUnit/ExitPolls/* and *www.gallup.com/poll/112132/Election-Polls-Vote-Groups-2008.aspx*

income, the unemployment rate, and consumer confidence—are certainly of great importance in the votes given the incumbent versus the challenger. Economic recessions played a major role in the defeat of incumbent presidents Herbert Hoover (1932), Jimmy Carter (1980), and George H. W. Bush (1992) and contributed to the defeat of candidates from the party of a president not running for re-election in 1968 and 2008. The 2012 election was an exception to this with President Obama being re-elected in 2012 by a small margin despite continuing unemployment of over eight percent and essentially flat overall employment compared to when he took office.

Generally, it is not the voter's *personal* economic well-being that affects his or her vote but rather his or her perception of *general* economic conditions. People

| IN BRIEF | DETERMINANTS OF VOTER CHOICE |

- Elections are not policy mandates. The vast majority of voters do not base their electoral choices on candidates' stands on issues.
- Party identification remains a strong influence over voter choice.
- Different social groups give disproportionate support to Democratic and Republican

- candidates. This is a strong argument for a pluralist interpretation of politics.
- Voters tend to retrospectively hold the incumbent party responsible for hard economic times.
- Media campaigning emphasizes candidate image in voter choice.

who perceive the economy as getting worse are likely to vote against the incumbent party, whereas people who think the economy is getting better support the incumbent.

The focus on economic voting is problematic in that most voters have little understanding of economics. Several biases toward economics taint their decision making: (1) an anti-market bias, or "a tendency to underestimate the economic benefits of the market mechanism" and assume profit motives must always be anti-social; (2) an anti-foreign bias, or "a tendency to underestimate the economic benefit of interaction with foreigners" and to see trade as exploitation of domestic workers; (3) a make-work bias, or a tendency to underestimate the economic benefits of conserving labor and to see preserving unneeded and inefficient jobs as preferable to making disruptive change; and (4) a pessimistic bias, or "a tendency to overestimate the severity of economic problems and underestimate the economic performance of the recent past, present, and future."[11]

War can be another issue over which the masses vote retrospectively: voters prefer quick military victories. The 1968 election was shaped by President Lyndon Johnson's decision not to seek re-election, a choice driven by the prolonged war in Vietnam. The U.S. experience in Vietnam remained a haunting reminder for presidents to avoid the quagmire of a protracted guerrilla war. In 2004, voters were almost equally divided over whether the war in Iraq was "worth it." After the quick successes of U.S. and allied troops in overthrowing the dictatorship in Iraq, an insurgency by Baathist elements and widespread terrorist attacks by Al Qaeda resulted in continuing U.S. casualties that eroded public support for the war, as well as Bush's approval ratings. Voters in the 2006 congressional elections appear to have rejected Bush's Iraq policy of "stay the course." Confidence in his handling of the war in Iraq waned: 25 percent of poll respondents in November 2006 approved it and 70 percent disapproved.[12] Yet while it was clear what voters opposed, there was no way to determine what they preferred. Democrats in general offered no real alternative policies. At best, retrospective voting can only indicate what policies voters object to; it says little about the voters' preferences for new policy directions.

CANDIDATE IMAGE VOTING

Today's media-oriented campaigning, emphasizing direct candidate communication with individual voters, reduces the mediating function of parties and interest or identity groups. Media campaigning emphasizes *candidate image*—personal qualities such as leadership, compassion, character, humor, attractiveness, and charm. As more voters identify as independents, the personal characteristics of candidates have become central to many. Indeed, these qualities are most important in the decisions of less partisan, less ideological voters. They will choose moderate candidates who generally share most policy views. Only image remains to keep them apart. Candidate image is more important in presidential than congressional contests, inasmuch as presidential candidates are more visible to the voter than candidates for lesser offices.

It is difficult to identify exactly what personal qualities appeal most to voters. Warmth, compassion, strength, confidence, honesty, sincerity, good humor, and appearance all seem important. "Character" has become a central feature of media coverage of candidates (see Chapter 5). Reports of adultery, drug and/or alcohol abuse, shady financial dealings, conflicts of interest, or lying or misrepresenting facts receive heavy media coverage because they attract large audiences. But it is difficult to estimate how many voters are swayed by "character" issues.

Attractive personal qualities can win support from opposition-party identifiers and people who disagree on the issues. In 1960, John Kennedy's handsome and youthful appearance, charm, self-confidence, and good humor defeated the heavy-jowled, defensive, and ill-humored Richard Nixon. Ronald Reagan's folksy mannerisms, warm humor, and comfortable rapport with television audiences justly earned him the title "the Great Communicator." Reagan disarmed his critics by laughing at his own flubs—falling asleep at meetings, forgetting names—and telling his own age jokes. His personal appeal won more Democratic voters than any other Republican candidate in modern history, and he earned the votes of many people who disagreed with him on the issues. Barack Obama's youth, vigor, and relaxed persona were more appealing to many voters than the elderly McCain.

POLITICAL PARTIES AND ELECTIONS

Elitism asserts that the elites share a consensus about the fundamental values of the political system. This does not mean elite members never disagree or never compete with one another for preeminence. But competition centers on a narrow range of issues, and elites agree on more matters than they disagree on. Our elite model suggests they agree about the general direction of public policy and limit their disagreement to relatively minor matters or symbolic issues.

Traditional political science asserted that parties were necessary instruments of popular control of government. But party organizations are oligarchic and dominated by ideological activists largely out of touch with the more moderate voters. Candidates are selected in primary elections in which personal organization and financial assets, not party organizational support, are crucial to victory. Television and Internet have replaced party organizations as a means of linking candidates to voters. In short, the party system fails to provide the masses with an effective means to direct public policy.

POLITICAL PARTIES AS OLIGARCHIES

It is something of an irony that the parties, as the agents of democratic decision making, are not themselves democratic in their structures. They are skeletal organizations,

| FOCUS | IMAGES OF OBAMA AND ROMNEY, 2012 |

Democrat Barack Obama projected the image of someone who "connects well with ordinary Americans," according to survey respondents during the fall campaign of 2012. Mitt Romney, his Republican challenger, was seen as being better on reducing the budget deficit. On no other issues did either candidate get over 50 percent. Obama benefited from his incumbency, while Romney gained sharply after a weak performance from Obama in the first debate. The public did not seem particularly enthusiastic about either candidate. In a pre-debate survey, the four words most given for Obama were *good, trying, failure*, and *incompetent* (compared to 2008's *confident, inexperienced, intelligent*, and *presidential*). For Romney, the four words were *honest, rich, business(man)*, and *good*. Physical appearance did not make a significant impact in 2012: the younger Obama looked as if he had aged considerably in the four years of his first term, while Romney did not appear particularly old, although cartoonists often focused on his hair and chin. Obama's racial background did not seem to have the same impact as it had in the "historic" election of 2008.

CHARACTER TRAITS THAT DESCRIBE ...

	Obama	Romney
Has new ideas	40%	47%
Is honest and truthful	44	39
Is a strong leader	44	44
Connects well with ordinary Americans	59	30
Is a strong leader	44	44
Takes more moderate positions	49	39
Would do better on the job situation	41	49
Would do better making wise decisions about foreign policy	47	43

Source: Data from Pew Center for the People and the Press, October 2012. *www.people-press.org/2012/10/08/romneys-strong-debate-performance-erases-obamas-lead/1 and www.people-press.org/2012/09/07/obama-romney-biden-and-ryan-in-one-word/obamaoneword social/.*

Republican Party
Website of the Republican National Committee (RNC). With news, press releases, policy positions, etc. *www.rnc.org*

Democratic Party
Website of the Democratic National Committee (DNC). With news, press releases, policy positions, etc. *www. democrats.org*

"manned generally by small numbers of activists and involving the great masses of their supporters scarcely at all."[13] Power in the parties rests in the hands of those who have the time and money to make it a full-time, or nearly full-time, occupation. Party activists—people who occupy party offices and committee posts, who attend local, county, state, or national party meetings and conventions, and who regularly solicit and/or contribute campaign funds to their party and its candidates—are no more than 3 or 4 percent of the adult population. They have the time and financial resources to be able to "afford" politics, the information and knowledge to understand it, and the organization and public relations skills to succeed in it.

Most Republican and Democratic primary voters pay little or no attention to candidates for *party* offices. Indeed, there is seldom much competition for these offices at the local level, with only a single name appearing on the ballot for each post.

Party affairs resemble a pyramid, with all eligible voters in the United States at the bottom (see Figure 6.2). Usually a bit over half of those vote in a general presidential election. Between 30 and 40 percent cast ballots in off-year congressional elections. Party primary elections, even in presidential years, draw only about 25 percent of eligible voters, yet these elections in effect choose the Democratic and Republican presidential candidates. At the top of the pyramid, party activists are no more than 3 or 4 percent of the electorate, and only a handful of elites actually run a party.

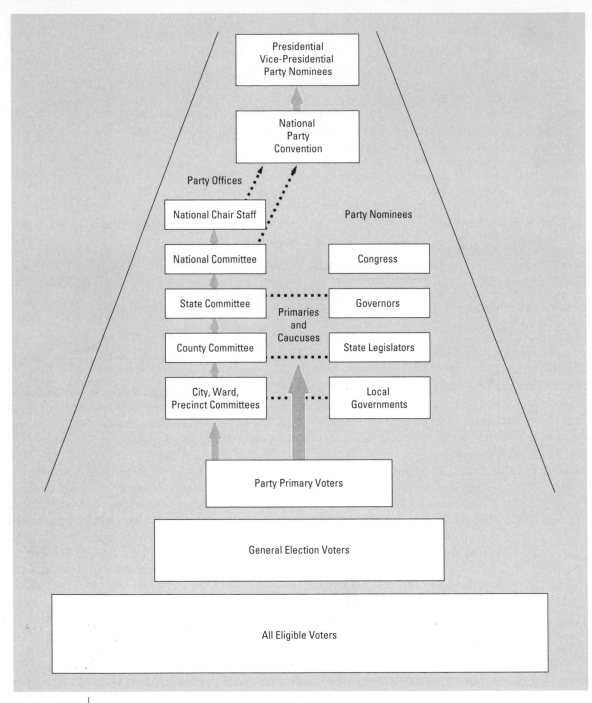

FIGURE 6.2 | PARTIES AS OLIGARCHIES

The Democratic and Republican party organizations formally resemble the U.S. federal system, with national committees, officers and staffs, and national conventions, 50 state committees, and more than 3,000 county committees with city, ward, and precinct levels under their supervision. Members of local and county party committees are usually elected in their party's primary election, although many of these posts across the country are vacant and/or filled with appointees. Both the Democratic and Republican parties have national committees with full-time staffs, and both parties have various policy commissions and caucuses that attract the attention of the energetic few.

FUNCTIONS OF THE POLITICAL PARTIES

Pluralist theory developed a "responsible party" model of the U.S. political system that viewed the parties as principal instruments of popular control of government. Responsible parties were supposed to

- develop and clarify alternative policy positions for the voters
- educate the people about the issues and simplify choices for them
- recruit candidates for public office who agreed with party policy positions
- organize and direct their candidates' campaigns to win office
- hold their elected officials responsible for enacting party policy positions once elected
- organize legislatures to ensure party control of policy-making

In carrying out these functions, responsible parties were supposed to modify the demands of special interests, build a consensus that could win majority support, and provide simple and identifiable, yet meaningful, choices for the voters on Election Day. In this way, disciplined, issue-oriented, liberal and conservative competitive parties would be the principal means by which the people would direct public policy.

There are some fundamental problems with this "responsible" model of the parties. First, in the two-party system, the parties have less incentive to offer strong liberal or conservative policy positions and more motivation to capture the broad center, where most voters can be found. So the parties mostly echo each other. And indeed, as we've seen, voter decisions are seldom based on policy anyway.

Second, the Democratic and Republican parties are organized as oligarchies, dominated by active, ideologically motivated elites. These party activists, including delegates to the national conventions, hold policy views that do not reflect the opinions of rank-and-file voters in either party. Democratic Party activists are far more liberal than Democratic voters, and Republican Party activists are more conservative than Republican voters.

Third, as we saw above, party loyalties among voters have been declining over time. Some people may remain registered as Democrats or Republicans in order to vote in primary elections, but increasingly people identify themselves as independents. Split-ticket voting, in which a voter casts his or her votes for candidates from both parties, is also increasing.

The mass media, particularly television, and the Internet, particularly social media, have replaced the party as a means of political communication. Campaigning is now largely a media activity. Candidates no longer need party workers to carry their message from block to block, although parties do work on get-out-the-vote (GOTV) activities.

The parties have no direct way to hold their elected officials responsible for enacting party positions, to carry out party platforms, or to ensure that legislators vote the party line. Party leaders within legislative bodies may give out prized committee assignments, consider preferences in bills, and use the occasional perks of office to round up votes for the parties' positions. But there are no significant disciplinary measures they can employ against wayward legislators. They can only occasionally deny re-nomination to rebellious officeholders, such as happened in 2006 to Connecticut Democratic Senator Joseph Lieberman and Rhode Island Republican Senator Lincoln Chafee, two moderates who were denied their parties' nomination for re-election (Lieberman was re-elected anyway, as an independent).

Finally, and perhaps most important, primary elections undermine the power of party organizations and party elites because they now determine nominees, not party organizations. The progressive reformers who introduced primary elections at the beginning of the twentieth century wanted to undercut the power of party machines in determining who runs for office, and they succeeded in doing so. Nominees now establish personal organizations for campaigning in primary elections; they are less obliged to negotiate with party leaders.

Despite these problems, political parties survive in the United States. They are important in selecting people for public office, if not selecting public policy. Few independents are ever elected to high political office. Except for a tiny handful, serious candidates must first win Democratic or Republican party nomination.

DECLINING MASS ATTACHMENTS TO PARTIES

A large majority of people in the United States (85 percent) see the two-party system as "seriously broken" or having "real problems"; only 12 percent feel it works fairly well.[14] In recent decades, two clear trends have appeared. First, the percentage of voters preferring neither party has roughly doubled and, second, Democratic Party loyalty has massively eroded (see Figure 6.3). (Republican Party numbers have remained steady for decades.) The rise of independents and the decline of Democratic partisans are two major developments that tend to complement one another.

Dealignment is the decline in the attractiveness of both parties. We can infer it from the growing number of people who have negative or neutral images of the parties and the growing belief that neither party can provide solutions for important problems. A majority also say they have voted for different parties in past presidential elections, and many have voted for an independent or a third-party candidate. However, only about a third register as independents. One reason, and another indicator of dealignment, may be that many states have "closed" primaries that allow only registered Democratic and Republican party members to vote in them. Political Scientist Russell Dalton has found that the newer "dealigned" voters are frequently educated, informed on political issues, concerned with politics generally, and willing to consider candidates from either party without partisan bias.[15]

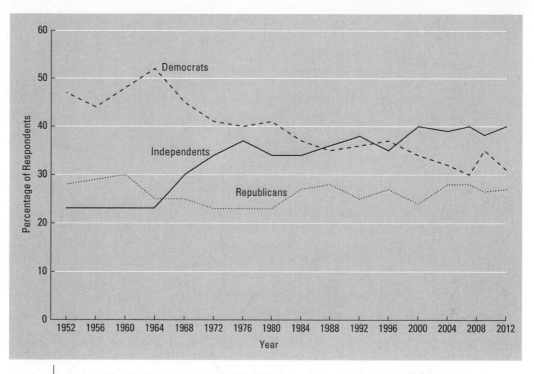

FIGURE 6.3 | PARTY IDENTIFICATION, 1952–2012

Source: Calculated from National Election Surveys data (Ann Arbor, MI: Center for Political Studies, University of Michigan) and Gallup Poll. *www.gallup.com/poll/151943/Record-High-Americans-Identify-Independents.aspx.*

Realignment is a longer-term change. Whenever an election is won or lost, political pundits will speculate on the possibility of a party realignment. Realignment occurs when

> social groups change their party alignment; the party system realigns when the partisan bias of groups changes in ways that alter the social group profile of the parties. The changes may result from a previously Democratic group becoming Republican, [they] may reflect the development of a partisan cleavage among a group of voters who had not displayed any distinctive partisan bias, [and they] might also come about as a highly aligned group begins to lose its partisan distinctiveness.[16]

The major party realignment in recent decades was the Democratic Party's loss of white southern and northern working-class voters, sometimes referred to as "Reagan Democrats." White southerners, generally conservative, drifted away from their traditional Democratic Party. The rising new middle class in the Sunbelt also tended to register Republican. Republican candidates swept the southern states in all presidential elections from 1972 to 2004, except in 1976, 1992, and 1996 when the Democrats ran a southerner as their candidate. The result appears to be a Republican L-shape on the map, with the Republican Party strongest in the South and the Rocky Mountain states, while the Democratic Party dominates the

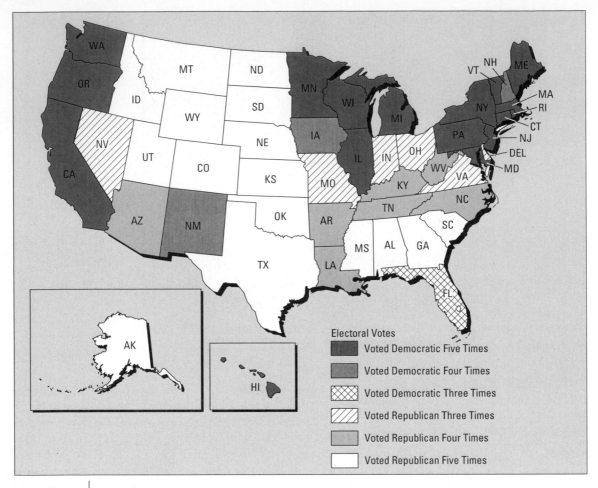

FIGURE 6.4 | STATE PARTY ALIGNMENT 1996–2012

Northeast and West Coast (see Figure 6.4). Still, while voters vote Republican, they did not join the party in any huge numbers, and Republican membership as a portion of the electorate is not significantly different than it was 50 years ago: roughly a third.

THE ATTRACTION TO THE CENTER

In a democracy where the strong majority of voters are in the center, parties have only two options to win elections: mobilize their partisan base and hope for a slight majority (as happened in 2004), or, more commonly, reach for the middle. Both parties' nominees, if they are to succeed, must appeal to the political center. With only two parties and an overwhelmingly non-ideological electorate, "consumer demand" requires that party ideologies be ambiguous and moderate. Therefore we cannot expect the parties, which seek to attract the maximum number of voters,

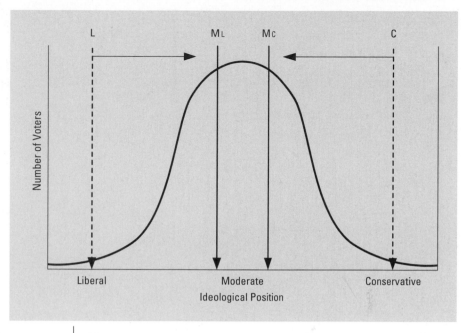

FIGURE 6.5 | VOTER IDEOLOGY

to take up liberal and conservative positions supported by only minorities in the population.

We can diagram the centrist tendencies of the party system as in Figure 6.5. Let us assume the parties seek to win public office by appealing to a majority of voters, and that voters choose the party *closest* to their own ideological position. If the voters distribute themselves along a normal curve on these liberal–conservative dimensions, with most voters occupying the moderate center and only small numbers occupying the far left and far right positions, both parties will have a strong incentive to move to the center. If the liberal party (L) took a strong ideological position to the left of most voters, the conservative party (C) would move toward the center, winning more moderate votes even while retaining its conservative supporters, who would still prefer it to the more liberal opposition party. Likewise, if the conservative party took a strong ideological position to the right of most voters, the liberal party would move to the center and win. Thus, both parties must abandon strong ideological positions and move to the center, becoming moderate in the fight for support of the majority of voters—the moderates.

In short, because the first goal of a party is to win elections, strong ideological and policy positions are counterproductive, except to mobilize strong partisans to turn out to vote. We note that the ideological distribution of the voters is a mirror image of that of the party elites and activists. Political scientist Morris Fiorina has studied how political and media elite present elite cleavage as a "culture war" among the masses, even though it is the elites who are most divided, and not the masses (see Figure 6.6).[17]

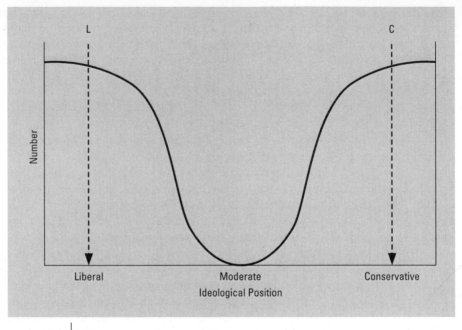

L C

Liberal   Moderate   Conservative

Ideological Position

Number

FIGURE 6.6 | ELITE AND ACTIVIST IDEOLOGY

Source: Fiorina, Morris, Samuel J. Abrams, and Jeremy C. Pope. *Culture War? The Myth of a Polarized America*, 3rd ed. (Upper Saddle River, NJ: Pearson Longman, 2010).

TWO-PARTY POLITICS

Dealignment from the parties would seem to create a favorable environment for independent candidates and third parties. However, the tradition of the two-party system, combined with winner-take-all elections for Congress and for presidential electors, works against the success of third parties. In addition, the laws of the 50 states governing access to the November general election ballot erect high barriers to third-party candidates who would challenge the Democratic and Republican nominees. The major parties' candidates are automatically included on general election ballots, but independents and third parties must meet varied requirements in the 50 states to get on the ballot.

Except for Republican Abraham Lincoln in 1860, no third-party candidate has ever made it to the White House. Still, independent presidential candidates have affected the outcome of the race between the major-party candidates. For example, Theodore Roosevelt's 1912 "Bull Moose" effort split off enough votes from Republican William Howard Taft to allow Democrat Woodrow Wilson to win. Democrat turned "American Independent" candidate George Wallace won 13.5 percent of the vote and 46 electoral votes in 1968, attracting mostly southern Democrats and moving the presidency to Republican Richard Nixon. In 1992, independent Ross Perot pulled 19 percent of the vote, allowing Democrat Bill Clinton to defeat incumbent George H. W. Bush. More recently, Green Party candidate Ralph Nader in 2000 pulled sufficient support from voters who likely otherwise would have voted for Democrat Al Gore in Florida and other states, allowing Republican George Bush a victory.[18] Still, the two-party system historically has discounted independent candidates, although a presidential election will draw dozens of parties and independent candidates.

WHY THIRD PARTIES FAIL

Mass distrust of parties, politicians, and politics in general would seem to create an environment for the success of a third party, perhaps an "antiparty party." In the 1990s, Ross Perot's Reform Party was partially successful in mobilizing dissatisfied voters. Yet the Reform Party eventually collapsed in 2000, as have all other third parties in modern times. Why do these parties fail?

Most "third parties," more accurately called minor parties, are formed not to win elections so much as to promote an ideology or register a protest. Running for office provides candidates visibility and free media coverage, so third parties use the electoral process to express their views and recruit activists to their cause. They measure success not by election victories but by their ability to bring their views to the public's attention. For example, socialist parties, advocating a government-run economy, the abolition of private property, eradication of religion, and similar Marxist hopes, have run candidates in virtually every presidential election in the last century. Opposite them on the ideological spectrum, the Libertarian Party promotes sharply limited government with a message of less economic regulation, less government control of social life, drug legalization, and opposition to U.S. involvement in international affairs. Libertarians generally win a few hundred thousand votes and are the most consistently "successful" minor party. The 1988 Libertarian presidential candidate, Ron Paul, a Republican member of the House of Representatives, has been the main voice for libertarian ideas in recent years.

Occasionally, issue activists will promote a separate party as a means to call attention to their concerns. Perhaps the most persistent was the Prohibition Party, which achieved temporary success with the 1919 passage of the Eighteenth Amendment to the Constitution, prohibiting the manufacture, sale, or transportation of alcohol. The Eighteenth Amendment did little more than inspire the growth of organized crime in the United States, however. What the Prohibitionists referred to as a "noble experiment" failed and was repealed by the Twenty-First Amendment in 1933. Today the Green Party provides an example of a single-issue party, with its original emphasis on environmental protection, although it contends it has a broader socialist agenda as "part of the worldwide movement that promotes ecological wisdom, social justice, grass-roots democracy, and nonviolence." Other examples of single-issue parties in the United States include the Right-to-Life Party (anti-abortion), the Taxpayers Party (anti-tax), the American Nazi Party (pro-hate), and the Marijuana Party (pro–drug legalization).

Libertarian Party
This website reflects the Libertarian Party's strong ideological commitments to individual liberty, free markets, and nonintervention in world affairs.
www.lp.org

Green Party
Although centered on the issue of "ecological wisdom," the Green party website also promotes various left-wing causes.
www.gp.org

STRENGTH OF THE TWO-PARTY SYSTEM

One explanation of the strength of the two-party system focuses on the broad *cultural consensus* in the nation's political culture. Both the elites and the masses express commitment to the values of democracy, individual rights, capitalism, free enterprise, religious freedom, and equality of opportunity. No party directly challenging these values has ever won much of a following. There is little support in the nation's political culture for avowedly fascist, Marxist, racist, communist, authoritarian, or other blatantly antidemocratic parties. Political parties with religious affiliations, common in European democracies, are absent from U.S. politics. Socialist parties radically opposed to liberal democracy and free enterprise consistently appear under various labels—the Socialist Party, the Socialist Labor Party, and the Socialist Workers Party. (The largest popular vote ever won by a socialist presidential candidate was the 6 percent earned by Eugene V. Debs in 1912.)

This cultural explanation also accounts for the influence of historical precedent. The two-party system has gained acceptance through *custom*. The nation's first party system developed from two coalitions, the Federalists and the Anti-Federalists, and this dual pattern has been reinforced over two centuries. As a result, both parties have become umbrella groups containing a variety of views and interests.

Yet another factor in the preservation of the two-party system is the difficulty third parties have in gaining access to the ballot. Democratic and Republican nominees are automatically included on all general election ballots, but third-party and independent candidates in presidential elections must spend a great deal of effort and money to meet the requirements of 50 separate states in order to appear. These requirements often include the filing of petitions signed by 5 or 10 percent of registered voters, which can be tens of thousands of signatures in smaller states and hundreds of thousands in larger states.

Another explanation of the continuing domination of the Republican and Democratic parties is the nature of the electoral system itself. Winners in presidential and congressional elections, as well as in state gubernatorial and legislative elections, are determined by a plurality, winner-take-all vote. Even in elections that require a majority (more than 50 percent)—which may require a runoff election— only one party's candidate wins. This **winner-take-all system** gives parties an overriding incentive to broaden their appeal to a plurality or majority of voters. In contrast, many other countries employ proportional representation, in which voters cast a single ballot for the party of their choice, and legislative seats are given out in proportion to the parties' percentage of the total vote. Minority parties with narrow membership can win legislative seats, perhaps with as little as 5 percent of the vote, necessitating unstable coalition governments that must then cater to extreme factions to stay in power.

PRIMARY ELECTIONS AND THE DETERIORATION OF THE PARTIES

Voters in party primary elections decide who will be their party's nominee for public office. Party primary elections decide state legislative candidates (in every state except nonpartisan Nebraska and since 2012 in open primary California), gubernatorial candidates, congressional candidates, and, in presidential party primaries, delegates pledged to support one or another of the candidates for the party's presidential nomination.

The institution of party primaries for nominating presidential and other candidates for office contributed a great deal to the decline in importance of party organizations. Primaries shifted power from party elites to candidates, interest groups and others donating to campaigns, and the media. In their efforts to make the parties' presidential nominations more "democratic," reformers forced states to use primary elections for selecting candidates and delegates to their national presidential nominating conventions. It was not until 1972 that a majority of party convention delegates were selected in presidential primary elections. The increased use of primaries was written into state laws and now generally applies to both parties.

Given the expanded role of primaries, do the voters now select the presidential nominees? Actual participation in presidential primaries is far lower than in general elections. Whereas the number voting for president in general elections varies between 50 and 65 percent of eligible voters, participation in presidential primaries usually does not exceed 20 to 30 percent. Clearly, with an average turnout this low, primaries do not represent the voice of the people. Further, in low-turnout elections, participants come disproportionately from the college-educated, professionally employed upper-middle classes. Conspicuously underrepresented in the primary electorate are working-class voters and ethnic minorities.

Primary elections strengthen the influence of the ideological activists in each party. Liberals are overrepresented among Democratic primary voters, and conservatives are overrepresented among Republican primary voters. These ideological voters generally give an advantage in Democratic presidential primaries to candidates with a liberal record and in Republican presidential primaries to candidates with a conservative record. However, image often triumphs over ideology: Primary voters are attracted to charismatic candidates regardless of their ideological leanings. Finally, some primary voters knowingly abandon their ideological preference to select a more moderate candidate who appears to have a better chance of winning in November, such as occurred in the Republican choice of Mitt Romney in 2012.

The nomination process begins with the Iowa caucuses in January, followed by a primary election in New Hampshire, a tiny state that jealously guards its position as the first to hold a primary in every presidential year. New Hampshire *is* crucial—but only as a media event. In order to increase their own clout, many states have moved their presidential primaries earlier in the year, and most convention delegates for both parties are now chosen by mid-March. This can mean that states holding later primaries are largely ignored unless the election is close, such as in 2008 when the battle between Barack Obama and Hillary Clinton raged through June.

Primaries provide an opportunity for the media to separate the serious candidates from the aspirants. Although the primary electorate is more heavily ideological than the electorate in general elections, early primaries are usually crowded with candidates, who rarely develop the issues well. Vague promises of "unity," "hope," or "change" help a candidate avoid upsetting any party faction. Thus a candidate's media image becomes crucial. Before the primary season, candidates seek to establish credibility as serious contenders of presidential caliber. They attempt first to generate name familiarity (as revealed in public opinion surveys) and thus recognition as serious candidates, not necessarily as front-runners. The proliferation of primaries and attendant media attention make it possible for a candidate to become well known quickly. A reputation can be created by a large campaign chest, an appealing campaign style, and a good image on television.

The consequence of the primary system is that political party elites cannot control the selection of candidates. Among voters within the same party, public opinion becomes more volatile, more susceptible to media manipulation, and even more issue-free than in the general election. The primary system has been a major factor in the demise of parties and the creation of the new media elite: "Because the competing candidates often share most ideological orientations, personal attributes such as appearance, style, and wit attain new importance (presidents today must be fit and not fat, amusing not dull, with cool not hot personalities)."[19]

MONEY DRIVES ELECTIONS

The high costs of media campaigning add to the political influence of wealthy contributors and thus to elitism in electoral politics. Campaign spending by all candidates, the parties, and independent political organizations runs $3 *billion* per election! The most important hurdle for any candidate for public office is raising the funds to meet campaign costs. Expenditures for congressional campaigns continue to reach new highs. The presidential elections of 2000, 2004, and 2008 each broke records for spending (see Figure 6.7). Expenditures seem to be almost doubling with each campaign. In 2008, Barack Obama spent more than double his opponent John McCain, $730 million versus $333 million.[20] Obama also set a record of over $160 million in small contributions. These exploited a loophole in the law, as these were in amounts under $200, so no disclosures were required under federal campaign finance law and the legitimacy of the donors went unknown.[21]

Center for Responsive Politics The website of an organization devoted to the study of campaign finance laws, the role of money in elections, PACs, "soft money," and special-interest groups. *www.opensecrets.org*

The typical winning campaign for the U.S. Senate can cost over $10 million. Senate campaign expenses vary greatly by state, mostly based on the costs in the local media market. The Senate race in New York in 2000, featuring First Lady Hillary Clinton (now Secretary of State), set a new spending record for a congressional election at more than $85 million. Senator Clinton spent $57 million in her 2006 re-election campaign. Both campaigns required advertising in the New York City media market, the largest and costliest in the country.

The typical winning campaign for a seat in the House of Representatives now costs more than $1.47 million.[22] House members seeking to retain their seats must raise this amount, which comes to over $14,000 a week, every two years! Even losers typically spend over $200,000.

FINDING AND FEEDING THE "FAT CATS"

Most campaign funds are raised from individual contributions. Only about one-half of 1 percent (0.46 percent) of the U.S. adult population contributes $200 or more to presidential or congressional campaigns.[23] Contributors are disproportionately high-income, well-educated professional people with strong partisan views. Networks of contributors exist in every state, and campaign staffs use sophisticated computerized mailing lists, e-mail appeals, and databases of regular contributors to solicit funds.

Small donors (people who give less than $200 in a single contribution) account for the largest number of contributors. But "fat cats," people who write checks for the legal maximum to candidates or parties for $2,400, $5,000, or more, are the

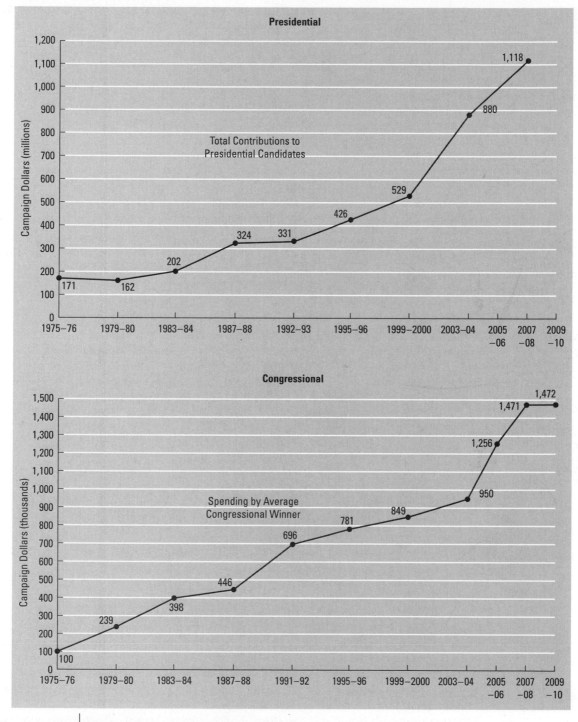

FIGURE 6.7 | THE GROWING COSTS OF CAMPAIGNS

Source: Center for Responsive Politics.

FOCUS   DIRTY POLITICS

Political campaigning frequently turns ugly with negative advertising that is vicious and personal. It is widely believed that television's focus on personal character and private life—rather than on policy positions and governmental experience—encourages negative campaigning. But personal attacks in political campaigns began long before television. They are nearly as old as the nation itself.

"If Jefferson is elected," proclaimed Yale's president in 1800, "the Bible will be burned and we will see our wives and daughters the victims of legal prostitution." In 1864, *Harper's Weekly* decried the "mudslinging" of the day, lamenting that President Abraham Lincoln was regularly referred to by his opponent as a "filthy storyteller, despot, liar, thief, braggart, buffoon, monster, ignoramus Abe, robber, swindler, tyrant, fiend, butcher, and pirate." Television's first memorable attack ad was the "Daisy Girl" commercial broadcast by Democrat Lyndon Johnson's presidential campaign in 1964 against Republican Barry Goldwater. Never mentioning Goldwater by name, the ad attempted to define Goldwater as a warmonger who would start a nuclear conflict.

What are the effects of negative advertising? First, it works more often than not. Controlled experiments indicate that targets of attack ads are rated less positively by people who have watched these ads. But another effect of negative advertising is to make voters more cynical about politics and government in general. Negative campaigning by opposing candidates helps reduce voter turnout. Imagine that advertising in other areas was negative—if airline ads focused on insulting each others' safety records or late arrival times, nobody would fly.

Source: Kathleen Hall Jamieson, *Dirty Politics: Deception, Distraction, and Democracy.* (Oxford University Press, 1992); Stephen Ansolabehere et al., "*Does Attack Advertising Demobilize the Electorate?*" *American Political Science Review*, 88 (December 1994): 829–838; Kim Fridkin Kahn and Patrick J. Kenney, "*Do Negative Campaigns Mobilize or Suppress Turnout?*" *American Political Science Review*, 93 (December 1999): 877–889.

most valued contributors. Despite their financial importance, these donors make up barely one-tenth of 1 percent (0.13 percent) of the adult population. A $2,500 check is only the entry fee for fat-cat status; a contribution of $100,000 is preferred. These are the donors whom candidates aggressively pursue. They are the ones in attendance when the president and other top politicians travel around the country for fundraisers. They are also the ones who are wined, dined, prodded, and cajoled in a ceaseless effort by the parties and candidates to raise funds for the next election. (The next chapter focuses on interest groups and their money.)

Fundraising occupies more of a candidate's time than any other campaign activity. Fundraising dinners (up to $2,500 per plate), cocktail parties, barbecues, fish fries, and so on are scheduled nearly every day of a campaign. The candidates are expected to appear personally to meet and greet big contributors. Movie stars, famous musicians, and other celebrities may also be asked to appear at fundraising affairs to increase attendance; tickets may be "bundled" to well-heeled individual contributors or sold in blocks to organizations. Fundraising continues to consume huge amounts of politicians' time once they are in office. Luckily for them, they are salaried, not hourly, employees of the people.

WEALTHY CANDIDATES

One way in which candidates can dispel concern over the possible corrupting influence of campaign donations is to fund their own campaign. They will often point out that this means they cannot be bought. Jon Corzine [D-New Jersey] won his

U.S. Senate seat in 2000 with $65 million of his *own* money. Candidates can put their own money into their campaigns through outright gifts or through personal loans to be paid back later from outside contributions.

The U.S. Supreme Court opened this loophole by declaring that, as an exercise of their First Amendment right of free speech, individuals can spend as much of their personal wealth on their own campaigns as they wish. Specifically, in *Buckley v. Valeo* in 1976, the Court held that the government could not limit individuals' rights to spend money to publish or broadcast their own views on issues or elections. This means not only that candidates can spend unlimited amounts of their own money on their own campaigns, but also that private individuals can spend unlimited amounts to circulate their own views on an election (although their contributions to candidates and parties can still be limited).[24] In 2009, New York Mayor Michael Bloomberg spent over $100 million to win a third term.

CAMPAIGN FINANCE REFORM

Federal Election Commission The most important website for campaign finance information! It contains ample information on all federal regulations and statutes. *www. fec.gov*

Periodically, the political system must deal with the potential threat to its legitimacy provoked by perceptions of corruption as billions of dollars flow through campaigns. Each reform measure only creates new loopholes in the law for creative minds to exploit. For example, before 2002, "soft money"—political contributions given directly to the Democratic and Republican parties—was unlimited as to the amount the parties could raise. Nearly all soft money was raised in large contributions—indeed, the reason it was so popular with parties was that it allowed big donors to give without having to abide by the limits imposed on direct campaign contributions. Direct contributions to the candidates were referred to as "hard money," and the amount any individual could contribute was limited. Technically, soft money was supposed to be used for party building, get-out-the-vote drives, or general party advertising. But in reality, both parties used their soft money in direct support of their candidates, which they interpret as "party-building."

By 2002, campaign finance reform, notably the proposed elimination of soft-money contributions, became a national issue. Senators John McCain and Russell Feingold introduced new legislation to close existing loopholes and strengthen the integrity of the system. The Bipartisan Campaign Reform Act (BCRA), better known as McCain-Feingold, was a major rewrite of campaign finance laws. Among its more important reforms:

- *Hard money:* Contributions from individuals to federal candidates are limited (initially to $2,000) and indexed to grow with inflation (to $2,500 in 2012). Individual contributions to political parties are limited to $30,800 per year.
- *Soft money:* Contributions from national party committees are limited to $5,000. Parties may no longer accept or spend unregulated soft money. State and local party committees can solicit contributions of up to $10,000 for get-out-the-vote activities and registration efforts in federal elections.
- *Advertising:* Ads by corporations, unions, and interest groups in support of a candidate for federal office cannot be run during the 60 days before a general election or the 30 days before a primary. (This provision was over-ruled by the U.S. Supreme Court in the 2010 *Citizens United v. Federal Election Commission* case.)

THE SUPREME COURT AND CAMPAIGN FINANCE

The U.S. Supreme Court has recognized that limitations on campaign *contributions* help further a compelling government interest—"preventing corruption and the appearance of corruption" in election campaigns. But the Court has been reluctant to allow governments to limit campaign *expenditures,* because paying to express political views is necessary in the exercise of free speech. In an important early case, *Buckley v. Valeo* (1976), the Court held that limiting a candidate's campaign expenditures violated the First Amendment's guarantee of free speech.[25]

When called on to consider the constitutionality of the McCain Feingold campaign reform act (BCRA; see above), the Court upheld limitations on contributions directly to candidates and to national parties.[26] It also upheld limits on soft-money contribution to state and local parties, recognizing that these provisions were designed to prevent circumvention of valid prohibitions on campaign contributions. And the Court upheld a prohibition on spending for "electioneering communications" by individuals and interest groups that are controlled by or coordinated with parties or candidates.

Later, the Supreme Court reconsidered the BCRA's provisions limiting individual and organization electioneering communications. It distinguished between "express advocacy" on behalf of a candidate or party and "issue ads" that are *not* the functional equivalent of express advocacy (in other words, ads that do not urge viewers or listeners to vote for or against a particular candidate or party). "When it comes to defining what speech qualifies as the functional equivalent of express advocacy, the Court should give the benefit of doubt to speech, not censorship."[27] The effect of the decision is to permit political contributors to support organizations unaffiliated with a candidate or party, including nonprofit organizations (see below), that air television ads not expressly endorsing a candidate, right up to Election Day.

LAST ELECTION CYCLE'S LOOPHOLE: INDEPENDENT GROUP EXPENDITURES (527s)

Expenditures by independent groups (referred to as "527s" based on the name of the authorizing provision in the U.S. Tax Code) are unregulated so long as they are not coordinated with a candidate's campaign. Contributions to these organizations are also unregulated. Big-money contributors who can no longer provide large amounts of cash to candidates or parties can establish independent 527 groups to produce and broadcast campaign advertisements. In the 2008 election cycle, 527s spent about $500 million.[28]

THIS ELECTION CYCLE'S LOOPHOLE: SUPERPACS

In 2010, the U.S. Supreme Court accepted an appeal from a group called Citizens United[29] which had been barred from advertising a political film that was critical of then-presidential candidate Hillary Clinton, based on restrictions in BCRA. On free speech grounds, the Court ruled that independent expenditures by corporations and unions could not be restricted (donations to campaigns and coordinated spending still could be regulated, however). The result was that by mid-2012 over 500 SuperPACs[30] had been created and had collected over $200 million. Liberal and conservative, Republican-leaning and Democrat-leaning, SuperPACs can raise and spend *unlimited* amounts promoting or attacking candidates. By mid-2012 most of the donations to these SuperPACs were coming from wealthy individuals, and not corporations.

ELECTIONS, PARTIES, AND DEMOCRACY | AN ELITIST INTERPRETATION

Elite theory contends that the masses do not participate in policy-making, and that the elites who do are subject to little direct influence from the apathetic masses. But many scholars who acknowledge that all societies are governed by elites seek to reaffirm democratic values by contending that voters can influence elite behavior in elections. In other words, modern pluralists sometimes challenge elitism on the ground that elections give the masses a voice in policy-making by holding governing elites accountable to the people.[31]

Our analysis suggests that elections are imperfect instruments of accountability. The first problem with the accountability thesis is that it applies at best only to elected government elites, and little to the elites who control the special interests that fund and guide the elected elites (see Chapter 7 for more on these). However, our analysis of elections also suggests that it is difficult for the voters to hold even government elites accountable.

1. Elections are primarily symbolic exercises that help tie the masses to the established order. They offer the masses an opportunity to participate in the political system, but voting does not enable the masses to determine public policy.
2. Elections are a means of selecting people, not policy. Voters choose on the basis of a candidate's personal image, filtered through partisan commitment. A candidate's election does not imply a policy choice by the electorate.
3. U.S. political parties do not present the U.S. voter with clear ideological alternatives. Both major parties are overwhelmingly middle class in organization, values, and goals. Deviation by either party from the shared consensus is more likely to lose than attract voters.
4. Voters are not well informed about the policy stands of candidates, and relatively few voters are concerned with policy questions. The masses cast their votes based on traditional party ties, candidates' personalities and "character," group benefits, and a host of other factors with little relationship to public policy.
5. Democratic and Republican party leaders differ over public policy more than do party mass followers or the general public. However, all observed party differences fall well within the range of elite consensus on the values of individual rights and liberal freedom.
6. Money drives elections. Elitism is strengthened by the increasing role of individual and interest-group donors to campaigns. Campaign finance laws have proven ineffective. The Supreme Court has held that campaign expenditures are protected as free speech. Expenditures by independent organizations, corporations, and unions are also protected speech.

7. Elections provide the masses with an opportunity to retrospectively judge the conduct of past administrations, but they do not help them direct the course of future events. A vote against the party or candidate in power does not automatically identify the policy being censured. Moreover, voters have no guarantee that a newly elected official will pursue any specific policy alternatives.

8. The parties are dominated by small groups of activists who formulate party objectives and try to select candidates for office. The masses play a passive role in party affairs.

9. Republican political party identification, as a portion of the electorate, has been reasonably stable over several decades. However, recent decades have seen dealignment from the Democratic Party and a corresponding increase in the overall number of independent voters, a decline in "strong" party identifiers, and more split-ticket voting.

10. Despite mass disenchantment with the two-party system, formidable barriers to other alternatives exist, including winner-take-all district and state elections and state laws limiting access to the ballot.

NOTES

1. Murray Edelman, *The Symbolic Uses of Power* (Urbana: University of Illinois Press, 1964), p. 17.

2. Gerald M. Pomper, *Elections in America: Control and Influence in Democratic Politics* (New York: Dodd, Mead, 1980), p. 51.

3. John Stuart Mill, *Considerations on Representative Government* (Chicago: Henry Regnery, Gateway, 1962), p. 144.

4. For an introduction to and discussion of the extensive political science literature on determinants of voter choice, see Richard G. Niemi and Herbert F. Weisberg, *Controversies in Voting Behavior*, 4th ed. (Washington, DC: CQ Press, 2001). Among the most important works: Angus Campbell et al., *The American Voter* (New York: Wiley, 1960); Norman H. Nie, Sidney Verba, and John R. Petrocik, *The Changing American Voter* (Cambridge, MA: Harvard University Press, 1976); Eric Smith, *The Unchanging American Voter* (Berkeley: University of California Press, 1989). See also Robert S. Erikson and Kent L. Tedin, *American Public Opinion*, 7th ed. (New York: Longman, 2007); William H. Flanigan and Nancy H. Zingale, *Political Behavior of the American Electorate*, 12th ed. (Washington, DC: CQ Press, 2009).

5. Geofrey C. Layman and Thomas M. Carsey, "Party Polarization and Conflict Extension in the American Electorate," *American Journal of Political Science*, 46 (October 2002): 786–802.

6. *CBS/New York Times* Polls, August 24 and 30, 2008. http://graphics8.nytimes.com/packages/pdf/politics/demdel20080824.pdf and http://graphics8.nytimes.com/packages/pdf/politics/20080901-poll.pdf

7. Real Clear Politics Horse Race Blog. "On the Party ID Numbers." May 19, 2009. http://www.realclearpolitics.com/horseraceblog/2009/05/on_the_bouncing_pid.html

8. Gallup Poll, July 13, 2009. http://www.gallup.com/poll/121571/Marriage-Remains-Key-Predictor-Party-Identification.aspx

9. Frank Newport. "Blacks as Conservative as Republicans on Some Moral Issues," Gallup Polls. December 3, 2008. www.gallup.com/poll/112807/Blacks-Conservative-Republicans-Some-Moral-Issues.aspx

10. See Morris P. Fiorina, *Retrospective Voting in American National Elections* (Princeton, NJ: Princeton University Press, 1988).

11. Bryan Caplan, "The 4 Boneheaded Biases of Stupid Voters (and We're All Stupid Voters)," *Reason*, Vol. 39, No. 5 (October 2007).

12. As reported in the *Washington Post*, December 12, 2006.

13. Mill, *Considerations*, pp. 130–131.

14. NBC *News/Wall Street Journal* Poll. December 7–11, 2011.

15. Russell J. Dalton, *The Apartisan American: Dealignment and Changing Electoral Politics* (Los Angeles: CQ Press, 2013).

16. Center for Responsive Politics, http://www.opensecrets.org (2009).

17. Morris P. Fiorina, Samuel J. Abrams, and Jeremy C. Pope, *Culture War? The Myth of a Polarized America*, 3rd ed. (Upper Saddle River, NJ: Pearson Longman, 2010). Classic analysis of how the idea of an ideologically divided electorate is really applicable only to activists and elites.

18. Using a basic formula from the Green Party for their 2000 voters, about half would have voted for Gore, about 20 percent for Bush, and the remainder not voted at all. The authors calculated that Nader's votes cost Gore Florida and New Hampshire. Had Gore won either, he would have had the electoral votes needed to win.

19. Center for Responsive Politics, http://www.opensecrets.org/bigpicture/DonorDemographics.php?cycle=2008

20. Center for Responsive Politics, http://www.opensecrets.org/pres08/index.php

21. Dan Morain and Doug Smith, "Obama's Fundraising Prowess Exposes Flaws in Law," *Los Angeles Times*, October 9, 2008. http://articles.latimes.com/2008/oct/09/nation/na-money9

22. Center for Responsive Politics (2012). http://www.opensecrets.org/bigpicture/stats.php?cycle=2010&display=A&type=W

23. Center for Responsive Politics (2009).

24. *Buckley v. Valeo*, 424 U.S. 1 (1976).

25. *Buckley v. Valeo*, 424 U.S. 1 (1976).

26. *McConnell, Senator, et. al. v. Federal Election Commission*, 540 U.S. 93 (2003).

27. *Federal Election Commission v. Wisconsin Right to Life* (June 25, 2007).

28. Center for Responsive Politics, http://www.opensecrets.org/527s/527contribs.php?cycle=2008

29. *Citizens United v. Federal Election Commission*, 558 U.S. 50 (2010).

30. SuperPACs did not come directly out of the *Citizens United* decision, rather *Speechnow.org v Federal Election Commission*, 599 F.3d 686 (D.C. Cir. 2010).

31. Frank J. Sorauf, *Party Politics in America* (Boston: Little, Brown, 1968), pp. 7–80.

When I have to choose between voting for the people or the special interests, I always stick with the special interests. They remember. The people forget.

—Henry Fountain Ashurst, U.S. Senator, 1912–1941

ELITES AND ORGANIZED INTERESTS

CHAPTER **7**

Organized interest groups, not "the people," have the most direct day-to-day influence over government. The public interest is a fiction, but organized interests are potent political realities in Washington, state capitals, and city halls. Interest group activity, including lobbying, is generally protected by the First Amendment to the U.S. Constitution—"the right of the people peaceably to assemble and to petition the government for redress of grievances." This is pluralism at work.

We see the original discussion of interest group politics in the United States in James Madison's *Federalist Number 10*, where the path to avoiding the "tyranny of the majority" is to encourage the existence of many factions, none of whom could bully the rest. Whereas Jean-Jacques Rousseau of France spoke of society having a single "general will," in the United States there was always the idea of a diversity of interests. Frequently, interest group politics is derided as a game of "special interests" versus the "common interest." Ultimately, all interests are special; some just appear a bit more special than others.

INTEREST GROUPS: PLURALIST OR ELITIST?

Pluralists contend that interest groups perform several important functions for their members and for a democratic society. First, the organized group links the individual and the government. Political scientists Gabriel A. Almond and Sidney Verba wrote:

> Voluntary associations are the prime means by which the function of mediating between the individual and the state is performed. Through them the individual is able to relate himself effectively and meaningfully to the political system.[1]

Pluralists also argue that interest groups enhance individual well-being. In a complex society, with primary associations to small groups, such as the family, diminishing in importance, secondary associations that are less intimate but more goal-oriented may help people overcome the sense of powerlessness characteristic of mass societies. Groups help integrate the individual with society.

Finally, pluralists assert that interest groups help reduce potentially divisive conflicts. According to the theory of overlapping group memberships, all citizens are members of interest groups, some organized, some not.[2] Each person develops through multiple group affiliations. A person may be, for example, a nurse, a Midwesterner, a military veteran, a motorcycle enthusiast, and a Roman Catholic, with each affiliation imposing its own values. No single group affiliation could claim the individual's total, undivided loyalty, but multiple affiliations help modify the demands of any one group and reduce social conflict.

In short, pluralists consider interest groups "good" because (1) they provide an effective voice for citizens competing for resources, (2) they reduce the anxiety of feeling powerless, and (3) they provide stability.

However, pluralist theory rests on several assumptions that may or may not be correct:

- Membership in organizations is widespread and represents all individual interests.
- Organized groups efficiently translate members' expectations into political demands and members gain by presenting demands through a representative association.
- Although some win and some lose, each group, whatever its demands, should have equal access to the political resources necessary for success.

While nominally articulating the demands of the masses, interest groups protect the values of the established elites, which includes their own leadership. Rather than advance social changes, they help maintain the status quo. Their influence is largely based on ability to mobilize financial resources, so all groups are not equal in their ability to compete for members.[3]

How democratic is interest group pluralism? Do interest groups represent "the people" fairly? Or is the interest group system another point of elite influence over government elites? The Iron Law of Oligarchy provides the answer: all organizations are run by elites.

THE ELITE BIAS OF INTEREST GROUPS

Most of the U.S. population belongs to at least one formal organization. Like voting and other forms of political participation, however, membership is linked to socioeconomic status. It is highest among the professional and managerial, college-educated, and high-income members of the upper-middle and upper classes.

Class Bias

The class bias of organized groups varies. Unions (in which membership frequently is not voluntary) recruit from the working class, although frequently their leaders have higher-status origins. But most other organizations challenge pluralist theories about representation in government by having a strong middle- and upper-class bias and accompanying policy goals. Upper-middle-class blacks lead civil rights organizations. Liberal causes draw disproportionately from the university-educated and academically connected liberal establishment and rarely appeal to the lower classes. The social bias in association membership is complemented by the high social origins of lobbyists and the predominance of business and professional organizations in effective lobbying.

Active participation—and holding formal office—also relates directly to social status. Whereas the majority in the United States are *members* of organizations, only a minority are *active* in them. Control typically rests with a small elite. The oligarchs, who help shape the goals of the organizations, come disproportionately from the upper social classes. The inherent biases of interest groups challenge pluralist theories about representation in government. Whether interest groups are or are not an effective link between citizens and government, many citizens do not avail themselves of the benefit. Even if the formal organization reduces anxiety or increases feelings of power, it does not serve the poor and uneducated, whose alienation from society is greatest and whose need for such political connection is most extreme.

THE DOMINANCE OF BUSINESS AND UNION ORGANIZATIONS

Economic organizations dominate interest group politics (see Table 7.1). In sheer number of organizations with offices and representatives in Washington, business and union groups and occupational and trade associations predominate.

Business interests are represented, first of all, by large inclusive organizations, such as the U.S. Chamber of Commerce, representing thousands of local chambers of commerce across the nation; the National Association of Manufacturers; the Business Roundtable, representing the nation's largest corporations; and the National Federation of Independent Businesses, representing small business. Specific business interests are also represented by thousands of trade associations that closely monitor their interests. Among the most powerful are the American Bankers Association, the American Gas Association, the American Iron and Steel Institute, the National Association of Real Estate Boards, the American Petroleum Institute, and the National Association of Broadcasters.

Professional associations rival business and trade organizations in lobbying influence. The American Bar Association and the American Medical Association are two of the most influential groups in Washington. For example, the American Bar Association, which includes virtually all the nation's practicing attorneys, and its more specialized offspring, the American Association for Justice (formerly the Association of Trial Lawyers), have successfully resisted efforts to reform the nation's tort laws. Former chief lobbyist and executive director of the Kansas Trial Lawyer's Association Kathleen Sebelius is now Secretary of the Department of Health and Human Services. The Motion Picture Association of America (MPAA), the movie industry trade group, is led by former Senator Christopher Dodd (D-Connecticut).

Business Roundtable Organization representing the largest U.S. corporations. *www. roundtable.org*

TABLE 7.1 | SIGNIFICANT ORGANIZED INTEREST GROUPS BY TYPE

Business-General

Business Roundtable

National Association of Manufacturers

National Federation of Independent Businesses

National Small Business Association

U.S. Chamber of Commerce

Business-Sectoral

American Bankers Association

American Gas Association

American Iron and Steel Institute

American Petroleum Institute

American Tobacco Institute

American Truckers Association

Automobile Dealers Association

Home Builders Association

Motion Picture Association of America

National Association of Broadcasters

National Association of Real Estate Boards

Pharmaceutical Research and Manufacturers of America

Union

AFL-CIO

American Federation of State, County, and Municipal Employees

American Federation of Teachers

International Brotherhood of Teamsters

International Ladies' Garment Workers Union

National Association of Letter Carriers

National Education Association

Service Employees International Union

United Auto Workers

United Steel Workers

Agricultural

American Farm Bureau Federation

National Cattlemen's Association

National Farmers Union

National Grange

National Milk Producers Federation

Age Related

AARP

Children's Defense Fund

Professional

American Bar Association

American Medical Association

American Association for Justice (Association of Trial Lawyers)

American Association of University Professors

Ideological

American Conservative Union

Americans for Constitutional Action (conservative)

Americans for Democratic Action (liberal)

MoveOn (liberal)

National Conservative Political Action Committee

People for the American Way (liberal)

Single Issue

Mothers Against Drunk Driving

National Abortion Rights Action League, Pro-Choice America

National Rifle Association

National Right-to-Life Committee

Planned Parenthood Federation of America

National Organization for the Reform of Marijuana Laws

National Taxpayers Union

Environmental

Environmental Defense Fund

National Wildlife Federation

Natural Resources Defense Council

Nature Conservancy

Sierra Club

Wilderness Society

Civil Rights and Identity

American Civil Liberties Union

American Indian Movement

Anti-Defamation League of B'nai B'rith

Christian Coalition

Electronic Freedom Foundation

Foundation for Individual Rights in Education

Mexican-American Legal Defense and Education Fund

National Association for the Advancement of Colored People

National Council of Churches

National Council of La Raza

National Urban League

Southern Christian Leadership Conference

U.S. Catholic Conference

Gender

American Association of University Women

EMILY's List

League of Women Voters

National Organization for Women

Gay & Lesbian Alliance Against Defamation

Veterans

American Legion

Veterans of Foreign Wars

Vietnam Veterans of America

Government

National Association of Counties

National Conference of State Legislators

National Governors Association

National League of Cities

U.S. Conference of Mayors

| FOCUS | SUPER LOBBY: THE BUSINESS ROUNDTABLE |

Arguably the most powerful lobby in Washington is the Business Roundtable. It was established in 1972 "in the belief that business executives should take an increased role in the continuing debates about public policy." The Roundtable is composed of the chief executives of the largest corporations in America and is financed through corporate membership fees.

The power of the Business Roundtable arises in part from its "firm rule" that a corporate chief executive officer (CEO) cannot send a substitute to its meetings. Moreover, corporate CEOs lobby the Congress in person rather than sending paid lobbyists. Members of Congress are impressed when the CEO of IBM appears at a congressional hearing on business regulation, or when the chair of Prudential Insurance talks to Congress about Social Security.

One congressional staff member explained, "If the Corporation sends his Washington representative to our office, he is probably going to be shunted over to a legislative assistant. But the chairman of the board is going to get to see the senator." Another aide echoed: "Very few members of Congress would not meet with the president of a Business Roundtable corporation." Among the current issues of concern to the Roundtable are support for free trade agreements and the World Trade Organization; driving down health insurance costs for employers; lowering the corporate income tax; support for federal efforts to improve the workforce with education and performance standards in schools; and reform of tort laws that allow businesses to be sued for product liability.

THE INFLUENCE OF ORGANIZED LABOR

While labor unions have declined in membership over the last several decades (see Chapter 4), they remain a major political influence in Congress and the Democratic Party. The American Federation of Labor–Congress of Industrial Organizations (AFL-CIO) is a federation of more than 50 separate unions with more than 11 million members. It has long maintained a large and capable lobbying staff in Washington, and it provides both financial contributions and campaign services (registration, get-out-the-vote, information, endorsements) for members of Congress it favors. Many of the larger industrial unions (the International Brotherhood of Teamsters, United Auto Workers, and United Steel Workers) maintain effective lobbying staffs in Washington.

A classic example of a union elite is the former president of the Service Employees International Union (SEIU), Andrew ("Andy") Stern. The SEIU was the fastest-growing union in the country, having gained 800,000 members in the last decade, focusing on government employees. The Ivy League-educated son of a suburban lawyer, Stern's main policy goal was health care reform, on which he had worked with fellow elite Lee Scott, then CEO of WalMart. He also pushed for controversial card check legislation, which would allow workers to unionize without a secret ballot. Stern's union was an early and active supporter of Barack Obama; as Stern stated in a 2009 interview, "We spent a fortune to elect Barack Obama— $60.7 million to be exact—and we're proud of it."[4] In return for this investment, Stern was the most frequent visitor to the Obama White House in its first nine months.[5] Stern resigned as SEIU president in 2010.

Power within the labor movement has shifted dramatically in recent years to government employee unions, notably the American Federation of State, County,

AFL-CIO
Union federation website with information on wages as well as executive salaries. *www.aflcio.org*

and Municipal Employees; the National Education Association; and the American Federation of Teachers. In 2005, the AFL-CIO lost a third of its membership when the SEIU and four other major unions broke away, later joining the Teamsters and others to form the Change to Win Coalition. The split was based on strategy in achieving shared goals, with the AFL-CIO focusing on lobbying and the new group on recruitment.

Ideological Groups

Many specific interests can be broadly categorized as "liberal" or "conservative," so these two labels provide the largest groupings of interests in the United States. Ideological organizations pursue liberal or conservative agendas, often with great passion and considerable financial resources provided by true-believing contributors.

These groups rely heavily on direct mail and the Internet to solicit funds from sympathizers. The oldest is the liberal Americans for Democratic Action, well known for its annual ratings of members of the Congress according to their support for liberal "social justice" policies. The American Conservative Union, which also rates politicians, focuses on free markets, traditional values, and a strong national defense. The arrival of SuperPACs has allowed ideologically motivated individuals and groups to spend millions on election campaigns.

Liberal and Conservative

Americans for Democratic Action
The ADA is the nation's oldest liberal organization. *www.adaction.org*

American Conservative Union
Conservative views and rankings of Congress. *www. conservative.org*

The terms *liberal* and *conservative* have been much misused and abused, and their meaning has changed over time. The basic distinction is between worldviews, with liberals seeking to cure society's imperfections while conservatives seek to maintain what actually does work in society.

Conservatism, in the contemporary sense of the term, includes classical liberal values of free markets, limited government, and individual self-reliance in economic affairs, combined with a classical conservative belief in the value of tradition, law, family, and faith. (See Chapter 2 for more detail.) For most of U.S. history, these two perspectives were opposed to each other, but both share a general distrust of government and a strong emphasis on checks and balances. Conservatives generally prefer limited government in *economic* affairs, preferring the free market to government regulation, private charity to social-welfare programs, and low taxes. They do see a role for government in regulating *social* conduct—fighting crime, encouraging faith, and strengthening families as the core social institution. Conservatives tend to believe in the idea that humans are imperfect and flawed creatures. Conservatives also believe political leaders are human.

Liberalism, in the contemporary sense, generally means belief in a strong government to provide economic security and protection for civil rights, combined with freedom from government intervention in personal conduct. The prevailing impulse is to use the power of government to solve society's troubles. Contemporary liberalism started with classical liberalism's view of government as protector from harm but expanded over time into an activist belief that powerful government can improve society by promoting "social justice," its vision of a "fair" society.

This includes working to end racism, sexism, homophobia, and poverty and providing medical care for all, as well as protecting the environment. Liberals prefer an active powerful government in *economic* affairs—a government that provides a broad range of public services, regulates the market, redistributes wealth, and provides generous social benefits. Liberals oppose government restrictions on certain *social* affairs such as sex and reproduction and drug use.

People may be strong or weak adherents to either ideology, and it is not uncommon to see them combined (see Focus: Are You a Liberal or a Conservative?). Libertarians prefer minimal government in all areas, whereas populists like strong government and traditional values.

SINGLE-ISSUE GROUPS

Single-issue groups appeal to principle and belief, but as their name implies, they concentrate their attention on a single cause. They attract the support of individuals with a strong commitment to that cause. The single largest and most powerful interest group in the United States is AARP, which focuses on issues relating to the elderly and retired. Other prominent single-issue groups include the National Rifle Association (opposed to gun control) and Mothers Against Drunk Driving. Environmental organizations have proliferated in recent decades; the most prominent are the Sierra Club, the Environmental Defense Fund, Greenpeace, the National Wildlife Federation, and the Natural Resources Defense Council.

Among the most vocal single-issue groups in recent years have been the organizations on both sides of the abortion issue. The National Abortion Rights Action League describes itself as pro-choice and promotes unrestricted access for a woman to obtain an abortion. The National Right-to-Life Committee describes itself as pro-life and promotes recognition of a fetus as a full human life. Both groups agree on the need to reduce the number of abortions.

CIVIL RIGHTS ORGANIZATIONS

NAACP
Civil rights issues and advocacy for African-Americans.
www.naacp.org

ADL
Civil rights advocacy with focus on fighting hate groups.
www.adl.org

La Raza
Civil rights and economic concerns of Hispanic Americans.
www.nclr.org

Most civil rights organizations grew out of early protest movements (see Chapter 13). The National Association for the Advancement of Colored People (NAACP) is the oldest civil rights organization in the United States, founded in 1909. Its Legal Defense Fund, headed by Thurgood Marshall, who later became the nation's first African-American Supreme Court Justice, won the historic case of *Brown v. Board of Education, Topeka, Kansas,* in 1954, declaring school segregation unconstitutional. The Southern Christian Leadership Conference (SCLC) was organized around the nonviolent protest efforts of Martin Luther King, Jr., in the 1960s and led to the landmark Civil Rights Act of 1964. The National Council of La Raza began in the 1960s as a group to advocate for the rights of Mexican-Americans, expanding its mission to all Latinos by the 1970s. The Anti-Defamation League is another civil rights group that focuses on fighting bigotry in all forms, exposing and educating the public on hate groups such as the Ku Klux Klan, neo-Nazi white supremacists, and anti-Jewish terrorists. It also promotes religious freedom and the separation of church and state.

FOCUS | ARE YOU A LIBERAL OR A CONSERVATIVE?

	You Might Be a *Liberal* if You Agree That	You Might Be a *Conservative* if You Agree That
Economic policy	Government should regulate business to protect the public interest.	Free-market competition is better at protecting the public than government regulation.
	The rich should pay higher taxes to support public services for all, especially the poor.	Taxes should be kept as low as possible to boost economic growth.
	Government spending for social welfare is a good investment in people and contributes to social justice.	Government welfare programs destroy incentives to work by reducing individual responsibility.
Crime	Government should emphasize alleviating social conditions such as poverty and joblessness that contribute to crime.	Government should place primary emphasis on individual responsibility of criminals and provide more police and prisons.
Social policy	Government should protect the right of women to choose abortion and fund abortions for poor women.	Government should protect the unborn by restricting abortions and not use taxpayer money for them.
	Government should pursue affirmative action programs on behalf of minorities and women in employment, education, and so on.	Government should be color blind and not grant preferences to anyone based on race or sex.
	Government should keep religious prayers and ceremonies out of schools and public places.	Government should allow prayers and religious observances in schools and public places.
Foreign policy	Government should support human rights throughout the world by engaging non-democratic nations.	Government should support human rights throughout the world by firmly promoting democracy.
	Terrorism is best countered by addressing underlying conditions that promote a terrorist mindset.	Terrorism is best countered by killing or capturing terrorists and disrupting their activities.

WOMEN'S GROUPS

NOW
National Organization for Women advocates feminist issues and supports women candidates.
www.now.org

Women's organizations date back to the antislavery societies in pre–Civil War America (see Chapter 13). The largest women's group is the League of Women Voters, which provides information to voters, backs registration and get-out-the-vote drives, and generally supports measures seeking to ensure honesty and integrity in government. EMILY's List is an organization to promote the campaigns of pro-choice Democratic women candidates (see Focus: EMILY's List). The most active feminist organization has been the National Organization for Women, founded in 1966.

GAY RIGHTS GROUPS

The Lambda Legal Defense and Education Fund promotes civil rights for the lesbian, gay, bisexual, transgender (LGBT) communities through litigation, education, and public policy work. In 2003, Lambda Legal brought *Lawrence v. Texas*, in which the United States Supreme Court invalidated the remaining state sodomy laws. Another organization, the Gay and Lesbian Alliance Against Defamation (GLAAD), promotes positive images of homosexuals in the media.

HOW WELL DO GROUPS REPRESENT THEIR MEMBERS?

The major test of pluralist group theory is how well interest groups translate members' demands into political action—if at all. *All* groups are afflicted with the curse of oligarchy. African-American civil rights organization leaders do not necessarily represent the views of black masses. Black leaders think black people are going backward, whereas followers think they are making progress. Leaders support racial preferences, but followers do not. Members tend to be social conservatives, but not their leaders.[6] In another case, environmental group leaders may hold that greater reliance on nuclear energy can quickly reduce carbon emissions, but members may be generally opposed to nuclear power.

The general public sees larger organizations as less reflective of the views of the people. In a 2011 Harris poll,[7] distrust of major interest groups was evident: A majority of respondents felt too much influence on Washington was held by "big companies" (88 percent), the news media (72 percent), trade associations (61 percent), and labor unions (55 percent). The big money sources were also seen as too powerful, such as political action committees or PACs (87 percent) and political lobbyists (84 percent). On the other hand, respondents felt local groups had too *little* power: that included churches and religious groups (49 percent), nonprofit organizations (65 percent), and small business (91 percent), along with public opinion itself (82 percent).

FOCUS | EMILY'S LIST

The greatest obstacle to challenging an incumbent is fundraising, and it is most difficult early in the campaign, when challengers have little name recognition and little or no standing in the polls.

Not too many years ago, most women candidates confronted incumbent men. These challengers needed early contributions to provide the initial credibility to their candidacy. EMILY's List is a politically adroit and effective effort, created by IBM heir Ellen Malcolm, to support liberal Democratic women candidates who favor abortion rights by infusing early money into their campaigns. (EMILY stands for Early Money Is Like Yeast, because it "makes the dough rise.") Each

contributor pays at least $100 to join and pledges to give at least another $100 to two women from a list of candidates prepared by EMILY's leaders. Most of the contributors are professional women who appreciate pre-screening of pro-choice, liberal women candidates around the country.

EMILY's List is also a political action committee (PAC). It claims to have helped drive the dramatic increase in women members of Congress over the last 20 years. In 2012, there were 88 women serving in the Congress—17 senators and 71 House members, although it is fair to assume EMILY's List did not fund the 29 of them who were Republicans.

LARGE VERSUS SMALL ORGANIZATIONS

The size of the group is an important variable in its leadership's political effectiveness. Because elected officials are sensitive to numbers, a large membership enhances a group's access to legislators. However, large groups find it difficult to commit themselves to an explicit position because their membership is so heterogeneous (see FOCUS: Size and Representation—AARP). The policy positions of mass membership organizations are often vague and broad, devoid of specific content—and thus harmless. The U.S. Chamber of Commerce, for example, seeks to represent "businesspeople" without regard for the nature of the business. Because intra-business disputes are frequent, the chamber cannot take a position on many of the legislative and administrative details that affect the economic health of the business community. For example, in 2009, several large companies such as PG&E, Apple, and Exelon left the organization over its opposition to climate change policy. Narrowly focused organizations, such as the American Petroleum Institute, which represents only the oil industry, are far more effective than the broad-based Chamber of Commerce.

Small and highly organized groups have attained tangible benefits. Those with narrow interests can concentrate their resources on a limited, tangible objective and act decisively and persistently based on precise information. Such organizations are most frequently business, professional, or industrial; they are also the major employers of lobbyists at the state and national levels. Many businesspeople organize into trade associations representing industrial and commercial activities. Because their membership represents a specific form of business activity—for example, the American Bankers Association—many trade associations are quite small; some have as few as 25 members. Their power to advocate specific issues is disproportionate to that of the business community as a whole, which is less focused.

SINGLE-INTEREST VERSUS TRADITIONAL INTEREST GROUPS

AARP
Largest membership organization in the U.S., focusing on seniors. *www.aarp.org*

The leadership of single-interest groups may reflect members' views better than larger, traditional, better-financed organizations. Because single-issue groups focus on one narrow concern (abortion or gun control, for example), their leaders do not have much flexibility for bargaining or compromise. Their strength lies almost solely in the intensity of their beliefs. This intense commitment has at least two important consequences. First, leaders have far less freedom of action than with a membership recruited for nonissue reasons. Second, dedication to the cause hampers leaders from fully using the traditional processes of political compromise. Clearly, a person who sees abortion as a form of murder cannot compromise by saying, "I would agree to 30,000 federally funded abortions and no more."

Why have single-issue groups proliferated in recent years? Much of the answer lies in the decline of political parties (see Chapter 6). Candidates turned to single-interest organizations, whose electoral influence grew. Such groups, of course, represent political minorities, but so do all other interest groups. The essential difference is that they are *more* representative of the views of their

| SIZE AND REPRESENTATION—AARP

There is little evidence to suggest members know or care very much about what their leaders are doing in their name.[a] The larger an organization, the more difficult representation becomes. Consider the largest interest group currently extant, AARP (formerly the American Association of Retired Persons), which claims over 40 million members. Because membership is open to anyone over age 50 who pays the modest dues, it is easy to imagine the cross-cutting cleavages that characterize its membership. Members have little in common other than age, making it difficult for AARP to speak for them on complex issues such as funding for home health care, coverage of prescription drugs, expansion of state Medicaid criteria, coverage of nursing home care, housing supplements for the aged, energy assistance, and—simultaneously—opposition to budget cuts designed to reduce national deficits. AARP led the successful fight in Congress against the Balanced Budget Amendment to the Constitution. It is doubtful that all 40 million members agree on even a portion of this expansive agenda.

Although common sense tells them such large groups cannot deliver a vote, Congress members still are frequently intimidated by them. After each election, myriad organizations claim to have been the decisive bloc. Legislators feel vulnerable and have no reliable defense against such an organization's demands.

In 1995, however, Senator Alan Simpson (R-WY) investigated the complex web of AARP's business enterprises. The organization earns more than $180 million annually from insurance, travel clubs, discount drugs, credit cards, and annuities. Troubled by AARP's tax-exempt status, Simpson cut to the heart of big-organization politics: "They're a huge cash flow operation, 38 million people paying $8 dues, bound together by a common love of airline discounts and automobile discounts and pharmacy discounts, and they haven't the slightest idea what the organization is asking for."[b]

Simpson described the interests of AARP members as "selective" economic advantages and "collective" advantages. If AARP and its allies persuade Congress to expand Medicare, all people over 65 benefit. These benefits are collective. Incentives to join are the selective benefits, and probably no organization can match AARP in providing them. For $16 a year (2012 dues), members have access to a mouthwatering list of savings: insurance discounts, savings on mail-order drugs, low-rate credit cards, discounted travel, and *Modern Maturity* magazine. Some members may, of course, develop a keen interest in the political aspirations of the organization, but most do not; they are there because it makes good economic sense.[c]

[a]Terry Moe, *The Organization of Interests* (Chicago: University of Chicago Press, 1980).

[b]These were Simpson's remarks of 1995, when he chaired a two-day hearing on AARP. See Charles R. Morris, *The AARP: America's Most Powerful Lobby and the Clash of Generations* (New York: Times Books, 1996).

[c]Mancur Olson, *The Logic of Collective Action* (Cambridge, MA: Harvard University Press, 1965).

members—because they cannot compromise—than are the established groups. They are not the functional equivalent of political parties, because their causes are limited. They are, however, more responsive to issues than parties and traditional interest groups. Interest groups also have the ability to mobilize blocks of voters, as well as assist in fundraising for candidates.

LOBBYING: HOW ORGANIZED INTERESTS INFLUENCE GOVERNMENT

Lobbying is any communication directed at a government decision maker with the hope of influencing decisions. For organized interests, lobbying is a continuous activity—in congressional committees, in congressional staff offices, at the White

House, at executive agencies, at Washington cocktail parties. If a group loses a round in Congress, it continues the fight in the agency in charge of executing the policy, or it challenges the policy in the courts. The following year it resumes the struggle in Congress: It fights for repeal of the offending legislation, for weakening amendments, or for budget reductions that would cripple enforcement efforts. The process can continue indefinitely.

The most heavily lobbied branch of government is Congress. Since 1998, over 507,000 clients have paid to lobby the House of Representatives, and almost the same number wanted to influence the Senate. Of the executive departments, the Department of Defense saw over 42,000 clients of lobbying firms seeking influence, the Department of Health and Human Services about 37,000, and the Treasury 30,000. The Departments of Transportation, Commerce, and Energy saw just under 30,000 lobbying clients show interest. The Environmental Protection Agency had almost 27,000 pay to try to get it to better understand their needs.[8]

ACCESS

To communicate with decision makers, an organized interest first needs access to them (see Focus: Lobbyists and Influence Peddlers). As a prominent Washington lobbyist explained: "Number 1 is the access—to get them in the door and get a hearing for your case ... knowing the individuals personally, knowing their staffs and how they operate and the kind of information they want ... that kind of personal knowledge can help you maximize the client's hearing."[9]

"Opening doors" is a major business in Washington. Individuals who have personal contacts with decision makers (or who say they do) sell their services at high prices. Washington law firms, public relations agencies, and consultants all offer their insider connections and their advice to potential clients. Many professional lobbyists are former members of Congress, White House aides, or congressional staff personnel who "know their way around." The personal prestige of the lobbyist, together with the group's perceived political influence, helps open doors in Washington. The nation's top lobbying firms are listed in Table 7.2. These firms are reported to have spent the most in direct lobbying. Those at the top—Patton Boggs, Cassidy & Associates, Akin Gump—compete each year for the coveted title of "the most powerful firm in Washington." All have more than 100 clients and together spend more than $150 million each year in lobbying (not including their PAC expenditures).

Generally, to gain an introduction to a decision maker, the person or group lobbying must have something to offer. All politicians wish to preserve their power, which in a democracy means getting re-elected. Therefore, being able to mobilize voters on behalf of a candidate is the greatest gift a lobbyist can offer, and it is a particular boon for groups with large memberships. Second to votes is money, which is used to finance campaigns to get votes. Money itself cannot vote, but since many interests do not have the ability to offer large blocks of voters to a legislator, money will have to do.

TABLE 7.2	TOP LOBBYING FIRMS BY TOTAL OFFICIALLY SPENT FOR LOBBYING 1998–2012

Firm	Total ($ millions)
Patton Boggs LLP	452
Akin, Gump et al.	369
Cassidy & Associates	349
Van Scoyoc Associates	291
Williams & Jensen	209
Ernst & Young	179
Holland & Knight	161
Quinn, Gillespie & Associates	158
Hogan & Hartson	155
Brownstein, Hyatt, et al.	137

Source: Center for Responsive Politics. *www.opensecrets.org/lobby/top.php?indexType=l.*

INFORMATION

Once lobbyists gain access, their knowledge and information become their most valuable resources. A lobbyist may contribute such information as (1) knowledge of the legislative process, (2) expertise on the issue under debate, and (3) information about the group's position on the issue. Because legislators and their aides value all three types of knowledge, lobbyists can often trade their knowledge for congressional support.

Lobbyists must spend considerable time and effort tracking information about bills affecting their interests. They must be thoroughly familiar with the ins and outs of the legislative process—the relevant committees and subcommittees, their schedules of meetings and hearings, their key staff members, the best moments to act, the precise language for proposed bills and amendments, the witnesses for hearings, and the political strengths and weaknesses of the legislators themselves.

The lobbyist's policy information must be accurate as well as timely. A successful lobbyist never supplies faulty or inaccurate information; his or her success depends on maintaining the trust and confidence of the decision makers. A reputation for honesty is as important as a reputation for influence. Lobbyists also provide the information and argumentation that members of Congress use in legislative debate and in speeches back home. In this role, they complement the functions of congressional staff. Testimony at legislative hearings is a common form of information exchange between lobbyists and legislators. Lobbyists also provide the technical reports and analyses used by congressional staffs in their legislative research.

DEMAND

After providing a legislator with information and perhaps hints of campaign funds or electoral support, a lobbyist must actually request the legislator's vote. One

| FOCUS | LOBBYISTS AND INFLUENCE PEDDLERS |

Washington is awash in lawyers, lobbyists, and influence peddlers. Their offices are concentrated on K Street near the Capitol, and they are often collectively referred to as simply "K Street." An elite few firms dominate the influence-peddling business.

Direct lobbying expenditures, in addition to PAC contributions to candidates, provide a reasonably good indicator of who is influential in Washington. Billions of dollars are spent each year on direct lobbying. At the industry group level, pharmaceutical and health products manufacturers spend the most. The insurance industry ranks second in direct lobbying expenditures, followed by telephone industries, the oil and gas industry, and the electric utilities. Of the top groups spending money on lobbying, only one might be considered non-economic: AARP.

Many individual corporations also spend millions of dollars each year in direct lobbying activities. Spending by industry tends to reflect the legislative agenda of Congress: When health insurance is being considered, insurance companies, health maintenance organizations, nurse's unions, and medical associations appear near the top of the lobbying spending lists; when tobacco legislation is considered, the American Tobacco Institute and tobacco companies spend heavily; and when tort reform is on the agenda, the Trial Lawyers' American Association for Justice and the nation's top law firms lobby heavily. Most large corporations, as well as industry, professional, and trade groups, have their own "in-house" lobbyists. But when particularly important legislation is considered by Congress, these organizations turn to the top Washington lobbying firms. In his classic book, *The Power Elite*, sociologist C. Wright Mills described these firms as "professional go-betweens … who act to unify the power elite."[10] They are active at all institutional levels—communicating, negotiating, and mediating among corporations, banks, and the wealthy; foundations and think tanks; and the president, Congress, administrative agencies, and the courts. They are the "insiders" and "fixers" "inside the Beltway" in Washington.

technique most experienced lobbyists shun is the threat. Amateur lobbyists may threaten legislators by vowing to defeat them at the next election, a tactic guaranteed to produce a defensive reaction and a vote against the threatening lobbyist. Moreover, experienced members of Congress know that such threats are empty; lobbyists can seldom deliver enough votes to influence the outcome of an election. Legislators can also ignore a particular lobbyist, knowing there is always another lobbying firm or interest group more willing to play the game.

GRASSROOTS MOBILIZATION

Many organized interests also lobby Congress by mobilizing constituents to apply pressure on their behalf. Many lobbyists believe legislators, especially insecure ones, pay close attention to letters, e-mails, and calls from "folks back home." The larger organized interests often have local chapters throughout the nation and can mobilize these local affiliates to apply pressure when necessary. Lobbyists encourage influential local elites to visit a Congress member's office personally or to make a personal phone call on behalf of the group's positions.

Of course, experienced lawmakers recognize attempts by lobby groups to orchestrate "spontaneous" grassroots outpourings of cards and letters. Such pressure mail is often identical in wording and content. Nevertheless, members of Congress dare not ignore a flood of letters and e-mails from home, because it shows constituents are aware of the issue and care enough to sign their names.

Another grassroots tactic is to mobilize the press in a Congress member's home district. Lobbyists may provide news, analyses, and editorials to local newspapers and then clip favorable articles to send to lawmakers. They may also buy full- or half-page advertisements in legislators' hometown newspapers, as well as the *Washington Post* or a national newspaper such as the *Wall Street Journal*.

DIRECT CONTACTS

Lobbying is expensive. Influential lobbyists make more money than the Congress members they are lobbying. Indeed, many former Congress members, as well as former White House staff and cabinet members, pursue lucrative careers in Washington as lobbyists after leaving office. Billions are spent on congressional lobbying activity each year, *in addition to* political campaign contributions, discussed later. These expenditures may seem high, but they pale in comparison to the many billions or perhaps trillions of dollars that hinge on congressional decisions. Among broad economic sectors, banking, finance, insurance, and real estate interests spend the most for lobbying, closely followed by oil and gas, communications and electronics, and the pharmaceutical and health care industry.

CAMPAIGN SUPPORT

However, the real key to success in lobbying is the campaign contribution. Interest-group contributions not only help lobbyists gain access and a favorable hearing, but also help elect people friendly to the group's goals. As the costs of campaigning increase, legislators must depend more heavily on these contributions.

Both the Democratic and Republican parties rely principally on large economic interests for their money. But their sources of money differ in significant

"A very special interest to see you, Senator."

ways. First, labor unions, especially government employee and teacher unions, are a major source of funding for the Democratic Party and give little to the Republican Party. The Democratic Party relies more heavily on lawyers, lobbyists, and law firms, receiving about four times as much money from this source as the Republican Party. Hollywood gives more than twice as much to the Democrats as to the Republicans. Banks divide their money fairly evenly between the parties. The Republican Party relies more heavily on real estate and home-building industries, the oil and gas industry, the pharmaceutical companies, and manufacturing.

It is illegal for a lobbyist to extract a specific vote pledge from a legislator in exchange for a campaign contribution. Such crude "vote buying" is usually (but not always) avoided. Instead, organized interests contribute to the campaign fund of a member of Congress over a long period of time and leave it to the lawmaker to figure out how to retain their support. When a legislator consistently votes against an organized interest, that interest may then contribute to the opposition candidate in the next election.

THE FAT CATS: TOP CAMPAIGN CONTRIBUTORS

The Center for Responsive Politics studies Federal Elections Commission (FEC) campaign records for all presidential and congressional contributions. Contributions from 1989 to 2012 have been combined in a list of the top donors (see Table 7.3). This list reflects the total contributions to candidates or political parties of the top givers, their political action committees (PACs), employees, and members of their immediate families, according to a study by the Center for Responsive Politics. Not included are independent expenditures, money for issue advertisements, or other indirect expenses. Of the top 20 donors through mid-2012, five were businesses, two were professional groups, one was an organization created to promote a single party, and 12 were unions.

REGULATING THE LOBBIES

Although the First Amendment protects lobbying, government can regulate lobbying activities. The principal method is disclosure: The law requires lobbyists to register as lobbyists and report how much they spend. But definitions of lobbying are unclear and enforcement is weak. Many of the larger lobby groups—for example, the National Association of Manufacturers, the National Bankers Association, and Americans for Constitutional Action—have never registered as lobbyists. These organizations claim that because lobbying is not their "principal" activity, they need not register under the law.

Financial reports of lobbyists grossly underestimate the extent of lobbying in Congress because the law requires reports only on money spent on direct lobbying before Congress, not on money spent for public relations or for campaign contributions. Another weakness in the law is that it applies only to attempts to influence Congress and does not regulate lobbying activities in administrative agencies or the executive branch. However, restrictive legislation might violate the First Amendment freedom to "petition the government for a redress of grievances."

Center for Responsive Politics Useful source for information about lobbying spending. *www.opensecrets. org/lobbyists*

TABLE 7.3 | ALL-TIME CAMPAIGN CONTRIBUTORS, 1989–2012

Rank	Organization Name	Total (millions)	Democrats (%)	Republicans (%)	Type of Organization
1	ActBlue	$62.8	99	0	Party-focused
2	AT&T	$48.8	43	55	Business
3	American Fed. of State, County and Municipal Employees	$48.0	92	1	Union
4	National Association of Realtors	$41.8	47	49	Business
5	National Education Association	$41.4	74	5	Union
6	Goldman Sachs	$38.3	58	39	Business
7	Service Employees International Union	$38.2	75	2	Union
8	American Association for Justice (American Trial Lawyers Assn.)	$35.8	88	8	Professional
9	Intl. Brotherhood of Electrical Workers	$35.2	96	2	Union
10	American Federation of Teachers	$33.6	87	0	Union
11	Laborers Union	$32.9	87	7	Union
12	Teamsters Union	$32.5	87	5	Union
13	Carpenters & Joiners Union	$31.6	86	10	Union
14	Communications Workers of America	$31.4	92	0	Union
15	Citigroup	$29.5	49	49	Business
16	American Medical Association	$28.0	40	59	Professional
17	United Food and Commercial Workers Union	$28.0	92	0	Union
18	United Auto Workers	$27.9	98	0	Union
19	National Auto Dealers Association	$27.7	32	67	Business
20	Machinists and Aerospace Workers Union	$27.6	98	1	Union

Source: Center for Responsive Politics. *www.opensecrets.org/orgs/list.php.*

IN BRIEF

Lobbying is any communication directed at government policymakers with the hope of influencing their decisions. Among the techniques of lobbying are the following:

- Gaining access to policymakers in Congress, the White House, and the bureaucracy
- Providing information to policymakers and their staffs, directly and by testifying at committee and administrative hearings

- Mobilizing the grassroots constituents of elected policymakers, inspiring letters, e-mails, and calls from "the folks back home"
- Direct contacts with policymakers, or schmoozing at social occasions, dinners, trips, outings, and the like
- Campaign contributions directly to candidates (especially incumbents) or through PACs

INTEREST GROUP INFLUENCE THROUGH CAMPAIGN SUPPORT

Political parties are large, disorganized, and largely focused on elections. A contributor wishing to support a specific political cause gets more for his or her money by contributing to a **political action committee**, or **PAC**. PACs are nonparty organizations that solicit voluntary contributions to disburse to political candidates. PACs have been organized by labor unions, trade and professional associations, corporations, environmental groups, and liberal and conservative ideological groups. However, the largest number of PACs is in the corporate sector.

PACs have become a major force in Washington politics in recent years. The increasing cost of television campaigning makes many legislators dependent on PAC contributions to run their campaigns. Interest groups generally channel their campaign contributions through political action committees. PACs are organized not only by corporations and unions, but also by trade and professional associations as well as single-issue and ideological groups. PAC contributions account for nearly half of all House campaign financing and about 25 percent of all Senate campaign financing.

PAC contributions come in larger lumps than most individual contributions. PACs are easier for Congress members to contact for contributions; only about 4,000 regularly contribute to congressional campaigns. Table 7.4 lists the top 10 PAC contributors in the 2010 congressional election.

PACS PREFER INCUMBENTS

When Democrats control Congress, business PACs split their dollars nearly evenly between Democrats and Republicans; when Republicans control Congress, they shift their dollars heavily to the GOP. Labor PACs, however, do not waver from

TABLE 7.4	BIG MONEY PACs: LARGEST PAC CONTRIBUTORS TO THE 2010 CONGRESSIONAL ELECTIONS		
PAC	Total (millions)	Democrat %	Republican %
National Association of Realtors	$3.8	55	44
Honeywell International	$3.7	54	45
National Beer Wholesalers Association	$2.9	53	47
AT&T Inc	$3.1	47	52
International Brotherhood of Electrical Workers	$3.0	98	2
American Bankers Association	$2.9	45	55
American Association for Justice (Trial Lawyers of America)	$2.8	97	3
Operating Engineers Union	$2.8	88	11
National Auto Dealers Association	$2.5	44	55

Source: Center for Responsive Politics. *www.opensecrets.org/pacs/toppacs.php?Type=C&cycle=2010.*

their traditional support of Democrats, even when Republicans control Congress. PAC money thus goes overwhelmingly to incumbent officeholders. Not only does this practice strengthen incumbents against their opponents, but it also makes incumbents less likely to change the law governing PAC contributions. The object is *access*.

PACs
For more
information on
PAC contributions.
*www.opensecrets.
org/pacs*

PACs even give money to officeholders not up for election in a particular year, in order to help them retire debts or prepare for a future election. In addition, PACs spend money in "indirect" expenditures, which include ads and endorsements not paid for directly by the candidates' campaign organizations.

INTEREST GROUP BIAS AGAINST CHANGE

In general, organizations gradually become more moderate as the goal of perpetuating themselves takes priority over their original goals. Of course, they do not stop seeking change or increased benefits, but the extent of change they seek is minimal. Political scientist Thomas Mann grieved that "when effective action on the country's most pressing problems requires the imposition of losses on organized interests, with benefits to all on the distant horizon, the odds of success in the U.S. political system are not very high."[11] Once they achieve even a few of their goals, they, and in particular the elites who run them, then have a stake in the ongoing system and a rational basis for pursuing more moderate politics. Social stability is a product of this organizational system.

Interest groups serve society by connecting their members to the established social system, so those who would seek to radically alter the system find interest-group politics an unsatisfactory mechanism. Radicals seek excluding other interests and thus breaking down pluralist democracy. True, some groups develop with radical change in mind, but the process of bureaucratization of leadership from outsiders to insiders gradually reduces any organization's commitment to substantial change. They become part of the pluralist system of competition, bargaining, and compromise. A group's leadership is then part of the elite who participate in running the system. Ironically, if disempowered people succeed in organizing themselves, the new organizations eventually will develop their own commitment to the status quo (see Chapter 13).

INTEREST GROUPS | AN ELITIST INTERPRETATION

Pluralism, as we discussed in Chapter 1, is the belief that democratic values are preserved in a system where multiple, competing elites determine public policy through bargaining and compromise, voters exercise meaningful choices in elections, and new elites can gain access to power. Pluralism asserts that organized interest groups provide the individual with an effective way to participate in the political system, by allowing diverse voices to be heard through membership in the organized groups that reflect different interests. Pluralists further believe that competition and negotiation among organized interests provides a balance of power that protects the individual from both competing interests and a "tyranny of the majority."

Our analysis of interest groups yields the following propositions:

1. Organized interest groups are governed by small elites whose values do not necessarily reflect those of most members.
2. Interest groups draw disproportionately from middle- and upper-class segments of the population. The pressure-group system is not representative of the entire community.
3. Business, labor, and professional organizations dominate among organized interest groups.
4. Considerable inequality exists among organized interest groups. Smaller, more cohesive, and focused groups with narrow memberships are able to achieve more tangible results than larger organizations with more diverse memberships seeking less tangible goals.
5. Business groups and unions are the most highly organized and active lobbyists in Washington and the state capitals.
6. The ability to offer campaign support, particularly in terms of money, increases the influence of interest groups. This is especially evident in the growth of PACs.
7. Organizations and their elites tend to become agents of social stability as they acquire a stake in the existing political order.

Notes

1. Gabriel A. Almond and Sidney Verba, *The Civic Culture: Political Attitudes and Democracy in Five Nations* (Boston: Little, Brown, 1965), p. 245.
2. David B. Truman, *The Governmental Process* (New York: Alfred A. Knopf, 1951). The classic description and defense of interest group pluralism.
3. Roberto Michels, *Political Parties: A Sociological Study of the Oligarchical Tendencies of Modern Democracy* (New York: Dover, 1959 [1915]), esp. p. 248.
4. Interview with Andrew Stern by Michael Mishak. http://www.lasvegassun.com/news/2009/may/10/stern-unplugged-seiu-chief-labor-movement-and-card/
5. Peter Nicholas, "Obama's Curiously Close Labor Friendship," *Los Angeles Times*, http://articles.latimes.com/2009/jun/28/nation/na-stern28
6. Linda S. Lichter, "Who Speaks for Black America?" *Public Opinion* (August/September 1985): 44.
7. Harris Interactive. April 12–18, 2011. N=l,010 adults nationwide, www.harrisinteractive.com/vault/HI-Harris-Poll-Power-and-Influence-2011-06-01.pdf
8. Center for Responsive Politics, 2012. http://www.opensecrets.org/lobby/top.php?indexType=a
9. Congressional Quarterly, *The Washington Lobby*, 4th ed. (Washington, DC: CQ Press, 1982), p. 5.
10. C. Wright Mills, *The Power Elite* (New York: Oxford University Press, 1956), p. 391.
11. Thomas E. Mann, "Breaking the Political Impasse," in Henry J. Aaron, ed., *Setting National Priorities: Policy for the Nineties* (Washington, DC: Brookings Institution, 1990), pp. 303, 313.

If the President is the head of the American body politic, Congress is its gastrointestinal tract. Its vast and convoluted inner workings may be mysterious and unpleasant, but in the end they excrete a great deal of material whose successful passage is crucial to our nation's survival. This is Congress's duty.

—Jon Stewart et al.

CONGRESS: THE LEGISLATIVE ELITE

The Founders intended that Congress be the first and most powerful branch of government. Article I of the Constitution describes the national government's powers as *powers given to Congress*. The Founders also intended that the House of Representatives represent "the people" in government. Among the governmental bodies created by the Constitution of 1787, only the House of Representatives was to be directly elected by the people. The Senate was to be elected by state legislatures (until the Seventeenth Amendment in 1913 provided for their direct election); the president was to be chosen by the Electoral College; and the Supreme Court was to be appointed for life. House members were to be elected every two years to ensure their responsiveness to the people. Indeed, even today House members fondly refer to their chamber as "the people's House."

But who are "the people" that Congress really represents? It is our argument that Congress members principally represent themselves. We contend that they are recruited from local elite structures; that the masses are largely inattentive to congressional affairs and elections; that the overriding interest of Congress members is their own re-election; that in pursuit of that goal they depend heavily on large campaign contributors; that Congress has structured itself as "an incumbent protection society," that is, a way to assist its members to remain in office; that even *within* Congress a leadership "establishment" controls legislation; and finally that Congress has largely ceded policy initiation to the president, the bureaucracy, the courts, and organized interest groups.

THE ELITE BIAS OF CONGRESSIONAL RECRUITMENT

The elite bias of Congress begins with the recruitment of its members. Senators and House members are seldom recruited from the masses; they are drawn from the well-educated, prestigiously employed, affluent, upper and upper-middle classes of their home constituencies. They are among the most ambitious, politically motivated, and skilled communicators in their communities. Their social ties are mainly to state and community elite structures; they retain their local contacts, business ties, and contributor networks. Members who sacrifice local ties and succumb to the attractions of Washington's "inside the beltway" social life do so at some risk ("the beltway" is a reference to the circle of interstate highways that surrounds Washington, DC). Most now spend a minimum time in the capitol, usually Tuesdays through Thursdays, and long weekends at home meeting with constituents and holding fundraisers.

POLITICAL ENTREPRENEURSHIP

U.S. House of Representatives Official website of the House, with schedule of floor and committee actions, legislative information, and links to every representative's website and every committee website. *www.house.gov*

The most important qualification for Congress is **political entrepreneurship**—the ability and desire to sell yourself to others as a candidate, to raise money from political contributors, to organize and motivate others to work on your campaign, and to communicate to others personally, in small groups and large audiences, and, most important, through the media.

For most members of Congress, politics is a career. "Citizen officeholders"—people with business or professional or commercial careers who get into politics part-time—have largely been driven out of political life in the United States by people who become career politicians early in life. Politically ambitious young people, fresh from college or law school, seek out internships or staff positions with members of Congress or congressional committees or in state capitols or city halls. Others volunteer to work in political campaigns. They find political mentors to guide them in learning to organize campaigns, contact financial contributors, and deal with the media. Then they prudently wait for open seats in their state legislatures, city councils, or perhaps Congress itself to launch their own initial campaigns for elective office.

U.S. Senate Official Senate website, with floor and committee schedules, Senate news, and links to each senator's website. *www. senate.gov*

Political parties seldom recruit candidates any more; candidates recruit themselves. Nor do interest groups recruit candidates; rather, candidates seek out interest groups in the hope of winning their support.

PROFESSIONALISM

Candidates for Congress have a better chance at election if their occupations are socially respectable and provide opportunities for extensive public contacts. Lawyers, bankers, and insurance and real estate brokers establish in their businesses the wide circle of friends necessary for political success. While professional backgrounds dominate the halls of Congress, in the 112th Congress 118 military veterans served as members.

Congress members are almost always of higher social standing than their average constituent. The overrepresentation of lawyers in Congress and other public offices is particularly marked. Lawyers have always played a prominent role in the political system. Twenty-five of the 52 signers of the Declaration of Independence and 31 of the 55 members of the Continental Congress were lawyers. The legal profession has also provided 70 percent of the presidents, vice presidents, and cabinet officers of the United States and about 40 percent of the U.S. senators and

House members. For example, in the 112th Congress, 167 Representatives and 55 Senators had law degrees. Lawyers are in a reasonably high-prestige occupation, but so are physicians, business executives, and scientists. Why, then, do lawyers dominate Congress?

Lawyers are trained in the law, legislators make laws, so the fit is natural. We must also recognize more personal factors. Lawyers represent clients in their work; therefore they can use the same skill to represent constituents in Congress. Also, lawyers deal with public policy as it is reflected in the statute books, so they may be reasonably familiar with public policy before entering Congress. But professional skills alone cannot explain the dominance of lawyers in public office. Of all the high-prestige occupations, only lawyers can really enhance their careers through political activities. Physicians, corporate managers, and scientists pay a high cost if they neglect their vocations for politics. But political activity can help boost lawyers' careers; free public advertising and contacts with potential clients are two important benefits. Moreover, lawyers have a monopoly on public offices in law enforcement and the court system, and the offices of judge or prosecuting attorney often provide lawyers with stepping-stones to higher public office, including Congress.

The 112th Congress saw lawyers eclipsed in the House of Representatives by businesspeople, 181 to 148. Both numbers were below the most common profession of politicians: politics. Over 200 (208, to be exact) members of the House gave that as their background. It is interesting to note that 78 representatives listed education as their profession. The Senate still reflects the older professional composition of Congress: 52 lawyers, 28 businesspeople, and 36 politicians.[1]

Congressional members are also among the most highly educated occupational groups in the United States. Their educational level is considerably higher than that of the populations they represent and reflects their occupational background and their middle- and upper-class origins.

RACE AND GENDER

The U.S. Congress has historically been almost entirely populated by European-American males. While this group continues to be overrepresented compared to the general population, women and minorities have made substantial inroads.[2] For an overview of the ethnic and gender make-up of Congress, see Table 8.1.

African-Americans make up 12 percent of the nation's population. In 2011 their membership in the House of Representatives reached 10 percent. The leap in black membership was a product of judicial interpretations of the Voting Rights Act, which requires that minorities be given maximum opportunity to elect minorities to Congress through redistricting. While large numbers of African-Americans served in Congress after the Civil War, it was not until 1966 that the first, Republican Edward Brooke of Massachusetts, was popularly elected to the Senate; he served until 1979. Carol Moseley Braun was the first black woman elected to the Senate in 1992; she was defeated for re-election in 1998. Barack Obama was elected to the Senate in 2004 (he was replaced by African-American Roland Burris in 2009). Two black Republicans were elected to the House in 2010.

TABLE 8.1 | GENDER AND RACE IN CONGRESS

	Women	African-Americans	Hispanics
House Members (435)			
1985–1987	22	19	11
1987–1989	23	22	11
1989–1991	25	23	11
1991–1993	29	25	10
1993–1995	48	38	17
1995–1997	49	39	18
1997–1999	51	37	18
1999–2001	58	39	19
2001–2003	59	36	19
2003–2005	59	37	23
2005–2007	65	40	23
2007–2009	71	40	23
2009–2011	76	42	27
2011–2013	71	42	25
2013–2015	81	44	28
Senators (100)			
1985–1987	2	0	0
1987–1989	2	0	0
1989–1991	2	0	0
1991–1993	2	0	0
1993–1995	6	1	0
1995–1997	8	1	0
1997–1999	9	1	0
1999–2001	9	0	0
2001–2003	13	0	0
2003–2005	14	0	0
2005–2007	14	1	3
2007–2009	17	1	3
2009–2011	17	1	1
2011–2013	16	0	2
2013–2015	20	0	3

Note: Final results for the 2012 election were not available at the time this text went to press. Numbers given are based on confirmed results with a few estimated results added. Note that numbers do not include delegates.

| FOCUS | REPRESENTATIVE PAUL RYAN |

Due to the national attention being given to the federal deficit and the national debt, Wisconsin Representative Paul Ryan found himself thrust into the spotlight in 2011. As Chair of the House Budget Committee, Ryan put forth a detailed alternative budget in challenge to President Obama's ongoing trillion-dollar deficits. Called the "Path to Prosperity: A Blueprint for American Renewal," Ryan's plan focused on closing the gap between federal spending and the nation's ability to pay. Ryan called for tax reform, freezing federal spending at 2008 levels, and recreating entitlements. His plan was viewed as enough of a threat that President Obama invited him to sit front and center at a budget reform speech where the president proceeded to attack him and his plan as "un-American." Paul Ryan had become the center of the politics of the debt and deficit.

Born in 1970, Ryan graduated from Miami University in Ohio. His early jobs included being an aide to Senator Bob Kasten, legislative director for Senator Sam Brownback, and then speechwriter for fiscal conservative hero Jack Kemp, the 1996 Republican candidate for the vice presidency. In 1999, at age 28, Paul Ryan entered the House of Representatives, sent by the First District of Wisconsin, the seat which he still holds.

Rising to Chair of the Budget Committee with the Republican Party recapture of the House in 2010, the data- and detail-driven Ryan saw the United States'

credit rating downgraded and no end in sight to a federal deficit of over a trillion dollars annually. His "Path to Prosperity" called for cutting business tax rates while eliminating corporate tax deductions to eliminate "crony capitalism," in which politically favored businesses get special tax treatment. In addition to a spending freeze, he proposed making Social Security means tested so that the wealthy would receive less, turning Medicaid into block grants to the states, and changing Medicare into a program to support the purchase of health insurance for the elderly. The political responses from both parties were predictable. His willingness to place entitlements on the table for discussion scared most politicians who did not want to be seen cutting funds for old people. Still, a budget based on his plan passed the House with 235 votes, after which it stalled in the Senate.

Due to his willingness to bring up difficult issues and his talent for explaining complex economics in common language, Paul Ryan was chosen by Mitt Romney as the Republican candidate for Vice President in 2012.

Source: David Von Drehe, "Paul Ryan: The Prophet," *Time Magazine*, December 14, 2011. *www.time.com/time/specials/packages/article/0,28804,2101745_2102133_2102332,00 .html*. Christian Schneider, "Mr. Ryan Goes to Wisconsin," *National Review*, April 21, 2011. *www.nationalreview.com/articles/265285/mr-ryan-goes-wisconsin-christian-schneider*. Official biography at *http://paulryan.house.gov/Biography/*.

Hispanics, or Latinos, make up 16.3 percent of the nation's population, the second largest group after whites. However, to date, Hispanics have not achieved the political power of African-Americans, making up only 7.4 percent of Congress. The primary reason is that only about two-thirds of Hispanic adults are citizens, which is the basic requirement for voting. In 2008, only 32 percent of Hispanics voted, so their representation in Congress is consistent with that. As more move to citizenship and as younger U.S.-born Hispanics reach adulthood, Hispanic influence in the political system will grow.

Asian-Americans are the fastest growing racial group in the United States, now almost 6 percent of the population. Asian-Americans mirror the relatively low representation of Hispanics, but from a smaller overall population. Only 12 Asian-Americans serve in the House and 2 in the Senate. This will likely change in the future as well. Congress also has several members born abroad, hailing from Taiwan, India, Japan, Pakistan, Peru, and Vietnam.

Women have made great strides in congressional representation. In 2011, 101 women took their seats in the House and in the Senate, roughly one-third of them Republicans. While parity would be a Congress evenly split between the two sexes, there is significant momentum in both parties to encourage female candidates. Women also are moving up the party hierarchy by achieving leadership positions in each house, notably Nancy Pelosi, former Speaker of the House, 2007–2011.

Party

For 60 years (1933–1994), except for four years Democrats controlled the House of Representatives, and for all but 10 years they also held a majority in the Senate (see Table 8.2). The Republican victory in the congressional election of 1994 was described as an "earthquake" in Washington and was widely attributed to Republican leader Newt Gingrich, who recruited Republican candidates to support a "Contract with America." Speaker Gingrich's platform incorporated many popular provisions, including term limits, tax reductions, reduced federal spending, a constitutional amendment to balance the budget, and welfare reform. The Republican surge was also aided by an elite deal to increase African-American representation by drawing "minority-majority" districts that concentrated not only likely Democratic voters, but Republicans as well. Gingrich and the Republicans worked reasonably well in negotiation and compromise with President Clinton over many issues. The main exception was the 1998 impeachment of Clinton.

The twenty-first century has seen party control of the House and Senate switch back and forth almost every election. With the election of George W. Bush in 2000, Republicans held sway over the government until the June 2001 party switch of one senator, which gave the Democrats a one-vote majority in the Senate. The Senate was recaptured by the Republicans in 2002. Both houses changed hands in the Democratic victory of 2006. By then, many Congressional Republicans had fallen to scandals and ethical lapses, the same issues that had led the Democrats to lose control of Congress only 12 years earlier. With the 2008 election of Barack Obama as president, the Democrats vastly increased their control of both houses of Congress; however, this control was short-lived, with the Senate majority falling to 53 and a complete loss of majority in the House. The 2010 midterm election saw Democrats suffer a historic loss of over 60 seats and control pass to the Republicans, who had just been voted out of the majority four years earlier.

While it is normal for a president's party to lose seats in the first midterm election (2002 having been a rare exception), the degree of rejection of the Democrats in 2010 was severe by historical standards. Several of Obama's major policy achievements were unpopular, especially the health care law, stimulus spending, and bank bailouts, leading voters to punish the Democrats at the polls, with Republicans picking up 65 seats and the majority. The 2012 election saw a split result: Democrats continued control over the Senate and White House, while Republicans kept control of the House of Representatives, losing only a few seats. Given the fiscal challenges facing the nation, the public appeared to want compromise.

Table 8.2 | Party Control of Congress

Year	Session	House		Senate	
		Democrat	Republican	Democrat	Republican
1961	87th	**263**	174	**64**	36
1963	88th	**259**	176	**66**	34
1965	89th	**295**	140	**68**	32
1967	90th	**248**	187	**64**	36
1969	91st	**243**	192	**57**	43
1971	92nd	**255**	180	**55**	45
1973	93rd	**243**	192	**57**	43
1975	94th	**291**	144	**61**	39
1977	95th	**292**	143	**62**	38
1979	96th	**277**	158	**58**	42
1981	97th	**243**	192	47	**53**
1983	98th	**269**	166	46	**54**
1985	99th	**253**	182	47	**53**
1987	100th	**258**	177	**55**	45
1989	101st	**260**	175	**55**	45
1991	102nd	**268**	167	**56**	44
1993	103rd	**259**	176	**56**	44
1995	104th	205	**230**	47	**53**
1997	105th	207	**228**	45	**55**
1999	106th	212	**223**	45	**55**
2001	107th	213	**222**	**51**	49
2003	108th	206	**229**	49	**51**
2005	109th	203	**232**	45	**55**
2007	110th	**233**	202	**51**	49
2009	111th	**257**	178	**60**	40
2011	112th	**192**	243	**53**	47
2013	113th	200	**235**	**55**	45

Note: Majority party in **bold**. Figures include self-described "independents" who align themselves with one or the other party.

Divided government, with one party in the White House and the other controlling the House and Senate, does not *necessarily* mean policy gridlock, as seen by the successful periods when Presidents Reagan and Clinton were able to work with opposition legislatures. George W. Bush was able to work with Democrats to pass education reform, homeland security reorganization, and counterterrorism legislation. Bush's immigration reform proposal—for a guest worker program with a

"Listen, pal! I didn't spend seven million bucks to
get here so I could yield the floor to you."

promise of citizenship for illegal immigrants who are here now, as well as increased border enforcement—failed despite Democratic cooperation, as it was opposed by many Congressional Republicans. President Obama has had a testier relationship with Congressional Republicans. In the end, divided government is an expression of checks and balances and the goal of limited power of elites.

The president is the Commander-in-Chief, and there is little Congress can do by itself to compel changes in military strategy. In theory, Congress can cut off funds for any war, but it is politically risky to vote to deny funds for troops in the field, so a Democratic Congress never denied funding for the war in Iraq. President Obama's 2009 decision to mirror Bush's Iraq "surge" strategy in Afghanistan was unpopular with more left-leaning Democrats in both houses, but it succeeded with Republican support.

Partisanship is a prohibitive barrier to cooperation between the president and Congress. After the 2006 election, Democratic majorities in both houses were major obstacles to policy initiatives by President Bush. In response, the president could veto or threaten to veto any major new Democratic programs passed in Congress. The level of partisan animosity increased noticeably under President Obama, with major Democratic initiatives, including the health care bill, passing with little or no Republican support. Bipartisanship is a popular term in political rhetoric, but it seldom describes what actually occurs in Washington, especially with divided party government. The rhetoric at the Capitol has grown more and more inflammatory.

PERSONAL WEALTH

The personal wealth of members of Congress is well above that of the average citizen. Members are required to submit annual financial statements that list their

TABLE 8.3	ESTIMATED* PERSONAL WEALTH OF THE 10 WEALTHIEST CONGRESS MEMBERS	
Rank	**Name**	**$ Millions**
1	Darrell Issa (R-Calif.)	448
2	Michael McCaul (R-Tex.)	380
3	Jane Harman (D-Calif.)	327
4	John Kerry (D-Mass.)	232
5	Mark Warner (D-Vir.)	193
6	Herb Kohl (D-Wis.)	173
7	Jared Polis (D-Colo.)	143
8	Vernon Buchanan (R-Fla.)	136
9	Nancy Pelosi (D-Calif.)	101
10	Jay Rockefeller (D-W.Va.)	99

*Estimates by Center for Responsive Politics based on official filings of Congress members for 2012. Figures represent estimated average net wealth (assets minus debts) based on reported ranges.

assets and liabilities as well as income, guests, and more. But it is difficult to gauge what lawmakers are worth based on what they file, inasmuch as disclosure forms do not require exact values but rather ranges of worth. The Center for Responsive Politics tries to estimate the personal wealth of members based on these filings.[3] The average personal wealth in the House of Representatives is $5.9 million and in the Senate $13.2 million. The 10 wealthiest members—with an estimated $100 million or more—are listed in Table 8.3.

WHOM DOES CONGRESS REALLY REPRESENT?

Over time, professional officeholders become isolated from the lives and concerns of average citizens; they acquire an "inside the beltway" mentality and have no direct feeling for how their constituents live. They respond instead to the media, to polls, and to interest groups, and their relevant constituencies are in fact small groups of political activists with the time, interest, and skill to communicate about political events. Even given mass public disapproval, as exhibited by antiwar rallies in 2003, the anti-government spending Tea Party beginning in 2009, and the Occupy movement in 2011, legislative elites are more likely to focus on the demands of the elite leaders of organized interests.

MASS INATTENTION

For the great mass of people, Congress is an institution with low visibility and low esteem. Opinion polls consistently report grim facts about the public's lack of awareness of Congress. Only 59 percent of citizens can identify one U.S. senator from their state; only 25 percent can name both of their state's senators. Members of the House of Representatives fare even worse; only 29 percent of the general public can identify their representative.[4]

Even when constituents know a congressional member's name, few know his or her specific policy positions or, for that matter, the member's overall political position. One study found that among those who offered a reason for candidate choice, only 7 percent indicated their choice had any "discernible issue content." As for detailed information about policy stands, only a "chemical trace" of the population qualifies as attentive to their congressional candidate's policy positions.[5]

ELITES AS THE RELEVANT CONSTITUENTS

A legislator's relevant constituents, then, are the home district's active, interested, and resourceful elites. In an agricultural district, they are the leaders of the American Farm Bureau Federation and the major agricultural producers—cotton producers, wheat growers, and so on; in the Southwest, oil producers or ranchers; in the mountain states, tourism and mining interests; in New England, the lumber, fishing, and insurance interests; in California, farmers, Hollywood, and the technology industry; in Appalachia, coal interests and leaders of the United Mine Workers. More heterogeneous urban constituencies may contain a variety of influential constituents—bankers and financial leaders, real estate owners and developers, owners and managers of large industrial and commercial enterprises, labor elites, and the owners and editors of media outlets. In certain big-city districts with strong, disciplined party organizations, the key congressional constituents may be the city's political and governmental elites—the city or county party chairpersons or the mayor. In the Washington, DC, metro area and in state capitals, leaders of government employees' unions are critical. And, of course, anyone who makes major financial contributions to a congressional candidate's campaign becomes a *very* important constituent.

HOME STYLE

Congress members spend as much time cultivating their home districts and states as they do legislating in Washington. **Home style** refers to the activities of senators and representatives in promoting their images among their constituents.[6] These activities include members' allocations of their personnel and staff resources to constituent services, personal appearances in their home district or state, and efforts to bring federally funded projects, grants, and contracts to their home district or state.

Constituent service, or casework, is a form of "retail" politics. Members of Congress win votes and campaign contributors one at a time by helping people on a personal level. Over time grateful voters and contributors accumulate, giving incumbents an advantage at election time. **Pork** describes the efforts of senators and representatives to "bring home the bacon"—to award federally funded roads, parks, post offices, and redevelopment projects to cities; research grants to universities; weapons contracts to local plants; demonstration projects of all kinds; and other "goodies" to each year's appropriations bills. On Capitol Hill much of this pork comes in the form of **earmarks**—special provisions for expenditures tucked inside larger appropriations bills. Only recently has Congress ruled that members must reveal their sponsorship of earmarks.

Roll Call
This online magazine covers a variety of current topics about Congress but is especially strong on stories dealing with running for Congress and campaign financing. *www.rollcall.com*

Members of Congress spend as much time in their home districts as they do in the capitol, "moving between two contexts, Washington and home, and between two activities, governing and campaigning."[7] It is important to be seen at home "pressing the flesh," giving speeches and attending dinners, attending civic meetings, and so on. A major portion of a legislator's time is spent in fundraising, which also allows more time with key local elite interests. Congress usually follows a Tuesday to Thursday schedule of legislative business, allowing members to spend long weekends at home, and also enjoys long recesses during the late summer and over holidays.

CONGRESS IN DISREPUTE

Congress is the least popular branch of government. Polls reveal that a majority of people in the United States believe (perhaps accurately) that members of Congress have low or very low standards of honesty and ethics[8] (see Figure 8.1). Rarely has the Congress achieved a 50 percent approval rating among the general public (see Figure 8.2), with approvals in recent years sharply lower, generally in the 10–20 percent range. Congress's approval rating is almost always well below that of the president.

THROW THE RASCALS OUT?

If Congress is so unpopular, we should reasonably expect voters to "throw the rascals out." The theory of representative democracy implies that dissatisfied voters will defeat incumbents running for re-election. But just the opposite occurs in congressional elections. Well over 90 percent of House members and usually over

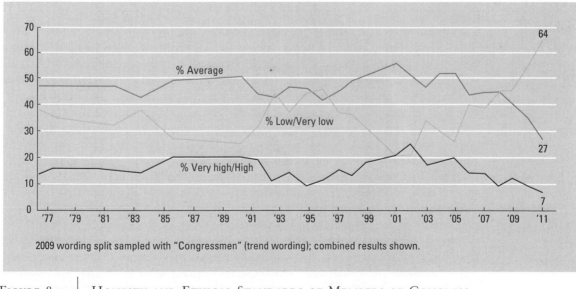

FIGURE 8.1 | HONESTY AND ETHICAL STANDARDS OF MEMBERS OF CONGRESS

Source: *www.gallup.com/poll/151460/record-rate-honesty-ethics-members-congress-low.aspx.*

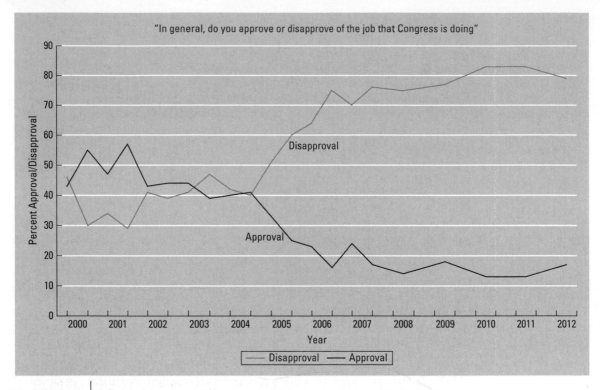

FIGURE 8.2 | CONGRESSIONAL APPROVAL RATINGS

Source: *www.gallup.com/poll/151460/record-rate-honesty-ethics-members-congress-low.aspx* at *www.gallup.com.*

75 percent of senators seeking re-election succeed in doing so (see Figure 8.3). Even when the Republican and Democratic parties switch control of Congress, incumbents prevail. In 1994, when Republicans gained control of Congress, 90 percent of House incumbents running for re-election won, as well as 92 percent of Senate incumbents. In 2006, when Democrats regained control, the incumbent re-election rate was 97 percent in the House and 85 percent of Senate incumbents won. In 2010, when the House reverted to Republican control, 87 percent of incumbents were reelected (and 90 percent in the Senate). Incumbents facing difficult re-election races often decline to run again. When a change in control is likely, older members of Congress also choose to retire rather than continue without their committee chair positions. The failure of voters to throw the rascals out, despite mass disapproval of the performance of Congress, is thus more consistent with elite theory than with democratic theory.

In an apparent paradox, most voters approve of their own representative yet disapprove of the Congress as a whole. Individual members of Congress are generally popular in their districts, even though Congress itself is an object of distrust and even ridicule. Obviously, if most incumbents are popular in their home districts, incumbents will continue to be reelected. The real question is, how do they maintain their popularity?

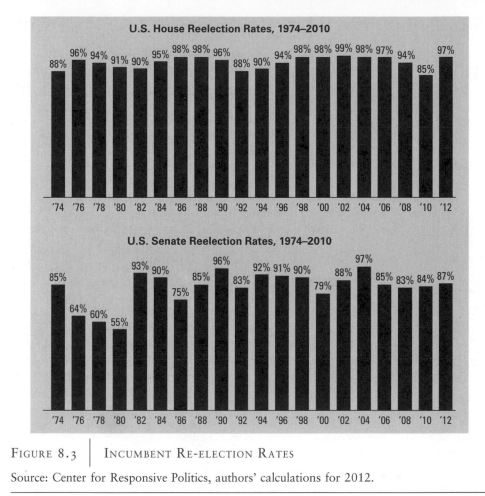

FIGURE 8.3 | INCUMBENT RE-ELECTION RATES

Source: Center for Responsive Politics, authors' calculations for 2012.

INCUMBENT ADVANTAGES

Why do incumbents win? First of all, name familiarity—in the absence of any knowledge of issues—can be a powerful advantage. The average voter, even if only vaguely aware of the incumbents, is likely to recognize their names on the ballot and vote for them. Even during a political campaign, an incumbent enjoys much higher name recognition than a challenger. This advantage builds over time. For the 112th Congress, the *average* length of service in the House was 9.8 years (4.9 terms) and in the Senate 11.4 (1.9 terms).[9] This reflects that in 2010 many incumbents were defeated in heated party primary elections.

More importantly, incumbents use the resources of their office—an effective political organization with staff time, travel funds, perks, and privileges—to tend to the needs of their key constituents. They use their franking privilege for mailing newsletters, polls, and other information; they appear at various public events, call news conferences, address organizational meetings, and, in general, make themselves as visible as possible, largely at taxpayers' expense. They will use earmarking privileges to bring money for visible projects to their state or district, which has the added benefit of generating positive press coverage.

Finally, because the smart money backs a winner, incumbents attract heavy campaign contributions and thus enjoy an enormous financial advantage over challengers. In the 2010 election cycle, House incumbents raised an average of $1,439,997 to get reelected, compared to the challengers' average of $688,632. The gap in the Senate is also huge: an average of $9,782,702 for incumbents to "only" $6,528,077 for challengers.[10] (See Chapter 6 for more on campaigning.)

TERM LIMITS?

Mass distrust of politicians fueled a national grassroots movement to limit the terms of public officials—notably members of Congress and state legislators. Proponents of term limits rely on anti-elitist arguments: Citizen legislators have largely been replaced by career professional politicians, and term limits would increase competition in the electoral system. Creating "open-seat" races on a regular basis should encourage more people to seek public office.

However, the enthusiasm of the mass public for term limits is more than matched by the intense opposition the proposal meets on Capitol Hill. It is unlikely members of Congress will ever vote to limit their own terms of office. Elites argue such limits infringe on the freedom of choice enjoyed by voters who, if upset with the performance of Congress or their state legislature, can always limit their terms by not reelecting them. Many states have enacted term limits for state legislators. Results are mixed—the move introduces regular change among holders of elite legislative positions, but it sharply reduces the overall experience level and induces lawmakers to calculate their future jobs, often as lobbyists, while still representing the people.

THE ELABORATE PROCEDURES OF LEGISLATIVE ELITES

The customs, rules, and procedures of Congress are elaborate but important to the functioning of legislative elites. They make the legislative process fair and orderly. Without them, 535 men and women could not arrive at collective decisions about the thousands of items submitted to them during a congressional session. Yet the same rules also delay or obstruct proposed changes in the status quo. In congressional procedures, legislation faces many opportunities for defeat and many obstacles to passage.

IN BRIEF | INCUMBENT ADVANTAGES

Incumbent advantages include:

- Name recognition
- "Home style" service to constituents and contributors
- "Pork" for the home district or state
- Overwhelming advantage in campaign contributions

KILL BILL

The elaborate procedures of Congress ensure that few of the bills introduced are ever passed. In a typical two-year congressional session, more than 10,000 bills will be introduced, but fewer than 800 will be enacted. This is a kill ratio of well over 90 percent. Recent sessions have produced far fewer laws, with the 111th Congress passing only 383 laws. Rather than viewing the cumbersome process of Congress as a poorly functioning way to legislate, it is perhaps more accurate to refer to the lawmaking process in Congress as a highly efficient mechanism for *preventing* legislation.

THE LAWMAKING PROCESS: HOW A BILL BECOMES A LAW

I'm Just a Bill
Beloved classic cartoon from *Schoolhouse Rock* explaining the legislative process can be found on various websites, including iTunes and YouTube.

Congress follows a fairly standard pattern in the formal process of making laws; Figure 8.4 describes briefly some of the most important procedural steps.[11] Bills generally originate in the president's office, in executive departments, or in the offices of interested elites, but a member of the House or Senate must formally introduce them into Congress. Except for bills raising revenue, which must begin in the House of Representatives according to the Constitution, bills can be introduced in either house. On introduction, a bill moves to one of the standing committees of the House or Senate. Most are shuffled down to subcommittees, but it is the full committee that eventually decides a bill's fate. The committee may (1) recommend it for adoption with only minor changes, (2) virtually rewrite it into a new policy proposal, (3) ignore it and prevent its passage through inaction, or (4) kill it by majority vote. The full House or Senate *may* overrule a committee decision, but they do so rarely. Most members of Congress are reluctant to upset the prerogatives of the committees and the desires of recognized leaders. Therefore committees have virtually life-or-death power over every legislative measure.

STANDING CONGRESSIONAL COMMITTEES

Library of Congress
The Thomas system allows the tracing of bills from their introduction through the committee system, floor schedule vote, and so on. *http://thomas.loc.gov*

Neither the House nor the Senate as a body could hope to review all the measures put before it. This problem is solved by creating specialized working groups, each called a **committee**, to focus on specific policy issues. (Table 8.4 lists standing committees in the House and Senate.) As early as 1885, Woodrow Wilson described the U.S. political process as "government by the standing committees of Congress."[12] Although it reduces legislative work to manageable proportions, the committee system also allows a minority of the legislators, sometimes a single committee chair, to delay and obstruct the legislative process.

In the Senate, the most prestigious committees are Foreign Relations, Appropriations, and Finance; in the House, the most powerful are the Rules Committee, Appropriations, and Ways and Means. The Senate Foreign Relations Committee has a particularly significant role in providing "advice and consent" to presidents on foreign issues; the House Rules Committee is a unique bottleneck in the legislative process in which House bills must have rules of debate attached to them. In both the House and the Senate, Appropriations Committees have a say in all federal spending; the Ways and Means Committee (known as Finance in the

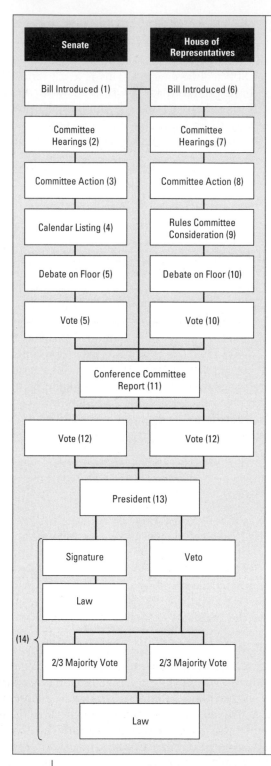

1. **Introduction.** Bills can be introduced in either house; often "Companion" bills are introduced in both houses. (In this example, a bill is first introduced in the Senate.) It is given a number and referred to the proper committee.

2. **Hearings.** The subcommittees and/or full standing committees may hold public hearings on the bill.

3. **Committee action.** The full committee meets in executive (closed) session. It may kill the bill, approve it with or without amendments, or draft a new bill. It is here that most bills "die."

4. **Calendar.** If the committee recommends the bill for passage, it is listed on the calendar.

5. **Debate, amendment, vote.** In the Senate, the majority and minority leader decide when the bill goes to the floor for debate. Amendments may be added. The bill is voted on. (A "filibuster" may prevent a vote; 60 votes are needed to halt a filibuster.)

6. **Introduction to the second house.** If the bill passes, it goes to the House of Representatives, where it is referred to the proper committee.

7. **Hearings.** Hearings may be held again, by subcommittees and/or full standing committees.

8. **Committee action.** The committee rejects the bill, prepares a new one, or accepts the bill with or without amendments. Most bills "die" in committee.

9. **Rules Committee consideration.** If the committee recommends the bill, it is listed on the calendar and sent to the Rules Committee. The Rules Committee can block a bill or clear it for debate before the entire House. Bills are given "rules" that determine length of debate, whether amendments will be considered. etc.

10. **Debate, amendment, vote.** The bill goes before the entire body and is debated and voted on.

11. **Conference Committee.** If the bill as passed by the second house contains major changes, either house may request a conference committee. The conference—persons from each house, representing both parties—meets and tries to reconcile its differences.

12. **Vote on conference report.** When committee members reach an agreement, they report back to their respective houses. Their report is either accepted or rejected.

13. **Submission to the president.** If the report is accepted by both houses, the bill is signed by the speaker of the House and the president of the Senate and is sent to the president of the United States.

14. **Presidential action.** The president may sign or veto the bill within ten days. If the president does not sign and Congress is still in session, the bill automatically becomes law. If Congress adjourns before the ten days have elapsed, it does not become law. (This is called the pocket veto.) If the president returns the bill with a veto message, it may still become a law if passed by a two-thirds majority in each house.

FIGURE 8.4 | HOW A BILL BECOMES A LAW

TABLE 8.4 | THE STANDING COMMITTEES OF CONGRESS

Senate

Agriculture, Nutrition, and Forestry	Homeland Security and Environmental
Appropriations	Affairs
Armed Services	Judiciary
Banking, Housing, and Urban Affairs	Rules and Administration
Budget	Small Business and Entrepreneurship
Commerce, Science, and Transportation	Select Aging
Energy and Natural Resources	Select Ethics
Environment and Public Works	Select Indian
Finance House	Select Intelligence
Foreign Relations	Veterans Affairs
Health, Education, Labor, and Pensions	

House

Agriculture	Judiciary
Appropriations	Resources
Armed Forces	Rules
Budget	Science
Education and the Workforce	Select Intelligence
Energy and Commerce	Small Business
Financial Services	Standards of Official Conduct
Government Reform	Transportation and Infrastructure
Homeland Security	Veterans Affairs
House Administration	Ways and Means
International Relations	Veterans Affairs

Joint Committees

Joint Economic Committee	Joint Committee on Printing
Joint Taxation	Joint Committee on the Library

Senate) has sway over tax policy. Given that many interests want to claim federal money and/or avoid taxation, membership on either of these committees means considerable attention. To expedite business, most standing committees create subcommittees to handle particular matters falling within their jurisdiction, further concentrating power in the hands of a few congressional members. Interested elites cultivate the favor of powerful subcommittee and committee chairpersons.

Public Hearings

In examining legislation, a committee or subcommittee often holds public hearings on bills deemed worthy by the chairperson or, in some cases, by the majority of the committee. Influenced by the legal profession, the committees tend to look upon public hearings as trials in which contestants present their sides of the argument to the committee members, who act as judges. Presumably, skillful judges (the legislators) will sift through facts on which to base their decisions. In practice, however, committees use public hearings primarily to influence public opinion or executive action or, occasionally, to discover the position of major elite groups on the measure under consideration. Committee hearing can also make for excellent political theater. Major decisions take place in secret executive sessions.

Committee Membership

The membership of the standing committees on Agriculture, Energy, Banking, and Judiciary generally reflects the interest of particular elite groups in the nation. Legislators representing farm interests sit on the Agricultural committees; representatives of land, water, and natural resource interests serve on Resources committees; those representing financial centers will serve on Banking and Financial Services committees, and lawyers dominate the Judiciary committees of both houses.

Given the power of congressional committees, the assignment of members is one of the most significant activities of Congress. In the House of Representatives, the Republicans assign their members to committees through the Committee on Committees, which consists of one representative from each state that sends a Republican to Congress. But the real business of this committee is conducted by a subcommittee appointed by the Republican party leader. The subcommittee fills committee vacancies with freshman members and those who request transfer from other committees. Both consider the career backgrounds of members, their seniority, their support for the party leadership, and how membership might help re-election. Often the chairperson of a standing committee tells the Committee on Committees his or her preferences for committee members. Democrats in the House make committee assignments through the Steering and Policy Committee, composed of the party leadership.

In the Senate, the Committee on Committees fills Republican committee positions, and a steering committee appointed by the Democratic leader selects Democratic committee members. Usually only senators with seniority are eligible for positions on the major Senate committees, but there are exceptions, such as when Senate Democratic leaders wanted to showcase a rising new star in the party and put Barack Obama on the Foreign Relations committee as a freshman.

The Power of the Chair

Committee and subcommittee chairpersons are powerful. They usually determine the bills the committee will consider, select issues for public hearings, and establish the agenda. Governmental and nongovernmental interests officially must consult the chairperson on all questions relating to his or her committee; this procedure gives the chairperson standing with the executive branch and with interested non-governmental elites. Only occasionally does a majority within the committee-subcommittee overrule a chairperson's decision on a committee matter.

THE SENIORITY SYSTEM

Traditionally, the member of the majority party with the longest continuous service on the committee becomes chairperson; the member of the minority party with the longest continuous service on the committee is the ranking minority member. Thus chairpersons are chosen not by their own committees, by their own party, or by the House and Senate as a whole. They are chosen by the voters of noncompetitive or "safe" congressional districts where voter participation is low and representatives are likely to stay in office the longest. In both House and Senate, the seniority system works against the politically competitive districts and guarantees polarization in the legislative process.

As their influence within Congress grows, high-seniority legislators tend to identify with Congress as an institution, weakening the possible influence of their constituencies. Two factors are at work here. Legislators get to know each other well (they see one another more regularly than they see constituents), and older legislators probably have learned from experience that an unpopular vote will not bring the vigorous constituency response from voters they once thought was inevitable. They develop a more realistic view of the electorate, expressed well in one senator's remarks: "After several terms, I don't give a damn anymore. I'm pretty safe now and I don't have to worry about reaction in the district."[13] Legislators also specialize in certain kinds of legislation, thus developing expertise that draws their colleagues to them as credible sources of information. As one put it, "That's the beauty of the seniority system—there are informed, experienced people on each Committee you can consult."[14]

DECENTRALIZATION: SUBCOMMITTEES AND "IRON TRIANGLES"

Over time, the specialized subcommittees of Congress have gained power. At present, the House has about 150 subcommittees and the Senate about 90. Each develops its own specialized policy network, the "iron triangle" of interest groups, executive bureaucracies, and congressional subcommittee members and staff (see Chapter 11). These "sub-governments" develop to the benefit of all participants: legislators benefit from campaign contributions by interest groups; lobbyists benefit from personal working relationships with committees and their staffs; administrative agencies benefit from interest groups' and congressional committees' support of their budget requests. Gradually, legislators, lobbyists, and bureaucrats develop a common bond whose strength frequently exceeds that of loyalty to the party.

THE HOUSE RULES COMMITTEE

After a standing committee reports a bill in the House (see Figure 8.4), the Rules Committee must issue a special rule or order before the bill can go before the House membership for consideration. Consequently, each bill must go through two committees. (The only exceptions are bills reported by the House Appropriations and Ways and Means committees; the House may consider their bills at any time as privileged motions.) The Rules Committee can kill a bill by shelving it indefinitely. It can insist the bill be amended as the price of permitting it on the floor and can even substitute a new bill for the one framed by another committee. The Rules Committee determines how much debate will be permitted on any bill and the number and kind of amendments that may be offered from the floor. The only formal limits on Rules Committee authority are the discharge petition (rarely used and hardly ever successful) and calendar Wednesday, a cumbersome procedure that permits standing committees to call up bills the Rules Committee has blocked. The Rules Committee, clearly the most powerful committee in Congress, is dominated by senior members elected from noncompetitive districts.

Senate Filibusters

In the Senate, control of floor debate rests with the majority leader. But the majority leader does not have the power to limit debate; a senator who has the floor may talk without limit and may choose to whom he or she yields the floor. This gives each individual senator the power to slow or block a bill's passage. If senators wish to talk a bill to death, they may do so in what is known as a **filibuster**. This device permits a minority to tie up the business of the Senate and prevent it from voting on a bill. Debate can be limited only by a process called **cloture vote**. Sixteen members' signatures on a petition will bring cloture to a vote; a three-fifths vote of the full Senate (60 votes) is required to end debate. *This means 41 senators can, if they choose, block legislation by voting against cloture.* The filibuster is a means by which a minority can defend itself against the "tyranny of the majority."

The Floor Vote

Fewer than one in ten bills introduced into Congress every year become law. After approval of a bill by the standing committee in the Senate or by the standing committee and the Rules Committee in the House, the bill moves to the floor for a vote. Usually the most crucial votes come on the amendments to the bill that are offered to the floor (however, the Rules Committee may prevent amendments in the House). Once the membership defeats major amendments or incorporates them into the bill, the bill usually picks up support, and the final vote is usually heavily in favor of it.

Conference Committees

One of the features most limiting to the power of elites in the U.S. government is its division of the legislature into two houses; after following a complicated path in one house, a bill must repeat the process in the other. A bill must pass both branches of Congress in *identical form* before it goes to the president for signature. However, the Senate often amends a House bill, and the House usually amends Senate bills. And every time one house amends a bill, it must resubmit the bill to the originating house for concurrence with the changes. If either house declines to accept changes in the bill, an ad hoc joint committee, called a *conference committee,* must iron out specific differences. Disagreements between the houses are so frequent that one-third to one-half of all public bills, including virtually all important ones, must go to conference committees after passage by both houses.

Conference committee members, appointed by the presiding officers of each house, usually come from the two standing committees that handled the bills in each house. Because the final bill produced by the conference committee is generally accepted by both houses, these committees have tremendous power in determining the final form of legislation. Both houses must accept or reject conference committee reports as a whole; they cannot further amend them. Most conference committee meetings are closed and unrecorded; the committees hold no hearings and listen to no outside testimony.

The bill that emerges from their deliberations may not represent the view of either house and may even contain items never considered by either one. Some people have dubbed conference committees a "third house" of Congress, whose members are not elected to them by the people, keep no record of their work, and usually operate behind closed doors—with no debate about their products allowed. Astute lobbyists know that trying to influence conference committee members can give them one more chance to impact legislation.

ELITES WITHIN ELITES: THE CONGRESSIONAL ESTABLISHMENT

The power hierarchy among federal government elite is supported by protocol, by the distribution of formal constitutional powers, by the powers associated with party office, by the committee and seniority systems of Congress, and by the "informal folkways" of Washington. According to the protocol of Washington society, the president holds the highest social rank, followed by former presidents and their widows, the vice president, the Speaker of the House, members of the Supreme Court, foreign ambassadors and ministers, cabinet members, U.S. senators, state governors, former vice presidents, and, finally, House members. This is reflected in the practice of representatives referring to themselves as "Congressperson" or "member of Congress" and trying to catch some of the glow of the more prestigious Senate, rather than being merely a member of the House.

SENATORIAL POWER

The Constitution grants greater formal powers to senators than to House members. Numbering only 100, individual senators are more visible than House members in the social and political life of Washington, as well as in their home states. Senators also have special authority in foreign affairs not accorded to House members, because the Senate must advise and consent by a two-thirds vote to all treaties entered into by the United States. The threat of Senate repudiation of a treaty makes it desirable for the president to solicit Senate views on foreign affairs; in general, the secretary of state works closely with the Senate Foreign Relations Committee on such matters. Influential senators undertake personal missions abroad and serve on delegations to international bodies. Another constitutional power afforded senators is to advise and consent on executive appointments, including Supreme

---

| FOCUS | Senator Al Franken |

There have been many paths to the political elite, but starting with stand-up comedy and writing for *Saturday Night Live* (SNL) is among the most unusual. Former comedian Al Franken takes public policy and legislation very seriously as Senator from Minnesota since 2009.

Born in 1951, Alan Stuart Franken graduated with honors from Harvard with a degree in political science. His talent was political satire and he began a career in comedy. In 1975 he became one of the original writers of Saturday Night Live, where he continued until 1995 (except 1981–1984). His performances on SNL included the character Stuart Smalley, and Franken went on to write and star in the film *Stuart Saves His Family*. Franken won three Emmy awards for television writing and performing.

After television, Franken turned to writing, producing five books, three of which went to number one on the *New York Times* Best Seller List, including *Rush Limbaugh Is a Big, Fat Idiot and Other Observations* and *Lies and the Lying Liars Who Tell Them: A Fair and Balanced Look at the Right*. His politics was clearly on the left.

On the more serious side, Al Franken was a regular performer starting in 1999 for the United Service Organizations (USO), visiting troops in Kosovo, Iraq, Uzbekistan, and Afghanistan, as well as military hospitals. He was awarded the USO's Merit Award for his 10 years of service in 2009. Franken also was a Fellow at Harvard's Kennedy School of Government in 2003.

In 2004, Franken turned his attention to talk radio, becoming host of *The Al Franken Show* on left-wing Air America for three hours a day. On his last day in 2007, Franken announced his candidacy for the U.S. Senate. In 2005, he and his family moved to Minneapolis to prepare for this political run. Also in 2005, Franken started his Midwest Values PAC (political action committee), which raised over $1 million in about a year. The election in 2008 was very close and ballot issues resulted in its being decided by the courts. On June 30, 2009, Franken was declared the winner.

In the Senate, Franken's first legislation was the bipartisan Service Dogs for Veterans Act. He often filled in for a missing president pro tempore, and presided over the confirmation hearings for Supreme Court Justices Sotomayor and Kagan. To the disappointment of many, Senator Franken takes his duties very seriously.

Court justices, cabinet members, federal judges, ambassadors, and other high executive officials. Although the Senate generally approves the presidential nominations, the added potential for power contributes to the difference between the influence of senators and of House members. Finally, senators serve six-year terms and represent broader and more heterogeneous constituencies. Thus, they have a longer guaranteed tenure in Washington, more prestige, and greater freedom from minor shifts in opinion among nongovernmental elites in their home states (see Focus: Senator Al Franken).

Senators can enhance their power through their political roles; they often wield great power in state parties and can usually control federal patronage dispensed in their state. The power of the Senate to confirm nominations has given rise to the important political custom of **senatorial courtesy**: Senators of the same party as the president have virtual veto power over major appointments—federal judges, postmasters, customs collectors, and so on—in their states. Presidential nominations that go to the Senate are referred to the senator or senators from the relevant state. If the senator declares the nominee personally obnoxious to him or her, the Senate usually respects this declaration and rejects the appointment. Thus, before submitting a nomination to the Senate, the president usually makes sure the nominee will be acceptable to the party's senator or senators from that state.

The position of senator combines a high degree of power with a relatively minimal level of responsibility. If a senator misses a vote while campaigning or ill, the Senate still functions. If a policy turns out to be unpopular, a senator can hide behind the fact that up to 99 others shared the decision. It is perhaps the optimal elite position, with substantial power, high prestige, and minimal accountability.

THE SPEAKER OF THE HOUSE

Party leadership roles in the House and the Senate are major sources of power in Washington. (See Table 8.5 for a list of Senate and House leaders for the 112th Congress, 2011–2013.) The Speaker of the House of Representatives, elected by the majority party of the House, exercises more power over public policy than any other single member of either house. Before 1910, the speaker appointed all standing committees and their chairs, possessed unlimited discretion to recognize members on the floor, and served as chair of the Rules Committee. But in 1910, progressives severely curtailed the speaker's authority. Today the speaker shares power over committee appointments with the Committee on Committees; committee chairs are selected largely by seniority, not by the speaker; and the speaker no

TABLE 8.5 | LEADERSHIP IN THE 112TH CONGRESS, 2011–2013

House of Representatives	Senate
Speaker of the House—John Boehner, R-Ohio	President—Joseph Biden, D. U.S. Vice President
	President pro tempore—Daniel Inouye, D-Hawaii
Democrats	**Democrats**
Minority leader—Nancy Pelosi, Calif.	Majority leader—Harry Reid, Nev.
Minority whip—Steny Hoyer, Md.	Majority whip—Richard J. Durbin, Ill.
Assistant minority leader—James Clyburn, S.C.	Chief deputy majority whip—Barbara Boxer, Calif.
Caucus chair—John Larson, Conn.	Democratic Senatorial Campaign Committee chair and Conference secretary—Patty Murray, Wash.
Caucus vice chair—Xavier Becerra, Calif.	
Democratic Congressional Campaign Committee chair—Chris Van Hollen (D-Md.)	Policy Committee chair and Conference vice chair—Charles Schumer, N.Y.
Republicans	**Republicans**
Majority leader—Eric Cantor, Vir.	Minority leader—Mitch McConnell, Ky.
Majority whip—Kevin McCarthy, Calif.	Minority whip—Jon Kyl, Ariz.
Conference chair—Jeb Hensarling, Tex.	Conference vice chair—Lisa Murkowski, Alaska
Conference vice chair—Roy Blunt (R-Mo.)	Policy Committee chair—John Thune, S.Dak.
Conference secretary—John Carter, Tex.	National Republican Senatorial Committee chair—John Cornyn, Tex.
Policy chair—John Barrasso (R-Wyo.)	
National Republican Congressional Committee chair—Peter Sessions, Tex.	

longer serves as chair of the Rules Committee. However, the speaker retains considerable authority by referring bills to committees, appointing all conference committees, ruling on all matters of House procedure, recognizing those who wish to speak, and generally directing the business of the floor. More important, the speaker is the principal figure in House policy formulation, leadership, and responsibility. Although sharing these tasks with standing committee chairs, the speaker is generally "first among equals" in relation to them. The speaker is also third in line for the presidency.

FLOOR LEADERS AND WHIPS

Next to the speaker, the most influential party leaders in the House are the majority and minority floor leaders and party whips. These are chosen by their respective party caucuses at the beginning of each congressional session. The party caucus, composed of all the party's members in the House, usually does little more than elect these officers; it makes no major policy decisions. The floor leaders and whips have little formal authority; their role is to influence legislation through persuasion. Party floor leaders must combine parliamentary skill with persuasion, maintain good personal relationships with party members, and cultivate close ties with the president and administration. They cannot deny party re-nomination to members who are disloyal to the party, but because they can control committee assignments and many small favors in Washington, they can prevent a maverick from becoming an effective legislator.

A **whip**, or assistant floor leader, keeps members informed about legislative business, sees that members are present for important floor votes, and communicates party strategy and position on particular issues. Whips also serve as the eyes and ears of the leadership, counting support before important votes. Party whips should know how many votes a particular measure has, and they should be able to get the votes to the floor when the roll is called.

SENATE LEADERSHIP

The vice president of the United States, who serves as president of the Senate, has little control over Senate affairs and votes only in case of a tie. This made the vice president particularly needed in 2001, when the Senate was split evenly between Republicans and Democrats. The majority party in the Senate also elects from its membership a president *pro tempore,* traditionally the longest-serving member, who presides in the absence of the vice president. Senators must be recognized in the order in which they rise. In actuality, presiding over the Senate is such a tedious task that it often falls to junior senators.

The key power figures in the Senate are the majority and minority leaders, chosen by their respective parties. The majority leader usually has great personal sway within the Senate and is influential in national affairs. When of the same party as the president, he or she is in charge of getting the president's legislative program through the Senate. Although possessed of somewhat less formal authority than the Speaker of the House, the Senate majority leader has the right to be the first senator to be heard on the floor and, with the minority floor leader, determines the Senate's agenda. But on the whole, the majority leader's influence rests on powers of persuasion.

COMMITTEE CHAIRS

The committee system and the seniority rule also create powerful congressional figures: the chairs of the most powerful standing committees. The standing committee system is self-sustaining because an attack on the authority of one committee or committee chairperson is much like a threat to all; members know that if they allow one committee or committee chairperson to be bypassed on a particular measure, they open the door to similar infringements of power. Hence, committee chairs and ranking committee members tend to stand by one another and support one another's authority over legislation assigned to their respective committees.

Committee chairs and ranking committee members also earn respect because of their seniority and experience in the legislative process. They are often experts in parliamentary process as well as in the substantive area covered by their committees. Finally, and perhaps most important, committee chairs and ranking committee members acquire power through their close relationships with the bureaucratic and interest-group elites within their committee's jurisdiction.

LEADERSHIP PACs

Money is another source of power for congressional leaders of both parties. They, as well as some individual members of Congress, maintain their own **leadership PACs**. Contributors to these PACs increase their influence with the leadership, and the congressional leaders increase their influence with members by distributing PAC money to supporters in Congress, thus making it more likely to be elected to leadership and key committee chair positions. Leadership PACs are separate from the leaders' personal campaign funds (see Table 8.6).

POLARIZATION ON CAPITOL HILL

Politics on Capitol Hill has become increasingly highly polarized. The Republicans are more uniformly opposing government growth and spending than ever, and the Democrats are more committed to federal government expansion than in previous years. The proportion of political moderates—conservative Democrats or liberal Republicans—hovered at about 30 percent in the 1960s and 1970s, but the number has plummeted. Few of today's lawmakers fall into this centrist category.[15] The result is more conflict, less bipartisan cooperation, more gridlock, and more acrimony in the halls of Congress.

The most common explanation for this increased polarization is the dealignment of southern conservative voters from the Democratic Party. Southern conservatives began voting almost en bloc for the Republican Party in the 1980s, although most retained Democratic Party membership. As the South advanced economically, its new middle class tended to register Republican. As conservatives gained strength in the Republican Party, liberal Republicans, mostly from the Northeast, lost ground. Geographically, the Republican Party became centered in

TABLE 8.6 | Top 10 Congressional Leadership PACs, 2010 Cycle

Every Republican is Crucial PAC	Eric Cantor (R-Vir.)	House majority leader
Freedom Project	John A. Boehner (R-Ohio)	Speaker of the House
AmeriPAC	Steny H. Hoyer (D-Md.)	House minority whip
PAC to the Future	Nancy Pelosi (D-Calif.)	House minority leader
Keep Our Majority	Dennis Hastert (R-Ill.)	Former speaker of the House
Victory Now PAC	Chris Van Hollen (D-Md.)	Democratic Congressional Campaign Committee chair
Continuing a Majority Party Action Committee	David Camp (R-Mich.)	Chair, Ways and Means Committee
Majority Committee PAC	Kevin McCarthy (R-Calif.)	House majority whip
Democrats Win Seats PAC	Debbie Wasserman-Schultz (D-Fla.)	Chair, Democratic National Committee
Prosperity PAC	Paul Ryan (R-Wis.)	Chair, House Budget Committee

Source: Center for Responsive Politics. *www.opensecrets.org/pacs/industry.php?txt=Q03&cycle=2010.*

the Mountain States and the South, while the Democratic Party held on to the Northeast and the West Coast. Voters have also sorted themselves by moving to areas with like-minded political views.

PARTY VOTING

Party votes, those roll-call votes in which a majority of voting Democrats oppose a majority of voting Republicans, occur on more than half the roll-call votes in Congress. Indeed, roll-call voting follows party lines more often than it follows sectional, urban–rural, or any other divisions that have been studied. How much cohesion exists within the parties? Members of both parties vote with their party majority more than 80 percent of the time.

However, party-line votes are the result more of members' personal predispositions than of explicitly formulated party policy. We can make the distinction between party "regularity," which is strong, and party organization and discipline, of which there is very little.

CONFLICT

Conflict between parties occurs most frequently over taxation, social-welfare programs, health care, the environment, "values" issues, and the regulation of business and labor. It is particularly apparent on spending and taxing proposals in the budget. The budget is the president's product and carries the label of the president's party. By 2012, the strongest divide was on the issue of the size and role of government. On some issues, voting generally follows party lines during roll calls on preliminary motions and amendments but swings to a bipartisan vote on the final legislation. In such situations the parties disagree on certain aspects of the bill but compromise on its final passage, as long as bills are amended to provide sufficient benefits to legislators voting for it to provide political cover.

CONGRESS AND THE PRESIDENT: AN UNSTABLE BALANCE OF POWER

How do the roles of Congress and those of the other governmental elites differ? Policy proposals are usually initiated outside Congress with the president, bureaucratic elites, and interested nongovernmental elites. Congress does not merely ratify or rubber-stamp decisions; it plays an independent role in the policy-making process. But that role is essentially deliberative; Congress accepts, modifies, or rejects the policies initiated by others. For example, the annual federal budget, perhaps the most important policy document of the national government, is written by executive elites and modified by the president before Congress receives it. Congress is the critical conduit through which appropriations and revenue measures must pass, but sophisticated lawmakers are aware that they function largely as arbiters rather than initiators of public policy.

However, the relationship between Congress and other policy-making elites is not necessarily stable. Whether Congress merely ratifies the decisions of others or asserts its voice independently depends on many factors, such as the aggressiveness and political skills of the president, the strength of congressional leadership, and whether there is divided party control of the White House and Capitol Hill. A politically weakened president, combined with opposition party control of the Congress, provides the environment for congressional assertions of power.

MASS PREFERENCE FOR DIVIDED GOVERNMENT

The masses do not appear to want "responsible-party government"—in which the winning party in an election is fully responsible for public policy. When asked, "Which is better for the country—one political party running both the White House and Congress or each being run by a different political party?" 30 percent said one party and 45 percent favored different parties. Among Democrats, who controlled Congress and the White House at the time of the poll, only 46 percent preferred single-party control. Among Republicans and Independents the majority preferred split control.[16]

THE POWER OF THE PURSE

Budget

Theoretically, Congress can control the president through its power over government spending. The Constitution (Article I, Section 9) states that "no money shall be drawn from the Treasury, but in consequence of appropriations made by law." Congress can withhold funds or place elaborate restrictions on the use of funds to work its will over the president. But even through the use of budgetary power, its most effective tool, Congress has *not* been able to dominate the presidency. More often than not, the president's budget recommendations are accepted by Congress with relatively minor changes (see Chapter 11).

PRESIDENTIAL SUPPORT

The president generally receives greater support from his own party than from the opposition party in Congress. Thus, the presidents who have run up the highest legislative "box scores"—victories for bills they supported—are those whose party has controlled one or both houses of Congress (see "The President and Congress" in Chapter 9).

Occasionally, Congress and the president have engaged in highly publicized budgetary battles. Most famously, President Clinton twice vetoed budget resolutions passed by the Republican-controlled Congress in late 1995. The federal government temporarily shut down because appropriations acts had not been passed. But when opinion polls showed that more people blamed Congress than the president for the gridlock, Congress relented and sent the president a budget that more closely reflected his preferences. George W. Bush vetoed four appropriations bills in 2007 and 2008, which Congress then modified for his approval.

CONGRESSIONAL INVESTIGATIONS

Congress retains the power to embarrass a presidential administration and occasionally even to force it to change course through congressional investigations. Such investigations, with the cooperation of the television media, can compel presidents to abandon unpopular actions. The Watergate hearings of 1973–1974 and the Iran-Contra hearings in 1987 remain two of the most historically prominent. Congress is also supposed to police itself (see Focus: Congressional Ethics: An Oxymoron?)

Most congressional investigations are conducted by standing committees of Congress. Occasionally, however, investigations are deemed so important as to merit the appointment of independent commissions. This was the case in 1963, when President Lyndon Johnson appointed a President's Commission on the Assassination of President John F. Kennedy, chaired by Supreme Court Chief Justice Earl Warren; its findings were distributed as the "Warren Report." In 2002 the president and Congress created the National Commission on Terrorist Attacks upon the United States; this Commission issued its widely read *9/11 Commission Report* in 2004.

IMPEACHMENT

The ultimate congressional power over the president is the threat of **impeachment**. It is a two-part process in which the House investigates and votes on whether to impeach an executive or judicial officer, followed by a trial in the Senate. Despite the Constitution's admonition that impeachment can be voted only for "Treason, Bribery, and other high Crimes and Misdemeanors" (Article II, Section 4), all impeachment movements in U.S. history have developed on political grounds (see Chapter 9).

Despite pious rhetoric in Congress about the "search for truth," "impartial investigation," and "unbiased constitutional judgment," the impeachment process, whatever the merits of the charges against a president, is political, not judicial. The 1998 House vote to impeach President Clinton (which passed 228 to 206) followed partisan lines, with all but five Republicans voting yes and all but five Democrats voting no. The subsequent Senate trial of the President was perfunctory. Although Republicans held a slim majority in the Senate, they lacked the necessary two-thirds vote to remove Clinton from office. Indeed, Republican leaders failed even to obtain a majority vote for conviction.

CONGRESSIONAL ETHICS: AN OXYMORON?

Congressional ethics has long simmered as an issue on Capitol Hill, occasionally boiling over into well-publicized scandals.

Bribery is a criminal act: It is illegal to solicit or receive anything of value in return for the performance of a governmental duty. Congress members are expected to perform services for their political contributors, but a direct quid pro quo—receiving a financial contribution specifically for the performance of a particular service—is illegal. Few Congress members would be so foolish as to openly quote a potential contributor a price for a specific service, and most contributors know not to state a dollar amount for performing such a service.

Yet scandals have tarnished the image of Congress. During its notorious Abscam investigation in 1980, the FBI set up a sting operation with agents posing as wealthy foreign Arabs offering bribe money to legislators while secretly videotaping the transactions. Six representatives and one senator were convicted; only one member of Congress approached by the FBI turned down the bribe.

Rep. Randy Cunningham resigned in 2005 after pleading guilty to charges of accepting $2.4 million in bribes from lobbyists. In 2006, Rep. Tom DeLay was forced to step down as Republican majority leader and later resigned from Congress over campaign finance violations (he did, however, go on to compete on TV's *Dancing with the Stars*), and Rep. Bob Ney was convicted of conspiracy to commit fraud. Rep. William Jefferson was forced to resign his committee posts after an FBI raid found $90,000 in alleged bribe money in his home freezer (he lost his re-election bid in 2008).

Other representatives and senators have resigned following charges of sexual misconduct, including Senator Robert Packwood, who faced official expulsion following a Senate Ethics Committee report in 1995 charging him with numerous counts of sexual harassment of female staff, and Rep. Tom Foley in 2006 over a pending investigation into sexually inappropriate e-mail messages to teenage congressional pages.

Congress has an interest in maintaining the integrity of the institution itself. Its rules of ethics include the following: All members must file personal financial statements each year; members cannot accept fees for speeches or personal appearances; surplus campaign funds cannot be put to personal use; members may not accept gifts worth more than $50; former members may not lobby Congress for at least one year after retirement. In 2007, the House strengthened the rules: Members and staff may not accept *any* gifts or meals from lobbyists; lobbyists cannot pay for members' travel; and requests for earmarks require the disclosure of their sponsors as well as justifications and certification that they will not benefit lawmakers or their spouses.

The Constitution (Article I, Section 5) gives Congress the power to discipline its own members. "Each House may … punish its Members for disorderly Behavior, and, with the Concurrence of two thirds, expel a Member." This is seldom done. In 1994 the powerful chair of the House Ways and Means Committee, Dan Rostenkowski, was indicted by a federal grand jury for misuse of congressional office funds. He refused to resign and Congress did not expel him, but his Chicago constituents voted him out of office. Only 20 members of Congress have ever been expelled: 17 for supporting the Confederacy during the Civil War period, one in 1797 for treason, one of the Abscam bribe takers in 1980, and in 2002 Representative James A. Traficant, who was expelled from the House *after* his conviction on 10 federal corruption charges.

A lesser punishment then expulsion is official censure. Censured members are obliged to "stand in the well" and listen to charges read against them. It is supposed to be a humiliating experience and fatal to the member's political career. Rep. Barney Frank was censured for sexual misconduct with congressional pages in 1983, but he was regularly reelected by his Massachusetts constituents until his retirement in 2013. In 2010, House Ways and Means Committee Chair Charles Rangel was forced to step down from that key position when the full House voted to censure him for a series of ethical violations including misuse of rent-controlled apartments, not paying taxes on rental income of his villa in the Dominican Republic, and improper fundraising. Still lesser forms of punishment include a public reprimand by the Ethics Committee and orders to repay funds improperly received.

Why is the impeachment of a president so rare, even during periods of divided government? Opinion polls clearly indicated that most U.S. adults did not believe Clinton's misconduct should result in his removal from office. (See Focus: Sex, Lies, and Impeachment, in Chapter 9.) A public backlash appeared to develop: Clinton's approval ratings actually *rose* after the House action, and his high popular approval ratings appeared to be the key to his acquittal by the Senate.

CONGRESS | AN ELITIST INTERPRETATION

Congress was designed to be the most powerful branch of government and the House of Representatives to represent "the people." This is not an accurate description of Congress today. Rather, elite theory suggests several contrary propositions regarding Congress.

1. Congress tends to represent locally organized elites, who inject a strong parochial influence into national decision making. Members of Congress are responsible to national interests that have a strong base of support in their home constituencies.

2. A member's relevant political constituency is not the general population of the home district but its elite. Less than half the general population of a district knows its legislator's name; fewer still have any idea how their representative voted on any major issue. Only a tiny fraction ever express their views to their legislators.

3. Congress seldom initiates changes in public policy. Instead, it responds to policy proposals initiated by the president, executive, and interested nongovernmental elites. The congressional role in national decision making is usually deliberative: Congress responds to policies initiated by others.

4. Congressional committees are important to communication between governmental and nongovernmental elites. "Iron triangles" consisting of alliances of leaders from executive agencies, congressional committees, and private business and industry tend to develop in Washington. Committee chairs are central because of their control over legislation in Congress.

5. The elaborate rules and procedures of Congress delay and obstruct proposed new laws, making Congress more a mechanism for stopping legislation than for passing it.

6. An elite system within Congress places effective control over legislation in the hands of relatively few members. Most of these congressional establishment members from both parties come from heavily partisan "safe" districts and have acquired seniority and control key committee chairs.

7. Most bills that do not die before the floor vote pass unanimously. The greatest portion of the national budget passes without debate. Conflict in Congress tends to follow party lines more often than any other factional division. It centers on the details of domestic and foreign policy but seldom on its major directions.

NOTES

1. Jennifer E. Manning, "Membership of the 11th Congress: A Profile," Congressional Research Service. March 1, 2011. http://www.senate.gov/resources/pdf/R41647.pdf
2. Ibid.
3. Center for Responsive Politics. "Personal Finances: Overview," 2011. http://www.opensecrets.org/pfds/averages.php
4. Michael X. DelliCarpini and Scott Keeter, "The U.S. Public's Knowledge of Politics," *Public Opinion Quarterly*, 55 (May 1991): 583–612.
5. Warren Miller and Donald Stokes, "Constituency Influence in Congress," *American Political Science Review*, 57 (March 1963).
6. Richard Fenno, *Home Style* (Boston: Little, Brown, 1978). The classic description of how attention to constituency by members of Congress enhances their reelection prospects. Home-style activities, including casework, pork-barreling, travel and appearances back home, newsletters, and surveys, are described in detail.
7. Richard Fenno, *The Making of a Senator* (Washington, DC: CQ Press, 1989), p. 119.
8. Jeffrey M. Jones, "Record 64% Rate Honesty, Ethics of Members of Congress Low" Gallup.

December 12, 2011. http://www.gallup.com/poll/151460/record-rate-honesty-ethics-members-congress-low.aspx
9. Manning, "Membership of the 112th Congress."
10. Center for Responsive Politics, "Election Stats," 2011. http://www.opensecrets.org/bigpicture/elec_stats.php?cycle=2010
11. Barbara Sinclair, *Unorthodox Lawmaking*, 3rd ed. (Washington, DC: CQ Press, 2007). A description with case studies of the various detours and shortcuts a major bill is likely to take in Congress.
12. Woodrow Wilson, *Congressional Government* (1885; reprint, New York: Meridian Books, 1956), p. 178.
13. John W. Kingdon, *Congressmen's Voting Decisions* (New York: Harper & Row, 1973), p. 62.
14. Kingdon, *Voting Decisions*, p. 88.
15. See Juliet Eilperin, *Fight Club Politics* (Lanham, MD: Rowen & Littlefield, 2006).
16. Rasmussen Reports, "30% Favor One Party Running the White House and Congress," November 7, 2009. http://www.rasmussenreports.com/public_content/politics/general_politics/november_2009/30_favor_one_party_running_the_white_house_and_congress

The Presidency is the focus for the most intense and persistent emotions....
The President is ... the one figure who draws together the people's hopes
and fears for the political future.

—James David Barber

THE PRESIDENCY

Governmental elites in the United States do not command; they seek consensus with other elites. Decision making thus is a process of bargaining, accommodation, and compromise among the dominant interests in society. The presidency stands at the center of this elite interaction. For the elite, the president proposes policy initiatives, mobilizes influence within the political system, and supervises the management of government and the economy. For the masses, the president is a symbol of national unity, the most visible member of the elite, an outlet to express their emotions toward government, and a vicarious means of taking political action. For *both* elites and masses, the presidency provides a means of handling national crises—taking whatever actions necessary in an emergency to stabilize the nation, protect its security, and calm its citizens (see Table 9.1).

The president of the United States has two primary jobs: **head of government** and **chief of state**. As head of government the president functions as the chief of the executive branch, the pinnacle of the vast system of federal government including the military, wielding power and making decisions that can affect the lives of millions. Still, presidential power is constrained; the role exists within the system of checks and balances set up by the Founders, who feared each president was a potential tyrant. (In many other nations, these two roles are handled by two different people; for example, in Great Britain, the prime minister heads the government while the monarch serves as chief of state.) Some chief of state duties are formal, such as representing the nation in receiving foreign rulers, but it is mostly a symbolic function: the president is the living symbol of the nation. Yet in this role the president's impact is potentially greater than in the formal executive job; this is the president as celebrity-in-chief.

TABLE 9.1 | PRESIDENTS OF THE UNITED STATES

	Name	Dates Served	Party
1	George Washington	1789–1797	Federalist
2	John Adams	1797–1801	Federalist
3	Thomas Jefferson	1801–1809	Democratic-Republican
4	James Madison	1809–1817	Democratic-Republican
5	James Monroe	1817–1825	Democratic-Republican
6	John Quincy Adams	1825–1829	Democratic-Republican
7	Andrew Jackson	1829–1837	Democrat
8	Martin Van Buren	1837–1841	Democrat
9	William Henry Harrison	1841	Whig
10	John Tyler	1841–1845	Whig
11	James Polk	1845–1849	Democrat
12	Zachary Taylor	1849–1850	Whig
13	Millard Fillmore	1850–1853	Whig
14	Franklin Pierce	1853–1857	Democrat
15	James Buchanan	1857–1861	Democrat
16	Abraham Lincoln	1861–1865	Republican
17	Andrew Johnson	1965–1869	Democrat
18	Ulysses Grant	1869–1877	Republican
19	Rutherford Hayes	1877–1881	Republican
20	James Garfield	1881	Republican
21	Chester Arthur	1881–1885	Republican
22 & 24	Grover Cleveland	1885–1889 & 1893–1897	Democrat
23	Benjamin Harrison	1889–1893	Republican
25	William McKinley	1897–1901	Republican
26	Theodore Roosevelt	1901–1909	Republican
27	William Taft	1909–1913	Republican
28	Woodrow Wilson	1913–1921	Democrat
29	Warren Harding	1921–1923	Republican
30	Calvin Coolidge	1923–1929	Republican
31	Herbert Hoover	1929–1933	Republican
32	Franklin Roosevelt	1933–1945	Democrat
33	Harry Truman	1945–1953	Democrat
34	Dwight Eisenhower	1953–1961	Republican
35	John Kennedy	1961–1963	Democrat
36	Lyndon Johnson	1963–1969	Democrat

TABLE 9.1 | PRESIDENTS OF THE UNITED STATES *continued*

	Name	Dates Served	Party
37	Richard Nixon	1969–1974	Republican
38	Gerald Ford	1974–1977	Republican
39	James Carter	1977–1981	Democrat
40	Ronald Reagan	1981–1989	Republican
41	George H. W. Bush	1989–1993	Republican
42	William Clinton	1993–2001	Democrat
43	George W. Bush	2001–2009	Republican
44	Barack Obama	2009–2017	Democrat

THE PRESIDENT AS SYMBOLIC LEADER

More than any other political figure, the president attracts the attention and emotion of the masses in the United States and even worldwide. The people look to the presidency for leadership and reassurance. They want a president who will personalize government, simplify political issues, and symbolize the protective as well as the compassionate role of the state. They want someone who seems concerned about their safety and welfare. This is the president as chief of state, or national symbol.

The presidency possesses enormous symbolic significance and affects popular images of authority, legitimacy, and confidence in the political system. The incumbent can arouse feelings of patriotism or cynicism, hope or despair, honor or dishonor. Political scientist James David Barber wrote:

> The Presidency is the focus for the most intense and persistent emotions ... The President is ... the one figure who draws together the people's hopes and fears for the political future. On top of all of his routine duties, he has to carry that off—or fail.[1]

PRESIDENTIAL APPROVAL RATINGS

The people look for toughness, competence, and decisiveness in the presidency. They are prepared to support a president who is willing to *do something,* whether "something" is a good idea or not. National surveys regularly gauge presidential popularity by asking, "Do you approve or disapprove of the way (___) is handling the job as president?"

All presidents begin their terms with broad public support; people *want* to support the country's leader and popular expectations far exceed the president's powers to meet them. Indeed, over time support wanes as troubles pile up and the president is unable to cope with them. The result is an inevitable decline in public support until a new crisis occurs or dramatic action is necessary. President

Obama began in January 2009 with considerable mass goodwill based on his campaign for bipartisanship, fiscal responsibility, and "hope." His approval rating fell faster in his first year than that of any president since Truman due to inflated expectations.

A brief overview of presidential popularity ratings over time confirms the pattern. Figure 9.1 compares approval ratings of eight presidents. Each took office with broad popular support. Over time this support declined. But dramatic action—peace in Vietnam for Nixon, the assassination attempt on Reagan, victory in the Persian Gulf War for the elder Bush, and the terrorist attack of September 11 early in George W. Bush's presidency—produced dramatic increases in presidential support.

Presidential Approval RealClearPolitics.com uses averaging to bring together multiple polls for the president, Congress, and other public opinion information. *www.realclearpolitics.com/epolls/latestpolls/*

Nothing inspires elite support among the masses more than *decisive* military victory. President George H. W. Bush achieved nearly 90 percent public approval ratings following victory in the Persian Gulf War. This unprecedented peak was followed by a rapid slide as the nation turned its attention to the economic recession at home. George W. Bush at first matched his father's historic peak in approval ratings following the terrorist attack on the United States of September 11, 2001, and the successful ousting of the terrorist-supporting Taliban regime in Afghanistan. But his ratings gradually slumped with continuing insurgent attacks, almost daily casualties, and no end to the conflict in sight. They did not recover even when the Iraq "surge" strategy introduced in 2007 proved successful.

The Vietnam War brought down Lyndon Johnson and led to his decision not to run for re-election in 1968, and Iran's holding of U.S. embassy employees hostage for more than a year battered Jimmy Carter's popularity. Only during World War II (1941–1945) did approval of the president—Franklin D. Roosevelt—remain high for the duration of the conflict.

Recessions also erode presidential popularity. Arguably, presidents can do little about economic cycles, but the masses hold them responsible anyhow. Early in Ronald Reagan's term, a recession undercut the well-liked president's approval ratings. The steepest decline in presidential approval ever recorded came after the elder President Bush's victory in the Persian Gulf War and the onset of a recession (and a broken promise not to raise taxes). Barack Obama's first year saw unemployment increase to over 10 percent, which weighed heavily on the decline in his approval ratings; the lack of job growth after the recession's end kept his ratings down, usually below 50 percent.

Scandals in a presidential administration usually undermine presidential popularity. Indeed, the Watergate affair (see Focus: Watergate and the Limits of Presidential Power) brought Richard Nixon to a new low in presidential polls just before his resignation. Gerald Ford suffered for pardoning Nixon. Reagan was hurt by the Iran-Contra scandal in his second term. Paradoxically, Bill Clinton's popularity benefitted from the sex scandal that engulfed him in his second term. His approval ratings went *up* when the scandal broke and when the House of Representatives voted for impeachment, due to the public's perception that the matter was private and unrelated to his presidential duties (see Focus: Sex, Lies, and Impeachment).

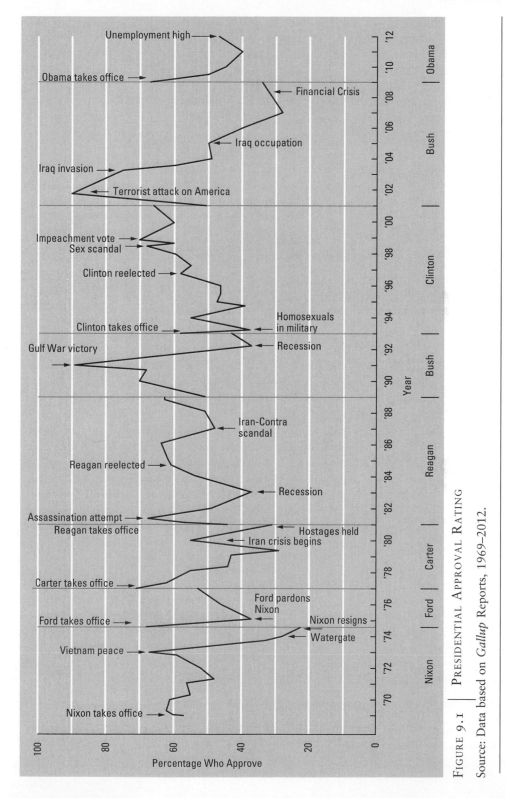

FIGURE 9.1 | PRESIDENTIAL APPROVAL RATING

Source: Data based on *Gallup* Reports, 1969–2012.

www.politicalcartoons.com/cartoon/43f78db3-a6ea-45ed-88bb-4cd6a2281ea5.html

CELEBRITY-IN-CHIEF

The president is the leading celebrity in the nation and possibly the world, with instant name and face recognition. Television networks cancel their regular programming and provide free air time when the president chooses to address the nation, and the media chronicle life in the White House down to the name of the president's dog and favorite sports and personal details about the First Family.[2] President Clinton was seen as a rock star and referred to as Elvis, Reagan had already been a successful movie star before entering political life, Teddy Roosevelt had a toy named after him, and Kennedy cultivated a fashionable, sexy modern image. Obama also became a star, with 63.2 million U.S. viewers watching him debate McCain and 37.8 million tuning in for his inauguration.[3] His books sold millions, and the audio version won two Grammy awards. Obama entered the popular culture in an unprecedented manner as the focus of countless "collectible" merchandise from clothing to comic books (see Focus: President as Superhero).

IN BRIEF | PRESIDENTIAL APPROVAL

- Presidential approval among the masses is high:
  - During the "honeymoon" period at start of a term.
  - During crises.
  - When decisive military action is taken.

- Presidential approval erodes:
  - Over time in office.
  - During military stalemates.
  - In economic recessions.
  - During political scandals.

FOCUS | PRESIDENT AS SUPERHERO

The 2008 election saw the creation of the world's newest, most famous celebrity: Barack Obama. In addition to his appealing slogans of "hope" and "change," the young new president was cast as a specially gifted politician who could right the wrongs of the nation. The image of political leader as more than human reflects the mass desire to be rescued from economic, political, and personal woes. Posters and T-shirts of Obama as Superman began to appear widely. His appearance in issue #583 of *The Amazing Spider-Man* went through five printings, joining the vast quantity of Obama collectibles including trading cards, dolls and action figures, and clothing. As with almost all celebrities, the peak of fame was followed by a decline to "normal" human levels of popularity.

http://marvel.com/comics/onsale/lib/view2.htm?filename=/i/content/st/6546new_storyimage-1430468_full.jpg

The president frequently will capture the Zeitgeist of the nation, the "spirit of the times."[4] This can be a sense of optimism such as Kennedy, Reagan, and Obama brought, or a feeling of pessimism such as Nixon and Carter enveloped. When the masses seek an expression of the Zeitgeist and their mood, it can be a real reflection of the times or sometimes just an aspiration to feel better.

THE PRESIDENT AND MASS PSYCHOLOGY

The White House Official presidency site with news and information, presidential policy views, speeches, etc., plus links to all executive agencies. *www.whitehouse.gov*

Political scientist Fred Greenstein classified five "psychological functions of the presidency."[5] First, the president functions as a cognitive tool for the masses, helping them better understand the government and its function. For example, the legislative process (see Chapter 8) can be convoluted and difficult to follow, but anyone can understand the president giving a signature. Second, a president provides an outlet for emotional expression, like a movie screen on which people can project their feelings and frustrations. If times are hard, the president often gets blamed even though he or she has little to no power over the economy. Conversely, presidents benefit from being the national symbol when times are good. Usually, neither the blame nor the praise is merited.

Third, the president is a symbol of unity and nationhood. When a national tragedy such as the 2001 terrorist attacks occurs, people fly flags and support their president, as both are national symbols. Fourth, a president will provide the masses with a "vicarious means of taking political action" by acting decisively and effectively while they cannot. Each individual can think "If I were president …" Lastly, the president is a symbol of social stability, providing the masses with a feeling of security and guidance.

A classic illustration of the psychological role of the president came on the evening of September 11, 2001, when President George W. Bush spoke to the nation's people from the Oval Office in a nationally televised address:

> The pictures of airplanes flying into buildings, fires burning, huge structures collapsing, have filled us with disbelief, terrible sadness, and a quiet, unyielding anger. These mass murders were intended to frighten our citizens into chaos and retreat. But they failed, our country's strong …. These deliberate and deadly attacks were more than acts of terror. They were acts of war.

Later the president spoke standing side by side with firefighters and rescue workers at the site of the World Trade Center. Both words and pictures were designed to reassure the people that the president and the U.S. government were committed to dealing effectively with this new crisis.

Presidential Character

Traditionally, the public expected presidents to be exemplary in their personal lives. James David Barber, in his book *The Presidential Character*, observed:

> The President is expected to personify our virtuousness in an inspiring way, to express in what he does and is (not just what he says) a moral idealism which, in the public mind, is the very opposite of politics.[6]

In the past the news media protected the president by not reporting on private moral conduct. John Kennedy's encounters with a number of women, including movie star Marilyn Monroe and mobster girlfriend Judith Exner, were widely known during his term in office but not revealed publicly until after his death.[7]

The masses appear to distinguish between private morality and public trust in the president. Even before President Clinton's admission of "inappropriate behavior" with Monica Lewinsky, the overwhelming majority believed he had engaged in a sexual affair with the 21-year-old White House intern. Yet although the public held a negative opinion about Clinton "as a person" (58 percent), people continued to give him strong support in his handling of his job as president (68 percent).[8]

Presidential Powers of Persuasion

The presidency's real power depends not on formal authority but on the power to persuade.[9] In a system of checks and balances, while responsibility for initiating public policy falls principally on the president and White House staff and executive departments, Congress does not necessarily follow a president's wishes. The president must persuade others in the political system, through charm, reason, or threats, that what he or she wants is what they want as well.

IN BRIEF | PSYCHOLOGICAL ROLES OF PRESIDENTS

According to Fred Greenstein, the president

- "Simplifies perception of government and politics" by serving as the main cognitive tool for providing citizens insight into their government.
- Provides "an outlet for emotional expression."
- Is a "symbol of unity" and of nationhood (as national shock and grief over the death of a president clearly reveal).

- Provides the masses with a "vicarious means of taking political action" in that the president can act decisively and effectively while they cannot do so.
- Is a "symbol of social stability" in providing the masses with a feeling of security and guidance.

The status and authority of the office work to reinforce a president's arguments and ability to charm and threaten. Through the power to initiate policy alone, the president's influence on the nation is considerable. The president sets the agenda for public decision making, frames the issues, and decides their timing by presenting programs to Congress in various presidential messages, including the annual State of the Union message and the draft of the annual government budget. The president thereby largely determines the business of Congress in any session, and few major undertakings get off the ground without White House initiation. But none of this means a president gets what he or she wants.

As celebrity and media star, a president can also work to influence the political system by appealing directly to the people.[10] Reagan referred to this as "going over the heads" of Congress when he tried to get legislative support for his measures by appealing to public opinion. The idea was first clearly laid out by Theodore Roosevelt who viewed the presidency as a "bully pulpit."

THE PRESIDENT'S FORMAL POWERS

The president has many sources of formal power as chief executive, chief legislator, party leader, chief diplomat, commander-in-chief, and crisis manager. But despite the great powers of the office, no president can control policy-making. The president functions within an established elite system and can exercise power only within the framework of that system, and its checks and balances. The choices are only those alternatives for which elite consensus can be mobilized. The president must be sensitive to the interests of major elites—business, agriculture, military, education, bureaucracy, and so on.

CHIEF EXECUTIVE

The president is the chief executive of the nation's largest bureaucracy: 15 departments, 60 independent agencies, 2.8 million civilian employees, and a large executive office. An organizational chart of the federal government (see Figure 11.1 in Chapter 11) places the president at the head of this giant bureaucracy. But the president cannot really govern this bureaucracy in the fashion of a military officer or corporate president. The Constitution gives the president authority to appoint principal officers of the government, but only "by and with the Advice and Consent of the Senate." And as we saw in Chapter 8, the Senate can and does constrain the president's appointment powers. Moreover, Congress can establish or abolish executive departments and regulate their operations by law. And Congress's "power of the purse" allows it to determine the budget of each department and thereby limit or broaden or even "micromanage" the activities of these departments. The president is responsible for developing the federal budget each year and sending it to Congress for its consideration (see "The Budget Maze" in Chapter 11), but Congress has the last word on spending.

The president can issue executive orders directing specific federal agencies to carry out policies or directing all federal agencies to pursue a preferred course of action. Presidents regularly issue 50–100 executive orders each year. In 1948, Harry Truman issued Executive Order 9981 to desegregate the U.S. armed forces. In 1965, Lyndon Johnson's Executive Order 11246 instituted affirmative action programs in the federal government. Executive orders have legal force. They can be overturned only by an act of Congress or, of course, by the federal courts if unconstitutional. Executive orders can also be overturned by later executive orders, as seen in the reversals on abortion funding policy begun in 1984 when Reagan ordered that no federal funds be used for international or foreign organizations that provided abortions or abortion counseling, only to have Clinton overturn that in 1993, Bush reverse Clinton and reinstate the ban in 2001, and Obama reverse Bush in 2009.

Presidents rely heavily on their White House staff to exercise their powers. The senior staff normally includes a chief of staff, the national security adviser, the press secretary, a legal counsel, a director of personnel (in charge of appointments), and assistants for political affairs, legislative liaison, and domestic policy. Staff organization depends on each president's personal taste. Some organize their staffs hierarchically, concentrating power in the chief of staff. Others maintain direct contact with several staff members.

White House Staff
Current staff positions and members can be found at the White House website. *www.whitehouse. gov*

Center for the Study of the Presidency & Congress
Studies of the office of the president and publication of the journal *Presidential Studies Quarterly. www. thepresidency.org*

CHIEF LEGISLATOR

The president has principal responsibility for the initiation of national policy, and about 80 percent of the bills considered by Congress originate in the executive branch. The Constitution requires the president to "recommend to their Consideration such Measures as he shall judge necessary and expedient" (Article II, Section 3). Each year the principal policy statement of the president comes in the State of the Union message to Congress. Originally a written report, it is now a major television event, normally in late January. It is followed by the president's budget, which sets forth the president's programs and their cost. Many other policy proposals are developed by executive departments and agencies, transmitted to the White House for the president's approval, and then sent to Congress.

Presidents are expected to be the chief lobbyist on behalf of the administration's bills as they make their way through Congress. Presidents may exchange many favors, large and small, for the support of individual members; they may help direct "pork" to a member's district or promise White House support for a member's pet project. They may also issue or withhold invitations to the White House for prestigious ceremonies, dinners with visiting heads of state, and other glittering social occasions—an effective resource because most members of Congress value prestige. Presidents may also agree to campaign for Congress members, bringing the star power of the presidency to local media markets when they appear.

Congressional leaders must decide whether they can get a two-thirds vote in both houses to override the threat of a veto, another powerful legislative tool the president wields. Presidents need the loyalty of more than one-third of either the House or the Senate to sustain a veto and have a long history of successfully preventing Congress from overriding them. Most presidents will issue a few dozen vetoes, although George W. Bush served over five years before sending his first of 11 vetoes to Congress.

Another way presidents can influence the legislative process is through **signing statements**. In a practice used by incumbents from James Madison through Barack Obama, a president signs a bill but adds a statement regarding its interpretation, sometimes objecting to included provisions or adding details when the law is unclear. Signing statements have found greater use since the 1980s after then-Justice Department attorney (now Supreme Court Justice) Samuel Alito wrote that since the Constitution includes the president in the legislative process, a president should be able to present his understanding of a law just as the Congressional Record explains that of the Congress.[11] All presidents since the 1980s have been frequent users of signing statements, even Obama who promised not to use them during his campaign.

CHIEF DIPLOMAT

The president leads the world's most powerful democracy and, as its chief diplomat, has principal responsibility for formulating U.S. foreign policy. Presidents have the constitutional authority to make treaties with foreign nations "with the Advice and Consent of the Senate." They may "appoint Ambassadors and other public Ministers, and Consuls" and "receive Ambassadors and other public ministers." But presidents have expanded on these modest constitutional powers to dominate foreign policy-making. Although nations may also watch the words and actions of the Congress, the president's statements are generally taken to represent the official position of the U.S. government. Most importantly, presidents have come to dominate U.S. foreign policy as a by-product of their role as commander-in-chief of the armed forces. Military force is the ultimate diplomatic language.

COMMANDER-IN-CHIEF

In 1775, George Washington was commissioned Commander-in-Chief by the Continental Congress and given command of all regular troops and militia called to duty in the Revolutionary War. Washington later chaired the Constitutional Convention of 1787, and his prestige convinced the Convention to add the title Commander-in-Chief to the presidency. "The President shall be the Commander in Chief of the Army and Navy of the United States" (Article II, Section 2), although Congress retained the power to "declare war" (Article I, Section 8).

Defenselink
Official website of
the Department of
Defense, with
news, data, and
links to all service
branches. *www.
defense.gov*

Since 1789, U.S. forces have participated in military actions overseas on more than 200 occasions (see Chapter 14), but Congress has declared war only five times: in the War of 1812, the Mexican War, the Spanish-American War, World War I, and World War II. In response to the terrorist attacks of 2001, President Bush outlined a broad "war on terrorism" to be fought at home and abroad through diplomatic, military, financial, investigative, homeland security, and humanitarian means. He warned that the war would require a long-term sustained effort and got congressional approval for the invasions of Afghanistan and Iraq. Congress, whether controlled by Republicans or Democrats, also renewed funding each year for the two wars and other counterterrorism actions around the globe.

While Congress retains the formal power to declare war, in modern times wars are not declared.[12] Instead, they begin with direct military actions as determined by the president as commander-in-chief of the armed forces. Over the years, Congress has generally recognized the supremacy of the president in military affairs. (The Supreme Court has generally refused to take jurisdiction in cases involving the war powers of the president and Congress.) John Adams fought a war against the French without a congressional declaration, Thomas Jefferson fought the Barbary pirates, and presidents throughout most of the nineteenth century fought various Native American nations. Abraham Lincoln carried presidential war-making powers further than any president before or since in his prosecution of the Civil War, including curtailing civil rights. In the twentieth century, Woodrow Wilson sent troops to Mexico and a dozen Latin American nations, Franklin Roosevelt sent naval destroyers to protect British convoys in the North Atlantic before Pearl Harbor and had Nazi saboteurs executed after a military tribunal found them guilty, and Harry Truman committed U.S. forces to a major war in Korea. Lyndon Johnson ordered bombing attacks on North Vietnam in 1965 and eventually committed more than half a million soldiers to the Vietnam War. Richard Nixon withdrew U.S. troops from Vietnam following the Paris Peace Agreement in 1973, but not before he expanded the geographic scope of the war into Cambodia and Laos. Finally, the suitcase with the launch codes for the nation's nuclear arsenal is always in the president's presence.

In 1973, over Nixon's veto, Congress passed the War Powers Act to restrict presidential war-making powers. The act states that in the absence of a congressional declaration of war, the president can commit armed forces to hostilities or circumstances of imminent hostilities only to repel an armed attack on the United States or its armed forces or to forestall the "direct and imminent threat of such an attack," or to protect and evacuate U.S. citizens and nationals in another country if their lives are threatened. The president must report promptly to Congress the commitment of U.S. forces, which cannot be deployed for over 60 days unless Congress authorizes their continued use. Finally, Congress asserted that it could end a military deployment without requiring the president's signature.

The War Powers Act raises serious constitutional questions. Congress cannot constitutionally command troops, yet that is what the act attempts to do by specifying that troops must come home if Congress orders them to or fails to endorse the president's decision to commit them. No president can allow Congress to usurp this presidential authority. Carter did not notify Congress before deploying U.S. military forces in a failed attempt to rescue U.S. embassy employees held hostage in Iran. George H. W. Bush also ignored the War Powers Act in ordering the invasion of Panama in 1989 and sending troops to protect Saudi Arabia in 1990 following Saddam Hussein's invasion of Kuwait. Bush also claimed he had the constitutional power to order U.S. military forces to liberate Kuwait from Iraqi occupation, whether or not Congress authorized the action. (Congress voted to authorize the use of force a few days before U.S. air attacks began.) Without mentioning the War Powers Act, Clinton ordered U.S. troops into Bosnia to end the genocide there in 1995; later, he ordered extensive bombing of Serbia to force its president to withdraw troops that were starting another genocide in Kosovo. In 2011, Obama argued that his air war against Libyan dictator Muammar Qaddafi was not really a war and thus did not need congressional approval.

CHIEF OF LAW ENFORCEMENT AND GRANTOR OF PARDONS

The president's responsibility to "take care that the laws be faithfully executed" grants the incumbent authority and appointment power over the Justice Department and the Federal Bureau of Investigation (FBI), the nation's main law enforcement institutions. The president also leads the nation's intelligence community, which focuses on counterintelligence (protecting the United States from foreign spies) and counterterrorism (protecting the citizenry from attacks by terrorists).

The Constitution gives the president broad power to grant pardons and reprieves for offenses against the United States, from minor crimes to terrorism and drug trafficking, excepting only impeachment. Presidents need not explain pardons, which are irreversible. The most famous is Gerald Ford's pardon of Richard Nixon for any crimes he "may have committed against the United States while President." Presidents may also "grant reprieves," reducing a sentence or fine for a crime.

PARTY LEADER

Though it is not a formal part of the job, presidents are the recognized leaders of their party. They usually control the national committee and its Washington staff and largely direct the national party convention. More important, perhaps, presidents enjoy much stronger support in Congress from members of their own party than from

---

IN BRIEF | ## FORMAL PRESIDENTIAL POWERS

The formal powers of the president include the following:

- Chief executive—supervise the executive branch of government; appoint and remove policy officials; prepare executive budget
- Chief legislator—initiate policy; veto legislation passed by Congress
- Chief diplomat—make treaties ("with the advice and consent of the Senate"); make executive

agreements; exercise power of diplomatic recognition—"receive ambassadors and other public ministers"

- Commander-in-chief—command U.S. armed forces; appoint military officials; initiate military actions; exercise broad war powers
- Chief of law enforcement—"take care that the laws be faithfully executed"; grant pardons and reprieves for federal offenses
- Chief of state—represent the nation formally

members of the opposition (see "Presidential Support" in Chapter 8). Since they have the power to nominate people to thousands of federal government jobs, presidents also control federal patronage through which party supporters can be rewarded.

THE VICE PRESIDENT

Historically, the office of the vice president has been extremely limited, with little role beyond the constitutional job description of acting as president of the senate. The first person to hold the office, John Adams, said, "My country has in its wisdom contrived for me the most insignificant office that ever the invention of man contrived or his imagination conceived." Later, John Nance Gardner (Vice President, 1933–1941) described the office as "not worth a bucket of warm [spit]" (*spit* is generally substituted for what he actually said). Vice President Richard Nixon did perform as a stand-in for President Eisenhower in meetings during times of illness, but the expansion of the responsibilities of the vice president began in earnest with Walter Mondale, who was used as a trusted advisor and given broad access to the White House and included in key meetings. This trend continued with vice presidents George H. W. Bush, Dan Quayle, Al Gore, and Joe Biden. Gore was given significant responsibility for major initiatives, such as the Reinventing Government program and environmental policy.

No vice president ever achieved the degree of power and influence enjoyed by Richard Cheney, vice president to George W. Bush. Cheney's role in formulating policy was unprecedented. He was a central decision maker on the critical issue of national security and counterterrorism, as well as on domestic issues including taxation and energy. "The Cheney vice presidency developed in the unique way it did because of a variety of factors which maximized vice presidential power while minimizing vice presidential accountability."[13] Circumstances particular to Cheney included his very close relationship with President Bush, Cheney's experience with the executive branch and the political process, and his ability to move trusted staff into key White House and executive branch positions.

Cheney was also not a political threat, for while most vice presidents want the top job (as did Mondale, Bush, Quayle, Gore, and Biden), Cheney was notable for his lack of presidential ambitions. This meant the president did not need to recognize him as a rival and also allowed Cheney to pretty much ignore his pubic approval ratings (which were very low). Cheney brought to the office of vice president a commitment to restore presidential power to where it had been before post-Watergate laws diminished it, particularly in national security matters. Cheney was also to vastly expand the power of his own office, since he had the special attention of the president, little accountability in a period of acute national emergency and war, and a unique insight into the details of political functioning. It is unlikely this confluence of factors will be repeated.

THE PRESIDENT AND CONGRESS

The people expect their president to take the lead in initiating national policy and hold him or her responsible even for results the office does not grant the authority or capacity to change. Presidents have every incentive not only to propose policy initiatives but also to get them enacted by the Congress.

WHITE HOUSE LOBBYING

Presidents do not simply send their bills to Congress and then await the outcome. The White House staff includes "legislative liaisons"—lobbyists for the president's programs. They organize the president's legislative proposals, track them through committee and floor proceedings, arrange committee appearances by executive department and agency representatives, count votes, and advise the president on when and how to cut deals and twist arms. The president may contact wavering Congress members individually by telephoning and meeting with them, but direct arm-twisting is generally reserved for the most important legislative battles. There is seldom time to contact individual members of Congress personally about many bills in various stages of legislative process in both the House and Senate.

Presidents are far more successful when Congress is controlled by their own party. Democrats John Kennedy and Lyndon Johnson enjoyed the support of Democratic-controlled Congresses and averaged success scores over 80 percent. Jimmy Carter was hardly a popular president, but with a supportive Democratic Congress, he also recorded high box scores. Republicans Richard Nixon and Gerald Ford fared poorly with Democratic-controlled Congresses.

Republican Ronald Reagan was very successful in his first term with a Democratic House and a Republican Senate, but after Democrats took over both houses, his success rate plummeted. In Bill Clinton's first two years in office a Democratic Congress helped him get 86 percent of his legislative proposals enacted. When the Republicans took control in 1994, his box scores declined dramatically. Republicans controlled Congress for much of the first six years of George W. Bush's two terms; with the election of a Democratic Congress in 2006, his success in Congress ended abruptly. Barack Obama saw great success in his first year getting his agenda through a Congress controlled by his party, packaging many initiatives into the stimulus legislation and seeing a 95 percent success rate in 2009. This plummeted with the passing of control of the House to the Republicans in 2011.

THE VETO POWER

The **veto** is the president's most powerful weapon in dealing with Congress, especially a Congress controlled by the opposition. Even the *threat* of the veto enhances the president's bargaining power. Congressional leaders must muster a two-thirds vote of both houses to override the veto. The president needs only one-third, plus one of either the House or the Senate, in order to sustain it. This usually forces opposition party leaders to bargain with the president: "What will the president accept?" From George Washington to George Bush, more than 96 percent of all presidential vetoes have been sustained (see Table 9.2).

For many years, both Democratic and Republican presidents petitioned Congress for a "line-item veto"—the ability to veto some provisions of a bill while accepting others. Presidents would then be able to veto specific pork-barrel items from major spending bills without losing the entire appropriation. When Congress finally granted a form of the line-item veto in 1996, the Supreme Court held it to be unconstitutional, because it "authorizes the president himself to elect to repeal laws, for his own policy reasons" and therefore violates the law-making provisions

TABLE 9.2 | PRESIDENTIAL VETOES

President	Total Vetoes*	Vetoes Overridden	Percentage of Vetoes Sustained
F. Roosevelt	635	9	99
Truman	250	12	95
Eisenhower	181	2	99
Kennedy	21	0	100
L. Johnson	30	0	100
Nixon	43	7	84
Ford	66	12	85
Carter	31	2	94
Reagan	78	9	88
G. H. W. Bush	44	1	98
Clinton	37	2	95
G. W. Bush	12	4	67
Obama	2	0	100

*Regular vetoes plus pocket vetoes.

Source: Harold W. Stanley and Richard G. Niemi, *Vital Statistics on American Politics*, 2005–2006 (Washington, DC: CQ Press, 2006), p. 256. Updated by authors.

set forth in Article I of the Constitution. Presidential signing statements may in some cases be an attempt to exercise a line-item veto.

LIMITS ON PRESIDENTIAL EXECUTIVE POWER

The Constitution declares that "executive Power" shall be vested in the president, but it is unclear whether this statement grants any powers not specified elsewhere in the Constitution or given to the president by acts of Congress. In other words, does "executive Power" give presidents constitutional authority to act as they deem necessary *beyond* the powers granted in the Constitution or by laws of Congress?

VIEWS ON PRESIDENTIAL POWER

Different presidents have had different perspectives on the nature of the executive power. William Howard Taft, later U.S. Chief Justice, held a strict constructionist view of the presidency: "the President can exercise no power which cannot be fairly and reasonably traced to some specific grant of power" or justly included in such a grant as necessary.[14] Theodore Roosevelt saw a stewardship presidency, in which the president has "not only a right but a duty to do anything the needs of the nation demanded unless such action was forbidden by the Constitution or by the laws."[15] In the most expansive view of presidential power, Abraham Lincoln wrote in 1864 that "I felt that measures otherwise unconstitutional might become lawful by becoming indispensible to the preservation of the constitution through the preservation of the nation."[16]

Historically, U.S. presidents have indeed acted beyond specified constitutional powers or laws of Congress. Among the most notable instances:

- George Washington issued a Proclamation of Neutrality during the war between France and Britain following the French Revolution, helping establish the president's power to make foreign policy.

- Thomas Jefferson, who prior to becoming president argued for a narrow interpretation of presidential powers, purchased the Louisiana Territory although the Constitution contains no provision for the acquisition of territory, nor authorizes presidential action to do so.

- Andrew Jackson ordered the removal of federal funds from the national bank and removed his secretary of the treasury from office, establishing the president's power to *remove* executive officials, a power not specifically mentioned in the Constitution.

- Abraham Lincoln, asking, "Was it possible to lose the nation yet to preserve the Constitution?" established the precedent of vigorous presidential action in national emergencies. He blockaded southern ports, declared martial law in parts of the country, and ended slavery with the Emancipation Proclamation, all without constitutional or congressional authority.

- Franklin Roosevelt, battling the Great Depression during the 1930s, ordered the nation's banks to close temporarily. Following Imperial Japan's attack on Pearl Harbor in 1941, he ordered the incarceration without trial of 120,000 Japanese Americans.

- George W. Bush ordered that "enemy combatants" captured by U.S. forces in Afghanistan and Iraq be detained at the naval base in Guantanamo Bay, Cuba, and be subject to military tribunals. (This was later approved by Congress, but only after the Supreme Court required it.)

- Barack Obama asserted the right to kill American citizens anywhere overseas without due process if they are deemed part of a terrorist group fighting the United States. The case was concerning Al Qaeda leader Anwar Alwaki, who was born in the U.S. but killed by drone in Yemen in 2010. He was behind several terror attacks in the United States, including the Fort Hood attack which killed 13.

EXECUTIVE PRIVILEGE

What powers are implied by **executive privilege**—the right of the president to keep confidential communications from other branches of government? Traditionally presidents have argued that the Constitution's establishment of separate branches entitles them to conduct affairs of the executive branch without interference by Congress or the courts. Public exposure of internal executive communications would inhibit the president's ability to obtain candid advice from subordinates, hamper negotiations with foreign governments, and interfere with command of military operations.

Congress has never recognized executive privilege. It frequently tries to compel the testimony of executive officials at congressional hearings, though presidents have regularly refused to appear and seldom allow other executive officials to appear or divulge information, citing executive privilege. The federal courts have generally refrained from interfering in this dispute between the executive and legislative branches. Still, President Nixon was not immune from court orders when illegal acts were under investigation. Although the Court acknowledged he might legitimately claim executive privilege in military or diplomatic matters, he could not do so in a criminal investigation.[17] The Court ordered Nixon to surrender tape recordings of White House conversations between himself and his advisors during the Watergate scandal (see Focus: Watergate and the Limits of Presidential Power).

IMPEACHMENT

The most significant safeguard against abuse of presidential power is **impeachment**. The Constitution grants Congress this power over the president, the vice president, and "all civil Officers of the United States" (Article II, Section 4). Technically, impeachment is a charge similar to a criminal indictment brought against an official. The power to bring the charges is given to the House of Representatives. The power to try all impeachments belongs to the Senate, which needs a two-thirds vote to convict. Impeachment and conviction only remove an official from office; a subsequent criminal trial is required to inflict any other punishment.

The Constitution specifies that impeachment and conviction can be only for "Treason, Bribery, or other High Crimes and Misdemeanors." These words indicate that Congress is not to impeach presidents, federal judges, or any other officials simply because it disagrees with their decisions or policies. Indeed only serious criminal offenses, not political conflicts, can result in impeachment. Nevertheless, politics was at the root of the impeachment of President Andrew Johnson in 1867. (Johnson was a southern Democrat who remained loyal to the Union, and whom Lincoln had chosen as vice president in 1864 as a gesture of national unity. A Republican House impeached him on a party-line vote, but after a month-long trial in the Senate, the "guilty" vote fell one vote short of the two-thirds needed for removal.) Partisan politics also played a key role in the House impeachment of Bill Clinton (see Focus: Sex, Lies, and Impeachment).

JUDICIAL CHECKS ON PRESIDENTIAL POWER

President Harry Truman believed the president had broad authority "to keep the country from going to hell," and he was willing to use means beyond those specified in the Constitution or authorized by Congress. In 1952, while U.S. troops were fighting in Korea, steel workers at home were threatening to strike. Rather than offend organized labor by forbidding the strike under the terms of the Taft-Hartley Act of 1947 (which he and the unions had opposed), Truman chose to seize the steel mills by executive order and continue their operation under

| FOCUS | WATERGATE AND THE LIMITS OF PRESIDENTIAL POWER |

Richard Nixon was the only president ever to resign the office. His tenure included a number of historic successes, including the limitation of nuclear weapons agreement with the USSR. He changed the global balance of power in favor of democracy by opening relations with the People's Republic of China and dividing the communist world. His administration implemented stronger environmental protection and workplace safety. He withdrew U.S. troops from Vietnam, negotiated a peace agreement, and ended a long and unpopular war. But his remarkable record is forever tarnished by his failure to understand the limits of presidential power.

In 1972, five burglars were arrested in the offices of the Democratic National Committee in the Watergate Building in Washington, DC. Also arrested were key personnel of the Committee to Re-Elect the President (CREEP). All pleaded guilty and were convicted. Although there is no evidence that Nixon himself ordered or had prior knowledge of the break-in, he discussed with his advisors the advisability of payoffs to buy the defendants' silence. Nixon hoped his landslide electoral victory in November of that year would put the matter to rest. However, a series of revelations by reporters Bob Woodward and Carl Bernstein in the *Washington Post* kept the story alive. Using an inside source known only as Deep Throat (since revealed to be FBI Associate Director Mark Felt), Woodward and Bernstein alleged that key members of Nixon's re-election committee including its chairman, then attorney general John Mitchell, and White House staff were actively involved in the break-in and,

more important, in the subsequent attempts at a cover-up.

In February 1973 a special Senate committee began to investigate Watergate and related activities. The committee's nationally televised hearings enthralled millions of viewers. White House counsel John Dean testified that he had earlier warned Nixon the cover-up was "a cancer growing on the presidency." The committee and the nation learned of a secret audio tape-recording system in the Oval Office. Hoping the tapes would prove or disprove charges of Nixon's involvement in the cover-up, the committee subpoenaed them. Nixon refused to turn them over, arguing that the constitutional separation of powers gave the president an "executive privilege" to withhold his private conversations from Congress. However, the U.S. Supreme Court, voting 8 to 0 in *United States v. Nixon,* ordered Nixon to comply.[a]

Despite the rambling nature of the tapes, committee members interpreted them as confirming Nixon's involvement in the payoffs and cover-up. Informed by congressional leaders of his own party that impeachment by a majority of the House and removal from office by two-thirds of the Senate were assured, on August 9, 1974, Richard Nixon resigned his office. On September 8, 1974, new president Gerald Ford pardoned Nixon "for all offenses against the United States which he, Richard Nixon, has committed or may have committed or taken part in" during his presidency. Upon his death in 1994, Nixon was eulogized for his foreign policy successes.

[a]*United States v. Nixon* 418 U.S. 683 (1974).

U.S. government control. But the U.S. Supreme Court ordered the steel mills returned to their owners. The Court acknowledged that the president may have inherent powers to act in a national emergency but argued that Congress had provided a legal remedy in the Taft-Hartley Act. The president can act to keep the country from "going to hell," but if Congress has already acted to do so, the president must abide by the law.[18] Nonetheless, presidents have interpreted both the Constitution and the laws of Congress in ways that give them great power.

The president is not above the law or immune from judicial scrutiny. His or her official conduct must be lawful; federal courts may reverse presidential actions found to be unconstitutional or in violation of the laws of Congress. Nor are

FOCUS | SEX, LIES, AND IMPEACHMENT

William Clinton was only the second president in the nation's history (following Andrew Johnson in 1867) to be impeached by the House of Representatives. (Richard Nixon resigned just before an impeachment vote in 1974.) The 1998 vote split along partisan lines (228 to 106, with all but five Republicans voting yes and all but five Democrats voting no). It followed a report to the House by Independent Counsel Kenneth Starr that recommended impeachment for perjury, obstruction of justice, witness tampering, and "abuse of power."

The Starr Report describes in graphic and lurid detail Clinton's sexual relationship with young White House intern Monica Lewinsky.[a] It cites as impeachable offenses Clinton's lying about their relationship to his staff, friends, and the nation; his misleading testimony in a sworn statement in the Paula Jones case; his conversations with close friend Vernon Jordan about finding Lewinsky a job; his attempts to impede Starr's investigation; and his evasive testimony before Starr's grand jury.

Perjury—knowingly giving false testimony in a sworn legal proceeding—is a criminal offense. But does the Constitution envision more serious misconduct— crimes that undermine the Constitution or abuse presidential power? Is lying about sex serious enough to warrant impeachment and removal of a president elected by the people? In *Federalist Paper No. 65*, Alexander Hamilton wrote that impeachment should deal with "the abuse or violation of some public trust." Polls showed people did *not* believe Clinton's misconduct should have resulted in his impeachment or removal from office:

QUESTION: "Do you approve or disapprove of the House decision to vote in favor of impeaching Clinton and sending the case to the Senate for trial?" Yes–35%, No–63%

QUESTION: "Do you think Bill Clinton should resign now and turn the presidency over to Al Gore?" Yes–30%, No–69%

QUESTION: "Should the Senate vote in favor of convicting Clinton and removing him from office or vote against convicting?" Vote to convict–29%, Vote against convicting–68%[b]

But the decision about what is impeachable is entirely in the hands of the House of Representatives, and the decision about whether to remove the president from office is entirely in the hands of the Senate. There is no appeal from these decisions. They are political as well as judicial, partisan as well as legal, and personal as well as driven by public opinion.

The Senate impeachment trial ended in acquittal. Indeed, the strongest charge, obstruction of justice, failed to win even a majority of Senate votes, far less than the required two-thirds. All 45 Democrats were joined by five Republicans to create a 50–50 tie on the obstruction charge, while 55 senators voted not guilty on the perjury charge, leaving Clinton tarnished but still in office.

[a]Kenneth Starr, *Official Report of the Independent Counsel's Investigation of the President*, 1998, *http://icreport.access.gpo.gov/report/ lcover.htm*

[b]Gallup poll reported in *USA Today*, December 21, 1998.

presidents immune from criminal prosecution; they cannot ignore demands to provide information in criminal cases.

The Supreme Court has held that the president has "absolute immunity" from civil suits "arising out of the execution of official duties." The president cannot be sued for damages caused by actions or decisions within his constitutional or legal authority. But the president can be sued for private conduct beyond the scope of his or her official duties. The Supreme Court rejected the notion of presidential immunity from civil claims in a sexual harassment suit by a former Arkansas employee against President Bill Clinton for alleged actions while he was governor.[19]

GEORGE W. BUSH: A TURBULENT PRESIDENCY

George Walker Bush suffered an especially turbulent presidency. From the disputed election of 2000, to terrorist organization Al Qaeda's mass murders in 2001, to the wars in Afghanistan and Iraq, to the financial crisis that began in 2007, Bush experienced the dramas of his office. In domestic affairs he succeeded in tax reform, guiding the economy through 25 quarters of growth, making major education reforms, and expanding Medicare. His approval ratings skyrocketed after 9/11 but later plunged to near-record lows as casualties mounted in Iraq and the economy declined. His average approval was 49 percent, mid-range among presidents.

BACKGROUND TO THE PRESIDENCY

George Walker Bush was born into his family's tradition of wealth, privilege, and public service. His grandfather, investment banker Prescott Bush, was a U.S. senator from Connecticut. His father, George Herbert Walker Bush, had served as Congressman, Ambassador to the United Nations, Envoy to China, Director of the CIA, Vice President, and President. George W. Bush grew up in Midland, Texas, where his father had established himself in the oil business before going into politics. He followed in his father's footsteps to Yale University, on graduation joined the Texas Air National Guard, and earned an MBA from the Harvard Business School. He unsuccessfully followed his father into the oil business. He sold his oil interests and reinvested the money in the Texas Rangers baseball team, eventually selling his interest for a profit of over $15 million.

In 1994 George W. Bush was elected governor of Texas. He had gained valuable political experience serving as an unofficial advisor during his father's presidential campaigns and in the White House. Bush improved public services yet kept Texas among the few states without an income tax. He supported educational reform by opposing the practice of "social promotion" and requiring pupils to pass statewide tests before advancing to the next grade. Bush's style was to meet frequently and privately with his Democratic opponents and remain on friendly terms with them, and he won many legislative battles. He was willing to accept legislative compromises and tried to avoid controversies wherever possible; he was overwhelmingly reelected governor of Texas in 1998.

In 2000, he won the presidency in a close race against Democratic Vice President Al Gore. Due to a series of technical and legal issues in Florida, Bush came to the Oval Office with the legitimacy of his election in question by many.

TERRORIST STRIKE: 9/11

The terrorist attack on the United States on September 11, 2001, became the defining moment in the Bush presidency. Bush grew in stature, respect, and decisiveness with public appearances and statements that reassured the U.S. people. He promptly declared a "war on terrorism" against both the Al Qaeda and related terrorist organizations themselves and the nations that harbor and support them. Bush also repeatedly condemned ignorant attacks on Arabs and Muslims in the United States, quickly squashing a brief rise in hate crimes. Congress rushed to approve money for homeland defense and to support the president's use of force.

Bush explained to an anxious nation the "war on terrorism": attack prevention through heightened security, redirection of law enforcement, strengthening of intelligence capabilities, creation of an international coalition to hunt down terrorists and seize their assets, and direct military attacks on terrorist networks and the governments that shelter them. Military action in Afghanistan followed quickly. Bush showed no hesitation, no indecision, and no willingness to appease terrorists. His public approval ratings skyrocketed: fully 90 percent of U.S. adults approved of the way he was handling his job. The rapid collapse of the hated Taliban government in Afghanistan seemed to confirm Bush's actions. It would be his finest hour.

BUSH POLICY INITIATIVES

During his first term, Bush generally enjoyed the support of a Republican Congress (although the Democrats held the Senate from mid-2001 to the end of 2002). He set forth an ambitious policy agenda:

Tax reductions: The centerpiece of Bush's domestic policy was a 2001 tax cut that reduced the top marginal income tax rate to 35 percent and boosted investment through preferential treatment on capital gains and dividends. While running a deficit and increasing the national debt, Bush argued that these tax cuts strengthened the economy.

Education reform: The 2002 No Child Left Behind Act redefined the federal government's role in education to include setting performance standards, requiring measures of achievement based on testing, and threatening sanctions including the transfer of pupils out of failing schools. This law, co-sponsored by liberal Democrat Ted Kennedy, was passed with overwhelming bipartisan support.

Health care: The 2003 addition to Medicare of prescription drug coverage for seniors was the largest expansion of federal entitlements since the 1960s.

Homeland security: The USA PATRIOT Act extended federal government powers for wiretapping, surveillance, investigation, and the arrest of terrorist suspects. (Many of its provisions were already present in the 1996 Anti-Terrorism Act, while others had been used previously to fight organized crime and child pornography.) In 2002 Bush asked Congress to create a new Department of Homeland Security as part of a major reorganization of the federal bureaucracy.

Foreign policy: In his 2002 National Security Strategy, Bush spelled out a focused commitment to basic liberal ideals, including democracy, women's rights, religious freedom, property rights, and free speech and press. He saw the United States as having a mission to promote such values even in countries where local elites saw them as threats, such as Iraq. He expressed a willingness to use military force preemptively to achieve national security goals, particularly counterterrorism. Bush also talked about a willingness to act alone, although the war in Afghanistan was a NATO operation and over 30 other nations joined the war to remove Saddam Hussein from power in Iraq. Although many in the media scoffed at Bush's portrayal of the war on terrorism as a struggle between good and evil, most people heralded what they saw as Bush's "moral clarity" and the firmness of his convictions.

THE WAR IN IRAQ

Bush's legacy will be defined by the Iraq War. "Operation Iraqi Freedom" enjoyed widespread public support at its onset in March 2003. Saddam Hussein's regime had violated over a dozen United Nations resolutions regarding inspections for **weapons of mass destruction** (WMDs). Bush stated that the main purpose of military action in Iraq was to counter a medium-term threat by eliminating the Iraqi WMD capacity and enact a "regime change" to ensure Hussein would not aid terrorists. Iraq was a brutal dictatorship that committed genocide, killing hundreds of thousands of its own people, especially Shi'ite Arabs and Kurds. Congress voted overwhelmingly to support military action. The U.S. military and its 34 allies captured Baghdad in just 21 days.

The quick victory over Hussein marked the end of the war, but also the start of a difficult occupation. Although Iraq was able to transition to a functioning democracy, high levels of violence and unrest kept the new freedom fragile. Hussein and his Baathists had set up weapons and support for "insurgents" before the invasion, hoping that by attacking coalition forces and killing Iraqi civilians they would discourage the invaders from remaining.

Bush had also designated Iraq as the front line in the battle against terrorism, prompting Osama bin Laden and Al Qaeda to pour the bulk of their resources and thousands of terrorists into Iraq with the goal of killing foreign invaders as well as Shi'a Muslims, whom Al Qaeda's ideology views as heretics. Shi'a Iraqis formed militias to defend themselves and a civil war seemed to be brewing, egged on by Iran, which supplied weapons and training.

U.S. casualties began to mount into the thousands and the war became a national ordeal. Bush seemed to have no realistic strategy for exiting the deepening quagmire. Voters responded by electing a Democratic-controlled Congress in 2006, a clear negative retrospective judgment on Bush's performance. His presidential approval ratings fell to 35 percent.

In early 2007, Bush implemented the plan General David Petraeus recommended, to deploy a "surge" of combat troops into Iraq. Bush sent over 20,000 additional troops to clear out and hold Iraqi territory to make it safe for civilians. The new counterinsurgency model also included engaging local leaders and providing more services for the population. The surge was successful and Iraqi security was handed over to Iraqi forces trained by the coalition. Bush negotiated a Status of Forces Agreement with the Iraqi government calling for the removal of U.S. forces from Iraq by the end of 2011, a process completed under Obama.

THE FINANCIAL CRISIS

Bush's presidency ended amid the worst financial crisis in decades. Years of easy credit, spurred by low interest rates from the Federal Reserve, created a bubble in housing and other asset prices. People got used to living on easy credit and borrowing: credit cards, student loans, auto loans, and mortgages. Housing market lenders gave hundreds of thousands of dollars to NINJA (no income no job, application) borrowers. These debts were bundled together and sold to investors around the world, with the assumption that the U.S. government would guarantee the mortgages through former federal agencies Fannie Mae and Freddie Mac. Risk was ignored and assets grossly mispriced. In a wave of greed, bankers, insurers, lenders, and home buyers all assumed housing prices would continue to rise. The bubble burst in 2007. Millions of houses became "underwater," worth less than the amount owed on them. Mortgage-backed securities plummeted in value. The stock market dropped by nearly half.

Commercial banks, investment banks, and insurance companies took billions in losses and sought assistance from the Treasury Department and the Federal Reserve. The Fed acted to stave off the bankruptcy of investment banker Bear Stearns, and the Treasury took over Fannie Mae and Freddie Mac. The government nationalized the country's largest insurance company, American International Group (AIG). But the hemorrhaging continued and the nation tumbled into recession for the last quarter of 2008 and the first of 2009.

In September 2008, the Treasury and the Fed went before Congress to plead for a massive $700 billion bailout of banks and insurance companies. The Troubled Asset Relief Program (TARP) was set up to buy illiquid assets held by financial institutions. The government also made loans secured by preferred stock shares. Government owning shares of financial institutions, that is, "nationalization" of the banks, would have been unthinkable before the crisis. "I've abandoned free market principles to save the free market system," Bush stated in a December 2008 interview on CNN.[20]

THE OBAMA PRESIDENCY

The presidency of Barack Hussein Obama II cannot be reviewed except in hindsight, so serious analysis of his tenure cannot begin until after he has completed a full term. Whatever the final outcome of his presidency may be, his presence in the Oval Office as the nation's first African-American president has been historic. His arrival at the pinnacle of the nation's elite marks a fundamental change in the nation, where "a man whose father less than 60 years ago might not have been served in a local restaurant can now stand before you to take a most sacred oath"[21] and become leader of the most powerful nation in history. Handsome, youthful, eloquent, and charismatic, Obama swept into the White House on a slogan of "change" and "hope."

OBAMA'S RISE TO POWER

Barack Obama Senior was born in Nyanza, Kenya, and came to the University of Hawaii as a foreign student. He met and married a fellow student, Ann Durham of Wichita, Kansas. Born in Honolulu, Barack Junior was two years old when his parents separated and divorced. His mother then married a student from Indonesia, and the family moved to Jakarta where Barack attended elementary school. At age 10 he returned to Honolulu to live with his maternal grandparents. In his memoir, *Dreams from My Father,* Obama describes his experiences growing up in a white, upper-middle class family. He reflects on his struggles to reconcile social perceptions of others with his multiracial background.[22]

Obama attended Occidental College in Los Angeles for two years before transferring to Columbia University where he majored in political science and international relations. Upon graduation in 1983, he went to Chicago to work as a community organizer in a low-income area. In 1988 he was admitted to Harvard Law School and there was elected president of the *Harvard Law Review,* the first African-American to hold that position. Media attention to this resulted in a contract for a book that became *Dreams from My Father.* After graduating Harvard in 1991, Obama returned to Chicago where he taught constitutional law at the University of Chicago Law School, practiced law representing community organizations and civil rights groups, and served on several foundations' board of directors, including the Chicago Annenberg Challenge of which he was chair. He married fellow Harvard Law graduate Michelle Robinson in 1992; they have two daughters.

Obama was elected to the Illinois State Senate in 1996, representing Chicago's South Side neighborhood of Hyde Park. He served two terms but often voted "present" on controversial legislation, including anti-abortion bills. Obama's only political failure came in 2000 when he challenged a Chicago veteran politician, Bobby Rush, for his seat representing Illinois' predominately black First Congressional district. Rush was the co-founder of the Illinois Black Panther Party in 1968 and had held the seat since 1993. The Chicago Machine and Mayor Richard Daley supported Rush, and Obama was soundly defeated. But the defeat taught him to work with the Machine rather than against it. He made peace with Mayor Daley and won the confidence of Illinois State Senate President Emil Jones. He sought the financial backing of white liberals including the Pritzkers, owners of Hyatt hotel chain. He lined up the support of powerful Illinois unions with mostly black membership—teachers, government employees, and service workers. By 2004 he was ready to reach for higher office.

In March 2004, Obama won the Democratic primary for an open U.S. Senate seat, gaining 53 percent of the vote in a three-way race. He attracted national attention when he was chosen to deliver the keynote address at the 2004 Democratic National Convention, the same honor that launched the presidency path of Bill Clinton in 1998. Obama's compelling call for unity earned him instant national celebrity: "Well, I say to them tonight, there's not a liberal America and a conservative America; there's the United States of America," and "We worship an awesome God in the blue states, and we don't like federal agents poking around our libraries in the red states. We coach little league in the blue states and, yes, we've got some gay friends in the red states."[23] He went on to win 70 percent of the vote to be elected to the Senate.

RUNNING FOR PRESIDENT

In early 2007, Obama stood at the Old State Capitol Building in Springfield, Illinois, where Abraham Lincoln had delivered his 1858 "House Divided" speech, and announced his candidacy for the presidency. He chose "Change you can believe in" as his campaign theme and stayed "on message" throughout the long primary battle with New York Senator Hillary Clinton. Democratic primary voters and caucus-goers had a historic choice of either the first woman or the first African-American presidential nominee. Clinton claimed she won more primary votes than Obama, but the Obama campaign wisely focused on gathering convention delegates. In the end, the unelected superdelegates chose to support the candidate with the most elected delegates, Barack Obama.

Obama carried his message of change into the general election campaign. As a young, handsome, athletic, African-American he personified change, physically contrasting with the 72-year-old Republican candidate John McCain. He skillfully steered his campaign around the rocks of racial division, distancing himself from the extreme statements of his Chicago pastor Jeremiah Wright. Race never really emerged as a hindrance in the campaign, and perhaps it helped Obama mobilize voters seeking an "historic" change. Obama led McCain in the polls from the beginning. Only in the few weeks immediately after his selection of Alaska Governor Sarah Palin as his running mate did McCain pull ahead in the polls. McCain's slim chances for victory evaporated with the financial meltdown in September, and Obama won 53 percent of the popular vote.

THE OBAMA ADMINISTRATION

Obama's new administration was off to a quick start, even before his formal inauguration. President Bush had included Obama and his economic team, led by Treasury Secretary designate Timothy Geithner, in decisions for dealing with the financial crisis. Obama chose a diverse team as his cabinet: primary opponent Hillary Clinton became the new Secretary of State, Bush's Secretary of Defense Robert Gates was asked to stay on, and several Democratic governors were brought aboard, including Kathleen Sebelius, Gary Locke, Tom Vilsack, and Janet Napolitano. Obama began with strong public goodwill and a 67 percent approval rating.

OBAMA'S POLICY INITIATIVES

In his first two years, Obama was able to secure some major policy successes. Among his key policy achievements were:

- *Equal pay:* The Lilly Ledbetter Fair Pay Act extended the statute of limitations for unequal pay lawsuits.
- *The economic stimulus plan:* In February 2009, Obama secured passage of the $787 billion American Recovery and Reinvestment Act, but the economy exited recession before more than a quarter of the money had been spent. Obama claimed that this measure "saved or created" millions of jobs.
- *Health care:* Obama's signature achievement was his Patient Protection and Affordable Health Care Act of 2010, which was designed to expand health insurance coverage to millions previously uninsured. Its requirement that all individuals must purchase health insurance or face various penalties saw multiple legal challenges.
- *Financial market reform:* The Dodd-Frank Wall Street Reform and Consumer Protection Act of 2010 was designed to address some of the causes of the 2007–2009 financial crisis and to protect borrowers from "predatory" lending.
- *Fighting terrorism:* Obama continued to vigorously pursue the fight against Al Qaeda and terrorism. He dramatically expanded the use of drone aircraft to make "targeted assassinations" of terrorist leaders, he expanded further federal surveillance powers through several extensions of the PATRIOT Act that were due to expire but were necessary to defend the nation against the

terrorist threat, and he maintained military tribunals and the detention center at Guantanamo Bay. (Many of these actions upset the political left.)

- *Foreign policy:* Obama's foreign policy showed a great deal of flexibility, but had at its core the idea of improving worldwide public opinion of the United States. His leadership of a multinational military attack on Libya to remove dictator Qaddafi demonstrated his focus on coalitions.
- *Killing Osama bin Laden:* Obama ordered a U.S. Navy SEAL team to kill the leader of Al Qaeda and the mastermind behind the 9/11 attacks as well as the deaths of tens of thousands of others worldwide.

In foreign policy a variety of disparate events and actions took place under Obama. Obama's personal highlight was winning the Nobel Peace Prize in 2009, for which he was nominated only a few weeks into office. His Nobel Speech on just war theory was seen as an impressive summary of when military action is necessary. Beyond the aggressive use of drones, Obama's major military action was the introduction of a surge of troops in Afghanistan to stabilize that nation before withdrawing U.S. forces. He also worked to maintain China's cooperation and the flow of Chinese capital into the U.S. economy.

The ultimate issue faced by Obama was unemployment, an issue on which he was able to do very little. The country was in recession when he took office, with an unemployment rate of 7.8 percent. In the next year it climbed to over 10 percent and stubbornly remained over eight percent through 2012, higher than it had been when he took office. Despite the creation of millions of jobs, these were not enough to make up for the larger number lost in the recession and the financial crisis, or the new jobs needed as the population grew and new graduates entered the work force. In the end, the number of Americans working fell from 145 million when Obama was elected in 2008 to 144 million at his re-election in 2012.

THE PRESIDENCY | An Elitist Interpretation

The president is the popular symbol of governmental authority. However, presidents are substantially less able to control decisions than they would like.

1. Governmental elites in the United States do not command; they seek consensus. Governmental decision making involves bargaining, accommodation, and compromise among government and nongovernment elites. Our examination of the presidency provides clear evidence of the consensual nature of elite interaction and the heavy price a president must pay for failure to accommodate other elites.
2. Presidential power depends ultimately not on any formal authority but on his or her personal abilities of persuasion. Good economic times raise presidential popularity.
3. For the masses, the president is the symbol of the government and the nation itself. Presidential popularity with the masses depends on their perception of dynamic leadership in the face of crises. Economic recessions erode presidential popularity, as do prolonged wars.

4. Presidents have an important psychological role for the masses, connecting them with their political system. Presidents are also celebrities who reflect the Zeitgeist and the popular culture.

5. A president must govern within the boundaries of checks and balances with other elites in government and outside it.

6. The president is expected to be commander-in-chief and diplomatic leader as well as leader in domestic policy.

NOTES

1. James David Barber, *The Presidential Character*, 3rd ed. (Englewood Cliffs, NJ: Prentice-Hall, 1985), p. 2.

2. For Obama, it is, respectively, Bo, basketball, and Sasha and Malia.

3. Neilsen ratings, see http://blog.nielsen.com/nielsen wire/media_entertainment/632-million-watched-mccain-and-obamas-second-debate/ and http://blog.nielsen.com/nielsenwire/media_entertainment/nearly-378-million-watch-president-obamas-oath-and-speech/

4. Benjamin Svetkey, "Barack Obama: Celebrity in Chief," *Entertainment Weekly*, November 21, 2008. http://www.ew.com/ew/article/0,20241874,00.html

5. Fred I. Greenstein, "The Psychological Functions of the Presidency for Citizens," in *The American Presidency: Vital Center*, Elmer E. Cornwell, ed. (Chicago: Scott, Foresman, 1966), pp. 30–36.

6. Barber, "The Presidential Character," p. 25.

7. Thomas Reeves, *John F. Kennedy* (New York: Kreiger, 1990), p. 190.

8. Gallup poll, as reported in *USA Today*, September 14, 1998.

9. Richard Neustadt, "Presidential Power and the Modern Presidents: The Politics of Leadership from Roosevelt to Reagan" (New York: Free Press, 1990).

10. Samuel Kernell, *Going Public: New Strategies of Presidential Leadership*, 4th ed. (Washington, DC: CQ Press, 2006).

11. Samuel Alito, "Using Presidential Signing Statement to Make Fuller Use of the President's Constitutionally Assigned Role in the Process of Enacting Law," United States Department of Justice, Office of Legal Counsel, February 5, 1986. http://www.archives.gov/news/samuelalito/accession-060-89-269/Acc060-89-269-box6-SG-LSWG-AlitotoLSWG-Febl986.pdf

12. Max Boot, *The Savage Wars of Peace: Small Wars and the Rise of American Power*. (New York: Basic, 2003).

13. Joel K. Goldstein, "Cheney, Vice Presidential Power, and the War on Terror," *Presidential Studies Quarterly* 40, no. 1 (March 2010), p. 134.

14. William Howard Taft, *Our Chief Magistrate and His Powers* (New York: Columbia University, 1916), pp. 138–145, reprinted as "The Strict Constructionist President" in *Understanding the Presidency*, 2nd ed. James P. Pfiffner and Roger H. Davidson, eds (New York: Longman, 2000), p. 28.

15. Theodore Roosevelt, *The Autobiography of Theodore Roosevelt* (New York: Charles Scribner's Sons, 1913), pp. 197–200, reprinted as "The Stewardship Presidency" in *Understanding the Presidency*, 2nd ed. James P. Pfiffner and Roger H. Davidson, eds (New York: Longman, 2000), p. 31.

16. Abraham Lincoln, "Letter to A.G. Hodges," April 4, 1864, from *The Complete Works of Abraham Lincoln*, vol. 10 (New York: Francis D. Tandy, 1894), pp. 65–68, reprinted as "The Prerogative Presidency" in *Understanding the Presidency*, 2nd ed. James P. Pfiffner and Roger H. Davidson, eds (New York: Longman, 2000), pp. 35–37.

17. *United States v. Nixon* 418 U.S. 683 (1974).

18. *Youngstown Sheet and Tube Co. v. Sawyer* 393 U.S. 579 (1952).

19. *Clinton v. Jones* 520 U.S. 681 (1997).

20. George W. Bush, Interview on CNN, December 16, 2008. http://www.edition.cnn.com/TRANSCRIPTS/0812/16/cnr.04.html

21. Barack H. Obama, "Inaugural Address," January 21, 2009. http://www.whitehouse.gov/blog/inaugural-address/

22. Barack Obama, *Dreams from My Father: A Story of Race and Inheritance* (New York: Times Books Random House, 1995).

23. Barack Obama, "Keynote Address, Democratic National Convention," July 27, 2004. http://www.washingtonpost.com/wp-dyn/articles/A19751-2004Jul27.html

Scarcely any political question arises in the United States that is not resolved, sooner or later, into a judicial question.

—Alexis de Tocqueville

COURTS: ELITES IN BLACK ROBES

CHAPTER **10**

The Supreme Court and the federal court system compose the most elitist institution in U.S. government. Nine justices—none of whom is elected and all of whom serve for life—possess ultimate authority over all the other institutions of government. These people have the power to declare void the acts of popularly elected presidents, Congresses, governors, state legislators, school boards, and city councils. No appeal is possible from their determination of what is the "supreme law of the land," short of undertaking the difficult task of amending the Constitution itself.[1]

The Supreme Court, rather than the president or Congress, has made many of the nation's most important domestic policy decisions. The Court took the lead in eliminating segregation from public life, ensuring separation of church and state, defining rights of criminal defendants and the powers of law enforcement officials, ensuring voter equality in representation, defining the limits of free speech and a free press, and declaring abortion a fundamental right of women. At other times, it upheld segregation, the internment of Japanese-Americans in World War II, and the forced sterilization of the poor. Sooner or later, the most important policy questions come before these justices—who cannot be removed for reasons other than "treason, bribery, or high crimes and misdemeanors." In a paradox for democratic theory, polls regularly report that the masses have more trust and confidence in the Supreme Court, the most elitist, nonelected branch of the government, than in the presidency or Congress. Among government institutions, only the U.S. military (even more hierarchical and more removed from popular control) inspires more mass confidence than the Supreme Court.

JUDICIAL REVIEW AS AN ELITIST PRINCIPLE

Recognition of the undemocratic character of judicial power in the United States is not new. The Founders viewed the federal courts as the final bulwark against mass threats to principle and property:

> Limited government ... can be preserved in practice no other way than through the medium of courts of justice, whose duty it is to declare all acts contrary to the manifest tenor of the Constitution void.[2]

In *Marbury v. Madison,* the historic 1803 U.S. Supreme Court decision establishing the power of judicial review, Chief Justice John Marshall argued persuasively that (1) the Constitution is "the supreme law of the land" and U.S. and state laws must be congruent with it; (2) Article III of the Constitution gives the Supreme Court the judicial power, which includes the power to interpret the meaning of laws and, in case of conflict between laws, to decide which law shall prevail; and (3) the courts are sworn to uphold the Constitution, so they must declare void a law that conflicts with the Constitution. Since 1803, the federal courts have struck down more than 100 laws of Congress and countless state laws that they believed conflicted with the Constitution. Judicial review and the power to interpret the meaning and decide the application of law are judges' major sources of power.

The Founders' decision to grant federal courts the power of judicial review over *state* court decisions and *state* laws is easy to understand. Article VI states that the Constitution and national laws and treaties are the supreme law of the land, "anything in the Constitution or laws of any state to the contrary notwithstanding." Federal court power over state decisions is probably essential in maintaining national unity, because 50 different state interpretations of the meaning of the Constitution or of the laws and treaties of Congress would create unimaginable confusion. Thus, the power of federal judicial review over state constitutions, laws, and court decisions is seldom questioned.

However, at the *national* level, why should an appointed court's interpretation of the Constitution prevail over the views of an elected Congress and an elected president? Members of Congress and presidents swear to uphold the Constitution, and we should be able to assume they do not pass laws they believe to be unconstitutional. Because both houses of Congress and the president must approve laws before they become effective, why should federal courts be allowed to set aside these decisions?

The answer is that the Founders distrusted popular majorities and the elected officials subject to their influence. They believed government should be prevented from attacking classical liberal principles and individual rights, particularly the right of property, whether to do so was the will of the majority or not. The Founders created a republic to avoid the potential excesses of mob rule, as the term democracy was then understood. So they deliberately insulated the courts from popular majorities; by appointing judges for life terms, they sought to ensure their independence. The Founders originally intended that the president (who was not to be directly elected) would appoint judges and that the Senate (also originally not to be directly elected) would confirm the president's appointments. Only in this way, the writers of the Constitution believed, would judges be sufficiently protected from the masses to permit them to judge courageously and responsibly.

Supreme Court Cases
Cornell Law School's Legal Information Institute website contains up-to-date information about important legal decisions rendered by federal and state courts, along with an exhaustive online law library available to researchers. *www. law.cornell.edu*

THE MAKING OF A SUPREME COURT JUSTICE

All federal judges are appointed by the president and confirmed by a majority vote of the Senate. The recruitment process is highly political. The U.S. Attorney General's office assists the president in screening candidates for all federal judgeships. For positions on the Supreme Court, presidents usually nominate judges who share their political philosophy. We might assume this practice is a democratizing influence on the Court, given that the people elect a president because they agree with his or her political philosophy. But Supreme Court justices frequently become independent once they reach the Court. Former Chief Justice Earl Warren, as Republican governor of California, had swung critical delegate votes to Eisenhower in the 1952 Republican convention. When the grateful president rewarded him with the chief justiceship, little in Warren's background suggested that he would lead the most liberal era in the Court's history. Later, Eisenhower complained the Warren appointment was "the biggest damn mistake I ever made."[3]

SOCIAL BACKGROUND

Justices' social backgrounds generally reflect close ties with the upper social strata. Historically, more than 90 percent of the Supreme Court justices have been from socially prominent, politically influential, upper-class families, although the trend has been to greater representation from among the middle class and even the poor. While five of nine current justices are worth over $1 million, and Justice Ginsberg's wealth exceeds $10 million,[4] most started from modest or even severely disadvantaged backgrounds. Justice Thomas grew up in a house with a dirt floor and Justice Sotomayor grew up in a public housing project. The diversity of the Court continues to expand from its historic profile, with three female members (Ginsberg, Kagan, and Sotomayor), one African-American (Thomas), one Latina (Sotomayor), three Jews (Breyer, Kagan, and Ginsberg), two Italian-Americans (Scalia and Alito), and six Roman Catholics (Roberts, Scalia, Kennedy, Thomas, Alito, and Sotomayor). In 2012, for the first time in the nation's history, there was not a single White Anglo-Saxon Protestant on the Supreme Court. Still, one traditional pattern has held steady: more than two-thirds of the justices ever and all those currently serving attended Ivy League or other prestigious law schools (see Table 10.1). One justice, Elena Kagan, actually once was Dean of the Harvard Law School.

Social background does not necessarily determine judicial philosophy. However, "if ... the Supreme Court is the keeper of the American conscience, it is essentially the conscience of the American upper-middle class, sharpened by the imperative of individual social responsibility and political activism, and conditioned by the conservative impact of legal training and professional legal attitudes and associations."[5]

POLITICIZING THE CONFIRMATION PROCESS

Historically, the Senate Judiciary Committee, which holds hearings and recommends confirmation to the full Senate, has consented to nominations by the president with a minimum of dissent; the Senate has rejected only 29 of the 132

Table 10.1 | Backgrounds of U.S. Supreme Court Justices

Justice	Year of Birth	Law School	Position at Time of Appointment	Appointed by (Year)
John Roberts, Chief Justice	1955	Harvard	Judge, U.S. Court of Appeals	Bush (2005)
Antonin Scalia	1936	Harvard	Judge, U.S. Court of Appeals	Reagan (1986)
Anthony Kennedy	1936	Harvard	Judge, U.S. Court of Appeals	Reagan (1987)
Clarence Thomas	1948	Yale	Judge, U.S. Court of Appeals	Bush (1991)
Ruth Bader Ginsburg	1933	Columbia	Judge, U.S. Court of Appeals	Clinton (1993)
Stephen Breyer	1938	Yale	Judge, U.S. Court of Appeals	Clinton (1994)
Samuel Alito	1950	Princeton	Judge, U.S. Court of Appeals	Bush (2006)
Sonia Sotomayor	1954	Yale	Judge, U.S. Court of Appeals	Obama (2009)
Elena Kagan	1960	Harvard	U.S. Solicitor General	Obama (2010)

Supreme Court nominations ever sent to it. The prevailing ethos had been that a popularly elected president deserves the opportunity to appoint judges; that the opposition party will have its own opportunity to appoint judges when it captures the presidency; and that partisan bickering over judicial appointments is undesirable. But in 1987, the U.S. Senate's rejection of President Reagan's nomination of Judge Robert Bork ended the traditional confirmation ethos. Bork, a highly respected legal scholar and experienced judge, was denied a seat on the Supreme Court not because he was not qualified, but because of his political philosophy. The term "**bork**" entered the lexicon to describe the blocking of qualified nominees on political grounds. Securing the Senate's confirmation of a Supreme Court nominee now depends on a highly partisan political campaign (see Focus: Senate Confirmation as Sleazy Spectacle).

Rejection by Filibuster

The Constitution requires only a majority consent of the Senate for presidential nominees to federal courts. However, in recent years, minority parties in the Senate have used the filibuster and cloture rules to hold up presidential nominees, notably nominees to federal Appeals Court seats. This has resulted in an unusually large number of vacancies on the bench, delaying trials and hearings and affecting the rights of citizens to a speedy resolution of their legal cases. Senators can filibuster the nomination, and the filibuster cannot be ended without a successful cloture motion, which itself requires a three-fifths vote of the Senate. This means the opposition party can defeat cloture with only 41 votes (see Chapter 8) and leave a president's judicial nominee unconfirmed. Senate leaders of the majority party have complained bitterly that the filibuster and cloture rules undermine the Constitution's requirement of only majority consent of the Senate. Both parties play this game when they do not hold the majority.

RECENT SUPREME COURT NOMINATIONS

In 2005, President George W. Bush was successful in his first Supreme Court nomination. John Roberts was eminently qualified to replace William Rehnquist as Chief Justice: B.A., Harvard; J.D., Harvard Law School; editor of the *Harvard Law Review;* assistant to the attorney general; and since 2003 judge on the D.C. Circuit Court of Appeals. At the Senate Judiciary Committee hearings he was pleasant, courteous, and extraordinarily knowledgeable about the law. He testified for days without any notes. He promised judicial restraint—to interpret the law, not to make it—but appeared more moderate than conservative in judicial philosophy. His nomination was confirmed by 72 to 22, with all Republicans and half the Democrats supporting him. Notably among those who opposed him was then-Senator Barack Obama.[6]

Also in 2005, upon the resignation of Sandra Day O'Connor, President Bush nominated Harriet Miers, a longtime personal friend serving as counselor to the president. Miers received her B.A. and law degrees from Southern Methodist University and served two years on the Dallas City Commission and was appointed Texas Lottery Commissioner. She had never served in a judicial capacity. Neither Republicans nor Democrats in the Senate were impressed with these meager credentials. After weeks of personal visits with senators, Miers was obliged to withdraw her nomination.

U.S. Courts
This is "a clearinghouse for information from and about the Judicial Branch of the U.S. government." It covers the U.S. Supreme Court, U.S. Courts of Appeals, U.S. District Courts, and U.S. Bankruptcy Courts. *www. uscourts.gov*

President Bush promptly nominated Samuel Alito, a judge with 15 years of experience on the Circuit Court of Appeals. Alito received his law degree from Yale and became a Justice Department official who wrote many memos in support of Reagan policies. Liberals would accuse him of personally endorsing these policies, but Alito responded that he was only serving his client as any lawyer would. He declined to say whether he supported *Roe v. Wade* but acknowledged that it was established precedent. Overall he gave the impression that he would be a moderate on the Court, rather than a regular member of the conservative block. His nomination was confirmed by the Senate on a 58 to 42 vote.

President Obama has made two Supreme Court nominations. In 2009, he chose U.S. Appeals Court Judge Sonia Sotomayor, a woman with 18 years of experience as a district court judge, before which she had been a criminal prosecutor and a corporate litigator. Her parents had moved from Puerto Rico, making her the Court's first Latina member. Her life story of growing up in a public housing project with a widowed mother, combined with her legal and judicial experience, made her a compelling nominee. She was confirmed by a vote of 68 to 31. In 2010, U.S. Solicitor General Elena Kagan was confirmed by a 63 to 37 vote. Before joining the Obama Justice Department, Kagan had been Associate White House Counsel and a policy advisor in the Clinton Administration as well as Harvard Law School Dean. An earlier appointment in 1999 to the federal Appeals Court expired without having had a Senate hearing scheduled.

SENATE QUESTIONING OF COURT NOMINEES

Senators on the Judiciary Committee, questioning presidents' nominees, have traditionally been frustrated by the refusal of nominees to comment on issues that are likely to come before the court in future cases. The nominees have argued that

| FOCUS | SENATE CONFIRMATION AS SPECTACLE |

The battle over the nomination of Clarence Thomas to be only the second African-American on the U.S. Supreme Court marked the Senate's collapse into disgraceful spectacle. Indeed, the Senate Judiciary Committee's performance in the Thomas confirmation established a new low in using prurient material politically.

Clarence Thomas, as President George H. W. Bush's nominee to replace Thurgood Marshall, the first African-American Supreme Court justice, reflected a generally conservative judicial philosophy. Born to a teenage mother who earned $10 a week as a maid, Clarence Thomas lived in a dirt-floor shack in Pin Point, Georgia, where he was raised by strict, hardworking grandparents. They taught young Clarence the value of education and sacrificed to send him to a Catholic school. He excelled academically and went on to mostly white Immaculate Conception Seminary College in Missouri to study for the Catholic priesthood. When in 1968 he overheard a fellow seminarian express satisfaction at the assassination of Martin Luther King, Jr., Thomas left the seminary in anger and enrolled at Holy Cross College in Washington, DC, where he helped found the college's Black Student Union. He graduated with honors and went on to Yale Law School.

Thomas began his legal career as an assistant Missouri attorney general under future Senator John C. Danforth. Thomas came to Washington with Danforth and was appointed assistant secretary for civil rights in the U.S. Department of Education and later chairman of the U.S. Equal Employment Opportunity Commission. In the latter role, Thomas spoke out against racial quotas, in favor of individual rights, and against welfare programs that create permanent dependency.

Bush White House strategists believed Thomas provided them with an opportunity to push a strong conservative past the liberal, Democratic-controlled Senate Judiciary Committee and win confirmation by the full Senate. They reasoned that liberal groups who had blocked the earlier nomination of conservative Robert Bork would be reluctant to launch personal attacks on an African-American.

But behind the scenes, liberal interest groups, including the National Abortion Rights Action League,

People for the American Way, and the National Organization for Women, were searching for evidence to discredit Thomas. On the third day of the hearings, a University of Oklahoma law professor, Anita Hill, a former legal assistant to Thomas both at the Department of Education and later at the Equal Employment Opportunity Commission, contacted the staff of the Judiciary Committee with charges that Thomas had sexually harassed her in both jobs. Initially, Hill declined to make her charges public, but when Chairman Joseph Biden (now U.S. vice president) refused to circulate anonymous charges, she agreed to be interviewed by the FBI and went on to give a nationally televised press conference, elaborating on her charges against Thomas. Her bombshell became a media extravaganza and sent the Senate into an uproar.

The televised hearings captured the nation's attention, touching directly on emotional issues of race and sex. Feminist groups cast the issue as one of sexual harassment and male insensitivity to women's concerns. But Clarence Thomas fought back hard, denying all charges and accusing the committee of conducting a "high-tech lynching" of an "uppity" black man who dares to have conservative opinions.

The mass public may not know or care much about judicial philosophy. Yet race and sex elicited strong opinions. And the "truth" in Washington is all too often determined by opinion polls. An astonishing 86 percent of the general public said they had watched the televised hearings. A majority of blacks as well as whites and a majority of women as well as men sided with the nominee. (In response to the question "Who do you believe more—Anita Hill or Clarence Thomas?" 54 percent said Thomas and 27 percent said Hill. Black opinion was even more heavily weighted in Thomas's direction, 61 to 19.[a]) The final Senate confirmation vote was 52 to 48, the closest vote in the history of Supreme Court confirmations.

[a]*Gallup Opinion Reports* (October 15, 1991), p. 209. A year later these percentages would shift in Hill's favor, following widespread attention in the media on the issue of sexual harassment.

giving specific opinions may impinge upon their judicial impartiality when faced with specific cases. A true judicial approach requires that they examine specific facts in each case, listen to the arguments on both sides, and confer with their colleagues on the Court before rendering an opinion. Thus in 2005, when asked whether he supported the controversial ruling in the 1973 abortion case *Roe v. Wade*, John Roberts said, "I should stay away from issues that may come before the Court again." But then-Democratic Senator Joseph Biden insisted that Roberts should at least discuss his views about abortion and the right of privacy as well as other general legal views: "Without any knowledge of your understanding of the law, because you will not share it with us, we are rolling the dice with you, judge." Samuel Alito was respectful of questioning senators but stopped short of providing any views on pending cases that might later come before the Court, as is common practice. In the Senate Judiciary committee in 2009, Republican senators repeatedly asked Sonia Sotomayor about whether some personal views she had expressed over the years would influence her court rulings. She matched her now fellow justices' skill in her ability to avoid answering specific questions.

THE STRUCTURE OF THE FEDERAL COURT SYSTEM

The federal court system consists of three levels of courts with general jurisdiction, together with various special courts (such as the Court of Claims, the Customs Court, the Patent Court, and the Court of Military Appeals). The Constitution establishes only the Supreme Court, although Congress determines the number of Supreme Court justices—traditionally nine. Article III authorizes Congress to establish "such inferior courts" as it deems appropriate. Congress has designed a hierarchical court system consisting of nearly 100 U.S. federal district courts and 11 U.S. circuit courts of appeals, in addition to the Supreme Court of the United States (see Figure 10.1).

FEDERAL DISTRICT COURTS

Federal **district courts** are the trial courts of the federal system. Each state has at least one district court, and larger states have more. (New York, for example, has four.) More than 600 judges, appointed for life by the president and confirmed by the Senate, preside in these courts. The president also appoints U.S. marshals for each district court to carry out orders of the court and maintain order in the courtroom. Federal district courts hear criminal cases prosecuted by the U.S. Department of Justice, as well as civil cases. As trial courts, the district courts use both grand juries (juries composed to hear evidence and, if warranted, to indict a defendant by bringing formal criminal charges against that person) and petit, or regular, juries (juries that determine guilt or innocence). District courts may hear as many as 300,000 cases in a year.

CIRCUIT COURTS OF APPEALS

Circuit courts of appeals are appellate courts. They do not hold trials or accept new evidence but consider only the record of the trial courts and oral or written arguments (briefs) submitted by attorneys. Federal law provides that every

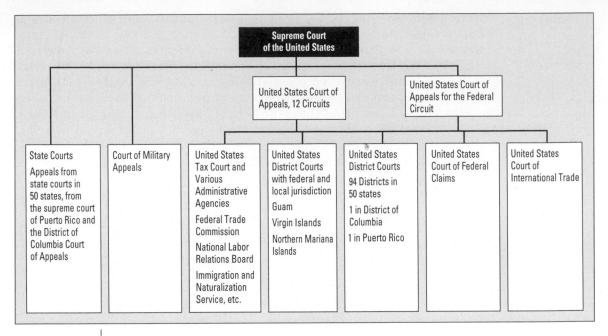

FIGURE 10.1 | THE U.S. COURT SYSTEM

individual has a right to appeal his or her case, so appellate courts have little discretion in hearing appeals. (Appellate judges themselves estimate that more than 80 percent of all appeals are "frivolous"—that is, without any real basis.) These courts require nearly 100 circuit court judges, appointed for life by the president and confirmed by the Senate. Normally, three circuit judges serve together on a panel to hear appeals. More than 90 percent of the cases they decide end at this level. Further appeal to the Supreme Court is not automatic; the Supreme Court itself decides what appeals it will consider. Hence, for most cases, the decision of the circuit court of appeals is final.

THE U.S. SUPREME COURT

The Supreme Court of the United States is the final interpreter of all matters involving the U.S. Constitution and federal laws and treaties, whether the case began in a federal district court or in a state court. The Supreme Court technically must hear *writs of appeal,* but only a few matters qualify. Among them are cases involving clear constitutional issues (for example, a finding that a federal law is unconstitutional, that a state law is in conflict with federal law, or that a state law is in violation of the U.S. Constitution). *Writs of certiorari* are granted when four members agree that an issue involves a "substantial federal question." However, the Supreme Court denies most cases submitted to it and need not give any reason for denying appeal or certiorari. Each year the Court receives about 8,000 appeals, usually submitted as *writs of certiorari* (literally "to make more certain"), but it

The U.S. Supreme Court
Official website provides recent decisions, case dockets, oral arguments, public information, etc. *www. supremecourt.gov*

accepts fewer than 150. The Supreme Court determines for itself whether to accept an appeal and consider a case.

In the early days of the republic, the size of the Supreme Court fluctuated, but since 1869 its membership has remained at nine: the chief justice and eight associate justices. The Supreme Court is in session each year from October through June, hearing oral arguments, accepting written briefs, conferring, and rendering opinions.

THE JURISDICTION OF THE FEDERAL COURT SYSTEM

In the U.S. federal system, each state maintains its own court system. The federal courts are not necessarily superior to state courts; both state and federal courts operate independently. But because the U.S. Supreme Court has appellate jurisdiction over state supreme courts as well as over lower federal courts, the Supreme Court oversees the nation's entire judicial system.

State courts have general jurisdiction in all criminal and civil cases. According to Article III of the U.S. Constitution, federal court jurisdiction extends to

- Cases arising under the Constitution, federal laws, or treaties
- Cases involving ambassadors, public ministers or counsels, or maritime laws
- Cases in which the U.S. government is a party
- Cases between two or more states
- Cases between a state and a citizen of another state
- Cases between citizens of different states
- Cases between a state or a citizen and a foreign government or citizen of another nation

Obviously, it is not difficult "to make a federal case out of it," regardless of what "it" might be. The Constitution contains many vaguely worded guarantees—"due process of law," "equal protection of the laws," protection from "cruel and unusual punishment" and "unreasonable searches and seizures," and so forth—which allow nearly every party to any case to claim a federal question is involved and a federal court is the proper forum (see Focus: "Make It a Federal Crime!")

APPEALS FROM STATE COURTS

The great bulk of the national caseload begins and ends in state court systems. The federal courts do not intervene once a state court has started hearing a case, except in rare circumstances. Congress has stipulated that legal disputes between citizens of different states must involve $75,000 or more to be heard in federal court. Moreover, parties to cases in state courts must "exhaust their remedies"—that is, appeal their case all the way through the state courts—before the federal courts will hear their appeal. Appeals from state supreme courts go directly to the U.S. Supreme Court and not to federal district or circuit courts. Usually these appeals are made on the grounds that they raise "a federal question"—that is, a question on the application of the U.S. Constitution or federal law. The U.S. Supreme Court reviews only a small fraction of appeals from state court decisions.

FEDERAL COURT CASELOADS

Of the 10 million civil and criminal cases begun in the nation's courts each year, fewer than 3 percent (250,000) are filed in federal district courts. State and local courts hear the great bulk of legal cases. The U.S. Constitution reserves general police powers to the states so that crimes and civil disputes are generally matters of state and local concern. Murder, robbery, assault, and rape are normally state offenses rather than federal crimes. Federal crimes generally center on offenses that (1) were committed against the U.S. government or its property; (2) were committed against U.S. government officials or employees while they are on duty; (3) cross state lines (such as nationally organized crime, unlawful escape across state lines, taking kidnapping victims across state lines); (4) interfere with interstate commerce; and/or (5) occur on federal territories or on the seas.

JUDICIAL POWER: ACTIVISM VERSUS SELF-RESTRAINT

Great legal scholars have argued the merits of activism versus self-restraint in judicial decision making for more than a century.[7] Proponents of **judicial self-restraint** argue that because justices are not popularly elected, the Supreme Court should move cautiously and avoid direct confrontation with legislative and executive authority. Justice Felix Frankfurter wrote, "The only check upon our own exercise of power is our own sense of self-restraint. For the removal of unwise laws from the statute books, appeal lies not to the courts but to the ballot and to the processes of democratic government."[8]

However, Frankfurter was arguing a minority position. The dominant philosophy of the Supreme Court under Chief Justice Earl Warren (1953–1969) was one of **judicial activism**. The Warren Court believed it should shape constitutional meaning to fit its estimate of the needs of contemporary society. By viewing the Constitution as a deliberately broad and flexible document, we can avoid making dozens of new constitutional amendments to accommodate a changing society. The idea here is that the strength of the U.S. Constitution lies in its flexibility.[9]

This Supreme Court posture of judicial activism, combined with its lifetime appointments, greatly strengthens its elitist character. If a nonelective institution such as the federal judiciary assumes a strong, activist role in national policymaking, the result is an even more elitist political system. This is true whether the Supreme Court is active on behalf of liberal or conservative policies. Liberals who praise the virtues of judicial activism, who urge the Court to stand against the misguided policies of an elected president and Congress, must recognize the elitist nature of their argument.

RULES OF RESTRAINT

Even an activist Supreme Court adheres to some general rules of judicial self-restraint. These include the following:

- The Court will decide on the constitutionality of legislation only in an actual case. Thus, it will not advise the president or Congress on constitutional questions.

- The Court will not anticipate a question on constitutional law; it does not decide hypothetical cases.
- The Court will not formulate a rule of constitutional law broader than required by the precise facts to which it must be applied.
- The Court will not pass upon a constitutional question if some other ground exists upon which it may dispose of the case.
- When doubt exists about the constitutionality of a law, the Court will try to interpret the law so as to give it a constitutional meaning and avoid the necessity of declaring it unconstitutional.
- A complainant must have exhausted all remedies available in lower federal courts or state courts before the Supreme Court accepts review.
- Occasionally the Court defers to Congress and the president, classifies an issue as a political question, and refuses to decide it. The Court has stayed out of foreign and military policy areas.
- If the Court holds a law unconstitutional, it will confine its decision to the particular section of the law that is unconstitutional; the rest of the statute stays intact.[10]

FOCUS | ## "MAKE IT A FEDERAL CRIME!"

Washington politicians are continually pressured to make "a federal crime" of virtually every offense in society. Neither Democrats nor Republicans, liberals nor conservatives, are willing to risk their political futures by telling their constituents a particular crime is a state responsibility and not an important enough subject for federal attention. So Washington lawmakers continue to add offenses to the ever-lengthening list of federal crimes.

Traditionally, the federal government's criminal responsibilities were limited to enforcement of a relatively narrow range of federal laws, including laws dealing with counterfeiting, tax evasion, bank fraud and embezzlement, robbery or theft of federally insured funds, interstate criminal activity, and murder or assault of a federal official. Although some federal criminal laws overlapped state laws, most criminal activity—murder, rape, robbery, assault, burglary, theft, auto theft, drug offenses, and sex offenses—fell under state jurisdiction. Indeed, the *police power* was believed to be one of the reserved powers of the states referred to in the Tenth Amendment.

Today, federal crimes range from drive-by shootings to obstructing sidewalks in front of abortion clinics. Any violent offense motivated by animosity based on race, religion, or ethnicity is a "hate crime" subject to federal prosecution. Racketeering and conspiracy (organizing and communicating with others about the intent to commit a crime) are federal crimes. Federal involvement in law enforcement has its greatest impact on drug-related crime. Drug offenders may be tried in either federal or state courts or both. Federal drug laws carry heavier penalties than those of most of the states.

Only recently has the U.S. Supreme Court recognized that federalizing crime may impinge on the reserved powers of the states. In 1994, Congress passed a popular Violence Against Women Act that allowed victims of gender-motivated violence, including rape, to sue their attackers for monetary damages in federal court. Congress defended its constitutional authority to involve itself in crimes against women by citing the commerce clause, arguing that crimes against women interfered with interstate commerce, a legislative power given to the federal government in Article I of the Constitution. But in 2000, the Supreme Court said, "The Constitution requires a distinction between what is truly national and what is truly local, and there is no better example of the police power, which the Founders undeniably left reposed in the states and denied the central government than the suppression of violent crime."[a]

[a] *United States v. Morrison*, 529 U.S. 598 (2000).

STARE DECISIS

Courts are also limited by the principle of ***stare decisis***, which means the issue has already been decided in earlier cases and the decision stands. Reliance on precedent is a fundamental notion in law. Indeed, the underlying common law of England and the United States is composed simply of past decisions. Students of the law learn through the case-study method: the study of previous decisions. Reliance on precedent gives stability to the law; if every decision were new law, then no one would know what the law is from day to day. The Supreme Court continues to use precedents from English common law going back to Magna Carta of 1215.

Despite the *stare decisis* principle, judicial activists are frequently willing to discard precedent. Former Justice William O. Douglas, who seldom felt restrained by legal precedent, justified disregard of precedent as follows:

> The decisions of yesterday or of the last century are only the starting points.... A judge looking at a constitutional decision may have compulsions to revere the past history and accept what was once written. But he remembers above all else that it is the Constitution which he swore to support and defend, not the gloss which his predecessors may have put on it. So he comes to formulate his own laws, rejecting some earlier ones as false and embracing others. He cannot do otherwise unless he lets men long dead and unaware of the problems of the age in which he lives do his thinking for him.[11]

ORIGINAL INTENT

Should the Constitution be interpreted in terms of the intentions of its original writers, or according to the morality of society today? Many legal scholars hold that the Constitution is a living document, that each generation must interpret it in the light of current conditions, and that to do otherwise would soon render it obsolete. But in interpreting the Constitution, whose values should prevail—those of the judges or of its writers?

The doctrine of **original intent** takes the values of the Founders as expressed in the text of the Constitution and applies them to current conditions. Defenders of original intent argue that the words in the document must be given their historical meaning, and that meaning must restrain courts as well as the legislative and executive branches of government. They see this originalism as important to the system's checks and balances. The Supreme Court should not set aside laws made by elected representatives unless they conflict with the original intent of the Founders. Setting aside laws because they do not accord with today's moral standards is simply substituting the Court's morality for that of elected bodies. Such decisions lack democratic legitimacy, because there is no reason why judges' moral views should prevail over those of elected representatives.

WISDOM VERSUS CONSTITUTIONALITY

Distinguished jurists have long urged the Supreme Court to exercise self-restraint. A law may be unwise, unfair, or even stupid and yet still be constitutional. We cannot equate the wisdom of the law with its constitutionality, and the Court should decide only the constitutionality and not the wisdom of a law. Justice Oliver

Wendell Holmes once lectured his colleague, 61-year-old Justice Harlan Stone, on this point:

> Young man, about 75 years ago I learned that I was not God. And so, when the people … want to do something I can't find anything in the Constitution expressly forbidding them to do, I say, whether I like it or not, "Goddamn it, let 'em do it."[12]

However, the actual role of the Supreme Court in the nation's power struggles suggests that the Court indeed equates wisdom with constitutionality. People frequently cite broad phrases in the Fifth and Fourteenth Amendments, establishing constitutional standards of "due process of law" and "equal protection of the laws," when attacking laws they believe are unfair or unjust. Most have come to believe that laws that are simply unwise must also be unconstitutional and that the courts have become the final arbiters of fairness and justice.

The debate between the straight constitutionality of the originalists and a more activist approach based on the "wisdom" of judges and justices had a public airing during the Senate confirmation hearings for Sonia Sotomayor in 2009. In earlier speeches she had talked about the relative merit of personal experience and judicial rulings: "I would hope that a wise Latina woman with the richness of her experiences would more often than not reach a better conclusion than a white male who hasn't lived that life." (Her comment is better understood in context.)[13] The school of thought arguing that personal experience of judges, including gender, race, and ethnicity, can matter in making decisions is known as legal realism. It dates back to the early twentieth century and the time of Justice Benjamin Cardozo.

SUPREME COURT POLITICS

Once appointed to lifetime positions, the jobs of Supreme Court justices do not depend on public opinion, partisan shifts in Congress or the presidency, or indeed the outcome of democratic politics. Supreme Court justices make decisions based on their own political and judicial philosophies.

IN BRIEF | JUDICIAL ACTIVISM VERSUS JUDICIAL SELF-RESTRAINT

Arguments over the merits of judicial activism versus self-restraint continue:

- Activism argues that constitutional meaning must be fitted to the needs of contemporary society; the strength of the Constitution is its flexibility. (Judicial activism adds to the power of the nonelected judiciary and results in an even more elitist political system.)
- Self-restraint recognizes that the federal judiciary is nonelective and it should leave lawmaking to elected officials.

- The Supreme Court follows some rules of restraint, for example, not deciding hypothetical questions and not giving advisory opinions.
- The courts recognize the principle of *stare decisis*—relying on past decisions and thus giving stability to the law.
- The doctrine of original intent requires interpretation of the Constitution according to the intent of the Founders, not the current moral views of judges.

Most cases do not present a clear liberal–conservative dimension, and even fewer present a partisan—Democratic versus Republican—dimension. (However, see Focus: The President versus the Supreme Court.) Each case presents a separate set of facts, and even justices who share a general philosophy may perceive the central facts of a case differently. So ideological blocs are not always good predictors of voting outcomes on the Supreme Court, as demonstrated in 2012 when conservative Chief Justice John Roberts voted to uphold President Obama's health care law.

CHANGING LIBERAL AND CONSERVATIVE BLOCS ON THE SUPREME COURT

Over time, the ideological composition of the Supreme Court changes (see Table 10.2). A liberal bloc, headed by Chief Justice Earl Warren, dominated Court decision making from the mid-1950s through the end of the 1960s. The liberal bloc gradually weakened following President Richard Nixon's appointment of

---

| FOCUS | THE PRESIDENT VERSUS THE SUPREME COURT |

The U.S. system of checks and balances sets up a basic rivalry between the branches of government. President Barack Obama has shown a willingness to make his irritation with the judicial branch public, even pre-emptively, on issues that are politically important. In his 2010 State of the Union address, Obama singled out the Supreme Court's ruling in the case of *Citizens United v. the Federal Election Commission* (see Chapter 7), berating the justices sitting before him by stating "Last week, the Supreme Court reversed a century of law that I believe will open the floodgates for special interests—including foreign corporations—to spend without limit in our elections." A shocked-looking Justice Samuel Alito frowned and mouthed the words "not true." A few weeks later at a speech at the University of Alabama, Chief Justice John Roberts commented that "The image of having the members of one branch of government standing up, literally surrounding the Supreme Court, cheering and hollering while the court—according the requirements of protocol—has to sit there expressionless, I think is very troubling." Roberts also said he felt the event had "degenerated into a political pep rally."[a]

In 2012, Obama used a press conference to comment on his views of the Supreme Court as an "unelected group of people" who could strike down

as unconstitutional his health care law: the Affordable Care Act. "Ultimately, I am confident that the Supreme Court will not take what would be an unprecedented, extraordinary step of overturning a law that was passed by a strong majority of a democratically elected Congress," he said. A former constitutional law professor, Obama was inaccurate in describing judicial review as "unprecedented," and the health care law's passage by seven votes was hardly a "strong majority." The president, like all other Americans, has the right to comment on the court. In June 2012, the Court ruled on this matter that the most controversial aspect of the law, an individual mandate forcing individuals to purchase health insurance or face a fine, was in fact a tax and thus allowed under the Constitution. It also ruled that states could not be coerced by the federal government to expand the federal-state Medicaid program, as that violated the constitutional separation of powers. These rulings were made by an independent judiciary which remains immune to political control due to lifelong tenure and a constitutional separation of powers.

[a]Politico, "Roberts Questions SOTU Attendance," March 9, 2010. *www.politico.com/politico44/perm/0310/very_troubling_f90ec36f-c19d-4360-81c8-f72bdd227b3a.html.*

| TABLE 10.2 | LIBERAL AND CONSERVATIVE VOTING BLOCS ON THE SUPREME COURT |

	The Warren Court	The Burger Court	The Rehnquist Court	The Roberts Court*
	1968	1975	2004	2011
Liberal	Earl Warren Hugo Black William Douglas Thurgood Marshall William Brennan Abraham Fortas	William Douglas Thurgood Marshall William Brennan Harry Blackmun	John Paul Stevens Ruth Bader Ginsburg Stephen Breyer David Souter	Ruth Bader Ginsburg Stephen Breyer Sonia Sotomayor Elena Kagan
Moderate	Potter Stewart Byron White	Potter Stewart Byron White Lewis Powell	Anthony Kennedy Sandra Day O'Connor	Anthony Kennedy
Conservative	John Harlan	Warren Burger William Rehnquist	William Rehnquist Antonin Scalia Clarence Thomas	John Roberts Samuel Alito Clarence Thomas Antonin Scalia

*All blocs have been designated by the authors.

Warren Burger as chief justice in 1969, but Nixon's appointees did not all join the conservative bloc; Harry Blackmun and Lewis Powell frequently voted with the liberal bloc and only William Rehnquist consistently adopted conservative positions. President Gerald Ford's only appointee to the Court, John Paul Stevens, began as a moderate but later joined the liberal bloc. As a result, the Burger Court, although generally not as active as the Warren Court, still did not reverse any earlier liberal decisions.

President Ronald Reagan campaigned on a pledge to restrain the liberal activism of the Court. His first appointee, and the first woman on the Court, Sandra Day O'Connor, turned out to be less conservative than expected, especially on women's issues and abortion rights. When Chief Justice Burger retired in 1986, Reagan seized the opportunity to strengthen the conservative bloc by elevating Justice Rehnquist to chief justice and appointing a strong conservative, Antonin Scalia, to the Court. If Reagan had succeeded in getting the powerful conservative voice of Robert Bork on the Court, the Court might have reversed some of its earlier liberal decisions. But the Democratic Senate rejected Bork, and Anthony Kennedy, the man ultimately confirmed, compiled a generally liberal voting record.

New faces on the Supreme Court can either change or reinforce the overall balance of the institution. George H. W. Bush's appointment of the conservative Clarence Thomas as a replacement for the liberal Thurgood Marshall gave the conservative bloc a strong voice on the Court. President William Clinton's appointees, Ruth Bader Ginsburg and Stephen G. Breyer, predictably reinforced the liberal bloc. President George W. Bush replaced conservative Chief Justice William Rehnquist with John Roberts and the generally conservative Sandra Day O'Connor with Samuel Alito, holding the conservative bloc together. President Barack Obama replaced liberals with other liberals.

DO THE COURTS RULE THE NATION?

George C. Wallace once put the argument bluntly: "Thugs and federal judges have just about taken charge of this country."[14] Others have also worried about the increasing role of the judiciary—the ability of courts to intrude into people's lives in ways unprecedented in history. Elite theory is interested in the extent to which we now rely on a nonelected judiciary to solve our problems, rather than on democratically elected executives and legislators.

GROWING RELIANCE ON THE COURTS

Harvard Law School professor Archibald Cox, who became famous as the first Watergate prosecutor, warned that "excessive reliance upon courts instead of self-government through democratic processes, may deaden the people's sense of moral and political responsibility for their own future, especially in matters of liberty, and may stunt the growth of political capacity that results from the exercise of the ultimate powers of decision."[15] For good or for ill, we have come to rely on courts to solve problems once handled by legislatures, local officials, school boards, teachers, parents, or other social organizations. On the most controversial issues, such as abortion, elected politicians seem to abandon their charge to govern and leave it to the courts (see Focus: The Supreme Court and Abortion).

COURT CONGESTION

Nearly one million lawyers practice in the United States. Each year the nation's courts try more than 10 million cases, mostly in state and local courts. Over 250,000 cases begin in federal courts each year. Most will be settled before trial, but about 25,000 (or 10 percent) go to trial. People appeal more than 50,000 cases to U.S. courts of appeal each year. And the U.S. Supreme Court receives about 8,000 appeals each year, although it accepts and decides on fewer than 200 of them.

FOCUS | THE SUPREME COURT AND ABORTION

It is ironic indeed that a democratic nation calls on a nonelective, lifetime elite to decide its most contentious issues.

Historically, abortions for any purpose other than saving the life of the mother were criminal offenses under most state laws. A few states permitted abortions in cases of rape or incest or to protect the health of the woman. Then in 1970, a few states enacted laws that in effect permitted abortion at the request of the woman and the concurrence of her physician. A growing pro-abortion coalition formed, including the American Civil Liberties Union (ACLU), the National Association for the Repeal of Abortion Laws (NARAL), Planned Parenthood, and feminist organizations including the National Organization for Women (NOW). These groups went under the name "pro-choice," referring to a woman's choice to have a baby.

In this period, the Supreme Court was developing a new constitutional right of privacy, partly in response to the 1965 case *Griswold v. Connecticut*. When Estelle Griswold opened a birth control clinic on behalf of Planned Parenthood, the state of Connecticut found her in violation of a state law prohibiting the use of contraceptives. She challenged the constitutionality of the statute, and the Supreme Court, seeing a right to privacy between a patient and her doctor, struck down the law by a vote of 7 to 2.[a]

The right to privacy is nowhere specifically stated in the Constitution. Justice William Douglas found it in "the penumbras formed by emanations from" the First, Third, Fourth, Ninth, and Fifteenth Amendments. Other justices found it in the Ninth Amendment: "The enumeration of the Constitution of certain rights, shall not be contrived to deny or disparage others retained by the people." The fact that *Griswold* dealt with reproduction gave encouragement to interest groups advocating abortion rights.

When Norma McCorvey sought an abortion in Texas in 1969, her doctor refused, citing a state law prohibiting abortion except to save a woman's life. McCorvey bore the child and gave it up for adoption but then challenged the Texas law in federal courts on a variety of constitutional grounds, including the right to privacy. *Amicus curiae* briefs were filed by a wide assortment of interest groups on both sides of the issue. McCorvey became "Jane Roe," and *Roe v. Wade* became one of the most controversial cases in the Court's history.[b] The Supreme Court ruled in 1973 that the constitutional right to privacy as well as the Fourteenth Amendment's guarantee of "liberty" included a woman's decision to bear or not to bear a child. The Court said the word *person* in the Constitution did *not* include the unborn child; therefore the Fifth and Fourteenth Amendments' guarantee of "life, liberty and property" did not protect the fetus. The Court also ruled that a state's power to protect the health and safety of the mother could not justify *any* restriction on abortion in the first three months of pregnancy. Between the third and sixth months of pregnancy, a state could set standards for abortion procedures to protect the health of women but could not prohibit abortions. Only in the final three months could a state prohibit or regulate abortion to protect the unborn.

Roe v. Wade set off a political conflagration. A new movement, known as "pro-life" (referring to the life of the unborn), was mobilized to restrict the scope of the decision and to seek its overturn. Congress defeated efforts to pass a constitutional amendment restricting abortion or declaring that life begins at conception. However, Congress did ban the use of federal funds under Medicaid (medical care for the poor) for abortions except to protect the life of a woman. The Supreme Court upheld the ban, holding that there was no constitutional obligation for governments to pay for abortions.[c]

Initial efforts by some states to restrict abortion ran into Supreme Court opposition.[d] But opponents of abortion won a victory in *Webster v. Reproductive Health Services* in 1989.[e] In this case, the Supreme Court upheld a Missouri law denying public funds for abortions that were not necessary to preserve the life of the woman and denying the use of public facilities or employees in performing or assisting in abortions. More important, the justices recognized the state's "interest in the protection of human life when viability is possible," and they upheld Missouri's requirement for a test of "viability" after 20 weeks and prohibition on abortions of a viable fetus except to save a woman's life. *Webster* gave pro-life groups hope that the Supreme Court might eventually overturn *Roe v. Wade.*

Since then, the Supreme Court appears to have chosen a policy of affirming a woman's right to abortion while upholding modest restrictions, as evidenced by its ruling in *Planned Parenthood of Pennsylvania v. Casey* in 1992.[f] In this case, the Supreme Court upheld a series of restrictions on abortion enacted by Pennsylvania: that physicians must inform women of risks and alternatives; a 24-hour wait period; and that minors must have the consent of parents or a judge. The majority also upheld a state's right to protect any fetus that reached the point of "viability." The Court went on to establish a new standard for constitutionally evaluating restrictions: They must not impose an "undue burden" on women seeking abortion or place "substantial obstacles" in her path. All Pennsylvania's restrictions that met this standard were upheld.

A number of states have attempted to outlaw an abortion procedure known as "intact dilation and evacuation" or "partial birth" abortion. This rare procedure involves partially delivering the fetus/baby feet-first, then vacuuming out the brain and crushing the skull to ease complete removal. Congressional bans of this procedure in the 1990s were vetoed by President Clinton. In 2004, Congress again voted to ban "partial birth" abortions and President Bush signed the ban into law. In 2007, the Supreme Court found 5 to 4 that the federal ban did *not* create an "undue burden" on a woman's right to an abortion and was constitutional.[g]

[a]*Griswold v. Connecticut,* 381 U.S. 479 (1965).

[b]*Roe v. Wade,* 400 U.S. 113 (1973).

[c]*Harris v. McRae,* 448 U.S. 297 (1980).

[d]*Planned Parenthood of Missouri v. Danforth,* 418 U.S. 52 (1976); *Belloti v. Baird,* 443 U.S. 662 (1979); *Akron v. Akron Center for Reproductive Health,* 103 S. Ct. 2481 (1983).

[e]*Webster v. Reproductive Health Services,* 492 U.S. 111 (1989).

[f]*Planned Parenthood of Pennsylvania v. Casey,* 505 U.S. 110 (1992).

[g]*Gonzales v. Earhart,* April 18, 2007.

The growing number of legal cases not only raises questions about the increasing power of a nonelected, lifetime judicial elite but also burdens the court system and creates many injustices. Cases may be backed up on court dockets for years. As a result, injured parties in civil cases must suffer long delays before receiving compensation. Criminal defendants who are free on bail may deliberately delay the trial, hoping witnesses will move away or forget important details or victims will grow frustrated and give up trying to prosecute. Most lawsuits require attorneys on both sides, and attorneys are expensive. The longer a case drags on, the more expensive it is likely to be, thus disproportionately favoring the wealthy and well-funded organizations.

PLEA BARGAINING

Congestion forces prosecuting attorneys in criminal cases to **plea bargain** with defendants—that is, to make special arrangements for criminal defendants to plead guilty in exchange for reduced charges. For example, a prosecutor may reduce the charge of rape to sexual assault, which usually carries a lighter penalty. The prosecutor enters into such a bargain to avoid the delays and costs of a trial; the defendant accepts to escape serious penalty for the crime. Estimates suggest that 90 percent of all criminal cases are now plea bargained. Plea bargains are more likely to be accepted by accused who cannot afford a lawyer and receive their representation from a court-appointed attorney, who likely has a large caseload that might be managed more easily through multiple plea bargains.

JUDICIAL REFORMS

Federal courts are so well insulated from popular, congressional, and presidential pressures that reform will probably have to come from within. If federal judges are slow in handling cases, if their decisions are arbitrary, if congestion and confusion reign in their courtrooms, if they bog down in details of managing school districts or prisons or hospitals, if they are lazy or poorly trained in the law, if they are in poor health or senile, no one can do much about it. Only five federal court judges have ever been impeached and convicted by Congress. In 1989, Federal District Court Judge L. C. Hastings became the first sitting judge in more than 50 years to be impeached, tried, and found guilty by the Congress. (Ironically, the politically popular and flamboyant Hastings was elected to the House of Representatives in 1992 and has won reelection ever since.) Other judges have resigned under fire: federal judge Otto Kerner (former governor of Illinois) resigned his judicial post in 1974 only five days before he was scheduled to enter prison for income tax evasion, perjury, bribery, and mail fraud. In short, the U.S. citizenry has little control over the judiciary, despite the control it exercises over all of us.

THE COURTS | AN ELITIST INTERPRETATION

The Supreme Court determines many of the nation's most important policies. Indeed, most political questions sooner or later end up in the courts. Any fair examination of the court system in the United States will reveal the elitist character of judicial decision making.

1. The Supreme Court is the most elitist branch of the national government. Nine justices—none of whom is elected and all of whom serve for life—can void the acts of popularly elected presidents, Congresses, governors, legislatures, school boards, and city councils.
2. The principle of judicial review of congressional acts grew out of the Founders' distrust of popularly elected officials subject to influence by popular majorities. Judicial review enables the courts to protect constitutional principles against attacks by elected bodies.
3. Presidents may attempt to influence court decisions through their selection of judges, but life terms make judges independent of presidential or congressional influence once they are appointed.
4. Because justices are not popularly elected, some scholars and jurists have urged self-restraint in judicial policy-making. They argue that the Supreme Court should decide only the constitutionality of a law, not its wisdom; the Court should not substitute its own judgment for the judgment of elected representatives. But over the years judicial activism has augmented the power of judges. Justices have used broad phrases in the Constitution such as "due process of law" and "equal protection of the law" to strike down laws they believe are unfair or unjust.

5. Even an activist Supreme Court adheres to some rules of restraint. It does not give advisory opinions or decide hypothetical cases or decide on the constitutionality of a law until an actual case directly involving the law comes before it.

6. U.S. citizens have come to rely on courts to resolve key conflicts in society. There are more lawyers and more court cases in the United States than in any other nation in the world.

NOTES

1. U.S. Supreme Court decisions are available at http://www.supremecourtus.gov. Court opinions are cited by the names of the parties, e.g., *Brown v. Board of Education of Topeka, Kansas,* followed by a reference number, such as 347 U.S. 483 (1954). The first number in the citation (347) is the volume number, "U.S." refers to *United States Reports;* the subsequent number is the page on which the decision begins; the year the case was decided is in parentheses.

2. James Madison, Alexander Hamilton, and John Jay, *The Federalist* (New York: Modern Library, 1937), p. 505.

3. Joseph W. Bishop, "The Warren Court Is Not Likely to Be Overruled," *New York Times Magazine,* September 7, 1969, p. 31.

4. Seth Cline, "Ruth Bader Ginsburg, Steven Breyer Wealthiest Judges on U.S. Supreme Court," September 6, 2011. http://www.opensecrets.org/news/2011/09/ruth-bader-ginsburg-steven-breyer.html

5. John R. Schmidhauser, *The Supreme Court* (New York: Holt, Rinehart & Winston, 1960), p. 59.

6. Barack Obama, "Senate Speech on Nomination of John Roberts." *Congressional Record,* September 22, 2005 (Senate), pp. S10365–S10367. From the Congressional Record online via GPO access [wais.access.gpo.gov] [DOCID:cr22se05-143].

7. Frank Jerone, *Law and the Modern Mind* (New York: Coward-McCann, 1930); Benjamin N. Cardozo, *The Nature of the Judicial Process* (New Haven, CT: Yale University Press, 1921); Roscoe Pound, *Justice According to Law* (New Haven, CT: Yale University Press, 1951).

8. *West Virginia State Board of Education v. Barnette,* 319 U.S. 624 (1943).

9. Archibald Cox, *The Warren Court* (Cambridge, MA: Harvard University Press, 1968), p. 2.

10. Henry Abraham, *The Judicial Process* (New York: Oxford University Press, 1968), pp. 310–326.

11. Justice William O. Douglas, "*Stare Decisis,*" *Record* (April 1947).

12. Quoted by Charles P. Curtis, *Lions Under the Throne* (Boston, MA: Houghton Mifflin, 1947), p. 281.

13. Sonia Sotomayor, "A Latina Judge's Voice" (Berkeley, CA: UC Berkeley School of Law, 2001). For transcript see http://www.berkeley.edu/news/media/releases/2009/05/26_sotomayor.shtml

14. *Newsweek,* January 10, 1977, p. 42.

15. Archibald Cox, *The Role of the Supreme Court in American Government* (New York: Oxford University Press, 1976), p. 103.

The problem is not conspiracy or corruption, but unchecked rule.
And being unchecked, the rule reflects not the national need but the
bureaucratic need.

—John K. Galbraith

THE BUREAUCRATIC ELITE | CHAPTER 11

Power in the United States continues to shift from those who control economic and political resources to those who control technology, information, and expertise. The Washington bureaucracy has become a major base of power in U.S. society— independent of Congress, the president, the courts, and the people. Government bureaucracies pervade every aspect of modern life: the home, communications, transportation, the workplace, schools, the community, the air, and the water.

By definition, **bureaucracy** refers to the vast bulk of the executive branch of government, whether at the federal, state, or local level. In government, bureaucracy focuses on career civil servants, but it also includes the thin stratus of political appointees nominally in charge of these millions of government employees. The word is derived from the French word *bureau* meaning "office" and refers to the idea that society is ruled not by elected officials, but rather by men and women inhabiting offices who make regulations and decisions. While this notion may sometimes be taken to extremes, this often-overlooked portion of government does have powerful influence over life in the United States.

In theory, a bureaucracy is a form of social organization that the German sociologist Max Weber described as having (1) a chain of command (hierarchy); (2) a division of labor among subunits (specialization); (3) specification of authority for positions and units by rules and regulation (span of control); (4) impersonality in executing tasks (neutrality); (5) adaptation of structure, authority, and rules to the organization's goals (goal orientation); and (6) predictability of behavior based on maintenance of records and assurance of rules (standardization).[1] If we use Weber's definition, then both corporations and governments, and many other organizations in society such as universities, are bureaucracies.

In practice, bureaucracy has become a negative term. People view it as bringing with it "red tape," paper shuffling, duplication of effort, waste and inefficiency, impersonality, insensitivity, and overregulation. Many of us have had frustrating experiences dealing with various faces of the bureaucracy, such as a state Department of Motor Vehicles or perhaps a college's registration office during the first week of classes. More important, since bureaucracies are not subject to market demands for quality customer service, people have come to view governmental bureaucracy as unresponsive to the needs of the nation or the people. A General Social Survey poll in 2006 found that when asked whether "most government administrators can be trusted to do what is best for the country," a meager 27 percent of respondents agreed.

Certainly, "the people" have no direct means of altering bureaucratic decisions. Even the president, the White House staff, and cabinet officials have great difficulty establishing control over the bureaucracy. Congress and the courts can place only the broadest restrictions on bureaucratic power. The bureaucrats control information and technology, and they almost invariably outlast their political superiors in office. Often, in fact, the bureaucrats feel a certain contempt for their superiors because political leaders do not have the information, technical expertise, and experience of the bureaucrats.

SOURCES OF BUREAUCRATIC POWER

The power of bureaucracies grows with advances in technology, increases in information, and growth in the size and complexity of society. A large, complex, technological society cannot be governed by a single president and 535 members of Congress who lack the expertise, time, and energy to look after nuclear power or environmental protection or occupational safety or communications or aviation or fair employment. So the president and Congress create bureaucracies, appropriate money for them, and authorize them to draw up detailed rules and regulations to govern us. The bureaucracies usually receive only vague and general directions from the elected leaders. Actual governance is in the hands of Immigration and Customs Enforcement, the Environmental Protection Agency, the Occupational Safety and Health Administration, the Federal Communications Commission, the Federal Aviation Administration, the Equal Employment Opportunity Commission, and about 2,000 similar bureaucratic agencies. One estimate suggests that the bureaucracies announce *20* rules or regulations for every *one* law of Congress. Currently, federal regulations run to over 80,000 pages. In this way, the power to make policy has passed from the president and Congress to the bureaucratic elite.

CIVIL SERVICE REFORM ESTABLISHED INDEPENDENCE

In 1883, the Pendleton Civil Service Reform Act established a bureaucracy whose membership should be based on expertise or merit. Before that, government jobs were regularly handed out to reward political support, with each new administration dumping the civil servants of the previous one. This patronage use of civil service positions came to be seen as a form of corruption and the high turnover as disruptive to the function of government.

Today, only the top positions are given to political supporters, while the vast majority of the bureaucracy is allowed to develop some form of competency independent of political change at the top.

ORGANIZED EXPERTISE

Policy-making shifted to the bureaucracy in part because elected officials do not have the time, energy, or expertise to handle the details of policy-making. A related explanation is that the increasing complexity and sophistication of technology require technical experts, or **technocrats**, to actually carry out the intent of elected officials. No single bureaucrat can master the complex activities of even a single large governmental agency—from budgeting, purchasing, personnel, accounting, planning, communication, and organization to the complexities of nuclear plants, energy transmission, the tax code, or information technology. Each bureaucrat has relatively little knowledge of overall policy. But each person's narrow expertise, when combined with that of thousands of other bureaucrats, creates an organized base of power that political leaders find difficult to control. This elite is diffuse, but no less powerful.

SHIFTS IN RESPONSIBILITY

Another reason policy-making is shifted to the bureaucracy is that Congress and the president deliberately pass vague and ambiguous laws, largely for symbolic reasons—to protect the environment, ensure occupational safety, allocate broadcasting channels, guarantee flight safety, prevent unfair interstate charges, guarantee equal employment opportunity, and so on. Bureaucrats must give meaning to symbolic measures; their role is to use the authority of these symbolic laws to decide what actually will be done. Frequently, Congress and the president do not want to take public responsibility for unpopular policies. They find it easier to blame the bureaucrats and pretend unpopular policies are a product of an ungovernable Washington bureaucracy. This explanation allows elected officials to impose regulations without accepting responsibility for them.

BUREAUCRATIC EXPANSIONISM

The bureaucracy itself is now sufficiently powerful to have its own laws passed—laws that allow agencies to expand in size, acquire more authority, and obtain more money. Bureaucracy has become its own source of power. Political scientist James Q. Wilson commented on "the great, almost overpowering, importance of the existing government and professional groups in shaping policy":

> I am impressed by the extent to which policy making is dominated by the representatives of those bureaucracies and professions having a material stake in the management

---

IN BRIEF | SOURCES OF BUREAUCRATIC POWER

Bureaucratic power arises from the following sources:

- Political elites do not have time or expertise to handle the details of policy.
- Economic and social institutions are complex and sophisticated.

- Political elites deliberately shift responsibility to bureaucrats.
- Bureaucratic elites seek to expand their own power and budgets.
- Government size and cost have expanded overall.

and funding of the intended policy and by those political staffs who see in a new program a chance for publicity, advancement, and a good reputation for their superiors.[2]

GOVERNMENT SIZE AND COST

For an overview of the Executive Branch of Government, see www.whitehouse. gov/our_government/executive_branch/

How big is the government? All governments in the United States—the federal government together with 50 state governments and over 80,000 local governments, including cities, counties, and school and special districts—collectively spend an amount equivalent to about 40 percent of U.S. gross domestic product (GDP), the sum of all the goods and services produced in the nation. The federal government alone accounts for about 29 percent of GDP, and all state and local governments combined account for another 11 percent. Government continues to grow (see Focus: The Growth in Executive Departments).

ORGANIZATION OF THE WASHINGTON BUREAUCRACY

The executive branch of the U.S. government includes 15 departments, more than 60 independent executive agencies operating outside these departments, and the large Executive Office of the President (EOP) (see Figure 11.1).

CABINET

Internal Revenue Service
The tax-collecting I.R.S. is potentially the most powerful of all government agencies, with financial records on every tax-paying individual and business. www.irs.gov

The **cabinet** rarely functions as a group. It consists of the secretaries of the 15 executive departments and the vice president, with the president as its head. From time to time, presidents grant "cabinet level status" to other officials, for example, the United Nations (UN) ambassador, the Central Intelligence Agency (CIA) director, national security adviser, U.S. trade representative, and administrator of the Environmental Protection Agency (EPA). Cabinet officers in the United States are powerful because they head giant administrative organizations. The secretary of state, the secretary of defense, the secretary of the treasury, the U.S. attorney general, and to a lesser extent the other departmental secretaries are all people of power and prestige. But the cabinet, as a council, does not make policy.[3] Presidents do not hold cabinet meetings to decide important policy questions. More frequently, they know what they want and hold cabinet meetings only to help sell their views.

FOCUS | THE GROWTH IN EXECUTIVE DEPARTMENTS

The size of the federal government has expanded steadily since the nation's founding, but much of the growth took place in the mid- to late twentieth century. Five new departments were created between 1966 and 1989 alone. Only two departments have ever been eliminated: the Department of the Navy was combined with the old War Department to form the Defense Department in 1947, and the U.S.

Post Office lost its cabinet rank in 1972 when it became a "quasi-governmental corporation."

The EOP works directly for the president and can largely escape congressional oversight. This bureaucracy has grown from a few dozen employees in the early days of the United States to well over 2,000 today. The growth of the EOP in size and cost has largely mirrored the expansion of the rest of the executive branch.

FOCUS | THE GROWTH IN EXECUTIVE DEPARTMENTS *continued*

1789	1797	1849	1889	1903	1913	1947	1953	1966	1967	1977	1980	1989	2002
State	State	State	State	State	State	State	State	State	State	State	State	State	State
Treasury	Treasury	Treasury	Treasury	Treasury	Treasury	Treasury	Treasury	Treasury	Treasury	Treasury	Treasury	Treasury	Treasury
War	War	War	War	War	War	Defense	Defense	Defense	Defense	Defense	Defense	Defense	Defense
Justice	Justice	Justice	Justice	Justice	Justice	Justice	Justice	Justice	Justice	Justice	Justice	Justice	Justice
Post Office	Post Office	Post Office	Post Office	Post Office	Post Office	Post Office	Post Office	Post Office	Post Office[a]				
	Navy	Navy	Navy	Navy	Navy								
		Interior	Interior	Interior	Interior	Interior	Interior	Interior	Interior	Interior	Interior	Interior	Interior
			Agriculture	Agriculture	Agriculture	Agriculture	Agriculture	Agriculture	Agriculture	Agriculture	Agriculture	Agriculture	Agriculture
				Labor & Commerce	Labor	Labor	Labor	Labor	Labor	Labor	Labor	Labor	Labor
					Commerce	Commerce	Commerce	Commerce	Commerce	Commerce	Commerce	Commerce	Commerce
							Health, Education and Welfare	Health, Education and Welfare	Health, Education and Welfare	Health, Education and Welfare	Health, and Human Services	Health, and Human Services	Health, and Human Services
								Housing and Urban Development	Housing and Urban Development	Housing and Urban Development	Housing and Urban Development	Housing and Urban Development	Housing and Urban Development
									Transportation	Transportation	Transportation	Transportation	Transportation
										Energy	Energy	Energy	Energy
											Education	Education	Education
												Veterans' Affairs	Veterans' Affairs
													Homeland Security

[a]The U.S. Post Office loses cabinet status in 1972 and becomes a "quasi-governmental corporation."

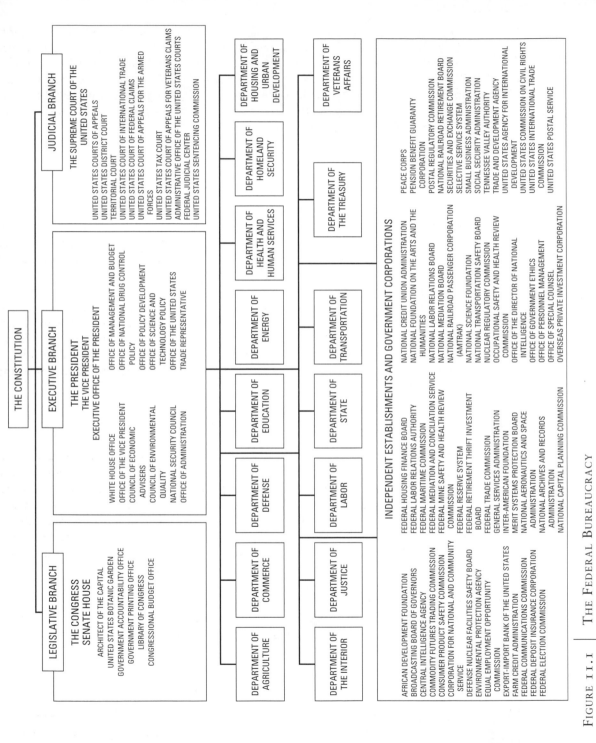

Figure 11.1 | The Federal Bureaucracy

Source: http://frwebgate.access.gpo.gov/cgi/nl/getdoc.cgi?dbname=2008_government_manual&docid=214669tx_xxx-3.pdf

NATIONAL SECURITY COUNCIL

National Security Council
Official NSC website. *www. whitehouse.gov/ administration/ eop/nsc/*

The National Security Council (NSC) resembles an inner cabinet; the President is chair, and the Vice President, Secretary of State, Secretary of Defense, and Secretary of the Treasury are participating members. The Chair of the Joint Chiefs of Staff and the Director of National Intelligence (DNI) are advisors to the NSC. A special assistant to the president for national security affairs heads the NSC staff. The purposes of the council are to advise the president on security policy and to coordinate the foreign, military, and domestic policies.

OFFICE OF MANAGEMENT AND BUDGET

The Office of Management and Budget (OMB) is the largest agency in the EOP. Its function is to prepare the budget of the United States for the president to submit to Congress. The federal government cannot spend money without appropriations by Congress, and all requests for congressional appropriations must clear the OMB first, a requirement that gives the OMB great power over the executive branch. Because all agencies request more money than they can receive, the OMB has primary responsibility for reviewing, reducing, and approving estimates submitted by departments and agencies (subject to appeal to the president). It also continuously scrutinizes the organization and operations of executive agencies to recommend changes promoting efficiency and economy. Like members of the White House staff, the top officials of the OMB are responsible solely to the president; thus, they must reflect the president's goals and priorities in their decision making.

PRESIDENTIAL CONTROL OF THE BUREAUCRACY

The president's formal powers over the bureaucracy center on appointments, reorganization, and the budget they derive from the Constitution. We should, however, consider the *real* limitations on these powers (see Focus: Bureaucratic Maneuvers).

Constitutional Basis of Executive Authority: Constitutionally, the president has formal Constitutional authority over the federal bureaucracy, in that Article II, Section 2, gives presidents the power to "require the Opinion, in writing, of the principle Officer in each of the executive Departments, upon any Subject relating to the Duties of their respective Offices." The Constitution also gives presidents formal power to appoint all secretaries (subject to Senate confirmation), undersecretaries, and deputy secretaries and most bureau chiefs in the federal government. The president also has the power to reorganize the federal bureaucracy, subject to congressional veto. And, of course, the president exercises formal control over the budget. The OMB works directly under presidential supervision.

APPOINTMENTS

Although the federal bureaucracy consists of 2.8 million civilian employees, the president actually appoints only about 2,500 people. Approximately 600 are policy-making positions; the rest are subordinate positions often used by presidents

**Federal Depart-
ments and Agencies**
Most federal
departments can be
accessed directly by
using their initials
followed by .gov,
for example the
Department of
Justice—*www.doj.
gov*, Federal Bureau
of Investigation—
www.fbi.gov.
Where other
forms of address
are employed,
for example,
Department of
Defense—*www.
defenselink.mil*,
this book identifies
these websites in the
margins of
appropriate
chapters.

USA Jobs
Why not join
the bureaucracy!
This website is the
official source for
federal employment
information. *www.
usajobs.gov*

for patronage. Many patronage positions go to professional bureaucrats by default because a president cannot find qualified political appointees. Political appointees are often baffled by the career bureaucrats in the agencies, who have the knowledge, skills, and experience to continue existing programs with little or no supervision from their nominal chiefs. Political heads sometimes **"go native"**; they yield to the pressure of these career bureaucrats and become their captives instead of taking control.

In as much as a majority of bureaucrats are career civil servants, exercising policy control over the bureaucracy is particularly difficult for a president after the other party has held the White House a long time. Some presidents have turned to creative solutions. Richard Nixon increased the power of his immediate White House staff and placed control of major programs in their hands, at the expense of the cabinet departments.[4] Barack Obama gave "czars" oversight of specific policy areas; some appointments did not require Senate confirmation. Obama's controversial "Green Jobs" czar, a former communist named Van Jones, resigned in 2009. Still, the practice of placing White House figures into policy positions apart from the bureaucracy is clearly at the heart of presidential attempts to exercise control over the bureaucratic process.[5]

Several recent presidents have dealt with the power of bureaucracy by bringing in people with experience. George H. W. Bush experienced less conflict with the bureaucracy in part because he himself had held a variety of bureaucratic posts during his career—U.N. ambassador, CIA director, and ambassador to the People's Republic of China. The Washington bureaucracy was generally supportive of Bill Clinton's policy activism, with its initial promise of expanded governmental services and budgets. The only serious bureaucratic opposition Clinton encountered arose in the 1996 battle with the Department of Health and Human Services over welfare reform and his "reinventing government" program, which reduced the federal payroll substantially and helped streamline some processes such as purchasing.

George W. Bush's cabinet appointees were more experienced in government affairs than those of previous administrations. Vice President Richard Cheney, Secretary of Defense Robert Gates, Secretary of State Colin Powell, and Secretary of Defense Donald Rumsfeld, among others, all served in high positions in previous administrations. Their experience gave them greater knowledge and power over the Washington bureaucracy than top political elites in previous administrations. Barack Obama followed this model with a cabinet heavy in government experience, such as U.S. Attorney General Eric Holder's 20 years in Washington, or Secretary of State Hillary Clinton's 15 years.

REORGANIZATION

Presidents can choose to reorganize the bureaucracy to reflect their priorities. However, most limit this practice to one or two key programs, because presidential reorganizations are subject to legislative veto. For example, in the 1960s, President Kennedy created the National Aeronautics and Space Administration (NASA) as an independent agency to carry out his commitment to a national space program. President Carter created the Department of Education to fulfill his campaign pledge to emphasize educational matters (and to please a major campaign supporter, the teachers' unions), even though the department's parent organization, the Department of Health, Education, and Welfare, bitterly opposed it. President Reagan promised in his 1980 campaign to eliminate the Department of Education (for essentially the same reason that Carter created it) as well as the Department of Energy.

However, nothing arouses the fighting instincts of bureaucrats as much as the rumor of reorganization. Reagan was eventually forced to drop his plans to eliminate the two departments. Instead, he ended his administration by creating a new cabinet-level department—the Department of Veterans Affairs—in response to demands for greater status and prestige by veterans' interests.

Department of Homeland Security This DHS website shows the many agencies that were consolidated under DHS. *www.dhs. gov/xabout/ history/editorial_ 0133.shtm*

To reassure the public of the government's efforts to prevent further terrorist attacks after September 11, 2001, President George W. Bush first created an Office of Homeland Security inside the EOP, with high-profile Pennsylvania Governor Tom Ridge as its first director. Continued criticism of security arrangements forced Bush to propose a more thorough reorganization of the executive branch. He proposed and Congress created a new Department of Homeland Security, which would not only coordinate domestic and international antiterrorist efforts but also exercise direct responsibility over 22 agencies such as the Transportation Security Administration, Immigration and Customs Enforcement, Border Patrol, the U.S. Coast Guard, the Secret Service, and the Federal Emergency Management Agency.

THE BUDGET

The president exercises budgetary power over the bureaucracy through the OMB. Thus, the OMB director must be a trusted ally of the president, and the department must support the president's programs and priorities if presidential control over the bureaucracy is to be effective. But even the OMB must accept the budgetary base of each department (the previous year's budget, adjusted for inflation) and engage in budgeting that provides increases based on previous years' requests, known as "incremental" budgeting. Despite its own expertise, the OMB rarely challenges the budgetary base of agencies but instead concentrates its attention on requested increases.

Any agency that feels shortchanged in the president's budget can leak the fact to its supporting interest groups and congressional subcommittee. Any resulting public outcry may force the president to restore the agency's funds. Or Congress can appropriate money not requested by the president. The president may go along with the increased expenditures simply to avoid another confrontation with Congress.

THE BUDGET MAZE

The budget is the most important policy statement of any government. The expenditure side of the budget shows who gets what from government, and the revenue side shows who pays the costs. The budget lies at the heart of the policy-making process.

FOCUS | BUREAUCRATIC MANEUVERS

How can bureaucrats outmaneuver the president? One illustration of bureaucratic leeway and discretion in implementing presidential decisions has been widely quoted:

> Half of a President's suggestions, which theoretically carry the weight of orders, can be safely forgotten by a cabinet member. And if the President asks about a suggestion the second time, he can be told that it is being investigated. If he asks a third time, the wise cabinet officer will give him at least part of what he suggests. But only occasionally do Presidents ever get around to asking three times.[a]

Bureaucratic maneuvers can become even more complex. Morton Halperin, former staff member of the National Security Council under Henry Kissinger (Halperin later charged Kissinger and others with bugging his telephone), describes "ten commandments" of bureaucratic infighting.[b] These suggest the power of the bureaucracy and the frequently bitter nature of bureaucratic warfare:

1. Never play "politics" with security. But use your own notions of politics to screen out information from the president that conflicts with your own objectives.
2. Tell the president only what is necessary to persuade him of the correctness of your own position. Avoid giving him "confusing" information. Isolate the opposition by excluding them from deliberations.
3. Present your own policy option in the middle of two other obviously unworkable alternatives to give the president the illusion of choice.
4. If the president selects the "wrong" policy anyhow, demand "full authority" to deal with the undesirable consequences, which you say are sure to arise.
5. Always predict the consequences of not adopting your policy in terms of worst cases, making predictions of dire consequences that will follow.
6. If the president chooses your own policy, urge immediate action; if he selects another policy, you may agree in principle but argue that "now is not the time."
7. If the opposition view looks very strong, "leak" damaging information to your supporters in the press or Congress and count on "public opposition" to build.
8. Fully implement orders that result from the selection of your own policy recommendation; circumvent or delay those that do not.
9. Limit the issues that go to the president. Bring up only those favorable to your position or that he is likely to favor.
10. Never oppose the president's policy in such extreme terms that you lose his trust. Temper your disagreements so that you can live to argue another day.

Bureaucrats do not really consider these "commandments" cynical. Indeed, they may not realize when they are following them. They often sincerely believe their own policies and projects are in the nation's best interest.

[a]Graham T. Allison, *Essence of Decision* (Boston, MA: Little, Brown, 1971), p. 172.

[b]Leslie H. Gelb and Morton H. Halperin, "The Ten Commandments of the Foreign Policy Bureaucracy," *Harper's* (June 1972): 28–36.

THE PRESIDENTIAL BUDGET

The president is responsible for submitting the annual federal budget, with estimates of revenue and recommendations for expenditures, to Congress. Congress controls the purse strings; no federal monies may be spent without congressional appropriation. The president relies on the OMB to prepare a budget for Congress. The president's budget is usually submitted in late January of each year. The federal fiscal year (FY) begins October 1; this gives Congress about eight months

---

| IN BRIEF | PRESIDENTIAL CONTROL |

Presidential control over the bureaucracy derives primarily from

- Presidential power over appointments to the White House, Cabinet, and other high offices, most, however, requiring Senate approval.
- Presidential power over reorganization and the creation of new bureaucracies, subject to congressional approval.

- Presidential power over budget recommendations to Congress.
- Formal Constitutional authority to "require the Opinion, in writing, of the principle Officer in each of the executive Departments, upon any Subject relating to the Duties of their respective Offices" (Article II, Section 2).

Office of Management and Budget
Official OMB website; includes latest presidential budget. *www. whitehouse.gov/ omb*

to consider the president's budget and pass the appropriations acts for the coming fiscal year.

Preparation of the budget by the OMB starts more than a year before the beginning of the fiscal year for which it is intended. (Fiscal years are named for the year in which they *end*, so, for example, the OMB prepares FY 2014 in 2012 for presentation to Congress in January 2013 and passage before October 1, 2013; FY 2014 ends September 30, 2014.) The OMB considers budget requests by all executive departments and agencies, adjusting them to fit the president's overall policy goals. It prepares the Budget of the United States Government for the president to submit to Congress. Table 11.1 summarizes the steps in the overall schedule for budgetary preparation.

CONGRESSIONAL CONSIDERATION

The Constitution gives Congress authority to decide how the government should spend its money: "No money shall be drawn from the Treasury but in consequence of appropriations made by law" (Article I, Section 9). The president's budget is sent initially to the House and Senate budget committees, whose job it is to draft a budget resolution for Congress, setting future target goals for appropriations in various areas. The House and Senate budget committees rely on their own bureaucracy, the Congressional Budget Office (CBO), to review the recommendations made by the president and the OMB. Congress is supposed to pass a budget resolution by late spring. The resolution should guide the House and Senate appropriations committees and their subcommittees in writing the appropriations acts.

There are usually 13 separate appropriations acts each year. Each one covers a broad area of government—for example, defense, labor, human services and education, commerce, justice, state, and judiciary. These appropriations bills must pass both the House and the Senate in identical form, just as any other legislation must. All the acts are supposed to be passed before the start of the fiscal year, October 1. These procedures were mandated in the Congressional Budget and Impoundment Control Act of 1974. However, Congress rarely follows its own timetable or procedures.

TABLE 11.1 | THE BUDGET PROCESS

Approximate Schedule	Actors	Tasks
Presidential Budget Making		
January–March	President and OMB	The OMB presents long-range forecasts for revenues and expenditures to the president. The president and the OMB develop general guidelines for all federal agencies. Agencies are sent guidelines and forms for their budget requests.
April–July	Executive agencies	Agencies prepare and submit budget requests to the OMB.
August–October	OMB and agencies	The OMB reviews agency requests and holds hearings with agency officials. The OMB usually tries to reduce agency requests.
November–December	OMB and president	The OMB presents revised budget to the president. Occasionally, agencies may appeal OMB decisions directly to the president. The president and the OMB write budget messages for Congress.
January	President	The president presents budget for the next fiscal year to Congress.
Congressional Budget Process		
February–May	CBO and congressional committees	Standing committees review taxing and spending proposals for reports to House and Senate budget committees. The CBO also reviews the entire presidential budget and reports to budget committees.
May–June	Congress; House and Senate budget committees	House and Senate budget committees present first concurrent resolution, which sets overall total for budget outlays in major categories. Full House and Senate vote on resolution. Committees are instructed to stay within budget committee's resolution.
July–September	Congress; House and Senate appropriations committees and budget committees	House and Senate appropriations committees and subcommittees draw up detailed appropriations bills. Bills are submitted to House and Senate budget committees for second concurrent resolution. Budget committees may force reductions through "reconciliation" provisions to limit spending. The full House and Senate vote on "reconciliations" and second (firm) concurrent resolution.
September–October	Congress and president	The House and Senate pass various appropriations bills (between 9 and 16 bills, by major functional category, such as "defense"). Each is sent to the president for signature. (If vetoed by the president, the appropriations bills go back to the House and Senate, which must override veto with two-thirds vote in each body or revise bills to gain president's approval.)
Executive Budget Implementation		
After October 1	Congress and president	Fiscal year for all federal agencies begins October 1. If no appropriations bill has been passed by Congress and signed by the president for an agency, Congress must pass and the president must sign a continuing resolution to allow the agency to spend at last year's level until a new appropriations act is passed. If no continuing resolution is passed, the agency must officially cease spending government funds and must officially shut down.

The common goal of the congressional budget procedures, the House and Senate budget committees, and the CBO is to allow Congress to consider the budget in its entirety rather than in separate segments. But after the budget resolution has been passed, the 13 separate appropriations bills begin their tortuous journeys through specialized appropriations subcommittees. Agency and department leaders from the administration are frequently called to testify before these subcommittees to defend the president's request. Lobbying activity is heavy in these subcommittees.

If the appropriations committees report bills that exceed the ceilings established by the budget resolution, Congress must prepare a reconciliation bill to reconcile the amounts set by the budget resolution and the amounts set by the appropriations committees. This procedure tends to match the power of the House and Senate budget committees against the House and Senate appropriations committees. When passed, the reconciliation bill binds the appropriations committees and Congress to ceilings in each area. However, all this congressional infighting generally runs beyond the October 1 deadline for the start of the fiscal year.

CONTINUING RESOLUTIONS AND GOVERNMENT SHUTDOWNS

All appropriations acts *should* be passed by both houses and signed by the president into law before October 1, but Congress rarely meets this deadline. Government agencies frequently find themselves beginning a new fiscal year without a budget. Constitutionally, any U.S. government agency for which Congress does not pass an appropriations act may not draw money from the Treasury and thus is obliged to shut down. To get around this problem, Congress usually adopts a **continuing resolution** that authorizes government agencies to keep spending money for a specified period at the same level as in the previous fiscal year.

A continuing resolution is supposed to grant additional time for Congress to pass, and the president to sign, appropriations acts. But occasionally this process has broken down in the heat of political combat over the budget: The time period specified in a continuing resolution has expired without agreement on appropriations acts or even on a new continuing resolution. Shutdowns occurred during the bitter battle between President Clinton and the Republican-controlled Congress over the FY 1996 budget. In theory, the absence of either an appropriations act or a continuing resolution should cause a federal agency to shut down, that is, to cease all operations and expenditures for lack of funds. But in practice, such shutdowns have been only partial, affecting only "nonessential" government employees and causing relatively little disruption.

PRESIDENTIAL VETOES OF APPROPRIATIONS BILLS

Presidents can veto an appropriations bill, but they cannot veto specific provisions in the bill. As a result, presidents rarely veto appropriations bills, even those with spending provisions they dislike. Still, a veto threat can help a president assert his agenda, as did Barack Obama's 2009 threat to veto any military appropriations bill that funded the F-22 fighter airplane, which resulted in the project's being cut off without the veto. However, presidents can send Congress a list of "rescissions," and Congress by resolution (which cannot be vetoed by the president) must approve a rescission; otherwise, the government must spend the money.

Presidents, both Democratic and Republican, have long struggled to obtain the **line-item veto**—the ability to veto some spending items in a bill while accepting others. The governors of many states hold this power. In 1996, Congress finally agreed to allow it to presidents, but the U.S. Supreme Court held the line-item veto unconstitutional, arguing that it gave the president the power to amend bills, a legislative power reserved for Congress in Article I of the Constitution.

ELITE FISCAL RESPONSIBILITY?

Over the years, total federal spending has grown dramatically. In 1962, federal spending amounted to only $92 billion; in 2012, this figure was $3.8 trillion (see Figure 11.2). The growth of federal spending is being driven primarily by entitlement programs, notably Social Security, now the single largest item in the budget, and Medicare and Medicaid, the fastest-growing items. National defense, 56 percent of all federal spending in 1960, declined to 15 percent after the end of the Soviet Cold War threat in the 1990s and then grew back to 20 percent with the war on terrorism.

OVERALL FEDERAL SPENDING

The enormous growth of federal spending in billions of dollars is partly offset by the United States' dynamic economy. Expressed as a percentage of the gross domestic product (GDP)—the sum of all the goods and services produced in the United States in a year—federal spending remained basically steady at about 20 percent from the early 1960s to the mid-2000s, until hitting 28 percent in 2009 and 23 percent in 2011 (see Figure 3.2). In other words, both total dollar spending by Washington and its relative share of the economy have grown enormously, particularly under Presidents George W. Bush and Barack Obama.[6]

ENTITLEMENT SPENDING

Accounting for over 60 percent of all federal spending, **entitlements** are items determined by past decisions of Congress that represent commitments in future budgets. They provide classes of people with legally enforceable rights to benefits, such as Social Security and Medicare benefits for seniors, which make up the bulk of entitlement spending. Neither of these programs is directed at the poor. Welfare payments, food stamps, and Medicaid are "means tested"—that is, benefits are limited to lower-income families. In addition to entitlements, other mandatory spending (including interest payments on the national debt, federal employees' retirement, unemployment compensation, veterans' benefits, and so on) together with spending for national defense leaves only about 12 percent of the budget for "nondefense discretionary" spending.

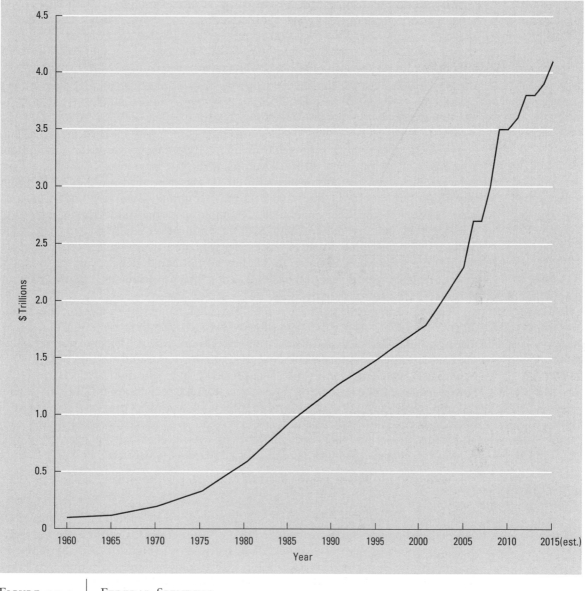

FIGURE 11.2 | FEDERAL SPENDING

Source: *www.whitehouse.gov/omb/budget/Historicals*. 2012–2015 are OMB estimates.

Capping entitlements is widely recognized by economists as the only way to rein in future federal spending. But few in Washington—president, Congress members, bureaucrats, Republicans, or Democrats—are willing to challenge the powerful senior citizen lobby (see Focus: Size and Representation—AARP in Chapter 7). George W. Bush's 2005 attempt to address the looming crisis in Social Security by promoting the adoption of a Swedish-style model mixing a public plan with private savings accounts was quickly blocked.

BALANCING THE BUDGET

Washington regularly spends more than it receives in revenue. Annual deficits have put the U.S. government almost *$16 trillion in debt*, a figure equal to over $50,000 for every man, woman, and child in the nation.[7] The debt is larger than the size of GDP and is owed to banks, insurance companies, investment firms, and anyone else who buys U.S. government bonds. International investors own about 20 percent of the national debt. Government interest payments to holders of the debt amounted to about $250 billion in 2010. The debt need not ever be paid off, but future generations of U.S. taxpayers must continue to pay the annual interest on it as long as it is not paid. The booming economy and fiscal discipline of the late 1990s briefly enabled the federal government to finally end its more than 30 years of annual deficits in 1998. (Deficits refer to the *annual* excess of expenditures over revenues; debt refers to the accumulated deficits of the national government over the years.) For four years, the government actually incurred surpluses (see Figure 11.3).

The terrorist attacks of September 11, 2001, ended all hopes of continuing federal surpluses—hopes that had already been eroded by a recession that began in early 2001. The recession resulted in lower than expected federal revenues, and the terrorist attack inspired additional spending for homeland security and military operations. President Bush's fiscal response to the recession was to push the Republican-controlled Congress to enact major tax reductions in 2001 and again in 2003. Democrats correctly argued that these reductions contributed to the return of deficit spending. Republicans correctly argued that tax reductions would stimulate the economy and that economic growth would eventually increase revenues. However, spending also grew, so no deficit reduction was forthcoming.

TAX POLITICS

The federal government finances itself primarily from individual income taxes (45 percent) and Social Security payroll taxes (36 percent). Corporations currently pay only about 12 percent of total federal revenues (see Figure 11.4), although corporate profits distributed to shareholders or employees and executives are taxed again by the government as personal income.

Social Security and Medicare taxes (also known as FICA) are paid by wage earners (15.3 percent of total payrolls, paid about half by employers and about half by employees). The Social Security tax (12.4 percent combined employer–employee rate) is considered a **regressive tax**—that is, it captures a larger share of the income of lower-income workers than of higher-income workers. The reason is that, first of all, Social Security taxes are imposed on only the first $110,100 of *wage* income (in 2012, rising slightly every year); wages above that amount are not subject to these taxes. (Medicare taxes, 2.9 percent combined rate, are levied against all wage income.) Second, Social Security taxes are not levied against *non-wage* and investment income (interest, dividends, rents, profits from the sale

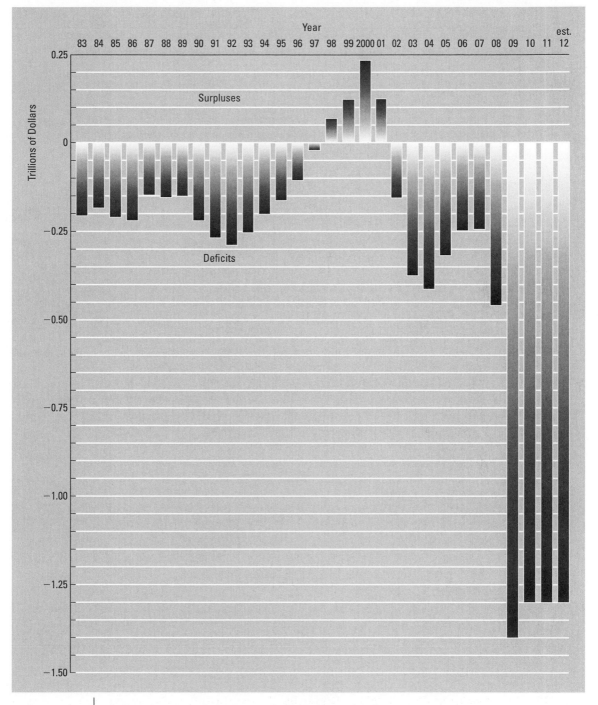

FIGURE 11.3 | ANNUAL FEDERAL DEFICITS AND SURPLUSES

Source: *www.whitehouse.gov/omb/budget/Historicals.*

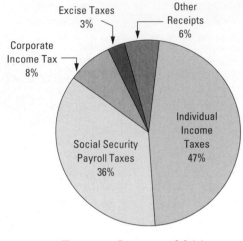

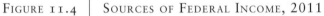

Figure 11.4   Sources of Federal Income, 2011

Source: *www.whitehouse.gov/omb/budget/*.

of stocks and bonds, and so on)—sources of income concentrated among high-income taxpayers.

In contrast, the federal individual income tax is a highly **progressive tax**—that is, it captures a larger share of the income of higher-income workers than of lower-income workers (see Figure 11.5). Personal income in 2012 was taxed at six separate rates—10, 15, 25, 28, 33, and 35 percent. These rates are applied progressively to levels of income, or "brackets," indexed annually to reflect inflation.

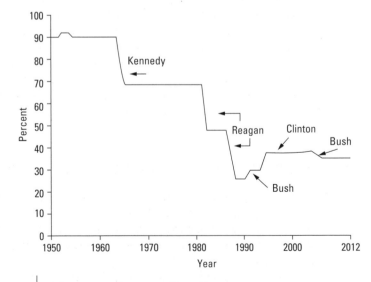

Figure 11.5   Maximum Income Tax Rates

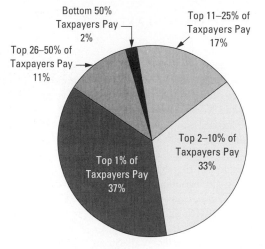

FIGURE 11.6 | WHO PAYS THE FEDERAL INDIVIDUAL INCOME TAX?

Source: *www.irs.gov/pub/irs-soi/09inratesnap.pdf.*

Social Security
The Social Security Administration website provides information as well as access to individual accounts. *www.ssa.gov*

The progressive nature of the federal individual income tax and the personal and standard exemptions for families and earned income tax credits for low-income earners combine to remove most of the tax burden from middle- and low-income taxpayers. Indeed, the lower 50 percent of U.S. income earners pay less than 2 percent of all federal income taxes (see Figure 11.6).

Pluralists frequently cite the progressive nature of the federal individual income tax as evidence of the political influence of low- and middle-income citizens. However, Social Security payroll taxes provide almost as much revenue to the federal government as the individual income tax, and Social Security taxes are decidedly regressive. Moreover, the corporate income tax, set at 35 percent of net profits, produces relatively little revenue owing to a host of exemptions, deductions, and special treatments written into the lengthy and complex U.S. Tax Code. Finally, capital gains, income on investments such as profits from the sale of stocks, bonds, real estate, and so on, are currently taxed at only 15 percent, a rate less than half the top marginal rate on earned income of 35 percent (see Focus: Capital Gains Taxes and the Economy).

BUREAUCRATIC POWER, IRON TRIANGLES, AND REVOLVING DOORS

Traditionally, voters assumed that when Congress passed a law and then created a bureaucracy and appropriated money to carry out the intent of the law, this was the end of the political process. Congress's intent would be carried out—the political battle having been resolved—and government would get on with the job of "administering" the law.

It turns out, however, that political battles do not end with a victory or defeat in Congress. Organized interests do not abandon the fight and return home simply because the site of the battle shifts from the political arena to an administrative one.

FOCUS | CAPITAL GAINS TAXES AND THE ECONOMY

Why should some types of income be given preferential treatment in the tax laws? Preferential treatment for capital gains has been supported by both Democratic and Republican presidents. In the words of President John Kennedy in 1963, "The tax on capital gains directly affects investment decisions, the mobility and flow of risk capital ... the ease or difficulty experienced by new ventures in obtaining capital, and thereby the strength and potential for growth in the economy." Lowering taxes on investment gains encourages investment, resulting in more economic growth and more jobs.

Preferential tax treatment for capital gains appeals to a wide variety of elites—especially Wall Street investment firms and the real estate industry. Reducing taxes on capital gains increases the turnover (buying and selling) of stocks, bonds, and real estate, and hence the income of investment and real estate firms. And, of course, it significantly reduces the tax burden on high-income taxpayers—those most likely to have income from the sale of these assets.

Capital gains taxes also affect the masses. First, roughly a quarter of capital gains are earned by persons making under $75,000 a year in income, notably elderly retirees living off their investments. The greater benefit comes from the increased jobs that come with economic growth. A stronger economy will also see more capital gains and thus revenues from capital gains taxes. When President George W. Bush and a Republican Congress reduced the capital gains tax to 15 percent in 2003, capital gains tax revenues doubled, rising from $50 billion in 2003 to $103 billion in 2006.[a] Unhappiness about the different treatment of income from investments and that of income from work may be common, but since Alexander Hamilton's day, elites have seen the wisdom of promoting investment. Elites may have enjoyed the largest share of over two centuries of economic growth, but the masses have also benefited.

[a]Congressional Budget Office, The Budget and Economic Outlook. Fiscal Years 2008 to 2017. January 2007.

Source: *www.cbo.gov/ftpdocs/77xx/doc7731/01-Budget-Outlook.pdf.*

We tend to think "political" questions are the province of the president and Congress and "administrative" questions are the province of the bureaucracy. Actually, "political" and "administrative" questions do not differ in content; they differ only in who decides them.

IMPLEMENTATION, REGULATION, AND ADJUDICATION

Bureaucracies are not constitutionally empowered to decide policy questions. But they do so, nevertheless, as they perform their tasks of implementation, regulation, and adjudication.

Budget implementation is the development of procedures and activities to carry out policies legislated by Congress. It requires bureaucracies to translate laws into operational rules and regulations and to allocate resources—money, personnel, offices, supplies—to functions. All these tasks involve decisions by bureaucrats—decisions that drive how the law will actually affect society. In some cases, bureaucrats delay the development of regulations based on a new law, assign enforcement responsibility to existing offices with other higher-priority tasks, and allocate few people with limited resources to the task. In other cases, bureaucrats act forcefully in making new regulations, insist on strict enforcement, assign responsibilities to newly created aggressive offices with no other assignments, and allocate a great deal of staff time and agency resources to the task. Interested groups have a strong stake in these decisions, and they actively seek to influence the bureaucracy.

Regulation relies on the development of formal rules for implementing legislation. The federal bureaucracy publishes about 80,000 pages of rules in the *Federal Register* each year. Regulatory battles are important because regulations that appear in the *Federal Register* have the effect of law. Congress can amend or repeal a regulation only by passing new legislation and obtaining the president's signature. Controversial bureaucratic regulations often remain in place because Congress is slow to act, because key committee members block corrective legislation, or because the president refuses to sign bills overturning the regulation.

In adjudication, bureaucrats decide whether a person or firm is failing to comply with laws or regulations and, if so, what penalties or corrective actions are to be applied. Regulatory agencies and commissions—for example, the National Labor Relations Board, the Federal Communications Commission, the Equal Employment Opportunity Commission, the Federal Trade Commission, and the Securities and Exchange Commission—are heavily engaged in adjudication. Their elaborate procedures and body of previous decisions closely resemble the court system. Some agencies authorize specific hearing officers, administrative judges, or appellate divisions to accept evidence, hear arguments, and decide cases. Individuals and firms engaged in these proceedings usually hire lawyers specializing in the field of regulation. Administrative hearings are somewhat less formal than a court trial, and the "judges" are employees of the agency itself. Losers may appeal to the federal courts, but the record of agency success in the federal courts discourages many appeals.

BUREAUCRATIC GOALS

Bureaucrats generally believe strongly in the value of their programs and the importance of their tasks. Senior military officers and civilian officials of the Department of Defense favor a strong national defense, and top officials in the Social Security Administration are committed to maintaining the integrity of the retirement system and serving the nation's senior citizens. Beyond these public-spirited motives, bureaucrats, like everyone else, seek higher pay, greater job security, and added authority and prestige for themselves. Like all elites, bureaucratic elites wish to maintain their power. These public and private motives motivate bureaucrats to seek to expand the powers, functions, and budgets of their departments and agencies.

IRON TRIANGLES

Once an issue has been shifted to the bureaucracy, three major power bases—the **iron triangles**—come together to decide its outcome: the executive agency administering the program; the congressional subcommittee charged with overseeing it; and the most interested groups, generally those directly affected by the agency (see Figure 11.7). Agency–subcommittee–interest-group relationships become established; even the individuals remain the same over fairly long periods of time, as senior members of Congress retain their subcommittee memberships. Frequently these iron triangles can be connected into **issue networks** by individuals who hold positions in multiple triangle relationships.

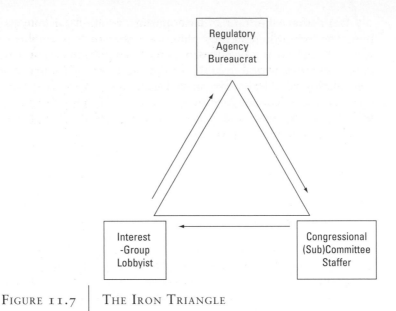

FIGURE 11.7 | THE IRON TRIANGLE

Note that the parts of this triumvirate do *not* compete as pluralist ideology suggests. Instead, bureaucratic agency, congressional subcommittee, and organized interest come together to "scratch each other's back" in bureaucratic policy-making. Bureaucrats get political support from interest groups in their requests for expanded power and authority and increased budgetary allocations. Interest groups get favorable treatment of their members by the bureaucracy. Congressional committee members get political and campaign support from interest groups as well as favorable treatment for their constituents and contributors who are served or regulated by the bureaucracy.

REVOLVING DOORS

Center for Public Integrity
Reform organization committed to "exposing" corruption, mismanagement, and waste in government. *www. iwatchnews.org/*

Washington insiders—bureaucrats, lobbyists, former members of Congress, White House and congressional staffers—frequently change jobs. They may move from a government post (where they acquired experience, knowledge, and personal contacts) to a job in the private sector as a consultant, lobbyist, or salesperson. Defense contractors may recruit high-ranking military officers or Defense Department officials to help sell weapons to their former employers. Trade associations may recruit congressional staffers, White House staffers, or high-ranking agency heads as lobbyists, or these people may leave government service to start their own lobbying firms. Attorneys from the Justice Department, the Internal Revenue Service, and federal regulatory agencies may be recruited by Washington law firms to represent clients in dealings with their former employees. Following retirement, many members of Congress turn to lobbying their former colleagues.

Concern about **revolving doors** centers not only on individuals cashing in on their knowledge, experience, and contacts obtained through government employment but also on the possibility that some government officials will be tempted to tilt their decisions in favor of corporations, law firms, or interest groups that promise them well-paid jobs after they leave government employment. The Ethics in Government Act limits post-government employment: Former members of Congress are not permitted to lobby Congress for one year after leaving that body; former employees of executive agencies are not permitted to lobby their agency for one year after leaving government service, and they are not permitted to lobby their agency for two years on any matter over which they had any responsibility while employed by the government.

THE REGULATORY QUAGMIRE

The Washington bureaucracy has become the regulator of the national economy, the protector of business against its rivals, and the guardian of the U.S. people against everything from tainted foods to rickety stepladders. Federal regulatory bureaucracies began in 1887 with the creation of the Interstate Commerce Commission to regulate railroad rates. Since then, thousands of laws, amendments, court rulings, and executive orders have expanded the powers of the regulatory commissions over every aspect of our lives. (See Figure 11.1 for a list of independent commissions and agencies.)

Federal regulatory bureaucracies are legislatures, investigators, prosecutors, judges, and juries—all wrapped into one. They issue thousands of pages of rules and regulations each year; they investigate thousands of complaints and conduct thousands of inspections; they require businesses to submit hundreds of thousands of forms each year; they hold hearings, determine "compliance" and "noncompliance," issue corrective orders, and levy fines and penalties. Most economists agree that overregulation adds greatly to the cost of living, that it is an obstacle to innovation and productivity, and that it hinders economic competition. Most regulatory commissions are *independent;* they are not under an executive department, and

Code of Federal Regulations
All 50 titles of federal regulations can be found at the Cornell Law School website. *www.law.cornell. edu/cfr/text*

IN BRIEF | BUREAUCRATIC POWER

- Bureaucracies make policy when they perform their tasks of implementation, regulation, and adjudication.
- Implementation is the development of procedures and activities to carry out laws passed by Congress.
- Regulation is the development of formal rules for implementing congressional legislation. Adjudication is decision making about individual cases, whether or not individuals or firms are complying with laws and regulations, and what penalties or corrective actions are to be applied. Bureaucratic policy-making generally aspires to the expansion of the powers, functions, and budgets of departments and agencies.

- Iron triangles—executive bureaucracies administering a program, the congressional subcommittee charged with overseeing it, and the interest groups most directly affected by the program—contribute to the power of bureaucrats.
- Issue networks are interconnected iron triangles.
- Revolving doors allow bureaucrats, as well as lobbyists, former members of Congress, and White House and congressional staffers, to move from one post to another, often cashing in on their knowledge, experience, and contacts to obtain government employment or government contracts for private employers.

their members are appointed for long terms by a president who has little control over their activities. The most independent of all federal regulatory agencies is the Federal Reserve System (see Focus: The Fed: Money Is Too Important to Be Left to Elected Officials).

THE CAPTURED REGULATORS

Over the years, the reform movements that lead to the establishment of many of the older regulatory agencies diminish in influence. Regulatory agencies become more closely identified with their regulated industries. The **capture theory of regulation** describes how regulated industries come to benefit from government regulation and how regulatory commissions come to represent the industries they are supposed to regulate rather than "the people." From time to time, various regulatory commissions have behaved as if "captured" by their industry. These have included the (now extinct) Interstate Commerce Commission with railroads and trucking, the Federal Reserve Board with banking, the Federal Communications Commission (FCC) with television and radio, the Securities and Exchange Commission (SEC) with the stock market, and the Federal Power Commission with the natural gas industry.

FOCUS | THE FED: MONEY IS TOO IMPORTANT TO BE LEFT TO ELECTED OFFICIALS

Money is too important to be left to democratically elected officials. It became apparent a century ago that the control of money would have to be removed from government and placed in the hands of bankers themselves. Moreover, it was generally agreed that bankers' power over money would have to be unrestricted by Congress or the president. Elected officials repeatedly have demonstrated a general tendency to try to inflate a currency, thus making it possible to pay debt with devalued money and minimize the pain of overspending. Only an independent central bank can be immune from such political pressures.

The Federal Reserve was created in response to the Panic of 1907, in which the U.S. banking system narrowly averted collapse due to the extraordinary action of a single individual, J. P. Morgan. Morgan used his personal wealth and considerable influence with other financiers to support the financial system. Political pressures to weaken the financial system had been continuing since the battle against Alexander Hamilton's central bank and had once again led to financial crisis. The elite provided a rescue.

The Federal Reserve Act of 1913 created the Federal Reserve System, popularly known as "the Fed." Its purpose is to decide the nation's monetary policy and credit conditions, to supervise and regulate banking activity, and to provide various services to banks. Federal Reserve banks are banks' banks; only banks can open accounts at Federal Reserve banks.

Controlling the Money Supply
To stabilize the banking system and control the supply of money, the Fed requires all banks to maintain a reserve in currency or in deposits with a Federal Reserve bank. If the "reserve ratio" is set at 5 percent, for example, a bank may create demand deposits only up to 20 times the amount of its reserve. (So, if it has $100 million in reserve, its total demand deposits cannot exceed $2 billion.)

If the Fed decides there is too much money in the economy (inflation is occurring), it can raise the reserve requirement, for example, from 5 to 10 percent, reducing what a bank can create in demand deposits to only 10 times its reserve. (Then if a bank has $100 million in reserve, its total demand deposits will be limited to $1 billion.) In this way the Fed can expand or contract the money supply as it sees fit.

The Fed can also alter the money supply by changing the interest it charges member banks to borrow reserve. A bank can expand its deposits by borrowing reserve from the Fed, but it must pay the Fed an interest rate, called the "discount rate," in order to do so. The Fed regularly raises and lowers the discount rate, thereby making it easier or harder for banks to borrow reserve. Raising the discount rate tends to contract money supply; lowering it expands the money supply.

The Fed is also authorized to buy and sell U.S. Treasury bonds and notes in what it calls open-market operations. Indeed, the assets of the Fed consist of U.S. debt. Each day the Open Market Desk of the Fed buys and sells billions of dollars worth of government bonds. If it sells more than it buys, it reduces its own reserve and hence its ability to lend reserve to banks; this contracts the money supply. If it buys more than it sells, it adds to its own reserve, enabling it to lend reserve to member banks and expand the money supply. This ability to expand the money supply was used aggressively in 2008 and 2009 under the name "quantitative easing."

Fed Governance

The Federal Reserve System is fully independent—its decisions need not be ratified by the president,

Congress, the courts, or any other governmental institution. It does not depend on annual federal appropriations but instead finances itself. Theoretically, Congress could amend or repeal the Federal Reserve Act of 1913, but to do so would now be economically unthinkable. The only changes made to the Act throughout the century have *added* to the powers of the Fed. Several new powers are likely to be added in response to the financial crisis of 2007–2009.

The governance of the Fed ensures its isolation from democratic politics. The primary check and balance on the Fed elite comes from its seven-member board of governors, who are appointed by the president and confirmed by the Senate. A full term of a member is 14 years, and appointments are staggered so that one expires in each even-numbered year. The chairperson of the board is appointed for a four-year term, starting midway through each presidential term, ensuring that the new president cannot immediately install a new chairperson. Each Federal Reserve bank has its own board of nine directors chosen by member banks and is accountable to those banks. The Fed's accounts are regularly audited by the Government Accountability Office (GAO). All meetings of the Fed are held in secret, although under Chairman Benjamin Bernanke, more transparency into Fed operations and deliberations has taken place.

Historically, regulatory commissions have acted against only the most wayward members of an industry. By attacking the businesses giving the industry bad publicity, the commissions actually help improve the public's opinion of the industry as a whole. Regulatory commissions provide symbolic reassurance to the public that the behavior of the industry was proper.

ELITE BENEFIT FROM REGULATION

Perhaps the most powerful benefit of regulation for economic elites is that by limiting entry into an industry by smaller firms, the regulatory commissions reduce competition. They can do this directly by denying access to necessary infrastructure such as travel routes or broadcast channels. More frequently they act indirectly by making the requirements for entry into a business too costly. This function is an important asset to larger, established businesses that can more easily absorb regulatory costs by spreading them over existing production; they no longer fear new competitors that cannot afford the regulatory burden. Smaller businesses cannot absorb increased or new regulatory costs as easily, and many thus are unable to compete, giving the biggest players a greater market share. The primary losers are the masses, who pay higher prices due to reduced competition and who lose the employment provided by small businesses.

THE ACTIVIST REGULATORS

Congress has created several regulatory agencies to cover areas in which its members have little or no expertise. Their jurisdiction extends to *all* industries rather than specific ones. Prime examples are the Equal Employment Opportunity Commission (EEOC), the Occupational Safety and Health Administration (OSHA), and the Environmental Protection Agency (EPA). The business community widely resents the burden of regulations created by these agencies. Rules developed by the EEOC to prevent discrimination in employment and promotion (affirmative action guidelines) have been awkward, and EEOC enforcement of these rules has been nearly chaotic. Many businesses do not believe the EEOC has the expertise to understand their industry or their labor market. The same is true of OSHA, which has issued thousands of safety regulations that appear costly and ridiculous to those in the industry. Industry representatives contend that the EPA should weigh the costs of its regulations against the benefits, as starkly seen in 2011–2012 when the EPA moved against the hydraulic fracturing, or "fracking," of shale to extract natural gas, a process which had already massively expanded domestic energy production and created tens of thousands of new jobs, and promised much more.

The EEOC, EPA, and OSHA have general responsibilities across all business and industry. Thus, these agencies are unlikely to develop expertise like that of the FCC, SEC, or other single-industry regulators. They also are unlikely to be captured by industry. Rather, they are bureaucratic extensions of civil rights (EEOC), consumer (OSHA), and environmental (EPA) interest-group lobbies to whom they owe their existence. These are a different set of interests than the more clearly economic interests in other areas, but the process of capture is essentially the same.

The Federal Reserve
The Fed's website covers recent developments as well as history. *www.federal reserve.gov*

THE HIDDEN COSTS OF REGULATION

The costs of government regulation do not appear in the federal budget. Rather, they are paid for by businesses, employees, and consumers. Indeed, politicians prefer a regulatory approach to the environment, health, and safety precisely because it forces costs on the private sector—costs that are largely invisible to voters and taxpayers.

Occupational Safety and Health Administration
This website covers news and information directly related to OSHA's mission "to ensure safe and healthful workplaces in America." *www. osha.gov*

How large is the regulatory bill? Proponents of a regulatory activity usually object to estimating its cost. Politicians who wish to develop an image as protectors of the environment, of consumers, of the disabled, and so on do not want to call attention to the costs of their legislation. Only recently has the OMB even attempted to estimate the costs of federal regulatory activity. Overall, regulatory activity cost the United States about $1.75 trillion in 2012, an amount equal to 48 percent of the total federal budget or 11.7 percent of Gross National Product (GNP).[8] This means each inhabitant of the United States pays about $5,600 per year toward the hidden costs of regulation. Paperwork requirements consume more than five billion hours of people's time, mostly to comply with the administration by the IRS of the tax laws. However, the costs of environmental controls, including the EPA's enforcement of clean air and water and hazardous waste disposal regulations, are the fastest-growing regulatory costs. All such costs are eventually passed on to consumers. While many regulations clearly provide benefits to the health, safety, and well-being of the masses, the process by which these costs and benefits are allocated is almost entirely closed to the people.

DEREGULATION AND REREGULATION

The demand for deregulation has echoed in Washington for many years. Complaints about excessive regulation include the following:

1. The increased costs to businesses and consumers of complying with many separate regulations, issued by separate regulatory agencies, are excessive. Environmental regulation alone may be costing the country over $200 billion a year (not including new carbon regulations), but the costs never appear in a federal budget because businesses and consumers absorb them.

2. Overregulation hampers innovation and productivity. For example, the United States lags behind all other advanced nations in the introduction of new drugs because of lengthy testing by the Food and Drug Administration (FDA). Most observers feel the FDA would not approve aspirin if it were proposed for marketing today. The costs and delays in winning permission for a new product tend to discourage invention.

3. Regulatory bureaucracies' oversight of licensing and business start-up reduces competition. The red tape required—the cost of complying with federal reporting requirements—is in itself an obstacle to small businesses and has promoted inefficient businesses and a lack of competitiveness.

4. Regulatory agencies do not weigh the costs of complying with their regulations against the benefits to society. Regulators generally introduce controls with little regard for the cost–benefit trade-offs.

In 1978, Congress acted for the first time to significantly reduce the burden of regulation. Over the objections of the airline industry, which wanted continued regulation, Congress stripped the Civil Aeronautics Board (CAB) of its power to allocate airline routes to various companies and to set rates. The CAB went out of existence in 1985. Against their will, airlines were set free to choose where to fly and what to charge and to compete openly with one another. Higher costs before deregulation had limited mass access to air travel.

Airline deregulation thus brought about a huge increase in affordable flight. The airlines doubled their seating capacity and made more efficient use of their aircraft through the development of hub-and-spoke networks. Air safety continued to improve. Fatalities per millions of miles flown declined, and, because travelers were diverted from far more dangerous highway travel, overall transportation safety improved. But these favorable outcomes were overshadowed by complaints about congestion at major airports and increased flight delays, especially at peak hours.

Deregulation threatens to diminish politicians' power and eliminate bureaucrats' jobs. It forces industries to become competitive and diminishes the role of interest-group lobbyists. Thus, in the absence of strong popular support for continued deregulation, pressures for reregulation remain strong in Washington.

Public scandals in any sector of the economy frequently result in Congress's acting to impose new regulations. A series of accounting scandals, including the collapse of Enron, once the nation's seventh-largest corporation, with evidence that top executives falsified information and hid assets in private accounts, led to new SEC oversight in the form of the Sarbanes-Oxley Act, which required stronger corporate accounting and transparency control, as well as expensive compliance measures. In 2009, mass outrage over executive compensation in the financial industry led to moves to control pay, particularly in companies that had accepted federal bailout money. The 2010 Wall Street Reform and Consumer Protection Act, known by its main authors' names as Dodd-Frank, added considerable complexity to financial regulation in response to the 2007–2009 financial crisis. Many of its costs have been passed along to consumers.

CONTROLLING THE BUREAUCRACY: CHECKS AND BALANCES?

The bureaucracy exists within the framework of the overall federal government and is subject to some checks and balances by other parts of government. Presidential appointments (made with Senate approval) are designed to give policy direction from an elected leader to the bureaucrats technically under the direction of these political patronage positions. Congress or the courts can overturn the decisions of bureaucracies if sufficient opposition develops. But such opposition is unlikely if bureaucracies work closely with their congressional subcommittees and their interest groups.

PRESIDENTIAL CONSTRAINTS

Presidents can constraint the bureaucracy by

1. Appointing political nominees to oversight positions in the executive branch.
2. Presenting Congress with budget requests that increase, decrease, or eliminate agency spending.
3. Vetoing appropriations legislation that funds unwanted programs and agencies.

Still, political appointees' short duration in office weakens their ability to control a permanent bureaucracy, and appropriation bills are usually package deals that a president is highly reluctant to veto for the sake of some relatively small portion of overall spending.

CONGRESSIONAL CONSTRAINTS

Congress can restrain the bureaucracy by

1. Passing direct legislation that changes rules or regulations or limits bureaucratic activity.
2. Altering or threatening to alter the bureau's budget.

3. Retaining specific veto powers over certain bureaucratic actions. (Agencies must submit some proposed rules to Congress; if Congress does not act within a specified time, the rules take effect.)
4. Conducting investigations, usually during legislative or appropriations hearings, that publicize unpopular decisions, rules, or expenditures by bureaus.
5. Making direct complaints to the bureaucracy through formal contacts.

Yet it is difficult for Congress to use these powers as a truly effective check on the bureaucracy, because at the level of the Iron Triangle, House and Senate staffs are close to the bureaucrats who inform the decision-making process in Congress.

JUDICIAL CONSTRAINTS

Decisions by executive agencies usually can be appealed to federal courts. Moreover, federal courts can issue injunctions or court orders to executive agencies before they institute their rules, regulations, projects, or programs. Thus the federal courts exercise more direct control over the bureaucracy than Congress does. Judicial control of the bureaucracy has its limitations, however:

1. Judicial oversight usually emphasizes *procedural* fairness rather than policy content.
2. Bureaucracies have set up elaborate administrative processes to protect their decisions from challenge on procedural grounds.
3. Lawsuits against bureaucracies are expensive; the bureaucracies have armies of attorneys paid for out of tax monies to oppose anyone who attempts to challenge them in court.
4. Excessive delays in federal courts add to the time and expense of challenging bureaucratic decisions.

In fact, citizens have not had much success in court cases against bureaucracies. The courts rarely reverse the decisions of federal regulatory commissions, and bureaucrats win most court cases challenging their regulations.

THE BUREAUCRACY | AN ELITIST INTERPRETATION

The federal bureaucracy is a major base of power in the United States, largely independent of the other branches of government and not very responsive to public pressure. Bureaucracy pervades every aspect of modern life, and its power continues to grow. Bureaucratic elites both formulate and implement public policy. Elitism in bureaucracy takes several forms:

1. Bureaucratic power increases with the size and technological complexity of modern society. Congress sets forth only general policy statements. Bureaucracies write tens of thousands of rules and regulations and actually undertake the tasks of government.
2. Bureaucratic power increases because (a) Congress and the president do not have the time or expertise to master policy details; (b) Congress and the president deliberately pass vague laws for symbolic reasons, then turn over actual

governance to bureaucracies; and (c) the bureaucracy has amassed sufficient power to influence the president and Congress.

3. Although the president is officially in charge of the executive branch of government, presidential control is limited by (a) the relatively small number of policy-making patronage positions appointed by the president versus the large numbers of professional civil service bureaucrats, (b) the difficulty of achieving meaningful reorganization, and (c) the difficulty of vetoing large spending bills to address specific agency spending in the budget.

4. The budget is the most important policy statement of a government. The president, through the OMB, is responsible for the preparation of the Federal Budget each year for submission to Congress. But only Congress can authorize the expenditure of federal funds; it does so through annual appropriations acts for major areas of government spending.

5. Federal spending has grown dramatically over the years, driven largely by "entitlement" spending, notably Social Security and Medicare. While the 1990s produced four years of balanced budgets, deficits resumed with a vengeance due to the financial crisis, increased spending on "stimulus" and war, and tax reductions. Future generations are already burdened with an accumulated national debt of almost $16 trillion (and growing).

6. Once a political question shifts to the bureaucracy, an "iron triangle" of power bases comes together to decide its outcome: the executive bureaucracy, the congressional subcommittee, and the organized interest groups.

7. The federal regulatory commissions are investigators, prosecutors, judges, and juries—all wrapped into one. Members of these commissions serve long, overlapping terms, and they do not report to executive departments. They are relatively free from mass influence.

8. The Federal Reserve Board (the Fed), which governs the Federal Reserve System, is the most independent of all federal agencies. It controls the nation's supply of money and directly influences interest rates.

9. Regulations hide the true costs of government by shifting them from the government itself to businesses, employees, and consumers. Bureaucrats seldom weigh the costs of their actions against the benefits. For 2012 the cost of federal regulation was $1.75 trillion.

10. Congress can restrain the bureaucracy directly by ordering changes in rules, altering the budget, retaining veto powers over bureaucratic action, conducting investigations, and registering complaints. In practice, Congress rarely reverses bureaucratic decisions and seldom tampers with "uncontrollable" budget items. The courts can also restrain the bureaucracy, but rarely do they reverse administrative decisions. Checks and balances are at best weak in controlling the bureaucracy.

NOTES

1. Max Weber, *The Theory of Social and Economic Organization*, A. M. Henderson and Talcott Parsons, trans. (New York: Oxford University Press, 1947).

2. James Q. Wilson, "Social Science: The Public Disenchantment, a Symposium," *American Scholar* (Summer 1976): 358; also cited by Aaron Wildavsky,

Speaking Truth to Power (Boston, MA: Little, Brown, 1979), p. 69.

3. *Clinton v. City of New York*, 524 U.S. 417 (1998).

4. Richard P. Nathan, *The Plot That Failed: Nixon and the Administrative Presidency* (New York: John Wiley and Sons, 1975).

5. Dunn Anita, "Reality Check: The Truth about Czars." White House Briefing Room, The Blog. http://www.whitehouse.gov/blog/The-Truth-About-Czars/. Dunn includes links to administration critics.

6. Congressional Budget Office, *The Budget and Economic Outlook: Fiscal Years 2008 to 2017*. January 2007. http://www.cbo.gov/ftpdocs/77xx/ doc7731/01-24-BudgetOutlook.pdf

7. For a current report on the debt of the United States, see "Debt to the Penny and Who Holds It" at http://www.treasurydirect.gov/NP/BPDLogin?application=np.

8. Clyde Wayne Crews, Jr., *Ten Thousand Commandments: An Annual Snapshot of the Federal Regulatory State*, 2012 edition. Competitive Enterprise Institute. http://cei.org/studies/ten-thousand-commandments-2012

The importance of denationalizing conflicts can hardly be overestimated, particularly in a large country like the United States where there is great diversity in resources and local problems.

—Robert A. Dahl

FEDERALISM: STATE AND COMMUNITY ELITES

CHAPTER **12**

Elites exist at numerous levels. Although those at the national level have more power, in the United States, state and local elites, or **subelites**, cumulatively hold considerable power themselves. This decentralization allows decision making by subelites, thus reducing strain on the national political system and on national elites by keeping many issues out of the national arena. Subelites pursue their own policies within the separate states and communities; they need not battle for a single national policy to be applied uniformly throughout the land. For example, subelites who wish to raise taxes to increase educational spending can do so in their own states and communities, and those who wish to reduce taxes and maintain or cut spending levels can also do so at the subnational level.

The United States is a federal republic, in which political power is divided between the national, or federal, government and the 50 states. It was the states that agreed with each other to form a central government and give it specified powers that had belonged exclusively to the states or the people. The Constitution divided authority between the central and state governments, although the balance of this division has changed significantly over time. States are in turn divided into counties, cities, and towns. The states each have a government system of checks and balances similar to that of the federal government: an executive branch headed by an elected governor, an elected legislative branch divided into two houses (except unicameral Nebraska), and an independent judiciary. Counties generally are run by an elected county commission, although there is considerable variation between states. Cities generally have a government divided into an executive branch, headed by a mayor, and a legislative branch, known by some variation of the term city council. (For a picture of each level of government's executive elite, see Focus: Rising Star, twice in this chapter.)

The people have more confidence in state and local government than in the federal government (see Figure 12.1). Moreover, the masses would prefer that governmental power be concentrated at the state rather than the federal level, and they

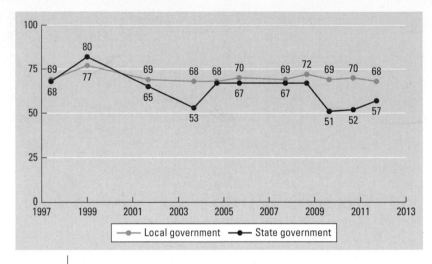

FIGURE 12.1 | TRUST AND CONFIDENCE IN GOVERNMENT ENTITIES

Source: Lydia Saad, "In U.S., Local and State Governments Retain Positive Ratings,"
Gallup.com. October 3, 2011. *www.gallup.com/poll/149888/Local-State-Governments-Retain-Positive-Ratings.aspx.*

believe local and state governments do the best job (see Figures 12.2 and 12.3). Yet over the nation's history, *power has shifted over time to Washington and away from states and communities.*

FEDERALISM: THE DIVISION OF POWER BETWEEN NATIONAL AND STATE GOVERNMENTS

The U.S. Constitution divides power between two separate authorities, the nation and the states, each of which can directly enforce its own laws on individuals through its own courts. There are more than 86,000 separate governments in the United States, of which more than 60,000 have the power to levy their own taxes. *The Constitution reserves for states all governmental powers not vested specifically in the national government or reserved to the people.* All other governmental jurisdictions are subdivisions of states. States may create, alter, or abolish these other units of government by amending state laws or constitutions. Finally, only the states have the power to amend the Constitution.

Federalism differs from a "unitary" political system in that in federalism the central government has no constitutional authority to determine, alter, or abolish the power of the states. At the same time, U.S. federalism differs from a confederation of states, in which the national government depends on its states for power. Authority and power are shared constitutionally and practically.

The U.S. Constitution originally defined federalism in terms of (1) the powers exercised by the national government (delegated powers) and the national supremacy

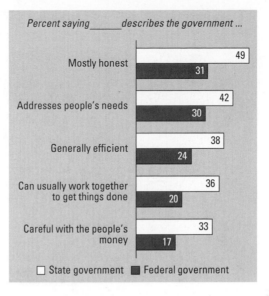

FIGURE 12.2 | STATE GOVERNMENTS GET HIGHER MARKS

Source: Pew Center for People and the Press, "Growing Gap in Favorable Views of Federal, State Governments," April 26, 2012. *www.people-press.org/2012/04/26/ growing-gap-in-favorable-views-of-federal-state-governments/.*

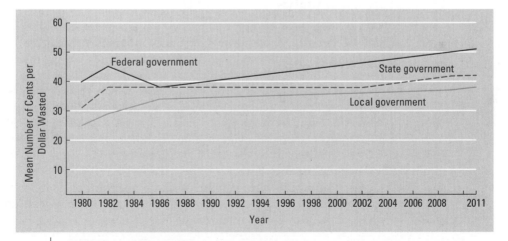

FIGURE 12.3 | PERCEIVED WASTE BY LEVEL OF GOVERNMENT

For almost 30 years, poll respondents have consistently seen local spending as the least wasteful and Federal spending as the most wasteful. By 2009 they believed half of Federal spending was wasted. State spending fell in between.

Source: Adapted from *www.gallup.com/poll/149543/Americans-Say-Federal-Gov-Wastes-Half-Every-Dollar.aspx*

"Look, the American people don't want to be bossed around by federal bureaucrats. They want to be bossed around by state bureaucrats."

clause; (2) the powers reserved to the states; (3) the powers denied by the Constitution to both the national government and the states; and (4) the constitutional provisions giving the states a role in the composition of the national government.

CONSTITUTIONAL POWERS AND FEDERAL AND STATE AUTHORITY

The U.S. Constitution lists 18 grants of power to Congress, including authority over war and foreign affairs, authority over the economy ("interstate commerce"), control over the money supply, and power to tax and spend "to pay the debts and provide for the common defense and general welfare." Finally, after 17 specific grants of power comes the power "to make all laws which shall be necessary and proper for carrying into execution the foregoing powers and all other powers vested by this Constitution in the government of the United States or in any department or officer thereof." This is known as the "necessary and proper" clause, frequently referred to as the "elastic" clause because it has been stretched dramatically over the nation's history.

Federalist Society
The Federalist Society advocates for the original interpretation of the Constitution on issues of federal and state powers.
www.fed-soc.org

These delegated powers, when coupled with the assertion of "national supremacy" in Article VI, ensure a powerful national government. The national supremacy clause is specific in asserting the supremacy of federal laws:

> The Constitution, and the laws of the United States which shall be made in pursuance thereof; and all treaties made or which shall be made under the authority of the United States, shall be the supreme law of the land; and the judges in every state shall be bound thereby, anything in the constitution or laws of any state to the contrary notwithstanding.

The Constitution denies the states some powers in order to safeguard national unity: the powers to coin money, enter into treaties with foreign nations, interfere with the "obligations of contracts," levy taxes on imports and exports, and engage in war, among others.

Despite these broad grants of power to the national government, the states retained considerable governing power from the beginning of the republic, referred to as the *reserved powers*. The Tenth Amendment reassured the states that "the powers not delegated to the United States ... are reserved to the states respectively, or to the people." The states generally retain control over property and contract law, criminal law, marriage and divorce, the provision of education, highways, and social welfare activities. The general police power was seen as one of the "reserved powers." The states control the organization and powers of their own local governments. Finally, the states, like the federal government, retain the power to tax and spend for the general welfare.

The Constitution denies some powers to both national and state government, namely, the powers to abridge individual rights. The first eight amendments to the U.S. Constitution originally applied only to the national government, but the Fourteenth Amendment, passed by Congress in 1866, provided that the states must also adhere to fundamental guarantees of individual liberty.

THE STATES' ROLE IN NATIONAL GOVERNMENT

The states are also basic units in the organizational scheme of the national government. States determine voter eligibility (within federal civil rights guidelines). The House of Representatives apportions members to the states by population, and state legislatures draw up their districts. Every state has at least one House representative, regardless of its population. Each state elects two U.S. senators, regardless of its population. The president is chosen by the electoral votes of the states; each state has as many electoral votes as it has senators and House representatives. Finally, three-fourths of the states must ratify amendments to the U.S. Constitution.

POWER FLOWS TO THE NATIONAL ELITE

Over time, governmental power has become centralized in Washington. Although the formal constitutional arrangements of federalism remain in place, power has flowed relentlessly toward the national government since the earliest days of the nation. The legal basis of this shift centers on Article I, Section 8, of the Constitution.

THE "NECESSARY AND PROPER" CLAUSE

Chief Justice John Marshall added immeasurably to national power in *McCulloch v. Maryland* (1819) when he broadly interpreted the "necessary and proper" or elastic clause. In approving the establishment of a national bank (a power not specifically delegated to the national government in the Constitution), Marshall wrote:

> Let the end be legitimate, let it be within the scope of the Constitution, and all means which are appropriate, which are plainly adopted to that end, which are not prohibited but consistent with the letter and the spirit of the Constitution, are constitutional.

Since then, the elastic clause has been called the "implied powers" clause, suggesting that the national government can stretch out its authority to anything not specifically prohibited by the Constitution. Given this tradition, the courts are unlikely to hold an act of Congress unconstitutional solely because no formal constitutional grant of power gives Congress the power to act.

THE CIVIL WAR

The Civil War was the nation's greatest crisis in federalism. Could a state leave the union? Did a state have the right to oppose federal action by force of arms? The issue was decided in the nation's bloodiest war, and the answer was "no." Combined military and civilian casualties in the Civil War exceeded U.S. casualties in World War II, even though the U.S. population in 1860 was only one-quarter of the population in 1940.

PROHIBITION AND REPEAL

The Eighteenth Amendment to the Constitution in 1919 banned the manufacture, sale, or transportation of alcoholic beverages in the United States. This forced the federal government to regulate an area of life previously seen as under the authority of state power—the health, safety, and morals of the community. A major impetus for this Progressive Era law was to protect women from domestic violence. The Eighteenth Amendment was repealed by the Twenty-first Amendment in 1933, which was ratified at the nadir of the Great Depression. Today, some counties in the United States still ban alcohol and many states restrict its sale.

CIVIL RIGHTS

Over the years, the U.S. Supreme Court has built a national system of civil rights based on the Fourteenth Amendment. This amendment rose out of the Civil War: "No *state* shall ... deprive any person of life, liberty, or property, without due process of law; nor deny to any person within its jurisdiction the equal protection of the laws." In early cases, the Supreme Court held that the general guarantee of "liberty" in the first phrase (the "due process" clause) prevents states from interfering with free speech, the press, religion, and other personal liberties. Later, particularly after the school segregation case of *Brown v. Board of Education of Topeka, Kansas* in 1954, the Supreme Court also used the "equal protection" clause to ensure fairness and equality of opportunity throughout the nation. The issue of states refusing federal orders was at stake when the federal government sent troops to Little Rock, Arkansas, in 1957 and to Oxford, Mississippi, in 1962 to enforce desegregation.

THE INTERSTATE COMMERCE CLAUSE

The growth of national power under the interstate commerce clause is also an important development in federalism. The Industrial Revolution created a national economy governable only by a national government. The Constitution placed many

---

IN BRIEF | THE SHIFT OF POWER

Over time, power in the U.S. federal system has shifted to the national government. The most important developments in this shift have been the following:

- A broad interpretation of the "necessary and proper" clause, obscuring the notion of "delegated powers."
- The victory of the national government in the Civil War, demonstrating that states cannot successfully resist federal power.

- The establishment of a national system of civil rights based on the Fourteenth Amendment, which brought the federal government into the process of defining and enforcing civil rights, even in state-level matters. The growth of federal power under the "interstate commerce" clause as a national industrial economy emerged.
- The growth of federal grants-in-aid to state and local governments.

---

obstacles in the way of federal government regulation of the economy. In *National Labor Relations Board v. Jones & Laughlin Steel Corporation* (1937), an activist Supreme Court recognized the principle that Congress could regulate production and distribution of goods and services for a national market under the interstate commerce clause. As a result, the national government gained control over wages, prices, production, marketing, labor relations, and all other important aspects of the national economy.

MONEY AND POWER

Money and power go together. It is usually a useful research technique to "follow the money." Federal land grants to the states began as far back as the famous Northwest Ordinance in 1787, when Congress gave federal land to the states to assist in building public schools. Again, under the Morrill Land Grant Act in 1862, Congress made land grants to the states to promote higher education, and many universities across the nation began with these grants. In 1913, the Sixteenth Amendment gave the national government the power to tax incomes, and financial power shifted from the states to Washington. The income tax gave the federal government the authority to raise large sums of money, which it spent for the "general welfare" as well as for national security. The first major federal *money* grants to the states began shortly after enactment of the federal income tax. Grant programs began in agricultural extension (1914), highways (1916), vocational education (1917), and public health (1918).

The federal government rapidly expanded its power in states and communities by the use of grants-in-aid, federal money given to states for specific purposes. During the Great Depression of the 1930s, the national government used its taxing and spending powers in a number of areas formerly reserved to states and communities. Congress began grant-in-aid programs to states and communities for public assistance, unemployment compensation, employment services, child welfare, public housing, and urban renewal. A second major expansion of federal money to the states came with the 1960s Great Society programs. Since the 1980s, the states have had greater discretion in how they disburse federal grants.

Urban Institute
Washington think tank offers viewpoints on federalism and issues confronting state and local governments.
www.urban.org

THE EVOLUTION OF U.S. FEDERALISM

U.S. federalism has undergone many changes during its more than 200 years of existence, with state and local governments becoming increasingly dependent on federal grant money. State and local dependency on federal grants increased dramatically in the 1960s and 1970s, declined under President Reagan in the 1980s, crept up again under Presidents Bill Clinton and George W. Bush,[1] and expanded even further under President Obama's economic stimulus programs in 2009 and 2010.

DUAL FEDERALISM

The pattern of federal–state relations during the nation's first 100 years has been described as **dual federalism**. The states and the nation divided most governmental functions. The national government concentrated its attention on the delegated powers—national defense, foreign affairs, tariffs, commerce across state lines, coining money, establishing standard weights and measures, maintaining a post office and building post roads, and admitting new states. State governments decided the important domestic policy issues—property (including slaves until the Civil War), education, welfare, health, and criminal justice. This separation of policy responsibilities is often compared to a layer cake, with local governments at the base, state governments in the middle, and the national government at the top.

COOPERATIVE FEDERALISM

The Industrial Revolution and the resulting development of a national economy, the income tax that shifted financial resources to the national government, and the challenges of two world wars and the Great Depression all combined to end the strict distinction between national and state concerns. The new pattern of federal–state relations was labeled **cooperative federalism**. Both the nation and the states exercised responsibilities for welfare, health, highways, education, and criminal justice. This merging of policy responsibilities is compared to a marble cake: "As the colors are mixed in a marble cake, so functions are mixed in the American federal system."[2]

The Great Depression of the 1930s left states financially helpless. Tax revenue declined dramatically and the states had few alternatives for income. The federal government, under the Constitution, controlled the money supply and had a far greater capacity to borrow. The Depression forced states to ask for federal financial assistance in dealing with poverty, unemployment, and old age. Governors welcomed massive federal public-works projects. In addition, the federal government intervened directly in economic affairs, labor relations, business practices, and agriculture. Through the grant-in-aid device, the national government cooperated with the states in public assistance, employment services, child welfare, public housing, urban renewal, highway building, and vocational education.

Yet even during this period when the nation and the states shared responsibility, the national government emphasized cooperation in achieving common national and state goals. Congress generally acknowledged that it had no direct constitutional authority to regulate public health, safety, or welfare. It relied primarily on its powers to tax and spend for the general welfare in providing financial assistance to state and local governments to achieve shared goals and did not usually legislate directly on local matters.

INCREASED CENTRALIZATION AND NEW FEDERALISM

Over the years, it became increasingly difficult to maintain the fiction that the national government was merely assisting the states in performing their domestic responsibility. By 1964 and the inauguration of President Lyndon Johnson's Great Society programs, the federal government was clearly setting forth its own national goals. Virtually all problems confronting U.S. society—from poverty and pollution to consumer safety, home insulation, and noise abatement—were declared national problems. Congress legislated directly on any matter it chose. The Supreme Court no longer concerned itself with the reserved powers of the states; the Tenth Amendment lost most of its meaning. The pattern of federal–state relations became centralized.

The term **new federalism** refers to efforts to return power and responsibility to states and communities. The term was first used by President Nixon for his general-revenue-sharing proposal: the direct allocation of federal tax revenues to state and local governments to use for general purposes without restrictions. Later, the term referred to a series of proposals by President Reagan to provide greater flexibility in the use of federal funds and allow state and local officials to exercise more power over projects and programs within their jurisdictions. Reagan consolidated many **categorical grants** (by which the federal government specifies individual projects or programs in cities and states) into a few large **block grant programs** (by which the federal government provides funds for use by states and cities for broad purposes, such as law enforcement and community development, with state and local officials deciding on specific projects or programs). These efforts succeeded for a time in slowing the growth of federal grant money to the states and even in reducing state and local reliance on federal funds. Under President Clinton, the Welfare Reform Act of 1996 replaced a 60-year-old federal entitlement program of cash aid to low-income mothers and children. The act granted greater responsibility to the states by allowing them broad flexibility in determining eligibility for cash aid. These mixtures of power, funding, and responsibility are sometimes referred to as "salad bowl" federalism.

REPRESENTATIONAL FEDERALISM

The main direction of the flow of power is toward national elites. In 1985, the U.S. Supreme Court ended all pretense of constitutional protection of state power in its *Garcia v. San Antonio Metropolitan Authority* decision.[3] Before this case it was generally believed that the states were constitutionally protected from direct congressional coercion in matters traditionally reserved to them. Congress could bribe states with grant-in-aid money to enact federal programs—or threaten them with the loss of such aid if they failed to conform to federal rules—but it was careful to avoid direct orders to state and local governments. In theory, at least, state and

| FOCUS | RISING STAR: GOVERNOR BOBBY JINDAL |

Born in Baton Rouge to parents from India, Bobby Jindal was elected governor of Louisiana in 2007 at the age of 36. His birth name is Piyush, but he goes by Bobby based on his identification with a character on the TV series *The Brady Bunch*. Turning down Yale and Harvard, he graduated from Brown University with honors in biology and public policy and received a graduate degree in political science from Oxford University in 1994, where he was a Rhodes scholar.

In 1996, Jindal was appointed secretary of the Louisiana Department of Health and Hospitals, where he was able to move the department from a massive deficit into a surplus and save the Medicaid program. He was 25 years old when he ran the state's largest department, with a $4 billion budget. For this he became executive director of the National Bipartisan Commission on the Future of Medicare. In 1999, he became president of the University of Louisiana system. President Bush nominated him to be assistant secretary

of Health and Human Services in 2001. After this federal service, he returned to Louisiana for an unsuccessful run for governor. In 2004, he was elected to the U.S. House of Representatives.

Jindal, a social conservative, was elected governor of Louisiana in 2006. His primary focus as governor has been ethics reform, as Louisiana has been notorious for corruption. He has also pushed economic development. In February 2009, Jindal gave the official Republican response to President Obama's address to Congress, an appearance that brought national attention as well as some criticism. He was viewed as a possible vice presidential candidate in 2008 and is frequently mentioned as a potential Republican presidential candidate in the future. Jindal achieved further national recognition in 2010 for his criticism of the federal response to the Gulf of Mexico oil spill. Declaring it to be unconstitutional, Jindal also has been a national leader in opposing President Obama's health care legislation.

local governments were free to forgo the money and ignore the strings attached to it. However, in the *Garcia* case, the Supreme Court upheld a federal law requiring state and local governments to obey federal wage and hour rules. The Court dismissed the constitutional argument that the nature of federalism and the reserved powers clause of the Tenth Amendment prevented Congress from legislating directly in state and local affairs. The Court declared there were no constitutionally protected state powers and the only protection given the states is in congressional and presidential elections. This view of federalism—that there is no constitutional protection for state power other than the states' role in electing the members of Congress and the president—has been labeled **representational federalism**.

COERCIVE FEDERALISM

Over time, Congress has undertaken to issue direct regulations in areas traditionally reserved for the states. **Federal mandates** are direct orders to state and local governments to perform a particular activity or service to comply with federal laws and performance of their functions. They occur in a wide variety of areas, for example:

> *Age Discrimination Act* (1986): Outlaws mandatory retirement ages for public as well as private employees, including police, firefighters, and state college and university faculty.

> *Clean Air Act* (1990): Prohibits municipal incinerators and also requires additional inspections in certain urban areas.

Americans with Disabilities Act (1990): Requires all state and local government buildings to provide access for the disabled.

National Voter Registration Act (1993): Requires states to register voters at motor vehicle, social benefit, and unemployment compensation offices.

No Child Left Behind Act (2001): Requires states and their school districts to test public school pupils.

Help America Vote Act (2003): Requires states to modernize registration and voting procedures.

Many of these mandates impose heavy costs on state and local governments. When no federal monies are provided to cover these costs, the mandates are said to be **unfunded mandates**. The Unfunded Mandates Reform Act of 1995 was passed to address the issue, including having the Congressional Budget Office (CBO) calculate the costs forced on states and localities by federal mandates. Governors, mayors, and other state and local officials frequently complain about unfunded mandates. For example, the Real ID Act (2005) set a national standard for drivers' licenses and requires states to link their records to a national database. All 50 states needed extensions of the May 2008 deadline. The Department of Homeland Security estimated the costs of state compliance to be about $3.9 billion but provided only $150 million in assistance. (In 2009, Congress cut the budget severely, making full implementation unlikely.)

THE SUPREME COURT'S REASSERTION OF FEDERALISM

Several recent Supreme Court decisions appear somewhat more respectful of the powers of the states. In 1995, the Court held that the politically popular Gun Free School Zone Act exceeded the constitutionally delegated powers of Congress, its first opinion in more than 60 years that recognized limits on the national government's power over interstate commerce. The Justice Department had argued that keeping schools gun free would reduce crime and that reducing crime would facilitate interstate commerce. The Court held that such tenuous reasoning would remove virtually all limits to federal power: "To uphold the Government's contention here, we would have to pile inference upon inference in a manner that would convert congressional authority under the Commerce Clause to a general police power of the sort retained by the states."[4]

Other victories for federalism include the Supreme Court's invalidating a provision of the Brady Handgun Violence Protection Act. The Court decided in 1997 that this law's requirement that local law enforcement officers conduct background checks on gun purchasers violated "the very principle of separate state sovereignty."[5] In 1999, the Supreme Court said states were shielded in their own courts from lawsuits in which private parties seek to enforce federal mandates. In an opinion that surveyed the history of U.S. federalism, Justice Kennedy wrote: "Congress has vast power but not all power.... When Congress legislates in matters affecting the states it may not treat these sovereign entities as mere prefectures or corporations."[6] In 2000, the Supreme Court surprised Congress and challenged public opinion by holding that the Violence Against Women Act also invaded the reserved police powers of the states.

"The Constitution requires a distinction between what is truly national and what is truly local."[7]

However, all these rulings reaffirming federalism came in narrow 5 to 4 decisions and contrast with more than half a century of Court support for national power. There is no guarantee the Court or the nation will move toward stronger federalism.

Perhaps the most dramatic response of the states to a federal government expansion of power came after the passage of President Obama's Patient Protection and Affordable Care Act of 2010 (often referred to as Obamacare). The case of *Florida v. United States Department of Health and Human Services* was heard by the U.S. Supreme Court in March 2012 over two days. The lawsuit against the federal government had 26 states, a majority, join in asking for the law to be declared unconstitutional. The Supreme Court narrowed this and some related lawsuits to a few central questions:

1. Does Congress exceed its enumerated powers and violate basic principles of federalism when it coerces states into accepting onerous conditions that it could not impose directly by threatening to withhold all federal funding under the single largest grant-in-aid program, or does the limitation on Congress's spending power that this Court recognized in *South Dakota v. Dole*, 483 U.S. 203 (1987), no longer apply?
2. May Congress treat states no differently from any other employer when imposing invasive mandates as to the manner in which they provide their own employees with insurance coverage, as suggested by *Garcia v. San Antonio Metropolitan Transit Authority*, 469 U.S. 528 (1985), or has *Garcia*'s approach been overtaken by subsequent cases in which this Court has explicitly recognized judicially enforceable limits on Congress's power to interfere with state sovereignty?
3. Does the Affordable Care Act's mandate that virtually every individual obtain health insurance exceed Congress's enumerated powers and, if so, to what extent (if any) can the mandate be severed from the remainder of the Act?[8]

National Conference of State Legislatures This website provides information on 50 state legislatures and the issues they confront. *www. ncsl.org*

While the third question is clearly about the ability of the federal government to expand its power over individuals, the core question of federal reach is shared by both states and individuals. In its ruling on case in June 2012, the Supreme Court supported the Obama Administration's assertion that the individual mandate was constitutional, although on grounds of it being a tax (which had not been the reason the federal government felt it was acceptable). However, on the first question above dealing with federal coercion of states into adopting programs, the Court ruled that the Affordable Care Act was unconstitutional.

MASS INFLUENCE IN THE STATES

The masses can exercise more direct influence in state politics than in national politics. This is true despite the fact that voters are less knowledgeable about state and local politics than about national politics, and voter participation in state and local elections is lower than that in national elections. But the masses in state and local politics have access to the initiative and referendum—provisions found in the constitutions of 18 states. They also have access to the recall—provisions found in the constitutions of 16 states (see Table 12.1).

TABLE 12.1 | INITIATIVE AND RECALL IN THE STATES

Initiative for Constitutional Amendments (Signatures Required to Get on Ballot)*	Recall (Signatures Required to Force a Recall Election)**
Arizona (15%)	Alaska (25%)
Arkansas (10%)	Arizona (25%)
California (8%)	California (12%)
Colorado (5%)	Colorado (25%)
Florida (8%)	Georgia (15%)
Illinois (8%)	Idaho (20%)
Massachusetts (3%)	Kansas (40%)
Michigan (10%)	Louisiana (33%)
Mississippi (12%)	Michigan (25%)
Missouri (8%)	Montana (10%)
Montana (10%)	Nevada (25%)
Nebraska (10%)	North Dakota (25%)
Nevada (10%)	Oregon (15%)
North Dakota	Rhode Island (15%)
(4% of state population)	Washington (25%)
Ohio (10%)	Wisconsin (25%)
Oklahoma (15%)	
Oregon (8%)	
South Dakota (10%)	

*Figures expressed as percentage of vote in last governor's election.
**Figures are percentages of voters in last general election of the official sought to be recalled.
Source: *Book of the States*, 2005–2006.

The U.S. Constitution has no provision for national referenda. There is no national direct vote on federal laws or amendments to the U.S. Constitution. The Founders were profoundly skeptical of direct democracy, in which the people themselves initiate and decide policy questions by popular vote. The Founders believed government ultimately rested on the consent of the governed, foreseeing a republic with decision making by representatives of the people, not the people themselves.

THE POPULIST MOVEMENT IN THE STATES

At the beginning of the twentieth century, a strong populist movement in the midwestern and western states attacked railroads, banks, corporations, and the political institutions that were said to be in their pockets. The people believed their elected representatives were ignoring the needs of family farmers, debtors, and laborers. They wished to bypass governors and legislatures and directly enact popular laws for railroad rate regulation, relief of farm debt, and monetary expansion. The populists were largely responsible for replacing party conventions with the primary elections still used today. They were also successful in bringing about the Seventeenth Amendment to the U.S. Constitution, which requires that U.S. senators be directly elected by the voters rather than chosen by state legislatures. Finally, the populists were responsible for the widespread adoption of three forms of direct democracy: the initiative, the referendum, and the recall.

THE INITIATIVE

The initiative is a device by which a specific number or percentage of voters, through the use of a petition, can have a proposed state constitutional amendment or state law placed on the ballot for adoption or rejection by the voters of a state. This process bypasses the legislature and allows citizens to propose laws and constitutional amendments.

THE REFERENDUM

The referendum is a device by which the electorate must approve either a decision of the legislature or a citizen-proposed initiative before it becomes law. The initiative and the referendum go hand in hand to allow citizens to directly alter the laws or constitution of their state.

THE RECALL

The recall election allows voters to remove elected officials before their term expires. It is initiated by a petition with a required number of signatures, usually expressed as a percentage of the votes cast in the last election for the official being recalled. Recall petitions are rarely successful, but one of the most celebrated was the 2003 recall of California Governor Gray Davis and his replacement by actor Arnold Schwarzenegger. In 2012, the failed attempt to recall Wisconsin Governor Scott Walker became a nationally significant showdown over the pension costs of government employees.

THE POLITICS OF STATE INITIATIVES

The masses overwhelmingly support the initiative process, and state initiatives have generally reflected their attitudes rather than elite preferences. Popular initiatives in recent years have limited terms for public officials, banned same-sex marriages, limited taxes of various kinds, made English the official language, allowed gambling, allowed marijuana use for medicinal purposes, prohibited state funds for abortion, and permitted physician-assisted suicide. Most elites bitterly oppose the initiative process, and legislators in a majority of states have managed to stave off granting initiative rights to their citizens.

Of course, citizen initiatives are often backed by special interests—specific businesses or industries, labor unions, government employees, religious organizations, the gambling industry, and so on. In other words, many initiative movements are not really initiated by "the people." Paid workers gather the necessary signatures and promote the initiative on television and radio and in newspaper advertisements. The Center for Governmental Studies report on the California initiative noted that

> Despite its widespread use and popularity, the initiative process faces many criticisms: that it undermines legislative power and procedures, generates poorly-drafted or ill-considered proposals, encourages high-spending and deceptive campaigns, permits excessive special interest influence, has become too professionalized, encourages single issue politics, generates voter confusion and overload, discourages compromise and invites corruption and manipulation.
>
> Supporters of the initiative process defend it, arguing that it allows the public to circumvent the governor and legislature when necessary, neutralizes the power of special interests, overcomes resistance to government and political reforms, stimulates public involvement in state issues and exerts pressure on the legislature to act responsibly.[9]

Perhaps the state with the greatest use of the initiative process, California has seen direct democracy run amok. In 1997, a successful ballot initiative made it a felony to sell horsemeat for human consumption. California Chief Justice Ronald George asserted in 2009 that the ease of getting measures on the ballot had "rendered state government dysfunctional." It has placed vast restrictions on the ability of the state legislature to budget, resulting in nearly chronic budget crises. Initiatives can also produce strange contradictions, as in 2008 when voters passed two measures: one to regulate the confinement of poultry and another banning gay marriage. Chief Justice George commented that "Chickens gained valuable rights in California on the same day that gay men and lesbians lost them."[10]

THE OLD-COMMUNITY ECONOMIC ELITES

Most of the nation's economic resources are controlled by *national* institutions— industrial corporations, banks, utilities, insurance companies, investment firms, and the national government. Most of the forces shaping life in U.S. communities arise outside these communities; the Constitution denies community leaders the power to make war or peace or cause inflation or recession or determine interest rates or the money supply. But one economic resource—land—is controlled by *community* elites. Land is valuable because capital investment, labor and management, and production must be placed somewhere.

Traditionally, community power structures were composed primarily of landed interests whose goal was to intensify the use of their land and add to its value. These community elites sought to maximize land values, real estate commissions, builders' profits, rent payments, and mortgage interest and to increase revenues to commercial enterprises serving the community. Communities were traditionally dominated by mortgage lending banks, real estate developers, builders, and land-owners. They were joined by owners or managers of local utilities, department stores, attorneys and title companies, and others whose wealth is affected by land use. Local bankers who financed the real estate developers and builders were often at the center of the elite structure. Unquestionably, these community elites competed among themselves for wealth, profit, power, and preeminence. But they shared a consensus about intensifying the use of land.

| FOCUS | CORPORATE ELITE STRUCTURES IN THE STATES |

State elites fall into different patterns, largely based on the degree of diversification of their economies, but also on the degree of competitiveness between the political parties. States with more unity or cohesion among dominant interests will tend to be states where one party dominates; a smaller number of industries are present; and/or the state economy relies on resource extraction, such as oil, mining, or timber. This matches what James Madison noted in *Federalist Paper* Number 10, "the smaller the society, the fewer the number of interests, and the greater the likelihood that a single interest will dominate."

Cohesive elite structures are more likely to emerge in states in which relatively few major industrial corporations have their home offices, a proxy variable for diversity of large industries. The following table lists the number of corporations in the Fortune 500 in each state. Some states have none: Alaska, Hawaii, Montana, New Mexico, North Dakota, Vermont, and Wyoming. Because of their mostly rural, mostly resource-based, and non-diversified economies, these states are likely to have fairly cohesive elite structures. Likewise, the states with only a few major corporations (e.g., Arkansas with headquarters for Walmart's retail store and Tyson's chicken processing) are also likely to have relatively unified elite structures.

In contrast, states with large numbers of corporations engaged in a wide variety of industrial activities are likely to have plural elite structures. California and New York, for example, are large and diversified and house too many top-ranked corporations to be dominated by a unified elite.

TYPES OF ELITE STRUCTURES (RANKED BY NUMBER OF MAJOR INDUSTRIAL HEADQUARTERS LOCATED IN THE STATE)

Likely Plural Elite Structures

New York	57	California	53	Texas	51	Illinois	31
Ohio	27	Pennsylvania	23	Michigan	22	New Jersey	20
Virginia	20	Minnesota	20				

Likely Increasingly Diversified Elite Structures

Florida	16	North Carolina	15	Georgia	14	Massachusetts	13
Connecticut	12	Missouri	10	Wisconsin	10		

Likely Dominant Elite among Lesser Elites

Wisconsin	9	Colorado	9	Tennessee	8	Washington	8
Arizona	7	Kentucky	5	Indiana	5	Maryland	5
Nebraska	5	Arkansas	4	Oklahoma	4		

Likely Unified Elite Structures

Louisiana	3	Kansas	3	South Carolina	3	Nevada	3
Iowa	2	Oregon	2	Rhode Island	2	Delaware	2
Alabama	1	Idaho	1	Utah	1	North Dakota	0
Mississippi	0	West Virginia	0	Alaska	0	Vermont	0
Maine	0	Montana	0	New Mexico	0	South Dakota	0
Wyoming	0	New Hampshire	0	Hawaii	0		

Source: Locations taken from: *http://money.cnn.com/magazines/fortune/fortune500/2011/states/CA.html*.

| FOCUS | RISING STAR: MAYOR CORY BOOKER |

While he may have first come to national attention for his comedic "feud" with *Tonight Show* host Conan O'Brien,[a] Newark, New Jersey's mayor Cory Booker had already gained the notice of media pundits and political scientists for his effectiveness in dealing with the social and economic issues in one of the nation's most downtrodden cities.

Son of two of the first African-American executives at IBM, Booker attended Stanford University, where he was a football star. He received a BA in political science in 1991 and an MA in sociology in 1992 from Stanford before going to Oxford University as a Rhodes scholar, where he earned a history degree in 1994. In 1997, he graduated from Yale Law School with a JD. He had moved to Newark in his third year and decided to build his future there.

The year after graduating, Booker was elected to Newark's city council, where he staged such theatrical moves as going on a hunger strike, living in a tent in a housing project, and living in a motor home parked in areas heavy with drug traffic. He lost election to mayor in 2002, but the documentary film of his effort, *Street Fight*, was nominated for an Academy Award in 2005. In 2006, Booker won the race for mayor with 72 percent of the vote. Just before he took office, New Jersey law enforcement stopped a plot by the Bloods gang to assassinate him.

As mayor, Booker has focused on reducing crime, which dropped substantially and stayed low despite the recession that began in 2008. He has also brought considerable investment to the city, as well as non-profit development money, notably getting Facebook founder Mark Zuckerberg to donate $100 million of his own money to Newark schools in 2010. In 2009, the Obama administration offered Booker a position as head of a new White House Office of Urban Affairs Policy, but he turned it down.

Booker is also a master of the use of social media, in 2010 responding to a twitter request to help an elderly man shovel snow from his driveway. He currently stars in a Peabody-winning documentary series on the Sundance Channel called *Brick City*, which features his efforts as mayor. In 2012 he saved a woman's life in a house fire, suffering second-degree burns in the process.

[a]See, for example, *Conan O'Brien v. Cory Booker* on *www.youtube. com*. The feud was negotiated to an end by Secretary of State Clinton, with O'Brien agreeing to donate money to Newark for each joke he made about the city.

Growth was the shared elite value. The old-community elite was indeed a "growth machine."[11] Its members believed capital investment in the community would raise land values, expand the labor force, generate demand for housing and commercial services, and enhance the local tax base. Attracting investors required the provision of highways, rail and water access, airport facilities, utilities, and fire and police protection. It also meant eliminating onerous business regulations, reducing taxes on new investments to the lowest feasible levels, supplying a capable and cooperative labor force, and providing enough cultural, recreational, and aesthetic amenities to give corporate managers a desirable lifestyle.

Traditional community elites strove for consensus on the belief that economic growth benefited the entire community, elites and masses alike. Community residents share a common interest in the economic well-being of the city: "Policies and programs can be said to be in the interest of cities whenever the policies maintain or enhance the economic position, social prestige, or political power of the city as a whole."[12]

Local government elites were expected to share in this consensus. Economic prosperity was necessary to protect the fiscal base of local government, as well as local budgets, public employment, and governmental services. Moreover, growth was usually good politics. Governmental growth expanded the power, prestige, and status of local government officials. Growth-oriented candidates for public office usually had larger campaign treasuries than antigrowth candidates. Finally, most local politicians had a sense of community responsibility: They knew that if the economy of the community declined, "local business will suffer, workers will lose employment opportunities, cultural life will decline, and city land values will fall."[13]

THE NEW-COMMUNITY POLITICAL ELITES

In many U.S. communities, most of the old economic elites have sold their businesses to national corporations and chain stores and been replaced as community leaders by new political elites. Community loyalties in the business sector are therefore weaker than in the past. New corporate managers can easily decide to close the local plant or store with minimal concern for the impact on the community. Local banks have merged into national banking corporations and are operated by executives with few community ties. City newspapers once independently owned by families who lived in the communities have been bought by giant media chains, staffed with people who hope to move up in the corporate hierarchy and advance their own careers, not the interests of the local community.

The nationalization of the economy and the resulting demise of locally owned enterprises created a vacuum of leadership in community affairs. Professional politicians moved into this vacuum in city after city, largely replacing the local bankers, real estate developers, chambers of commerce, and old-style newspaper editors who had dominated community politics for generations. The earlier economic elites were only part-time politicians who used local government to promote their economic interests. The new professional political elites work at local politics full-time. They are drawn primarily by personal political ambition, not so much for the wealth as for the power and celebrity that accompany running for and winning public office. They are not "screened" by economic elites or political parties; rather, they nominate themselves, raise their own funds, organize their own campaigns, and create their own publicity.

These political elites are independent entrepreneurs. They win office "by selling themselves to the voters, in person, one at a time, day after day. People who do not like to do this, people who do not like to knock on strangers' doors or who find it tedious to repeat the same thirty-second personal introduction thousands of times, are at a severe disadvantage."[14] Thus, over time, these full-time political elites drive out the part-time economic elites.

The new political elites seldom have a large financial stake in the community, aside from their homes. They are not local business leaders or bankers or developers. They may be lawyers, but they are not lawyers from prestigious local law firms; rather, they are "political activists with law degrees."[15] These elites are strongly committed not to the community's economic growth but mainly to advancing their own political power. They do not necessarily seek community consensus on behalf of prosperity.

On the contrary, new political elites complain about the problems of economic growth, including traffic congestion, pollution, noise, "unsightly" development, or the replacement of green spaces by concrete slabs. These issues are frequently referred to as LULUs—locally unwanted land uses—again connecting to the local power of land. Opposition to such unwanted consequences of economic growth may be quite reasonable, but it also carries with it a political overtone of exclusion sometimes referred to as NIMBYism (Not In My Back Yard). No-growth movements appeal to people who already own their houses and do not intend to sell them, such as people whose jobs are secure in government bureaucracies or tenured professorships, people who may be displaced from their homes and neighborhoods by new facilities, and people who see no direct benefit to themselves from growth. These "growth-management" movements are not mass movements. They do not express the aspirations of workers for jobs or renters for their own homes. Instead, they reflect the upper-middle-class lifestyle preferences of educated, affluent, articulate homeowners. This group would prefer boutique shops, fine restaurants, and preserving "green space." Growth brings unattractive factories, discount commercial outlets (such as Walmart), fast-food franchises, and "undesirable" residents. Even if new growth helped hold down local taxes, some affluent citizens would prefer to retain the appearance or lifestyle of their communities.

No-growth political elites challenge traditional economic elites in many large and growing cities in the West and South. The no-growth leaders may themselves have been beneficiaries of earlier community growth, but they quickly perceive their own political interest in slowing or halting additional growth, as the homeowners most concerned about growth are also the most likely to vote.

Opposing growth serves the financial interest of homeowners, apartment owners, and owners of already developed commercial property. Curtailing growth serves to freeze out competition from new homes, apartment complexes, and commercial centers. It allows owners of existing homes and properties to raise real estate prices and rents to new residents. It is no surprise that "neighborhood associations" led by upper- and upper-middle-class homeowners are at the forefront of no-growth politics. In some ways this echoes the nation's ongoing argument about money and credit—those elites who have it want to keep it more exclusive,

---

IN BRIEF | THE SHIFT IN COMMUNITY POWER

Community power has been shifting from traditional economic elites to newer political elites.

Traditional community power structures included mortgage lending banks, real estate developers, builders, and landowners, along with attorneys and title companies and others whose wealth was affected by land use decisions. Growth was the shared elite value. Consensus existed on community economic growth—it brought increased capital investment, more jobs, and improved business conditions, all assumed to benefit the entire community. Governmental elites reflected the consensus of economic elites.

Today, in many U.S. communities, old economic elites are being replaced by new political elites.

Traditional local economic elites are being displaced by national managers of plants and chain stores, weakening the community loyalties of the business sector. Aside from the value of their own homes, these new professional politicians seldom have much financial stake in the community. They are frequently opposed to economic growth and the problems it creates—congestion, pollution, noise, unsightly development, and environmental problems. No-growth movements appeal to people who already own their own houses, whose jobs are secure, and who see no direct benefit to themselves from economic growth.

those masses who want it desire greater availability, even if it cheapens its value. Alexander Hamilton would have recognized these motivations.

Municipal government offers the tools to challenge the old growth elites. Communities may restrict growth through zoning laws, subdivision control restrictions, utility regulations, building permits, and environmental regulations. Opposition to street widening, road building, or tree cutting can slow or halt development. Public utilities needed for development—water lines, sewage disposal facilities, fire houses, and so on—can be postponed indefinitely. High development fees, "impact fees," utility hookup charges, and building permit fees can all be used to discourage growth. Environmental laws and even historic preservation laws can be employed aggressively to halt development.

FEDERALISM | AN ELITIST INTERPRETATION

The existence of political subelites within the larger U.S. political system permits some decentralization of decision making. Decentralization, or decision making by subelites, reduces potential strain on the consensus of national elites. Each subelite group sets its own policies in its own state and community, without battling over a single national policy to be applied uniformly throughout the land. The following propositions summarize our consideration of U.S. federalism and our comparative analysis of elites in states and communities.

1. Federalism in the United States divides power constitutionally between national and state governments, each of which can directly enforce its own laws on individuals through its own courts. The Constitution itself cannot be amended without the consent of three-fourths of the states.

2. Over time power has centralized in Washington owing to (a) a broad interpretation of the "necessary and proper" clause granting the national government the power to do anything not specifically prohibited by the Constitution, (b) the victory of the national government in the Civil War, (c) the establishment of a national system of civil rights, (d) the growth of national power under the interstate commerce clause, and (e) the growth of federal grants-in-aid to state and local governments.

3. The principal instrument of national power in states and communities is the federal grant-in-aid. Federal grants provide about a quarter of all state and local government revenue. Federal rules, regulations, and guidelines accompanying the grants give the federal government great power over the activity of local governments.

4. The federal government also orders states to make changes or makes demands on states that require states to expend large amounts of money to comply. These are known as unfunded mandates.

5. Despite some efforts to return power to states and communities, power continues to flow toward national elites. The Supreme Court, in its *Garcia* decision, removed all constitutional protections for state power, other than the states' role in electing the members of Congress and the president.

6. The Supreme Court reversed direction on expanding federal power in several recent cases in which it held that Congress had exceeded its delegated powers. It remains to be seen whether these trends toward restoring federalism will continue.

7. Traditional community power structures concern themselves with economic growth. These community power structures are land and real estate interests, which mobilize mass support for local growth policies by promising more jobs.

8. New community political elites have arisen in many cities to replace old community economic elites. As the economy nationalized, locally owned businesses, banks, and newspapers were replaced by national corporations and chains, whose managers have fewer ties to community affairs. Local political elites moved into the vacuum of power. These new elites are self-nominated, full-time professional politicians.

9. The new political elites are not necessarily committed to economic growth. They frequently endorse "growth management" proposals designed to halt or curtail growth. These new elites reflect not mass interests but rather the preferences of upper-middle-class, educated, articulate homeowners to avoid locally unwanted land uses.

NOTES

1. Ben Canada, *Federal Grants to State and Local Governments: A Brief History.* Report for Congress, Congressional Research Service, 2003. http://lugar.senate.gov/services/pdf_crs/Federal_Grants_to_State_and_Local_Governments_A_Brief_History.pdf

2. Morton Grodzins, *The American System* (Chicago, IL: Rand McNally, 1966), p. 265.

3. *Garcia v. San Antonio Metropolitan Authority*, 469 U.S. 528 (1985).

4. *United States v. Lopez*, 514 U.S. 549 (1995).

5. *Printz v. United States*, 521 U.S. 890 (1997).

6. *Alden v. Maine*, 67 U.S.L.W. 1401 (1999).

7. *Brzonkala v. Morrison* (May 15, 2000).

8. The court documents on this case have been given their own page on the U.S. Supreme Court website: http://www.supremecourt.gov/docket/PPAACA.aspx

9. Center for Governmental Studies, *Democracy by Initiative: Shaping California's Fourth Branch of Government*, 2nd ed., 2008, p. 55. www.cgs.org/images/publications/cgs_dbi_full_book_f.pdf

10. Maura Dolan, "California Chief Justice Criticizes Initiative Process," *Los Angeles Times*, October 11, 2009.

11. See Harvey Molotch, "The City as Growth Machine," *American Journal of Sociology*, 82 (September 1976): 309–330; and "Capital and Neighborhood in the United States," *Urban Affairs Quarterly*, 14 (March 1979): 289–312.

12. Paul E. Peterson, *City Limits* (Chicago, IL: University of Chicago Press, 1981), p. 20.

13. Peterson, *City Limits*, p. 29.

14. Alan Ehrenhalt, *The United States of Ambition* (New York: Time Books, 1991), p. 15.

15. Ehrenhalt, *Ambition*, p. 16.

But what we know—what we have seen—is that America can change.
That is the true genius of this nation.

—Barack Obama

CIVIL RIGHTS: DIVERSIFYING THE ELITE

CHAPTER **13**

Pluralist theory explains that people seeking power will form interest groups, exercising the right to express shared views and the right of assembly. In U.S. history, significant portions of the population were denied these rights based on race, gender, or other identity basis. Some excluded people created protest movements, which sometimes led to the establishment of protest organizations designed to represent and shape mass movements. Movements and organizations will of course have elites. Protest leaders find that by moderating their demands, they can gain a significant portion of their original goals through accommodation and also achieve a stake in the elite system for themselves personally and for their organization. Thus, they come to share the elite consensus.

HOW ELITES DIVERSIFY

Established elites do not ignore identity-based interest groups that protest conditions. Rather they may (1) make symbolic gestures to pacify the active protesters, particularly by co-opting them through programs that bring protest leaders into the system; (2) limit protests through repression, which may include violence; or (3) do both simultaneously. Often elite response is a combination of accommodation and repression, with heavier doses of accommodation handed out to movements whose goals are within the general framework of elite consensus. In the United States, while repression was common in the more distant past, in contemporary times the system has preferred bringing promising members of minority or disempowered groups into the ruling elite. The result has been a rapidly diversifying elite.

We can identify two approaches to organization leadership: challengers to the system and bargainers with the system. Challengers speak with moral authority as members of disempowered groups and can apply or withhold negative labels (racist or sexist or whatever term is relevant) that ruling elites wish to avoid. However, because their power is based on decrying the system, challengers cannot fully enter the system. Bargainers, on the other hand, offer to the ruling elite goodwill and the assumption of innocence; in return, they want acceptance regardless of their group membership. Bargainers become part of the system and can achieve considerable power.[1] Barack Obama, clearly a bargainer, commented on such differences in his famous "Race Speech" on March 18, 2008:

> On one end of the spectrum, we've heard the implication that my candidacy is some-how an exercise in affirmative action; that it's based solely on the desire of wide-eyed liberals to purchase racial reconciliation on the cheap. On the other end, we've heard my former pastor, Reverend Jeremiah Wright, use incendiary language to express views that have the potential not only to widen the racial divide, but views that denigrate both the greatness and the goodness of our nation; that rightly offend white and black alike.[2]

Protest movements tend to be cyclical. Many fail, but others successfully travel the road from protest to organization to accommodation, though the price is high. Movement toward political success requires not only accommodation to the acceptable norms of established elites but also organizational leadership by talented and patient people with negotiating skills and the willingness to sustain activity for long periods of time. Group leaders without these characteristics will either quit or be tempted by the use of violence or other antidemocratic expressions. Regardless of the movements they represent, leaders seldom come from the lower strata of society, but usually from the upper-middle or upper classes.

Absorption into the elite is not a quick process. Since running the system is not an entry-level position, most members of the elite are older, mainly in their late 50s and 60s. To understand the level of diversity within the elite it is necessary to look not at the level of equality of opportunity today, but rather at the conditions prevailing when today's elites were just starting their careers. In 1965, Title VII of the Civil Rights Act stated that:

> It shall be unlawful for any employer or labor union to discriminate against any individual in any fashion in employment because of his race, color, religion, sex, or national origin, and that an Equal Employment Opportunity Commission shall be established to enforce this provision by investigation, conference, conciliation, persuasion, and if need be, civil action in federal court.

While this did not immediately end all discrimination (which sadly can still be found), it did make it *illegal*. The graduating high school class of 1966 became the first age cohort in U.S. history that did not face legal discrimination. This group turned 60 years old in 2008, prime age for elite membership. With each passing year, the starting conditions in terms of equality of opportunity for persons from disempowered groups saw improvement. As a result, while there was little visible change at the top of the system for several decades after the civil rights successes of the 1960s, the passage of time has produced the chance for a much more diverse group to rise to elite power positions at the pinnacle of their careers.

MINORITIES ACQUIRING ELITE STATUS

Today's elite is changing rapidly, reflecting changes 30 and 40 years ago when opportunities finally began to open for women and minorities. It is still disproportionately white and male, compared to the national demographic (see Table 13.1).

Still, political and economic elites are diversifying, as reflected by leadership in the White House, Congress, and corporate boardrooms.

In 2012, the United States had an African-American president, attorney general, and Supreme Court justice; the former Speaker of the House and the secretary of state were women; there are Hispanics on the Supreme Court, in two governor's offices (Nevada and New Mexico) and in Los Angeles city hall; and Louisiana and South Carolina have Asian-American governors. President Bush's cabinet had four women and five minorities and Obama's four women and six minorities (although some such as Elaine Chao and Hilda Solis meet both categories). By 2012, 42 African-Americans were serving in the House (10 percent) but none in the U.S. Senate (Obama resigned to become president). Hispanics are the nation's largest minority (15 percent), but they occupy only 25 House seats (6 percent); one serves in the Senate (see Figure 13.1). There are nine Asian-Americans in the House and two in the Senate.

The dramatic increase in minority representation in the House of Representatives followed the 1990 census redistricting. Congress's 1982 strengthening of the Voting Rights Act of 1965 outlawed any electoral arrangement that has the *effect* of weakening minority voting power (replacing an earlier *intent* test). In the 1986 *Thornburg v. Gingles* case, the Supreme Court interpreted the *effects* test to require that state legislatures redistrict their states to maximize minority

TABLE 13.1 | RACIAL AND ETHNIC GROUPS IN THE UNITED STATES

	Number	Percentage of Population
White, not Hispanic	196,817,552	63.7
Hispanic-Americans	50,477,594	16.3
African-Americans	37,685,848	12.2
Asian	14,465,124	4.7
Native Hawaiian and other Pacific Islander	481,576	0.2
American Indian and Alaska Native	2,247,098	0.7
Multiracial (two or more of the above)	9,009,073	2.9
Total population	308,745,538	100.0*

*The sum of populations is larger than the total because some people belong to more than one racial group.

Source: U.S. Census Bureau, *www.census.gov*.

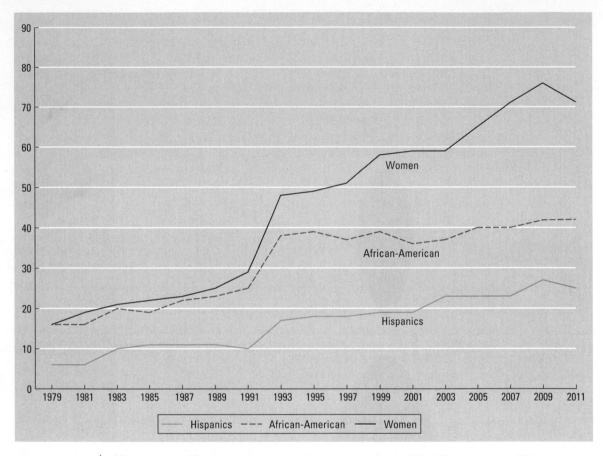

FIGURE 13.1 | NUMBER OF WOMEN, AFRICAN-AMERICANS, AND HISPANICS IN THE HOUSE OF REPRESENTATIVES

representation—creating "majority–minority" districts wherever possible.[3] (Later in the racial gerrymandering cases of *Shaw v. Reno* [1993] and *Hunt v. Cromartie* [2001] the Court held that bizarre-shaped districts based solely or predominantly on race were unconstitutional.[4]) These actions clearly strengthened African-American and Hispanic representation in Congress. The rise of women to political power has continued over the past 30 years.

Among business chief executives, by 2008 about 23.4 percent were women, 4.8 percent Hispanics, 4.0 percent Asian-Americans, and 3.9 percent African-Americans.[5] African-Americans have headed Citibank (Richard Parsons) and American Express (Kenneth Chenault). Hispanics have run CBS (Nina Tassler) and Fox News (Emiliano Calenzuk). Asian-Americans have headed PepsiCo (Indra Nooyi) and Yahoo! (Jerry Yang). Ellen Kullman runs DuPont, Meg Whitman is head of Hewlett-Packard, and African-American woman Ursula Burns heads Xerox. In 2012 Yahoo! chose a seven-month pregnant Marissa Mayer as its new CEO. These are some of the most powerful business positions in the nation and mark the arrival of a diverse business elite.

THE HISTORY AND DECLINE OF MINORITY EXCLUSION

The ability to achieve elite status begins with the opportunity to move upward in society. Upward mobility is almost impossible, however, when law and custom block basic rights. For African-Americans, this meant the institution of slavery and, after abolition, segregation and other civil rights limitations. For Hispanics, it meant denial of citizenship rights and immigration restrictions. For Asian-Americans, exclusionary laws and legal discrimination also denied basic democratic rights.

While the struggle for perfect civil rights continues (for example, over same-sex marriage), the distance traveled shows a journey close to its goal. In the words of President Obama:

> The profound mistake of Reverend Wright's sermons is not that he spoke about racism in our society. It's that he spoke as if our society was static; as if no progress has been made; as if this country—a country that has made it possible for one of his own members to run for the highest office in the land and build a coalition of white and black; Latino and Asian, rich and poor, young and old—is still irrevocably bound to a tragic past.[6]

THE AFRICAN-AMERICAN STRUGGLE FOR FREEDOM

The condition of African-Americans has marked the greatest gap between the nation's ideals and its reality. Most appalling was the institution of slavery, the nation's "birth defect." The U.S. founding creed was that "all men are created equal," yet some were slaves, so the twisted logic of slavery thus defined blacks as less than human, officially three-fifths of a person. This "American dilemma" also reflects the larger issue of the masses' attitudes toward democracy: commitment to abstract ideals with substantially less commitment to their practice.[7] We can view the struggle of African-Americans for full citizenship as a dialogue—sometimes violent, usually peaceful—between the demands of black counterelites and the response of dominant whites.

ABOLITION AND AFTERMATH

The Thirteenth Amendment (1865) abolished slavery in the United States. The Fourteenth (1867), written by a Republican Congress that intended to reconstruct southern society after the Civil War, made "equal protection of the laws" a command for every state. The Fifteenth Amendment (1869) prohibited federal and state governments from abridging the right to vote "on account of race, color, or previous condition of servitude." Congress also passed a series of civil rights statutes guaranteeing newly freed African-Americans protection in the exercise of their constitutional rights—for example, the Civil Rights Act of 1875 specifically outlawed segregation by private businesses. Between 1865 and the early 1880s, the imposition of civil rights by northern elites was evident in widespread voting by blacks throughout the South, the presence of many blacks in federal and state offices, and the almost equal treatment afforded blacks in public facilities.

These freedoms were preserved by a military occupation that protected black citizens and fought terrorist groups such as the Ku Klux Klan. Federal commitment ended with the Compromise of 1877, when the national government agreed to end military occupation of the South, give up its efforts to rearrange southern society, and lend tacit approval to white supremacy in that region. In return, southern elites pledged support to the Union, accepted national supremacy, and agreed to resolve a disputed election.

The Supreme Court adhered to the terms of this compromise. In the Civil Rights Cases of 1883, it declared unconstitutional those federal civil rights laws preventing discrimination by private individuals. This paved the way for the imposition of segregation as the prevailing social system in almost every sector of private and public life in the South. In *Plessy v. Ferguson*, in 1896, the Supreme Court upheld state laws requiring segregation, holding that it did not violate the equal protection clause of the Fourteenth Amendment so long as people in each race received equal treatment. Schools and other public facilities that were "separate but equal" won constitutional approval:

> The object of the Amendment was undoubtedly to enforce the absolute equality of the two races before the law, but in the nature of things it could not have been intended to abolish distinctions based upon color or to enforce social, as distinguished from political, equality, or a commingling of the two races upon terms unsatisfactory to either.[8]

The pattern of race relations at the turn of the century was clearly one of violent repression, exclusion of blacks from jobs and labor unions, and rigid segregation. African-Americans lost much of what they had gained after the Civil War.

ELITES AND DESEGREGATION

Freed slaves and their descendents became politically active (see Focus: The Early Black Elite: Booker T. Washington). The first African-American organizations emerged in response to this repression, notably the National Association for the Advancement of Colored People (NAACP) in 1909 and the National Urban League in 1910. Dominated by middle-class blacks and upper-class whites, they sought black equality and meaningful change within the system through court action and other legal means. Their techniques required commitment to the institutional status quo. They disavowed attempts to change or overthrow the basic political and economic structure; they simply sought to integrate blacks into it. They took literally the ideology and premises of the U.S. democratic system, that "all men are created equal."

NAACP Legal Defense Fund Founded in 1940 by Thurgood Marshall to provide legal assistance to poor African-Americans. *www. naacpldf.org*

The process of desegregation took time, largely due to opposition from southern political elites. The first major step came in 1948, when President Harry Truman issued Executive Order 9981 desegregating the U.S. military. Combat in the Korean War then brought white and black soldiers together. Truman also made it illegal to discriminate based on race for civil service positions. Then in the historic 1954 *Brown v. Board of Education of Topeka, Kansas* decision, the Supreme Court reversed the earlier doctrine of "separate but equal."[9]

This great step toward racial justice was taken by the *nonelective* branch of the federal government. Nine men, secure with lifetime appointments, responded to the legal arguments of highly educated black elites, one of whom—Thurgood Marshall—would later become a Supreme Court justice himself.

| FOCUS | THE EARLY BLACK ELITE: BOOKER T. WASHINGTON |

The predominant black leader at the turn of the twentieth century was Booker T. Washington. Born a slave, he rose to elite status through a strong belief that practical education could allow the black masses to build wealth to demonstrate to whites they should have eventual equality. He founded numerous educational institutions and in 1901 was the first African-American to receive a White House dinner invitation (from Theodore Roosevelt). His best-selling autobiography, *Up from Slavery*, solidified his position as popular spokesperson for African-Americans. His supporters in the black community were widespread, especially among businessmen, educators, and clergy. He also had support from liberal northern whites, among them were political and economic elites such as William H. Taft, Andrew Carnegie, and John D. Rockefeller. He was criticized by leaders of the NAACP, especially W. E. B. DuBois, as an accommodationist, but Washington believed confrontational activism would not improve conditions for blacks. (DuBois focused on creating an educated black elite.)

MASS RESISTANCE TO DESEGREGATION

Although the Supreme Court had spoken forcefully in the *Brown* case, almost all blacks in the South remained in segregated schools. From a political and enforcement viewpoint, the battle over segregation was just beginning. Frustrations intensified as southern blacks saw the discrepancy between the Supreme Court's intent and the behavior of local officials. Unless the national political elite directly challenged the political power of the southern elite, the pattern was unlikely to change.

The *Brown* decision might in fact have been rendered meaningless had President Dwight Eisenhower not decided to use military force in 1957 to enforce a federal court order to desegregate Little Rock's Central High School. Arkansas Governor Orval Faubus had posted state National Guardsmen at the high school to prevent federal marshals from carrying out federal court orders to admit black students. Eisenhower called the Guard units into federal service, ordered them to leave the high school, and replaced them with units of the U.S. 101st Airborne Division under orders to enforce desegregation. Eisenhower had not publicly spoken on behalf of desegregation, but the direct threat to national power by a state governor caused him to assert the power of the national elite. President Kennedy also used federal troops to enforce desegregation at the University of Mississippi in 1962.

MARTIN LUTHER KING, JR.: NONVIOLENT PROTEST ELITE

In 1955, an African-American woman, Rosa Parks, refused to ride in the back of a bus in Montgomery, Alabama. Her act inspired blacks to boycott the city's public transportation system. This action was the first significant step away from the NAACP's legalism. It also required mass-oriented leadership. A young minister named Martin Luther King, Jr., gained instant national prominence through the bus boycott and its eventual success and later led the struggle to eliminate discrimination and segregation. King, the son of an influential Atlanta minister, had received his doctorate from Boston University and began his ministry in Montgomery. In 1957,

The King Center
Biography of
Martin Luther
King, Jr., together
with news and
information from
the Atlanta King
Center. *www.
thekingcenter.org*

he created the Southern Christian Leadership Conference (SCLC), substantially more militant than the older black organizations and also explicitly nonviolent. The youngest person ever to receive the Nobel Peace Price, King was assassinated in 1969 in Memphis, Tennessee, and is honored by a national holiday in his name.

Under King's leadership, the civil rights movement developed political techniques that included breaking "unjust" laws in an open, nonviolent fashion, "bearing witness," and with a willingness to accept the penalty to help emphasize the injustice. King said civil disobedience "seeks to dramatize the issue so that it can no longer be ignored."[10] This dramatization of injustice made news and won sympathy.

King's tactics relied primarily on an appeal to the conscience of white elites. King did *not* urge black masses to remedy injustice themselves "by any means necessary," and he did *not* urge the overthrow of established elites. He asked for nothing radical, only that African-Americans be able to exercise their existing rights under the U.S. Constitution. In 1963, at a mass march on Washington, King delivered his appeal, titled "I Have a Dream":

> I have a dream. It is a dream deeply rooted in the American dream. I have a dream that one day this nation will rise up and live out the true meaning of its creed: "We hold these truths to be self-evident; that all men are created equal."

> I have a dream that my four little children will one day live in a nation where they will not be judged by the color of their skin but by the content of their character.

This appeal was based on existing law and classical liberal belief in the equality of individual rights. In response, President Kennedy sent a civil rights bill to Congress that became the Civil Rights Act of 1964.

HISPANIC-AMERICAN SEARCH FOR RIGHTS

Hispanic-Americans are the largest minority group in the United States. Officially, Hispanic, or Latino, refers to an ethnicity and can include persons of any race. This population is very diverse, reflecting different national origins and periods of entering U.S. society: in New York City, Puerto Ricans and Dominicans predominate; Miami holds largely Cuban refugees; Los Angeles and the Southwest are home to many people of Mexican origin; and San Francisco has drawn immigrants from Central America. Cuban and Nicaraguan immigrants are mostly middle class; Mexican immigrants generally have lower socioeconomic status.

The Hispanic population became a significant minority after the 1848 Treaty of Guadalupe Hildago, which ended the Mexican-American War with Mexico's ceding of land that is now California, Arizona, Nevada, New Mexico, and parts of other states (Texas had already joined the United States). The treaty granted citizenship rights to 65,000 Mexicans who wished to remain once the border was moved, although in practice numerous loopholes were used to deny full status to many. The United States next acquired Puerto Rico through the defeat of the Spanish Empire in the 1898 Spanish-American War; under the Jonas Act of 1919, Puerto Ricans have full citizenship rights when in the United States. Later, as the Cold War brought fighting through local proxies with the Soviet Union, refugees from civil wars in Latin America sought safety in the United States.

With the West underpopulated, immigration from Mexico was fairly open until the 1920s. During the Depression, however, some 35,000 illegal immigrants were deported and 350,000 Mexicans and Mexican-Americans "volunteered" to repatriate to Mexico. By World War II, the United States faced labor shortages and introduced the Bracero guest labor program, which imported Mexican laborers and lasted until 1964. In 1954 the Border Patrol launched "Operation Wetback" to repatriate illegal Mexican immigrants; the government claimed over a million people were returned to Mexico in this period.

The dominant early rights organization for Hispanics was the League of United Latin American Citizens (LULAC), established in Texas in 1929 and modeled after the NAACP. The group advocated assimilation and patriotism and lobbied against the Bracero program. Among its biggest legal victories was the 1947 *Mendez v. Westminster School District* case,[11] which ended the segregation of Mexican and Mexican-American schoolchildren. In response to this Circuit Court ruling, California Governor Earl Warren repealed segregation provisions remaining in California law. (Later, as chief justice of the U.S. Supreme Court, Warren wrote the majority polls in the *Brown* decision; see above.) LULAC also lobbied to shape the 1985 Immigration Reform and Control Act, which granted amnesty to about three million illegal immigrants. Other significant Hispanic rights groups in the 1960s were the Mexican American Legal Defense and Education Fund (MALDEF) and the National Council of La Raza (NCLR), both now more prominent than LULAC. César Chávez of the United Farm Workers union is the best-known Hispanic activist leader.

ASIAN-AMERICAN SEARCH FOR RIGHTS

Asian-Americans have been a significant presence in the United States since the mid-1800s, when immigrants came from China, Japan, and Korea to help develop the West, particularly California. Asian immigrants were prevented by law from becoming citizens and for long periods of time were denied entry to keep the nation from being "overwhelmed" by the "mongoloid race." Chinese "argued that the Chinese had no special interests other than seeing the rights and privileges enjoyed by others in the country."[12]

The 1790 Naturalization Act, which made citizenship available only to a "free white person" and set up the question of whether Asians were "white," was overturned only in 1952 by the McCarran-Walter Act, removing racial restrictions on citizenship. In the 1878 case *In re Ah Yup*, a federal court in California had ruled that Ah Yup could not naturalize due to his race. The Chinese Exclusion Act of 1882 made Chinese immigrants ineligible for citizenship and was not repealed until 1943. Numerous state laws denied property rights to Asian-Americans. In 1898, however, the U.S. Supreme Court ruled in *United States v. Wong Kim Ark* that Wong was a citizen by birth.[13] In *Yick Wo v. Hopkins*, an 1886 case about a San Francisco ordinance discriminating against Chinese persons, the Court ruled that even if a law appears to be race-neutral, if applied in a prejudicial manner it violates the Fourteenth Amendment's equal protection clause.[14]

In two later cases, Asian-Americans petitioned the Supreme Court to establish their status as "white." In *Takao Ozawa v. United States* (1922), Ozawa argued that as a Japanese-American he was not black and therefore white. The Court ruled that "black" means "not white," so he was "black."[15] In the 1923 case *United States v. Bhagat Singh Thind*, Thind produced elaborate evidence that showed ethnologic experts considered a person from India such as himself to be Caucasian, but the Court denied his petition, ruling that a "common man" would not consider him white.[16]

The issue of racial exclusion and immigration was finally ended by the Immigration and Nationality Act of 1965, abolishing national origin quotas on immigration that had favored European immigration and sharply restricted Asian and Latin-American arrivals.

MULTIRACIAL RIGHTS MOVEMENT

Historically, persons of mixed heritage were classed in whichever of the groups from which they descended had the lower social status. The "one drop" rule held that even a single black ancestor made a person black, an approach used by slaveholders to claim mixed-race children as slaves.

Multiracial persons do not wish to have to choose with which parent or grandparent they identify. The most recent civil rights movement to begin in the United States was the multiracial quest for recognition. Since the 1967 Supreme Court decision in *Loving v. Virginia*[17] struck down all remaining laws banning interracial marriage, the number of persons from multiple race backgrounds has steadily increased. Interracial dating is now supported by over 80 percent of the public, including over 90 percent of young people.[18] However, before 2000 the number of multiracial persons was not clearly known, because following regulations formulated under the one-drop rule, the U.S. Census Bureau did not allow respondents to choose more than one racial category.

An umbrella group of multiracial rights organizations, the Association of Multi-Ethnic Americans (AMEA), was formed in 1988 with the primary purpose of recognition. In 1996, the group organized a march on Washington. In 1997, it began increased lobbying to have the 2000 census allow people to "mark one or more" race or ethnic identity categories.

With billions of government dollars and political clout dependent on census counts of minorities, however, traditional civil rights elites felt multiracial recognition could dilute their numbers.[19] Claiming that some 70 percent of African-Americans have mixed ancestry, NAACP President Kweisi Mfume said, "No one should be forced to choose or reject any aspect of their heritage, but no category should be allowed to weaken others." The 2000 census did allow respondents to check more than one box, but for purposes of allocating federal funds, each individual who did so was counted in the traditionally least empowered group selected.

The president of the United States is biracial: Barack Obama's father was an African from Kenya, his mother a white woman from Kansas. In a poll taken in 2006, before he was a household name, respondents were told Obama's racial heritage and asked what race he was. The majority of whites (55 percent) said he was biracial or multiracial; almost two-thirds of blacks saw him as black.[20] Each group saw themselves in him. However, on the 2010 census form, Obama checked only "black," to the disappointment of multiracial activists.

THE CIVIL RIGHTS ACT OF 1964

The Civil Rights Act of 1964 passed both houses of Congress by better than a two-thirds favorable vote; it won the overwhelming support of both Republican and Democratic members of Congress. Among its most important provisions was the following (note the use of the commerce clause):

> Title II: It is unlawful to discriminate or segregate persons on the grounds of race, color, religion, or national origin in any public accommodation, including hotels, motels, restaurants, movies, theaters, sports arenas, entertainment houses, and other places that offer to serve the public. This prohibition extends to all establishments whose operations affect interstate commerce or whose discriminatory practices are supported by state action.

U.S. Commission on Civil Rights Federal agency monitoring discrimination and prejudice. *www.usccr.gov*

The Act brought about tangible gains for blacks as well as for other minorities and women. Its Title VI provided for the withdrawal of federal money as a sanction, a remarkable innovation in federal enforcement of civil rights.

RACIAL INEQUALITY AND AFFIRMATIVE ACTION

The gains of the civil rights movement were primarily in **equality of opportunity**, a central concept in the liberal creed of individual freedom to pursue "happiness," however it may be defined. Due to the gap between legal change and social outcomes, activists on the left began to focus their attention on a different notion, **equality of outcome**. Much contemporary identity politics centers on the outcome inequalities between groups in incomes, jobs, housing, health, education, and other material conditions of life (see Table 13.2). In this chapter we look at both: equality of opportunity to enter the elite, and the outcome of diversity in the elite.

OPPORTUNITY VERSUS OUTCOME

Most U.S. adults are concerned more with equality of opportunity than with equality of results. Equality of opportunity refers to the ability to make of yourself what you can; to develop your talents and abilities; and to be rewarded for work, initiative, and achievement. It means that everyone comes to the same starting line with basically the same chance of success, that whatever differences develop over time are a result of abilities, talents, initiative, hard work, and perhaps luck. Equality of outcome refers to the proportionally equal sharing of income, jobs, and material rewards, regardless of ability, talent, initiative, work, or luck.

How should society define equality? What public policies should be pursued to achieve it? Is it sufficient to eliminate discrimination, guarantee equality of opportunity, and apply color-blind standards to all? Or should government act to overcome the lingering results of past unequal treatment through preferential or compensatory measures that favor some minority or female applicants for university admission and scholarships, job hiring and promotion, and other opportunities for advancement?

Increasingly, the civil rights movement has shifted from the traditional goal of equality of opportunity to affirmative action to achieve equality of outcome. Although usually avoiding the term *quota*, affirmative action tests the success of equal opportunity by observing whether certain groups achieve admissions, jobs,

TABLE 13.2 | MINORITY LIFE CHANCES

	1975	1985	1995	2005	2010
Median Income of Families					
White	$14,260	$29,152	$36,822	$63,314	$68,822
Black	8,747	16,786	23,059	35,680	38,451
Hispanic	9,523	19,027	23,535	37,759	39,625
Percentage of Persons below Poverty Level (age 18 to 64)					
White	6.8%	8.4%	7.5%	7.8%	9.9%
Black	23.1	24.3	22.5	20.4	23.3
Hispanic	20.1	22.6	24.9	18.3	22.4
Unemployment Rate					
White	7.8%	6.2%	4.7%	4.4%	7.2%
Black	14.8	15.1	10.5	10.0	14.4
Hispanic	12.2	10.5	8.9	6.0	10.4

Source: Statistical Abstract of the United States, *www.census.gov*, *www.bls.gov*.

and promotions in proportion to their numbers in the population, and it allows for preferential or compensatory treatment to overcome the legacy of past discrimination.

AFFIRMATIVE ACTION

The constitutional question posed by affirmative action programs is whether they discriminate and thus violate the equal protection clause of the Fourteenth Amendment. The Supreme Court has failed to develop a clear-cut answer. In an early case, *Regents of the University of California v. Bakke* (1978), the Court struck down a special admissions program for minorities at a state medical school on the grounds that it excluded a white applicant because of his race and violated his rights under the equal protection clause.[21] The Court ordered Bakke's admission to medical school and elimination of the special program. It recommended that the state of California develop an admissions program that considered disadvantaged racial or ethnic backgrounds as a "plus" in an overall evaluation of an application but did not set numerical quotas or exclude any persons from competing for all positions.

The Supreme Court has been willing to approve affirmative action programs where there is evidence of past discriminatory actions. In *United States v. Paradise* (1987), the Court upheld a rigid 50 percent black quota system for promotions in the Alabama Department of Safety, which had excluded blacks from the ranks of state troopers before 1972 and had not promoted any blacks higher than corporal before 1984. In a 5 to 4 decision, the majority stressed the long history of

| FOCUS | "DIVERSITY" IN HIGHER EDUCATION |

Educational elites, such as university administrators, identify "diversity" as an institutional goal, referring to racial and ethnic representation in the student body and the faculty. They argue that students benefit educationally when they interact with peers from diverse backgrounds. However, despite numerous efforts to develop scientific evidence that racial or ethnic diversity on the campus improves learning, no definitive conclusions have emerged. Educational research on this topic is clouded by political and ideological conflict and a dearth of data beyond anecdotal reports and small samples.

Diversity and Affirmative Action

Even if diversity provides educational benefits, the question is how to achieve it. When affirmative action programs are designed as special efforts to recruit and encourage qualified minority students to attend college, they enjoy widespread public support. But when they include preferences for minority applicants over equally or better qualified whites (and especially Asian-Americans), public support falters and constitutional questions arise.

Diversity as a Constitutional Question

The U.S. Supreme Court held in 2003 that diversity may be a compelling government interest because it "promotes cross-racial understanding, helps to break down racial stereotypes, and enables [students] to better understand persons of different races."[a] In a case involving the University of Michigan Law School's affirmative action program, Justice Sandra Day O'Connor, writing for the 5-4 majority, said the Constitution "does not prohibit the law school's narrowly tailored use of race in admissions decisions to further a compelling interest in obtaining the educational benefits that flow from a diverse student body." However, in a companion case involving the university's affirmative action program for undergraduate admissions, the Court held the admissions policy was "not narrowly tailored to achieve respondents' asserted interest in diversity" and therefore violated the equal protection clause of the Fourteenth Amendment.[b] The Court again recognized that diversity may be a compelling interest but rejected a plan that made race the decisive factor for even minimally qualified minority applicants. Yet the Court restated its support for limited affirmative action programs that use race as a "plus" factor—the position it has held since the *Bakke* case in 1978. "Diversity" has become the conceptual framework through which institutions of higher learning have tried to secure identity-based admissions preferences.[c]

[a]*Gratz v. Bollinger*, 539 U.S. 244 (2003).

[b]*Grutter v. Bollinger*, 539 U.S. 306 (2003).

[c]Peter Wood, *Diversity: The Invention of a Concept* (San Francisco, IL: Encounter Books, 2003), pp. 228–229.

discrimination in the agency as a reason for upholding the quota system. Whatever burdens were imposed on innocent parties were outweighed by the need to correct the effects of past discrimination.[22]

In the absence of past discrimination, the Supreme Court has expressed concern about white individuals directly and adversely affected by government action solely because of their race. In *Firefighters Local Union v. Stotts* (1984), the Court ruled that a city could not lay off white firefighters in favor of black firefighters with less seniority.[23] In *Richmond v. Crosen* (1989), it held that a minority set-aside program, which mandated that 30 percent of all city construction contracts must go to "blacks, Spanish-speaking, Orientals, Indians, Eskimos, or Aleuts," violated the equal protection clause of the Fourteenth Amendment.[24]

The Court has held that the equal protection clause requires racial classifications to be subject to "strict scrutiny." This means race-based actions by government—any disparate treatment of the races by public agencies—must be found necessary to remedy past proven discrimination or necessary to advance a "compelling government interest" and "narrowly tailored" to further that interest (see Focus: "Diversity" in Higher Education). In striking down a federal construction contract set-aside program for small businesses owned by racial minorities, the Court expressed skepticism about governmental racial classifications: "There is simply no way of determining what classifications are 'benign' and 'remedial' and what classifications are in fact motivated by illegitimate notions of racial inferiority or simple racial politics."[25]

ELITE VERSUS MASS RESPONSE TO CIVIL RIGHTS

Progress in civil rights policy—from *Brown v. Board of Education of Topeka, Kansas* through the Civil Rights Act of 1964 to affirmative action programs today—has been a response by the national elite to conditions affecting minorities. It has *not* come about because of demands by the (white) majority of citizens. On the contrary, advances in civil rights have met with varying degrees of resistance from the masses.

MASS OPINION ABOUT DISCRIMINATION AND AFFIRMATIVE ACTION

The attitudes of white masses toward blacks in the United States are ambivalent. In 2009, 35 percent of whites and 30 percent of blacks agree that "discrimination against blacks is rare."[26] Public feeling about which groups see "a lot" of discrimination varies: 52 percent feel Hispanics see it, 49 percent say blacks see it, and 37 percent agree women do. (For comparison, 64 percent polled think gays and lesbians see "a lot" of discrimination.)[27] Affirmative action to help blacks, women, and other minorities get better jobs and education is supported by 70 percent of the public, including 65 percent of whites.[28]

At the same time the public opposes racial preferences in hiring, promotion, and admissions. Sixty-five percent, including 76 percent of whites, disagreed with the statement "we should make every effort to improve the position of blacks and minorities, even if it means giving them preferential treatment." This number has been stable over two decades. Favoring preferential treatment were a majority of blacks (58 percent) and a slight majority of Hispanics (53 percent).[29]

AFFIRMATIVE ACTION IN MASS REFERENDA

White masses have turned to citizens' initiatives to battle racial preferences. We have already suggested that elites generally consider popular referenda votes to be a threat to democratic values as well as to elite governance (see Chapter 4). In 1994, California's Proposition 187 was approved by voters to deny social services, including medical care, to illegal immigrants, although judicial elites overturned it before implementation. Such mass votes clearly can be a threat to civil rights.

The California Civil Rights Initiative, "Prop 209," was placed on the ballot by citizens' initiative in 1996 and was approved by 54 percent of voters. The initiative added the following phrase to the state's constitution:

> Neither the state of California nor any of its political subdivisions or agents shall use race, sex, color, ethnicity or national origin as a criterion for either discriminating against, or granting preferential treatment to, any individual or group in the operation of the State's system of public employment, public education or public contracting.

FOCUS | SECRETARY OF STATE HILLARY CLINTON

Hillary Rodham grew up in suburban Chicago, the daughter of wealthy parents who sent her to prestigious Wellesley College. After serving as local president of the Young Republicans, by 1969 she was an honors graduate with a counterculture image. Chosen by her classmates to give a commencement speech, she spoke of "more immediate, ecstatic, and penetrating modes of living."

At Yale Law School Rodham met Bill Clinton, a long-haired, bearded Rhodes scholar from Arkansas who was just as politically ambitious as she was. Both received their law degrees in 1973. Clinton returned to Arkansas to build a career in state politics, and Rodham went to Washington as an attorney—first for a liberal lobbying group, the Children's Defense Fund, and later on the staff of the House Judiciary Committee seeking to impeach President Richard Nixon. Rodham and other Yale grads travelled to Arkansas to help Clinton run, unsuccessfully, for Congress in 1974. In 1975, she went to a U.S. Marine Corps recruiting station and tried to enlist but was turned down as too old, female, and wearing glasses. Rodham decided to stay with Clinton in Little Rock, and they married before his next campaign, a successful run for state attorney general in 1976. She remained Hillary Rodham, even as her husband went on to the governorship in 1978.

Her husband's 1980 defeat for re-election as governor was blamed on his liberal leanings; in his 1982 comeback Clinton repackaged himself as a moderate and centrist. Rodham cooperated by changing her name to Clinton and echoing her husband's more moderate line. These tactics helped propel them back into the governor's mansion. Hillary Clinton soon became a full partner in Little Rock's Rose law firm, regularly earning more than $200,000 a year (her husband earned only $35,000 as governor). She won national recognition as one of the "100 most influential lawyers in the United States" according to the *American National Law Journal* and chaired the American Bar Association's Commission on Women and the Profession.

Her steadfast support of her husband during his impeachment by the House of Representatives in all likelihood saved his presidency, and her approval ratings in public opinion polls skyrocketed. Whatever she thought in private, Hillary Clinton never chastised her husband in public and blamed much of the scandal on "a vast right-wing conspiracy." Her Senate race attracted national media attention as well as campaign contributions from supporters throughout the nation. She studied New York problems diligently and overwhelmed her opponent in the then most expensive congressional campaign in history (the candidates spent over $85 million). She crushed the Republican challenger in her 2006 re-election bid, spending a mere $57 million.

Clinton announced her intention to run for president in 2008 and became the instant front-runner. Caught by surprise by the early primary successes of Illinois senator Barack Obama, she refocused on a long game in which she and Obama fought for Democratic delegates until June. After being elected, Obama offered his rival the prized cabinet position of Secretary of State. She is considered by many a potential 2016 candidate for the White House.

American Civil Rights Institute
Ward Connerly's organization focused on banning racial or gender preferences.
www.acri.org

The key words are "or granting preferential treatment to." Opponents challenged the California Civil Rights Initiative in federal courts, arguing that by preventing minorities and women from seeking preferential treatment under law, the initiative violated the equal protection clause of the Fourteenth Amendment. But a circuit court of appeals held, and the U.S. Supreme Court affirmed, that a

> ban on race or gender preferences, as a matter of law or logic, does not violate the Equal Protection Clause in any conventional sense. ... Impediments to preferential treatment do not deny equal protection.[30]

The success of the California initiative inspired mass movements in other states; Washington adopted a similar state constitutional amendment in 1998. In

Michigan, 58 percent of voters approved a statewide ban on affirmative action programs in public education, employment, and state contracts in 2006. The referendum effort was spearheaded by Ward Connerly, a multiracial businessman who had led the California Civil Rights Initiative in 1996, together with Jennifer Gratz, who had been denied admission to the University of Michigan Law School and was the plaintiff in an unsuccessful Supreme Court challenge to "diversity" as a justification for affirmative action programs.[31] Following voter approval of the referendum banning affirmative action, the president of the University of Michigan still announced her intention "not to allow our University" to end its affirmative action efforts.[32]

WOMEN'S RIGHTS IN THE UNITED STATES

The election of 2008 marked both the degree of success women have achieved in the United States and the persistence of a "glass ceiling" that slows their progress. As the year began, the common assumption was that former First Lady Senator Hillary Clinton would be the Democratic Party nominee for president, and, with a strong current against the Republicans, would win the White House. Instead, the nomination went to a historic candidate of a different sort. Barack Obama proceeded to lead his Republican challenger in the polls for all except one period: the weeks after McCain chose Alaska Governor Sarah Palin as his vice presidential running mate.

Clinton and Palin demonstrated the changing place of women in politics. As Clinton set out in politics after law school, including a stint on the staff of the House Judiciary Committee during the Watergate hearings, she understood the nation was not yet ready to let a woman reach the top. Working within the limitations of the system, she developed as a legal professional and saw political success through her husband, a governor and president. By 2000, times had changed and she ran for office (see Focus: Secretary of State Hillary Clinton). Sarah Palin, a generation younger than Clinton, saw few barriers to being a woman and politically powerful. In fact, Palin sees the roles of mother, wife, and political elite as mutually supportive. As a concerned "hockey mom," she ran for local office and rose to mayor and then governor of her state. She took on the "old boys' network" and confronted Republican male elites, including the state party head and the incumbent governor, over issues of corruption. In 2008, when John McCain asked her to be the Republican candidate for vice president, she had an infant child and a pregnant teenage daughter—a situation she used to describe herself as "normal." The news media were particularly harsh on both women during the campaign. When Clinton appeared to shed a tear in a debate, the press pounced on her display of "feminine weakness." Palin was criticized for giving insufficient time to her baby and family.[33] Both received extensive coverage of their clothing and hair that male candidates did not merit. Despite their ultimate lack of electoral success, however, Clinton and Palin showed women are serious contenders for the pinnacle of the elite.

THE WOMEN'S MOVEMENT

The first wave of feminist politics grew out of the antislavery movement. The first generation of feminists, whose elite included Lucretia Mott, Elizabeth Cady Stanton, and Susan B. Anthony, learned to organize, hold public meetings, and conduct petition campaigns as abolitionists. After the Civil War, women successfully changed many state laws abridging the property rights of married women. Activists also won some protection in the workplace, including laws limiting women's hours and working conditions. The most successful feminist efforts of the 1800s centered on protections for women in families. The perceived threats were husbands' drinking, gambling, and consorting with prostitutes. Women led the Anti-Saloon League and succeeded in outlawing gambling and prostitution in every state except Nevada and provided the major source of moral support for the Eighteenth Amendment (the prohibition of alcohol).

League of Women Voters
Oldest women's organization focuses on "making democracy work," with information about voting rights, campaign finance, lobbying, ethics, etc. *www.lwv.org*

In the early twentieth century, the feminist movement concentrated on women's suffrage—the right to vote. Suffragettes used mass demonstrations, picketing, and occasional civil disobedience. Success came with the 1920 passage of the Nineteenth Amendment: "The right of citizens of the United States to vote shall not be denied or abridged by the United States or by any state on account of sex." The suffrage movement also spawned the League of Women Voters. The goal of this first wave of feminist activity was legal equality.

EQUITY FEMINISM

Equity feminism continues in the classic liberal tradition of seeking equal opportunity for individuals regardless of sex and equal treatment under the law. The principles of equity feminism remain the vision of the vast majority of women in the United States. While 69 percent say the women's movement has made their life better, fewer than half say a strong women's movement is still needed to guarantee equality of opportunity. Seventy percent of women also decline to call themselves "feminists"; in fact, 17 percent see the term as an insult.[34] This reluctance to identify with the term may derive from views currently expressed by the elites of national women's organizations. When given a definition of feminism as believing in social, political, and economic equality of the sexes, most men (58 percent) and women (68 percent) accept the term as describing their views.[35] There is clearly a problem in how the word has come to be understood.

GENDER FEMINISM

The "second wave" of feminism of the 1960s and 1970s focused on the more radical **gender feminism**, which continues to prevail in elite circles in leading feminist organizations such as the National Organization for Women (NOW). NOW founder Betty Friedan eventually became marginalized within the group and cautioned young women against "bra-burning, anti-man feminists."[36] Gender feminism goes beyond a demand for equality and becomes "a call for liberation."[37] Women must not look to men to grant their freedom; they must liberate themselves from the patriarchal family and the male-dominated society. This requires, first of all, that women become conscious of the oppression inherent in sex roles, family structure, education, religion, the economy, and other social roles. The next imperative is for women to transform themselves personally and collectively from powerlessness to power and in so doing to reform and restructure society's institutions to reflect feminist values.[38]

NOW
Leading second-wave feminist organization, with information and argument on issues relating to women. *www.now.org*

Gender feminism includes diverse camps with differing views of both the source of women's oppression and strategies for its elimination. "Radical feminism" perceives male dominance in virtually all social institutions and seeks their revolutionary restructuring. Rape, pornography, sexual harassment, and domestic violence are visible products of a deeper "phallocentric" culture. Men are portrayed as largely unaware of the devaluation and repression in women's experience. "Liberal feminism" focuses on the socialization of children into differentiated sex roles and seeks reform measures, including nonsexist education. "Postmodern feminists" seek to reconstruct "sexist" philosophy, history, and language to liberate them from the "masculinist modes and patriarchal ideology" of "dead white European males." None of these submovements have significant support from the masses of women, but they have elite followings in academic and some political circles.

WOMEN AND WORK

Modern feminism has been driven by the changing role of women in the U.S. workforce. In 1960, fewer than one-third of married women worked outside the home. Today economic pressures have sent more than 70 percent of married women into the workforce, including women with children. In 1970, about 26.6 percent of family income came from working mothers; by 2005 that had climbed to 35.1 percent.[39] Working outside the home is an economic necessity for most but is seen as an option for wealthier women who are more likely to be in the elite. By 2010, the majority of the U.S. workforce was female.

THE DUAL LABOR MARKET AND THE EARNINGS GAP

Despite increases in the number and proportion of working women, the nation's occupational fields are still significantly divided between traditionally male and female jobs. The existence of this dual labor market, with male-dominated blue-collar jobs distinguishable from female-dominated pink-collar jobs, such as nursing and teaching, continues to be a major obstacle to economic equality between men and women (see Table 13.3). Women have made inroads in traditionally male white-collar occupations—doctors (from 10 percent in 1960 to 30 percent in 2008), lawyers (4 percent in 1960 to 34 percent in 2008), and architects (3 percent in 1960 to 25 percent in 2008), for example—although men still remain in the majority. However, women have only begun to break into the blue-collar occupations usually dominated by men and paying more than pink-collar jobs.

In the economic downturn that began in 2007, over 80 percent of the jobs lost were held by men, especially manufacturing, financial, and construction jobs, while careers dominated by women, particularly in health care and education, were more stable. These jobs also were more likely to be government positions. By November 2009, the unemployment rate for men was 10.5 percent and 7.9 percent for women. For some groups of women, employment numbers actually rose during the downturn: for black and white women employment rose from 2006 to 2008, although it declined in 2009; for Hispanic women the number working rose from 7,437,000 in 2006 to 7,838,000 in 2009.[40] What meager job growth took place in 2010 to 2012 did favor males.

TABLE 13.3 | THE GENDERED LABOR MARKET

	Percent who are women	Percent who are African-Americans	Percent who are Asian-Americans	Percent who are Hispanics
Total U.S. Workforce (age 16+)	46.7	11.0	4.8	14.0
Male-Dominated Occupations				
Chief Executives	23.4	3.9	4.0	4.8
Construction Managers	8.2	3.7	1.4	9.1
Financial Analysts	38.8	6.0	12.9	9.8
Architects	24.8	3.3	6.1	8.2
Aerospace Engineers	10.3	6.1	11.1	5.0
Computer Hardware Engineers	19.4	3.0	30.7	4.1
Chemists and Material Scientists	33.1	4.7	22.3	6.9
Lawyers	34.4	4.6	2.9	3.8
Physicians and Surgeons	30.5	6.2	16.6	5.8
Firefighters	4.8	8.2	0.3	9.4
Police and Sheriffs	14.7	13.6	1.8	11.6
Construction and Extraction	2.5	6.3	1.4	29.6
Farming, Fishing, Forestry	21.1	4.5	1.7	39.3
Production Occupations	29.7	12.2	5.2	21.1
Female-Dominated Occupations				
Accountants and Auditors	61.1	8.3	10.2	7.6
Insurance Underwriters	80.3	13.3	5.5	7.1
Advertising and Promotion Managers	62.1	7.6	5.8	9.7
Human Resource Managers	66.3	8.2	4.0	7.3
Psychologists	66.9	7.2	3.1	6.6
Social Workers	79.4	24.5	2.9	10.0
Teachers	81.2	9.9	2.2	6.8
Librarians	83.5	6.7	3.5	3.7
Registered Nurses	91.7	10.0	7.8	4.7
Healthcare Support Occupations	88.8	25.8	4.2	13.6
Child Care Workers	95.6	17.4	2.7	20.0
Secretaries and Admin Assts	96.1	8.1	2.3	9.6
Gender-Neutral Occupations				
Financial Managers	54.8	7.9	5.7	8.6
Physical Scientists	40.7	6.1	27.8	1.7
Food Preparation and Serving	56.0	12.1	5.4	21.0
Building and Ground Cleaning and Maintenance	40.2	15.0	2.8	33.4

Source: Adapted from Bureau of Labor Statistics, "Employment by Detailed Occupation, Sex, Race, and Hispanic or Latino Ethnicity." *www.bls.gov/cps/cpsaatl l.pdf.*

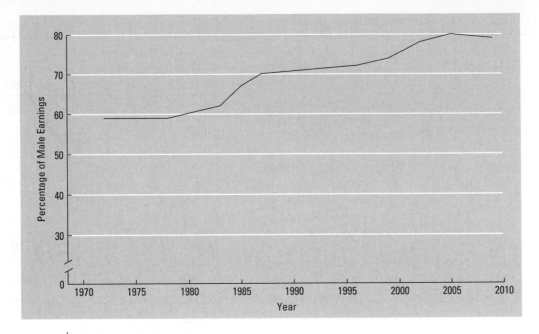

Figure 13.2 | The Earnings Gap

Median Annual Earnings of Women as a Percentage of Median Annual Earnings of Men

Source: *Statistical Abstract of the United States* 2006, p. 428, and Bureau of Labor Statistics.

Despite protection under federal laws, overall women continue to earn substantially less than men. Today they earn on average about 80 percent of what men do (see Figure 13.2). This earnings gap is *not* primarily due to direct discrimination, which is illegal; in fact, women are generally paid the same as men in the same job with the same skills, qualifications, experience, and work record. Rather, the earnings gap is a product of the division between traditionally male and female jobs, and of lower salaries in traditionally female occupations. What is missing is equality of opportunity (and willingness) for women to enter more renumerative "male" professions.

Gender Equality in Civil Rights Laws

Title IX of the Education Act Amendment of 1972 deals with sex discrimination in education. This federal law bars discrimination in admissions, housing, rules, financial aid, faculty and staff recruitment and pay, and athletics. The last category has proven the most troublesome because men's football and basketball programs have traditionally brought in the money to finance all other sports and have received the largest share of school athletic budgets.

By 2008, the strong majority of undergraduates were female, with 57 percent of bachelor's degrees going to women, including 67 percent of BAs given to African-Americans, 60 percent of those to Hispanics, and 55 percent of those for

Asian-American graduates.[41] Still, even when controlling for undergraduate major, female graduates tended to earn less than their male counterparts. And while there clearly is equal opportunity for college admission, women are less likely to choose high-paying majors such as engineering and finance.

FEMINISM AND ELITISM

Equal Employment Opportunity Commission Federal agency website with information on what constitutes discrimination by age, disability, race, ethnicity, religion, gender; how to file a charge; and guidance for employers. *www. eeoc.gov*

The gender feminist ideology and political activists are concentrated among women elites—politically active, often university-based, highly educated women. "They hold the keys to many bureaucratic fiefdoms, research centers, women's studies programs, tenure committees, and para-academic organizations."[42] They claim to speak for all women, but not all women, or even all feminists, share the view that women's oppression is a product of a male culture that exalts individualism, competition, and violence. Black feminist bell hooks (who spells her name without capital letters) famously described the women's movement as primarily concerned with middle class and wealthier white women, while ignoring women of color.[43] The more moderate female majority is "not temperamentally suited to activism.... They do not network. They do not ally. They do not threaten their opponents with loss of jobs or loss of patronage. They are not especially litigious."[44] Most women wish to work within the system, merely demanding equality.

The women's movement thus suffers from the perception that it is more upper class, more liberal, and indeed more elitist than the mainstream. To combat this elitist image, feminist organizations in recent years have tried to become more family friendly. They were strong supporters of the Family and Medical Leave Act of 1993, for instance. Yet even so, the leading women's lobbying groups in Washington—NOW, the Women's Legal Defense Fund, the American Nurses Association, the National Federation of Business and Professional Women, the American Association of University Women—tend to emphasize the concerns of well-educated, professionally employed women.

WOMEN ACQUIRING ELITE STATUS

Increasing numbers of women and minorities are moving into elite positions in business, finance, the media, and government. Today most boards of directors of Fortune 500 corporations include at least two or three women and minorities among their 14 to 16 directors. A generation ago these directors were usually symbolic figures, but increasingly women are breaking the "glass ceiling" to head major corporations. Women have recently served as chief executive officer of PepsiCo, Xerox, eBay, Yahoo!, Hewlett-Packard, Archer Daniels Midland, Kraft Foods, Sara Lee, Avon, and Harpo Inc. (led by Oprah Winfrey, the richest self-made U.S. woman). Other corporations in which women serve as chief financial officer or vice chair include Citigroup, Procter & Gamble, Johnson & Johnson, Disney ABC, Hewlett-Packard, and Time Inc. However, women, who constitute over half the population, remain underrepresented in the elite.

A generation ago, women cabinet members were appointed largely for symbolic representation, and to second-level cabinet positions. But there is no doubt that Secretary of State Condoleezza Rice exercised real power in the Bush administration, as did Secretary of State Hillary Clinton in the Obama administration. The change is visible in this snapshot from the Pentagon:

> Kathleen Hicks, deputy undersecretary of defense for strategy, plans, and forces, has served at the Pentagon off and on since 1993. But it was not until last February that she walked into a Defense Department office and found herself in a meeting in which all of the attendees were women. "It was the under secretary, a deputy, a military officer, and some career civilians. And, to a person, everyone around the table was female," says Hicks. After 15-plus years in the defense field, "it was absolutely stunning."[45]

Women occupy 71 seats in the House of Representatives in the 112th Congress, with former Speaker Nancy Pelosi as Minority Leader. The Senate has 17 female members. By 2012, the governors of six states were women, including Indian-American Republican Nikki Haley in South Carolina and Hispanic Republican Susana Martinez in New Mexico.

There are many explanations for the glass ceiling, and all are controversial: Women may choose staff assignments rather than fast-track operating-head assignments. Women may have lower expectations about peak earnings and positions, and these expectations become self-fulfilling. Women bear children, and even during relatively short maternity absences they may fall behind their male counterparts. Women may be less willing to change locations than men, and immobile executives are worth less to a corporation than mobile ones. Female executives believe they get much more scrutiny than men and must work harder to succeed. Finally, affirmative action efforts by governments—notably the Equal Employment Opportunity Commission—are directed primarily at entry-level positions rather than senior management posts.

GAY RIGHTS

Rights for homosexuals have advanced considerably in the 40 years since the gay rights movement began. The first issue was basic recognition of gays as legitimate members of society, despite religious and medical definitions of homosexuality as abnormal. The religious stance is based on prohibitions on homosexuality stated in the Bible and Koran[46] and incorporated into secular law. Homosexual intercourse, under the rubric of sodomy, remained illegal in parts of the United States until the 2003 U.S. Supreme Court decision in *Lawrence v. Texas* overturned all remaining state laws banning it. Once again the unelected branch of government decided for society what the status of a minority group would be. This decision in turn upset an earlier ruling in 1986's *Bowers v. Hardwick*, which had upheld a state's right to criminalize homosexual consensual sex between adults.[47] California legalized homosexuality in 1975.

By 2009, less than half the public saw homosexuality as "morally wrong," and most of the rest felt it was not a moral issue.[48] In the past, homosexuality was seen as a medical problem. The medical issue was the concept of homosexuality as a form of mental illness, which formally ended when the American Psychiatric Association voted in 1974 to remove homosexuality from its *Diagnostic and Statistical Manual of Mental Disorders* (DSM). Here a narrow group of medical experts made a decision to fundamentally reclassify gays and lesbians as not insane but within the normal range of human sexuality.

National Gay and Lesbian Task Force is the oldest homosexual rights group. *www. thetaskforce.org*

Most observers agree the gay rights movement began with the 1969 Stonewall Riots in New York City, when gays assaulted by police in a routine raid on a gay bar fought back. In 1970, a Gay Liberation March was held in the same city. A major step forward came with the 1977 election of openly gay Harvey Milk to the San Francisco Board of Supervisors. He briefly became the public face of the movement, leading a successful effort to stop an anti-gay rights ballot initiative. Milk was killed (along with Mayor George Moscone) by a fellow Board member in 1978, propelling him to iconic status within the civil rights community.

In 1983, Congressman Gary Studds (D-Mass.) "came out" and revealed his homosexuality on the floor of the House of Representatives after he was censured for having sex with an underage Congressional page; he was reelected six times. Representative Barney Frank, from 2007 to 2011 the chair of the powerful House Financial Services Committee, was first elected in 1980 and admitted his sexual orientation in 1987. (The current House has two other homosexuals, both of whom were public when elected.)

The gay rights movement includes a diverse group of organizations. Perhaps the best known is ACT UP, founded in 1987, with its slogan "We're Queer! We're Here! Get Used to It!" The National Gay and Lesbian Task Force is the oldest major gay rights group, founded in 1973 and focused on training activists, lobbying, and working to defeat initiatives hostile to gay and lesbian rights. The Gay & Lesbian Alliance Against Defamation (GLAAD), founded in 1985, is a media watch group best known for its annual awards to the entertainment industry for positive portrayals of gays and lesbians. Both political parties have gay organizations, the Alice B. Toklas Democratic Club and the Log Cabin Republicans. Most gay rights organizations have expanded their purview to include seeking better treatment for bisexuals and transsexuals as well, making the acronym LGBT (lesbian, gay, bisexual, transgendered) common.

After the successful 2009 passage of the Matthew Shepard Act, which made violence against LGBT community members a hate crime, gay rights organizations have made same-sex marriage their main goal. It is legal in five states, but the 1996 federal Defense of Marriage Act defines marriage as between a man and a woman. Nationally, people now support same-sex marriage (46 percent favor, 44 percent oppose).[49]

CIVIL RIGHTS | AN ELITIST INTERPRETATION

Elite theory helps us understand the development of protest movements and organizations, and their accommodation by governing elites through symbolic victories granted in exchange for the moderation of their demands and their support for the system. The masses frequently resist even these accommodationist policies. Progress in civil rights is an elite response to minority appeals, not to mass demands.

1. Members of all dominated groups who show a willingness to work within the system have been able to join the elite. Elimination of legal discrimination and guaranteed equality of opportunity have largely resulted in equal access to political and economic power, but there has been a lag in equal representation

in the elite as minorities and women with a decent starting chance to move up to elite status move forward in their careers.

2. Historically, the first governmental institution to act for equality of opportunity has been the Supreme Court. The Court, structurally the furthest removed from the influence of the masses, was the first to apply constitutional protections to blacks, Asians, Hispanics, and women. Elected elites were slower to act.

3. Elites and masses have not responded to demands that go beyond accepted social and political consensus, for example, radical demands for equality of outcome that have replaced demands for equality of opportunity.

4. Affirmative action—defined as preferential treatment for minorities and women in employment and education—is more likely to be supported by elites than by the masses. Mass opposition to such preferential treatment is widespread and growing over time as continuing success by women and minorities makes it seem less necessary.

5. Leaders of the civil rights movements are generally professional, educated, upper-middle-class men and women whose views are not universally shared by the masses, making it difficult to mobilize the masses on behalf of elite goals.

6. Differences prevail even among activist elites regarding whether civil rights movements should focus primarily on achieving equality of opportunity, securing special protections, or radically restructuring society.

NOTES

1. Shelby Steele, *A Bound Man: Why We Are Excited by Obama and Why He Can't Win* (New York: Free Press, 2008), pp. 73–77.
2. Barack Obama, "Race Speech," March 18, 2008. http://www.cnn.com/2008/POLITICS/03/18/obama.transcript/index.html
3. *Thornburg v. Gingles*, 478 U.S. 30 (1986).
4. *Shaw v. Reno*, 125 L. Ed. 2d 511 (1993); *Hunt v. Cromartie*, 532 U.S. 234 (2001).
5. Bureau of Labor Statistics. Household Data 2008. http://www.bls.gov/cps/cpsaat11.pdf
6. Barack Obama, "Race Speech."
7. Gunnar Myrdal, *An American Dilemma* (New York: McGraw-Hill, 1964), vol. 1, p. xxi.
8. *Plessy v. Ferguson*, 163 U.S. 537 (1896).
9. *Brown v. Board of Education of Topeka, Kansas*, 347 U.S. 483 (1954).
10. Martin Luther King, Jr., "Letter from Birmingham City Jail," April 16, 1963.
11. *Mendez v. Westminster School District;* 64 F. Supp. 544 (CD. Cal. 1946) affirmed 161 F. 2d 774 (9th Cir. 1947).
12. Gordon H. Chang, "Asian-Americans and Politics: Some Perspectives from History," in *Asian-Americans and Politics: Perspectives, Experiences, Prospects*, Gordon H. Chang, ed. (Washington, DC: Woodrow Wilson Center; Stanford, CA: Stanford University, 2001).
13. *United States v. Wong Kim Ark*, 169 U.S. 649 (1898).
14. *Yick Wo v. Hopkins*, 118 U.S. 356 (1886).
15. *Takao Ozawa v. United States*, 260 U.S. 178 (1922).
16. *United States v. Bhagat Singh Thind*, 261 U.S. 204 (1923).
17. *Loving v. Virginia*, 388 U.S. 1 (1967).
18. Pew Center for People and the Press, "Independents Take Center Stage in Obama Era: Trends in Political Values and Core Attitudes: 1987–2009," May 21, 2009. http://people-press.org/report/517/political-values-and-core-attitudes
19. Kim M. Williams, *Mark One or More: Civil Rights in Multiracial America* (Ann Arbor, MI: University of Michigan, 2006), pp. 90–104. An excellent introduction to the multiracial rights movement and civil rights organizations in general.
20. Zogby International, "Williams/Zogby Poll: Americans' Attitudes Changing Towards Multiracial

Candidates," December 20, 2006. http://www.zogby.com/NEWS/ReadNews.cfm?ID=1227

21. *Regents of the University of California v. Bakke*, 438 U.S. 265 (1978).

22. *United States v. Paradise*, 480 U.S. 149 (1987).

23. *Firefighters Local Union v. Stotts*, 467 U.S. 561 (1984).

24. *Richmond v. Crosen*, 109 S. Ct. 706 (1989).

25. *Adarand Construction v. Pena*, 132 L. Ed. 2d 158 (1995).

26. Pew Center for People and the Press, "Independents Take Center Stage in Obama Era: Trends in Political Values and Core Attitudes: 1987–2009," May 21, 2009. http://people-press.org/report/517/political-values-and-core-attitudes

27. Pew Center for the People and the Press/Pew Forum on Religion & Public Life, "Religion & Public Life Survey," August 2009. http://people-press.org/questions/?qid=1747222&pid=51&ccid=50#top

28. Pew Center for People and the Press, "Public Backs Affirmative Action, but Not Minority Preferences," June 2, 2009. http://pewresearch.org/pubs/1240/sotomayor-supreme-court-affirmative-action-minority-preferences

29. Pew Center for People and the Press, "Public Basics Affirmative Action."

30. *Coalition for Economic Equity v. Pete Wilson*, Ninth Circuit Court of Appeals, April 1997.

31. *Guatz v. Bollinger*, 539 U.S. 244 (2003).

32. *Detroit Free Press*, November 9, 2006.

33. Jodi Kantor, Kate Zernike, and Catrin Einhorn, "Fusing Politics and Motherhood in a New Way," *New York Times*, September 7, 2008. http://www.nytimes.com/2008/09/08/us/politics/08baby.html?_r=1&pagewanted=2

34. Sean Alfano, "Poll: Women's Movement Worthwhile: Women Divided on Whether Strong Women's Movement Is Still Needed," CBS News Poll, http://www.cbsnews.com/stories/2005/10/22/opinion/polls/main965224.shtml

35. Sean Alfano, "Poll."

36. Ariel Levy, "Lift and Separate: Why Is Feminism Still So Divisive?", *The New Yorker*, November 11, 2009.

37. Marilyn Pearsall, *Women and Values*, 2nd ed. (Belmont, CA: Wadsworth, 1993), pp. xi, 18.

38. Alison M. Jaggar, *Feminist Politics and Human Nature* (Totowa, NJ: Rowman & Littlefield, 1988). See also Maggie Homm, ed., *Modern Feminism* (New York: Columbia University Press, 1992).

39. Bureau of Labor Statistics, http://www.bls.gov/cps/wlf-table16-2007.pdf

40. Bureau of Labor Statistics, http://www.bls.gov/schedule/archives/empsit_nr.htm

41. Katharin Peter and Laura Horn, *Gender Differences in Participation and Completion of Undergraduate Education and How They Have Changed over Time*, February 2005. U.S. Department of Education, Institute of Education Sciences. http://nces.ed.gov/das/epubs/2005169/gender_l.asp

42. Christina Hoff Sommers, *Who Stole Feminism?* (New York: Simon & Schuster, 1994), p. 273. Critique of gender feminism by an equity feminist.

43. bell hooks, *Ain't I a Woman: Black Women and Feminism* (Boston, MA: South End, 1981).

44. Sommers, *Who Stole Feminism?*, p. 274.

45. Anna Mulrine, "A Woman's Place Is at the Pentagon," *U.S. News and World Report*, November 2009. http://www.usnews.com/news/articles/2009/11/03/a-womans-place-is-at-the-pentagon.html

46. Leviticus 18:22 and 20:13, Romans 1:26–27; also Koran Sura 7:80–81.

47. *Lawrence v. Texas*, 539 U.S. 558 (2003); *Bowers v. Hardwick*, 478 U.S. 186 (1986).

48. Pew Research Center for People and the Press, "Majority Continues to Support Civil Unions: Most Still Oppose Same-Sex Marriage," October 9, 2009. http://people-press.org/report/553/same-sex-marriage

49. Pew Research Center for People and the Press, http://www.people-press.org/2012/05/23/changing-views-of-gay-marriage-a-deeper-analysis/

Where is the help? Where are the Americans?

Unnamed survivor of the Indian Ocean tsunami, December 2005[1]

THE UNITED STATES AS GLOBAL ELITE

CHAPTER **14**

The United States is the most powerful nation on the planet. By almost any measure—political, diplomatic, economic, cultural, or military—it leads all others. The term for this position is **hegemony**: preeminent power and dominance by one nation in the global system. The United States is not an empire, in which a central state drains conquered territory of treasure and denies self-rule; rather, it has a history of asserting its might to generate economic growth and democratization for "conquered" lands. This chapter examines the United States as military and economic world leader.

With great power comes great responsibility, so as global hegemon the United States carries the greatest burden in maintaining the security and soundness of the global system, both politically and economically. Recognizing this unique position, the United States set out its goals:

> Today, the United States enjoys a position of unparalleled military strength and great economic and political influence. In keeping with our heritage and principles, we do not use our strength to press for unilateral advantage. We seek instead to create a balance of power that favors human freedom: conditions in which all nations and all societies can choose for themselves the rewards and challenges of political and economic liberty. In a world that is safe, people will be able to make their own lives better. We will defend the peace by fighting terrorists and tyrants. We will preserve the peace by building good relations among the great powers. We will extend the peace by encouraging free and open societies on every continent.[2]

This role carries many costs—being hegemon is financially expensive (Great Britain's economy was drained by this role before the United States assumed it) and the cost in blood is beyond measure. There is considerable political ambivalence at home and abroad about the country's serving in this capacity.

The common term **global cop** implies that in times of emergency, the United States is the first responder, expected to be able and willing to rectify problems.

337

It has provided emergency services, such as after the Indian Ocean tsunami and the earthquakes in Pakistan in 2005 and Haiti in 2010, when its military brought quick relief and medical treatment to the victims. In times of famine, the United States delivers food, as it did in Somalia in 1992–1993. When a country is invaded by a neighbor, it can intervene, as it did militarily for Kuwait in 1991 and diplomatically for Lebanon in 2005. The U.S. Navy has played a leading role in fighting piracy, from the war with Tripoli in 1803 to stopping Somalia-based raiders today. If a nation seeks help in ending terrorist insurgencies, the United States provides assistance, training, and equipment, as it has in Columbia, Mali, and the Philippines. It will act to prevent or end genocide, as it did in Bosnia in 1995 and Kosovo in 1999. And it is criticized when it fails to act, such as in the genocide in Rwanda in 1994 or the bloody Civil War in Liberia in 2003. The world's largest military has the world's largest responsibilities (see Table 14.1).

In his 2009 Nobel Peace Prize acceptance speech, President Obama explained:

> But the world must remember that it was not simply international institutions—not just treaties and declarations—that brought stability to a post–World War II world. Whatever mistakes we have made, the plain fact is this: The United States of America has helped underwrite global security for more than six decades with the blood of our citizens and the strength of our arms. The service and sacrifice of our men and women in uniform has promoted peace and prosperity from Germany to Korea, and enabled democracy to take hold in places like the Balkans. We have borne this burden not because we seek to impose our will. We have done so out of enlightened self-interest—because we seek a better future for our children and grandchildren, and we believe that their lives will be better if others' children and grandchildren can live in freedom and prosperity.[3]

The ability to protect human rights and global system stability can come only from a position of strength.

TABLE 14.1 | MILITARY EXPENDITURES BY COUNTRY, 2011

Rank	Nation	Military Expenditures (in billions US$)
1	United States	711.0
2	China	143.0
3	Russia	71.9
4	Great Britain	62.7
5	France	62.5
6	Japan	59.3
7	India	48.9
8	Saudi Arabia	48.5
9	Germany	46.7
10	Brazil	35.4

Source: Stockholm International Peace Research Institute (SIPRI). *www.sipri.org/research/armaments/milex/*.

The United States is also looked to as the guarantor of the global financial system. It fills this role mainly in cooperation with other nations through multilateral institutions such as the International Monetary Fund (IMF) or the G-7 and G-20 organizations. The United States will also act directly, such as in the bailout of Mexico during its currency crisis in 1994. The decisions undertaken by U.S. elites about the world's largest economy affect the entire globe.

APPROACHES TO FOREIGN RELATIONS IN THE UNITED STATES

As a large, free, and diverse nation, the United States is not always consistent in its views on the nature and purpose of its interactions with the rest of the globe. We can observe three philosophies at work in its actions; usually all three are operating to some degree. **Idealism** assumes the United States has a moral duty to spread democracy, human rights, religious freedom, freedom of the press, and economic freedom. This generally means upsetting entrenched elites in places without such rights and generating considerable criticism.

The opposing philosophy is **realism**, the idea that the country should act abroad only to protect a clearly defined national interest, whether economic or security related. Frequently proponents of realism combine these interests, such as in the justification that the Iraq war protected national security as well as promoting democracy.

Lastly, a solid undercurrent of isolationism in the United States sometimes bubbles to the surface. **Isolationism** is the idea that the United States is big enough not to need to engage in "foreign entanglements" (in George Washington's words), and that it should place domestic priorities first. Isolationism is usually linked to populism, whether on the left or the right, and focuses on preserving jobs "for Americans," restricting trade and immigration, and opposing globalization.

IDEALISM

The idealist school of U.S. foreign policy is sometimes called "Wilsonianism," after President Woodrow Wilson and his goal to "make the world safe for democracy." The foreign policy of George W. Bush was clearly in the idealist tradition:

> Freedom is the non-negotiable demand of human dignity; the birthright of every person—in every civilization. Throughout history, freedom has been threatened by war and terror; it has been challenged by the clashing wills of powerful states and the evil designs of tyrants; and it has been tested by widespread poverty and disease. Today, humanity holds in its hands the opportunity to further freedom's triumph over all these foes. The United States welcomes our responsibility to lead in this great mission.[4]

Idealists base their view on the classical liberal perception that human rights are universal, meaning people have rights because they are human, not because rights are granted by a government. They see the United States as fortunate, or even "blessed" (with deliberate use of religious terminology), and therefore morally obligated to use its power and wealth to spread individual rights, women's rights, religious freedom, and property rights.

Idealist approaches often argue a moral case. President George W. Bush argued that the war on terrorism is "a monumental struggle of good versus evil." In his 2002 State of the Union message he identified an "axis of evil" (Iraq, Iran, and North Korea), oppressive dictatorships that violate core liberal principles such as human rights. Under Bush, some referred to that incarnation of idealism as neo-conservatism. President Ronald Reagan referred to the former Soviet Union as an "evil empire," seeing the communist genocide of tens of millions of its own citizens and the brutal repression by secret police as the kind of moral wrong the United States should fight. "For make no mistake: Evil does exist in the world. A nonviolent movement could not have halted Hitler's armies. Negotiations cannot convince Al Qaeda's leaders to lay down their arms," in the words of President Obama.

REALISM

Realists see the elite struggle for power as universal. International politics, like all politics, is a struggle for power—a struggle among global elites. International relations scholar Hans Morgenthau once observed:

> Whatever the ultimate aims of international politics, power is always the immediate aim. Statesmen and peoples may ultimately seek freedom, security, prosperity or power itself. They may define their goals in terms of a religious, philosophic, economic, or social ideal. ... But whenever they strive to realize their goal by means of international politics they are striving for power.[5]

Realists see the use of force in the pursuit of the national interest as a "realistic" acceptance of the world and human nature. This could mean imposing stability in key areas or securing access to vital natural resources, such as oil. As President Obama phrased it, "We must begin by acknowledging the hard truth: We will not eradicate violent conflict in our lifetimes. There will be times when nations—acting individually or in concert—will find the use of force not only necessary but morally justified."[6]

Ideology is secondary in realist politics, which can often make for strange alliances. In World War II, after Nazi Germany and the Soviet Union ceased being allies, the United States welcomed the genocidal Joseph Stalin as an ally, for "the enemy of my enemy is my friend." After the defeat of the Axis power, the greatest threat to the United States was the Soviet Union, so during the Cold War the United States allied itself to a series of nasty dictators whose primary merit was

---

IN BRIEF | U.S. APPROACHES TO FOREIGN POLICY

Three major approaches appear in foreign policy perspectives in the United States:

- Idealism—the belief that the United States has a moral obligation to spread classical liberal values such as individual rights and freedoms to other parts of the world

- Realism—the belief that national power should be used only to promote the national interest
- Isolationism—the belief that the United States should focus on internal and not foreign matters

their willingness to help contain Soviet expansion. These included Mobutu Sésé Seko in Zaire, Ferdinand Marcos in the Philippines, Anastasio Somoza Debayle in Nicaragua, and Francisco Franco in Spain. Such alliances are sometimes referred to as "lesser evil" politics, in which compromises are made to further national interest goals and avoid the "greater evil," such as the destruction of human freedom associated with Soviet expansion.

ELITES DEBATE THE USE OF MILITARY FORCE

Council on Foreign Relations
Most influential elite foreign policy organization, developing, discussing, and publishing (in *Foreign Affairs*) policy prescriptions.
www.cfr.org

All modern presidents acknowledge that the most agonizing decisions they have made were to send U.S. military forces into combat. These decisions cost lives. The masses are willing to send their sons and daughters into danger—and even to see some of them wounded and killed—but only if convinced the outcome "is worth dying for." Elites must be able to explain and justify why lives must be sacrificed. Elite policy organizations such as the Council on Foreign Relations play a major role in developing U.S. foreign policy (see Focus: Council on Foreign Relations). Masses respond to idealist appeals of a "greater good," "fighting for freedom," and "stopping evil."

WAR AS POLITICS

Military elites argue that U.S. forces should be used only to protect vital national interests, be given clear military objectives, employ overwhelming strength, have the support of Congress and the people, and be deployed only as a last resort. In contrast, political elites often reflect the view that "war is a continuation of politics by other means"—a sentiment attributed to nineteenth-century German theorist of war Karl von Clausewitz. Economic interests, such as maintaining the flow of crucial natural resources such as oil, require physical security, and diplomatic efforts to protect such interests often depend on the express or implied threat of military force. Political elites have thus demonstrated a willingness to use military force for a variety of missions in addition to the conduct of conventional war (see Table 14.2):

- Demonstrating U.S. resolve in crisis situations (Kuwait, 1991)
- Demonstrating U.S. support for democratic governments (Haiti, 1993)
- Ending genocide (Bosnia, 1996)
- Protecting U.S. citizens living abroad (Grenada, 1983)

Global Security
Information about weapons, forces, and military conflicts around the world. *www.globalsecurity.org*

- Securing peace among warring factions or nations (Kosovo, 1999; Libya, 2011)
- Maintaining a peace agreement (Korea, 1952–present)
- Providing humanitarian aid under emergency conditions (Somalia, 1992; Haiti, 2010)
- Assisting in the war against drug trafficking (Panama, 1989)

DEFENSE POLICY-MAKING

In theory, the formulation of defense policy begins with an assessment of the range of threats to the nation and its interests. Once major threats such as Al Qaeda have been identified, strategies have to be devised, and defense policy-making must

FOCUS	ELITE FOREIGN POLICY-MAKING: THE COUNCIL ON FOREIGN RELATIONS

The influence of the Council on Foreign Relations (CFR) has been so pervasive that it can be difficult to distinguish its actions from government programs.[a] Of course, the CFR denies such influence. Indeed, its by-laws declare that "the Council shall not take any position on questions of foreign policy and no person is authorized to speak or purport to speak for the Council on such matters."[b] But policy initiation and consensus building do not require the CFR to officially adopt policy positions.

Its roster includes an impressive group of major figures in foreign policy. Current directors include Secretaries of State Colin Powell and Madeleine Albright, Treasury Secretary Robert Rubin, journalist Tom Brokaw, and Fed Vice Chair Alan Blinder. Current members include Presidents George H.W. Bush, Bill Clinton, and Jimmy Carter; Secretaries of State Condoleezza Rice, Zbigniew Brzezinski, and Henry Kissinger; Homeland Security Secretary Janet Napolitano; Fed Chairs Paul Volker and Alan Greenspan; World Bank Presidents Robert Zoellick, James Wolfensohn, and Paul Wolfowitz; Secretary of Defense Robert Gates, Vice Presidents Richard Cheney and Walter Mondale, Supreme Court Justices Stephen Breyer and Ruth Bader Ginsberg, New York City Mayor Michael Bloomberg, Senator John McCain, and UN Goodwill Ambassador Angelina Jolie.

The history of CFR policy accomplishments is dazzling. It developed the Kellogg Peace Pact in the 1920s and designed major portions of the United Nations (UN) charter. The Council takes pride in the success of the Cold War containment policy to halt Soviet expansion after World War II, outlined by CFR member George Kennan in his 1947 "X" article in CFR's *Foreign Affairs*. It laid the groundwork for the North Atlantic Treaty Organization (NATO) agreement and devised the Marshall Plan for European recovery. In the 1960s, the Council took the lead in formulating the initial decision to intervene militarily in Vietnam, the later decision to withdraw, and the basis of the 1973 Paris Peace Agreement. The CFR supported the initial invasion of Iraq, but as the occupation grew more costly, it felt Bush's goal of democracy for Iraq was unrealistic.

Above all, the Council seeks to keep the United States actively engaged in international politics, that is, to avoid isolationism, trade barriers, and xenophobia. It strongly supports multinationalism in U.S. foreign policy and continues to warn that the United States must not "retreat into our own borders or into any kind of isolationism."[c] It believes in international institutions: Its members actively support North American Free Trade Agreement (NAFTA), the World Trade Organization, and other efforts to stimulate global trade; an active U.S. role in peace efforts in the Middle East and the Balkans; and the development of a strategy for dealing with Salafist terrorism such as Al Qaeda.

[a]Lester Milbraith, "Interest Groups in Foreign Policy," in *Domestic Sources of Foreign Policy*, James Rosenau, ed. (New York: Free Press, 1967), p. 247.

[b]Council on Foreign Relations, *Annual Report* (1992), p. 174.

[c]*www.cfr.org/publications/Iraq.*

National Security Council
NSC membership, functions, press releases, and information about national security issues. *www.whitehouse.gov/nsc*

determine the appropriate requirements (military units, weapons, training, and readiness) to implement them. Finally, budgets must be calculated to finance the required force levels. Differences among elites arise at each step in this policy-making process—from differing assessments of the threats facing the nation to the right strategies to confront these threats, the force levels necessary to implement strategies, and the funds required to provide these forces. Indeed, elites sometimes reverse the process, deciding first on the defense budget, then structuring strategies and forces to stay within budget limits, and then estimating threats based on the forces available to meet them. Of course, this reversal of rational policy-making can place the nation in peril.

TABLE 14.2 | MAJOR DEPLOYMENTS OF U.S. MILITARY FORCES SINCE 1950

Year	Area	President	Year	Area	President
1950–1953	Korea	Truman, Eisenhower	1989	Panama	Bush
1958	Lebanon	Eisenhower	1990–1991	Iraq, Kuwait	Bush
1961–1973	Vietnam	Kennedy, Johnson, Nixon	1992–1993	Somalia	Bush, Clinton
1962	Cuban waters	Kennedy	1994–1995	Haiti	Clinton
1965	Dominican Republic	Johnson	1995–2000	Bosnia	Clinton
1970	Laos	Nixon	1999–2000	Kosovo	Clinton
1970, 1975	Cambodia	Nixon, Ford	2001–	Afghanistan	Bush, Obama
1982–1983	Lebanon	Reagan	2003–2011	Iraq	Bush, Obama
1983	Grenada	Reagan	2011	Libya	Obama

ORGANIZING THE NATION'S DEFENSES

The chain of command extends from the president to the secretary of defense, to the chief of the Joint Chiefs of Staff, to the various regional commands (see Figure 14.1). Each command encompasses all military forces in its region. Central Command—CENCOM—is responsible for all military activity in the Middle East. Since the start of the global war on terror, three new regional commands have been created: Northern Command in 2002 to run the military aspects of homeland security,[7] Africa Command in 2007 to give greater attention to that continent, and Cyber Command in 2010.

CURRENT FORCES AND MISSIONS

The United States has about 1.4 million men and women in uniform, with an equal number in the reserve. The Army has 15 active and reserve combat divisions, and the Air Force contains 12 fighter wings. The Navy now possesses 11 carrier strike forces (a carrier strike force typically includes one aircraft carrier with 75 to 85 aircraft, plus defending cruisers, destroyers, frigates, attack submarines, and support ships). Of 22 aircraft carriers in service worldwide, half are in the U.S. Navy, including all full-size vessels. The United States has unsurpassed numbers of stealth technology fighters and bombers and is the world leader in the use of combat robots and aerial drones.

Department of Defense
Official DoD website has information about all branches of the U.S. military.
www.defense.gov

U.S. military forces are currently deployed in more than 120 countries around the world. The largest deployments are in South Korea and Afghanistan, but U.S. forces are also stationed in Saudi Arabia and the Persian Gulf region, the Balkans, the Philippines, Japan, Colombia, and the NATO countries. U.S. military forces are trained for combat as well as for peacekeeping and nation-building missions.

Note: Cyber Command not shown

Figure 14.1 | U.S. Military Commands

This means there are significant numbers of military police, civil affairs units, local force trainers, and humanitarian relief supply units.

Current numbers of Army, Marine, Navy, and Air Force combat units and the limited transport and support services available to the military are inadequate to deal with more than a single major regional conflict. They were fighting two wars to 2011. Potential regional foes—for example, Iran and North Korea—possess heavy armor and artillery forces. The United States does not have the military capability to confront two of these regional enemies simultaneously. Moreover, commitments of U.S. troops to peacekeeping and humanitarian missions divert resources, training, and morale away from war-fighting. Physical and mental health can be affected when U.S. military forces are stationed abroad for long periods of time, especially for multiple deployments.

THE UNITED STATES IN THE INTERNATIONAL SECURITY SYSTEM

While having a military capacity far beyond that of any single rival, the United States generally prefers to rely on international alliances and partnerships for military action. It is a member of more than 80 international organizations,[8] most of which it helped found. The classic example is the 1990–1991 coalition created by President George H. W. Bush, in which 70 nations came together to forcibly liberate Kuwait from Iraqi occupation. Despite the fact that the United States had the military capacity to accomplish this goal by itself, the commitment of allies ranging from Britain and France to Egypt, China, and the Soviet Union made the end of Saddam Hussein's invasion absolutely inevitable. Similarly, U.S. military actions in Iraq and Afghanistan both have included an array of other nations. While the United States is a member of numerous alliances, the two organizations most significant for military operations have been the United Nations Security Council and NATO.

UNITED NATIONS SECURITY COUNCIL

The United States and its allies created the United Nations (UN) in 1945 to replace the ineffectual League of Nations as a global body that could provide a forum for nations to maintain diplomatic connections and avoid a third World War. The UN's primary goals are peace and human rights. However, since membership is by country regardless of the type or form of government, the institution (headquartered in New York City) quickly became overwhelmed by dictatorships and other non-democratic governments, often led by the Soviet Union. The only institution within it that has any real power is the Security Council (UNSC). With a focus on international security, the UNSC has these functions:

- To maintain international peace and security in accordance with the principles and purposes of the UN
- To investigate any dispute or situation which might lead to international friction
- To recommend methods of adjusting such disputes or the terms of settlement
- To formulate plans for the establishment of a system to regulate armaments
- To determine the existence of a threat to the peace or act of aggression and to recommend what action should be taken
- To call on members to apply economic sanctions and other measures not involving the use of force to prevent or stop aggression
- To take military action against an aggressor
- To recommend the admission of new members
- To exercise the trusteeship functions of the UN in "strategic areas"
- To recommend to the General Assembly the appointment of the Secretary-General and, together with the Assembly, to elect the Judges of the International Court of Justice[9]

The UN Security Council's ability to take military action against aggressors has been the basis of the United States' actions in Korea, Kuwait, Iraq, and Afghanistan. The Security Council has 15 members, five with extraordinary veto power: China, Russia, Great Britain, France, and the United States. This veto power can sometimes block U.S. action, but it also means the United States has the capacity to prevent any meaningful UN actions to which it may object.

NATO

The preservation of democracy in Western Europe was the centerpiece of U.S. foreign and military policy for most of the twentieth century. In response to Soviet aggression during World War II, beginning with the annexation of eastern Poland and Finland, coupled with numerous postwar conquests and installation of puppet regimes, the United States, Canada, Britain, and most of the remaining democracies joined in NATO. Each nation pledged that "an armed attack against one ... shall be considered an attack against them all." To give this pledge credibility, a joint military command was established with a U.S. commanding officer (the first being Dwight Eisenhower) to bind the United States to the defense of Europe against Soviet aggression. After the formation of NATO, the Soviets made no further advances in Western Europe. NATO now has 28 members, including almost all of Europe (another 22 countries, including Russia, are NATO "partners").

THE COLLAPSE OF COMMUNISM

The dramatic collapse of communism in 1989 vastly reduced the threat of a military attack on Western Europe. It came about as a direct result of Soviet President Mikhail Gorbachev's decision to renounce the use of military force that for 40 years had kept in power Eastern Europe's communist governments, in Hungary and Czechoslovakia, for example. The fall of the Soviet Union also resulted in a dramatic decline in conflicts around the world. As Soviet sponsorship for war by Marxist guerillas and terrorist groups ended, peace broke out. The dismantling of the Berlin Wall in 1989 and the reunification of Germany in 1990 further rearranged the balance of military power in Central Europe. The threat NATO was created to meet had ended.

NATO AND THE BALKAN CONFLICTS

NATO forces had never been deployed outside Western Europe until the genocide against Bosnian Muslims during the breakup of Yugoslavia in 1995. NATO intervened to halt the violence after 600,000 people had been killed. The United States had preferred to leave the matter to Europeans but eventually took action through NATO, providing about one-third of the troops deployed as peacekeepers. Yet some argued that U.S. national security interests were not at stake in southeastern European ethnic conflicts and therefore U.S. troops should not be exposed to the dangers of intervention. When a second Balkan genocide sponsored by Serbian ruler Slobodan Milošević began in 1999, NATO undertook an air campaign against Serbian targets that ended aggression against the Muslim Kosovar Albanians, who gained their independence in 2008.

NATO IN AFGHANISTAN

The only time the NATO alliance was called to respond to an attack on a member came after the 2001 terrorist attacks on the United States by Al Qaeda, based in Afghanistan. Subsequent attacks on NATO members Turkey (2003), Spain (2004), and Britain (2005) underscored the importance of denying safe haven to terrorists. After a military victory over Al Qaeda and its Taliban ally, the United States turned over command of its military forces in Afghanistan to NATO in 2003. NATO created an International Security Assistance Force, officially under UN auspices, "to assist the Islamic Republic of Afghanistan in creating a stable and secure environment for the people of Afghanistan." Some 37 nations contributed troops to this force, but the United States contributed the largest number. To date, NATO forces have failed to eliminate Al Qaeda or Taliban forces from Afghanistan's mountainous regions along the Pakistan border. The success of President Obama's 2009–2012 tripling of U.S. combat troops to enact a "surge" strategy, as had been successful in Iraq, remains to be seen.

NATO over Libya

NATO forces also worked together to enforce UN resolutions calling for protection for Libyan civilians who were rebelling against longtime dictator Muammar Gaddafi. Initially the operation was commanded by a U.S. Navy admiral, but the actions to support Libyan rebels soon passed to NATO command under an American general. The operation was an air mission.

SECURITY THREATS TO THE UNITED STATES

While the United States faces no serious threat from any conventional military force, two varieties of threat challenge the security of the nation: nuclear weapons and terrorism. Due to the incredible destructive capacity of nuclear weapons, security for the United States requires that it be able to prevent, deter, or intercept any possible nuclear attack on it or its allies. On a very different scale and far from traditional military conflict, the use of "asymmetrical" warfare techniques by small groups, and their willingness to target civilians in violation of all codes of the conduct of war, makes terrorism the nation's most critical security threat. Of course, a nuclear terrorist attack is the nightmare the nation's military and security services endeavor daily to prevent.

NUCLEAR THREATS TO SECURITY

Nuclear weapons are the most destructive forces ever created by humans. A single device can destroy a city and leave the surrounding area uninhabitable for millennia. A full nuclear war could end civilization and kill billions. Paradoxically, the destructiveness of nuclear weapons causes elites on both sides to exercise extreme caution in relations with each other. During the Cold War U.S. and Soviet troops never engaged in direct combat against each other, largely for fear of an escalation into global nuclear war. In 1999, India and Pakistan were able to defuse a military conflict when both these nuclear powers recognized the devastating threat of escalation.

Only nine nations have nuclear weapons. The United States came first in 1945 and remains the only country to have used them in war—on Imperial Japan to force a quick end to World War II and avoid a devastating invasion of Japan.

The Soviet Union followed in 1949, U.S. allies Britain and France became nuclear powers in 1952 and 1960, respectively, and China, then a Soviet ally, did so in 1964.

In 1968, most nations signed the Treaty on the Non-Proliferation of Nuclear Weapons, but four nuclear nations have not: India (acquired nuclear status in 1974), Pakistan (1998), North Korea (2006), and Israel (which neither confirms nor denies having nuclear weapons). Four nations that had nuclear weapons have given them up voluntarily: South Africa and three former Soviet republics, Belarus, Kazakhstan, and Ukraine. Many other nations have the technological capacity to quickly develop a nuclear arsenal, but they do not because they are covered by the United States' "nuclear umbrella," meaning U.S. willingness to retaliate on their behalf gives them deterrence without need to have the weapons themselves.

DETERRENCE AND ARMS REDUCTIONS

To avoid nuclear war, elites relied primarily on a policy of **deterrence**. Deterrence is based on the idea that *rational* elites in other countries can be dissuaded from launching a nuclear attack by the threat of a devastating retaliatory strike. A nuclear "balance of terror" existed between the United States and the Soviet Union, in effect holding each nation's population hostage against **mutual assured destruction** or MAD. To reduce this risk further, U.S. and Soviet leaders engaged in negotiations over nuclear arms control. From the SALT agreement between Nixon and Breshnev in 1972, to treaties made by Reagan and Gorbachev (START), Bush and Yelstin (START II), and George W. Bush and Vladimir Putin in 2002 (Treaty of Moscow), the former adversaries' nuclear arsenals have been reduced by over 80 percent from Cold War levels. A negotiation of the expiring START Treaty under Presidents Obama and Medvedev was completed in 2010. Deterrence is maintained.

There is no threat to the United States from responsible state actors, especially fellow democracies such as India, France, Israel, and Britain. Pakistan's nuclear weapons are a threat only if government stability degrades to the point where leaders lose control over their arsenal. But today nuclear threats are arising from "non-deterrable" sources: rogue nations led by an irrational elite or by terrorist groups. The biggest threats today are North Korea and Iran.

The regime in North Korea is considered capable of irrational actions, and thus it is the focus of "Six-Party talks," including all neighbors, to exchange economic benefits for nuclear disarmament. North Korea has continued to test nuclear weapon delivery rockets, particularly flying them over nearby Japan. The change in leadership in 2011 saw power pass from deceased leader Kin Jong Il to his son Kim Jong Eun, making a full understanding of the dictatorship's goals less clear.

Despite sharp economic sanctions led by the United States and an arms embargo ordered by the UN, the Iranian government has continued to develop nuclear materials. The International Atomic Energy Agency (IAEA) has sent inspectors under the Treaty on the Non-Proliferation of Nuclear Weapons and found significant levels of activity, but was repeatedly denied full access to nuclear facilities. The Iranian government has successfully used the ploy of agreeing to negotiations, then delaying them, and finally withdrawing from them repeatedly over the past decade. Iran's government regularly produces statements glorifying death, causing some to doubt whether it could be a rational actor. Moderate Iranian leader Akbar Hashemi Rafsanjani (Chairman of the Expediency Council, which has supervisory power over all branches of government) offers the official view that nuclear war could be acceptable despite mass losses:

> If one day, the Islamic world is also equipped with weapons like those that Israel possesses now, then the imperialists' strategy will reach a standstill because the use of even one nuclear bomb inside Israel will destroy everything. However, it will only harm the Islamic world. It is not irrational to contemplate such an eventuality.[10]

Missile Defense
Missile Defense Agency website in the Department of Defense. *www. mda.mil*

Iranian President Mahmoud Ahmandinejad has repeatedly embraced mass martyrdom and genocide.

ANTIBALLISTIC MISSILE DEFENSES

As early as 1983, President Ronald Reagan urged that the United States seek a technological defense against nuclear missiles. His Strategic Defense Initiative (SDI) was a research program to explore means of destroying enemy nuclear missiles from the Soviet Union in space before they could reach their targets. The media dubbed it "Star Wars." The end of the Cold War refocused this ballistic missile defense against more limited but more likely threats from rogue nations. Technological breakthroughs and the successful launch of nuclear-capable missiles by North Korea inspired President George W. Bush to announce a limited deployment of missile interceptors in 2004. Bush also notified the Russians that the United States was withdrawing from the provisions of the SALT I Anti-Ballistic Missile Treaty of 1972 in order to set up a missile defense system for Europe, primarily due to the Iranian threat. Facing Russian objections, President Obama abandoned plans to build anti-missile bases in Poland and the Czech Republic in 2009.

NUCLEAR TERRORISM

The greatest security threat to the United States is nuclear terrorism. Al Qaeda has been particularly interested in acquiring nuclear weapons. North Korea sold its nuclear technology to Libya and Syria, both recognized state sponsors of terrorism, although the Syrian facility was destroyed by an unexplained explosion in 2007, while Libya declined to pursue its program fearing a U.S. invasion. Iran is also a major state sponsor of terrorism, particularly by the organization Hezbollah, which it created to "export the revolution." The prospect of a catastrophic attack on the United States or its allies forms the greatest fear of security planners.

THE TERRORIST THREAT

The terrorist attack of September 11, 2001, resulted in almost 3,000 civilian deaths at the World Trade Center in New York and the Pentagon in Washington. It awakened the nation to the threat of **terrorism**—"premeditated, politically motivated violence perpetrated against noncombatant targets by subnational groups or clandestine agents, usually intended to influence an audience."[11] While other nations including democratic allies such as Britain, India, Colombia, Israel, and the Philippines had seen terrorism on a frequent basis, the United States had been largely immune to large-scale terrorism (the 1995 domestic terror attack in Oklahoma City had been the largest since the 1920 Wall Street bombing by anarchists). The world's largest military power had been attacked by 19 men with box cutters! A new approach to security was needed, including both domestic and foreign responses.

The terrorist threat worldwide remains high. In 2010, there were about 11,500 terrorist attacks against noncombatants, resulting in over 50,000 victims, including over 13,000 deaths. About three-quarters of the attacks took place in the Middle East or South Asia; the overwhelming majority of the victims were Muslims.[12]

Currently, the Department of Defense, the FBI, and the Department of Homeland Security view catastrophic terror as the most serious threat to the nation's security. According to the 2006 *Quadrennial Defense Review*, "The enemies in this war are not traditional conventional military forces but rather dispersed, global terrorist networks that exploit Islam to advance radical political plans. These enemies have the avowed aim of acquiring and using nuclear and biological weapons to murder hundreds of thousands of Americans and others around the world." Al Qaeda has proven itself eager to inflict mass civilian causalities in New York, Bali, Iraq, Nairobi, and Pakistan and has worked to acquire weapons of mass destruction to increase its capacity to kill.

MASS RESPONSE TO THE WAR ON TERRORISM

On the evening of September 11, President George W. Bush spoke to the U.S. people from the Oval Office in a nationally televised address:

> The pictures of airplanes flying into buildings, fires burning, huge structures collapsing, have filled us with disbelief, terrible sadness, and a quiet, unyielding anger. These mass murders were intended to frighten our nation into chaos and retreat. But they failed, our country is strong. These deliberate and deadly attacks were more than acts of terror. They were acts of war.[13]

The president outlined a broad "response to terrorism" to be fought both at home and abroad through diplomatic, military, financial, homeland security, and humanitarian means.

The masses' initial response to the terrorist attack was precisely the opposite of the terrorists' intentions. National pride and confidence in national leadership soared in the aftermath, and flags flew throughout the country. Since 9/11 almost two million U.S. adults have volunteered to serve their country and been sent to Iraq or Afghanistan. Trust in government rose to levels not seen since the 1960s, presidential approval ratings reached dramatic highs, and support for military action was overwhelming. But over time this "rally 'round the flag" effect diminished. Trust in government and support for the president returned to their pre-9/11 levels.

ELITE RESPONSE TO TERRORISM: DOMESTIC LAW

Elites typically respond to perceived threats to national security with repressive measures: from Lincoln's suspension of the writ of habeas corpus during the Civil War through the Sedition Act of 1918 during World War I that outlawed "disloyal" speech, the internment of 120,000 Japanese Americans during World War II, laws placing additional prohibitions on communists during the Cold War, and expanded government surveillance powers following the 1995 and 2001 terrorist attacks.

In response to the deadly Oklahoma City bombing of a federal building by right-wing terrorists, Congress passed the 1996 Antiterrorism and Effective Death Penalty Act. This law made it a crime to aid foreign-country supporters of terrorism, defined terrorist financing as money laundering and thus a crime, specifically addressed concerns about weapons of mass destruction (WMDs), expanded the reach of U.S. law to terrorist threat conspiracies whether in the United States or abroad, increased penalty limits on habeas corpus appeals, and speeded the deportation of alien terrorists.

An even more sweeping enactment followed: the USA PATRIOT Act of 2001. This act was passed nearly unanimously in the Senate (98 to 1) and overwhelmingly in the House (337 to 66), with bipartisan support. Its key provisions covered the following:

- *Roving wiretaps.* As already permitted for fighting organized crime, law enforcement may tap any telephones suspects might use without the need for separate warrants for each line.
- *Internet tracking.* Law enforcement authorities may track Internet communications without obtaining warrants.
- *Business records.* Investigators may obtain information from credit cards, bank records, consumer purchases, libraries, schools, and colleges.
- *Foreign Intelligence Surveillance Court.* A special court may issue search warrants on an investigator's assertion that the information sought is relevant to a terrorist investigation. The warrant is not made public, to avoid alerting the subject.
- *Property seizure.* Authorities may seize the property of suspected terrorists. To secure its return, owners bear the burden of proving it was not used for terrorist purposes.
- *Detention.* Suspected terrorists may be detained for lengthy periods without judicial recourse.
- *Alien reporting and detention.* Aliens of selected nations must report to the government, and illegal aliens suspected of terrorist connections can be indefinitely detained.
- *Harboring of terrorists.* Knowingly harboring persons who have committed, or are about to commit, a terrorist act was made a crime.

Central Intelligence Agency CIA official website, with history, news, and links to its *World Fact Book*, with information on every nation. *www.cia.gov*

The Patriot Act was extended in 2006 with relatively few technical changes. The wiretap, business records, and terrorist monitoring provisions were set to expire in 2009 but have been renewed several times at the behest of President Obama.

THE WAR ON TERRORISM

In addition to domestic steps it can take to secure the homeland from terror attacks, the United States also has the capacity to go worldwide to counterattack terrorist groups and their state sponsors. In the "global war on terrorism"

(GWOT) the United States would prefer to battle terrorists on their own turf, not in the United States. The war on terrorism has also brought a new emphasis on nonconventional forces and tactics to meet asymmetrical threats and created new conditions for the use of military force. These include the following:

- Direct attacks against terrorist forces to capture or kill them, operations usually carried out by highly trained Special Operations Forces or aerial drones, but can be raids like the 2011 mission to kill Osama bin Laden.

- Attacks on nations that harbor terrorists, allow terrorist to maintain bases, or supply and equip terrorist organizations, such as Libya (1986), Afghanistan (2001), and Iraq (2003).

- Preemptive attacks on regimes that threaten to use weapons of mass destruction—chemical, biological, or nuclear—against the United States or its allies, or to supply terrorist organizations with these weapons. The Bush administration argued that the war in Iraq is a part of the war on terrorism. The argument for preemptive military action was summarized by Bush's Secretary of State Condoleezza Rice: "We cannot wait until the smoking gun becomes a mushroom cloud."

Under the Obama administration, the term "War on Terror" has been replaced with "overseas contingency operations" against "man-caused disasters," but the fight has continued.

Counterterrorism operations also require extensive intelligence gathering. The scale of the United States' information gathering is global. All U.S. intelligence agencies were placed under the direction of the Director of National Intelligence (DNI) in 2005 to better promote inter-agency communication. The DNI acts as principal advisor to the president, National Security Council, and Homeland Security Council for intelligence matters. The Central Intelligence Agency (CIA), the Defense Intelligence Agency (DIA), National Reconnaissance Office, the National Geo-Spatial Intelligence Agency, the National Security Agency, and the intelligence-gathering portions of other departments and the military are all under the DNI.[14]

INTELLIGENCE GATHERING AND THE WAR ON TERROR

Two programs illustrate the global reach of U.S. intelligence services. The Terrorist Finance Tracking Program analyzes the SWIFT (Society for Worldwide Interbank Financial Telecommunication) database, the global clearinghouse for financial transactions based in Belgium. The program was key in helping capture the Al Qaeda mastermind of the 2002 terror attacks in Bali, Indonesia, which killed over 200 people. Its existence was revealed by the *New York Times* in June 2006,[15] damaging its usefulness in monitoring the money flow on which terrorism depends.

The signals intelligence network known as ECHELON, shared by several nations including the United States, monitors most global communications, including phone, fax, and e-mail, that travel by satellite transmission, microwave links, or telephone networks. In 2005, after holding the information for a year at the administration's request on national security grounds, the *New York Times* reported that

President Bush had authorized the National Security Agency to monitor international telephone calls to track possible terrorist communications.[16] The administration felt it did not need a warrant because the communications were not entirely domestic. The *Times* story alerted the terrorists that their communications were not secure, prompting a shift to other methods.

AFGHANISTAN: "OPERATION ENDURING FREEDOM"

The military phase of the war on terrorism began on October 7, 2001, when U.S. aircraft attacked Al Qaeda bases in Afghanistan. Simultaneously, U.S. Special Forces began to organize and lead Afghan fighters, including several tribal groups calling themselves the Northern Alliance, in a campaign against the ruling Taliban. Coming so soon after the 9/11 attack on the United States, this military effort enjoyed widespread international support. A coalition of nations participated in "Operation Enduring Freedom"; some, including Britain and Canada, contributed combat troops, while others, including Pakistan, Saudi Arabia, and Uzbekistan, allowed U.S. forces to base operations in their territory. Kabul, the Afghan capital, was occupied by anti-Taliban forces on November 13.

By April 2002, Al Qaeda and Taliban forces had been either destroyed or scattered into small groups in the mountainous areas of Afghanistan and neighboring Pakistan. However, Al Qaeda leader Osama bin Laden escaped to live in Pakistan (until 2011). A new government was installed in Kabul, but various tribal chiefs throughout Afghanistan continued to exercise independent power, and the Taliban remained a strong force in the mountainous regions of southern Afghanistan and across the border in Pakistan. President Obama tripled the number of U.S. forces in Afghanistan in 2009–2012 in an effort to re-create the successful "surge" strategy used in Iraq; results are still pending.

ENEMY COMBATANTS

At Guantanamo Bay, Cuba, and abroad, the U.S. military has detained hundreds of persons captured in the fighting in Afghanistan and Iraq, as well as some captured in other nations. Traditionally, prisoners of war are not entitled to rights under the U.S. Constitution, but they are to be afforded humane treatment under the international Geneva Convention. Because captured Al Qaeda fighters do not meet the traditional definition of soldier (fights in uniform, is part of a clear chain of command, serves in a national military), they have been classified differently, although the category "enemy combatant" appears analogous to "prisoner of war." They may be detained for the duration of a war. However, the war on terrorism does not appear to have a specific duration (its start is generally dated either to Al Qaeda's 1998 "Declaration of War" against the United States or to the 9/11 attacks of 2001). Due to this controversy, the Obama administration retired the term "unlawful enemy combatant" in 2009, replacing it with "alien unprivileged enemy belligerent." Obama still endorsed the "indefinite detention" of some detainees at the Guantanamo facility in May 2009.[17]

In 2004, the U.S. Supreme Court had held that enemy combatants captured on the battlefield and "imprisoned in territory over which the United States exercises an exclusive jurisdiction and control" are entitled to constitutional rights, including habeas corpus—the right to bring their case to U.S. courts.[18] President Bush then established special military commissions to try detainees. The Supreme Court struck these down because Congress had not established them by law, and they did not operate under the rules of the Uniform Code of Military Justice. The Court said the president's powers as commander-in-chief did not grant him the power to hold and try detainees without congressional legislation.[19] Bush then asked Congress for the power to establish special military tribunals with special rules to try detainees, which Congress granted. After suspending them early in his term, President Obama quietly restarted military commissions in December 2009.[20]

DRONE WARFARE

The United States has increasingly adopted the use of unmanned aerial drones as a major instrument for the projection of military power. Begun under President George W. Bush, the drones have been used to locate and attack targets in the fight against the Taliban, and Al Qaeda and its affiliates. Due to policies against the detention and interrogation of captured terrorists, the Obama administration was instead focused on a policy of targeted killing, with thousands of enemy fighters killed in hundreds of drone attacks by Predator and Reaper drones over Afghanistan and Pakistan. Many attacks resulted in civilian casualties due to Taliban and Al Qaeda preference to hide among noncombatants. While the Pakistani government has vociferously objected to drone use over its territory, the Pakistani military has aided in target selection and provided intelligence. Numerous reports from civilians living in the areas of Pakistan with a heavy Taliban or Al Qaeda presence indicated that because drones are a more precise weapon than ground combat operations, drones were tolerated. President Obama was actively involved in approving drone targets. In 2012, Obama joked about the issue after saying that his daughters were fans of the pop group the Jonas Brothers, warning "Boys, don't get any ideas. I have two words for you—Predator drones. You will never see it coming."[21]

THE WAR IN IRAQ

Elites lose the support of the masses when they fail to produce victories in war or cannot agree on a course of action. Once the 2008 surge strategy in Iraq began to work and the situation improved (see Focus: David Petraeus), mass interest in the war in Iraq faded quickly.

"OPERATION IRAQI FREEDOM"

At the end of the Gulf War in 1991, in which the United States led a seventy-nation coalition to expel Iraqi armies from neighboring Kuwait, the Iraqi dictator Saddam Hussein agreed to UN conditions including the destruction of all his chemical and biological weapons and the end of efforts to acquire nuclear weapons. UN inspectors were to verify Iraqi compliance and sanctions were imposed when he refused to allow full inspection. In 1998, Hussein ordered the inspectors out of the country. In response, Congress passed the Iraqi Liberation Act of 1998, which made it the policy of the United States to support "regime change" and a transition to democracy in Iraq.

Over the next several years Iraq violated at least a dozen UN resolutions. Faced with a U.S. military buildup in the region in late 2002, Hussein allowed UN inspectors to return but continued to obstruct their work. On March 19, 2003, after warning him to leave Iraq, the United States and Great Britain launched air strikes and then a ground offensive. U.S. and British troops took just 21 days to capture Baghdad. Hussein was captured and turned over to the new Iraqi government, which tried and convicted him of mass murder for the deaths of over one million Iraqis and others. He was executed by hanging.

At different times President Bush stated the purpose of "Operation Iraqi Freedom" as (1) eliminating Iraq's weapons of mass destruction, (2) ensuring Hussein would not harbor or assist terrorist organizations, (3) effecting a "regime change" for Iraq to end the threat he posed for his neighbors and free Iraqis from his oppressive rule, and (4) bringing democracy to Iraq. The first two have clear national interest, and realist, grounds; the latter two are idealist.

Given Iraq's numerous violations of UN resolutions, the United States ensured the successful adoption in 2002 of Security Council Resolution 1441, which called for "serious consequences" for Iraq's continued non-compliance.[22] Still, Secretary of State Colin Powell lobbied for yet another resolution, which failed due to

---

FOCUS | **DAVID PETRAEUS**

The most influential counterterrorism official in the world today is former U.S. Army General David H. Petraeus, Director of the Central Intelligence Agency (CIA). Before that he commanded international forces in Afghanistan, a position he took after being commander of the U.S. Central Command. Petraeus was in charge of fighting two wars, Operation Enduring Freedom in Afghanistan and Operation Iraqi Freedom, as well as overseeing regional security with allied governments in Pakistan, Yemen, India, Israel, and Saudi Arabia as well as two major state supporters of terrorism with Iran and Syria.

Petraeus achieved these commands after being commander of coalition forces in Iraq from 2007 to 2008. He was mocked by left-wing critics MoveOn as "General Betray-Us." There he devised and implemented the "surge" strategy that successfully broke Al Qaeda and the Baathist insurgency in Iraq. Earlier, as commanding officer of the 101st Airborne Division, he had been in Mosul, the northern Iraqi city of nearly two million people, where he used a spectrum of counterinsurgency techniques that focused on providing security for the local people, including applying military force, building public works, invigorating the local economy, and setting up local elections. These ideas had all been featured in the U.S. Army's *Counterinsurgency* Field Manual, written under his direction.

Before being deployed to Iraq, Petraeus made his military career in nation-building and peacekeeping operations in Bosnia and Haiti. He held leadership positions in combat units including airborne, armor, and infantry; staff positions such as Military Assistant to the Supreme Allied Commander in Europe and Executive Assistant to the Chairman of the Joint Chiefs of Staff; and appointments in both NATO and the UN. He holds a Ph.D. in International Affairs from Princeton University.

Source: Official biography at *www.cia.gov/about-cia/leadership/david-h.-petraeus.html*, and Steve Coll, "The General's Dilemma: David Petraeus, the Pressures of Politics, and the Road Out of Iraq," *The New Yorker*, September 8, 2008. *www.newyorker.com/reporting/2008/09/08/080908fa_fact_coll?currentPage=all*.

opposition from French, Chinese, and Russian elites, who had significant commercial interests with the Hussein regime, mostly concerning oil.

Among the permanent members of the Security Council, only the British were prepared to offer significant military support for Operation Iraqi Freedom. Poland lent thousands of troops and one region in occupied Iraq was placed under command of a Polish general. However, elites and mass opinion in Western Europe, led by France and Germany, generally opposed military action, and Bush's critics at home and abroad increasingly complained of his "unilateralism," or willingness for the United States to take actions alone. In the end, 35 countries, including most of Europe, contributed military support, much of it modest help from smaller formerly communist nations. No weapons of mass destruction were found despite an intensive search, leading critics to charge that faulty intelligence on Iraq was somehow Bush's plan to mislead Congress, the UN, and the people about their existence.

United Nations
United Nations' mission, member states, issues of concern, institutions, and history. *www.un. org*

THE OCCUPATION OF IRAQ

The coalition occupation of Iraq started out as ineffectual in providing security for Iraqis. Two prominent errors at the onset were the dismissals of the entire Iraqi Army and of virtually all Iraqi managers and technicians who had been members of the Baath ruling party. Iraq held its first democratic election in 50 years in 2003, however, and despite violence and threats of violence nearly 60 percent of the population participated, many proudly displaying their blue-inked thumbs to show they had voted. A new constitution was approved in a second vote that year. The United States officially turned over sovereignty to a new Iraqi government in 2004, continuing its military presence through negotiated "status of forces agreements."

Attacks on civilians, as well as on U.S., coalition, and Iraqi forces, grew in intensity and deadliness. Most came from disaffected Sunni Arabs, especially former members of the Hussein regime. Al Qaeda was responsible for significant violence, including suicide attacks, truck bombs, and attacks on religious and political targets. The insurgency brought in thousands of foreign radical Islamic fighters. The Shiites organized their own militia, the strongest being the Iranian-supported Mahdi Army. Large areas of Iraq came under the control of one or another of these insurgent groups.

U.S. forces suffered a gruesome toll in lives and limbs. By 2010 over 4,400 troops had been killed and tens of thousands wounded, many by "improvised explosive devices." Nearly every Army and Marine combat unit and several National Guard and Reserve units were rotated into Iraq more than once, bringing forces to the breaking point.

Al Qaeda poured the bulk of its resources and people into Iraq, and President Bush continued to argue that the war was central to the worldwide war against terrorism. He felt an abrupt withdrawal ("cut and run") would encourage radical Salafist Islamic terrorists around the world.

> Failure is not an option. Iraq would become a safe haven from which terrorists could plan attacks against American interests abroad, and our allies. Middle East reformers

would never again fully trust American assurances of support for democracy in human rights in the region. Iraq is the central front in the global war on terror.[23]

President Bush ordered a "surge" in U.S. troops in Iraq in 2007, adding about 30,000 to bring the U.S. total to over 168,000. Under the command of General David Petraeus (see Focus: David Petraeus), the United States engaged in successful counterinsurgency tactics and built on widespread Iraqi resentment of both the Hussein regime and the radicalism of Al Qaeda. It became U.S. policy to provide security and economic expansion, train Iraqi security forces, and allow ethnic factions to reach national reconciliation. Elections in 2010 solidified Iraqi democracy. As Iraq achieved greater stability, U.S. combat forces withdrew in 2011.

THE GLOBAL ECONOMIC ELITE

In terms of economic might, the United States remains the world's largest economy by a substantial margin. Its 2010 gross domestic product (GDP) of $14.5 trillion was almost triple that of the next largest economies, China ($5.9 trillion) and Japan ($5.5 trillion) (see Table 14.3). The United States makes up almost a third of the global economy (30 percent of a gross world product of $47.8 trillion). Of the 2,000 largest companies in the world (according to *Forbes* magazine), 524 are based in the United States, vastly more than in any rival economy (see Table 14.4). U.S. consumers drive the global system of production, purchasing over $10 trillion worth of goods and services in 2008.

THE UNITED STATES AND GLOBAL TRADE

International trade—the buying and selling of goods and services between individuals and firms located in different countries—has expanded rapidly. Today, almost one-fourth of the world's total output is sold in a country other than the one that produced it. The United States exports about 10 percent of the value of its GDP and imports about 15 percent (see Figure 14.2). Global interconnectedness heavily shapes the U.S. economy. For example, in the 2007–2009 financial crisis, the United States found itself rescuing not only its own institutions but foreign banks as well.[24] Two of the first banks to collapse due to the U.S. mortgage meltdown were in Germany and Britain. When the U.S. economy catches cold, the world sneezes.

Globalization has created a global elite—the leaders of the world's largest banks and industrial corporations, whose economic power challenges the notion of national sovereignty. This elite can move or threaten to move economic resources such as industrial plants, sales and inventory, and capital investment across national boundaries and thus shape the economic policies of national governments. Foreign direct investment and cross-national ownership of economic resources continue to rise.

Due to its economic predominance, the United States has written the rules on international trade since the 1940s, mostly to the benefit of the nations that participate. About two-thirds of all foreign currency reserves worldwide are in relatively stable U.S. dollars, for instance, although that number was higher before the

TABLE 14.3	NATIONS OF THE WORLD BY GDP, 2010	
Rank	Nation	GDP (in billions US$)
1	United States	14.5
2	China	5.9
3	Japan	5.5
4	Germany	3.3
5	France	2.6
6	Great Britain	2.3
7	Brazil	2.1
8	Italy	2.1
9	India	1.6
10	Canada	1.6

Source: International Monetary Fund, *www.imf.org/external/pubs/ft/wed/2012/01/weodata.*

TABLE 14.4	COMPANIES IN THE *FORBES* GLOBAL 2000, BY NATION	
Rank	Nation	Number of Companies
1	United States	536
2	Japan	258
3	China	136
4	Great Britain	93
5	Korea (Republic of)	68
6	Canada	66
7	France	63
8	India	61
9	Germany	53
10	Switzerland	45

Source: Forbes Global 2000, *www.forbes.com/global2000.*

adoption of the European Union currency, the euro. Almost all commodities, such as barrels of oil and ounces of gold, are priced in U.S. dollars, helping create a constant demand for dollars, which have only one supplier: the U.S. government. To provide greater liquidity during the 2007–2009 financial crisis, the Federal Reserve Bank was able to add almost $2 trillion into the global financial system (coordinated with other countries' central banks). Because the world has a greater quantity of dollars than the United States itself requires, the nation has always been able to borrow its own currency and largely control the interest rate.

U.S. ECONOMIC WEAKNESSES

Continued high levels of borrowing by the U.S. government (the current national debt is $16 trillion), state and local government ($3 trillion), businesses ($12 trillion), and U.S. consumers ($13 trillion) have forced the United States to turn to foreign lenders to pay for public and private spending.[25] Total gross external debt in 2011 came to $15 trillion, of which only $1.2 trillion was not in U.S. dollars.[26] Of the public debt, in 2012 roughly $5.1 trillion was held by foreigners, with China ($1.2 trillion), Japan ($1.1 trillion), and Brazil ($237 billion) the single largest holders.[27] Some foreign Treasury bill holders have begun to worry about U.S. ability to repay its debt; in 2009, Luo Ping, a senior China Banking Regulatory Commission (CBRC) official, told a New York conference:

> U.S. Treasuries are the safe haven; it is the only option. We hate you guys. Once you start issuing $l–$2 trillion … we know the dollar is going to depreciate, so we hate you guys, but there is nothing much we can do.[28]

In a 2009 speech at Peking University, U.S. Treasury Secretary Timothy Geithner was laughed at by the audience when he tried unsuccessfully to reassure his Chinese

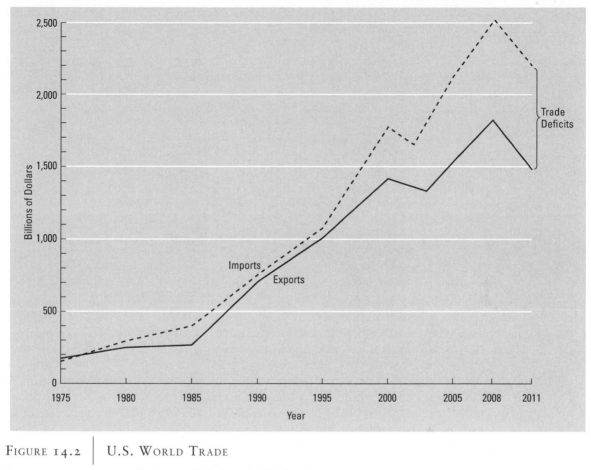

FIGURE 14.2 | U.S. WORLD TRADE

Source: *www.census.gov/foreign-trade/balance/c0004.html.*

audience that investments in U.S. debt were safe.[29] One response has been these nations slowly diversifying their foreign holdings into other currencies.

A variety of factors point to weakness in the U.S. economic system, beyond federal debt levels. The government's financial obligations to Social Security and Medicare, for instance, amount to $65 trillion if it measures this future commitment as businesses are required to do.[30] In 2008, the U.S. government found itself taking on several trillion in debt from the supposedly privatized enterprises Freddie Mac and Fannie Mae. Given "that the United States has a history of defaulting on its official debt via inflation" and "that countries holding U.S. bonds can sell them in a nanosecond," one economist asked, "Is the United States bankrupt?" in a Federal Reserve journal.[31]

INTERNATIONAL TRADE INSTITUTIONS

Both Democratic and Republican elites in the United States over the past half century have supported expanded world trade. The U.S. market is the largest in the world and the most open to foreign-made goods. U.S. policy has been to maintain an open market while encouraging other nations to do the same, reaping a global economic boom that began in the 1980s and has moved about two billion people worldwide out of poverty.

The shutdown of global trade that came with Depression-era tariffs could not be allowed to recur, so the United States began lowering tariffs after World War II and continued to press for freer trade, to the benefit of all. During the Cold War and today, the weakest economies in the world are those that exclude themselves from global trade. Domestic workers and labor unions assert that a benefit for workers abroad must diminish their own power; their opposition has been ignored. The United States continues to lead international efforts to further liberalize world trade, encourage the flow of investment capital around the world, and eliminate foreign market barriers to U.S. exports. It works toward these goals through multilateral institutions such as the World Trade Organization (WTO).

Office of the U.S. Trade Representative
Information about U.S. trade policy.
www.ustr.gov

THE WORLD TRADE ORGANIZATION

A multinational General Agreement on Tariffs and Trade organization (GATT) was created in 1947 to encourage international trade. Over the years, GATT has been dominated by banking, business, and commercial interests seeking multilateral tariff reductions and the relaxations of quotas. In 1993, the WTO was created to supersede GATT (which remains in place under the WTO). The WTO is the principal instrument for formulating global trade policy. Today, the WTO includes over 150 nations, covering 95 percent of global trade, that agree to global trade rules. It has power to adjudicate trade disputes among members and monitor and enforce trade agreements. Trade liberalization under GATT and the WTO has helped global trade and wealth explode; in 1985 gross world product was $22 trillion and by 2011 was almost $50 trillion.

THE INTERNATIONAL MONETARY FUND

The International Monetary Fund (IMF) is an organization of 186 nations that promotes trade and economic growth. It was created by the United States and its allies after World War II to stabilize currency exchange rates and set up a global payment system for international trade. When economically weak nations incur chronic balance-of-trade deficits and perhaps face deferral or default on international debts, the IMF may condition its rescue loans on changes in a nation's economic policies. It may require a reduction in a nation's government deficits through reduced public spending and/or higher taxes, or it may require a devaluation of the country's currency, making its exports cheaper and imports more expensive. It may also mandate the adoption of noninflationary monetary policies.

The IMF is run by a Board of Governors, although major actions require a vote by the membership. Different nations have different numbers of votes; the United States holds 16.75 percent of the votes. Since major decisions require an 85 percent supermajority, the United States has the ability to unilaterally block any action. No other nation has such a voice (Japan and Germany come next with about 6 percent of the votes each).

THE WORLD BANK

The World Bank, created at the same time as the IMF, provides capital to developing nations to assist in economic development and poverty reduction. Since the United States is the largest shareholder, the president of the bank is by tradition a U.S. citizen. The World Bank is headquartered in Washington, DC, and works closely with the IMF in investigating nations applying for loans and imposing IMF conditions on them. International Bank for Reconstruction and Development (IBRD) and International Development Association (IDA) are institutions within the World Bank.

The current president of the World Bank, Robert Zoellick, has had a long career in the elite. In the first Bush administration, he served as Undersecretary of State for Economic and Agricultural Affairs and White House Deputy Chief of Staff. During the Clinton years he was Vice President of Fannie Mae, an advisor to Goldman Sachs, and an academic. In the second Bush administration, he was U.S. Trade Representative and Deputy Secretary of State, before being appointed by Bush to the World Bank (and confirmed by the bank's executive board).

THE NORTH AMERICAN FREE TRADE AGREEMENT

In 1993, the United States, Canada, and Mexico signed the North American Free Trade Agreement (NAFTA). GNP in Mexico almost doubled in the 1990s as a result, from $600 billion to $1 trillion. Objections to NAFTA by labor unions and environmental groups in the United States were drowned out by support by the three nations' business communities, both parties in Congress, President Bill Clinton, and former President George Bush. NAFTA aims to remove tariffs on virtually all products traded among the three nations, as well as on banking, insurance, and other financial services. In 2012, the Mexican economy was stronger than the U.S.'s, with only 5 percent unemployment. Net immigration from Mexico approached zero.

GLOBALIZATION AND DEMOCRACY

The economic power of the United States is rooted in its political principles, particularly property rights, freedom of expression, and rule of law. These principles are the requirements not just of successful capitalist economies but of liberal democracies as well. Property rights are essential, for unless individuals securely own their own land, tools, and businesses, they remain dependents on the state and generally uninspired to achieve their best. The rise of modern democracy came with the growth of an economic middle class. Nations with a tiny elite and a huge mass of poor are unlikely to democratize. Since the days of Aristotle it has also been recognized that a mass made up mostly of a middle class is required for a stable, participatory political system.

The United States is also a world leader in innovation (see Table 14.5). U.S. popular culture dominates global markets for entertainment, including television, music, and books, and a worldwide audience makes Hollywood's products

TABLE 14.5	TOTAL PATENTS GRANTED, 2010	
1	Japan	285,044
2	United States	186,189
3	China	84,554
4	Republic of Korea	75,533
5	Germany	55,046
6	France	27,734
7	Russian Federation	22,370
8	Great Britain	13,786
9	Switzerland	12,798
10	The Netherlands	9,916

Source: Data from World Intellectual Property Organization, *www.wipo.int/ipstats/en/statistics/patents/*.

blockbusters. In technology, the United States is second only to Japan in patents granted. Intellectual property rights are even included in the Constitution (Article I, Section 8): Congress shall have the power "to promote the Progress of Science and useful Arts, by securing for limited times to Authors and Inventors the exclusive Right to their respective Writings and Discoveries." The WTO frequently adjudicates intellectual property disputes, a major source of trade conflict for the United States.

The United States leads in higher education. Of the 10 most prestigious universities in the world, eight are in the United States. Of the top 50 universities globally, 35 are in the United States (five are in Britain, no other country has more than two in the ranking; see Table 14.6). The United States is also the most popular destination for students studying abroad.

While globalization of trade is promoting greater freedom worldwide, globalization of corporate power is moving economic elites further away from the values, beliefs, and concerns of the masses and even from the restraints of national governments. Social historian Christopher Lasch observes of the U.S. elite:

> It is a question whether they think of themselves as Americans at all. Patriotism, certainly, does not rank very high in their hierarchy of virtues. "Multiculturalism," on the other hand, suits them to perfection, conjuring up the agreeable images of a global bazaar. ... The new elites are at home only in transit, en route to a high-level conference, to the grand opening of a new franchise, to an international film festival, or to an undiscovered resort. Theirs is essentially a tourist's view of the world—not a perspective likely to encourage a passionate devotion to democracy.[32]

The long-term results of globalization on the relationship between elites and masses remain to be seen.

TABLE 14.6 | ACADEMIC RANKING OF WORLD UNIVERSITIES

Rank	University	Location
1	Harvard University	United States
2	University of California, Berkeley	United States
3	Stanford University	United States
4	Massachusetts Institute of Technology	United States
5	University of Cambridge	Great Britain
6	California Institute of Technology	United States
7	Princeton University	United States
8	Columbia University	United States
9	University of Chicago	United States
10	Oxford University	Great Britain
11	Yale University	United States
12	Cornell University	United States
13	University of California, Los Angeles	United States
14	University of California, San Diego	United States
15	University of Pennsylvania	United States
16	University of Washington	United States
17	University of Wisconsin, Madison	United States
18 (tie)	University of California, San Francisco	United States
18 (tie)	Johns Hopkins University	United States
20	University of Tokyo	Japan

Source: Center for World-Class Universities and the Institute of Higher Education of Shanghai Jiao Tong University, *www.arwu.org/ARWU2010.jsp*.

IN BRIEF | GLOBALIZATION

- The world's 2,000 largest corporations include 536 U.S.-based firms. European Union nations and Japan also heavily populate the global elite, joined by new elites from rapidly emerging economies.
- Global elites support open markets—the elimination of tariffs and trade barriers—to encourage nations to open their doors to products and services. The WTO is the principal instrument for formulating global trade policy.
- Globalization of corporate power moves economic elites even further from the people and increasingly removes the restraints of national governments from worldwide corporate activities.

UNITED STATES AS GLOBAL HEGEMON | AN ELITIST INTERPRETATION

U.S. elites hold great power in the international arena. The United States is preeminent in both economic and military power: it is the global hegemon.

1. The United States' superior military capabilities have allowed it to act as "global cop": providing emergency responses to disasters, maintaining system order, and fighting a "war on terrorism." The biggest security concern is nuclear proliferation, particularly to terrorist groups and/or nations who do not appear responsive to rational deterrence approaches.

2. Political elites argue that military force may be used for important political and humanitarian goals such as support of democratic governments, peacemaking, peacekeeping, counterterrorism, and humanitarian aid.

3. The United States is central to most international institutions, most of which it helped found. It holds a United Nations Security Council veto, the presidency of the World Bank, and leads in the WTO, IMF, and NATO.

4. The U.S. accounts for about a fourth of world economic activity. The U.S. dollar is the predominate foreign reserve currency. The United States is the leader in education, business, and innovation.

NOTES

1. Atika Shubert reporting on CNN Sunday Morning. Christmas around the World. December 25, 2005. http://transcripts.cnn.com/TRANSCRIPTS/0512/25/sm.01.html

2. George W. Bush, "Introduction," *National Security Strategy*, 2002. http://georgewbush-whitehouse.archives.gov/nsc/nss/2002/nssintro.html

3. Barack Obama, "Nobel Peace Prize Lecture," 2009. http://nobelprize.org/nobel_prizes/peace/laureates/2009/obama-lecture_en.html

4. George W. Bush, "Introduction," *National Security Strategy*, 2002. http://georgewbush-whitehouse.archives.gov/nsc/nss/2002/nssintro.html

5. Hans Morgenthau, *Politics among Nations*, 5th ed. (New York: Alfred A. Knopf, 1973), p. 27.

6. Barack Obama, "Nobel Peace Prize Lecture," 2009. http://nobelprize.org/nobel_prizes/peace/laureates/2009/obama-lecture_en.html

7. United States Northern Command, http://www.northcom.mil/about/index.html

8. The organizations are: ADB, AfDB, ANZUS, APEC, Arctic Council, ARF, ASEAN (dialogue partner), Australia Group, BIS, BSEC (observer), CBSS (observer), CE (observer), CERN (observer), CP, EAPC, EBRD, FAO, G-20, G-5, G-7, G-8, G-10, IADB, IAEA, IBRD, ICAO, ICC, ICCt (signatory), ICRM, IDA, IEA, IFAD, IFC, IFRCS, IHO, ILO, IMF, IMO, IMSO, Interpol, IOC, IOM, ISO, ITSO, ITU, ITUC, MIGA, MINUSTAH, NAFTA, NATO, NEA, NSG, OAS, OECD, OPCW, OSCE, Paris Club, PCA, PIF (partner), SAARC (observer), SECI (observer), SPC, UN, UN Security Council, UNCTAD, UNESCO, UNHCR, UNITAR, UNMIL, UNRWA, UNTSO, UPU, WCL, WCO, WFTU, WHO, WIPO, WMO, WTO, and ZC. http://www.cia.gov/library/publications/the-world-factbook/geos/us.html

9. United Nations Security Council, http://www.un.org/Docs/sc/unsc_functions.html

10. Akbar Hashemi Rafsanjani, *Qods Day Speech*, December 14, 2001. Voice of the Islamic Republic of Iran, translated by BBC Worldwide Monitoring. http://www.globalsecurity. Org/wmd/library/news/iran/2001/011214-text.html

11. Title 22 of the *U.S. Code*, Section 2656 (d).

12. National Counter Terrorism Center, *2010 Report on Terrorism*, April 30, 2011. http://nctc.gov/wits banner/docs/2010_report_on_terrorism

13. George W. Bush, *Presidential Address to the Nation*, September 11, 2001.

14. Office of the Director of National Intelligence, http://www.dni.gov/who.htm

15. Eric Lichtblau and James Risen, "Bank Data Is Sifted by U.S. in Secret to Block Terror," *New York Times*, June 23, 2006. http://www.nytimes. com/2006/06/23/washington/23intel.html?_r=l&hp &ex=1151121600&en=18f9ed2cf 37511d5&ei=5094&partner=homepage

16. James Risen and Eric Lichtblau, "Bush Lets U.S. Spy on Callers without Courts," *New York Times*, December 16, 2005. http://www.nytimes.com/2005/ 12/16/politics/16program.html?pagewanted=print

17. Peter Finn, "Obama Endorses Indefinite Detention without Trial for Some," *Washington Post*, May 21, 2009. http://www.washingtonpost.com/wp-dyn/ content/article/2009/05/21/AR2009052104045. html

18. *Rasul v. Bush*, 524 U.S. 466 (2004).

19. *Hamden v. Rumsfeld*, June 29, 2006.

20. Peter Finn, "Resumed Military Panels Face New Challenges," *Washington Post*, December 4, 2009. http://www.washingtonpost.com/wp-dyn/content/ article/ 2009/12/03/AR2009120303409.html

21. Adam Entous, "Special Report - How the White House Learned to Love the Drone," Reuters, May 19, 2012. http://uk.mobile.reuters.com/article/ idUKTRE64H5U720100519?irpc=932

22. United Nations Security Council Resolution 1441. http://daccess-dds-ny.un.org/doc/UNDOC/GEN/ N02/682/26/PDF/N0268226.pdf?OpenElement

23. President George W. Bush, *National Strategy for Victory in Iraq*, November 1, 2005. http:// www.whitehouse.gov

24. Pallavi Gogoi and Barbara Hagenbaugh, "Billions in AIG's Federal Aid Went to Foreign Banks," *USA Today*, March 17, 2009. http://www.usatoday. com/money/companies/management/2009-03-16- some-aig-billions-went-to-banks_N.htm

25. Federal Reserve Bank. The website http://www. Federalreserve.gov/releases/zl/current will show the current amount.

26. U.S. Treasury, Treasury International Capital System. "U.S. Gross External Debt," 2012. http:// www.treasury.gov/resource-center/data-chart- center/tic/Pages/external-debt.aspx

27. U.S. Treasury, Treasury International Capital System. "Major Foreign Holders of Treasury Securities," 2012. http://www.treasury.gov/resource- center/data-chart-center/tic/Documents/mfh

28. Geoff Dyer, "China's Dollar Dilemma," *Financial Times*, February 23, 2009. http://www.ft.eom/cms/ s/0/07e696a0-014a-llde-8f6e-000077b07658.html

29. Glenn Somerville, "Geithner Tells China its Dollar Assets are Safe," Reuters, June 1, 2009. http://www. reuters.com/article/2009/06/01/us-usa-china- idUSTRE54U0W320090601

30. Alvene Senger, "Side Effects: Obamacare Adds $17 Trillion to Long-Term Unfunded Government Spending," April 2, 2012. http://blog.heritage.org/ 2012/04/02/side-effects-obamacare-adds-17-trillion- to-long-term-unfunded-government-spending/

31. Lawrence J. Kotlikoff, "Is the United States Bank- rupt?" *Federal Reserve Bank of St. Louis Review* Vol. 80 no. 4 (July/August 2006), pp. 235–249. http://research.stlouisfed.org/publications/review/ 06/07/Kotlikoff.pdf

32. Christopher Lasch, *The Revolt of the Elites* (New York: W.W. Norton, 1995), p. 6.

The kind of elitists I admire are those who ruthlessly seek out and encourage intelligence and who believe that competition—and, inevitably, some measure of failure—will do more for character than coddling ever can. My kind of elitist does not grade on a curve and is willing to flunk the whole class.

—William A. Henry III

WHAT CAN STUDENTS DO?

Regardless of what students are told by graduation speakers about their ability to reshape the world, elites—not students—govern the nation. It will be a long while before anyone in college today occupies a position of power allowing him or her to shape the country. In the meantime, what can students do to help preserve democratic values?

1. *Avoid being exploited or used by demagogues of the left or right.* It is wise to lower your expectations about short-term possibilities for change. Excessive idealism, coupled with impatience to change society now, leads only to bitterness and disillusionment. In the long run, these feelings may reduce rather than increase your political effectiveness. Excessive idealism can also expose you to the demagogic appeals of those politicians who exploit others' idealism for their own advantage. Understanding your personal limits in shaping the world and resolving society's problems is important. It is time to reexamine adolescent optimism about "changing the world."

2. *Develop your powers to think critically.* You will benefit from reexamining the "truths" taught to you by looking beyond the bumper-sticker slogans of easy democracy (and of prepackaged alternatives such as socialism, anarchism, and hate) to the realities of power in contemporary society. Just as this book has tried to reexamine traditional teachings about U.S. government, concerned students should also critically reexamine the economic system, the social system, the communications system, and even the accepted "truths" of the physical and biological sciences. Developing your independent powers of social and political analysis can help you resist the flood tide of popular rhetoric, the symbolic posturing of politicians, and the pseudoscience of the bureaucratic social engineers. You can learn to be wary of politicians who promise to solve society's problems with a magic stroke of the pen: to end racism, eliminate

poverty, cure the sick, prevent crime, clean the air and water, provide new energy, all without imposing any new taxes or further restricting individual freedom. You will learn that society's problems have no simple solutions.

3. *Master technological tools rather than letting them master you.* Technology makes many things easier, such as communication and finding information, but it also facilitates the destruction of privacy and the spread of falsehoods. You should endeavor to learn about one or more aspects of information technology in the pursuit of your education. If computers are going to direct your life, why not learn some computer technology yourself? The same applies to social institutions. If laws regulate your life, why not master some aspects of the law yourself, even as an undergraduate? If you are going to be the object of the administrative, managerial, and budgetary practices of large bureaucracies, why not learn something about these subjects, for self-defense if nothing else? If you are not majoring in any of the natural sciences or engineering, why not explore some of these courses—perhaps on a pass-fail basis if your school permits it? The more you know about today's technology, the less impressed you will be when someone tells you that certain policies are "technological requirements."

4. *Become familiar with the meaning of individual freedom and dignity throughout the ages.* Read about and understand the human quest for freedom in many times and cultures—from Socrates to St. Thomas More to Aleksandr Solzhenitsyn, from Moses to Galileo to Aung San Suu Kyi. You should also learn to view U.S. democracy from a world perspective, comparing the personal freedoms we enjoy with those existing in other nations. It is one thing to struggle against mindless corporate and governmental bureaucracies in this country but quite another to conclude that the United States is "not worth saving"—especially when viewing the personal liberties in the United States in the context of the personal restrictions in many other nations.

5. *Maintain a healthy distrust of government and assume responsibility for your own life.* Personal freedom is most endangered when we place too much trust in government, see great idealism in its actions, and have unquestioning faith in our public leaders. Democratic values—individual dignity, freedom of speech and the press, rights of dissent, personal liberty—are safer when we are suspicious of government and its power and worry about its size and complexity. Perhaps the most important danger to a free people is that they "politicize" all the problems confronting them as individuals, blame government and "society" for their problems, and therefore excuse themselves from personal efforts to confront these problems. If we look to government to resolve all our problems, our social dependency will increase, and we will assume less responsibility for our lives. The traditional democratic value is to encourage individuals to shape their own destinies.

We the People of the United States, in Order to form a more perfect Union, establish Justice, insure domestic Tranquility, provide for the common defense, promote the general Welfare, and secure the Blessings of Liberty to ourselves and our Posterity, do ordain and establish this Constitution for the United States of America.

Preamble to the Constitution of the United States of America

THE CONSTITUTION OF THE UNITED STATES OF AMERICA

ARTICLE I

Section 1 All legislative Powers herein granted shall be vested in a Congress of the United States, which shall consist of a Senate and House of Representatives.

Section 2 The House of Representatives shall be composed of Members chosen every second Year by the People of the several States, and the Electors in each State shall have the Qualifications requisite for Electors of the most numerous Branch of the State Legislature.

No Person shall be a Representative who shall not have attained to the age of twenty-five Years, and been seven Years a Citizen of the United States, and who shall not, when elected, be an Inhabitant of that State in which he shall be chosen.

Representatives and direct Taxes shall be apportioned among the several States which may be included within this Union, according to their respective Numbers, *which shall be determined by adding to the whole Number of free Persons, including those bound to Service for a Term of Years, and excluding Indians not taxed, three-fifths of all other persons.*[†]

The actual Enumeration shall be made within three Years after the first Meeting of the Congress of the United States, and within every subsequent Term of ten Years, in such Manner as they shall by Law direct. The Number of Representatives shall not exceed one for every thirty Thousand, but each State shall have at Least one Representative, and until such enumeration shall be made, the State of New

---

[†]Superseded by the Fourteenth Amendment. Throughout, italics indicate passages altered by subsequent amendments.

Hampshire shall be entitled to chuse three, Massachusetts eight, Rhode-Island and Providence Plantations one, Connecticut five, New York six, New Jersey four, Pennsylvania eight, Delaware one, Maryland six, Virginia ten, North Carolina five, South Carolina five, and Georgia three.

When vacancies happen in the Representation from any State, the Executive Authority thereof shall issue Writs of Election to fill such Vacancies.

The House of Representatives shall chuse their Speaker and other Officers; and shall have the sole Power of Impeachment.

Section 3 The Senate of the United States shall be composed of two Senators from each State, *chosen by the Legislature thereof,** for six Years; and each Senator shall have one Vote.

Immediately after they shall be assembled in Consequence of the first Election, they shall be divided as equally as may be into three Classes. The Seats of the Senators of the first Class shall be vacated at the Expiration of the second Year, of the second Class at the Expiration of the fourth Year, and of the third Class at the Expiration of the sixth Year, so that one-third may be chosen every second Year; *and if Vacancies happen by Resignation, or otherwise, during the Recess of the Legislature of any State, the Executive thereof may make temporary Appointments until the next Meeting of the Legislature, which shall then fill such Vacancies.*** No Person shall be a Senator who shall not have attained to the Age of thirty Years, and been nine Years a Citizen of the United States, and who shall not, when elected, be an Inhabitant of the State for which he shall be chosen.

The Vice President of the United States shall be President of the Senate, but shall have no Vote, unless they be equally divided.

The Senate shall chuse their other Officers, and also a President pro tempore, in the Absence of the Vice President, or when he shall exercise the Office of President of the United States.

The Senate shall have the sole Power to try all Impeachments. When sitting for that Purpose, they shall be on Oath or Affirmation. When the President of the United States is tried, the Chief Justice shall preside: And no Person shall be convicted without the Concurrence of two-thirds of the Members present.

Judgment in Cases of Impeachment shall not extend further than to removal from Office, and disqualification to hold and enjoy any Office of Honor, Trust or Profit under the United States: but the party convicted shall nevertheless be liable and subject to Indictment, Trial, Judgment and Punishment, according to Law.

Section 4 The Times, Places and Manner of holding Elections for Senators and Representatives, shall be prescribed in each State by the Legislature thereof; but the Congress may at any time by Law make or alter such Regulations, except as to the Places of chusing Senators.

---

*See the Seventeenth Amendment.

**See the Seventeenth Amendment.

The congress shall assemble at least once in every Year, and such Meeting shall be on the first Monday in December, unless they shall by Law appoint a different Day.*

Section 5 Each House shall be the Judge of the Elections, Returns and Qualifications of its own Members, and a Majority of each shall constitute a Quorum to do Business; but a smaller Number may adjourn from day to day, and may be authorized to compel the Attendance of absent Members, in such Manner, and under such Penalties as each House may provide.

Each House may determine the Rules of its Proceedings, punish its Members for disorderly Behaviour, and, with the Concurrence of two-thirds, expel a Member.

Each House shall keep a Journal of its Proceedings, and from time to time publish the same, excepting such Parts as may in their Judgment require Secrecy; and the Yeas and Nays of the Members of either House on any question shall, at the Desire of one-fifth of those Present, be entered on the Journal.

Neither House, during the Session of Congress, shall, without the Consent of the other, adjourn for more than three days, nor to any other Place than that in which the two Houses shall be sitting.

Section 6 The Senators and Representatives shall receive a Compensation for their Services, to be ascertained by law, and paid out of the Treasury of the United States. They shall in all Cases, except Treason, Felony and Breach of the Peace, be privileged from Arrest during their Attendance at the Session of their respective Houses, and in going to and returning from the same; and for any Speech or Debate in either House, they shall not be questioned in any other Place.

No Senator or Representative shall, during the Time for which he was elected, be appointed to any civil Office under the Authority of the United States, which shall have been created, or the Emoluments whereof shall have been increased during such time; and no Person holding any Office under the United States, shall be a Member of either House during his Continuance in Office.

Section 7 All Bills for raising Revenue shall originate in the House of Representatives; but the Senate may propose or concur with Amendments as on other Bills.

Every Bill which shall have passed the House of Representatives and the Senate, shall, before it become a Law, be presented to the President of the United States; If he approves he shall sign it, but if not he shall return it, with his Objections to that House in which it shall have originated, who shall enter the Objections at large on their Journal, and proceed to reconsider it.

If after such Reconsideration two-thirds of that House shall agree to pass the Bill, it shall be sent, together with the Objections, to the other House, by which it shall likewise be reconsidered, and if approved by two-thirds of that House, it shall become a Law. But in all such Cases the Votes of both Houses shall be determined

---

*See the Twentieth Amendment.

by Yeas and Nays, and the Names of the Persons voting for and against the Bill shall be entered on the Journal of each House respectively. If any Bill shall not be returned by the President within ten Days (Sundays excepted) after it shall have been presented to him, the Same shall be a Law, in like Manner as if he had signed it, unless the Congress by their Adjournment prevent its Return, in which Case it shall not be a Law.

Every Order, Resolution, or Vote to which the concurrence of the Senate and House of Representatives may be necessary (except on a question of Adjournment) shall be presented to the President of the United States; and before the Same shall take Effect, shall be approved by him, or being disapproved by him, shall be re-passed by two-thirds of the Senate and House of Representatives, according to the Rules and Limitations prescribed in the Case of a Bill.

Section 8 The Congress shall have Power To lay and collect Taxes, Duties, Imposts, and Excises, to pay the Debts and provide for the common Defense and general Welfare of the United States; but all Duties, Imposts, and Excises shall be uniform throughout the United States; To borrow Money on the credit of the United States; To regulate Commerce with foreign Nations, and among the several States, and with the Indian Tribes; To establish a uniform Rule of Naturalization, and uniform Laws on the subject of Bankruptcies throughout the United States; To coin Money, regulate the Value thereof, and of foreign Coin, and fix the Standard of Weights and Measures; To provide for the Punishment of counterfeiting the Securities and current Coin of the United States; To establish Post Offices and post Roads; To promote the Progress of Science and useful Arts, by securing for limited times to Authors and Inventors the exclusive Right to their respective Writings and Discoveries; To constitute Tribunals inferior to the Supreme Court; To define and punish Piracies and Felonies committed on the high Seas, and Offences against the Law of Nations; To declare War, grant Letters of Marque and Reprisal, and make Rules concerning Captures on Land and Water; To raise and support Armies, but no Appropriation of Money to that Use shall be for a longer Term than two Years; To provide and maintain a Navy; To make Rules for the Government and Regulation of the land and naval Forces; To provide for calling forth the Militia to execute the Laws of the Union, suppress Insurrections and repel Invasions; To provide for organizing, arming, and disciplining the Militia, and for governing such Part of them as may be employed in the Service of the United States, reserving to the States respectively, the Appointment of the Officers, and the Authority of training the Militia according to the discipline prescribed by Congress; To exercise exclusive Legislation in all Cases whatsoever, over such District (not exceeding ten Miles square) as may, by Cession of particular States, and the Acceptance of Congress, become the Seat of the Government of the United States, and to exercise like Authority over all Places purchased by the Consent of the Legislature of the State in which the Same shall be, for the Erection of Forts, Magazines, Arsenals, Dockyards, and other needful Buildings;—And To make all Laws which shall be necessary and proper for carrying into Execution the foregoing Powers, and all other Powers vested by this Constitution in the Government of the United States, or in any Department or Officer thereof.

Section 9 The Migration or Importation of such Persons as any of the States now existing shall think proper to admit, shall not be prohibited by the Congress prior to the Year one thousand eight hundred and eight, but a Tax or duty may be imposed on such Importation, not exceeding ten dollars for each Person.

The Privilege of the Writ of Habeas Corpus shall not be suspended, unless when in Cases of Rebellion or Invasion the public Safety may require it.

No Bill of Attainder or ex post facto Law shall be passed.

No Capitation, or other direct, Tax shall be laid, unless in Proportion to the Census or Enumeration herein before directed to be taken.

No Tax or Duty shall be laid on Articles exported from any State.

No Preference shall be given by any Regulation of Commerce or Revenue to the Ports of one State over those of another: nor shall Vessels bound to, or from, one State be obliged to enter, clear, or pay Duties in another.

No Money shall be drawn from the Treasury, but in Consequence of Appropriations made by Law; and a regular Statement and Account of the Receipts and Expenditures of all public Money shall be published from time to time.

No Title of Nobility shall be granted by the United States: And no Person holding any Office or Profit or Trust under them, shall, without the Consent of the Congress, accept of any present, Emolument, Office, or Title, of any kind whatever, from any King, Prince, or foreign State.

Section 10 No State shall enter into any Treaty, Alliance, or Confederation; grant Letters of Marque and Reprisal; coin Money; emit Bills of Credit; make any Thing but gold and silver Coin a Tender in Payment of Debts; pass any Bill of Attainder, ex post facto Law, or Law impairing the Obligation of Contracts, or grant any Title of Nobility.

No State shall, without the Consent of the Congress, lay any Imposts or Duties on Imports or Exports, except what may be absolutely necessary for executing its inspection Laws: and the net Produce of all Duties and Imposts, laid by any State on Imports or Exports, shall be for the Use of the Treasury of the United States; and all such Laws shall be subject to the Revision and Control of the Congress.

No State shall, without the Consent of Congress, lay any Duty of Tonnage, keep Troops, or Ships of War in time of Peace, enter into any Agreement or Compact with another State, or with a foreign Power, or engage in War, unless actually invaded, or in such imminent Danger as will not admit of delay.

ARTICLE II

Section 1 The executive Power shall be vested in a President of the United States of America. He shall hold Office during the Term of four Years, and, together with the Vice President, chosen for the same Term, be elected, as follows: Each State shall appoint, in such Manner as the Legislature thereof may direct, a Number of Electors, equal to the whole Number of Senators and Representatives to which the State may be entitled in the Congress: but no Senator or Representative, or Person holding an Office of Trust or Profit under the United States, shall be appointed an Elector.

*The Electors shall meet in their respective States, and vote by Ballot for two Persons, of whom one at least shall not be an Inhabitant of the same State with themselves. And they shall make a List of all the Persons voted for, and of the Number of Votes for each; which List they shall sign and certify, and transmit sealed to the Seat of the Government of the United States, directed to the President of the Senate. The President of the Senate shall, in the Presence of the Senate and House of Representatives, open all the Certificates, and the Votes shall then be counted. The Person having the greatest Number of Votes shall be the President, if such Number be a Majority of the whole Number of Electors appointed; and if there be more than one who have such Majority, and have an equal Number of Votes, then the House of Representatives shall immediately chuse by Ballot one of them for President, and if no Person have a Majority, then from the five highest on the List the said House shall in like Manner chuse the President. But in chusing the President, Votes shall be taken by States, the Representation from each State having one Vote: A quorum for this Purpose shall consist of a Member or Members from two-thirds of the States, and a Majority of all the States shall be necessary to a Choice. In every Case, after the Choice of the President, the Person having the greatest Number of Votes of the Electors shall be the Vice President. But if there should remain two or more who have equal Votes, the Senate shall chuse from them by Ballot the Vice President.**

The Congress may determine the Time of chusing the Electors, and the Day on which they shall give their Votes; which Day shall be the same throughout the United States.

No Person except a natural born Citizen, or a Citizen of the United States, at the time of the Adoption of this Constitution, shall be eligible to the Office of President; neither shall any Person be eligible to that Office who shall not have attained to the Age of thirty-five Years, and been fourteen Years a Resident within the United States.

*In Case of the Removal of the President from Office, or of his Death, Resignation, or Inability to discharge the Powers and Duties of the said Office, the Same shall devolve on the Vice President, and the Congress may by Law provide for the Case of Removal, Death, Resignation or Inability, both of the President and Vice President, declaring what Officer shall then act as President, and such Officer shall act accordingly, until the Disability be removed, or a President shall be elected.***

The President shall, at stated Times, receive for his Services, a Compensation which shall neither be encreased nor diminished during the Period for which he shall have been elected, and he shall not receive within the Period any other Emolument from the United States, or any of them.

Before he enter on the Execution of his Office, he shall take the following Oath or Affirmation:—"I do solemnly swear (or affirm) that I will faithfully execute the Office of President of the United States, and will to the best of my Ability, preserve, protect and defend the Constitution of the United States."

---

*Superseded by the Twelfth Amendment.
**See the Twenty-fifth Amendment.

Section 2 The President shall be the Commander in Chief of the Army and Navy of the United States, and of the Militia of the several States, when called into the actual Service of the United States; he may require the Opinion, in writing, of the principal Officer in each of the executive Departments, upon any Subject relating to the Duties of their respective Offices, and he shall have Power to grant Reprieves and Pardons for Offences against the United States, except in Cases of Impeachment.

He shall have Power, by and with the Advice and Consent of the Senate, to make Treaties, provided two-thirds of the Senators present concur; and he shall nominate, and by and with the Advice and consent of the Senate, shall appoint Ambassadors, other public Ministers and Consuls, Judges of the Supreme Court, and all other Officers of the United States, whose Appointments are not herein otherwise provided for, and which shall be established by Law: but the Congress may by Law vest the Appointment of such inferior officers, as they think proper, in the President alone, in the Courts of Law, or in the Heads of Departments.

The President shall have Power to fill up all Vacancies that may happen during the Recess of the Senate, by granting Commissions which shall expire at the End of their next Session.

Section 3 He shall from time to time give to the Congress Information of the State of the Union, and recommend to their Consideration such Measures as he shall judge necessary and expedient; he may, on extraordinary Occasions, convene both Houses, or either of them, and in Case of Disagreement between them, with Respect to the Time of Adjournment, he may adjourn them to such Time as he shall think proper; he shall receive Ambassadors and other public Ministers; he shall take Care that the Laws be faithfully executed, and shall Commission all the Officers of the United States.

Section 4 The President, Vice President, and all civil Officers of the United States, shall be removed from Office on Impeachment for, and Conviction of, Treason, Bribery, or other high Crimes and Misdemeanors.

ARTICLE III

Section 1 The judicial Power of the United States, shall be vested in one supreme Court and in such inferior Courts as the Congress may from time to time ordain and establish. The Judges, both of the supreme and inferior Courts, shall hold their Offices during good Behaviour, and shall, at stated times, receive for their Services, a Compensation, which shall not be diminished during their Continuance in Office.

Section 2 The judicial Power shall extend to all Cases, in Law and Equity, arising under this Constitution, the Laws of the United States, and Treaties made, or which shall be made, under their Authority;—to all Cases affecting Ambassadors, other public Ministers and Consuls;—to all Cases of admiralty and maritime

Jurisdiction;—to Controversies to which the United States shall be a Party;—to Controversies between two or more States;—*between a State and Citizens of another State;**—between Citizens of different States;—between Citizens of the same State claiming Lands under Grants of different States, and *between a State or the Citizens thereof, and foreign States, Citizens, or Subjects.*†

In all Cases affecting Ambassadors, other public Ministers and Consuls, and those in which a State shall be Party, the supreme Court shall have original Jurisdiction. In all the other Cases before mentioned, the supreme Court shall have appellate Jurisdiction, both as to Law and Fact, with such Exceptions, and under such Regulations as the Congress shall make.

The Trial of all Crimes, except in Cases of Impeachment, shall be by Jury; and such Trial shall be held in the State where the said Crimes shall have been committed; but when not committed within any State, the Trial shall be at such Place or Places as the Congress may by Law have directed.

Section 3 Treason against the United States, shall consist only in levying War against them, or in adhering to their Enemies, giving them Aid and Comfort. No Person shall be convicted of Treason unless on the Testimony of two Witnesses to the same overt Act, or on Confession in open Court.

The Congress shall have Power to declare the Punishment of Treason, but no Attainder of Treason shall work Corruption of Blood, or Forfeiture except during the Life of the Person attained.

ARTICLE IV

Section 1 Full Faith and Credit shall be given in each State to the public Acts, Records, and judicial Proceedings of every other State. And the Congress may by general Laws prescribe the Manner in which such Acts, Records, and Proceedings shall be proved, and the Effect thereof.

Section 2 The Citizens of each State shall be entitled to all Privileges and Immunities of Citizens in the several States.

A Person charged in any State with Treason, Felony, or other Crime, who shall flee from Justice, and be found in another State, shall on Demand of the executive Authority of the State from which he fled, be delivered up, to be removed to the State having Jurisdiction of the Crime.

No Person held to Service of Labour in one State, under the Laws thereof, escaping into another, shall, in Consequence of any Law or Regulation therein, be discharged from such Service or Labour, but shall be delivered up on Claim of the Party to whom such Service of Labour may be due.***

---

*See the Eleventh Amendment.

†See the Eleventh Amendment.

***See the Thirteenth Amendment.

Section 3 New States may be admitted by the Congress into this Union; but no new State shall be formed or erected within the Jurisdiction of any other State; nor any State be formed by the Junction of two or more States, or Parts of States, without the Consent of the Legislatures of the States concerned as well as of the Congress.

The Congress shall have Power to dispose of and make all needful Rules and Regulations respecting the Territory or other Property belonging to the United States; and nothing in this Constitution shall be so construed as to Prejudice any claims of the United States, or of any particular State.

Section 4 The United States shall guarantee to every State in this Union a Republican Form of Government, and shall protect each of them against Invasion; and on Application of the Legislature, or of the Executive (when the Legislature cannot be convened) against domestic Violence.

ARTICLE V

The Congress, whenever two-thirds of both Houses shall deem it necessary, shall propose Amendments to this Constitution, or, on the Application of the Legislatures of two-thirds of the several States, shall call a Convention for proposing Amendments, which, in either Case, shall be valid to all Intents and Purposes, as Part of this Constitution, when ratified by the Legislatures of three-fourths of the several States, or by Conventions in three-fourths thereof, as the one or the other Mode of Ratification may be proposed by the Congress; Provided that no Amendment which may be made prior to the Year One thousand eight hundred and eight shall in any Manner affect the first and fourth clauses in the Ninth Section of the first Article; and that no State, without its Consent, shall be deprived of its equal Suffrage in the Senate.

ARTICLE VI

All debts contracted and Engagements entered into, before the Adoption of this Constitution, shall be as valid against the United States under this Constitution, as under the Confederation.

This Constitution, and the Laws of the United States which shall be made in Pursuance thereof; and all Treaties made, or which shall be made, under the Authority of the United States, shall be the supreme Law of the Land; and the Judges in every State shall be bound thereby, any Thing in the Constitution or Laws of any State to the Contrary notwithstanding.

The Senators and Representatives before mentioned, and the Members of the several State Legislatures, and all executive and judicial Officers, both of the United States and of the several States, shall be bound by Oath or Affirmation, to support this Constitution; but no religious Test shall ever be required as a Qualification to any Office or public Trust under the United States.

ARTICLE VII

The Ratification of the Conventions of nine States, shall be sufficient for the Establishment of this Constitution between the States so ratifying the Same.

Done in Contention by the Unanimous Consent of the States present the Seventeenth Day of September in the Year of our Lord one thousand seven hundred and eighty seven and of the Independence of the United States of America the Twelfth. In witness whereof We have hereunto subscribed our Names.

Articles in Addition to, and Amendment of, the Constitution of the United States of America, Proposed by Congress, and Ratified by the Several States, Pursuant to the Fifth Article of the Original Constitution.

AMENDMENT I

(Ratification of the first ten amendments was completed December 15, 1791.)

Congress shall make no law respecting an establishment of religion, or prohibiting the free exercise thereof; or abridging the freedom of speech, or of the press; or the right of the people peaceably to assemble, and to petition the Government for a redress of grievances.

AMENDMENT II

A well regulated Militia, being necessary to the security of a free State, the right of the people to keep and bear Arms, shall not be infringed.

AMENDMENT III

No Soldier shall, in time of peace be quartered in any house, without the consent of the Owner, nor in time of war, but in a manner to be prescribed by law.

AMENDMENT IV

The right of the people to be secure in their persons, houses, papers, and effects, against unreasonable searches and seizures, shall not be violated, and no Warrants shall issue, but upon probable cause, supported by Oath or affirmation, and particularly describing the place to be searched, and the persons or things to be seized.

AMENDMENT V

No person shall be held to answer for a capital, or otherwise infamous crime, unless on a presentment or indictment of a Grand Jury, except in cases arising in the land or naval forces, or in the Militia, when in actual service in time of War or public danger; nor shall any person be subject for the same offence to be twice put in jeopardy of life or limb; nor shall be compelled in any criminal case to be a witness against himself, nor be deprived of life, liberty, or property, without due process of law; nor shall private property be taken for public use, without just compensation.

AMENDMENT VI

In all criminal prosecutions, the accused shall enjoy the right to a speedy and public trial, by an impartial jury of the State and district wherein the crime shall have been committed, which district shall have been previously ascertained by law, and to be informed of the nature and cause of the accusation; to be confronted with the witnesses against him; to have compulsory process for obtaining witnesses in his favor, and to have the Assistance of Counsel for his defense.

AMENDMENT VII

In Suits at common law, where the value in controversy shall exceed twenty dollars, the right of trial by jury shall be preserved, and no fact tried by a jury, shall be otherwise reexamined in any Court of the United States, than according to the rules of the common law.

AMENDMENT VIII

Excessive bail shall not be required, nor excessive fines imposed, nor cruel and unusual punishments inflicted.

AMENDMENT IX

The enumeration in the Constitution, of certain rights, shall not be construed to deny or disparage others retained by the people.

AMENDMENT X

The powers not delegated to the United States by the Constitution, nor prohibited by it to the States, are reserved to the States respectively, or to the people.

AMENDMENT XI (1795)

The Judicial power of the United States shall not be construed to extend to any suit in law or equity, commenced or prosecuted against one of the United States by Citizens of another State, or by Citizens or Subjects of any Foreign State.

AMENDMENT XII (1804)

The Electors shall meet in their respective states and vote by ballot for President and Vice President, one of whom, at least, shall not be an inhabitant of the same state with themselves; they shall name in their ballots the person voted for as President, and in distinct ballots the person voted for as Vice President, and they shall make distinct lists of all persons voted for as President, and of all persons voted for as Vice President, and of the number of votes for each, which lists they shall sign and certify, and transmit sealed to the seat of the government of the United States, directed to the President of the Senate;—The President of the Senate shall, in the presence of the Senate and House of Representatives, open all the certificates and the votes shall then be counted;—the person having the greatest number of votes for President, shall be the President, if such number be a majority of the whole number of Electors appointed; and if no person have such majority, then from the persons having the highest numbers not exceeding three on the list of those voted for as President, the House of Representatives shall choose immediately, by ballot, the President. But in choosing the President, the votes shall be taken by states, the representation from each state having one vote; a quorum for this purpose shall consist of a member or members from two-thirds of the states, and a majority of all the states shall be necessary to a choice. And if the House of Representatives shall not choose a President whenever the right of choice shall devolve upon them, *before the fourth day of March next following,** then the Vice President shall act as President, as in the case of the death or other constitutional disability of the President.—The person having the greatest number of votes as Vice President shall be the Vice President, if such number be a majority of the whole number of Electors appointed, and if no person have a majority, then from the two highest numbers on the list, the Senate shall choose the Vice President; a quorum for the purpose shall consist of two-thirds of the whole number of Senators, and a majority of the whole number shall be necessary to a choice.

But no person constitutionally ineligible to the office of President shall be eligible to that of Vice President of the United States.

AMENDMENT XIII (1865)

Section 1 Neither slavery nor involuntary servitude, except as a punishment for crime whereof the party shall have been duly convicted, shall exist within the United States, or any place subject to their jurisdiction.

Section 2 Congress shall have the power to enforce this article by appropriate legislation.

AMENDMENT XIV (1868)

Section 1 All persons born or naturalized in the United States, and subject to the jurisdiction thereof, are citizens of the United States and the State wherein they reside. No State shall make or enforce any law which shall abridge the privileges or immunities of citizens of the United States; nor shall any State deprive any person of life, liberty, or property, without due process of law; nor deny to any person within its jurisdiction the equal protection of the laws.

Section 2 Representatives shall be apportioned among the several States according to their respective numbers, counting the whole number of persons in each State, excluding Indians not taxed. But when the right to vote at any election for the choice of electors for President and Vice President of the United States, Representatives in Congress, the Executive and Judicial officers of a State, or the members of the

*Altered by the Twentieth Amendment.

Legislature thereof, is denied to any of the male inhabitants of such State, being twenty-one years of age, and citizens of the United States, or in any way abridged, except for participation in rebellion, or other crime, the basis of representation therein shall be reduced in the proportion which the number of such male citizens shall bear to the whole number of male citizens twenty-one years of age in such State.

Section 3 No person shall be a Senator or Representative in Congress, or elector of President and Vice President, or hold any office, civil or military, under the United States, or under any State, who, having previously taken an oath, as a member of Congress, or as an officer of the United States, or as a member of any State legislature, or as an executive or judicial officer of any State, to support the Constitution of the United States, shall have engaged in insurrection or rebellion against the same, or given aid or comfort to the enemies thereof. But Congress may by a vote of two-thirds of each House, remove such disability.

Section 4 The validity of the public debt of the United States, authorized by law, including debts incurred for payment of pensions and bounties for services in suppressing insurrection or rebellion, shall not be questioned.

But neither the United States nor any State shall assume or pay any debt or obligation incurred in aid of insurrection or rebellion against the United States, or any claim for the loss or emancipation of any slave; but all debts, obligations, and claims shall be held illegal and void.

Section 5 The Congress shall have power to enforce, by appropriate legislation, the provisions of this article.

AMENDMENT XV (1870)

Section 1 The right of citizens of the United States to vote shall not be denied or abridged by the United States or by any State on account of race, color, or previous condition of servitude.

Section 2 The Congress shall have power to enforce this article by appropriate legislation.

AMENDMENT XVI (1913)

The Congress shall have power to lay and collect taxes on incomes, from whatever source derived, without apportionment among the several States, and without regard to any census or enumeration.

AMENDMENT XVII (1913)

The Senate of the United States shall be composed of two Senators from each State, elected by the people thereof, for six years; and each Senator shall have one vote. The electors in each State shall have the qualifications requisite for electors of the most numerous branch of the State legislature.

When vacancies happen in the representation of any State in the Senate, the executive authority of such State shall issue writs of election to fill such vacancies: *Provided,* That the legislature of any State may empower the executive thereof to make temporary appointments until the people fill the vacancies by election as the legislature may direct.

This amendment shall not be so construed as to affect the election or term of any Senator chosen before it becomes valid as part of the Constitution.

AMENDMENT XVIII (1919)

Section 1 After one year from the ratification of this article the manufacture, sale, or transportation of intoxicating liquors within, the importation thereof into, or the exportation thereof from the United States and all territory subject to the jurisdiction thereof for beverage purposes is hereby prohibited.

Section 2 The Congress and the several States shall have concurrent power to enforce this article by appropriate legislation.

Section 3 This article shall be inoperative unless it shall have been ratified as an amendment to the Constitution by the legislatures of the several States, as provided in the Constitution, within seven years from the date of submission hereof to the States by the Congress.[*]

AMENDMENT XIX (1920)

The right of citizens of the United States to vote shall not be denied or abridged by the United States or by any State on account of sex.

Congress shall have power to enforce this article by appropriate legislation.

AMENDMENT XX (1933)

Section 1 The terms of the President and Vice President shall end at noon on the 20th day of January, and the terms of Senators and Representatives at noon on the 3rd day of January, of the years in which such terms would have ended if this article had not been ratified; and the terms of their successors shall then begin.

Section 2 The Congress shall assemble at least once in every year, and such meeting shall begin at noon on the 3rd day of January, unless they shall by law appoint a different day.

---

[*]Repealed by the Twenty-first Amendment.

Section 3 If, at the time fixed for the beginning of the term of the President, the President elect shall have died, the Vice President elect shall become President. If a President shall not have been chosen before the time fixed for the beginning of his term, or if the President elect shall have failed to qualify, then the Vice President elect shall act as President until a President shall have qualified; and the Congress may by law provide for the case wherein neither a President elect nor a Vice President elect shall have qualified, declaring who shall then act as President, or the manner in which one who is to act shall be selected, and such person shall act accordingly until a President or Vice President shall have qualified.

Section 4 The Congress may by law provide for the case of the death of any of the persons from whom the House of Representatives may choose a President whenever the right of choice shall have devolved upon them, and for the case of the death of any of the persons from whom the Senate may choose a Vice President whenever the right of choice shall have devolved upon them.

Section 5 Sections 1 and 2 shall take effect on the 15th day of October following ratification of this article.

Section 6 This article shall be inoperative unless it shall have been ratified as an amendment to the Constitution by the legislatures of three-fourths of the several States within seven years from the date of its submission.

AMENDMENT XXI (1933)

Section 1 The eighteenth article of amendment to the Constitution of the United States is hereby repealed.

Section 2 The transportation or importation into any State, Territory, or possession of the United States for delivery or use therein of intoxicating liquors, in violation of the laws thereof, is hereby prohibited.

Section 3 This article shall be inoperative unless it shall have been ratified as an amendment to the Constitution by conventions in the several States, as provided in the Constitution, within seven years from the date of submission thereof to the States by the Congress.

AMENDMENT XXII (1951)

Section 1 No person shall be elected to the office of the President more than twice, and no person who has held the office of President, or acted as President for more than two years of a term to which some other person was elected President shall be elected to the office of President more than once. But this Article shall not apply to any person holding the office of President when this Article was proposed by the Congress, and shall not prevent any person who may be holding the office of President, or acting as President, during the term within which this Article becomes operative from holding the office of President or acting as President during the remainder of such term.

Section 3 This article shall be inoperative unless it shall have been ratified as an amendment to the Constitution by the legislatures of three-fourths of the several States within seven years from the date of its submission to the States by the Congress.

AMENDMENT XXIII (1961)

Section 1 The District constituting the seat of Government of the United States shall appoint in such manner as the Congress may direct: A number of electors of President and Vice President equal to the whole number of Senators and Representatives in Congress to which the District would be entitled if it were a State, but in no event more than the least populous State; they shall be in addition to those appointed by the States, but they shall be considered, for the purposes of the election of President and Vice President, to be electors appointed by a State; and they shall meet in the District and perform such duties as provided by the twelfth article of amendment.

Section 2 The Congress shall have power to enforce this article by appropriate legislation.

AMENDMENT XXIV (1964)

Section 1 The right of citizens of the United States to vote in any primary or other election for President or Vice President, for electors for President or Vice President, or for Senator or Representative in Congress, shall not be denied or abridged by the United States or any state by reason of failure to pay any poll tax or other tax.

Section 2 The Congress shall have the power to enforce this article by appropriate legislation.

AMENDMENT XXV (1967)

Section 1 In case of the removal of the President from office or of his death or resignation, the Vice President shall become President.

Section 2 Whenever there is a vacancy in the office of the Vice President, the President shall nominate a Vice President who shall take office upon confirmation by a majority vote of both Houses of Congress.

Section 3 Whenever the President transmits to the President pro tempore of the Senate and the Speaker of the House of Representatives his written declaration that he is unable to discharge the powers and duties of his office, and until he transmits to them a written declaration to the contrary, such powers and duties shall be discharged by the Vice President as Acting President.

Section 4 Whenever the Vice President and a majority of either the principal officers of the executive departments or of such other body as Congress may by law provide, transmit to the President pro tempore of the Senate and the Speaker of the House of Representatives their written declaration that the President is unable to discharge the powers and duties of his office, the Vice President shall immediately assume the powers and duties of the office as Acting President.

Thereafter, when the President transmits to the President pro tempore of the Senate and the Speaker of the House of Representatives his written declaration that no inability exists, he shall resume the powers and duties of his office unless the Vice President and a majority of either the principal officers of the executive departments or of such other body as Congress may by law provide, transmit within four days to the President pro tempore of the Senate and the Speaker of the House of Representatives their written declaration that the President is unable to discharge the powers and duties of his office. Thereupon Congress shall decide the issue, assembling within forty-eight hours for that purpose if not in session. If the Congress, within twenty-one days after the receipt of the latter written declaration, or, if Congress is not in session, within twenty-one days after Congress is required to assemble, determines by two-thirds vote of both Houses that the President is unable to discharge the powers and duties of his office, the Vice President shall continue to discharge the same as Acting President; otherwise, the President shall resume the powers and duties of his office.

AMENDMENT XXVI (1971)

Section 1 The right of citizens of the United States, who are eighteen years of age or older, to vote shall not be denied or abridged by the United States or any state on account of age.

Section 2 The Congress shall have the power to enforce this article by appropriate legislation.

AMENDMENT XXVII (1992)

No law, varying the compensation for the service of the Senators and Representatives, shall take effect, until an election of Representatives shall have intervened.[*]

---

[*]The Twenty-seventh Amendment (1992), proposed in 1789 by James Madison, became law more than two centuries later when ratified by the Michigan legislature on May 7, 1992.

GLOSSARY

A

Agenda setting the first step in policy-making: determining which issues are worthy of consideration.

Articles of Confederation the treaty between the American states as a loose group of sovereign nations "for their common defense, the security of their liberties, and their mutual and general welfare," effective from 1781 to 1789.

B

Block grant directed money in which the federal government provides funds for use by states and cities for broad purposes.

Bork a term that describes the blocking of qualified nominees on political grounds, named after the refusal of the Senate to confirm Judge Robert Bork to the Supreme Court.

Budget implementation the development of procedures and activities to carry out policies legislated by Congress; requires bureaucracies to translate laws into operational rules and regulations and to allocate resources.

Bureaucracy (derived from the French word *bureau,* meaning "office"); refers to the idea that society is ruled not by elected officials, but rather by people making regulations and decisions; the vast bulk of the executive branch of government, whether at the federal, state, or local level.

C

Cabinet an informal executive branch organization that consists of the secretaries of the 15 executive departments and the vice president, with the president as its head; may include others.

Candidate image the personal traits of the candidates; their ability to project charm, warmth, compassion, youth and vigor, honesty and integrity, and so forth.

Candidate image voters voters who cast their ballots based on superficial aspects of a candidate as projected through the media—charm, confidence, sincerity, humor, and looks.

Capture theory of regulation a theory that explains how regulated industries come to benefit from government regulation and how regulatory commissions come to represent the industries they are supposed to regulate rather than the masses.

Categorical grants directed money in which the federal government specifies individual projects or programs in cities and states.

Checks and balances a political system in which power is distributed among multiple portions and levels of government, all of whom must come to agreement to allow anything to happen; highly effective tool for limiting governmental corruption.

Chief of state the role of the president as the symbolic representative of the nation.

Circuit courts of appeals the appellate courts, which do not hold trials or accept new evidence but consider only the record of the trial courts and oral or written arguments submitted by attorneys.

Circulation of elites the movement of talented and ambitious individuals from the lower strata into the elite.

Classical conservatism a world view that relies on tradition and sees human nature as flawed and prone to weakness, rendering politics necessary to mitigate the worst of the potential damage.

Classical liberalism an ideology that holds that society is created by a social contract among rational individuals capable of thinking for themselves and determining what is in their own best interest, who then choose to give up some freedoms in exchange for some security.

Cloture vote a Senate rule device to limit debate; 16 members' signatures on a petition will bring cloture to a vote, and then 60 votes are needed to end debate.

Committee a specialized working group that focuses on a specific policy area.

Common law the British approach to a legal system, built up over generations and centuries of precedents, instead of springing from contemporary legislature.

Connecticut compromise the agreement reached during the framing of the U.S. Constitution by large and small states that provided for equal representation of states in the Senate and representation based on population in the House of Representatives.

Conservatism a contemporary political ideology that includes classical liberal values of free markets, limited government, and individual self-reliance in economic affairs, combined with a classical conservative belief in the value of tradition, law, family, and faith.

Conspiracy theories fanciful or irrational theories about power, the existence of which marks places in the political system where segments of the population feel powerless.

Constituent service (casework) a form of retail politics in which members of Congress help people in their district deal with the government on an individual level.

Continuing resolution an action adopted by Congress that authorizes government agencies to keep spending money for a specified period at the same level as in the previous fiscal year.

Cooperative federalism a pattern of federal–state relations in which both the nation and the states exercise responsibilities for policy.

Counterelites demagogues who wish to become elites without going through the existing system of achieving power, often by relying on an ability to agitate the masses into supporting them and trying to leverage this into a claim to power.

D

Dealignment term for the trend of American voters declining to register with either the Democratic or Republican parties.

Democracy a form of government by popular participation in the allocation of values in a society.

Deterrence the idea that rational elites can be dissuaded from launching a nuclear attack by the threat of a devastating retaliatory strike.

District courts the trial courts of the federal system.

Divided government a situation wherein one party controls the White House and the other controls Congress, or when the House and Senate are controlled by different parties.

Dual federalism the pattern of federal–state relations during the nation's first 100 years, wherein the states and the nation divided most governmental functions.

E

Earmark a special provision for expenditures tucked inside a larger appropriation bill.

Economic elite the few in positions of power in the private economy, as distinct from governmental elites.

Elite(s) the few in any organization or society who have power.

Elite distemper the condition arising when elites act in a self-serving manner, thus weakening faith in democracy.

Elite member anyone who participates in important decisions that allocate resources for society.

Elite theory (or elitism) an approach to describing society, focusing on the few with power, their values, their behavior, and their demographics.

Entitlements items determined by past decisions of Congress that represent commitments in future budgets.

Equality before the law theory that the law should treat all fairly without advantage, regardless of social position, economic class, creed, or race.

Equality of opportunity a central concept in the liberal creed of individual freedom to pursue "happiness," in which all individuals have a reasonably equal chance to develop their capacities to the fullest potential in many aspects of life: social, educational, economic, and political.

Equality of outcome a central concept in socialism based on the idea that in a socially just society the material conditions of life will be roughly equal.

Equity feminism a form of advocating for women's rights which seeks equal opportunity and equal treatment under the law for individuals regardless of sex.

Establishment colloquial term for the most influential institutions in society.

Executive privilege the right of the president to keep confidential communications from other branches of government.

F

Federal mandates direct orders to state and local governments to perform a particular activity or service to comply with federal laws in the performance of their functions.

Filibuster a device that permits a minority to tie up the business of the Senate and prevent it from voting on a bill, barring a cloture vote.

G

Gender feminism a form of advocating for women's rights which goes beyond a demand for equality and seeks liberation from the patriarchal family and the male-dominated society.

Global cop a term that refers to the idea that the United States is the world's first responder, expected to be able and willing to rectify problems in times of emergency.

"Go native" an expression that refers to political heads yielding to the pressure of career bureaucrats and becoming their captives instead of taking control.

Group benefits voters voters that evaluate parties and candidates by expected favorable or unfavorable treatment for specific social groups and favor candidates seen as sympathetic to a group with which they identify.

H

Halo effect the tendency among poll respondents to give socially approved responses to questions, regardless of their true feelings.

Head of government the role of the president as head of the executive branch.

Hegemony preeminent power and dominance by one nation in the global system.

"Home style" the activities of senators and representatives in promoting their images among their constituents.

Horse race reporting term for a style of news reporting which focuses on who is ahead or behind, how much money candidates are spending, and their current standing in the polls.

I

Idealism an approach to international relations based on the belief that there exists a moral duty to spread democracy, human rights, religious freedom, freedom of the press, and economic freedom.

"If it bleeds, it leads" slogan in the news business based on exploiting mass fascination with human tragedy to improve ratings or advertising rates.

Impeachment formal process of removing an executive or judicial officer from office for criminal activity; a two-part process in which first the House of Representatives must impeach (similar to indict) and then the Senate holds a trial.

Information overload condition that exists when so many communications are directed at people that they cannot possibly process them all.

Initiative an electoral device whereby voters, through the use of a petition, may place a proposed measure on the ballot for adoption or rejection by the electorate of a state, bypassing the legislature.

Interlocking directorates system in which a director of one corporation also sits on the boards of one or more other corporations, enabling key corporate elites to wield influence over a large number of corporations.

Iron Law of Oligarchy theory in political science stating that an elite is inevitable in any social organization, of any size, whether family, club, union, business, or society as a whole.

Iron triangles executive bureaucracies administering a program, the congressional subcommittee charged with overseeing it, and the interest groups most directly affected by it.

Isolationism an approach to international relations based on the idea of avoiding foreign entanglements and placing domestic priorities first.

Issue networks interconnected iron triangles.

J

Judicial activism the belief that the Supreme Court should shape constitutional meaning to fit its estimate of the needs of contemporary society.

Judicial review the legal principle that the courts have the power to review laws made by the legislature to determine their constitutionality.

Judicial self-restraint the argument that since justices are not popularly elected, the Supreme Court should move cautiously and avoid direct confrontation with legislative and executive authority.

L

Leadership PACs (political action committees) a form of PAC run by a congressional leader to accept donations which can then be spread around to others, building popularity and support.

Liberalism a contemporary political ideology that values a strong and active government to provide economic security and protection for civil rights, combined with freedom from government intervention in personal conduct.

Line-item veto the ability to veto some spending items in a bill while accepting others.

Lobbying any communication directed at a government decision maker with the hope of influencing decisions.

M

Managerialism business theory that general management skills are more important than detailed production-specific knowledge.

Masses the many in any organization that do not hold power.

Mutual assured destruction (MAD) a term for the idea that a mutual nuclear balance of terror would deter a nuclear war.

Myth of the policy mandate the belief among politicians that their positions were what brought electoral victory, when it was most likely some other factor, such as personality or weariness with the opponent.

N

New federalism a term that refers to the efforts to return power and responsibility to states and communities.

Noblesse oblige social theory that elites have a responsibility for the welfare of the masses.

O

Original intent (originalism) a doctrine that takes the values of the Founders as expressed in the text of the Constitution and applies them to current conditions.

P

Party polarization the tendency for Democratic and Republican party activists and leaders to grow further apart ideologically.

Party voters voters who are likely to rely on either liberal or conservative principles in evaluating candidates and issues and generally favor one party over the other.

Party votes roll-call votes in Congress in which a majority of one party votes opposing a majority of the other party.

Plea bargain special arrangements made for criminal defendants to plead guilty in exchange for reduced charges.

Plural elite model political model that views power as more widely shared among leadership groups representing different segments of society, which are competitive and held responsible by the masses through elections, party competition, and interest groups. This is the predominant model for the United States.

Pluralism an approach to politics based on the belief that democratic values can be preserved in a system where multiple, competing elites determine public policy through bargaining and compromise, voters exercise meaningful choices in elections, and new elites can gain access to power.

Policy voters or issues voters voters who base their decisions on the key issues of greatest importance to them, such as taxation, abortion, or environment.

Political action committee (PAC) non-party organization that solicits voluntary contributions to disburse to political candidates.

Political entrepreneurship the ability and desire to sell yourself to others as a candidate, to raise money from political contributors, and to organize and motivate others to work on your campaign.

Polity a political system in which the many participate, but in which the majority is restrained from becoming tyrannical by protecting minority rights.

Pork the efforts of senators and representatives to award federally funded projects to their home states or districts.

Power the ability to influence people and events by granting or withholding valuable resources.

Progressive tax a tax that captures a larger share of the income of higher-income workers than of lower-income workers.

R

Realignment a longer-term change of mass party affiliation from one major party to another.

Realism an approach to international relations based on the belief that nations should act abroad only to protect clearly defined national interests, whether economic or security-related.

Recall a petition for an election to decide whether or not an incumbent official should be removed from office before the end of his or her term.

Referendum an electoral device by which the electorate must approve decisions of the legislature before these become law or part of the state constitution, or by which the electorate must approve of proposals placed on the ballot by popular initiative.

Regressive tax a tax that captures a larger share of the income of lower-income workers than of higher-income workers.

Regulation formal rules for implementing legislation.

Relative autonomy of elites the theory that each segment of the elite is relatively independent and able to pursue its own interests.

Representational federalism a view of federalism in which there is no constitutional protection for state power other than the states' role in electing the members of Congress and the president.

Republic Latin-rooted term equivalent to polity.

Retrospective voters voters that base their judgment on their perception of the condition of the nation, usually the economy.

Revolving door term for when elites move from power positions in banking, industry, the media, law, the foundations, and education to power positions in government, then frequently return to prestigious private posts after a term of "public service."

Ruling elite model political model that views power as concentrated in the hands of relatively few people who make key decisions and are subject to little influence from the masses.

S

Selective perception the tendency that people have to mentally screen out information or images with which they disagree.

Separation of powers a system that divides responsibility and makes it difficult for the masses to hold government accountable for public policy, but also makes corruption more difficult.

Signing statements a practice used by presidents in which a bill is signed with an added statement regarding its interpretation, sometimes objecting to included provisions or adding details when the law is unclear.

Social contract theory a political theory that society exists because the free individuals who compose it have made the rational decision that forming it is in their self-interest.

Sound bites the short snippets of a sentence or phrase that receive media coverage.

Stare decisis a legal term that means that the issue has already been decided in earlier cases and the decision stands.

Subelites state- and local-level elites.

Sullivan Rule qualification allowing false reporting unless it can be shown that the media published or broadcast false and damaging statements knowing at the time their statements were false and damaging, or that they did so with "reckless disregard" for the truth or falsehood of their statements.

T

Technocrats technical experts that actually carry out the intent of elected officials.

Terrorism politically motivated violence perpetrated against noncombatant targets, usually intended to influence an audience.

Think tanks policy-planning groups that are central coordinating points in the policy-making process. They review or create research on topics of interest with the goal of developing policy recommendations.

Three-fifths compromise the concession made during the framing of the U.S. Constitution that three-fifths of the number of slaves of each state would be counted for the purposes of representation and apportioning direct taxes.

U

Unfunded mandates mandates which create costs to states and localities, but are not federally financed.

V

Veto when a president refuses to sign a bill into law and returns it to Congress instead.

W

Weapons of Mass Destruction (WMDs) nuclear, chemical, biological, and radiological weapons designed to cause mass casualties.

Winner-take-all system a system of determining the election winner by plurality.

INDEX